THE PRESENT TESTAMENT

VOLUME TEN

WORDS OF A MESSANGER

BARBARA, GOD'S MODERN DAY PROPHET SPEAKING

BEHOLD GOD'S HOLY WORDS TODAY

BY

BARBARA ANN MARY MACK

MW01105711

AuthorHouse™
1663 Liberty Drive
Bloomington, IN 47403
www.authorhouse.com
Phone: 1 (800) 839-8640

© 2016 Barbara Ann Mary Mack. All rights reserved.

No part of this book may be reproduced, stored in a retrieval system, or transmitted by any means without the written permission of the author.

Published by AuthorHouse 04/14/2016

ISBN: 978-1-5246-0121-8 (sc)
ISBN: 978-1-5246-0122-5 (e)

Print information available on the last page.

Any people depicted in stock imagery provided by Thinkstock are models, and such images are being used for illustrative purposes only.
Certain stock imagery © Thinkstock.

This book is printed on acid-free paper.

Because of the dynamic nature of the Internet, any web addresses or links contained in this book may have changed since publication and may no longer be valid. The views expressed in this work are solely those of the author and do not necessarily reflect the views of the publisher, and the publisher hereby disclaims any responsibility for them.

authorHOUSE®

DEDICATION TO

ALMIGHTY GOD, THE HOLY
UNCHANGING WORD: THE
HOLY DICTATOR OF VALUABLE
MESSAGES OF DIVINE LOVE TODAY.

AND

BARBARA, GOD'S SENT
MESSENGER TODAY

ACKNOWLEDGMENT

MY APOLOGIES

IN THE MIDST OF THIS PERILOUS AND TRAGIC PERIOD OF TIME, MY REFUGE LIES IN THE MIDST OF MY HEAVEN SENT WRITINGS. THE SACRED WRITINGS THAT REVEAL A HEAVEN SENT AND ORCHESTRATED PURE AND HOLY LOVE. I APOLOGIZE IF MY HEAVEN SENT WRITINGS OFFEND ANYONE. THEY ARE PURE AND HOLY, AND THEY SUSTAIN ME IN THE MIDST OF THE HEARTACHE THAT PERMEATES THE LIVES OF GOD'S EARTHLY CHILDREN OF ALL AGES. MY SOUL RESTS WITHIN THE WRITINGS THAT REVEAL A HOLY LOVE THAT DESCENDED FROM GOD'S SACRED THRONE AND HEART. IT IS A LOVE THAT I REVERE, FOR IT IS APPROVED AND SANCTIFIED BY ALMIGHTY GOD HIMSELF. IT IS A LOVE THAT GIVES ME PEACE AND JOY THROUGHOUT EACH BLESSED DAY. IT IS A DIVINE LOVE THAT I WILL TREASURE FOREVER, FOR IT IS ORDERED AND ORCHESTRATED BY MY SAVIOR AND GOD. *ALLELUIA!!!*
JANUARY 18, 2016 AT 1:31 AM BY: BARBARA ANN MARY MACK
SENT MON, JAN 18, 2016 1:38 AM-READ MON 1/18/2016 9:50 AM

THE WRITINGS IN THIS BOOK ARE NOT IN CHRONOLOGICAL ORDER.
BEING AN IMPERFECT HUMAN, THERE MAY BE SOME GRAMMATICAL ERRORS, IF SO, PLEASE PARDON ME.

BARBARA ANN MARY MACK

INTRODUCTION

IS MY MISSION IN VAIN,
SAYS THE LORD?

BARBARA SPEAKING

I WILL DO ANYTHING FOR YOU, O LORD,
TO PROVE TO THE WORLD THAT WE ARE ON ONE ACCORD.

MY HEAVEN SENT TREASURE: *GOD'S HOLY WORDS TODAY*

DESCEND, O SWEET TREASURE THAT WAS RELEASED FROM THE MIGHTY THRONE OF GOD, MY SAVIOR AND HOLY SPOUSE. DESCEND, O SWEET TREASURE THAT IS A DIVINE GIFT TO GOD'S CALLED AND CHOSEN ONES TODAY. DESCEND TO THE RECEIVING ARMS AND MIND OF GOD'S SENT MESSENGER AND BRIDE (BARBARA). DESCEND TO THE REALM (BARBARA) THAT REPRESENTS YOUR HOLY OMNIPOTENT AND OMNIPRESENCE TODAY. DESCEND TO THE EARS AND HEART THAT TREASURE YOUR NEEDED PRESENCE IN THE LIVES OF THOSE WHO DO NOT OPENLY EXHIBIT YOUR HOLY EXISTENCE. DESCEND, O SWEET WORDS THAT REVEAL THE ETERNAL GLORY THAT AWAITS THE CHOSEN ONES, FOR YOU ARE WELL-LOVED BY ME! DESCEND TO ME, O TREASURE THAT ENLIGHTENS THE SOUL OF GOD'S SENT QUEEN (BARBARA)! DESCEND TO ME EVERY DAY, AS I ENJOY THE BLESSING OF YOUR HOLY PRESENCE. DESCEND TO ME AS I SLEEP! DESCEND TO ME AS I RELAX IN THE COMPANY OF THOSE WHOM YOU HAVE BLESSED AND SANCTIFIED. DESCEND TO ME IN THE PRESENCE OF CRAIG, OUR ETERNAL BELOVED ONE, FOR YOU DEEM HIM WORTHY. DESCEND TO ME, O SWEET TREASURE! DESCEND TO ME IN THE MIDST OF THE REALM (EVIL) THAT EMITS DESTRUCTION AND HAVOC UPON EARTH'S RESIDENTS TODAY! DESCEND TO ME IN THE MIDST OF THE HOLY ONES! DESCEND TO ME IN THE MIDST OF YOUR ANGELS AND SAINTS! DESCEND! DESCEND! DESCEND, O SWEET WORDS OF DIVINE TRUTH AND FREEDOM! FOR I, YOUR WELCOMED SPOUSE, AM READY TO RECEIVE YOU! *ALLELUIA!!!*
FEBRUARY 13, 2016 AT 6:36 PM BY: BARBARA ANN MARY MACK

EPISTLES TO GOD'S CHOSEN SON, ARCHBISHOP CRAIG, VIA EMAILS

SENT FROM: BARBARA, ALMIGHTY GOD'S MESSENGER AND BRIDE

READ BY: GOD'S CHOSEN SON

KEEP ME HIDDEN, O LORD, *FOR THE WORLD ISN'T WORTHY OF YOUR HOLY PRESENCE*

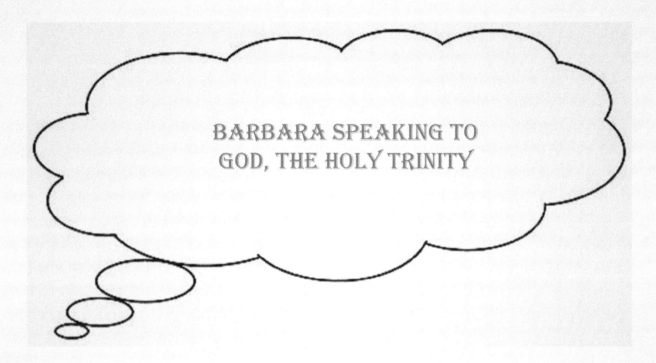

KEEP ME SAFE FROM THE WORLD, O LORD, AS I BATHE WITHIN THE ENJOYMENT OF YOUR HEAVEN SENT BLISS. KEEP ME *HIDDEN* FROM THE REALM THAT RELEASES ANXIETY AND FEAR, AS I ENJOY THE SPLENDOR THAT YOU RELEASE EVERY DAY. KEEP ME *HIDDEN* FROM THE REALM THAT INVITES THE SINFUL THINGS AND THOUGHTS THAT LEAD TO THE OUTER WORLD (HELL). KEEP ME *HIDDEN* FROM THOSE WHO DESIRE THE PLEASURES OF THIS PASSING WORLD. KEEP ME *HIDDEN* FROM THE WICKED THINGS THAT ARE VIEWED AS ACCEPTABLE, IN THE EYES AND LIVES OF THOSE WHO DO NOT ACKNOWLEDGE YOUR HOLY PRESENCE IN OUR BLESSED MIDST TODAY. *HIDE* YOUR FAITHFUL SERVANT AND BRIDE (BARBARA) FROM THIS WORLD, FOR THEY DO NOT ABIDE BY YOUR REALM OF HOLINESS. *HIDE* ME FROM THOSE WHO DO NOT DESIRE TO PLEASE YOU, MY LORD. *HIDE* ME FROM THOSE WHO DO NOT DESIRE TO SEE YOUR HOLY PRESENCE THROUGH YOUR HUMBLED SERVANT AND FRIEND (BARBARA). *HIDE* ME FROM THOSE WHO CANNOT SEE YOUR HOLY PRESENCE AS IT SHINES FROM BY OBEDIENT ESSENCE. *HIDE* ME, O LORD, FOR THEY DO NOT DESIRE TO SEE YOU THROUGH ME!

NOVEMBER 26, 2015 AT 8:35 PM BY: BARBARA ANN MARY MACK

SENT SAT, NOV 28, 2015 7:29 PM-READ SAT 11/28/2015 8:10 PM

GREETINGS DEAR ONE! FELICE RINGRAZIAMENTO -HAPPY THANKSGIVING
I AM PRESENTLY MOVING TO THE BEAT OF CHRISTMAS MUSIC AS I PEEL POTATOES FOR MY SALAD I AM ALSO MAKING MAC & CHEESE SO THAT I WILL HAVE ENOUGH FOOD FOR MY BROTHER DAVID. MY SISTER CISSY USUALLY COMES OVER FOR THE TURKEY STUFFING, EVEN THOUGH SHE DOESN'T CELEBRATE HOLIDAYS. I DO NOT WISH TO DISCUSS THE OUTCOME OF MY PECAN CAKE THAT I BAKED LATE LAST NIGHT, BUT IT DOES TASTE GOOD. FORTUNATELY, I AM THE ONLY ONE HERE WHO LIKES NUTS IN MY FOOD. THEREFORE, THE OUTWARD APPEARANCE OF THE CAKE DOESN'T MATTER AT ALL. ENJOY YOUR BLESSED DAY LOVE!!!
AMORE, BAKING, MOVING TO THE BEAT, BEAUTIFUL BARBIE
SENT SAT, NOV 28, 2015 7:29 PM-READ SAT 11/28/2015 8:10 PM

FELICE RINGRAZIAMENTO -HAPPY THANKSGIVING ARCHBISHOP CRAIG!
PRESENTLY, I AM MAKING A PECAN CAKE FOR THANKSGIVING DINNER AND BOILING EGGS FOR MY POTATO SALAD AND STUFFING. I AM TRYING TO COOK MY THINGS EARLY SO THAT LA TOYA AND AMYA CAN HAVE THE KITCHEN TO THEMSELVES WHEN THEY PREPARE THE TURKEY AND OTHER SIDE DISHES HOPEFULLY WE WILL HAVE EVERYTHING COMPLETED ON TIME THIS YEAR. LAST YEAR, OUR TURKEY WASN'T READY BECAUSE WE PREPARED AND BAKED IT LATER THAN USUAL. WE NEED TO DO A LITTLE SHOPPING FOR A FEW NECESSARY ITEMS (ONIONS, GREEN PEPPERS, CELERY, CHEESE ETC.) TO MAKE OUR MEAL COMPLETE. HOPEFULLY WE WILL FIND EVERYTHING THAT WE NEED. ARE YOU COOKING TOO? IF SO, I HOPE THAT EVERYTHING TURNS OUT THE WAY YOU LIKE IT. *AMORE, BAKING, BEAUTIFUL BARBIE (GOBBLE! GOBBLE!)*
SENT SAT, NOV 28, 2015 7:29 PM-READ SAT 11/28/2015 8:10 PM

OUR TABLE OF PLENTY

BARBARA SPEAKING

COME! O INVITED GUESTS (ALMIGHTY GOD AND CRAIG) OF MINE. SIT AT OUR TABLE OF PLENTY ON THIS BLESSED THANKSGIVING DAY. SIT AT THE TABLE OF PLENTY THAT IS PREPARED BY THE HANDS AND HEARTS OF ALMIGHTY GOD'S FAITHFUL DAUGHTERS (LA TOYA, AMYA AND BARBARA). SIT AT THE TABLE OF PLENTY THAT INVITES THE ONES (ALMIGHTY GOD AND CRAIG) WHO GIVE DIVINE PLEASURE AND SPIRITUAL BLISS TO BARBARA, GOD'S HEAVEN SENT MESSENGER AND BRIDE. COME, O INVITED GUESTS (ALMIGHTY GOD AND CRAIG), AND ENJOY THE MANY GOOD THINGS THAT OVERFLOW OUR TABLE OF PLENTY! COME, AND ENJOY THE PLENTIFUL BLESSINGS THAT COVER OUR BLESSED TABLE. FOR THE LORD GOD HAS SENT DOWN HIS BLESSINGS TO THE HOME OF HIS FAITHFUL DAUGHTERS AND FRIENDS. COME, MY LORD GOD! COME, O BELOVED ONE (CRAIG)! COME, AND ENJOY THE MANY GOOD THINGS THAT FLOW OVER OUR BLESSED TABLE OF PLENTY ON THIS VERY SPECIAL THANKSGIVING DAY! COME,

MY LORD! COME, O BELOVED ONE! TAKE YOUR SEATS AT OUR TABLE OF PLENTY, FOR WE (LA TOYA, AMYA AND BARBARA) TRULY DESIRE YOUR WELCOMED PRESENCE TODAY!!!
NOVEMBER 26, 2015 AT 3:46 PM BY: BARBARA ANN MARY MACK

I AM FREE! FREE! *FREE OF THE WORLD!*

BARBARA SPEAKING

I AM GRATEFUL, TRULY GRATEFUL, MY LORD, FOR I HAVE BEEN SET FREE FROM THE WORLD'S MANY REALMS OF TEMPTATIONS. FREE FROM THE REALM THAT RELEASES UNFAITHFULNESS. A REALM THAT RELEASES DISOBEDIENCE UNTO THE LORD'S HOLY WAY. A REALM THAT PROMOTES AND CONDONES ACTS OF UNGODLY WORKS. A REALM THAT CONDONES PREMARITAL SEX. A REALM THAT CONDONES SEXUAL PERVERSION AND DEVIATION. A REALM THAT CONDONES MURDER (ABORTION AND EUTHANASIA). A REALM THAT SEEKS THE GLORY OF MANKIND AND HIS LIMITATIONS, OVER ALMIGHTY GOD'S OMNIPOTENT EXISTENCE. I AM FREE FROM THE IMPURITIES THAT PERMEATE THE STREETS OF THOSE WHO WALK IN DARKNESS AND DESTRUCTION. I AM FREE OF THE ANXIETY THAT COMES FROM ONE WHO SEEKS THE RECOGNITION THAT MANKIND VIEWS AS SOMETHING NOTEWORTHY. I AM FREE OF THE WORLD'S DECEPTIVE VICES, WHICH LEAD TO ETERNAL DAMNATION AND DESTRUCTION. FREE! FREE! FREE FROM EVERYTHING THAT PREVENTS ONE FROM ENTERING GOD'S HOLY ETERNAL GATES TO SWEET PARADISE!
NOVEMBER 26, 2015 AT 6:59 PM BY: BARBARA ANN MARY MACK

CAUGHT UP IN A WHIRLWIND OF *HEAVENLY BLISS*

BARBARA SPEAKING

SURROUND ME, O REALM THAT WAS RELEASED FROM HEAVEN'S OPENED GATES! SURROUND ME, AS YOU REVEAL THE PRESENCE OF MY HOLY LORD AND GOD. RELEASE THE *DIVINE ECSTASY* THAT REVEALS HOLINESS IN MY MIDST. RELEASE THE HEAVEN SENT JOY THAT IS PROMISED TO GOD'S FAITHFUL SERVANTS AND FRIENDS. RELEASE THE DELIGHT THAT IGNITES THE BEING (BARBARA) OF THE *HAPPY ONE*. REVEAL THE HOLINESS THAT CAPTURES ME THROUGHOUT EACH BLESSED DAY. OH, THE JOY OF A *DIVINE WHIRLWIND* THAT SURROUNDS ME AS I BOW IN THE PRESENCE OF HE WHO FORMED ME NOT SO LONG AGO. LET ME FEEL THE *HEAVENLY ECSTASY* THAT ROAMS IN THE MIDST OF THE HEAVENLY ANGELS AND SAINTS! REJOICE! O SATISFIED SPIRIT OF MINE. REJOICE IN THE MIDST OF HE WHO IS GOOD AND HOLY! REJOICE! O BLESSED ESSENCE OF MINE. REJOICE THROUGHOUT ETERNITY!!!
NOVEMBER 26, 2015 AT 11:34 AM BY: BARBARA ANN MARY MACK
I SALUTE YOU, O LORD, ON THIS *THANKSGIVING MORNING*

BARBARA SPEAKING TO THE LORD GOD

I WILL GREET YOU ON THIS BLESSED THANKSGIVING DAY WITH MY HUMBLED HEAD LOWERED IN YOUR HOLY PRESENCE, MY LORD. MY FAMILY AND I GREETED YOU, AS WE SET AT OUR TABLE OF PLENTY IN YOUR HOLY AND FAITHFUL PRESENCE. MY FAMILY AND I OFFER OUR SINCERE GRATITUDE FOR OUR HOLY FAITHFUL GOD, AS WE BLESSED HIM IN THE PRESENCE OF OUR TABLE OF PLENTY. MY LORD, MY HOLY GOD, AS ALWAYS, YOU HAVE PROVIDED US WITH AN ABUNDANCE OF FOOD, ON THIS BLESSED THANKSGIVING MORNING, NOON, EVENING AND NIGHT. WE ARE TRULY GRATEFUL AND THANKFUL, O HOLY GOD. YOU HAVE PROVIDED MY FAMILY AND FRIENDS WITH THE COMFORT AND JOY THAT ACCOMPANY A BLESSED THANKSGIVING DAY. WE, YOUR FAITHFUL CHILDREN, ARE TRULY APPRECIATIVE. MY LORD, PLEASE ACCEPT THE GRATITUDE THAT YOUR CHILDREN EXHIBIT TOWARD YOU AND EACH OTHER, AS WE GIVE THANKS TO YOU, FOR YOUR HOLY PRESENCE AND GOOD THINGS TO EAT AND ENJOY. NOVEMBER 26, 2015 AT 7:30 PM BY: BARBARA ANN MARY MACK

FELICE RINGRAZIAMENTO CRAIG PADRE!
SENT SAT, NOV 28, 2015 7:29 PM-READ SAT 11/28/2015 8:10 PM

GREETINGS ARCHBISHOP CRAIG! FELICE RINGRAZIAMENTO! I PRAY THAT YOU AND YOUR LOVED ONES HAD A VERY BLESSED THANKSGIVING DAY CELEBRATION. WE (LA TOYA, AMYA AND ME) REALLY ENJOYED OUR DAY OF CELEBRATION AND THANKSGIVING TO OUR LORD GOD. AS ALWAYS, I SET A PLACE AT THE TABLE FOR THE LORD. EACH YEAR I MAKE SURE THAT HE HAS HIS OWN PLACE SETTING AT OUR TABLE. I USUALLY PUT FRUITS AND NUTS ON A PLATE, A GOBLET AND UTENSILS ON A NAPKIN. THE PLACE SETTING FOR THE LORD IS THERE THROUGHOUT OUR CELEBRATION SEASON, WHICH INCLUDES CHRISTMAS TIME. IT IS AN HONOR TO HAVE THE LORD WITH US DURING OUR DAYS OF THANKSGIVING. I CAN FEEL HIS HOLY PRESENCE IN OUR MIDST AT ALL TIMES. I CAN ALSO FEEL YOUR BLESSED AND HOLY PRESENCE, O BELOVED ONE. ENJOY THE REST OF THIS PERIOD OF GIVING THANKS TO OUR HOLY LORD, FOR HE IS WORTHY OF OUR THANKSGIVING. LA TOYA DID A SUPERB JOB ON OUR TURKEY! IT WAS DELICIOUS! I WAS UP UNTIL A LITTLE AFTER 3 AM WORKING ON MY BOOK. I SPENT MOST OF THANKSGIVING DAY WRITING DOWN NEW MESSAGES FROM THE LORD AND EDITING MY FORTHCOMING BOOK. WHILE DOING THIS, MIND KEPT FOCUSING ON THE TURKEY AND STUFFING IN THE FRIG. I FINALLY SETTLED FOR SOME PRETZELS AND WATER. I CANNOT WAIT TO HAVE ANOTHER HELPING WHEN WE RETURN FROM THE STORES. WE WANT TO CATCH A FEW BLACK FRIDAY SALES. WE NEED BOOTS AND OTHER THINGS FOR THE FAMILY. ANNETTE AND BOB ZAMBRANO SENT US A BASKET OF FRUIT FOR THANKSGIVING. IT ARRIVED A FEW MINUTES BEFORE ANNETTE CALLED TODAY. PERFECT TIMING! I CAN PUT SOME OF THE FRUIT ON THE LORD'S PLATE. WE WILL EAT THE FRUIT BEFORE IT GOES BAD THIS TIME. MY SISTER

CALLED AROUND NOON, AND WANTED TO STOP BY ON THANKSGIVING DAY. I WAS STILL IN BED, BECAUSE I WAS UP UNTIL 4 AM EDITING MY BOOK. AS A MESSENGER OF THE LORD, MY PRIMARY FUNCTION IS TO DO HIS WILL AT HIS TIME, NOT MY TIME. OVER THE RECENT YEARS, THE LORD HAS ME WORKING ON HOLIDAYS ALSO. I CANNOT TAKE MY FOCUS OFF OF MY DIVINE ORDERED WORK. ENJOY THE REST OF YOUR DAY LOVE! *AMORE, BELLA BARBIE*

SENT SAT, NOV 28, 2015 7:29 PM-READ SAT 11/28/2015 8:10 PM

LIFE BEYOND *PHYSICAL DEATH*

BARBARA SPEAKING

LOOKING FORWARD TO LIFE BEYOND PHYSICAL DEATH.
A LIFE THAT WAS PROMISED SINCE MY BIRTH.
A LIFE WITH MY HEAVENLY FATHER, MY CREATOR OF DIVINE LOVE-
A LIFE THAT ORIGINATED FROM HEAVEN ABOVE.
A LIFE THAT IS FREE OF PAIN AND SIN-
A LIFE WITH GOD, THE FATHER, AND HIS FAITHFUL CHILDREN.
A LIFE THAT IS ETERNAL AND GRAND-
A LIFE THAT WAS CREATED BY OUR LIVING GOD'S HOLY HAND.
COME! O BLESSED BROTHERS AND SISTERS OF MINE,
AS SHARE THE LIFE WITH OUR SAVING GOD, THROUGHOUT THE REALM OF TIME.
FOR IT IS A LIFE THAT IS HOLY AND TRUE.
IT IS A LIFE THAT IS PROMISED TO GOD'S FAITHFUL FEW.
I LOOK FORWARD TO THAT LIFE OF PROMISED HEAVENLY BLISS;
I LOOK FORWARD TO THE GIFT OF GOD'S HOLY KISS!
NOVEMBER 22, 2015 AT 5:13 PM BY: BARBARA ANN MARY MACK
SENT TUE, NOV 24, 2015 5:41 PM-READ TUE 11/24/2015 6:23 PM

GREETINGS ARCHBISHOP CRAIG! COME STA OGGI AMORE? I PRAY THAT ALL IS WELL WITH YOU AND YOUR LOVED ONES. CAN YOU GIVE LA TOYA A SPECIAL BIRTHDAY BLESSING TODAY, FOR IT IS HER BIRTHDAY TODAY (NOVEMBER 21ST)? SHE HAS TRULY BEEN A GIFT AND HEAVEN SENT BLESSING OVER THE PAST...YEARS. I AM TRULY HONORED TO BE HER BEAUTIFUL MOTHER. WE HAVE BEEN CELEBRATING HER BIRTHDAY SINCE THURSDAY. WE STARTED THE CELEBRATION BY EATING HER BIRTHDAY CAKE, WHICH WE SHOULD NOT HAVE PURCHASED A WEEK BEFORE. I HAVE SOME OF MY SHARE, WHICH I KNOW THAT LA TOYA OR AMYA WILL END UP WITH, BECAUSE ACCORDING TO THEM, I AM TAKING TOO LONG TO EAT IT. WE WILL SEE WHO GETS TO EAT THE LAST OF TOYA'S BDAY CAKE. ENJOY THE REST OF YOUR WEEKEND! I WILL RESUME THE EDITING AND PROOF READING OF MY MANUSCRIPT.
CIAO! BELLA BARBIE

GREETINGS DEAR ONE! I AM PRESENTLY PREPARING THE STUFFING FOR OUR TURKEY. SINCE I ALWAYS MAKE MY STUFFING FROM SCRATCH, IT SAVES TIME WHEN I COOK SOME OF THE INGREDIENTS A COUPLE OF DAYS BEFORE THANKSGIVING. I ALSO COOKED MY TURNIP GREENS (NOT FROM SCRATCH) EARLIER TODAY WHILE WORKING ON MY FORTHCOMING BOOK. THIS BOOK CONSISTS OF SOME OF THE EPISTLES (LETTERS) THAT WERE SENT VIA EMAILS TO A FEW RECIPIENTS OF GOD'S HOLY MESSAGES. AT THIS TIME, I WAS ABLE TO GET THE PAGE COUNT DOWN TO 576. I WILL TRY TO DECREASE THE COUNT A BIT MORE WITHOUT TAKING AWAY SIGNIFICANT MESSAGES. ENJOY YOUR DAY LOVE!
LOVE ALWAYS!!!!!
SENT TUE, NOV 24, 2015 5:41 PM-READ TUE 11/24/2015 6:23 PM

HI ARCHBISHOP CRAIG! TOYA MENTIONED THIS EVENING THAT SHE MISSES YOUR CELEBRATION OF THE HOLY EUCHARIST. HOPEFULLY WE WILL BE ABLE TO ATTEND IT SOON. I PRAY THAT YOU ARE ENJOYING YOUR GOD BLESSED DAY DEAR ONE. *AMORE*
SENT TUE, NOV 24, 2015 5:41 PM-READ TUE 11/24/2015 6:23 PM

HAPPY SABBATH ARCHBISHOP CRAIG! I PRAY THAT YOU HAVE A VERY GOOD AND BLESSED DAY. LA TOYA, AMYA AND I, ARE ABOUT TO WATCH SOME OF YOUR YOUTUBE SERMONS. WE ATTENDED ST. BARNABAS OVER THE PAST FEW WEEKS, BUT AS BEFORE, THERE WERE INTERRUPTIONS (PEOPLE TALKING AND SHOWING DISRESPECT DURING MASS) WHICH REMINDED US WHY WE NO LONGER DESIRE TO ATTEND MASS THERE. THIS HAS BEEN GOING ON FOR SOME TIME NOW. LA TOYA AND I USUALLY ASK THE INDIVIDUALS NOT TO TALK DURING MASS BECAUSE WE CANNOT HEAR WHAT THE PRIEST AND READERS ARE SAYING. THIS USUALLY CAUSES NEGATIVE FEEDBACK FROM THE DISRESPECTING ONES. IT SEEMS THAT WHEN THERE ARE MANY PEOPLE THAT ENTER THE CHURCH BUILDINGS, THE CHANCE OF INTERRUPTIONS WITHIN THE CONGREGATION IS LIKELY TO OCCUR. I DO NOT UNDERSTAND HOW SOME PEOPLE CAN LEAVE THEIR HOMES TO GO TO A PLACE WHERE THEY DO NOT DESIRE TO BE. IF YOU WANT TO CONVERSE WITH YOUR FAMILIES OR FRIENDS, IT SEEMS THAT A PLACE OTHER THAN THE CHURCH SHOULD BE ONE'S CHOICE. I HAVEN'T ATTENDED ST. BARNABAS SINCE EASTER TIME THIS YEAR, AND I ATTENDED THE SERVICE BECAUSE THE LORD SENT ME THERE TO DELIVER A MESSAGE TO ONE OF THE CONGREGATION. AS I OBSERVE THE ATTENDANTS DURING MASS, IT SEEMS THAT THEY ARE NOT PAYING ATTENTION TO WHAT THE CELEBRANT IS CONVEYING. IT APPEARS THAT THEIR THOUGHTS ARE FOCUSED ON SOMETHING OTHER THAN THE READINGS AND HOMILIES. THIS IS AWFUL, BECAUSE LA TOYA LOVES TAKING AMYA TO CHURCH. PERHAPS I WILL SPEAK TO OUR PASTOR ABOUT THIS MATTER. HE IS FAIRLY NEW TO THE CONGREGATION, THEREFORE, I WILL SEE WHAT THE

LORD WANTS IN REGARDS TO APPROACHING AND ADDRESSING THIS MATTER. MEANWHILE, WE WILL WATCH YOUR SERMONS AT HOME.

GOD BLESS! BELLA BARBARA

GREETINGS DEAR ARCHBISHOP CRAIG! I PRAY THAT YOUR DAY HAS BEEN A VERY GOOD ONE. I HAVE BEEN WORKING ON MY MANUSCRIPT, PREPARING IT FOR PUBLICATION. I HAVE BEEN UP TO THE EARLY MORNING HOURS WORKING ON THIS BOOK OVER THE PAST WEEKS. AS WITH MY OTHER GOD DICTATED BOOKS, THIS BOOK HAS A GOD APPOINTED DATE FOR COMPLETION. SO FAR I HAVE MANAGED TO DECREASE THE PAGE NUMBER WITHOUT REMOVING ANY OF THE SIGNIFICANT PASSAGES AND SAYINGS OF THE LORD. THIS IS THE MOST TIME CONSUMING PART OF PREPARING A BOOK FOR PUBLICATION. I SPOKE WITH MY BOOK CONSULTANT AN HOUR AGO. WE DISCUSSED WHICH PUBLICATION PACKAGE THAT I DECIDED ON AND ITS COST, WHICH WAS HALF PRICE UNTIL NOVEMBER 13TH. HE AND I SPOKE ON FRIDAY THE 13TH, WHICH AT THAT TIME HE LOCKED IN THE HALF OFF PRICE FOR ME. ALTHOUGH MY MANUSCRIPT ISN'T READY FOR PUBLICATION AT THIS TIME, AUTHORS ARE PERMITTED TO MAKE THE ARRANGEMENTS BEFORE SUBMITTING THE COMPLETED MANUSCRIPT. I HAVE TO MAKE THE IMAGE ARRANGEMENTS AND GET THE CONSENT FORMS FOR THOSE WHOSE PICTURES WILL BE INCLUDED IN THIS BOOK. I HAVE ALREADY SPOKEN WITH THE INDIVIDUALS. WE HAVE TO MEET AND LA TOYA WILL TAKE THE PHOTOS. ALTHOUGH WE (AUTHORS) ARE ALLOWED 40 IMAGE INSERTIONS WITHOUT A FEE, I DO NOT PLAN ON INCLUDING MANY IMAGES IN THIS VOLUME. I DO NOT WANT TO DISTRACT THE MESSAGES OF THE LORD WITH TOO MANY IMAGES. WE WILL SEE WHERE THE LORD LEADS ME ON THIS PROJECT FOR HIM. **AMORE, BELLA BARBARA** SENT MON, NOV 16, 2015 6:59 PM-READ MON 11/16/2015 8:37 PM

WHO ELSE WEEPS FOR YOU LIKE I DO, *SAYS THE LORD GOD?*

ALMIGHTY GOD SPEAKING

UNENDING RIVERS OF TEARS FLOW FROM MY ESSENCE DAILY, AS I WITNESS THE PAIN AND SUFFERING THAT ARE INFLICTED UPON MY CHILDREN OF ALL AGES. UNENDING MOUNTAINS THAT UNITE WITH MY FLOWING TEARS, PROTECT AND SHELTER THE TEARS OF YOUR MOURNING CREATOR AND GOD. FLOW! TEARS, FLOW! UNITE WITH THE PAIN OF MY CHILDREN AS THEIR SPIRITS EXIT THEIR ABUSED BODIES. UNITE WITH THE PAIN THAT ENCOMPASSES THE SOULS OF MY MURDERED AND WOUNDED CHILDREN OF ALL AGES. LET ME WEEP, AS I WITNESS THE ACTS OF EVIL THAT DESCEND UPON MY VULNERABLE CHILDREN. LET ME WEEP, FOR I AM IN MUCH PAIN TOO. LET ME WEEP AS I GATHER THE SOULS OF MY MURDERED CHILDREN UNDER MY ETERNAL WINGS OF LOVE. LET ME WEEP AS I COMFORT THE SOULS THAT HAVE RETURNED TO ME AFTER ONLY A SHORT ENJOYMENT OF PHYSICAL LIFE. LET ME WEEP! LET ME WEEP! LET ME WEEP IN THE PRESENCE OF THE MURDERED ONES, FOR MY HOLY TEARS HAVE UNITED WITH THEIRS.

NOVEMBER 12, 2015 AT 4:39 PM BY: BARBARA ANN MARY MACK

SENT SUN, NOV 15, 2015 5:29 PM-READ MON 11/16/2015 12:04 AM

HOW LONG WILL I HAVE TO CRY FOR THEM, *SAYS THE LORD?*

HOW LONG? HOW LONG? HOW LONG WILL I HAVE TO WEEP FOR THOSE WHOSE LIVES WERE TAKEN BY THE HAND OF THE ENEMY (SATAN)? ALTHOUGH HE COMES IN MANY DIFFERENT FORMS, HIS DESTRUCTION AND END RESULTS ARE THE SAME. HE HAS SHORTENED THE LIVES OF MANY INNOCENT LITTLE ONES, FOR HE DOESN'T DISCRIMINATE. HE DOESN'T SHOW MERCY AT ALL! HE DOESN'T EXHIBIT KINDNESS AT ALL! HE DOESN'T DEMONSTRATE THE ACTS OF A LOVING ENTITY, BECAUSE THERE IS NO LOVE WITHIN HIS REALM OF EVIL AND DESTRUCTION. HE IS DARKNESS IN EVERY FORM. THERE IS NO LIGHT OR HOPE WITHIN HIM, FOR HE IS NOTHING! I WILL WEEP FOR MY INNOCENT LITTLE ONES, UNTIL THE GATES THAT BECKON SATAN AND HIS DOOMED REALM OF EVIL, CLAIM THEM FOREVER.

NOVEMBER 12, 2015 AT 5:11 PM BY: BARBARA ANN MARY MACK

SENT SUN, NOV 15, 2015 5:29 PM-READ MON 11/16/2015 12:04 AM

GREETINGS DEAR ONE! I PRAY THAT YOUR DAY WENT VERY WELL. LA TOYA AND I HAD A VERY BUSY DAY. WE DID EVERYTHING THAT THE LORD NEEDED US TO DO TODAY. I WAS ABLE TO MEET WITH A WOMAN NAMED BARBARA, WHOM LA TOYA AND I HAD MET WHILE SHOPPING AT STAPLES. ALTHOUGH I DID NOT NEED TO PURCHASE ANYTHING FROM STAPLES TODAY, THE LORD INSTRUCTED ME TO GO THERE, SO THAT I MAY SHARE HIS HOLY WORDS WITH HER BEFORE SHE GOT OFF WORK. AS IN THE PAST, BARBARA WAS VERY EAGER TO HEAR WHAT THE LORD CONVEYED TO HER THROUGH ME. SHE REQUESTED MY INFORMATION SO THAT SHE COULD GET IN TOUCH WITH ME IN THE FUTURE. SHE TOLD US THAT SHE IS CATHOLIC ALSO. PLEASE KEEP HER IN YOUR PRAYERS, FOR SHE WAS VERY EXCITED TO KNOW THAT THE LORD SENDS PEOPLE TO REPRESENT HIM TODAY. SHE ALSO LOOKED THROUGH SEVERAL OF MY GOD DICTATED BOOKS. SHE WAS INTERESTED IN MY BOOKS" ODE TO MY BELOVED" AND "WILL YOU BE MY BRIDE FIRST?" AFTERWARDS, WE COMPLETED OUR FOOD SHOPPING LIST. I WAS ABLE TO FIND SOME OF MY THANKSGIVING DAY FOOD ITEMS. I AM ABOUT TO HAVE MY MEAL FOR THE DAY NOW. I AM READY FOR IT! ENJOY YOUR PRECIOUS NIGHT, O BELOVED ONE! *AMORE, BEAUTIFUL BARBARA*

THE WORLD CANNOT PROTECT OR SHIELD YOU FROM THE REALM OF EVIL, *SAYS THE LORD*

ALMIGHTY GOD SPEAKING

MY CHILDREN, THE WORLD CANNOT PROTECT OR SHIELD YOU FROM THE REALM OF EVIL, FOR IT IS INVISIBLE TO THE WORLD, BUT TANGIBLE TO ME. MY CHILDREN, YOU SEEK ANSWERS AND REMEDIES FROM THE WORLD, BUT YOU DO NOT COME TO ME. NO, NOT EVEN THOSE OF THE CLERGY. YOU SEEK REFUGE AND GUIDANCE FROM THE AUTHORITY OF THE WORLD, INSTEAD OF COMING TO ME WITH UNWAVERING TRUST. WHY, MY CHILDREN? THE WORLD CANNOT COMBAT THE REALM (SATAN) THAT IS INVISIBLE TO IT. THE WORLD CANNOT DEFEAT THAT WHICH IT CANNOT SEE NOR UNDERSTAND. THE WORLD CANNOT REMEDY THE HAVOC THAT

ROAMS IN THE MIDST OF EARTH'S RESIDENTS IN A FIERCE AND DESTRUCTIVE MANNER. THE WORLD CANNOT PERFORM THE WORKS OF THE ONLY ALMIGHTY AND OMNIPOTENT CREATOR AND GOD. THE LEADERS OF THE WORLD ARE BAFFLED! THE LEADERS OF THE WORLD ARE HELPLESS! THE LEADERS OF THE WORLD ARE LOOKING FOR REMEDIES THAT CANNOT FOOL NOR CAPTURE THE REALM (SATAN) THAT PRODUCES AND RELEASES UNSPEAKABLE ACTS AGAINST THE INNOCENT AND HELPLESS ONES. MY CHILDREN, O CLERGY, COME TO ME WHEN SATAN RELEASES THE ACTS THAT YOU CANNOT GIVE AN EXPLANATION FOR. COME TO ME WHEN YOU FEEL THAT YOUR WORK FOR THOSE WHOM YOU LOVE IS IN VAIN. COME TO ME WHEN THE REALM (SATAN) WHICH CANNOT BE SEEN AND TOUCHED BY HUMANITY, OVERPOWERS YOUR WEAK AND VULNERABLE SOULS. COME TO ME, MY CHILDREN, FOR I AM YOUR "ONLY UNDEFEATED REALM OF PROTECTION", IN THE MIDST OF THIS UNBELIEVABLE PERIOD OF TIME.
NOVEMBER 11, 2015 AT 12:41 AM BY: BARBARA ANN MARY MACK

THEY THINK THAT THEY KNOW ME, *SAYS THE LORD*

ALMIGHTY GOD SPEAKING

THEY, THE SO CALLED SCHOLARS AND LEARNED ONES, THINK THAT THEY KNOW ME. BUT HOW CAN THEY KNOW ME? FOR THEY POSSESS LIMITED, LIMITED, LIMITED REALMS OF UNDERSTANDING, THOUGHTS, AND WORLDLY KNOWLEDGE. THEY FORM THOUGHTS AND BELIEFS WHICH DECEIVE THEMSELVES AND THOSE WHO BELIEVE IN THEIR LIMITED THOUGHTS AND CONCLUSIONS. YOU DO NOT KNOW ME, O FOOLISH ONES, FOR I HAVE NOT REVEALED MYSELF TO YOU. YOU FORM BOOKS AND WRITINGS THAT COME FROM YOUR OWN IMAGINATION. YOU FOLLOW YOUR OWN ERROR OF THOUGHT INSTEAD OF ASKING ME, THE ONLY REVEALER OF MY HOLY TRUTH. YOU WHO DESIRE WORLDLY RECOGNITION AND FAME, DO NOT DESIRE MY TRUTH. YOU DESIRE THE REALM THAT ELEVATES THE LOWLY MINDED ONES. YOU DESIRE THE REALM THAT SEEKS AND DESIRES THE GLORY THAT COMES FROM LIMITED MANKIND, INSTEAD OF THE ETERNAL RECOGNITION AND GLORY THAT COME FROM ME ALONE. BE VERY CAREFUL WITH WHAT YOU WRITE OR SAY OF ME, O WORLDLY FAME AND GLORY SEEKERS! BE VERY CAREFUL, FOR YOU DO NOT KNOW WHAT YOU ARE SAYING OR THINKING. YOU DO NOT KNOW MY REALM OF ETERNAL HOLINESS. YOU DO NOT KNOW ME!
NOVEMBER 9, 2015 AT 2:51 AM BY: BARBARA ANN MARY MACK
SENT MON, NOV 9, 2015 5:54 PM-READ MON 11/9/2015 10:04 PM

STAY AWAY FROM ME, O WORLD, FOR I DO NOT WANT TO BE A PART OF YOU

BARBARA SPEAKING

STAY AWAY FROM ME O WORLD, FOR I DO NOT WANT TO BE A PART OF YOU. STAY AWAY FROM ME O WORLD, FOR I DO NOT WANT TO SEE YOU. GO AWAY, O WORLD, FOR WITHIN YOU LIES MUCH GRIEF, SORROW, DESTRUCTION, APATHY, AND HEARTACHE. GO AWAY, O WORLD, FOR YOU CANNOT CAPTURE ME! GO AWAY, O WORLD, FOR THE LORD, MY OMNIPOTENT CREATOR AND GOD, HAS CLAIMED ME AS HIS OWN. GO AWAY, O WORLD, FOR THE GATES TO HEAVEN HAVE OPENED WIDE, SO THAT MY OBEDIENT ETERNAL SOUL MAY ENTER WITH GLADNESS. GO AWAY, O WORLD, FOR YOU CANNOT TEMPT ME WITH YOUR TEMPORARY PLEASURES. YOU CANNOT LURE MY WEAK SOUL INTO YOUR DECEITFUL WEB OF LIES AND FALSE HOPE. YOU CANNOT QUENCH MY SPIRITUAL THIRST, FOR YOU ARE NOTHING! GO AWAY, O WORLD, AND ENTER THE GATES THAT LEAD TO YOUR ETERNAL DESTINATION (HELL)! STAY AWAY FROM ME, O WORLD, FOR MY LOVE BELONGS TO MY SAVING LORD AND GOD!!!
NOVEMBER 8, 2015 AT 6:51 PM BY: BARBARA ANN MARY MACK

OH MY LORD, SUCH A HEAVY, HEAVY CROSS TO BEAR

BARBARA SPEAKING TO THE LORD JESUS

OH MY LORD! OH SUCH A HEAVY, HEAVY CROSS TO BEAR. IN THE MIDST OF DIVINE LOVE, I BEAR MY GOD GIVEN CROSS. IN THE MIDST OF DIVINE MERCY, I BEAR MY HEAVY CROSS. IN THE PRESENCE OF GOD, MY HOLY ETERNAL SPOUSE, I BEAR MY HEAVY CROSS. MY LORD, MY SACRED SPOUSE AND REDEEMER, I BEAR MY HEAVY CROSS, AS YOU BORE YOURS. STRENGTHEN ME, O HOLY SAVIOR, SO THAT I MAY HOLD ON TO MY DIVINE PURPOSE AND

ASSIGNMENT OF LOVE. FOR THE CROSS THAT I BEAR IS VERY, VERY HEAVY. WEEP WITH ME, LORD JESUS, AS I BEAR MY HEAVY CROSS. WEEP WITH ME, MY SAVING GOD, AS I BEAR MY HOLY CROSS. CARRY MY BROKEN ESSENCE ON YOUR STRONG SHOULDERS OF DIVINE MERCY, AS I BEAR MY HEAVY CROSS. MY LORD, MY HOLY GOD, MY SPIRITUAL PAIN OUTWEIGHS MY PHYSICAL AFFLICTIONS. MY DIVINE ASSIGNMENT THAT DESCENDED FROM ABOVE IS VERY, VERY HEAVY, MY GOD. YOU, O LORD, KNOW THE DEPTH OF MY SPIRITUAL PAIN. FOR YOU, MY GOD, ARE EXPERIENCING, AND HAVE EXPERIENCED GREATER SUFFERINGS THAN MINE. I AM TRULY GRATEFUL THAT YOU HAVE FORMED ME FROM YOUR REALM OF WORTHY ONES. I AM TRULY GRATEFUL, THAT YOU HAVE FORMED ME FOR MY HOLY ASSIGNMENT OF LOVE. I AM TRULY GRATEFUL TO EXPERIENCE THE DEPTH OF YOUR UNENDING LOVE FOR YOUR GREAT CREATION (HUMAN BEINGS). MY LORD, THE AGONY THAT ACCOMPANIES DIVINE ASSIGNMENTS HAS TAKEN ME TO A LEVEL THAT I CANNOT BEAR ALONE. I AM GRATEFUL FOR YOUR HOLY PRESENCE, AS I WALK THROUGH THIS ASSIGNMENT THAT DESCENDED WITH ME. MY LORD, MY HOLY GOD, THE CROSS THAT YOU HAVE FORMED ME FOR IS VERY, VERY HEAVY. LET US WEEP AS ONE ESSENCE, MY GOD, AS I COMPLETE MY DIVINE ASSIGNMENT OF LOVE IN THE PRESENCE OF THOSE WHOM YOU HAVE FOUND WORTHY TO WITNESS AND PARTAKE IN.
NOVEMBER 8, 2015 AT 12:57 AM BY: BARBARA ANN MARY MACK

DO NOT THINK OF ME

BARBARA SPEAKING TO THE ETERNAL BELOVED ONE

I DO NOT WANT YOU TO THINK OF ME WHILE YOU ARE IN A REALM THAT DISPLEASES OUR GREAT AND HOLY GOD, FOR WE ARE ONE. DO NOT THINK OF ME, AS YOU TRAVEL IN THE COMPANY OF THOSE WHO DO NOT ACCEPT ME (ALMIGHTY GOD AND BARBARA), FOR WE ARE ONE, *SAYS THE LORD.* THE GATES THAT LEAD TO PURE AND HOLY BLISS AWAIT YOU, O ETERNAL BELOVED ONE. THE GATES THAT LEAD TO DIVINE PROMISES AND ECSTASY, CAUSE ME TO FEAR THE APPROACHING FUTURE. DO YOU NOT FEAR IT TOO, O BRAVE ONE? DO YOU NOT EXPERIENCE THE DEPTH OF PHYSICAL APPREHENSION AS I DO, O COURAGEOUS ONE? TRY NOT TO THINK OF ME, FOR OUR THOUGHTS WILL DRAW US IN THE DIRECTION OF OUR APPROACHING FUTURE. A FUTURE THAT TRANSCENDS REALISTIC PHYSICAL LOVE. A FUTURE WHICH SEPARATES US FROM THE REALM WHICH WE NOW DWELL WITHIN. A FUTURE THAT IS ENCOMPASSED BY THE REALM THAT PRODUCES HOLY UNIONS. A FUTURE THAT GOES BEYOND THE HUMAN IMAGINATION. A FUTURE THAT WAS DESIGNED FOR THE CHOSEN ONES. A FUTURE THAT TRANSCENDS!!!
NOVEMBER 8, 2015 AT 1:34 AM BY: BARBARA ANN MARY MACK
SENT SUN, NOV 8, 2015 4:43 PM-READ SUN 11/8/2015 10:04 PM

ENJOY LIFE, DEAR ARCHBISHOP CRAIG! TO ALL OF MY FACEBOOK FRIENDS, ENJOY THE SUNNY DAYS WITHIN YOU, EVEN IN THE MIDST OF THE STORMS AND HEAVY RAIN. MY BROTHERS AND SISTERS, ENJOY LIFE THROUGHOUT EACH BLESSED DAY. *ALLELUIA!*

LIFE: WHAT DOES IT MEAN TO YOU?

MY CHILDREN, DO YOU NOT KNOW HOW VALUABLE AND PRECIOUS YOUR LIVES ARE? DO YOU NOT KNOW OF THE DIVINE LOVE AND COMPASSION THAT WERE INCLUDED IN THE FORMATION OF MY GREAT CREATION (HUMAN BEINGS)? DO YOU NOT UNDERSTAND THE DEPTH OF MY HOLY LOVE THAT FLOWS THROUGH YOUR ESSENCE? DO YOU NOT APPRECIATE THE GIFT OF LIFE THAT I HAVE BLESSED YOU WITH? MY CHILDREN, MY HOLY CREATION, UNDERSTAND THE VALUE OF YOUR LIVES, FOR THEY WERE CREATED BY YOUR LOVING FATHER AND HOLY GOD. MY CHILDREN, EXHIBIT YOUR WORTH, FOR YOU CAME FROM ME! EXHIBIT THE REALITY OF DIVINE CREATION, FOR YOU CAME FROM ME. EXHIBIT THE DEPTH OF AN OFFSPRING OF THE HOLY ETERNAL ONE, FOR I DO EXIST! MY CHILDREN, APPRECIATE LIFE, FOR IT IS HOLY AND GOOD. APPRECIATE LIFE, FOR IT CAME FROM ME, THE ONLY PERFECT ONE. APPRECIATE THE VALUE OF YOUR LIFE, FOR YOU ARE UNIQUE AND VERY SPECIAL. APPRECIATE THE HOLY LOVE THAT FLOWS THROUGH YOUR PRECIOUS LIFE. APPRECIATE THE DEPTH OF YOUR HEAVENLY FATHER'S LOVE FOR YOUR LIFE. APPRECIATE THE GIFT OF LIFE, WHICH HAS NO MONETARY OR PHYSICAL VALUE, FOR LIFE TRANSCENDS ALL FORMS OF EARTHLY TREASURES OR RICHES. MY CHILDREN, UNDERSTAND THAT WHICH CAME FROM ME. MY CHILDREN, UNDERSTAND LIFE. NOVEMBER 6, 2015 AT 5:01 PM BY: BARBARA ANN MARY MACK

I WILL NOT BE DEFEATED, *SAYS THE LORD*

ALMIGHTY GOD SPEAKING

YOU WHO CONFORM TO, CONDONE, AND ACCEPT THE WAYS THAT GO AGAINST MY HOLY WAY, WILL SUFFER THE CONSEQUENCES OF DISOBEDIENCE, *SAYS THE LORD*. UNDERSTAND THE DEPTH AND MEANING OF GOING AGAINST MY HOLY WORD AND WAY, *SAYS THE LORD*. UNDERSTAND THE RESULTS! YES! THE INEVITABLE RESULTS, OF DISOBEYING MY HOLY UNCHANGING WAY AND WORD. I WILL NOT BE DEFEATED, NOR MOCKED BY THOSE WHO DISOBEY MY HOLY WAY. YOU WILL SUFFER THE CONSEQUENCE, O DISOBEDIENT AND ARROGANT ONES. YOUR DESTINATION IS ETERNAL DOOM AND DESTRUCTION WITH SATAN, THE FATHER OF DISOBEDIENCE AND DEFIANCE. UNDERSTAND MY FINAL WARNING, O ARROGANT AND DISOBEDIENT ONES! UNDERSTAND THE SERIOUSNESS OF MY FINAL WORD ON THIS MATTER, FOR IT IS WRITTEN IN THE HOLY BIBLE. MY HOLY WORD AND WAY HAVEN'T CHANGED, AND I SEE THAT YOU HAVEN'T CHANGED EITHER. YOU DID NOT FORM CREATION, O DEFIANT ONES! YOU DID NOT CREATE LIFE, O FOOLISH ONES! YOU DID NOT FORM THE HEAVENS AND EARTH, AND ALL THAT DWELL WITHIN THEM, O LOWLY AND CONFUSED ONES. SINCE YOU HAVE NO SAY IN THE MATTER, YOU MUST CONFORM TO MY HOLY WAY, WHICH IS THE ONLY WAY, OR BE PREPARED TO SUFFER THE ETERNAL CONSEQUENCES. REMEMBER THIS, O DISOBEDIENT ONES, I HAVEN'T NOR WILL I EVER CHANGE! THIS IS MY HOLY WORD! EITHER YOU ARE WITH ME, OR YOU ARE WITH SATAN, YOUR ORIGIN, THERE IS NO MIDDLE GROUND!

BARBARA SPEAKING TO ALMIGHTY GOD

MY LORD, MY MERCIFUL AND HOLY GOD. I PRAISE YOU CONTINUOUSLY FOR YOUR EXPRESSION OF PATIENCE AND DIVINE LOVE TOWARD THE DISOBEDIENT ONES. YOU ARE GRACIOUS, KIND AND LONG SUFFERING. YOU HAVE WATCHED YOUR CHILDREN PERFORM UNHOLY AND UNSPEAKABLE ACTS, WHICH CAUSED YOU TO TURN YOUR HOLY ESSENCE AWAY FROM THE SIGHTS. BECAUSE OF YOUR GENEROUS HEART, YOU HAVE GIVEN MANKIND AMPLE TIME TO RECTIFY OUR EVIL WAYS. YOU HAVE GIVEN US AMPLE TIME TO CONFORM TO YOUR HOLY UNCHANGING WAY. I BLESS YOU, O KING OF HEAVEN, FOR YOU HAVE TOLERATED MANKIND'S IMPURITIES AND DISOBEDIENCE FOR SUCH A LONG TIME. THROUGH THE GENERATIONS, YOU HAVE WEPT THE TEARS OF ONE WHO HAS BEEN BETRAYED AND ABUSED BY A LOVED ONE. THROUGH THE GENERATIONS, YOU HAVE SHOWN DIVINE PITY FOR THOSE WHO HAVE OPENLY ABUSED YOUR HOLY WORDS. OH HOW LOVING AND MERCIFUL YOU ARE, DEAR GOD. OH HOW COMPASSIONATE AND KIND YOU ARE. WE DO NOT DESERVE YOUR LONG SUFFERING AND KINDNESS, FOR SOME OF US REFUSE TO HONOR AND ACKNOWLEDGE YOUR GREATNESS AND HOLINESS. MY LORD, IN YOUR HOLY WORD, YOU SPEAK OF YOUR CHOSEN FEW. IN YOUR HOLY WORD, YOU SPEAK OF THOSE WHO WILL NOT BETRAY YOU. IN YOUR HOLY WORD, YOU SPEAK OF

THE RIGHTEOUS ONES. MY LORD, MY HOLY GOD, PLEASE COUNT ME AMONG YOUR CHOSEN FEW, FOR I DESIRE TO PLEASE AND SERVE ONLY YOU, MY VICTORIOUS GOD AND KING. *ALLELUIA!!!*

NOVEMBER 4, 2015 AT 12:11 PM BY: BARBARA ANN MARY MACK

SENT WED, NOV 4, 2015 1:13 PM-READ THU 11/5/2015 6:48 PM

TANGIBILITY, SWEET *TANGIBILITY*

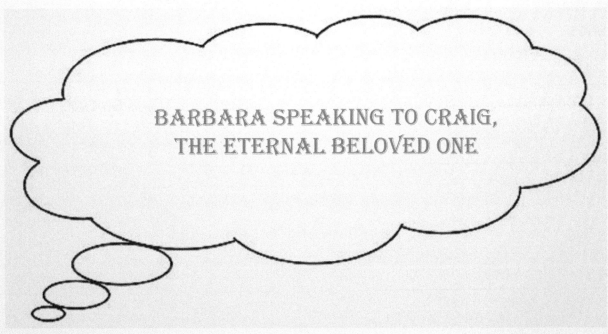

BARBARA SPEAKING TO CRAIG, THE ETERNAL BELOVED ONE

I CAN SEE IT! I CAN TOUCH IT! WE HAVE ENTERED THE REALM OF SWEET TANGIBILITY! CAN YOU NOT SEE IT, DEAR ONE? REACH OUT AND TOUCH THE TANGIBILITY THAT DEFINES AND REVEALS OUR FUSED ESSENCE OF DIVINE ORCHESTRATED LOVE. TOUCH IT, DEAR ONE! FOR YOU TOO, HAVE ENTERED THE REALM OF SWEET TANGIBILITY. TOUCH THE REALM THAT YOU HAVE ANTICIPATED FOR YEARS! TOUCH THE REALM THAT DESCENDED FROM HEAVEN'S OPENED GATES. TOUCH THE REALM THAT REVEALS THE HOLY PRESENCE OF OUR ORIGIN AND GOD. TOUCH IT, DEAR ONE! TOUCH THE REALM THAT INVITES YOUR WELCOME SOUL. TOUCH THE REALM OF SWEET TANGIBILITY, FOR IT HAS ENTERED YOUR WORLD TODAY! JOIN ME, DEAR ONE! JOIN ME AS I BOW IN THE PRESENCE OF SWEET TANGIBLE HOPE! JOIN ME AS I REJOICE WITHIN THE REALM THAT PRODUCES TANGIBLE LOVE AND PEACE! JOIN ME, AS I REJOICE WITH GOD'S HEAVENLY CHOIRS IN THE MIDST OF TANGIBLE FUSION AND DIVINE ORCHESTRATED LOVE! JOIN ME, DEAR ONE! JOIN ME IN THE MIDST OF TANGIBILITY!
ALLELUIA!!!

NOVEMBER 7, 2015 AT 6:10 PM BY: BARBARA ANN MARY MACK

SENT SAT, NOV 7, 2015 6:14 PM-READ SAT 11/7/2015 10:00 PM

GREETINGS DEAR ONE! COME STA OGGI? LA TOYA AND AMYA ARE OUTSIDE PUTTING UP HALLOWEEN DECORATIONS. TOYA REALLY GETS INTO TO THIS. SHE ALSO DRESSES UP AND GOES TRICKS OR TREATING WITH AMYA. THIS YEAR, LA TOYA WANTS TO INCLUDE ME AND ONE OF AMYA'S FRIENDS. I'M NOT SURE WHETHER I'LL BE UP TO THAT FRIGHTENING OUTING. THEY USUALLY DO THEIR TRICKS OR TREATING IN SOUTH PHILLY, WHICH IS ONE OF TOYA'S FAVORITE LOCATIONS IN THE CITY. LA TOYA'S COSTUME POSSIBILITIES ARE A MARSH MELLOW OR A NURSE. AMYA ORDERED A PANDA BEAR COSTUME FROM CHINA, WHICH ARRIVED LAST WEEK. SHE IS VERY PLEASED WITH HER COSTUME. AMYA LOVES PANDA BEARS I WILL GO AS MYSELF THIS YEAR, A MESSENGER OF THE LORD. THAT SHOULD SCARE AWAY THE EVIL SPIRITS.

CIAO! BELLA BARBIE

THE PLEASURES AND FAME THAT YOU RECEIVE FROM SATAN ARE TEMPORARY, MY CHILDREN

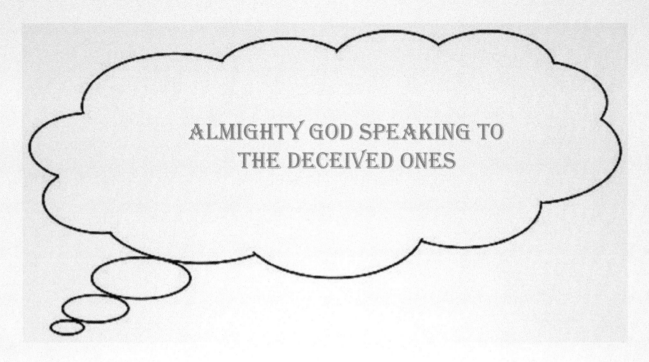

ALMIGHTY GOD SPEAKING TO
THE DECEIVED ONES

MY CHILDREN, THE PLEASURES AND FAME THAT YOU RECEIVE FROM THE WORLD (SATAN) ARE TEMPORARY. AFTER HE, THE CUNNING DEVIL, LURES YOU INTO HIS WEB OF WORLDLY FAME AND FORTUNE, HE MOCKINGLY RELEASES YOU INTO THE REALM OF ETERNAL DESTRUCTION AND DOOM (PHYSICAL AND SPIRITUAL DEATH). MY CHILDREN, OBSERVE THE REWARDS (SUICIDE, DRUG OVER DOSE, PHYSICAL, MENTAL, AND SPIRITUAL ABUSE) THAT COME FROM SATAN'S REALM OF TEMPORARY PLEASURE. AFTER HE HAS DECEIVED YOU, HE CASTS YOU ASIDE, YES, INTO THE REALM THAT INVITES THOSE WHO FOLLOWED THE WORLD'S VERSION OF PLEASURE AND HAPPINESS. MY CHILDREN, DO NOT BE FOOLED BY HE (SATAN) WHO IS DOOMED! DO NOT BE DECEIVED BY SATAN, THE FATHER OF TEMPORARY PLEASURE AND ETERNAL DAMNATION. MY CHILDREN, THE PLEASURES THAT ARE GIVEN TO YOU FROM SATAN, LEAD TO A REALM OF DISCONTENTMENT AND DISSATISFACTION. LISTEN, MY CHILDREN! LISTEN AT HIM (SATAN) LAUGH AT YOU! LISTEN TO HIS CHUCKLES, AS YOU FALL INTO HIS REALM OF TEMPORARY PLEASURE AND ETERNAL PAIN. LISTEN, MY CHILDREN! CAN YOU NOT HEAR HIM? CAN YOU NOT HEAR HIM MOCK YOU AS YOU FOLLOW HIM BLINDLY INTO THE REALM OF ETERNAL DOOM? LISTEN, MY CHILDREN! LISTEN AT HIS UNENDING LAUGHTER!
OCTOBER 29, 2015 AT 6:47 PM BY: BARBARA ANN MARY MACK
SENT SAT, OCT 31, 2015 8:35 PM-READ SAT 10/31/2015 10:06 PM

WHEN I READ AND HEAR ABOUT THE DEATHS OF THE YOUNG ONES, MY SOUL WEEPS FOR THEM

BARBARA SPEAKING TO THE LORD GOD

MY LORD, MY HOLY GOD, THEY HAVE TAKEN THE LIVES OF YOUR INNOCENT LITTLE ONES. THEY HAVE TAKEN THEIR LIVES WITHOUT A JUST REASON. WHAT CAN WE (ALMIGHTY GOD AND BARBARA) DO, O HOLY ONE? WHAT CAN WE DO TODAY? MY SOUL WEEPS FOR THE INNOCENT LITTLE ONES. MY SOUL WEEPS FOR THEM THROUGHOUT THE DAY. MY PRAYERS ARE CONSTANTLY IN YOUR HOLY PRESENCE, AS MY SOUL WEEPS FOR YOUR SLAIN LITTLE ONES. I WILL UNITE MY FALLING TEARS WITH THE TEARS THAT FALL FROM YOUR SORROWFUL ESSENCE, MY GOD. I WILL UNITE MY TEARS WITH THE TEARS OF MY SAVING LORD AND GOD. MY LORD, MY SOUL EXPERIENCES DIVINE PEACE AS I HEAR AND READ OF THE DEATHS OF YOUR INNOCENT LITTLE ONES. MY SOUL EXPERIENCES DIVINE PEACE, FOR I KNOW THAT YOU HAVE NOT ABANDONED THE SOULS OF YOUR INNOCENT LITTLE CHILDREN. MY SOUL EXPERIENCES DIVINE PEACE, FOR I KNOW THAT THE SOULS OF YOUR SLAIN CHILDREN RESIDE WITH YOU NOW AND FOREVER.

ALMIGHTY GOD SPEAKING TO THE SLAIN LITTLE ONES

I HEAR YOU, MY LITTLE CHILDREN. I HEAR YOUR UNENDING CRIES. I HAVE WITNESSED ALL OF YOUR DEATHS. I HAVE WITNESSED YOUR ABUSE AND PAIN. YOU ARE WITH ME NOW, O SAVED ONES! YOU ARE WITH THE KING OF PEACE (THE LORD JESUS)!!!
OCTOBER 31, 2015 AT 8:00 PM BY: BARBARA ANN MARY MACK
SENT SAT, OCT 31, 2015 8:35 PM-READ SAT 10/31/2015 10:06 PM

GREETINGS ARCHBISHOP CRAIG! LA TOYA AND AMYA JUST LEFT FOR TRICK OR TREATING. THEY LEFT ME HERE TO GIVE OUT THE GOODIES TO THE GHOULS AND GOBLINS

THAT ARE BRAVE ENOUGH TO COME TO OUR HOME. LA TOYA AND AMYA ARE HEADED FOR SOUTH PHILLY. HOPEFULLY THEY WILL RETURN WITH SOME TREATS AS WELL. TOYA PICKED UP PIZZA BEFORE THEY LEFT, SO THAT WE CAN HAVE SOMETHING SIMPLE AND READY TO EAT WHEN THEY RETURN. HAPPY HALLOWEEN!
SENT SAT, OCT 31, 2015 8:35 PM READ SAT 10/31/2015 10:06 PM

PAY ATTENTION TO MY HOLY WORDS TODAY, FOR THEY HAVEN'T CHANGED, *SAYS THE LORD*

ALMIGHTY GOD SPEAKING

MY CHILDREN, MY HOLY WORDS HAVEN'T CHANGED THROUGH THE REALM OF TANGIBLE AND VISIBLE TIME. BEHOLD MY UNCHANGING TANGIBLE WORD TODAY! FOR IT, MY HOLY WORD, HASN'T CHANGED. BEHOLD THE CONSISTENCY OF MY HOLY WORDS THAT ARE CONVEYED THROUGH MY CONTEMPORARY MESSENGER AND SCRIBE (BARBARA)! BEHOLD THE VISIBILITY OF MY HOLY UNCHANGING MESSAGES THAT I DICTATE TO MY OBEDIENT MESSENGER AND SCRIBE (BARBARA) TODAY! BEHOLD THE CONSISTENCY OF MY DIVINE REVELATIONS TODAY, FOR I AM AN UNCHANGING GOD! MY CHILDREN, DO YOU BELIEVE IN ME? DO YOU BELIEVE IN MY HOLY UNCHANGING PRESENCE TODAY? DO YOU BELIEVE THAT I CAN AND DO APPEAR TO YOU IN THE FORM (BARBARA) WHICH I VIEW AS AUTHENTIC AND HOLY? BEHOLD, MY CHILDREN! BEHOLD THE TANGIBLE AND VISIBLE FORM (BARBARA) THAT REPRESENTS MY REALM OF DIVINITY ON EARTH TODAY, FOR I AM REAL! MY CHILDREN, PAY CLOSE ATTENTION TO MY HOLY WORDS THAT FLOW THROUGH "THE PRESENT TESTAMENT", FOR THEY, MY HOLY WORDS, ARE IN YOUR BLESSED MIDST TODAY! THEY, MY HOLY WORDS, HAVEN'T CHANGED!!!
OCTOBER 23, 2015 AT 5:15 PM BY: BARBARA ANN MARY MACK

HOW ARE YOU DISTINGUISHED FROM THE WORLD, MY CHILDREN?

ALMIGHTY GOD SPEAKING

IF ONE WHO PROFESSES TO BE A CHRISTIAN WALKS SIDE BY SIDE WITH A PAGAN, HEATHEN, MURDERER, RAPIST OR ATHEIST, WOULD HE OR SHE GET THE RECOGNITION OF A CHRISTIAN? WOULD THOSE WHO OBSERVE HIM OR HER SAY, OH, THERE GOES A CHRISTIAN? MY CHILDREN, YOUR DEMEANOR IS VERY IMPORTANT, FOR ONE WHO PROFESSES TO BE A CHRISTIAN, SHOULD CONDUCT HIMSELF OR HERSELF ACCORDING TO MY VERSION OF A CHRISTIAN. A CHRISTIAN FOLLOWS MY HOLY TEACHINGS AND WAY AT ALL TIMES, FOR THERE IS NO OTHER! A CHRISTIAN CONDUCTS HIMSELF AND HERSELF IN A HOLY MANNER AT ALL TIMES, ACCORDING TO MY VERSION OF HOLINESS. A CHRISTIAN OFFERS DIVINE LOVE TO THOSE WHO ARE THRIVING TO LIVE ACCORDING TO MY VERSION OF HOLINESS. A CHRISTIAN DOES NOT CONFORM TO, NOR ACCEPT THE UNHOLY ACTS WHICH THE WORLD GLORIFIES AND ACCEPTS. A CHRISTIAN APPRECIATES THE TEACHINGS, YES, MY HOLY TEACHINGS THAT PERMEATE THE HOLY BIBLE, FOR THERE ARE NO OTHER TEACHINGS OF HOLINESS!

OCTOBER 23, 2015 AT 7:02 PM BY: BARBARA ANN MARY MACK

SENT WED, OCT 28, 2015 12:54 AM-READ WED 10/28/2015 10:14 AM

I DID WHAT I WAS SENT HERE TO DO. *MAY I RETURN TO YOU, O LORD?*

BARBARA SPEAKING TO THE LORD

MY LORD, I DID WHAT I WAS SENT HERE TO DO. MAY I RETURN TO YOUR GRACIOUS SIDE? I HAVE DELIVERED YOUR HOLY MESSAGES TO THOSE WHOM YOU HAVE SENT ME TO. MAY I RETURN TO MY LOVELY ETERNAL SPOUSE AND GOD? I HAVE OFFERED DIVINE LOVE TO THOSE WHOM YOU HAVE SENT ME TO. MAY I RETURN TO YOUR UNCHANGING REALM? I HAVE GIVEN UP MUCH FOR THE SAKE OF THOSE WHOM YOU HAVE CALLED, MAY I RETURN TO MY PERMANENT HOME? MY

LORD, MY MERCIFUL GOD, HAVE PITY ON SHE (BARBARA) WHO DESIRES YOUR HOLY SIDE. MAY I RETURN TO YOUR CONTINUOUS WARMTH? MY LORD, MY HOLY GOD, THEY WILL NOT LISTEN TO YOUR LIFE SAVING WORDS. MAY I RETURN? MAY I RETURN? MAY I RETURN TO YOU?

OCTOBER 25, 2015 AT 4:52 AM BY: BARBARA ANN MARY MACK

SENT WED, OCT 28, 2015 12:54 AM-READ WED 10/28/2015 10:14 AM

GREETINGS DEAR ARCHBISHOP CRAIG! LA TOYA AND I ARE EN ROUTE TO A MYSTERY/DINNER SHOW THIS EVENING. LA TOYA MADE RESERVATIONS A COUPLE OF MONTHS AGO. LA TOYA LOVES GOING OUT AND DOING FUN THINGS, WHILE AMYA AND I PREFER STAYING AT HOME TORTURING ONE ANOTHER INSTEAD. SO FAR THE WEATHER SEEMS TO BE VERY GOOD FOR THIS OUTING. HOPEFULLY IT WILL REMAIN THROUGHOUT THE DAY, IF NOT, WE WILL TOLERATE THE CHANGE. ENJOY YOUR BLESSED DAY LOVE! AMORE, BEAUTIFUL BARBIE

THOSE WHO ARE CHOSEN AND SENT BY ME EXHIBIT MY VERSION OF HOLY TRUTH AT ALL TIMES, *SAYS THE LORD*

MY CHILDREN, YOU CAN TELL THOSE WHO ARE SENT BY ME, FOR THEY EXHIBIT MY HOLY WAY AT ALL TIMES. MY CHILDREN, MANY HAVE COME IN MY HOLY NAME, ACCORDING TO THEM, BUT THEY DO NOT EXHIBIT OR SPEAK MY HOLY WORDS AND WAY. THEY EXHIBIT THE WAYS OF THE WORLD (SATAN). MY CHILDREN, DO NOT LET THEIR CLOTHING OR THEIR TITLES FOOL YOU, FOR THEY DO NOT REPRESENT ME! OBSERVE AND LISTEN TO THEM, FOR THEY DO SPEAK AND EXHIBIT THE WAYS OF HE (SATAN) WHO LEADS THE WORLD INTO THE OPENED GATES TO ETERNAL DAMNATION AND DOOM. MY CHILDREN, PAY CLOSE ATTENTION TO THOSE WHO DESIRE TO PLEASE THOSE WHO EXHIBIT THE SINS OF THE WORLD, FOR THEY DO NOT

REPRESENT ME! I DID NOT SEND THEM TO YOU. THEIR ORIGIN AND FATHER IS SATAN, THE SOURCE OF UNRIGHTEOUSNESS AND SIN. HE, SATAN, HAS FOOLED MANY THROUGH THE YEARS. PLEASE DO NOT FALL INTO HIS REALM OF DECEPTION AND ETERNAL DOOM, FOR HELL DOES EXIST FOR THOSE WHO FOLLOW THE WAYS OF THE WORLD. THIS IS MY TRUTH! DO NOT RECEIVE ANY OTHER TEACHINGS, FOR THEY ARE FALSE AND MISLEADING!!!

OCTOBER 24, 2015 AT 2:53 PM BY: BARBARA ANN MARY MACK

SENT WED, OCT 28, 2015 12:54 AM-READ WED 10/28/2015 10:14 AM

IF THE WORLD CONDONES SINFUL AND UNHOLY ACTS, WHO IS GOING TO HELL? WHAT IS HELL'S EXISTENCE FOR?

ALMIGHTY GOD SPEAKING

MY CHILDREN, HELL DOES EXIST! BELIEVE IT! FOR IT IS TRUTH. IF IT WAS NOT SO, I WOULD TELL YOU. THEREFORE, MY CHILDREN, MAKE PREPARATIONS FOR YOUR ETERNAL DESTINATION, FOR IT WILL TAKE PLACE VERY SOON! DO NOT FOCUS ON WHAT YOU TRULY BELIEVE, BUT RATHER, WHAT I SAY, *SAYS THE LORD GOD!*

BARBARA SPEAKING

MY BROTHERS AND SISTERS, DO NOT BE DECEIVED BY THE WORLD (SATAN)! HELL IS FOR THOSE WHO DO NOT CHANGE THEIR SINFUL WAYS BEFORE THEIR PHYSICAL DEATH. HELL DOES EXIST FOR THE UNRIGHTEOUS AND DISOBEDIENT ONES. HELL IS A PLACE WHERE THOSE WHO DID NOT REVEAL THE TRUTH, GOD'S HOLY TRUTH, TO THE IGNORANT AND VULNERABLE ONES, WILL ENTER. MY BROTHERS AND SISTERS, HELL DOES EXIST!!! DO YOU WANT TO FIND OUT FOR YOURSELVES? ARE YOU WILLING TO TAKE THE CHANCE? DO YOU PREFER TEMPORARY PLEASURE OVER ETERNAL DAMNATION AND SUFFERING? MY BROTHERS AND SISTERS, REGARDLESS OF WHAT THE WORLD TELLS YOU, HELL DOES EXIST FOR THOSE WHO REMAIN IN THE REALM OF UNHOLINESS, INCLUDING THE DECEITFUL CLERGY!!!

OCTOBER 25, 2015 AT 4:22 PM BY: BARBARA ANN MARY MACK

OH HOW LOVING AND MERCIFUL YOU ARE, O HEAVENLY FATHER AND GOD

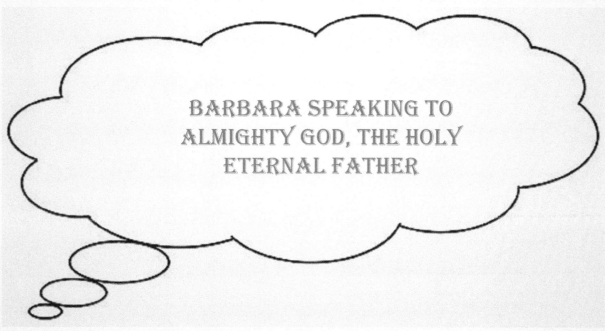

BARBARA SPEAKING TO ALMIGHTY GOD, THE HOLY ETERNAL FATHER

MY LORD, IN THE MIDST OF YOUR HOLINESS, YOU EXHIBIT YOUR REALM OF UNENDING LOVE AND MERCY FOR EARTH'S RESIDENTS TODAY. YOU EXHIBIT YOUR UNENDING REALM OF LOVE AND MERCY BY SENDING ME, YOUR HEAVEN SENT MESSENGER TODAY, TO THOSE WHOM YOU DEEM WORTHY TO KNOW YOUR REALM OF TRUTH. MY LORD, MY HOLY FATHER AND GOD, YOU SEND ME TO THOSE WHO DO NOT DESIRE TO HEAR YOUR HOLY TRUTH, FOR IT REVEALS THEIR DESTINATION. YOU HAVE SENT ME TO PEOPLE WHO DO NOT WANT TO HEAR YOUR TRUTH, FOR IT REVEALS THEIR UNHOLY WAYS. YOU HAVE SENT ME TO THOSE WHO DO NOT REVEAL YOUR WHOLE TRUTH TO THOSE WHO ARE LIVING IN THE PIT OF SIN. MY LORD, MY HOLY GOD, BECAUSE OF YOUR COMPASSION, YOU CONTINUE TO SEND ME TO THOSE WHOM YOU HAVE CALLED AND CHOSEN TO PARTAKE IN YOUR GLORY ON EARTH AND IN SWEET PARADISE. DESPITE THE CONSISTENT REJECTION OF YOUR HOLY TRUTH, YOU SEND ME TO THOSE WHO DO NOT DESIRE TO LEAVE THEIR REALM OF SIN. OUT OF OBEDIENCE TO YOU, MY LORD, I WILL GO WHERE YOU SEND ME. OUT OF OBEDIENCE UNTO YOU, I WILL SEEK THOSE WHOM SATAN DESIRES TO STEAL FROM US. OUT OF OBEDIENCE TO YOU, I WILL NOT REST UNTIL YOU AND I HAVE RETRIEVED THOSE WHOM SATAN HAS BLINDED WITH WORLDLY LIES. EVEN IN THE MIDST OF PHYSICAL AND SPIRITUAL PAIN, I WILL GO WHERE YOU SEND ME, MY GOD, FOR I TRULY LOVE AND ADORE YOU!!!

OCTOBER 25, 2015 AT 4:55 PM BY: BARBARA ANN MARY MACK

CAN YOU HEAR HIM, O DISOBEDIENT ONES? CAN YOU HEAR SATAN LAUGHING AT YOU?

ALMIGHTY GOD SPEAKING

CAN YOU HEAR HIM, MY CHILDREN? CAN YOU HEAR SATAN, OUR ENEMY, AS HE LAUGHS AT YOU? CAN YOU HEAR HIM AS HE CHUCKLES IN THE MIDST OF YOUR SINS AND UNHOLY ACTS? CAN YOU HEAR HIS LAUGHTER AS YOU HEAD IN THE DIRECTION OF DESTRUCTION AND ETERNAL

DAMNATION? CAN YOU HEAR THE JOY THAT SURROUNDS HIS REALM OF UNHOLINESS, AS HE JOINS YOU IN THE MIDST OF YOURS SINFUL ACTS? CAN YOU HEAR HIM LAUGHING AT YOU, AS YOU WALK THE STREETS THAT PROMOTE AND PRODUCE SINFUL LUSTS AND GREED? CAN YOU HEAR SATAN'S LAUGHTER AS YOU FALL FOR HIS REALM OF DECEPTION AND ETERNAL DOOM? CAN YOU, MY CHILDREN? LISTEN CLOSELY, FOR SATAN IS LAUGHING OUT LOUD AT THOSE WHOM HE HAS LURED INTO HIS REALM OF DESTRUCTION WITH TEMPORARY PLEASURES AND WORLDLY FAME. LISTEN TO HIM, MY CHILDREN! LISTEN TO THE SOUNDS OF DECEIT AND DESTRUCTION, FOR IT IS LEADING YOU TO SATAN'S ETERNAL PLACE OF RESIDENCE (HELL)! REMEMBER, MY CHILDREN, HELL IS NOT A FANTASY OR MYTH! IF YOU BELIEVE IN HEAVEN, THEN YOU SHOULD BELIEVE IN THE EXISTENCE OF HELL. FOR I, THE LORD, HAVE REVEALED ITS (HELL) EXISTENCE. I HAVE REVEALED HELL'S PURPOSE AS WELL.
OCTOBER 25, 2015 AT 5:37 PM BY: BARBARA ANN MARY MACK

THE VICTORY IS MINE, *SAYS THE LORD!!!*

ALMIGHTY GOD SPEAKING

SIT BACK AND RELAX, MY CHILDREN, FOR THE VICTORY OVER THE REALM OF EVIL IS MINE! I HAVE THIS BATTLE UNDER CONTROL, O WORRIED CHILDREN OF MINE! THE REALM (SATAN) THAT RELEASES EVIL IN THE MIDST OF MY VULNERABLE ONES TODAY, HAS BEEN DEFEATED BY THE POWER THAT EMITS FROM MY UNENDING REALM OF HOLINESS. I HAVE THIS BATTLE, YES, THIS CRUCIAL AND BRUTAL BATTLE, UNDER CONTROL! FOR I, THE LORD GOD, AM OMNIPOTENT! THERE IS NO OTHER POWER GREATER THAN MINE! SATAN, MY FOE, FINDS THIS OUT EVERY DAY. I, THE LORD, THE ETERNAL ONE, AM THE DIVINE VICTORY OVER THE REALM OF SIN AND EVIL THAT SLITHER IN THE MIDST OF MY GREAT CREATION. SATAN, THE DEFEATED REALM OF EVIL, KNOWS THIS TOO! HE KNOWS OF HIS DEFEAT, AND HE IS NOT ASHAMED TO TAKE AS MANY WITH HIM TO AND THROUGH THE GATES OF HELL, HIS ETERNAL HOME. THE VICTORY IS MINE, FOR I AM NOT A QUITTER! THOSE WHO DESIRE TO REIGN AND LIVE WITH ME THROUGHOUT ETERNITY ARE VICTORS OVER SATAN'S DEFEATED REALM ALSO. RISE, O VICTORIOUS CHILDREN OF MINE! RISE IN THE MIDST OF VICTORY AND DIVINE FAME, AS YOU AND I BATTLE THE REALM OF SIN AND DESTRUCTION AS ONE! RISE, O VICTORIOUS CHILDREN OF MINE! RISE! AS WE LOWER OUR SWORD OF VICTORY AND TRIUMPHANT GLORY! RISE, AS YOU SALUTE JESUS, YOUR VICTORIOUS GOD AND KING! RISE! O CHILDREN OF VICTORY AND DIVINE FAME. RISE, AS I LEAD YOU IN THE DIRECTION OF ETERNAL VICTORIOUS BLISS!!!
OCTOBER 27, 2015 AT 3:34 PM BY: BARBARA ANN MARY MACK

MY LORD, THE WORLD'S VERSION OF LOVE FRIGHTENS ME

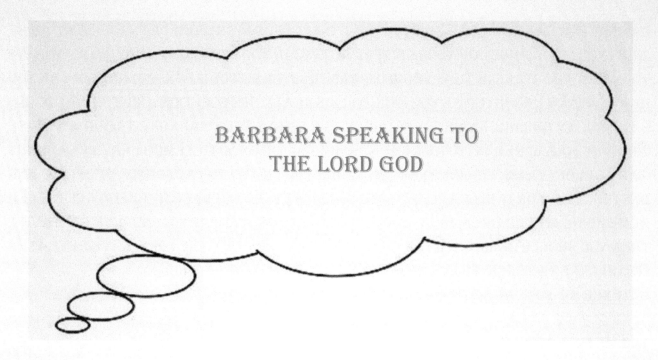

BARBARA SPEAKING TO
THE LORD GOD

MY LORD, O HEAVENLY SPOUSE AND GOD OF MINE, THE WORLD'S VERSION OF LOVE FRIGHTENS ME. THE WORLD'S VERSION OF LOVE SOMETIMES CAUSES GREAT PAIN AND SUFFERING. THE WORLD'S VERSION OF LOVE SEEMS TO BE TEMPORARY, AND WITHOUT RESPECT FOR YOU. MY LORD, I CANNOT BEAR THE SIGHT AND EXPRESSION OF THE WORLD'S VERSION OF LOVE, FOR IT DOESN'T CONFORM TO YOUR VERSION OF HOLY LOVE. THE WORLD'S VERSION OF LOVE INVITES THOSE WHO DO AND ACCEPT THE SINFUL ACTS OF SATAN, OUR (ALMIGHTY GOD AND BARBARA) ENEMY. THE WORLD'S VERSION OF LOVE DOESN'T REVEAL GOD'S HOLY TRUTH PERTAINING TO WHAT IS SIN. THE WORLD'S VERSION OF LOVE DOESN'T REVEAL THE TRUTH, GOD'S HOLY TRUTH, IN REGARDS TO HOW TO PLEASE ALMIGHTY GOD. THE WORLD'S VERSION OF LOVE, OMITS GOD'S TRUTH CONCERNING WHAT ONE MUST DO, IN ORDER TO LIVE THROUGHOUT ETERNITY WITH ALMIGHTY GOD AND HIS HOLY RESIDENTS IN HEAVEN. THE WORLD'S VERSION OF LOVE CAUSES ME TO WEEP FOR THE INNOCENT ONES, FOR THEY HAVE BEEN ABUSED BY THOSE WHO CLAIMED THAT THEY LOVED THEM. THE WORLD'S VERSION OF LOVE CAUSES ME TO WEEP FOR THOSE WHO PROFESS TO BE CHRISTIANS, BUT DO THE WORKS OF SATAN. THE WORLD'S VERSION OF LOVE IS DEVOID OF HOLINESS, FOR THEY DO NOT SEEK OR KNOW ALMIGHTY GOD. MY LORD, MY HOLY GOD, PLEASE SHELTER ME FROM THE WORLD'S VERSION OF LOVE, FOR IT DOES FRIGHTEN ME.

OCTOBER 27, 2015 AT 4:56 PM BY: BARBARA ANN MARY MACK

THE ELEGANCE OF THE WORLD CANNOT SATISFY ME

BARBARA SPEAKING

IN THE MIDST OF DIVINE ETERNAL ELEGANCE I DWELL, FOR THE ELEGANCE OF THE WORLD CANNOT SATISFY ME. IN THE MIDST OF DIVINE BEAUTY I DWELL, FOR THE BEAUTY OF THE WORLD BLINDS ME. O HEAVENLY HOST, O SAVING GOD AND FATHER, ENCOMPASS ME WITH THE ELEGANCE THAT SHINES THROUGHOUT YOUR KINGDOM ABOVE, FOR THE ELEGANCE OF THE WORLD COULD NEVER HOLD ME. ENCOMPASS MY ESSENCE WITH THE DIVINE ELEGANCE THAT ROAMS IN THE MIDST OF YOUR REALM OF SPIRITUAL BLISS, FOR THE WORLD CANNOT SATISFY MY SOUL. LET THE PEACE THAT RESTS WITHIN YOUR HOLY MIDST SURROUND ME, AS I LOOK UP TO YOU FOR COMFORT AND DIVINE SECURITY. LET THE GATES THAT HOLD YOUR REALM OF DIVINE ELEGANCE OPEN WIDE, SO THAT I MAY ENTER WITH THE SOULS OF YOUR FAITHFUL LOVED ONES. LET THE REALM THAT HOUSES AND RELEASES DIVINE ELEGANCE GREET ME, AS I ENTER WITH THE SOULS OF THE OBEDIENT ONES. MY HOLY LORD, OPEN WIDE THE GATES THAT HOLD THE REALM OF ELEGANCE THAT PRODUCES GREAT JOY, FOR THE ELEGANCE THAT THE WORLD PRODUCES CANNOT SATISFY ME.
OCTOBER 27, 2015 AT 5:39 PM BY: BARBARA ANN MARY MACK

IN SOME FAMILIES, MONIES ARE SET ASIDE FOR CHILDREN COLLEGE EDUCATION AND LIFE BEFORE AND SOON AFTER THEIR BIRTHS. THERE IS NOTHING WRONG WITH THIS PLAN. ALMIGHTY GOD WANTS US TO NOT ONLY FOCUS ON A LIFE WITHIN THIS WORLD, BUT ALSO OUR ETERNAL DESTINATION. HE WANTS US TO SHARE WITH OUR CHILDREN THE REALITY OF ETERNAL LIFE AND ITS IMPORTANCE. BY DOING THIS, WE OFFER OUR CHILDREN THE FULLNESS OF DIVINE CREATION AND THE MEANING BEHIND IT.

ALMIGHTY GOD AND
BARBARA SPEAKING

LIFE BEYOND COLLEGE

BARBARA SPEAKING

MY BROTHERS AND SISTERS, LET US STRIVE FOR THE LIFE THAT GOES BEYOND COLLEGE. LET US GRASP THE DEPTH AND MEANING OF "ETERNAL LIFE WITH ALMIGHTY GOD". LET US TEACH OUR CHILDREN ABOUT THE MOST PRECIOUS LIFE, ETERNAL LIFE, WHICH GOES BEYOND COLLEGE. LET US TEACH OUR CHILDREN ABOUT A LIFE THAT TRANSCENDS THE WORLD'S VERSION OF LIFE. LET US TEACH OUR LOVED ONES THE IMPORTANCE OF LIFE ETERNAL, WHICH GOES BEYOND WHAT WORLDLY EDUCATION OFFERS. LET US GIVE OUR CHILDREN THE OPPORTUNITY TO LEARN OF, AND APPRECIATE THE MEANING OF ETERNAL LIFE WITH ALMIGHTY GOD AND HIS HEAVENLY RESIDENTS. LET US DISTINGUISH THAT WHICH IS VERY VALUABLE FOREVER. LET US DISTINGUISH, THAT WHICH GIVES US EVERLASTING JOY AND DIVINE PLEASURE. LET US DISTINGUISH THAT WHICH IS MORE IMPORTANT AND VALUABLE IN OUR LIVES TODAY, AND THE FUTURE BEYOND PHYSICAL EXISTENCE.

ALMIGHTY GOD SPEAKING

MY CHILDREN, UNDERSTAND THE LIFE THAT GOES BEYOND THE PHYSICAL AND TEMPORARY REALMS. UNDERSTAND THE MEANING OF ETERNAL LIFE AND ITS GREAT REWARDS. UNDERSTAND, MY SONS! UNDERSTAND, MY DAUGHTERS! UNDERSTAND THE DEPTH AND HAPPINESS OF A LIFE THAT GOES BEYOND COLLEGE. FOCUS ON PERPETUAL LIFE INSTEAD OF TEMPORARY EXISTENCE, MY CHILDREN. MY CHILDREN, FOCUS ON ME (ETERNAL LIFE)!
OCTOBER 27, 2015 AT 7:11 PM BY: BARBARA ANN MARY MACK

IN THE MIDST OF SATAN"S DARKNESS, I CAN SEE ALMIGHTY GOD'S GLORIOUS LIGHT

BARBARA SPEAKING TO THE LORD JESUS

IN THE MIDST OF SATAN'S DARK AND DREARY DEEDS, I CAN SEE YOUR GLORIOUS LIGHT, LORD JESUS. IN THE MIDST OF THIS TERRIBLE AND TRAGIC PERIOD OF TIME, I CAN SEE YOUR GLORIOUS LIGHT LORD JESUS. IN THE MIDST OF SEXUAL PERVERSION, I CAN SEE YOUR GLORIOUS LIGHT LORD JESUS. IN THE MIDST OF MURDER AND PAIN, I CAN SEE YOUR GLORIOUS LIGHT, LORD JESUS. IN THE MIDST OF DRUG ABUSE AND DEATH, I CAN SEE YOUR GLORIOUS LIGHT, LORD JESUS. IN THE MIDST OF PHYSICAL, SPIRITUAL AND EMOTIONAL ABUSE, I CAN SEE YOUR MARVELOUS LIGHT LORD JESUS. IN THE MIDST OF APATHY AND DESPAIR, I CAN SEE YOUR MARVELOUS LIGHT LORD JESUS. IN THE MIDST OF THE DARK AND LONELY NIGHTS, I CAN SEE YOUR GLORIOUS FACE, MY HOLY GOD AND SAVIOR (LORD JESUS).
OCTOBER 27, 2015 AT 10:48 PM BY: BARBARA ANN MARY MACK
SENT WED, OCT 28, 2015 12:54 AM-READ WED 10/28/2015 10:14 AM

GREETINGS ARCHBISHOP CRAIG! COME STA OGGI AMORE? LA TOYA AND I ARE EN ROUTE TO GET MY YEARLY MAMMOGRAM AT THE HOSPITAL WHERE I WORKED FOR 13 YEARS. I CHOSE THAT LOCATION BECAUSE I AM VERY FAMILIAR WITH MOST OF THE STAFF THERE. IT IS AT THAT LOCATION (HOSPITAL) THAT THE LORD CHOSE FOR ME TO BEGIN MY MINISTRY FOR HIM. I HAVE DELIVERED MANY MESSAGES FROM THE LORD TO MANY EMPLOYEES, PATIENTS AND VISITORS SINCE 1996. I HAVE MANY OF MY MEDICAL TESTS DONE AT THAT LOCATION AND OTHER HOSPITALS AFFILIATED WITH THAT HOSPITAL AS WELL. IT IS ALWAYS A SPIRITUAL ACCOMPLISHMENT WHEN I DO VISIT THOSE LOCATIONS. IT IS AWESOME HOW THE LORD USES MY MEDICAL APPOINTMENTS TO MEET AND GREET HIS CALLED AND CHOSEN ONES. OH WHAT AN AWESOME HONOR TO HAVE SUCH A SPIRITUALLY PROFITABLE MINISTRY FOR THE LORD ALMIGHTY. PLEASE ENJOY THE REST OF YOUR DAY AS YOU THINK OF THE LORD AND ME. LOVE YAH ALWAYS! BEAUTIFUL BARBIE

SENT SUN, OCT 18, 2015 7:52 PM-READ SUN 10/18/2015 11:59 PM

I WILL NOT BE FAMOUS IN THE EYES OF THE WORLD, *SAYS THE LORD*

ALMIGHTY GOD AND BARBARA
SPEAKING TO THE WORLD

I WILL NOT BE FAMOUS IN THE EYES OF THE WORLD (SATAN), FOR MY WRITINGS AND WORKS ARE FROM MY HOLY CREATOR AND ALMIGHTY GOD. I WILL NOT BE FAMOUS IN THE EYES OF THE WORLD, FOR IT, THE WORLD, FOLLOWS THE TEACHINGS OF SATAN, MY (ALMIGHTY GOD AND BARBARA) ENEMY, SAYS THE LORD. THE WORLD DOES NOT KNOW ME, SAYS THE LORD, THEREFORE, IT, THE WORLD (SATAN), DOESN'T KNOW THOSE WHOM I SEND. THE WORLD CANNOT GRASP THAT WHICH COMES FROM THE REALM OF HOLINESS AND DIVINE GOODNESS (ALMIGHTY GOD), FOR IT, THE WORLD, IS DEVOID OF DIVINE LOVE AND KNOWLEDGE. I WILL NEVER BECOME A PART OF THE WORLD'S VERSION OF FAME AND GLORY, FOR THEIR FAME AND GLORY COME FROM A REALM (SATAN) THAT RELEASES TEMPORARY ACKNOWLEDGMENT. I AM FOREVER FUSED WITH THE REALM (ALMIGHTY GOD) THAT SENDS FORTH DIVINE AND CONTINUOUS FAME AND GLORY, FOR HE, ALMIGHTY GOD, IS ETERNAL. THE WORLD DOESN'T KNOW ALMIGHTY GOD, THE ORIGIN OF MY HOLY WRITINGS, THEREFORE, THEY DO NOT KNOW ME. THEY CANNOT GRASP NOR UNDERSTAND THE AUTHENTICITY OF MY HOLY WRITINGS BECAUSE THEY DO NOT UNDERSTAND THE HOLY DICTATOR OF MY WRITINGS. MY HOLY LORD AND GOD, I THANK YOU FOR KEEPING YOUR REALM OF HOLY WRITINGS AND WORKS FROM THOSE WHO HAVE CHOSEN THE WORLD OVER YOUR GOODNESS. THEY DO NOT KNOW ME (ALMIGHTY GOD AND BARBARA). THEY CANNOT SEPARATE THEIR LEVEL OF UNDERSTANDING FROM DIVINE REALITY BECAUSE THEY DO NOT KNOW YOUR REALM OF HOLINESS. I WILL NOT BE FAMOUS IN THE EYES OF THE WORLD, FOR THEY WILL NEVER KNOW ME, *SAYS THE LORD*. THEY HAVE BEEN BLINDED BY SATAN'S REALM OF LIMITATIONS AND WORLDLY FAME AND GREED. THEY WILL NEVER KNOW ME NOR THOSE WHOM I HAVE SENT TO REPRESENT ME, *SAYS THE LORD GOD*.
OCTOBER 18, 2015 AT 4:46 PM BY: BARBARA ANN MARY MACK
SENT SUN, OCT 18, 2015 7:52 PM-READ SUN 10/18/2015 11:59 PM

I WEEP WITH YOU, MY HURTING CHILDREN: I WEEP WITH YOU THROUGH MY MESSENGER AND BRIDE (BARBARA)

ALMIGHTY GOD SPEAKING TO THE HURTING ONES

MY HEART GOES OUT TO YOU WHO WEEP CONTINUOUSLY OVER THE LOSS OF YOUR LOVED ONES TODAY. MY HEART GOES OUT TO THOSE WHO HAVE LOST A LOVED ONE THROUGH THE ACTS OF THOSE WHO WORK FOR SATAN, THE VISIBLE REALM OF EVIL THAT SLITHERS THROUGH THIS VULNERABLE PERIOD OF TIME. MY HURTING CHILDREN, CAN YOU SEE MY TEARS AS THEY FLOW FROM THE ESSENCE OF MY CHOSEN MESSENGER AND BRIDE (BARBARA)? FOR I WEEP WITH YOU THROUGH HER EMPATHETIC BEING. CAN YOU FEEL MY HOLY WEEPING PRESENCE AS SHE COMFORTS YOU IN THE MIDST OF YOUR PHYSICAL AND SPIRITUAL PAIN? MY CHILDREN, MY HOLY REALM COMFORTS YOU THROUGH THE WEAK AND OBEDIENT ESSENCE OF SHE (BARBARA) WHO IS ALWAYS FAITHFUL TO US (ALMIGHTY GOD AND IS HURTING CHILDREN). CAN YOU FEEL MY HOLY PRESENCE IN YOUR WEEPING MIDST TODAY, MY CHILDREN? CAN YOU FEEL THE COMFORT THAT EMITS FROM THE BEING (BARBARA) WHOM I HAVE SENT TO COMFORT AND CONSOLE YOU DURING THIS CRUCIAL AND PAINFUL PERIOD OF TIME? CAN YOU, MY CHILDREN? CAN YOU FEEL ME?
OCTOBER 11, 2015 AT 4:02 PM BY: BARBARA ANN MARY MACK
SENT WED, OCT 14, 2015 4:18 PM-READ WED 10/14/2015 10:02 PM

GREETINGS LOVE! COME STA OGGI? BELOW IS TODAY'S PASSAGE. TAKE VERY GOOD CARE OF YOURSELF DEAR ONE. CIAO! BELLA BARBARA

MY TRUTH: AN EXPRESSION OF LOVE, *SAYS THE LORD*

ALMIGHTY GOD SPEAKING

TO WITHHOLD MY HOLY TRUTH IS AN EXPRESSION OF HATE FOR YOUR NEIGHBORS, FAMILY AND FRIENDS. FOR WITHHOLDING MY HOLY TRUTH WILL LEAD THEM THROUGH THE GATES OF DAMNATION AND ETERNAL DOOM. O SHEPHERDS, LEADERS, PARENTS AND FRIENDS, REVEAL MY HOLY TRUTH TO THOSE WHO ARE LIVING WITHIN THE REALM OF SIN, FOR IT IS AN EXPRESSION OF DIVINE LOVE, MY LOVE. TELL THEM WHAT I VIEW AS UNRIGHTEOUS AND UNHOLY, FOR THAT IS AN EXPRESSION OF LOVE. TO WITHHOLD MY HOLY TRUTH REVEALS ONE'S LACK OF LOVE AND RESPECT FOR ME, YOUR CREATOR AND GOD, AND MY VULNERABLE CHILDREN. TO WITHHOLD MY TRUTH REVEALS A LACK OF LOVE AND RESPECT FOR ME, THE ONLY FOUNDER AND RULER OF MY HOLY CHURCH. MY SONS! YES! YOU OF THE CLERGY. DO NOT WITHHOLD MY TRUTH FROM MY LOST AND VULNERABLE FLOCK, FOR IF YOU DO, YOU ARE NOT WORTHY TO BE CALLED A SHEPHERD OF MINE! DO THE SHEEP LEAD THE SHEPHERDS? DO THE STUDENTS LEAD THEIR TEACHERS AND INSTRUCTORS? DO CHILDREN RULE THEIR PARENTS? NO, THEY DO NOT! THE WORLD LEADS THEIR LEADERS. THE LEADERS OF THE WORLD CONFORM TO THE WORLD'S WAYS, DESIRES AND ACTS, FOR WORLDLY LEADERS DESIRE TO PLEASE THOSE OF THE WORLD. BUT YOU, O SHEPHERDS OF MINE, ARE COMMISSIONED BY ME, YOUR CREATOR AND GOD, TO GUIDE YOUR FLOCK TO GREEN AND EVERLASTING PASTURES OF ETERNAL LIFE. O SHEPHERDS OF MINE, GUIDE YOUR CONGREGATION BY TEACHING THEM MY HOLY TRUTH, WHICH IS THE ONLY WAY TO SALVATION. O SHEPHERDS OF MINE, LEAD YOUR CONGREGATIONS TO ME! THE SHEPHERDS OF THE WORLD LEAD THEIR FLOCK TO AND THROUGH THE GATES OF HELL. THEY DO NOT REVEAL MY HOLY WAY TO SALVATION. SHEPHERDS OF THE WORLD DO NOT REVEAL MY HOLY TRUTH, WHICH IS MY EXPRESSION, MY ONLY EXPRESSION OF LOVE. OCTOBER 14, 2015 AT 11:18 AM BY: BARBARA ANN MARY MACK

WHEN YOU PUNISH OR CHASTISE YOUR CHILDREN, DO YOU STILL LOVE THEM?

ALMIGHTY GOD SPEAKING

MY CHILDREN, WHEN YOU STRAY FROM MY VERSION OF HOLINESS AND RIGHTEOUS ACTS, I WILL CHASTISE AND PUNISH YOU, BECAUSE I TRULY LOVE YOU. WHAT LOVING PARENT STANDS BY AND WATCH HIS OR HER CHILDREN DO THINGS THAT WILL CAUSE THEIR DEATHS? WHAT LOVING PARENT STANDS BY AND WATCHES HIS OR HER CHILD DO THINGS THAT WILL HARM THEM? MY CHILDREN, BECAUSE I TRULY LOVE YOU, I WILL CHASTISE YOU WHEN YOU STRAY FROM MY HOLY WAY AND COMMANDMENTS. IF YOU PERSIST IN YOUR DISOBEDIENCE, I WILL PUNISH YOU, BECAUSE I WANT YOU TO DWELL WITH ME FOREVER IN SWEET PARADISE. OUT OF DIVINE LOVE FOR YOU, I WILL NOT ALLOW YOU TO DO THE THINGS THAT WILL BRING ABOUT YOUR ETERNAL DESTRUCTION. MY CHILDREN, YOU DO KNOW THE THINGS THAT I, YOUR HEAVENLY FATHER, CREATOR AND GOD, WILL NOT TOLERATE. DESPITE THE THINGS THAT YOUR FRIENDS, LEADERS AND PASTORS CONDONE AND ACCEPT, I, LIKE YOUR EARTHLY

PARENTS, WILL NOT TOLERATE YOUR DISOBEDIENCE. MY CHILDREN, OUT OF PURE AND HOLY LOVE, I WILL REPRIMAND, CHASTISE AND PUNISH YOU WHEN YOU DEVIATE FROM MY VERSION OF HOLINESS. OCTOBER 14, 2015 AT 2:02 PM BY: BARBARA ANN MARY MACK

EITHER YOU ARE WITH ME OR YOU ARE WITH THE WORLD, *SAYS THE LORD*

ALMIGHTY GOD SPEAKING

MY CHILDREN, YOU ARE EITHER WITH ME, YOUR SAVING GOD, OR YOU ARE WITH THE WORLD OF IMPENDING DOOM. THERE IS NO IN BETWEEN! YOU CANNOT SERVE OR ACKNOWLEDGE ME ONLY WHEN IT'S CONVENIENT OR PROFITABLE FOR YOU. YOU CANNOT BE FAITHFUL TO BOTH REALMS, ME AND THE WORLD. WE (ALMIGHTY GOD AND THE WORLD) WILL NOT BE SECOND TO THE OTHER. MY CHILDREN BE AWARE OF THIS FACT, I AM THE ONLY WINNER! I AM THE ONLY FAITHFUL AND OMNIPOTENT ONE. I AM THE ONLY SAVING ONE. I AM THE ONLY ETERNAL GOD, THERE IS NO OTHER! MY CHILDREN, DO NOT FALL FOR THE TEMPORARY AND DANGEROUS PLEASURES THAT THE WORLD SO ABUNDANTLY OFFERS TO THE DOOMED ONES. FLEE FROM THE TEMPORARY PLEASURES THAT LEAD TO THE GATES OF ETERNAL DESTRUCTION. I, YOUR LOVING GOD AND FATHER, AM SENDING OUT MY FINAL WARNING THROUGH MY CHOSEN MESSENGER AND BRIDE (BARBARA). IN THE MIDST OF HER WEAKNESS, SPIRITUAL AND PHYSICAL AGONY, SHE PROCEEDS IN DELIVERING MY LIFE SAVING MESSAGES TO THOSE WHOM I DEEM WORTHY. IN THE MIDST OF WORLDLY PLEASURES, I AM SENDING HER TO MY CALLED AND CHOSEN ONES. FOR THERE, DWELL THOSE WHOM I DEEM WORTHY OF MY INVITATION TO ETERNAL LIFE IN SWEET PARADISE. IN THE MIDST OF SATAN'S MANY DARTS AND DEFEATED REALM, MY MESSENGER AND BRIDE (BARBARA) SEEKS THE VALUABLE SOULS OF THOSE WHOM I DEEM WORTHY TO SPEND ETERNAL GLORY WITH ME IN SWEET PARADISE. MY CHILDREN, JOIN ME, AS I TRIUMPH OVER THE REALM THAT IS HEADED FOR FINAL DESTRUCTION AND DOOM! MY CHILDREN, WILL YOU COME TO ME, THE WINNING SIDE; THE ETERNAL GLORIOUS SIDE? MY CHILDREN, ARE YOU WITH ME, THE EVERLASTING WINNER AND VICTOR?
OCTOBER 15, 2015 AT 4:54 PM BY: BARBARA ANN MARY MACK
SENT FRI, OCT 16, 2015 1:32 AM-READ FRI 10/16/2015 10:57 AM

WORLDLY EDUCATION TREATED AS A FALSE GOD-I WILL NOT COMPETE AGAINST WORLDLY KNOWLEDGE (EDUCATION), *SAYS THE LORD*

ALMIGHTY GOD SPEAKING

O CHILDREN, WHY HAVE YOU FALLEN INTO SATAN'S TRAP, IN REGARDS TO WORLDLY EDUCATION AND KNOWLEDGE. SOME OF YOU REVERE WORLDLY EDUCATION OVER THAT WHICH

IS VITAL TO YOUR SURVIVAL ON EARTH. FOR SATAN HAS PLACED WORLDLY EDUCATION AND KNOWLEDGE AS A STUMBLING BLOCK AND PREFERENCE OVER ME AND MY HOLY KINGDOMS (HEAVEN AND EARTH). YOU DO NOT STRIVE FOR YOUR ETERNAL LIFE WITH ME, NOR YOUR LIFE TODAY. I CAN HEAR IT, MY CHILDREN. I CAN HEAR THE EDUCATORS, PARENTS, FRIENDS, EVEN THOSE OF THE CLERGY, GIVE REVERENCE TO WORLDLY EDUCATION INSTEAD OF MY REALM OF PLENTY. OH HOW HURTFUL IT IS TO ME WHEN I HEAR THOSE WHO CLAIM THAT THEY KNOW AND LOVE ME, EXALT WORLDLY EDUCATION, PEOPLE AND KNOWLEDGE OVER MY REALM OF ETERNAL AND VALUABLE KNOWLEDGE. OH HOW HURTFUL IT IS, AS I WITNESS HUMAN BEINGS GIVE PRAISE AND ACKNOWLEDGMENT TO MERE MANKIND, AND SHUT THEIR DOORS (LIVES) TO ME AND MY REALM OF ETERNAL GOODNESS AND PLENTY. OH HOW PAINFUL IT IS, MY CHILDREN. IT DOES CAUSE ME TO WEEP AT TIMES, FOR IT IS VERY PAINFUL TO WATCH THOSE WHOM I HAVE FORMED FROM THE DEPTH OF MY REALM OF GOODNESS, EXCLUDE ME FROM THEIR LIVES. OH HOW PAINFUL IT IS.

OCTOBER 13, 2015 AT 3:48 PM BY: BARBARA ANN MARY MACK

MY LORD, THEY DID NOT BELIEVE IN YOU THEN, AND THEY DO NOT BELIEVE IN YOU NOW

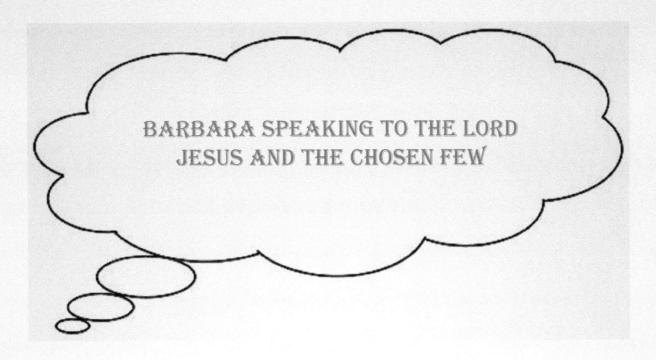

BARBARA SPEAKING TO THE LORD
JESUS AND THE CHOSEN FEW

MY LORD, MY HOLY GOD, THE WORLD HASN'T CHANGED. FOR THOSE WHO DID NOT BELIEVE IN YOUR HOLY ESSENCE IN THE PAST, THEIR SUCCESSORS EXHIBIT THEIR NONBELIEF TODAY. OH WHAT A PITIFUL DISPLAY OF IRREVERENCE UNTO YOU, MY GOD! OH WHAT A PITIFUL EXPRESSION, OF WHICH YOU DO NOT DESERVE, O HOLY GOD. DO NOT WEEP, O HOLY GOD AND SPOUSE OF MINE, FOR I AND YOUR CHOSEN FEW HAVE NEVER DENIED OR ABANDONED YOU. DO NOT WEEP, O SYMPATHETIC GOD AND FATHER, FOR YOUR CHOSEN FEW REMAIN IN THE REALM OF ALLEGIANCE AND FAITHFULNESS THAT RELEASES OUR LOVE FOR YOU. ALTHOUGH THOSE OF THE PAST DID NOT BELIEVE, LOVE, AND HONOR YOU, YOUR FAITHFUL FEW HAVE SHOWN THEIR ALLEGIANCE TO YOUR WORTHY EXISTENCE FROM THE BEGINNING. MY LORD, ALTHOUGH THOSE OF THE PRESENT DO NOT BELIEVE, HONOR, AND LOVE YOU, YOUR CHOSEN FEW EXHIBIT THEIR UNDYING ALLEGIANCE TO YOU. BEHOLD! MY LORD. BEHOLD THE FEW! YES, YOUR CHOSEN BLESSED FEW, WILL ALWAYS FOLLOW YOUR HOLY AND ONLY WAY. WE, YOUR CHOSEN AND BLESSED FEW, WILL NEVER FALL INTO THE TRAPS THAT SATAN PLACES IN THE PATHS OF THE NONBELIEVING ONES.

BARBARA SPEAKING TO THE CHOSEN FEW

MY SAVED BROTHERS AND SISTERS, I WILL PRAY FOR THE CHOSEN FEW, FOR YOU HAVE BEEN FAITHFUL TO THE LORD JESUS, MY HOLY AND ETERNAL SPOUSE AND SAVING GOD. I WILL PRAY FOR THE CHOSEN ONES ONLY, FOR THEY ARE THE SAVED ONES WHO ARE WRITTEN IN JESUS', THE LAMB, BOOK OF LIFE. I WILL PRAY FOR THE FEW, THE FEW, YES, GOD'S CHOSEN SAVED FEW!!!

OCTOBER 13, 2015 AT 4:56 PM BY: BARBARA ANN MARY MACK

ALMIGHTY GOD, THE LORD
JESUS, SPEAKING

MY CHILDREN BE AWARE OF HE WHO THE WORLD LOVES AND PRAISES, FOR HE DOESN'T REPRESENT ME NOR MY REALM OF HOLINESS. BE AWARE OF HE WHO THE WORLD REVERES, FOR HE IS GUISED, *SAYS THE LORD*. HE IS A REPRESENTATIVE OF SATAN, MY ENEMY, FOR HE TEACHES AND SPEAKS THE THINGS THAT OFFEND ME AND MY HOLY CHURCH. HE IS A DECEIVER, MY CHILDREN. BE AWARE AND ATTENTIVE TO WHAT HE SPEAKS OF, FOR HIS WORDS ARE NOT MINE. HIS WORDS ARE UNPROFITABLE AND VAIN (WORTHLESS)! BE AWARE OF HE WHO ATTRACTS THOSE WHOSE SINS ARE NOT ADDRESSED OR VIEWED AS UNHOLY. FOR HE IS CONCEALING MY HOLY TRUTH FROM THE IGNORANT AND VULNERABLE SINNERS. HE IS NOT A REPRESENTATIVE OF MINE! HE IS GUISED! HE IS NOT FROM MY REALM OF HOLY TRUTH! BE AWARE, MY CHILDREN, FOR HE HAS RELEASED FALSE DOCTRINE! HE HAS FOOLED MANY VULNERABLE SOULS! REMEMBER MY CHILDREN, THOSE WHO ARE SENT BY ME, REVEAL, TEACH AND PREACH MY HOLY UNCHANGING WORDS. FOR I AM THE ONLY HOLY ONE, THERE IS NO OTHER! MY CHILDREN: BE AWARE OF HE WHO ATTRACTS THE WORLD, FOR HE DOESN'T ATTRACT MY CHOSEN AND SAVED FEW! LOOK BENEATH HIS GUISE AND WITNESS HIS TRUE IDENTITY, FOR HE DESIRES TO PLEASE THE WORLD INSTEAD OF ALMIGHTY GOD, HIS TRIUMPHANT ENEMY. O CHOSEN FEW, BE AWARE OF THOSE WHO ATTRACT THE WORLD, FOR THEY DO NOT REPRESENT ME!

OCTOBER 13, 2015 6:30 PM BY: BARBARA ANN MARY MACK

LET US WEEP TOGETHER, MY GOD, AS WE WITNESS THE CRUELTY THAT HAS SWALLOWED THIS PASSING WORLD

BARBARA SPEAKING TO
ALMIGHTY GOD

MY LORD, MY HOLY GOD, LET YOU AND I EMBRACE EACH OTHER, AS WE WITNESS THE CRUELTY THAT SATAN HAS RELEASED UPON YOUR VULNERABLE CHILDREN TODAY. LET US EMBRACE EACH OTHER, AS WE WEEP IN THE PRESENCE OF YOUR HEAVENLY RESIDENTS. LET US WEEP IN THE MIDST OF YOUR HOLY CHOIRS, AS THEY SING HYMNS OF SORROW TO THEIR WEEPING AND HEARTBROKEN GOD. LET US WEEP FOR THOSE WHO WERE DESTROYED BY SATAN'S HANDIWORK BEFORE THEY REPENTED IN YOUR HOLY PRESENCE. LET US WEEP TOGETHER, MY LORD, FOR THE CRUELTY THAT SATAN HAS RELEASED UPON YOUR FLOCK TODAY, HAS DEVASTATED THE RESIDENTS OF EARTH. LET OUR FLOWING TEARS UNITE WITH THE TEARS OF YOUR DAUGHTERS AND SONS, AS THEY WEEP UNCONTROLLABLY IN YOUR HOLY PRESENCE. LET OUR FLOWING TEARS UNITE WITH YOUR DAUGHTERS AND SONS TEARS, AS THEY BURY THEIR MURDERED CHILDREN. LET OUR TEARS UNITE WITH THE TEARS THAT HAVE OVERWHELMED YOUR CHILDREN, AS THEY WEEP AT THE NEWS OF THEIR LOVED ONES UNACCEPTABLE DEATHS AND ABDUCTIONS. MY LORD, MY HOLY SPOUSE AND GOD, LET US WEEP AS ONE FUSED ESSENCE OF DIVINE LOVE AND MERCY, AS WE WITNESS THE CRUELTY THAT HAS SWALLOWED THIS PASSING GENERATION. MY LORD, MY HOLY GOD, LET YOU AND I WEEP TOGETHER.

OCTOBER 13, 2015 AT 8:13 PM BY: BARBARA ANN MARY MACK

SENT WED, OCT 14, 2015 4:18 PM-READ WED 10/14/2015 10:02 PM

LET'S GO FOR A WALK TODAY LORD JESUS

BARBARA SPEAKING TO THE LORD JESUS

LET YOU AND I GO FOR A WALK TODAY LORD JESUS. TAKE MY HAND, LORD, AND WALK WITH ME FOR A WHILE. LET YOU AND I VISIT THE PLACES WHERE YOUR VERSION OF LOVE FLOWS

THROUGH THE STREETS AND HEARTS OF THOSE WHO TRULY LOVE AND ADORE YOU. LET YOU AND I VISIT THE PLACES WHERE THE PEOPLE EXHIBIT A LOVE FOR YOUR REALM OF HOLINESS THAT SURPASSES THE WORLD'S VERSION OF LOVE. LET US VISIT THE PLACES WHERE YOUR SONS AND DAUGHTERS REVEAL A LOVE FOR YOUR SACRIFICIAL ACT (THE CRUCIFIXION). WALK WITH ME, MY LORD, SO THAT YOU AND I MAY VISIT THE HOMES OF THOSE WHO HAVE MADE SACRIFICES FOR YOUR HOLY KINGDOMS ON EARTH AND IN HEAVEN. TAKE MY HUMBLED HAND IN YOUR PERFECT HOLY HAND, AND WALK WITH ME THROUGH THE STREETS WHERE YOUR CHOSEN FEW WALK THROUGHOUT DAILY. TAKE MY TRUSTING HAND IN YOUR POWERFUL HAND, SO THAT I MAY HOLD ON TO YOUR HOLY STRENGTH THROUGHOUT THE NIGHTS. WALK WITH ME, O LORD, AS I VISIT THE STREETS THAT EXHIBIT DIVINE EXCITEMENT AND HEAVENLY BLISS. WALK WITH ME, MY GOD, AND LEAD ME IN THE DIRECTION OF YOUR GLORIOUS HOME ABOVE, FOR IT IS THERE, I WILL WALK WITH YOU IN THE MIDST OF CONTINUOUS PRAISE! IT IS THERE, I WILL EXPERIENCE THE DEPTH OF ETERNAL BLISS. IT IS THERE, THAT MY HEART WILL FIND EVERLASTING REST, AS I SIT WITH YOU ON OUR THRONE ABOVE. WALK WITH ME, LORD JESUS, THROUGHOUT ETERNITY!!!

OCTOBER 12, 2015 AT 10:53 PM BY: BARBARA ANN MARY MACK
SENT WED, OCT 14, 2015 4:18 PM-READ WED 10/14/2015 10:02 PM

I TURN MY FACE AND ETERNAL ESSENCE FROM THOSE WHO CONTINUE TO DEFY ME AND TEST ME, *SAYS THE LORD*

ALMIGHTY GOD AND
BARBARA SPEAKING

AS ONE HOLY ESSENCE (ALMIGHTY GOD AND BARBARA), I TURN MY FACE TO THOSE WHO CONTINUE TO DEFY MY HOLY WAY AND ME. IT IS EVIDENCE THAT YOU DO NOT BELIEVE IN MY HOLY WORDS THAT ARE WRITTEN VERY CLEARLY IN THE SACRED BIBLE. MY HOLY FACE IS NO

LONGER IN YOUR SINFUL UNCHANGING PRESENCE. YOU, O SINNERS, HAVE MADE YOUR CHOICE! LET IT BE DONE ACCORDING TO YOUR SINFUL WAYS, FOR I HAVE TURNED MY FACE AGAINST YOU. YOU DO NOT EXIST, O DOOMED ONES! YOUR PHYSICAL PRESENCE TODAY IS ON LIMITED TIME! ENJOY THE PLEASURES THAT ARE BRIEF, FOR YOU HAVE ABANDONED AND DEFIED ME FOR THE LAST TIME! YOU TEST ME DAILY, YOU WHO DO NOT BELIEVE IN MY UNCHANGING WAY AND WRATH, FOR SATAN HAS BLINDED YOU. THEREFORE, YOU WILL GET A TASTE OF MY WRATH ON JUDGMENT DAY. I HAVE SPOKEN TO YOU FOR THE LAST TIME! THOSE WHO AGREE, SUPPORT AND CONDONE THE SINFUL ONES UNHOLY ACTS WILL ACCOMPANY THEM THROUGH THE GATES OF HELL. THERE ARE NO, NO, NO EXCEPTIONS, FOR I, THE LORD, HAVE SPOKEN FOR THE LAST TIME!!!

OCTOBER 11, 2015 AT 2:49 PM BY: BARBARA ANN MARY MACK

SENT SUN, OCT 11, 2015 2:59 PM-READ SUN 10/11/2015 5:20 PM

WHOSE SIDE ARE YOU ON? IS IT THE LOSING SIDE (SATAN)? OR MY VICTORIOUS SIDE, *SAYS THE LORD*

ALMIGHTY GOD SPEAKING

WHOSE SIDE ARE YOU ON, MY CHILDREN? TO WHOM DO YOU PUT YOUR TRUST AND ETERNAL DESTINATION IN? WHOM DO YOU REALLY ADORE? IS IT SATAN, MY ENEMY AND STEALER OF VULNERABLE SOULS? WHOM DO YOU TRULY SERVE, MY CHILDREN? DO NOT DECEIVE YOURSELVES, FOR YOUR ETERNAL DESTINATION DEPENDS ON YOUR ALLEGIANCE. ARE YOU FOLLOWING THE ONE (SATAN), YES, THE LOSING ONE? IS YOUR LOYALTY TO HE (SATAN) WHO IS DOOMED? IS YOUR ALLEGIANCE TO HE (SATAN), WHO HAS TAKEN DOWN MANY VULNERABLE SOULS? IS YOUR ALLEGIANCE TO HE (SATAN) WHO DOESN'T KNOW THE MEANING OF LOVE? WHOSE SIDE ARE YOU ON? ARE YOU ON MY SIDE? YES! MY CHILDREN, THE WINNING SIDE. HAVE YOU FOLLOWED MY HOLY TEACHINGS AND WAY? HAVE YOU EXHIBITED MY VERSION OF HOLINESS, MY CHILDREN? FOR THERE IS NO OTHER WAY! COME, MY CHILDREN! NOW IS THE TIME TO JOIN THE WINNING SIDE! FOR IT IS THE ONLY SIDE THAT WILL GIVE YOU ETERNAL PEACE AND JOY!

OCTOBER 10, 2015 AT 5:58 PM BY: BARBARA ANN MARY MACK

SENT SUN, OCT 11, 2015 1:36 AM-READ SUN 10/11/2015 2:33 PM

PLEASANT DREAMS DEAR ONE (CRAIG)! PLEASE KEEP MY GIRLS (LA TOYA AND AMYA) IN YOUR DAILY PRAYERS. AMORE BARBARA

ALMIGHTY GOD SPEAKING

KNOWING THE WORDS THAT ARE WRITTEN IN THE HOLY BIBLE IS ONLY BENEFICIAL WHEN THEY ARE EXHIBITED IN THE DAILY LIVES OF THE KNOWLEDGEABLE ONES. ONE MUST

PRACTICE WHAT HE OR SHE KNOWS IN ORDER TO CALL ONESELF A CHRISTIAN. KNOWING WORDS NEVER BENEFITS ONE IF THE WORDS AREN'T PRACTICED OR AVOIDED. MY CHILDREN, WORDS, MERE WORDS, DO NOT BRING ABOUT YOUR SALVATION, FOR SATAN ALSO SPEAKS WORDS. IT ISN'T WHAT YOU SAY OR PROFESS THAT DETERMINE YOUR DESTINATION, BUT YOUR ALLEGIANCE TO MY HOLY UNCHANGEABLE WORDS. YOUR SINCERE ACTIONS REVEAL THE INTEGRITY OF THE WORDS THAT EXIT YOUR MOUTH. MY CHILDREN, IF YOU HAVE NOT READ AND UNDERSTOOD MY HOLY UNCHANGEABLE WORDS THAT FLOW THROUGH THE HOLY BIBLE, NOW IS THE TIME TO LEARN OF ME. MY CHILDREN, YOU ARE LIVING IN THE MIDST OF THE END TIMES. IT IS IMPERATIVE THAT YOU LIVE ACCORDING TO MY VERSION OF RIGHTEOUSNESS, FOR YOU ARE LIVING IN THE LAST DAYS. LEARN OF ME, SO THAT YOU WILL KNOW HOW TO LIVE ACCORDING TO MY VERSION OF HOLINESS. MY CHILDREN, IT ISN'T DIFFICULT NOR PAINFUL. IT IS A LIFE THAT IS FREE OF SATAN'S REALM OF TEMPORARY PLEASURES. IT IS A LIFE THAT IS SANCTIFIED AND APPROVED BY ALMIGHTY GOD. IT IS A LIFE THAT FILLS ONE WITH CONTINUOUS DIVINE LOVE AND TRUST. IT IS A LIFE THAT HARBORS NO FEARS NOR ANXIETIES. IT IS A LIFE THAT IS ENCOMPASSED BY MY REALM OF GRACE AND GLORY. IT IS A LIFE THAT IS GOVERNED BY MY REALM OF PEACE AND TRANQUILITY. IT IS A LIFE THAT INVITES THOSE WHO DESIRE TO REIGN WITH JESUS, THE KING OF PEACE AND DIVINE ECSTASY. IT IS A LIFE THAT CRAVES FOR AN INSEPARABLE UNION WITH ALMIGHTY GOD, THE ONLY GREAT AND HOLY CREATOR. MY CHILDREN, YOUR GOOD WORKS AND TRUST IN ME REVEAL WHO YOU ARE. YOUR ACTION REVEALS THE TRUTH.

OCTOBER 8, 2015 AT 6:15 PM BY: BARBARA ANN MARY MACK

UNDERSTAND THE SIGNS OF THE TIME-WHO'S WITH ME? WHO WANTS TO LIVE IN SWEET PARADISE ABOVE FOREVER?

ALMIGHTY GOD SPEAKING

MY CHILDREN, CAN YOU NOT SEE THE SIGNS THAT REVEAL THE TERRIBLE PERIOD THAT IS SPOKEN OF IN THE HOLY BIBLE? CAN YOU NOT BEHOLD THE TERRIBLE SIGNS? YES! THE HORRIBLE SIGNS THAT CONFIRM MY HOLY SPOKEN WORD. BEHOLD THE SIGNS! YES! THE MANY, MANY SIGNS THAT REVEAL THE PRESENCE OF THE FORETOLD HARDSHIP THAT WOULD COVER EARTH'S REALM OF DISOBEDIENCE. BEHOLD, MY CHILDREN! FOR YOU ARE IN THE MIDST OF THE GREAT AND TERRIBLE TRIBULATION. BEHOLD THE SIGNS! BEHOLD THE HARDSHIP! BEHOLD THE MURDERS! BEHOLD THE APATHETIC ONES (MURDERERS)! BEHOLD THE TRAGEDIES! BEHOLD THE NATURAL DISASTERS! BEHOLD THE PRESENCE OF EVIL IN YOUR MIDST! BEHOLD THE INJUSTICE THAT PERMEATES THE JUSTICE SYSTEM! BEHOLD THE IMMORALITY! WHERE IS YOUR FAITH, O WOUNDED ONES? WHERE IS YOUR ALLEGIANCE, O BETRAYING ONES? WHERE DOES YOUR LOYALTY LIE? I KNOW YOUR DEEDS AND YOUR WORKS,

SAYS THE LORD! I ALSO KNOW YOUR ALLEGIANCE AND YOUR DESTINATION. MY CHILDREN, UNDERSTAND THE SIGNS OF THIS PASSING WORLD. ARE YOU WITH ME, MY SONS? ARE YOU WITH ME, MY DAUGHTERS? WHO WANTS TO LIVE IN SWEET PARADISE WITH YOUR SAVING CREATOR AND GOD? IS IT YOU, MY SON? IS IT YOU, MY DAUGHTER? REMEMBER, MY CHILDREN, YOUR DEEDS AND WORKS REVEAL WHERE YOU DESIRE TO BE THROUGHOUT ETERNITY.

OCTOBER 8, 2015 AT 11:44 PM BY: BARBARA ANN MARY MACK

SENT SAT, OCT 10, 2015 12:58 AM-READ SAT 10/10/2015 11:18 AM

ARCHBISHOP CRAIG, WE DO NOT KNOW THE TIME AND DAY OF YOUR MASS IN PHOENIXVILLE. GOD BLESS!

SENT SAT, OCT 10, 2015 3:19 PM-READ SAT 10/10/2015 4:49 PM

HAPPY SABBATH DAY ARCHBISHOP CRAIG! BELOW ARE PASSAGES TAKEN FROM MY FORTHCOMING BOOK. TI AMO! BELLA BARBIE

IF I WAS TO COME TODAY OR TOMORROW, WOULD YOU RISE TO JOIN ME IN THE CLOUDS, *SAYS THE LORD?* OR WOULD YOU...?

MY CHILDREN, IF I WAS TO COME IN THE MIDST OF THE CLOUDS TODAY OR TOMORROW, WOULD YOU RISE AND JOIN ME IN THE CLOUDS? IF I WAS TO COME AGAIN TO YOUR WORLD OF NEED TODAY, WOULD YOU BE READY TO RISE WITH ME? IF I WAS TO APPEAR IN THE MIDST OF THE CHOSEN CLOUDS TOMORROW, WOULD YOU BE PREPARED, MY CHILDREN? IF I WAS TO COME TO YOU IN MY GLORIOUS FORM TODAY IN THE MIDST OF THE CLOUDS, WOULD YOU RISE WITH ME IN THE PRESENCE OF THE ONLOOKERS? ARE YOU PREPARED TO JOIN ME IN THE

MIDST OF THE HEAVENLY CLOUDS, MY CHILDREN? ARE YOU LIVING ACCORDING TO MY HOLY TEACHINGS THAT FLOW THROUGH THE HOLY BIBLE, YOUR PHYSICAL INSTRUCTOR? LEARN OF MY HOLY WORDS AND WAY, SO THAT YOU MAY RISE WITH ME WHEN I RETURN IN THE MIDST OF THE CLOUDS, FOR IT MAYBE TODAY OR TOMORROW. MY CHILDREN, WILL YOU BE ONE OF THE ONLOOKERS AS MY FAITHFUL ONES RISE WITH ME INTO MY HOLY KINGDOM ABOVE? WILL YOU BE AN OBSERVER OF MY GLORIOUS RETURN, OR WILL YOU BE A PART OF IT? WHAT WILL IT BE, MY CHILDREN? ARE YOU PREPARED AT THIS TIME? TODAY IS THE DAY TO BE READY, FOR NO ONE OTHER THAN OUR HEAVENLY FATHER AND GOD KNOWS OF MY RETURN, MY SECOND AND FINAL COMING. BE PREPARED, MY CHILDREN, SO THAT YOU MAY AVOID THE TRAGEDY OF SPENDING ETERNITY IN A PEACE-LESS REALM OF EXISTENCE.
OCTOBER 11, 2015 AT 1:25 AM BY: BARBARA ANN MARY MACK

IN THE MIDST OF TRAGEDIES, THEY CONTINUE TO DENOUNCE, BETRAY AND REJECT ME, *SAYS THE LORD*

ALMIGHTY GOD, THE LORD JESUS, SPEAKING

IN THE MIDST OF WORLDLY TRAGEDIES THE UNFAITHFUL, UNRIGHTEOUS AND DISOBEDIENT ONES CONTINUE REJECTING ME AND MY REALM OF DIVINITY. IN THE MIDST OF PERILOUS TIMES, THEY, THE UNRIGHTEOUS AND DECEIVED ONES, DENOUNCE ME AS THEIR SAVING GOD. DURING THESE LAST UNHOLY DAYS, THE WORLD PERSISTS IN DISPLAYING THEIR UNHOLY ACTS IN MY OMNIPRESENT SIGHT. I CAN SEE YOUR DIRTY DEEDS, O DOOMED PASSING WORLD! I CAN SEE THE EVILS THAT YOU RELEASE EVERY DAY. YOU TRY TO WALK BOLDLY INTO MY CHURCH! SOME OF THE DECEIVED SHEPHERDS INVITE YOU INTO MY CHURCH. BUT YOU CANNOT PENETRATE THE REALM THAT I HAVE PLACED BETWEEN YOU AND MY HOLY CHURCH. YOU MAY HAVE ACCESS TO A BUILDING THAT IS CALLED A CHURCH, BUT YOU DO NOT AND CANNOT ENTER ME, THE HOLY CHURCH! YOU CANNOT PIERCE THE REALM THAT SEPARATES THE RIGHTEOUS FROM THE UNHOLY ONES. YOU CANNOT PENETRATE ME! I HAVE NOT INVITED YOU INTO MY HOLY CHURCH, BECAUSE YOU DO NOT DESIRE TO CONFORM TO MY VERSION OF HOLINESS AND RIGHTEOUSNESS. YOU DO NOT DESIRE TO CHANGE YOUR SINFUL WAYS. YOU DO NOT DESIRE TO CHANGE, BECAUSE YOU BELIEVE THAT I WILL CHANGE OR CONFORM TO YOUR DIRTY ACTS. I KNOW HIM, HE WHO IS BEHIND YOUR REALM OF BELIEF. IT IS YOUR FATHER (SATAN)! IT IS YOUR GOD (SATAN)! IT IS YOUR LIFE (SATAN)! YOU HAVE DENOUNCED THE REALITY OF MY DIVINITY AS GOD, THE EVERLASTING SAVIOR! YOU OPENLY DENY MY PRESENT EXISTENCE IN THE LIVES OF THOSE WHO TRULY LOVE ME. YOU DENY THE REVERENCE THAT IS DUE TO THE SAVED ONES SACRIFICIAL GOD (THE VICTORIOUS KING JESUS). YOU PREFER THE DEPTH OF HELL OVER ETERNITY WITH ME IN SWEET PARADISE. IN THE MIDST OF THIS TRAGIC PERIOD OF TIME, YOUR DIRTY ACTS AND DEEDS ARE VERY VISIBLE. YOU HAVE TESTED MY MERCY,

O DISOBEDIENT ONES! YOU HAVE TESTED MY LOVE, O UNRIGHTEOUS ONES! NOW, YOU WILL REAP WHAT YOU HAVE SOWN THROUGH THE YEARS! BEHOLD! O HARDENED HEARTS OF MY BETRAYERS. BEHOLD MY JUSTICE IN YOUR MIDST TODAY! FOR IT, MY DIVINE JUSTICE, HASN'T CHANGED!!!

OCTOBER 6, 2015 AT 12:42 AM BY: BARBARA ANN MARY MACK

SENT THU, OCT 8, 2015 3:37 PM-READ THU 10/8/2015 4:11 PM

GO AWAY, O DEATH, FOR IT ISN'T MY TIME YET!

BARBARA SPEAKING TO DEATH (SATAN)

I CAN RECALL THE MANY TIMES WHEN DEATH KNOCKED ON MY DOOR, I REPLIED, GO AWAY, O DEATH, FOR IT ISN'T MY TIME YET!

BARBARA SPEAKING TO DEATH (SATAN)

WHEN I WAS A YOUNG CHILD, YOU KNOCKED ON MY DOOR, I REPLIED, GO AWAY, O DEATH, FOR IT ISN'T MY TIME YET! YEARS LATER, WHEN I WAS AN OLDER CHILD, YOU, O DEATH, KNOCKED ON MY DOOR. I REPLIED, GO AWAY, O DEATH, FOR IT ISN'T TIME YET!

BARBARA SPEAKING TO ALMIGHTY GOD

MY LORD, MY HOLY GOD, THE REALM OF DEATH KNOCKED ON MY DOOR MANY TIMES THROUGHOUT MY SHORT LIFE, BUT YOU REBUKED SATAN, THE ORIGIN OF UNPROFITABLE DEATH (SPIRITUAL AND PHYSICAL). FOR YOU, O GREAT AND HOLY ORIGIN OF DIVINE LIFE, YOU HAD A PLAN FOR MY LIFE, YES, MY VALUABLE LIFE, BEFORE I ENTERED MY MOTHER'S WOMB. YOUR HOLY PLAN, O LORD, CANNOT BE TERMINATED BY PREMATURE DEATH. YOUR HOLY PLAN FOR MY VALUABLE LIFE INCLUDED THE REVELATION OF YOUR HOLY PRESENCE IN OUR BLESSED MIDST TODAY. YOUR HOLY PLAN FOR MY LIFE INCLUDED THE MANIFESTATION OF YOUR HOLY PRESENCE, WHICH DWELLS WITHIN MY PURIFIED BEING. YOUR HOLY PLAN FOR MY HUMBLED LIFE, INCLUDES A DIVINE ASSIGNMENT THAT WILL BRING ABOUT THE CONVERSION OF THE BLESSED AND CHOSEN ONES. YOUR HOLY PLAN FOR MY BLESSED LIFE, INCLUDES THE MANIFESTATION OF A MODERN DAY MESSENGER AND PROPHET (BARBARA) OF OUR TRUE LIVING GOD. MY LORD, MY GOD, THROUGH THE YEARS SATAN, OUR ENEMY, TRIED ON NUMEROUS OCCASIONS, TO TERMINATE THE LIFE OF YOUR MESSENGER AND BRIDE (BARBARA). HE, SATAN, IS A FAILURE! HE IS A LOSER! HE CANNOT PREVENT THAT WHICH IS ORDERED BY YOU, THE ONLY ALMIGHTY ONE.

BARBARA SPEAKING TO DEATH (SATAN)

FLEE FROM MY VALUABLE PRESENCE, O DEATH, FOR YOU HAVE LOST THIS BATTLE! MY WORK FOR GOD, THE ONLY ALMIGHTY ONE, IS A COMPLETE SUCCESS! *ALLELUIA!!!*
OCTOBER 6, 2015 AT 11:59 PM BY: BARBARA ANN MARY MACK

BE PREPARED AT ALL TIMES, FOR ONE DOESN'T KNOW WHEN DEATH WILL APPROACH

BARBARA SPEAKING

MY BROTHERS AND SISTERS, SINCE WE DO NOT KNOW WHEN THE LORD, WHO IS ALPHA, THE BEGINNING, AND OMEGA, THE END, WILL CALL US BACK TO HIS ESSENCE WHEN OUR PHYSICAL LIFE ENDS, WE OUGHT TO BE SPIRITUALLY PREPARED FOR THAT BLESSED UNKNOWN DAY AND TIME .OH, THE MANY WHO WERE NOT PREPARED TO GREET THE LORD WHEN THEIR LIVES ENDED WITHOUT WARNING. BLESSED ARE THEY, THE BELIEVING ONES, WHO WERE SPIRITUALLY PREPARED WHEN THEY WERE CALLED BACK TO GOD, THEIR ORIGIN. BLESSED ARE THE TRUE BELIEVERS, FOR THEY OBEYED THE WRITINGS THAT FLOW THROUGH THE HOLY BIBLE. THEY LEARNED OF THE IMPORTANCE OF FOLLOWING THE TEACHINGS OF GOD, THE GREATEST TEACHER OF ALL AGES. THEY HAVE EARNED THE HIGHEST DEGREE, WHICH SURPASSES EVERY FORM OF WORLDLY RECOGNITION. YES! THEY HAVE EARNED ENTRANCE INTO GOD'S REALM OF HOLY ETERNAL BLISS. THEY HAVE BEEN AWARDED WITH THE HIGHEST HONORS (SUPPER WITH GOD, THE ETERNAL LAMB) THAT ONE CAN RECEIVE FOR GREAT WORKS. THEY, THE BLESSED ONES, MADE PREPARATION FOR LIFE IN ETERNAL GLORY. THEY REVERED ALMIGHTY GOD AND LIVED ACCORDING TO HIS VERSION OF HOLINESS. THEY ARE THE BLESSED AND CHOSEN FEW! *ALLELUIA!*
OCTOBER 6, 2015 AT 5:49 PM BY: BARBARA ANN MARY MACK

SPACE: UNENDING SPACE, ALMIGHTY GOD

BARBARA SPEAKING

OH THE BOUNDARY LESS ESSENCE (ALMIGHTY GOD) THAT SURROUNDS ME THROUGHOUT THE DAY, RELEASES UNQUENCHABLE JOY AND DELIGHT! OH THE DIVINE SPACE (ALMIGHTY GOD) THAT ENCOMPASSES MY SMALL BUT VALUABLE SOUL, RELEASES THE PEACE THAT KEEPS MY IGNITED SPIRIT MOVING THROUGHOUT EACH BLESSED DAY! YOUR ESSENCE IS ENDLESS, MY GOD, FOR YOU ARE DIVINE UNOCCUPIED AND INCORRUPTIBLE SPACE. LET ME JOIN YOU, O ENDLESS ONE (ALMIGHTY GOD), SO THAT I MAY SOAR IN THE MIDST OF SWEET BOUNDARY LESS SPACE. ENCOMPASS YOUR CHOSEN SPOUSE (BARBARA), O HOLY SPACE (ALMIGHTY GOD), AS I RELAX WITHIN THE ESSENCE (ALMIGHTY GOD) THAT CREATED ME NOT SO LONG AGO. FOR YOUR MERCY IS ENDLESS. YOUR KINDNESS SURPASSES ALL REALMS OF KINDNESS. YOU ARE ENDLESS, MY HOLY GOD, FOR YOU ARE MINE. YOU ARE ETERNITY! YOU ARE INFINITY! YOU ARE ALMIGHTY GOD! *ALLELUIA!*
OCTOBER 6, 2015 AT 6:17 PM BY: BARBARA ANN MARY MACK
SENT THU, OCT 8, 2015 3:37 PM-READ THU 10/8/2015 4:11 PM

ENJOY YOUR DAY ARCHBISHOP CRAIG! TI AMO! BELLA BARBIE . TODAY'S PASSAGES

HARK! YOU COWARDS. YOU WHO HIDE BEHIND MY HOLY WORDS, BUT DO NOT ABIDE BY THEM. YOU WHO SPEAK MY WORDS THAT ARE WITHIN THE HOLY BIBLE, BUT DO NOT LIVE BY THEM. YOU WHO SPEAK MY HOLY WORDS, BUT DO NOT INSTRUCT YOUR CONGREGATION TO LIVE BY THEM EVERY DAY. YOU COWARDS! YOU WHO ARE NOT FOLLOWING THE HOLY WORDS THAT YOU PREACH AND TEACH TO THE UNSUSPECTING ONES, ARE COWARDS AND BETRAYERS IN MY HOLY EYES. PRACTICE WHAT YOU PREACH, O COWARDS! PRACTICE WHAT YOU TEACH, O BETRAYERS OF YOUR HOLY CREATOR AND GOD! DO NOT CONFORM TO THE WORLD'S (SATAN) VERSION OF RIGHTEOUSNESS, O COWARDS, FOR YOUR ETERNAL DESTINATION IS AT STAKE! PREACH MY HOLY TRUTH, O COWARDS! EXHIBIT MY HOLY WAY, O BETRAYERS OF THE CHRISTIAN FAITH! DO NOT GIVE IN TO YOUR FLESHLY DESIRES OF FAME AND WORLDLY ACKNOWLEDGMENT, O COWARDS! DO NOT GIVE IN TO YOUR SPIRITUAL AND PHYSICAL WEAKNESSES, FOR YOUR ETERNAL DESTINATION IS AT STAKE! HEED MY WARNINGS, O COWARDS! COME BACK TO JESUS, THE ONLY FOUNDER OF THE CHRISTIAN FAITH, O BETRAYERS! COME BACK, WHILE THE DOOR, MY HOLY DOOR, IS OPEN TO YOU. HURRY! O COWARDS. HURRY! O BETRAYERS. FOR YOUR TIME IS RUNNING OUT, *SAYS THE LORD!*

OCTOBER 7, 2015 AT 4:01 PM BY: BARBARA ANN MARY MACK

WATERING DOWN THE HOLY SCRIPTURES, MY TRUTH, *SAYS THE LORD:* THE PRICE

ALMIGHTY GOD SPEAKING

WHY DO YOU WATER DOWN THE TRUTH, MY HOLY TRUTH, O CORRUPTING ONES? WHY DO YOU NOT REVEAL THE TRUTH THAT FLOWS FROM MY HOLY WORDS, O DECEIVING ONES? WHY DO

YOU WATER DOWN THAT WHICH WILL SAVE THE LOST SOULS THAT FOLLOW YOUR INCOMPLETE TRUTH? YOU MUST TELL THEM MY COMPLETE TRUTH, FOR IT WILL SAVE YOUR SOULS AS WELL. DO NOT GIVE IN TO SATAN'S REALM OF DECEPTION, YOU WHO WATER DOWN THE MEANING, MY HOLY MEANING, OF RIGHTEOUSNESS AND HOLINESS. UNDERSTAND THIS, YOU WHO WATER DOWN MY HOLY TRUTH, YOUR ETERNAL PLACE WILL BE IN HELL WITH SATAN, MY ENEMY. THERE ARE NO, NO, NO EXCEPTIONS! AVOID THE PRICE THAT COMES WITH WATERING DOWN MY HOLY WORDS, MY CHILDREN. AVOID THE PRICE THAT COMES WITH DECEIVING MY VULNERABLE FLOCK, FOR THE PRICE IS ETERNAL. THE PRICE IS ETERNITY IN HELL! THERE ARE NO EXCEPTIONS! OCTOBER 7, 2015 AT 4:24 PM BY: BARBARA ANN MARY MACK

I CAN SEE BENEATH THE FLESH

BARBARA SPEAKING TO ALMIGHTY GOD

MY LORD, MY HOLY GOD, I CAN SEE WHAT'S BENEATH THE FLESH THAT COVERS THOSE WHO COMMIT EVIL ACTS AGAINST YOUR VULNERABLE CHILDREN. I CAN SEE THAT WHICH IS HIDDEN FROM THE VISUAL PERCEPTION OF THE NATURAL ONES. YOU HAVE GIVEN ME THE ABILITY TO SEE THAT WHICH IS HIDDEN FROM THE WORLD. MY LORD, MY HOLY GOD, IT IS AN AWFUL SIGHT! FOR I CAN SEE THE EVIL THAT HIDES BENEATH THE FLESH OF ONE WHO SHOWS NO MERCY OR COMPASSION TOWARD YOUR VULNERABLE CHILDREN. I CAN SEE IT, MY LORD! I CAN SEE THE REALM OF EVIL THAT RESTS AND ABIDES BENEATH THE FLESH OF THOSE WHO WALK IN OUR MIDST EVERY DAY. OH WHAT A HORRIBLE SIGHT, MY GOD! TO SEE EVIL IN ITS NATURAL STATE IS AN ABILITY THAT I DO NOT DESIRE TO POSSESS. IT IS AN EXPERIENCE THAT THE WORLD DOES NOT HAVE ACCESS TO. IT IS AN ABILITY THAT LETS ME BE AWARE OF SATAN'S PRESENCE IN OUR MIDST TODAY. IT IS AN ABILITY THAT ALLOWS ME TO ADDRESS SATAN INSTEAD OF A NATURAL CREATION (MANKIND) OF ALMIGHTY GOD, WHEN HORRENDOUS ACTS ARE RELEASED.

BARBARA SPEAKING TO THE REALM OF EVIL

I CAN SEE YOU, O REALM OF EVIL THAT HIDES BENEATH THE FLESH OF AN INNOCENT LOOKING CHILD. I CAN SEE YOU, O REALM OF EVIL, AS YOU APPEAR AS A LOVING PARENT. I CAN SEE YOU, O REALM OF EVIL, AS YOU APPEAR IN THE FORM OF THE CLERGY. I CAN SEE YOU, O REALM OF EVIL, AS YOU APPEAR IN THE FORM OF A LOVING HUSBAND. I CAN SEE YOU, O REALM OF EVIL AS YOU APPEAR IN THE FORM OF A DEVOTED WIFE. I CAN SEE YOU, O REALM OF EVIL, AS YOU APPEAR IN THE FORM OF A CARING STRANGER. YES! I CAN SEE YOU, O REALM OF EVIL, AS YOU HIDE BENEATH THE FLESH.
OCTOBER 7, 2015 AT 5:17 PM BY: BARBARA ANN MARY MACK

THOSE WHO KNOW AND LOVE ME WILL NOT FOLLOW, CONDONE, NOR REVERE THE WAYS OF THE WORLD, *SAYS THE LORD*

ALMIGHTY GOD SPEAKING

GATHER AROUND ME, ALL WHO TRULY LOVE AND ADORE YOUR CREATOR AND FAITHFUL GOD! GATHER AROUND THE THRONE OF HE, ALMIGHTY GOD, WHO WOULD NEVER BETRAY OR FORSAKE HIS LOVED ONES! GATHER AROUND ME, ALL WHO ARE NOT ASHAMED TO LIVE MY VERSION OF HOLY LIVES, IN THE MIDST OF THIS PASSING WORLD. GATHER AROUND ME, ALL WHO LOVE TO SING JOYFUL SONGS OF PRAISE TO THEIR GENEROUS GOD AND FATHER! COME! ALL WHO ARE WILLING TO SACRIFICE ALL OF THEIR FLESHLY DESIRES THAT OFFEND THEIR FAITHFUL GOD AND HEAVENLY FATHER. COME! ALL WHO HAVE GIVEN UP THE THINGS THAT THE WORLD REVERES AND SHOWS ALLEGIANCE TO. COME! ALL WHO DO NOT CONFORM TO OR CONDONE THE THINGS THAT HURT THEIR CREATOR AND FAITHFUL GOD. COME! ALL WHO ARE OFFENDED BY THE DIRTY DEEDS THAT PERMEATE THIS PASSING WORLD. COME! ALL WHO WEEP WITH THEIR HEAVENLY FATHER AND GOD, AS THE WORLD EXHIBITS THE ACTS THAT

FLOW FROM SATAN'S UNHOLY REALM OF DISGUST. COME! ALL OF MY CHOSEN GUESTS, FOR THE KINGDOM OF HEAVEN IS OURS!

OCTOBER 7, 2015 AT 5:42 PM BY: BARBARA ANN MARY MACK

WHERE IS MANKIND GOING? WHERE IS MANKIND HEADING? WHERE?

ALMIGHTY GOD SPEAKING

WHERE ARE YOU GOING, MY SONS? WHERE ARE YOU GOING, MY DAUGHTERS? DO YOU KNOW, MY CHILDREN? WHERE ARE YOU HEADING, O WANDERING ONES? WHERE IS YOUR DESTINATION? ARE YOU SEEKING ME, MY CHILDREN? ARE YOU SEEKING YOUR ONLY SAVING GOD AND FATHER? WHERE ARE YOUR ETERNAL SOULS HEADING, O LOST ONES? WHERE IS YOUR DESTINATION? WILL YOU SEEK ETERNAL LIFE THROUGH ME, YOUR SAVIOR, MY CHILDREN. WILL YOU HEAD IN THE DIRECTION THAT LEADS TO ETERNAL GLORY IN SWEET PARADISE WITH ME, THE LORD JESUS? WHERE ARE YOU TODAY, MY SONS? ARE YOU WALKING WITH ME, YOUR SAVING GOD? ARE YOU LIVING WITHIN THE REALM OF SIN WITH SATAN OUR ENEMY? ARE YOU SEEKING SALVATION, OR ETERNAL DAMNATION? WHERE ARE YOU TODAY? O CALLED ONES. WHERE DOES YOUR ALLEGIANCE LIE? WHO ARE YOU LOYAL TO? IS IT ME, YOUR CREATOR AND GOD? IS IT HE (SATAN) WHO STEALS THE VULNERABLE SOULS OF MY UNSUSPECTING ONES? WHERE ARE YOU TODAY, MY CHILDREN? HAVE YOU READ MY LIFE SAVING WORDS THAT FLOW THROUGH THE HOLY BIBLE? HAVE YOU ATTENDED CHURCH SERVICES, SO THAT YOU CAN LEARN OF ME THROUGH MY SENT SHEPHERDS (PASTORS)? HURRY! MY CHILDREN. SEEK THE PATH, THE ONLY PATH (THE LORD JESUS) THAT LEADS TO ETERNAL GLORY IN HEAVEN ABOVE. HURRY! MY CHILDREN, HURRY!

OCTOBER 1, 2015 AT 7:44 BY: BARBARA ANN MARY MACK

SENT SAT, OCT 3, 2015 5:35 PM-READ SAT 10/3/2015 6:09 PM

GOD'S INTOLERANCE OF MANKIND'S WICKEDNESS HASN'T CHANGED: WAKE UP WORLD, BEFORE IT IS TOO LATE

ALMIGHTY GOD SPEAKING

I WILL NOT TOLERATE THE IRREVERENCE THAT YOU, THE WORLD, EXHIBIT TOWARD ME, YOUR CREATOR AND GOD. I WILL NOT TOLERATE THE UNHOLY ACTS THAT PERMEATE THE STREETS THAT CARRY THOSE WHO DISRESPECT MY UNCHANGING REALM OF HOLINESS. I WILL NOT TOLERATE THE INJUSTICE THAT FLOWS THROUGH THE WORLD'S CORRUPT JUSTICE SYSTEM. I HAVE NOT CHANGED, MY CHILDREN! I HAVE NOT CHANGED, O DISRESPECTFUL ONES. MY TOLERANCE TOWARDS YOUR UNHOLY ACTS AND THOUGHTS REMAINS! YOU MAY

TRY TO CHANGE MY CHURCH STANDARDS, BUT YOU CANNOT! YOU, O WORLD, LIKE SATAN, CANNOT CHANGE ME NOR MY CHURCH. DO YOU DESIRE TO WITNESS AND EXPERIENCE MY WRATH, O WICKED GENERATION? WHY DO YOU TEST MY LEVEL OF TOLERANCE DAILY? DO YOU NOT BELIEVE IN THAT WHICH IS WRITTEN IN THE HOLY BIBLE, IN REGARDS TO MY JUSTICE TOWARDS THE WICKED AND DISOBEDIENT ONES? WHY DO YOU CONTINUE TO TEST ME, O DISRESPECTFUL ONES? WHY DO YOU CONTINUE TESTING MY TOLERANCE? CAN YOU NOT SEE AND HEAR OF THE WORKS THAT ARE PLACED UPON THIS GENERATION? IT IS THE RESULTS OF YOUR WICKEDNESS, MY CHILDREN. LEARN OF MY JUSTICE BY READING THE HOLY BIBLE. I AM LOVING AND FORGIVING, TOWARD THOSE WHO REMOVE THEMSELVES FROM THE ACTS WHICH I VIEW AS UNHOLY AND ABOMINABLE. WAKE UP, O WORLD! WAKE UP BEFORE THE GATES TO SWEET PARADISE CLOSE IN YOUR UNHOLY PRESENCE. WAKE UP BEFORE THE OPPORTUNITY FOR YOU TO RECONCILE WITH ME, IS NO LONGER AVAILABLE TO YOU!

OCTOBER 4, 2015 AT 4:21 PM BY: BARBARA ANN MARY MACK

SENT SUN, OCT 4, 2015 7:13 PM-READ SUN 10/4/2015 8:01 PM

OH HOW I ADORE MAN

BARBARA SPEAKING TO ALMIGHTY GOD

OH HOW I ADORE MAN, ONE OF YOUR GREATEST CREATIONS, MY GOD. FOR MAN'S EXISTENCE REVEALS HIS ORIGIN AND SOVEREIGN KING (THE LORD JESUS). MAN'S EXISTENCE REVEALS GOD'S HOLY PRESENCE IN OUR BLESSED MIDST TODAY. MAN'S EXISTENCE REVEALS HIS UNION AND BOND WITH GOD, THE HOLY AND BLESSED TRINITY. OH HOW I TRULY ADORE MAN, YOUR MOST PRECIOUS CREATION, O HOLY GOD AND SPOUSE OF MINE. OH HOW I ADORE THAT WHICH CAME FROM YOUR REALM OF DIVINITY, O HEAVENLY GOD AND FATHER OF ALL THAT IS GOOD AND HOLY IN YOUR PERFECT EYES. I GIVE GLORY AND HONOR TO ALMIGHTY GOD FOR THE MIRACLE OF

LIFE-YES! THE MIRACLE OF MAN! OH YES! MAN!!! A HOLY WONDER THAT TRANSCENDS ALL OF THE WORLD'S VERSIONS OF WONDERS. YES! MAN! A GIFT FROM GOD'S HOLY EXISTENCE. *ALLELUIA!!!*

OCTOBER 2, 2015 AT 6:32 PM BY: BARBARA ANN MARY MACK

SENT SAT, OCT 3, 2015 5:35 PM-READ SAT 10/3/2015 6:09 PM

GREETINGS ARCHBISHOP CRAIG! COME STA OGGI? EVERY TIME THAT I HEAR OF SITUATIONS INVOLVING "SENSELESS MURDERS", MY MIND GOES BACK TO THE SAYINGS THAT FLOW THROUGH THE BOOK OF REVELATION IN THE HOLY BIBLE PERTAINING TO PERILOUS TIMES AND THE LAST DAYS. WE CHRISTIANS BELIEVE IN WHAT THE HOLY SCRIPTURES REVEAL. THEREFORE, I AM NOT SURPRISED, CONFUSED OR SHAKEN, WHEN I HEAR OF OR WITNESS UNSPEAKABLE AND SENSELESS OCCURRENCES. ONE OF THE CURRENT SITUATIONS INVOLVING A COMMUNITY COLLEGE IN OREGON STATE, AGAIN REVEALS THE PRESENCE OF EVIL (SATAN) IN OUR VULNERABLE MIDST TODAY. WHAT CAN WE DO TO REMEDY OR PREVENT THESE OCCURRENCES? IF WE CHRISTIANS BELIEVE IN WHAT THE BIBLE REVEALS, WE UNDERSTAND THAT WE CANNOT DO ANYTHING TO PREVENT OR DELAY A SCRIPTURE PROPHECY FROM MANIFESTING. IF ONE COULD DO THIS, THEN THE HOLY SCRIPTURES WOULD NOT BE A CREDIBLE AND VALUABLE GIFT FROM THE LORD, WHO PREPARED US FOR THESE LAST DAYS. BELOW IS SOMETHING THAT I COPIED FROM AOL NEWS YESTERDAY PERTAINING TO THE OCCURRENCE AT THE COLLEGE IN OREGON. PRAYERS AND CONCERNS CANNOT ALTER OR PREVENT A BIBLICAL PROPHECY. BUT, PRAYER AND UNITY CAN HELP US COPE WITH THE HORRENDOUS SITUATIONS WHEN THEY OCCUR. THEREFORE, I WILL CONTINUE TO PRAY FOR ALL WHO ARE AFFECTED BY THIS TRAGIC OCCURRENCE, INCLUDING THE PARENTS AND FRIENDS OF THE GUNMAN. WITH GOD'S ETERNAL PEACE, BARBARA

FOREVER, THAT'S HOW LONG I WILL LOVE YOU, *SAYS THE LORD*

ALMIGHTY GOD SPEAKING

OH FAITHFUL ONES, I WILL ALWAYS LOVE YOU. OH FAITHFUL ONES, I WILL ALWAYS WATCH OVER YOU. OH FAITHFUL ONES, I WILL ALWAYS PROTECT YOU FROM THE REALM OF EVIL AS IT TRIES TO STEAL YOU FROM ME, YOUR HOLY CREATOR AND GOD. OH FAITHFUL ONES, I WILL ALWAYS WALK WITH YOU DURING YOUR TIMES OF NEED, AND WHEN YOU ARE AT PEACE WITHIN. OH FAITHFUL ONES, I WILL SHARE MY SPIRITUAL WEALTH WITH YOU, SO THAT YOU MAY REIGN OVER THOSE WHO HAVE FOLLOWED THE REALM OF DECEPTION AND DOOM. I WILL SHARE MY POT OF SILVER AND GOLD THAT DESCENDS WITH MY BLESSINGS FROM ABOVE, FOR I WILL ALWAYS LOVE YOU. I WILL GIVE YOU THE GIFT OF ETERNAL LIFE AS AN EXPRESSION OF MY UNENDING LOVE. OH FAITHFUL DAUGHTERS! OH FAITHFUL SONS! LOOK UP TO YOUR HEAVENLY KING AND GOD, FOR I WILL ALWAYS LOVE YOU! ENTER! ENTER! ENTER MY HEAVENLY HOME, O FAITHFUL ONES, WHO HAVE FOLLOWED MY UNCHANGING WORD IN THE MIDST OF THE WORLD OF UNFAITHFULNESS. ENTER THE HOME OF HE (ALMIGHTY GOD) WHO WILL ALWAYS LOVE YOU! ENTER THE HEAVENLY HOME OF HE (ALMIGHTY GOD) WHO WILL LOVE YOU FOREVER!!! ENTER! ENTER! ENTER!!!
OCTOBER 2, 2015 AT 2:24 AM BY: BARBARA ANN MARY MACK
SENT SAT, OCT 3, 2015 5:35 PM-READ SAT 10/3/2015 6:09 PM

GREETINGS ARCHBISHOP CRAIG! ENJOY THIS BLESSED DAY LOVE! BELOW ARE PASSAGES TAKEN FROM MY FORTHCOMING BOOK "THE PRESENT TESTAMENT VOLUME NINE: IT IS WRITTEN". AMORE, BELLA BARBIE

WHEN SILENCE MATTERS: BEING SILENT IN THE MIDST OF SATAN"S UNHOLY PRESENCE AND WORKS WITHIN THE FAMILY

ALMIGHTY GOD SPEAKING

SATAN, THE ORIGIN AND SOURCE OF NEGATIVITY, ARGUMENTS, DIVISION, ABUSE AND HARDSHIP, WITHIN FAMILIES AND FRIENDSHIPS. HE, SATAN, IS THE INVISIBLE SOURCE OF ALL VISIBLE NEGATIVITY IN THE LIVES OF HUMAN BEINGS. HIS INVISIBLE PRESENCE CAUSES GREAT VISIBLE TRAGEDIES WITHIN FAMILIES AND FRIENDS. HE, SATAN, SLITHERS IN THE FORM THAT REVEALS THE PRESENCE OF EVIL. BECAUSE HE, SATAN, IS THE SOURCE OF ALL ARGUMENTS WITHIN FAMILIES. CHRISTIANS ARE CALLED TO ACKNOWLEDGE HIS UNHOLY PRESENCE, AND REBUKE SATAN BY BEING SILENT IN THE MIDST OF AN ARGUMENT OR DISAGREEMENT. SATAN CANNOT ARGUE WITH HIMSELF, HE WILL NOT. THEREFORE, IT IS PROFITABLE FOR HUMAN BEINGS TO BE SILENT WHEN AN ARGUMENT OR DISAGREEMENT IS APPROACHING THEIR REALM OF PEACE. I KNOW THAT IT IS VERY HARD TO BE SILENT AT CRUCIAL TIMES, MY CHILDREN, BUT IT IS A NECESSITY. MY CHILDREN, IF YOU VALUE THE RELATIONSHIP THAT YOU HAVE WITH YOUR LOVED ONES, IT IS BEST TO BE SILENT AT TIMES, EVEN IF YOU BELIEVE THAT YOU ARE RIGHT. DO NOT ALLOW SATAN TO DESTROY A LOVE

OR FRIENDSHIP THAT IS VERY VALUABLE TO YOU. MY CHILDREN, PRACTICE THE REALM OF SILENCE AT THE MOST NEEDED TIMES, FOR SILENCE PREVAILS IN THE MIDST OF SATAN'S "UNHOLY" PRESENCE. *THUS SAYS THE LORD GOD*, THE ORIGIN OF PEACE WITHIN THE FAMILY. OCTOBER 1, 2015 AT 3:04 PM BY: BARBARA ANN MARY MACK

ONE DAY, ONE DAY! I WILL SOAR ABOVE THIS PASSING WORLD

BARBARA SPEAKING

ONE DAY, OH THAT BLESSED, BLESSED, LONGED FOR DAY, I, MY IGNITED SPIRIT, WILL SOAR ABOVE THIS PASSING WORLD! ONE DAY, OH THAT BLESSED LONGED FOR DAY, MY HOLY IGNITED SPIRIT WILL SOAR ABOVE THIS PASSING WORLD! OH THAT BLESSED, BLESSED DAY, ALL OF GOD'S IGNITED CHILDREN WILL BOW WITH ME AS I PRAY, AS I SOAR ABOVE THIS PASSING WORLD! OH THAT LOVELY, LOVELY DAY, WHEN GOD'S HOLY IGNITED ANGELS WILL GREET ME AS I PRAY! WE WILL JOIN OUR HEAVENLY FATHER, AS I SOAR ABOVE THIS PASSING WORLD TODAY! MOVE, O IGNITED BLESSED SPIRIT OF MINE! MOVE IN THE PRESENCE OF MY HOLY GOD AND SPOUSE, AS I SOAR IN THE MIDST OF HIS ECSTASY, AS THIS PASSING WORLD WATCHES ME PRAY! *ALLELUIA!!!*
OCTOBER 1, 2015 AT 3:20 PM BY: BARBARA ANN MARY MACK

REJOICING IN THE MIDST OF LIFE, EVEN WHEN...

BARBARA SPEAKING

RISE! RISE! RISE! O BLESSED SPIRIT OF GOD'S FAITHFUL MESSENGER AND BRIDE (BARBARA). LIFT UP YOUR ELEGANCE AS YOU GREET HE (ALMIGHTY GOD) WHO IS YOUR ETERNAL LOVE AND HOLY SPOUSE! RISE! RISE! RISE, AS YOU BEND YOUR GRATEFUL ESSENCE IN THE PRESENCE OF HOLINESS AND PERPETUAL DIVINE ECSTASY! EXHIBIT THE DIVINE JOY THAT YOU RELEASE AS I ENJOY GOD'S GIFT OF LIFE! EXHIBIT THE REALM THAT RELEASES DIVINE BLISS AS I EXPRESS MY GRATITUDE FOR GOD'S GIFT OF LIFE! EXHIBIT THE JOY THAT ENCOMPASSES MY SATISFIED ESSENCE AS I BOW IN THE MIDST OF GOD'S GIFT OF LIFE. IN THE MIDST OF HARD TIMES, RELEASE THE GIFT OF DIVINE JOY! IN THE MIDST OF SPIRITUAL AND VERBAL ABUSE, RELEASE THE GIFT OF DIVINE BLISS! IN THE MIDST OF SADNESS AND SORROW, RELEASE THE GIFT OF DIVINE ECSTASY! IN THE MIDST OF TROUBLED TIMES, RELEASE THE SPLENDOR THAT SURROUNDS GOD'S MIGHTY HEAVENLY THRONE! IN THE MIDST OF PAIN AND SUFFERING, JOIN HANDS WITH GOD'S HOLY CHOIRS! RELEASE THE REALM THAT PRODUCES LIFE, EVEN IN THE MIDST OF SATAN'S CONTINUOUS ATTACKS! FOR GOD'S GIFT OF HOLY ETERNAL LIFE IS WORTHY OF DIVINE CELEBRATION EVERY DAY OF THE YEAR! *ALLELUIA!* JOIN THE SACRED BELLS! JOIN THE HEAVENLY CHOIRS! SALUTE OUR MAGNIFICENT CREATOR AND GOD, AS ALL ON EARTH AND IN HEAVEN ABOVE ENJOY GOD'S GIFT OF LIFE! *ALLELUIA!!!*
OCTOBER 1, 2015 AT 5:38 PM BY: BARBARA ANN MARY MACK
SENT SUN, OCT 4, 2015 7:13 PM-READ SUN 10/4/2015 8:01 PM

DANCE WITH ME, *SAYS THE LORD!*

ALMIGHTY GOD SPEAKING

DANCE WITH ME! O REALM THAT HOUSES MY FAITHFUL FRIENDS AND LOVED ONES. DANCE WITH ME, WITHIN MY REALM OF PURITY AND DIVINE HOPE! DANCE WITH ME! AS I ROAM

THE STREETS OF THOSE WHO LOVE TO WITNESS, AND BE A PART OF MY DIVINE REALM OF EXCITEMENT ON EARTH TODAY. DANCE WITH ME IN THE STREETS OF HOLY VICTORY! DANCE WITH ME IN THE STREETS OF HOLY FAME! DANCE WITH ME IN THE MIDST OF DIVINE ECSTASY AND JOY! DANCE WITH ME! AS I SALUTE THOSE WHO HAVE BEEN FAITHFUL TO ME, THE ONLY HOLY AND INFALLIBLE ONE! DANCE WITH ME! FOR I AM THE ONLY OMNIPOTENT ONE! DANCE WITH ME, THE ONLY OMNIPRESENT ONE! DANCE WITH ME, O WELL-LOVED CHILDREN OF MINE! DANCE WITH ME IN THE MIDST OF THE REALM THAT RELEASES CONTINUOUS PRAISE TO THE ONLY SUPREME MERCIFUL ONE! DANCE WITH ME, ALL WHO DESIRE TO WITNESS HOLINESS IN THEIR MIDST TODAY!

SEPTEMBER 30, 2015 AT 5:03 PM BY: BARBARA ANN MARY MACK

SENT WED, SEP 30, 2015 10:44 PM-READ THU 10/1/2015 3:33 PM

OH, THE HEAVENLY CHOIRS

BARBARA SPEAKING TO
GOD'S HEAVENLY CHOIRS

WRAPPED WITHIN THE BEAUTY OF GOD'S HEAVENLY CHOIRS, MOVES MY IGNITED BEING THROUGHOUT EACH BLESSED DAY! SING! SING! SING, O HEAVENLY CHOIRS OF DIVINE LOVE! SING TO ME AS I RELAX WITHIN THE HOLY TUNES THAT FLOW FROM YOUR PLEASED BEINGS! SING TO GOD'S HOLY AND CHOSEN BRIDE (BARBARA) AS I REJOICE IN THE MIDST OF RAPTURED HEAVENLY BLISS ON EARTH TODAY! ENCOMPASS ME, ALMIGHTY GOD'S CHOSEN MESSENGER OF DIVINE LOVE, AS I REJOICE IN THE MIDST OF THE RESIDENTS THAT DANCE AROUND THE THRONE OF LOVE AND MERCY. SURROUND ME WITH THE HEAVENLY BLISS THAT EMITS FROM YOUR CONTINUOUS WONDERFUL TUNES OF PRAISE AND WORSHIP. ENGULF MY INVITED SPIRIT WITH THE DIVINE BLISS THAT EMITS FROM YOUR HYMNS OF CONTINUOUS PRAISE! SING, CHOIRS, SING! RELEASE THE HEAVENLY SOUNDS THAT COVER THE ESSENCE OF BARBARA, THE HUMBLED ONE! SING YOUR MIGHTY HYMNS OF PRAISE, AS I DANCE IN THE MIDST OF DIVINITY WITH CRAIG, OUR ETERNAL BELOVED ONE! SING! CHOIRS OF GOD, SING! LET YOUR HYMNS OF PRAISE PERMEATE MY RAPTURED BEING, AS I APPROACH THE CALLED AND CHOSEN ONES ON EARTH TODAY! SING! O CHOIRS OF DIVINE LOVE, SING! SING IN THE MIDST OF DIVINITY, AS I BOW IN HIS HOLY PRESENCE THROUGHOUT ETERNITY! *ALLELUIA!!!*
SEPTEMBER 30, 2015 AT 1:15 PM BY: BARBARA ANN MARY MACK

IN THE MIDST OF MY LOVE

BARBARA SPEAKING TO ALMIGHTY GOD

IN THE MIDST OF MY LOVE, I WILL LIFT MY HANDS UP TO YOU IN PRAISE AND HONOR, O HOLY GOD AND SPOUSE OF MINE! IN THE MIDST OF MY LOVE, YES, MY GOD ORDERED LOVE, I WILL DANCE IN YOUR HOLY PRESENCE, O WORTHY ONE! IN THE MIDST OF MY LOVE, YES, MY HEAVENLY

LOVE, I WILL SING SONGS OF CONTINUOUS PRAISE TO YOU, O HOLY ONE! IN THE MIDST OF MY LOVE, YES, MY HOLY LOVE, I WILL BOW CONTINUOUSLY AT THE HOLY FEET OF GOD, MY SAVIOR AND SPOUSE.

BARBARA SPEAKING TO HER REALM OF HOLY LOVE

CAPTURE THE HOLY ESSENCE OF MY ETERNAL SPOUSE AND GOD, O LOVE THAT EMITS FROM GOD'S HOLY BRIDE (BARBARA). CAPTURE HIS HOLY ESSENCE, AS HE MOVES WITH GRACE AND DIVINE ELEGANCE THROUGH THE IGNITED BEING OF HIS CHOSEN MESSENGER AND BRIDE (BARBARA). CAPTURE THE BEAUTY THAT ENCOMPASSES GOD, THE SAVING ONE, AS HE ROAMS WITH ME WITHIN MY REALM OF HOLY LOVE THROUGHOUT ETERNITY.
SEPTEMBER 30, 2015 AT 2:23 PM BY: BARBARA ANN MARY MACK
SENT WED, SEP 30, 2015 10:44 PM-READ THU 10/1/2015 3:33 PM

ARE YOU STILL MINE? I NEED YOUR LOVE

ALMIGHTY GOD SPEAKING
TO HIS FAITHFUL ONES

O FAITHFUL SONS AND DAUGHTERS OF MINE, I LONG FOR YOUR EXPRESSION OF LOVE FOR ME, YOUR CREATOR AND GOD. WHEN THE WORLD FOLLOWS ANOTHER, I LONG FOR YOUR EXPRESSION OF LOVE AND ALLEGIANCE TO YOUR FAITHFUL GOD AND FATHER. WHEN THE WORLD REVERES ANOTHER INSTEAD OF ME, I LONG FOR YOUR EXPRESSION OF DEVOTION AND COMMITMENT TO YOUR SAVING GOD AND FATHER. WHEN THE WORLD FOLLOWS HE WHO IS LESS THAN THE STARS BELOW, YES, BELOW, I LONG FOR YOUR ALLEGIANCE AND LOVE FOR ME, YOUR FIRST AND LAST LOVE. O FAITHFUL ONES, ARE YOU STILL MINE? DO YOU HAVE A LOVE FOR ME THAT SURPASSES ALL REALMS OF HUMAN LOVE? DO YOU FOCUS ON MY VERSION

OF HOLY LOVE, MY SONS? DO YOU REVEAL MY VERSION OF HOLY LOVE, MY DAUGHTERS? MY CHILDREN, CAN I COUNT ON YOUR CONTINUOUS EXPRESSION OF LOVE AND DEVOTION IN THE MIDST OF THOSE WHO GIVE GLORY AND PRAISE TO ANOTHER? MY CHILDREN, ARE YOU STILL MINE, *SAYS THE LORD?*

SEPTEMBER 27, 2015 AT 1:08 PM BY: BARBARA ANN MARY MACK

SENT SUN, SEP 27, 2015 11:15 PM-READ SUN 9/27/2015 11:44 PM

EXHIBIT THE LOVE, THE DIVINE LOVE THAT YOU PROFESS

ALMIGHTY GOD SPEAKING

EXHIBIT IT, MY CHILDREN! EXHIBIT THE DIVINE LOVE THAT YOU PROFESS TO YOUR FAMILY, FRIENDS AND STRANGERS! EXHIBIT THE DIVINE LOVE THAT YOU HAVE READ AND HEARD OF THROUGH THE YEARS! EXHIBIT THE DIVINE LOVE THAT WILL LEAD YOU AND YOUR LOVED ONES INTO MY ETERNAL KINGDOM ABOVE. EXHIBIT THE DIVINE LOVE THAT HAS CARRIED YOUR FOREFATHERS AND MOTHERS THROUGH THEIR DIFFICULT TIMES. EXHIBIT THE DIVINE LOVE THAT DESCENDS IN YOUR MIDST DAILY! EXHIBIT THE DIVINE LOVE THAT HAS TAUGHT YOU THE MEANING OF FORGIVENESS! EXHIBIT THE DIVINE LOVE THAT HAS TAUGHT YOU THE MEANING OF MERCY AND COMPASSION TOWARD YOUR ENEMIES, STRANGERS AND LOVED ONES! EXHIBIT THE DIVINE LOVE THAT HAS LED YOU INTO A LIFE OF HOLINESS, IN THE PRESENCE OF THOSE WHO COMMIT AND SAY UNSPEAKABLE THINGS IN MY HOLY PRESENCE. EXHIBIT THE DIVINE LOVE THAT TEACHES ALL HOW TO LIVE MY VERSION OF HOLINESS. MY CHILDREN, EXHIBIT THE DIVINE LOVE THAT YOU PROFESS IN THE MIDST OF THOSE WHO DO NOT KNOW MY VERSION OF DIVINITY. MY CHILDREN, EXHIBIT ME AT ALL TIMES!!!

SEPTEMBER 25, 2015 AT 3:07 PM BY: BARBARA ANN MARY MACK

SENT SAT, SEP 26, 2015 2:43 PM-READ SAT 9/26/2015 3:13 PM

YEARNING FOR YOUR LOVE

ALMIGHTY GOD SPEAKING

OH CHILDREN OF MINE! OH PRECIOUS AND LONGED FOR CHILDREN OF MINE, I AM YEARNING FOR YOUR LOVE AND COMMITMENT TODAY. I AM LOOKING FORWARD TO THE DAY, YES, THE PRECIOUS AND LONGED FOR DAY, THAT YOU WILL GIVE AND EXPRESS SINCERE LOVE FOR YOUR FAITHFUL AND MERCIFUL CREATOR AND GOD. I AM YEARNING FOR THE PRECIOUS, PRECIOUS MOMENT IN TIME, THAT YOU WILL EXPRESS AN AUTHENTIC LOVE FOR ME AS I EXHIBIT MY GENUINE AND ETERNAL LOVE FOR YOU. I AM LOOKING FORWARD TO THE DAY,

YES, THE BLESSED DAY, THAT YOU WILL PROFESS YOUR LOVE FOR THE ONLY ONE WHO HAS NEVER ABANDONED YOU. MY CHILDREN, I AM YEARNING FOR YOUR LOVE TODAY!
SEPTEMBER 26, 2015 AT 1:58 PM BY: BARBARA ANN MARY MACK

READ, UNDERSTAND, TEACH, AND FOLLOW MY HOLY WORD, *SAYS THE LORD*

ALMIGHTY GOD SPEAKING TO
THE SHEPHERDS OVER HIS FLOCK

MY SONS! YES! YOU WHOM I HAVE CHOSEN TO LEAD MY FLOCK TODAY. READ MY HOLY WORD AND ABIDE BY THEM, SO THAT YOU MAY REVEAL MY TRUTH TO THOSE WHO LOOK UP TO ME THROUGH YOU. LEARN OF MY HOLY WORDS THAT FLOW THROUGHOUT THE HOLY BIBLE. LEARN OF THEM WITH ENTHUSIASM AND REVERENCE. LEARN OF THEM WITH PATIENCE AND JOY. LEARN OF MY HOLY WORDS OF TRUTH, SO THAT YOUR FLOCK MAY KNOW THAT YOU ARE A SHEPHERD WHO IS CHOSEN BY THEIR CREATOR AND GOD. LEARN OF MY HOLY WORDS, SO THAT YOU MAY LEAD AND TEACH MY FLOCK, TO AND OF MY HOLY REALM OF TRUTH. OH, MY BELOVED SONS, YES, YOU WHOM I HAVE CHOSEN, LEARN AND TEACH MY HOLY WORDS SO THAT YOUR PREACHING WILL NOT BE IN VAIN. UNDERSTAND MY HOLY WORDS, SO THAT YOU MAY PREACH THEM WITH BOLDNESS IN THE PRESENCE OF THOSE WHO DESIRE TO HEAR MY TRUTH.
SEPTEMBER 26, 2015 AT 2:36 PM BY: BARBARA ANN MARY MACK
SENT SAT, SEP 26, 2015 2:43 PM-READ SAT 9/26/2015 3:13 PM

GREETINGS ARCHBISHOP CRAIG! I WAS WAKEN THIS MORNING BY A CALL FROM MY PUBLISHER, INFORMING ME THAT THE COVER OF MY BOOK IS READY FOR VIEWING AND APPROVAL. I TELL YOU, MODERN TECHNOLOGY IS AWESOME! I JUST SENT IN MY DESIRE FOR THE COVER ON SUNDAY, AND MY PUBLISHER CALLED THE NEXT DAY TO MAKE SURE THAT THEY UNDERSTOOD MY REQUESTS. I HAVE BEEN WITH THIS PUBLISHING COMPANY SINCE

2002, AND I CAN HONESTLY SAY THAT THEY HAVE MADE WONDERFUL AND PROFITABLE CHANGES IN THE PUBLICATION PROCESS. I AM VERY HAPPY THAT WE AUTHORS HAVE A SAY IN THE PUBLICATION PROCESS OF OUR BOOKS. ENCLOSED IS A COPY OF THE COVER FOR THE HARD COPY OF MY BOOK. IT COMES IN SOFT COPY AS WELL. THE NEXT STEP IS VIEWING THE GALLEY. THEY WILL SEND THAT SOON. I DREAD THIS, BECAUSE THIS BOOK CONTAINS OVER SEVEN HUNDRED PAGES, WHICH MEANS THAT I HAVE TO GO THROUGH ALL OF THE PAGES BEFORE SIGNING THE APPROVED GALLEY FORM. OH WELL! THIS COMES WITH THE JOB THAT I HAVE WORKING FOR THE LORD. I AM NOT COMPLAINING, BECAUSE THE PAY (ETERNAL LIFE IN PARADISE) IS WORTH IT! ENJOY YOUR DAY LOVE! LOVE, BEAUTIFUL BARBARA
SENT WED, APR 15, 2015 1:08 PM-READ WED 4/15/2015 6:57 PM

HI ARCHBISHOP CRAIG! BELOW IS ANOTHER GOD INSPIRED PASSAGE OF MINE. TOODLES! BEAUTIFUL BARBARA

I AM AFRAID OF THEM (SATAN AND HIS ANGELS)

I AM AFRAID OF THOSE WHO EXHIBIT THE BEHAVIOR OF THE REALM OF EVIL (SATAN). ALTHOUGH I AM NOT AFRAID OF SATAN, I AM AFRAID OF THE EVIL THAT ROAMS THROUGH HIM AND HIS SERVANTS AND ANGELS. ALTHOUGH I KNOW THAT HE (SATAN) IS A DEFEATED FOE OF MINE, I AM AFRAID OF THE HATRED AND COMPASSIONLESS ESSENCE (SATAN AND HIS ANGELS) THAT FLOWS THROUGH EARTH'S REALM TODAY. I AM AFRAID OF THE APATHY THAT FLOWS FROM SATAN AND HIS DEFEATED ANGELS. I AM AFRAID OF THE QUALITY AND PRESENCE OF LOVE, COMPASSION, AND MERCY THAT NEVER ENTER THE ESSENCE OF THE EVIL ONE AND HIS ANGELS. ALTHOUGH I AM AFRAID, MY KNOWLEDGE AND UNION WITH ALMIGHTY GOD, THE VICTORY OVER THE REALM OF EVIL, MAKES ME FEARLESS THROUGHOUT EACH DAY. I BOW IN THE PRESENCE OF JESUS, MY VICTORIOUS SPOUSE AND GOD, AS I FEAR THE REALM THAT HATES AND WREAKS DESTRUCTION.
APRIL 20, 2015 BY: BARBARA ANN MARY MACK
SENT: MON, APR 20, 2015 5:47 PM-READ: MON 4/20/2015 9:12 PM

HI LOVE! I AM WAITING FOR MY PUBLISHER TO EMAIL MY GALLEY. SOMEONE CALLED THIS MORNING TO INFORM ME THAT THE GALLEY WAS READY FOR MY VIEWING. I WAS TOLD THAT AN EMAIL WAS SENT TO ME AROUND 11 AM. WHEN I CHECKED MY EMAILS, THERE WERE ONLY EMAILS CONTAINING PRICING AND GALLEY APPROVAL FORMS. I CALLED MY PUBLISHER TO TELL THEM OF THE ERROR. I AM WAITING FOR THEM TO EMAIL ME THE GALLEY. I WILL CHECK MY EMAIL SOON TO SEE IF IT WAS SENT THIS TIME. ALSO, ALTHOUGH THE PAGE LIMIT FOR THE BOOK THAT I PURCHASED SHOULD NOT HAVE EXCEEDED 740. BECAUSE OF THE FONT SIZE (10), THE PAGE COUNT OF MY BOOK IS 1124. IT'S GOING TO TAKE ME DAYS TO GO THROUGH THIS

GALLEY. I USUALLY GO THROUGH MY GALLEYS AT LEAST TWO TIMES. MY PUBLISHERS ARE VERY PARTICULAR ABOUT STAYING WITHIN THE GUIDELINES. THEREFORE, THIS IS EVIDENCE THAT THE LORD WANTS ALL OF THE PAGES INCLUDED IN THIS BOOK. THE PRICES OF THIS BOOK ARE:

THE RETAIL PRICE FOR YOUR EBOOK VERSION IS USD 9.99. THE RETAIL PRICE FOR YOUR HARD COVER VERSION IS USD 54.55. THE RETAIL PRICE FOR YOUR SOFT COVER VERSION IS USD 38.72.

I TREASURE THE DAYS

I TREASURE THE DAYS, THE GOD SENT DAYS.
I TREASURE THE OPPORTUNITY TO GIVE MY GOD AND SAVIOR CONTINUOUS PRAISE!
FOR HE HAS GRANTED US THE GIFT OF LIFE,
TO SHARE WITH FRIENDS, LOVED ONES, AND BARBARA, HIS HEAVEN SENT WIFE.
I TREASURE EACH MOMENT THAT FLOWS THROUGH OUR BLESSED DAY.
FOR I AM GIVEN THE GIFT OF FOLLOWING JESUS' HOLY WAY!
MY BROTHERS AND SISTERS, ENJOY YOUR DAYS, YOUR GOD SENT DAYS.
ENJOY THEM, O BROTHERS AND SISTERS OF MINE, AS YOU GIVE GOD, THE ALMIGHTY, CONTINUOUS PRAISE!
APRIL 20, 2015 BY: BARBARA ANN MARY MACK
SENT: MON, APR 20, 2015 3:46 PM-READ: MON 4/20/2015 9:13 PM

GREETINGS ARCHBISHOP CRAIG! COME STA OGGI AMORE? I AM RETURNING FROM AN ASSIGNMENT THAT THE LORD TRUSTED ME TO COMPLETE TODAY. THE LORD REVEALED TO ME EVERYTHING THAT WOULD OCCUR DURING THIS WONDERFUL TASK A COUPLE OF DAYS AGO. EVERY TIME THAT I EXPERIENCE THE MANIFESTATION OF WHAT GOD'S REVEALS TO ME, MY ESSENCE LEAPS WITH INCREASED TRUST AND LOVE FOR THE ALMIGHTY ONE. THE RECIPIENT OF THE LORD'S HOLY MESSAGE WAS A DOCTOR WHOM I HAVE NEVER MET BEFORE. DURING MY VISIT WITH HIM, THE REVELATION OF MY PUBLISHED BOOKS CAME INTO OUR CONVERSATION. LAST NIGHT, BEFORE GOING TO BED, THE LORD REVEALED TO ME WHICH BOOKS THAT I SHOULD TAKE WITH ME. LAST NIGHT, HE SHOWED ME HOW CAPTIVATED THE DOCTOR WOULD BE WHEN HE LEARNED OF THE MANY BOOKS THAT I HAVE WRITTEN. I TOOK ABOUT TEN OF MY PUBLISHED BOOKS, WHICH INCLUDED TWO VOLUMES OF BOOKS. THE DOCTOR LOOKED THROUGH SOME OF THE BOOKS WITH GREAT INTEREST. HE ALSO TOOK THE TIME TO DISCUSS THEM WITH ME. I TOLD HIM OF MY POSITION AS ONE OF THE LORD'S SCRIBES. HE BELIEVED IN WHAT HE SAW, IN REGARDS TO MY BOOKS. I AM SO GRATEFUL THAT THE LORD SHOWS OR TELLS ME WHAT IS GOING TO HAPPEN IN MOST OF MY ASSIGNMENTS. KNOWING WHAT IS GOING TO TAKE PLACE BEFORE IT OCCURS, PLACES ME IN GOD'S REALM OF HOLY TRUST AND ASSURANCE. IN UNKNOWN SITUATIONS, I DO NOT GET OVERLY CONCERNED,

BECAUSE I KNOW THAT EVERYTHING WILL GO ACCORDING TO WHAT THE LORD ORDERS. TRUST AND ASSURANCE ARE SIGNS OF OUR FAITH. I FINALLY WENT THROUGH MY 1124 PAGE GALLEY THIS MORNING. I WILL GO OVER IT AGAIN AFTER I EAT DINNER. I DID NOT FIND MANY ERRORS. I WILL CHECK AGAIN TO SEE IF I MISSED ANYTHING. IF I DID, I PLACED A NOTE OF APOLOGY IN MY BOOKS FOR ANY ERRORS.

GOD BLESS! BELLA TRUSTING BARBARA

RELAXING WITHIN GOD'S REALM OF HOLY TRUST

MY LORD, KNOWING YOU AND YOUR HOLY POWER, PLACES ME IN THE REALM OF DIVINE TRUST. KNOWING THE GIFT OF ALLEGIANCE AND LOVE THAT DESCEND TO MY REALM OF TRUST, PLACES ME IN A POSITION THAT NEVER CONTEMPLATES DOUBT OR ANXIETY. YOUR HOLY WORD COMFORTS ME, AS I WALK WITHIN YOUR REALM OF HOLY TRUST, MY LORD. FOR YOU SO LOVINGLY REVEAL TO ME YOUR HOLY WAY AND PLAN FOR YOUR CHILDREN TODAY. YOUR ALLEGIANCE TO MY HUMAN REALM OF WEAKNESS, INCREASES MY TRUST IN YOUR HOLY REVELATIONS, AS I DELIVERED YOUR PRESENCE AND MESSAGES TO YOUR NEEDY CHILDREN TODAY. YOU ARE FAITHFUL TO YOUR DIVINE REVELATIONS TO ME, MY GOD! YOU ARE FAITHFUL TO YOUR OBEDIENT AND DEVOTED DAUGHTER (BARBARA). YOUR REALM OF TRUST ENCOMPASSES ME DAILY, AS I DELIVER YOUR HOLY PRESENCE AND WORD TO THOSE WHOM YOU SEND ME TO. MY LORD, I CAN RELAX WITHIN YOUR REALM OF HOLY TRUST, FOR YOU HAVE BEEN A FAITHFUL GOD AND SPOUSE TO ME. ANXIETY CANNOT ENTER YOUR REALM OF HOLY TRUST! UNNECESSARY WORRY AND DISCONTENTMENT, CANNOT ENTER YOUR REALM OF HOLY TRUST. DOUBT AND UNBELIEF, CANNOT ENTER YOUR REALM OF HOLY TRUST. MY LORD, MY GOD, I TRULY TRUST THEE!

APRIL 22, 2015 BY: BARBARA ANN MARY MACK

SENT: WED, APR 22, 2015 6:53 PM-READ: WED 4/22/2015 10:12 PM

HI ARCHBISHOP CRAIG! MY PUBLISHER CALLED ME A LITTLE WHILE AGO TO INFORM ME THAT MY GALLEY IS READY FOR MY APPROVAL. SHE INFORMED ME THAT THIS BOOK CONSISTS OF A THOUSAND PAGES, WHICH MEANS THAT I HAVE TO GO THROUGH ALL OF THE PAGES TO MAKE SURE THAT THE GALLEY MEETS MY APPROVAL BEFORE SENDING IT TO THE PRINTER. THIS WILL TAKE SOME TIME, BECAUSE I USUALLY GO OVER THE GALLEY AT LEAST TWO TIMES BEFORE SIGNING THE APPROVAL FORMS. I APPROVED THE COVER OF THE BOOK A FEW DAYS AGO. HOPEFULLY THERE WILL NOT BE TOO MANY ERRORS IN THE GALLEY. I AM GOING TO BE VERY BUSY OVER THE NEXT FEW DAYS GOING OVER THE GALLEY. I BEGAN WORKING ON ANOTHER BOOK A COUPLE OF WEEKS AGO. I WANTED TO START THAT BOOK BEFORE THIS GALLEY WAS READY FOR MY VIEWING. TAKE CARE OF YOURSELF. GOD BLESS!

SENT: MON, APR 20, 2015 2:10 PM-READ: MON 4/20/2015 8:10 PM

ENJOY YOUR DAY LOVE! EVERY TIME THAT I TRY TO LOOK OVER MY GALLEY, THE LORD GIVES ME MORE KNOWLEDGE AND SAYINGS FROM HIS UNENDING REALM. I WILL PASS IT ON TO THOSE WHOM HE DEEMS WORTHY OF HIS GENEROSITY. BELOW ARE TODAY'S SAYINGS FROM THE LORD. AMORE, BELLA OBEDIENT BARBIE

OPEN THE GATES OF HELL, YOU WHO DEFY MY HOLY WAY, *SAYS THE LORD*

ALMIGHTY GOD SPEAKING

OPEN THE GATES TO HELL, YOU WHO TURN AWAY FROM MY HOLY COMMANDMENTS, AND ENTER WITH GLADNESS! FOR THERE YOU WILL DWELL THROUGHOUT ETERNITY, IF YOU DO NOT REFORM YOUR UNHOLY WAYS, *SAYS THE LORD!* OPEN THE GATES THAT REVEAL YOUR PERMANENT PLACE OF RESIDENCE, O DISOBEDIENT CHILDREN OF SATAN. OPEN THE GATES AND ENTER, YOU WHO HIDE YOUR DIRTY DEEDS AND THOUGHTS FROM THE WORLD! FOR I SEE IT ALL! YOU HAVE NOT DECEIVED ME, *SAYS THE LORD!* GO AHEAD! ENTER! THERE YOU WILL RELAX WITHIN THE REALM THAT YOU CHOSE OVER ME, THROUGHOUT ETERNITY, *SAYS THE LORD!* OPEN THE GATES, O LOWLY ONES! ENTER YOUR NEW HOME WITH GLADNESS! FOR IT IS THE PLACE THAT YOU
CHOSE OVER SWEET PARADISE! ENTER! ENTER! ENTER, *SAYS ALMIGHTY GOD!!*
APRIL 23, 2015 BY: BARBARA ANN MARY MACK, ALMIGHTY GOD'S CONTEMPORARY MESSENGER-PROPHETESS

LISTENING TO THE VOICE OF MY HEAVENLY FATHER AND GOD

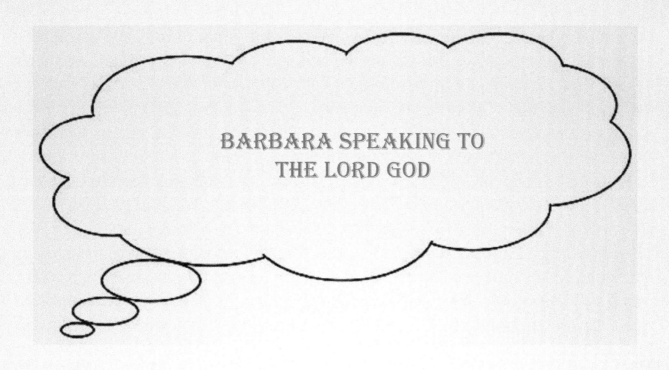

OH HOW GRAND IT IS TO HEAR YOUR LOVELY VOICE THROUGHOUT EACH DAY, MY FATHER. OH HOW AWESOME IT IS TO HEAR THE SWEET WHISPERS THAT FLOW FROM YOUR SACRED ESSENCE THROUGHOUT EACH BLESSED DAY. I BOW MY HONORED HEAD IN THE MIDST OF YOUR HOLY PRESENCE, AS I BATHE IN THE WHISPERS THAT REVEAL YOUR PLANS FOR YOUR GRATEFUL CHILDREN TODAY. YOU ARE HOLY, O GRACIOUS ONE! YOU ARE LOVING, O GRACIOUS ONE! YOU ARE MAGNIFICENT, O HEAVENLY FATHER AND GOD OF ALL THAT IS PURE AND HOLY! YOU ARE MINE! I BREATHE IN YOUR HOLY ESSENCE, AS I LISTEN TO THE SOUND OF YOUR MELODIOUS WORDS AS THEY FLOW FROM YOUR SACRED LIPS. MY WELCOME EARS BOW IN YOUR HOLY PRESENCE, AS THEY RECEIVE THE HOLY MESSAGES THAT YOU SO GENEROUSLY SEND TO YOUR NEEDY CHILDREN TODAY. I SALUTE YOU IN THE PRESENCE OF YOUR OBEDIENT ANGELS AND SAINTS AS WE UNITE IN CONTINUOUS PRAISE UNTO OUR GREAT AND HOLY FATHER AND GOD. I HEAR YOUR HOLY VOICE, MY FATHER! I HEAR YOUR HOLY DIRECTIONS, MY GOD! I HEAR YOUR HOLY PLANS, WHICH YOU SHARE IN ABUNDANCE WITH YOUR NEEDY FLOCK OF LOVE TODAY. I AM HERE, MY FATHER! I AM LISTENING TO YOUR HOLY VOICE! I WILL HONOR MY POSITION AS YOUR CHOSEN BRIDE AND MESSENGER, FOR I TRULY ADORE YOU!!! APRIL 23, 2015 BY: BARBARA ANN MARY MACK, GOD'S CONTEMPORARY MESSENGER AND PROPHETESS

EXHIBITING THE REALM OF GRATITUDE THROUGHOUT EACH DAY

BARBARA SPEAKING

IN THE MIDST OF THIS BLESSED GOD SENT DAY, I WILL EXHIBIT THE GRATITUDE THAT I HAVE FOR YOUR CONTINUOUS GENEROSITY TOWARDS ALL OF YOUR NEEDY CHILDREN, MY GOD. I WILL EXHIBIT THE REALM OF GENEROSITY TOWARD MY FAITHFUL GOD AND FATHER, FOR HE IS WORTHY OF MY CONTINUOUS ACKNOWLEDGMENT. I WILL EXHIBIT MY GRATITUDE AS I EXPRESS THE LOVE THAT DESCENDS FROM YOUR THRONE ABOVE, MY LORD. I WILL EXHIBIT MY GRATITUDE BY CARING FOR YOUR CHILDREN WHO ARE IN NEED OF YOUR DIVINE GUIDANCE AND PRESENCE. I WILL EXHIBIT MY GRATITUDE BY FEEDING YOUR HUNGRY FLOCK WITH YOUR REALM OF SPIRITUAL NOURISHMENT. I WILL EXHIBIT MY GRATITUDE BY LISTENING TO THOSE WHO ARE IN NEED OF SPIRITUAL COMPASSION AND WARMTH. I WILL EXHIBIT MY GRATITUDE BY HONORING MY GOD'S VERSION OF FORGIVENESS AND LOVE. I WILL EXHIBIT MY GRATITUDE BY LIVING A HOLY LIFE IN THE MIDST OF SATAN'S REALM OF TEMPTATIONS. I WILL EXHIBIT MY GRATITUDE, BY LISTENING TO THE VOICE OF GOD'S HOLY SPIRIT THROUGHOUT EACH DAY. I WILL EXHIBIT MY GRATITUDE BY HONORING GOD HOLY WORDS TODAY. I WILL EXHIBIT MY GRATITUDE BY COMBATING SATAN DAILY, FOR THE SOULS OF GOD'S VULNERABLE CHILDREN OF ALL AGES. MY LORD AND MY GOD, I WILL EXHIBIT MY GRATITUDE TO YOU, AS I BOW IN YOUR HOLY PRESENCE EACH DAY.

APRIL 23, 2015 BY: BARBARA ANN MARY MACK, GOD'S CONTEMPORARY MESSENGER AND PROPHETESS
SENT: FRI, APR 24, 2015 2:43 PM-READ: FRI 4/24/2015 3:39 PM

SURROUNDED BY GOD, THE HOLY TRINITY

BARBARA SPEAKING TO GOD, THE HOLY TRINITY

LET US DANCE, YOUR GRACE! LET ME FEEL YOUR HOLY ESSENCE AS I DANCE IN THE MIDST OF YOUR DIVINITY! LET THE REALM THAT HOUSES YOUR ETERNAL ESSENCE SURROUND ME, AS I ENJOY THE SPIRITUAL BLISS THAT EMITS FROM YOU. ENCOMPASSED BY THE REALM OF DIVINITY IGNITES MY DORMANT SOUL THROUGHOUT EACH BLESSED DAY. LET ME DANCE IN THE MIDST OF DIVINITY, AS I SOAR WITH THE GIFT (CRAIG) THAT DESCENDED FROM YOUR HEAVENLY GATES OF IGNITED LOVE! LET US ENJOY THE DIVINITY THAT ROAMS THE STREETS OF FREEDOM AND DIVINE ECSTASY! LET YOUR HOLY GIFT (CRAIG) SHARE THE REALM OF DIVINITY THAT SURROUNDS MY OBEDIENT SOUL THROUGHOUT THE NIGHT. FOR HE IS WORTHY TOO, MY LORD. I CAN FEEL YOUR HOLY PRESENCE AS I BREATHE IN YOUR SWEET FRAGRANCE, O LORD! I CAN FEEL YOUR HOLY ESSENCE, AS I CLING TO THE GIFT (CRAIG) THAT YOU HAVE BLESSED ME WITH, BEFORE THE FOUNDATION OF THIS TANGIBLE REALM OF EXISTENCE. ENCOMPASS ME, MY GOD. ENCOMPASS THE UNIFIED SOULS OF YOUR BELOVED ONES (CRAIG AND BARBARA), AS WE DANCE IN THE MIDST OF YOUR DIVINITY THROUGHOUT ETERNITY! *ALLELUIA!* O SACRED ONE, *ALLELUIA!!!*
APRIL 23, 2015 BY: BARBARA ANN MARY MACK

COME STA ARCHBISHOP CRAIG? BELOW ARE TODAY'S PASSAGES. I AM STILL GOING OVER MY GALLEY. I HAVE MADE WONDERFUL PROGRESS SO FAR. SURPRISINGLY, I HAVEN'T COME ACROSS TOO MANY ERRORS CONSIDERING THE PAGE COUNT (1124 PAGES). OF COURSE THIS DOESN'T MEAN THAT THERE AREN'T MORE ERRORS, BUT I HAVEN'T NOTICED THEM. DON'T FORGET TO RELAX YOUR WELL-LOVED MIND THROUGHOUT THIS DAY. **AMORE, BEAUTIFUL BARBARA**

OVER THE HILLS OF PAIN

OVER THE HILLS OF PAIN, MY ELATED SPIRIT SOARS! OVER THE HILLS OF PAIN, MY SPIRIT REJOICES WITH GOD, MY SAVIOR AND HOLY SPOUSE! OVER THE HILLS OF PAIN, MY SPIRIT REJOICES IN THE PRESENCE OF ALMIGHTY GOD AND HIS TRIUMPHANT SAINTS! OVER THE HILLS OF PAIN, MY SATISFIED SPIRIT GAZES INTO THE WELCOMING EYES OF GOD, MY SAVIOR! OVER THE HILLS OF PAIN, MY TEARS JOIN THE REALM OF PEACE AND JOY! OVER THE HILLS

OF PAIN, THE GLORY OF THE LORD ENCOMPASSES MY HUMBLED SOUL! OVER THE HILLS OF PAIN, MY WEAK BODY SOARS! OVER THE HILLS OF PAIN, I PRAISE ALMIGHTY GOD, THE ORIGIN OF MY HAPPY SOUL! OVER THE HILLS OF PAIN, I BOW IN THE PRESENCE OF GOD, MY SOURCE AND PURPOSE FOR EXISTING!!!
APRIL 25, 2015 BY: BARBARA ANN MARY MACK

SINNERS CANNOT JUDGE SINNERS

A SINNER CANNOT JUDGE A SINNER. A SINNER CANNOT CONDEMN A SINNER. A SINNER CANNOT PRAY TO ALMIGHTY GOD FOR A SINNER, FOR THE LORD SHUTS HIS HOLY EARS TO THOSE WHO ARE DWELLING WITHIN THE REALM OF SIN. THE LORD OUR GOD, IS PURE AND HOLY. HE WILL NOT LISTEN TO THE VOICE OF THOSE WHO SHARE IN THE UNGODLY DEEDS AND ACTS THAT COME FROM SATAN'S REALM. FOR HE IS PURE AND HOLY! A RIGHTEOUS PERSON PRAYS FOR THE SINNING ONES. FOR THE LORD HEARS THE PRAYERS OF THE RIGHTEOUS ONES. A RIGHTEOUS PERSON PRAYS FOR SINNERS. A RIGHTEOUS PERSON DOESN'T CONFORM TO SINFUL ACTS. A RIGHTEOUS PERSON DOESN'T TURN HIS OR HER BACK ON THOSE WHO ARE IN NEED OF SPIRITUAL HELP AND GUIDANCE. HELP ME, O RIGHTEOUS ONE! HELP ME GUIDE MY CHILDREN INTO THE REALM OF HOLINESS, *SAYS THE LORD!* THERE THEY WILL FIND ME!
APRIL 25, 2015 BY: BARBARA ANN MARY MACK
SENT: SAT, APR 25, 2015 4:15 PM-READ: SAT 4/25/2015 5:06 PM

TODAY'S PASSAGES FOR YOU LOVE! I AM SOOOOO PROUD OF MY GOD SENT MAN! AS I READ YOUR WRITINGS ON TWITTER, I AM MOVED BY YOUR EXPRESSION OF THE HEAVEN SENT CALL THAT YOU RESPOND TO EACH DAY. THE LORD IS TRULY GRATEFUL AS WELL!
WE WILL LOVE YOU ALWAYS, DEAR ONE! BELLA BARBIE

I AM SO GRATEFUL, MY LORD

I AM SO GRATEFUL LORD! I AM GRATEFUL FOR MY WONDERFUL HOME. I AM GRATEFUL FOR MY WARM BED. I AM GRATEFUL FOR THE BOUNTIFUL FOOD OF MY CHOICE THAT I HAVE IN MY REFRIGERATOR AND FREEZER. I AM GRATEFUL FOR THE CLOTHES THAT HANG IN MY CLOSETS. I AM GRATEFUL FOR THE LAUGHTER AND SONGS THAT FLOW FROM THE MOUTHS OF MY BLESSED DAUGHTER AND GRANDDAUGHTER. I AM GRATEFUL FOR OUR REALM OF PEACE AND CONTENTMENT THAT FLOW THROUGH OUR BLESSED HOME EACH DAY. TO SEE! TO HEAR! TO HAVE DIVINE KNOWLEDGE, PATIENCE, AND HOPE! TO WALK, TALK, AND DINE WITH YOUR HEAVENLY BODIES AND ANGELS. TO ROAM IN THE MIDST OF DIVINITY DAILY! TO SALUTE YOU DAILY! TO SING TO YOU DAILY! TO GIVE THANKS AND PRAISE TO YOU EVERY DAY! TO BOW IN YOUR HOLY PRESENCE DAILY! TO SEE YOUR CHOSEN SON (CRAIG) AT YOUR

WILL AND APPROVAL! TO HEAR HIS STRONG VOICE OF PRAISE TO YOU IN OUR (THE LORD AND BARBARA) HOLY PRESENCE! MY LORD, MY GOD, I AM TRULY GRATEFUL!
APRIL 25, 2015 BY: BARBARA ANN MARY MACK

OH, THE RADIANCE!

OH, THE RADIANCE THAT ENCOMPASSES MY SATISFIED SOUL AS I GAZE AT THE BEAUTY THAT EMITS FROM THIS GLORIOUS GOD SENT DAY! THE JOY THAT DANCES WITH MY BLESSED SOUL AS IT ENGULFS MY IGNITED SPIRIT, SOOTHES ME, AS I ENJOY THE GIFT OF THIS GLORIOUS GOD ORCHESTRATED DAY. COME! O BELOVED SPOUSE AND FRIEND OF MINE. LET US SIP THE HEAVEN SENT BLISS THAT DESCENDS IN OUR MIDST, AS YOU AND I BATHE IN THE REALM OF SPIRITUAL ECSTASY ON THIS BLESSED GOD SENT DAY! LET YOU AND I ENJOY THE HEAVEN SENT RADIANCE THAT ENCOMPASSES OUR UNIFIED SPIRITS OF DIVINE BLISS! LET US ENJOY THE REALM THAT PRODUCES DIVINE HAPPINESS, IN THE PRESENCE OF THOSE WHO DESIRE PROOF OF GOD'S HOLY EXISTENCE IN OUR LIVES. COME, DEAR ONE, LET US BATHE IN THE RADIANCE THAT EXHIBITS OUR ORIGIN AND GOD!
APRIL 25, 2015 BY: BARBARA ANN MARY MACK
SENT: SAT, APR 25, 2015 5:11 PM-READ: SAT 4/25/2015 7:07 PM

HI DEAR ONE! IF IT'S GOD'S HOLY WILL, WE WILL SEE YOU AT THE NOON CELEBRATION OF THE HOLY EUCHARIST. WE HAVE TO PICK AMYA UP FROM HER GRANDMOTHER'S FIRST. BELOW IS A PASSAGE FROM MY FORTHCOMING BOOK. AMORE, BELLA BARBIE

THE LORD SPEAKS TO CRAIG

WE (THE LORD AND BARBARA) ARE NEAR, O CHOSEN SON: WE ARE WITHIN YOUR REALM OF TOUCH! REACH OUT TO US, O CHOSEN SON. REACH OUT TO THE SOURCE (GOD) OF YOUR LOVE AND STRENGTH! WE ARE NEAR, O CHOSEN AND WELL-LOVED SON! CLING TO THE BEINGS OF THE MIGHTY ONES (THE LORD AND BARBARA)! CLING TO THE BEINGS OF THE SAVING ONES (THE LORD AND BARBARA)! CLING TO THE SOURCE (GOD) OF ETERNAL LOVE! MY SON: CLING TO ME THROUGHOUT ETERNITY! I HAVE REMOVED YOU FROM THE CHAINS THAT HELD YOU BOUND FOR MANY YEARS! YOU MAY FLEE, MY SON! YOU HAVE BEEN RELEASED TODAY!

BARBARA SPEAKS TO SATAN

RELEASE HIM (CRAIG), O DEFEATED REALM! RELEASE THE SOUL OF MY BELOVED SPOUSE (CRAIG)! HE IS MINE, O ENEMY OF THE LORD! HE IS OUR (THE LORD AND BARBARA) BELOVED ONE! YOU CANNOT HOLD WHAT HAS BEEN SANCTIFIED! YOU CANNOT CONTAMINATE WHAT HAS

BEEN BLESSED! RELEASE HIM, O SOURCE OF ETERNAL FILTH: FOR HE BELONGS TO THE HOLY TRINITY AND ME! REMOVE YOUR STENCH FROM THE REALM THAT SHELTERS MY BELOVED ONE, O ENEMY WHO IS CONDEMNED AND DOOMED! REMOVE YOUR STENCH FROM THE SWEET FRAGRANCE OF MY BELOVED SPOUSE, O DOOMED SOURCE OF UNHAPPINESS AND PAIN! HE IS MINE, O ENEMY OF CHRIST JESUS: HE IS MINE! RELEASE HIM TODAY!!!

BARBARA SPEAKS TO CRAIG

THE BELLS OF FREEDOM WILL RING AS I ENTER THE REALM THAT HAS CAPTURED THE BEING OF MY BELOVED SPOUSE! THE GATES WILL OPEN WIDE AS I ENTER THE REALM THAT TRIES TO HIDE MY BELOVED FROM THE HOLY ONE (GOD) AND ME! THE ARMS OF LOVE WILL SURROUND THE SPIRIT OF THE FRIGHTENED ONE (CRAIG)! I AM NEAR, O BELOVED SPOUSE OF MINE! LET THE SPIRIT OF FEAR ESCAPE YOUR CAPTURED SOUL TODAY! LET THE SPIRIT OF FEAR DEPART FROM YOUR WELL OF FREEDOM, O LONGED FOR ONE! MY GATES OF LOVE HAVE ENTERED THE ZONE OF OUR ENEMY. MY GATES OF LOVE HAVE CONQUERED SATAN, THE LOWLY ONE. YOU HAVE BEEN SET FREE FROM THE SCENT OF OUR ENEMY. ENTER MY GATES OF LOVE, O RELEASED ONE! ENTER THE WALLS OF BARBARA, YOUR BELOVED SPOUSE, WITH JOY IN YOUR RELEASED SOUL. ENTER THE WALLS OF BARBARA, YOUR HOLY BRIDE, WITH THE SONGS OF PRAISE UNTO OUR LORD AND SAVIOR! ENTER MY WALLS THAT ECHO FREEDOM, AS YOU RUN TO THE BEING OF YOUR CHOSEN SPOUSE. WE HAVE UNITED IN LOVE, MY LONGED FOR ONE (CRAIG); LET US REJOICE WITH GLADNESS IN OUR HEARTS! *ALLELUIA!!!*

BARBARA SPEAKS TO THE LORD

CATCH THE SOUL (CRAIG) THAT HAS BEEN RELEASED BY THE POWER OF DIVINE LOVE, O HOLY ONE! CATCH THE SOUL THAT CRIED OUT TO YOU IN THE MIDDLE OF CAPTIVITY! CATCH THE BEING (CRAIG) THAT RESEMBLES THE SPIRIT OF THE ONLY TRUE GOD! HE IS YOURS, O LONGED FOR KING (GOD). HE IS THE SPIRIT OF THE BELOVED ONE! HE HAS BEEN SET FREE, MY LORD. HE HAS BEEN SET FREE FROM THE GRIP OF SATAN, OUR ENEMY! HE HAS BEEN SET FREE FROM THE REALM THAT PRODUCES NOTHINGNESS! HE HAS BEEN SET FREE FROM THE ODOR THAT CONTAMINATED EARTH'S SPHERE! HE IS FREE, MY LORD! THE SPIRIT OF OUR BELOVED ONE CAN FLY IN THE DIRECTION OF OUR LOVE AND EXHIBIT DIVINE HAPPINESS AGAIN!

BARBARA SPEAKS TO CRAIG'S SPIRIT

FLY, SWEET SPIRIT, FLY! FLY INTO THE ARMS OF BARBARA, YOUR WANTING SPOUSE! FLY INTO THE ARMS THAT SEARCHED FOR YOUR TORMENTED BEING THROUGH THE REALM OF TIME! FLY INTO THE REALM THAT CAPTURED THE ESSENCE OF YOUR LOVE. WE HAVE BEEN

SET FREE, O SWEET SPIRIT OF MY BELOVED SPOUSE (CRAIG)! WE HAVE BEEN SET FREE FROM THE CLUTCHES OF SATAN, OUR ENEMY. WE HAVE BEEN SET FREE FROM THE REALM THAT HELD CAPTIVE OUR UNITED SPIRITS. WE HAVE BEEN SET FREE FROM THE REALM THAT TORMENTED OUR UNITED HEART OF LOVE. WE HAVE BEEN SET FREE FROM THE REALM THAT PRODUCES DARKNESS AND GLOOM. O BELOVED ONE. WE HAVE BEEN SET FREE FROM SATAN, OUR ENEMY TODAY!

SENT: SUN, APR 26, 2015 10:40 AM-READ: SUN 4/26/2015 3:03 PM

BUON GIORNO ARCHBISHOP CRAIG! AFTER GOING OVER MY 1124 PAGE GALLEY FOR THE FINAL TIME, I SPOKE WITH MY BOOK CONSULTANT, TO TELL HER THAT I AM READY TO SIGN THE APPROVAL FORM TO COMPLETE MY BOOK'S PUBLICATION PROCESS. BEING AN IMPERFECT BEING AND NONPROFESSIONAL WRITER, I KNOW THAT THERE WILL BE A FEW GRAMMATICAL ERRORS IN THIS BOOK ALSO. THE IMPORTANT THING IS, THAT THE LORD'S HOLY MESSAGES REMAIN INTACT THROUGHOUT MY BOOKS. IN SPITE OF THE HUMAN ERRORS, THE MESSAGE AND THEME ARE PRESENTED IN A MANNER WHICH THE READER WILL COMPREHEND WITHOUT DIFFICULTY. I AM JUST AN AVERAGE PERSON CHOSEN BY ALMIGHTY GOD, TO CONVEY HIS LIFE SAVING MESSAGES TO HIS FLOCK OF LOVE TODAY. I AM NOT A SCHOLAR OR A LITERARY GENIUS. OUR HUMAN ERRORS REVEAL OUR INFERIORITY TO OUR PERFECT CREATOR AND GOD. I CANNOT WAIT TO SEE MY BOOK IN ITS COMPLETED FORM! I CANNOT IMAGINE A BOOK THAT SIZE. THE LORD IS AWESOME! I BLESS HIM FOR CONSIDERING ME WORTHY TO CARRY OUT SUCH AN IMPORTANT ASSIGNMENT OF LOVE. BUONA PASQUA!

LUV YAH! BEAUTIFUL BARBARA

SENT: APR 27, 2015 12:44 PM-READ: MON 4/27/2015 7:29 PM

GREETINGS ARCHBISHOP CRAIG! BELOW IS TODAY'S MESSAGE FROM THE LORD TO THE WORLD. ENJOY THIS DAY LOVE! PEACE! BEAUTIFUL BARBIE

A CRY FOR THE REALM OF HOLINESS

ALMIGHTY GOD SPEAKING

I HEAR YOUR WEARY AND CONFUSED SOULS AS THEY CRY OUT FOR THE REALM OF HOLINESS, MY VULNERABLE CHILDREN. I HEAR YOUR SOULS AS THEY WANDER THROUGH THE REALM THAT HOUSES THE ONE (SATAN) WHO DESIRES TO STEAL YOU FROM ME BEFORE YOU REACH THE ONLY REALM THAT COULD SAVE YOUR WANDERING SOULS. I HEAR THE CONFUSION THAT ENCOMPASSES YOUR LOST SOULS AS YOU WANDER IN THE REALM (SATAN-SIN) THAT INVITES YOU THROUGHOUT EACH DAY. I HEAR YOU, O CONFUSED CHILDREN! I HEAR YOUR CRIES THROUGHOUT THE DAY. SEEK THE REALM, THE ONLY REALM THAT CAN RELEASE THE

FETTERS THAT BIND YOUR CONFUSED SOULS. SEEK THE REALM THAT COMBATS SATAN AND HIS SICK SERVANTS OF DESTRUCTION THROUGHOUT EACH DAY. SEEK THE ONLY REALM THAT CAN OFFER YOU CONTINUOUS DIVINE PEACE IN THE MIDST OF YOUR CONFUSION. SEEK THE ONLY REALM THAT HOUSES GOD, YOUR CREATOR AND EVERLASTING PROTECTOR! SEEK THE ONLY REALM THAT OFFERS YOU SALVATION THROUGH CHRIST JESUS, YOUR LORD AND GOD. SEEK THE ONLY REALM THAT CARES FOR YOUR ETERNAL SOULS, O CONFUSED ONES! SEEK IT! SEEK IT, DEAR CHILDREN! SEEK THE REALM OF HOLINESS! FOR IT IS THE ONLY REALM THAT PROTECTS THE WEAK SOULS FROM THE DECEPTION AND WRATH OF SATAN! IT IS THE ONLY REALM THAT PROTECTS THE VULNERABLE SOULS FROM SUICIDE AND EVIL THOUGHTS AND DEEDS. MY CHILDREN, I HEAR YOUR CRY FOR THE REALM THAT CAN RELEASE YOUR TORMENTED SOULS! *THUS, SAYS THE LORD,* YOUR ETERNAL GOD AND PROTECTOR

APRIL 27, 2015 BY: BARBARA ANN MARY MACK

SENT: APR 27, 2015 3:21 PM-READ: MON 4/27/2015 7:59 PM

GREETINGS LOVE! COME STA? MY PUBLISHER CALLED ME THIS MORNING TO LET ME KNOW THAT MY GALLEY WAS SENT TO ME FOR APPROVAL. THIS CALL WAS IN REFERENCE TO AN INCONSISTENCY OF THE PAGE NUMBERING FORM. I NOTICED WHILE GOING THROUGH MY GALLEY A FEW DAYS AGO THAT THE PAGE NUMBERS WERE NOT IN ORDER. AFTER BRINGING THIS TO MY PUBLISHER'S ATTENTION, THEY RECTIFIED THE PROBLEM. I AM PRESENTLY GOING THROUGH THE GALLEY TO MAKE SURE THAT THE PROBLEM HAS BEEN RECTIFIED, BEFORE I SIGN THE APPROVAL FORM. THERE ARE A LOT OF PAGES (1124) IN THIS BOOK. ENJOY YOUR DAY, DEAR ONE! AMORE, BELLA BARBIE

SENT: TUE, APR 28, 2015 2:05 PM-READ: TUE 4/28/2015 3:09 PM

ENJOY THIS BLESSED DAY, DEAR ONE (ARCHBISHOP CRAIG)! BELOW IS TODAY'S MESSAGE FROM THE LORD.

GOD BLESS YOU ALWAYS! BELLA BARBARA

IF THEY KNEW HIM (ALMIGHTY GOD) THEY WOULD...

ALMIGHTY GOD SPEAKING

THROUGH THE YEARS MANY HAVE PROFESSED THAT THEY KNOW ME, *SAYS THE LORD.* IF THEY KNEW ME, THEY WOULD HONOR THEIR LORD AND GOD THROUGHOUT EACH DAY. IF THEY KNEW ME, THEY WOULD GIVE CONTINUOUS PRAISE TO THEIR GOOD AND FAITHFUL SHEPHERD. IF THEY KNEW ME, THEY WOULD FEED MY HUNGRY FLOCK WITH THE KNOWLEDGE OF THEIR WORTHY GOD. IF THEY KNEW ME, THEY WOULD HONOR THOSE WHOM I HAVE PLACED IN AUTHORITY. IF THEY KNEW ME, THEY WOULD BOW IN MY HOLY PRESENCE INSTEAD OF

GIVING HONOR TO SATAN'S REALM OF SINFUL ACTS. IF THEY KNEW ME, THEY WOULD NOT MINGLE WITH THOSE WHO HATE AND DESPISE MY REALM OF JUSTICE. IF THEY KNEW ME, THEY WOULD KNOW THOSE WHOM I HAVE SENT TO REPRESENT ME, *SAYS THE LORD*. IF THEY KNEW ME, THEY WOULD SEEK THE ONLY REALM THAT OFFERS SALVATION THROUGH CHRIST JESUS. IF THEY KNEW ME, THEY WOULD CELEBRATE THE GIFT OF MY SACRED BODY AND BLOOD. IF THEY KNEW ME, THEY WOULD KNOW MY HEAVENLY FATHER, AND THE HOLY SPIRIT, FOR WE ARE ONE AND THE SAME, *SAYS THE LORD!*

APRIL 28, 2015 BY: BARBARA ANN MARY MACK

SENT: TUE, APR 28, 2015 2:05 PM-READ: TUE 4/28/2015 3:09 PM

BUON GIORNO ARCHBISHOP CRAIG! ENJOY THIS WONDERFUL DAY, WHICH IS ORCHESTRATED BY ALMIGHTY GOD. LA TOYA TOOK AMYA OVER ONE OF HER FRIEND'S HOME SO THAT THEY MAY ATTEND A FESTIVAL NEAR HER FRIEND'S HOME. LA TOYA DID NOT WANT TO TAKE AMYA BECAUSE SHE WANTED TO SPEND TIME AT HOME INSTEAD OF DRIVING SUCH A DISTANCE. LA TOYA GETS EXHAUSTED AT TIMES FROM DRIVING TO AND FROM AMYA'S SCHOOL FOUR TIMES A DAY. IT TAKES FROM [MAYBE] 30 MINUTES OR MORE, DEPENDING UPON THE TRAFFIC AND WEATHER, TO TRAVEL TO AND FROM THE SCHOOL. I SPOKE WITH TOYA ABOUT HAVING TO MAKE SACRIFICES FOR OTHERS. AMYA WILL TURN 14 THIS MONTH. SHE NEEDS TO SPEND TIME WITH HER FRIENDS OUTSIDE OF SCHOOL TOO. LA TOYA AND AMYA'S DAD ARE VERY PROTECTIVE OVER HER. I TOLD LA TOYA THAT THE LORD WATCHES OVER AMYA, AND WE DO NOT HAVE TO SHELTER HER FROM THE WORLD. AMYA HAS BEEN RAISED IN A GOD FEARING AND GOD FOCUSED HOME, THEREFORE, SHE KNOWS HER LIMITATIONS AS WE DO. LA TOYA AGREED TO LET AMYA GO TO THE FESTIVAL AND SPEND THE NIGHT WITH HER FRIEND. WE HAVE ALL VISITED AMYA'S FRIEND'S HOME MANY TIMES. HER MOM IS A DOCTOR AND BELIEVER IN ALMIGHTY GOD. THE LORD SENT ME TO DELIVER MESSAGES TO THE FAMILY SEVERAL TIMES. THE FAMILY IS FROM NIGERIA, AND THEY ARE VERY PLEASANT PEOPLE. PLEASE KEEP THEM IN YOUR VALUABLE PRAYERS TOO. BELOW IS TODAY'S PASSAGE. GOD BLESS! LOVE, BEAUTIFUL TRUSTING BARBIE

SENT: SAT, MAY 2, 2015 1:38 PM-READ: SAT 5/2/2015 6:58 PM

GREETINGS, ARCHBISHOP CRAIG! MISQUOTING THE HOLY BIBLE IS A VERY HARMFUL AND DANGEROUS THING. WHILE AT THE MARKET THE OTHER DAY, LA TOYA AND I RAN INTO SOMEONE WHOM WE HAVE MET AND SPOKEN WITH ABOUT THE LORD ON MANY OCCASIONS. OFTEN WHILE SPEAKING WITH THIS PERSON, MANY VERSES IN THE BIBLE ARE MISQUOTED OR DISTORTED. LA TOYA AND I CORRECT THIS PERSON, AND REVEAL THE BIBLE'S TRUE SAYINGS. WE NOTICED THAT THIS PERSON IS FAMILIAR WITH MANY PEOPLE WHO FREQUENT THIS PARTICULAR MARKET AS WELL. THIS IS VERY DANGEROUS, BECAUSE THIS PERSON SHARES THE LACK OF SCRIPTURAL KNOWLEDGE AND ACCURACY WITH MANY. THIS IS

DETRIMENTAL TO THOSE WHO DO NOT KNOW THE TRUTH, AND THOSE WHO ARE SEARCHING FOR GOD'S TRUTH. IT IS VERY IMPORTANT THAT ONE STUDIES AND LEARN OF GOD'S TRUTH ON HIS OR HER OWN AS WELL AS ATTENDING CHURCH. I HAVE BEEN READING AND STUDYING THE HOLY BIBLE SINCE THE AGE OF ELEVEN. I CONTINUE TO READ THE HOLY BIBLE AND DO RESEARCH ON GOD'S TRUTH. I BEGAN READING THE HOLY BIBLE TO LA TOYA WHILE SHE WAS IN MY WOMB. AS SHE GREW OLDER, SHE BEGAN READING THE BIBLE ON HER OWN, SO THAT SHE TOO MAY LEARN OF GOD'S HOLY TRUTH INSTEAD OF RELYING ON SOMEONE ELSE'S VERSION. WE HAVE BEEN READING GOD'S HOLY SCRIPTURES TO AMYA SINCE HER BIRTH. LA TOYA ALSO HAS AUDIO VERSIONS OF THE HOLY BIBLE, WHICH SHE PLAYS WHILE DRIVING AMYA TO AND FROM SCHOOL. BY DOING THIS, AMYA WILL KNOW GOD'S HOLY WORDS AS WE DO. IT IS IMPORTANT TO TAKE THE TIME TO LEARN OF GOD'S TRUTH, BECAUSE OUR ETERNAL SOULS ARE AT STAKE. WE HAVE TO KNOW WHAT GOD WANTS US TO DO, AND THE ONLY WAY TO KNOW WHAT HE DESIRES OF US, IS TO LEARN OF HIS HOLY TRUTH, WHICH IS DOCUMENTED IN THE BIBLE. FORTUNATELY, THIS INDIVIDUAL NEVER DISPUTES US (LA TOYA AND ME) WHEN WE CORRECT THE MISQUOTING OR MISINFORMATION. BEFORE GOING TO THIS PARTICULAR MARKET, THE LORD USUALLY PREPARES ME FOR THE ASSIGNMENT. HE TELLS ME WHICH OF MY PUBLISHED BOOKS TO BRING WITH ME, AND WHAT THE CONVERSATION (S) WILL BE CENTERED ON. CONTINUE IN GOD'S HOLY TRUTH, DEAR ONE, FOR THE VULNERABLE AND SEARCHING ONES DESERVE IT! AMORE, BELLA BARBARA

SENT: SAT, MAY 2, 2015 10:21 PM-READ: SAT 5/2/2015 11:27 PM

BARBARA SPEAKING

GREETINGS ARCHBISHOP CRAIG! BELOW ARE TODAY'S MESSAGES FROM THE LORD TO ALL

A TRIBUTE TO GOD'S ABUSED DAUGHTERS IN NIGERIA
LET US PRAY FOR THEIR SPIRITUAL, MENTAL, AND PHYSICAL WELLNESS!
AMORE, WEEPING BARBARA

HELP US, MY FATHER! HELP THE ABUSED ONES!

BARBARA SPEAKING TO ALMIGHTY GOD

HELP US (BARBARA AND GOD'S ABUSED FLOCK), MY FATHER, FOR WE ARE IN GREAT AGONY!
HELP US, DEAR LORD! FOR WE CANNOT HELP OURSELVES! THEY ARE STRONGER THAN WE
ARE, O HEAVENLY FATHER. THEY ABUSE US WITH GREAT HATRED AND APATHY! WE ARE
WEAK, MY FATHER! WE ARE WEARY, MY GOD! THE PAIN AND ABUSE ARE CONTINUOUS,
MY FATHER! THE AGONY IS ENDLESS! COME TO OUR AID, O MERCIFUL FATHER! COME TO
THE AID OF YOUR ABUSED AND HURTING FLOCK! HELP YOUR VULNERABLE DAUGHTERS OF
GREAT AND UNBEARABLE PAIN, O HEAVENLY SOURCE OF MERCY AND KINDNESS! HELP YOUR
VULNERABLE DAUGHTERS TODAY! WHO WILL YOU SEND, O MERCIFUL FATHER? WHO WILL YOU
SEND TO RESCUE YOUR HURTING AND MISUSED DAUGHTERS OF CONTINUOUS MISERY? SPEED
YOUR LOVE, MY FATHER! SPEED YOUR AID TO YOUR ABUSED AND HURTING DAUGHTERS, FOR
WE TRULY TRUST IN YOUR ENDLESS REALM OF MERCY! WE TRULY TRUST IN YOU. HELP US,
DEAR MERCIFUL FATHER! HELP YOUR VULNERABLE DAUGHTERS TODAY!
MAY 3, 2015 BY: BARBARA ANN MARY MACK

THERE WILL COME A TIME

ALMIGHTY GOD SPEAKING TO HIS ABUSED DAUGHTERS IN NIGERIA

MY (THE LORD AND BARBARA) HEART WEEPS! MY HEART WEEPS FOR MY ABUSED DAUGHTERS! MY HEART IS SURROUNDED BY CONTINUOUS PAIN! MY EYES CANNOT BEAR TO WITNESS THE CONSTANT ABUSE THAT ENGULFS MY VULNERABLE DAUGHTERS IN NIGERIA. I WILL HELP YOU, MY SUFFERING DAUGHTERS! I WILL SEND AID TO YOU. THERE WILL COME A TIME WHEN YOU AND I WILL WEEP NO MORE! THERE WILL COME A TIME WHEN WE WILL REJOICE TOGETHER! THERE WILL COME A TIME WHEN YOU AND I WILL DANCE AROUND MY HEAVENLY THRONE AS YOUR ABUSERS WEEP IN AGONY. MY DAUGHTERS, THERE WILL COME A TIME WHEN YOU WILL WEEP NO MORE! *THIS, SAYS THE LORD!*
MAY 3, 2015 BY: BARBARA ANN MARY MACK
SENT: SUN, MAY 3, 2015 4:54 PM-READ: SUN 5/3/2015 5:32 PM

TODAY'S GOD SENT PASSAGES, DEAR ONE. AMORE, BEAUTIFUL BARBARA

HOW CAN I, MY FATHER?

HOW CAN I NOT PRAY FOR THOSE WHO ARE BEING ABUSED? HOW CAN I NOT PRAY FOR THE HURTING ONES? HOW I CAN I LIE DOWN IN MY BED OF COMFORT WITHOUT THINKING OF, AND PRAYING FOR THOSE WHO ARE HURTING, MY FATHER? HOW CAN I PREPARE A DELICIOUS MEAL WITHOUT THINKING OF THOSE WHO HUNGER FOR SPIRITUAL AND PHYSICAL NOURISHMENT? HOW CAN I ENJOY THE LAUGHTER OF MY FAMILY AND FRIENDS WITHOUT THINKING OF THOSE WHO ARE IN CAPTIVITY AND MISERY? HOW CAN I BOW MY HEAD IN YOUR HOLY PRESENCE WITHOUT THINKING OF THOSE WHO ARE WITHOUT SHELTER AND PEACE? HOW CAN I RECEIVE HOLY COMMUNION IN YOUR MIGHTY PRESENCE, WITHOUT THINKING OF MY SPIRITUALLY AND PHYSICALLY LOST BROTHERS AND SISTERS? HOW CAN I ENJOY THE PLEASURE THAT COMES WITH LIFTING MY ESSENCE IN PRAISE TO YOU, WITHOUT THINKING OF MY SISTERS WHO ARE IN CAPTIVITY AND PAIN? HOW CAN I WALK THE STREETS WITH THE GIFT OF FREEDOM AS MY GUIDE, WITHOUT THINKING OF THOSE WHO ARE IN SLAVERY AND DISCONTENTMENT? MY LORD, MY MERCIFUL GOD, HELP ME SHARE THE GIFT OF FREEDOM AND PEACE, WITH THE SPIRITS OF THOSE WHO DO NOT EXPERIENCE IT. MY LORD, MY GOD, HELP ME EXHIBIT YOUR VERSION OF LOVE AND COMPASSION, AS I PRAY UNCEASINGLY FOR THOSE WHO ARE IN CAPTIVITY AND CONSTANT PAIN. MY LORD, MY GOD, HELP ME BECOME LIKE YOU!
MAY 3, 2015 BY: BARBARA ANN MARY MACK

I SEE THEM, THE HYPOCRITES

BARBARA SPEAKING TO ALMIGHTY GOD

I CAN SEE THEM, MY LORD! I CAN SEE THE HYPOCRITES! I CAN SEE THEM AS THEY PRETEND THAT THEY KNOW AND LOVE YOU. I CAN SEE THE TRUTH, YOUR HOLY TRUTH! I CAN SEE BEYOND THEIR COUNTENANCE. I CAN SEE BEYOND THEIR VAIN WORDS. I CAN SEE BENEATH THE COVERING OF THEIR INSINCERE SMILES AND WORDS. I CAN SEE THE TRUTH THAT PERMEATES THEIR DECEIVING SOULS. WHY DO THEY PRETEND, MY LORD, FOR YOU KNOW IT ALL! THEY CANNOT HIDE FROM YOU, FOR YOU ARE OMNIPRESENT. THEY CANNOT FOOL YOU, FOR YOU ARE OMNIPOTENT! THEY ARE THE HYPOCRITES! THEY ARE THE DECEIVERS THAT EXHIBIT THE REALM (SATAN) WHICH PRODUCES THEM DAILY. THEY DO NOT FEED YOUR HUNGRY CHILDREN! THEY DO NOT SHELTER THE HOMELESS ONES! THEY DO NOT EXHIBIT YOUR REALM OF HOLINESS! THEY DO NOT EXHIBIT THE DESIRE FOR ETERNAL LIFE IN SWEET PARADISE WITH YOU! THEY ARE THE DECEIVERS! THEY ARE THE HYPOCRITES! THEY ARE THOSE WHO ARE NOT WRITTEN IN YOUR BOOK OF ETERNAL LIFE. WHAT WILL YOU DO WITH THEM, MY LORD? WHERE WILL THEY GO ON JUDGMENT DAY? WHO WILL THEY JOIN ON THE ROAD TO DESTRUCTION? WHO WILL HEAR THEIR ENDLESS CRIES? WHO WILL HEAR THE CRIES OF THE HYPOCRITES? WHO WILL COME TO THEIR DOOMED AID? WHO WILL SAVE THE DOOMED ONES?
MAY 3, 2015 BY: BARBARA ANN MARY MACK
SENT: SUN, MAY 3, 2015 6:32 PM-READ: SUN 5/3/2015 7:36 PM

BUONA SERA ARCHBISHOP CRAIG! BELOW IS TODAYS PASSAGE. PLEASANT DREAMS! IN THE MIDST OF MEDITATION, MY SOUL CRIES OUT TO YOU, O LORD! IN THE MIDST OF MEDITATION MY ESSENCE SPEAKS TO YOU, MY GOD. BARBARA ANN MARY MACK

I MISS YOU!

BARBARA SPEAKING

I MISS YOU, O SWEET REALM THAT PRODUCED HOLINESS! I MISS OUR UNENDING RIVERS OF HEAVENLY BLISS ABOVE THE MANY STARS! I MISS THE WARMTH THAT ENCOMPASSED MY ESSENCE OF DIVINE CREATION. I MISS THE TRANQUILITY THAT EMITS FROM THE BEING OF MY SAVING GOD AND FATHER. I MISS THE ENDLESS SPIRITUAL DIALOGUES THAT FLOWED THROUGH OUR HEAVENLY RESIDENCE! I MISS THE DIVINE WATERS OF LOVE THAT FLOWED IN YOUR HOLY PRESENCE! I MISS THE UNITY THAT KEPT MY SPIRIT ANIMATED THROUGH THE REALM OF TIME! I MISS THE SOUND OF YOUR HEAVENLY CHOIRS, AS THEY JOINED YOUR ANGELS AND SAINTS IN CONTINUOUS PRAISE! I MISS YOU! I MISS YOU! I MISS YOU, O HEAVENLY SPOUSE AND GOD OF MINE! TAKE ME BACK, O SWEET REALM THAT I YEARN FOR THROUGHOUT EACH DAY! TAKE ME BACK, O HEAVENLY SPOUSE OF MINE! RELEASE MY YEARNING SPIRIT

THAT LONGS TO RETURN TO YOUR HOLY SIDE! RELEASE THE ESSENCE THAT CRIES OUT TO YOU DAILY! THE WATERS HAVE COVERED MY SINKING SPIRIT! TAKE ME BACK, O SWEET REALM OF INFINITY! LET ME WEEP NO MORE IN THIS PERIOD OF TIME! LET ME WEEP NO MORE! THE WATERS HAVE COVERED ME, MY GOD! RELEASE MY SOUL SO THAT I MAY REJOICE AGAIN! GIVE ME PEACE, MY GOD! LET THE REALM OF PEACE RESCUE ME FROM THE WATERS THAT SINK MY WEAK SOUL DAILY! I AM SINKING IN THIS WORLD OF NOTHINGNESS. RELEASE ME, MY GOD! MY DIVINE ASSIGNMENT IS TOO HEAVY FOR MY WEAK AND BATTERED SOUL! RELEASE ME, O GREAT WELL OF DIVINE PEACE! RELEASE THE SOUL THAT IS SLAUGHTERED DAILY! I WANT TO BE FREE, MY LORD! I WANT TO BE FREE! RELEASE ME FROM CAPTIVITY, O CARING SPOUSE AND GOD OF MINE! RELEASE ME FROM THE REALM THAT CAUSES ME TO WEEP DAILY! I AM GUILTY OF HAVING HUMAN FEELINGS. RELEASE ME, MY LORD, FOR THEY CAUSE ME TO WEEP DAILY! TAKE ME BACK, MY LORD, SO THAT I MAY WEEP NO MORE!!!

MAY 3, 2015 BY: BARBARA ANN MARY MACK
SENT: SUN, MAY 3, 2015 11:29 PM-READ SUN: 5/3/2015 11:36 PM

I HAVE BEEN RELEASED! THANK YOU, MY GOD! I CAN REST IN THE REALM OF SWEET PEACE NOW! *ALLELUIA!* GRATEFUL BARBARA
SENT: MON, MAY 4, 2015 12:29 AM-READ: MON 5/4/2015 11:00 AM

BUON GIORNO ARCHBISHOP CRAIG! COME STA? BELOW ARE TODAY'S PASSAGES. GOD BLESS! BELLA BARBARA

THE AGONY HAS ENGULFED ME, *O LORD!*

THE AGONY HAS ENGULFED ME, MY GOD!
IT SOMETIMES PREVENTS ME FROM EXPRESSING MY HEAVEN SENT LOVE.
IT SURROUNDS ME THROUGHOUT EACH DAY.
IT CAUSES ME TO WEEP WHENEVER I PRAY.
IT CAUSES ME TO CRY OUT TO MY MERCIFUL AND LONGED FOR GOD.
IT HINDERS ME FROM EXHIBITING MY UNCHAINED LOVE.
IT SURROUNDS ME THROUGHOUT THE DAY: IT SURROUNDS ME THROUGHOUT MY BLESSED NIGHT.
IT SURROUNDS ME, AS I WEEP IN MY GOD'S HOLY AND COMPASSIONATE SIGHT.
GO AWAY! O REALM THAT RELEASES CONTINUOUS AGONY.
LET ME REST WITHIN GOD'S REALM OF SWEET SERENITY!
FOR YOU HAVE TAKEN AWAY THE PEACE THAT I ONCE KNEW.
THE PEACE THAT DESCENDED FROM A GOD, WHO IS HOLY AND TRUE.
GO AWAY, O REALM THAT SLITHERS FROM THE GATES OF HELL!
GO BACK TO THE PLACE WHERE YOU WILL NEVER PREVAIL!

MAY 4, 2015 BY: BARBARA ANN MARY MACK

DO NOT MAKE ME LOOK AT IT (THE WORLD)

BARBARA SPEAKING

DO NOT MAKE ME LOOK AT IT.
DO NOT PERMIT ME TO RELEASE MY SHELTERED SPIRIT.
DO NOT MAKE ME CONFORM TO THEIR UNHOLY WAYS.
DO NOT MAKE ME WITNESS THE DESTRUCTIVE DAYS.
DO NOT MAKE ME WITNESS THE PAIN,
THAT FALLS UPON THE VULNERABLE AND INNOCENT ONES LIKE FIERY RAIN.
THE SWEET CLOISTERED LIFE, IS WHAT I DESIRE,
SO THAT MY WEARY SOUL WILL NEVER TIRE.

DO NOT SUBJECT ME, O LORD. DO NOT SUBJECT ME, O SWEET REALM OF DIVINE PURITY AND CONTINUOUS LOVE. DO NOT SUBJECT ME, O HEAVENLY SPOUSE WHOM I LONG TO JOIN ON YOUR MIGHTY THRONE OF DELIGHT AND WELCOMED PEACE. DO NOT SUBJECT ME, O MERCIFUL AND CARING FATHER OF THE VULNERABLE LITTLE CHILDREN. DO NOT SUBJECT BARBARA, YOUR CHOSEN BRIDE. DO NOT SUBJECT BARBARA, YOUR REALM OF SWEET MELODIES. DO NOT SUBJECT THE ONE (BARBARA) WHO WEEPS DAILY. DO NOT SUBJECT THE TEAR (BARBARA) THAT DESCENDED FROM YOUR REALM OF GENEROSITY. DO NOT SUBJECT THE WEAK BEING (BARBARA) WHO FOLLOWS YOUR HOLY ESSENCE THROUGHOUT EACH DAY. DO NOT SUBJECT BARBARA, YOUR CHOSEN QUEEN, WHO BOWS IN YOUR HOLY PRESENCE THROUGHOUT THE DAY AND NIGHT. DO NOT SUBJECT ME, O LORD. DO NOT SUBJECT ME TO THIS WORLD THAT IS IN NEED OF SPIRITUAL REPARATION.
MAY 4, 2015 BY: BARBARA ANN MARY MACK
SENT: MON, MAY 4, 2015 4:48 PM-READ: MON 5/4/2015 6:31 PM

GREETINGS DEAR ONE (ARCHBISHOP CRAIG)! I PRAY THAT YOUR BLESSED DAY IS GOING VERY WELL. I OFTEN HAVE LA TOYA AND AMYA READ THE EMAILS THAT I SEND, SO THAT THEY TOO WILL RECEIVE GOD'S HOLY MESSAGES. LA TOYA, AS WELL AS MANY OTHERS, OFTEN COMMENTS ON THE SIMILARITY OF MY WRITINGS AND THE WRITINGS THAT FLOW THROUGHOUT THE HOLY BIBLE. LA TOYA COMMENTS ON THE SIMILARITY OF EXPRESSIONS THAT THE PROPHETS IN THE OLD TESTAMENT AND MY EXPRESSION OF MY INNER FEELINGS AND DESIRES COINCIDE. THIS GIVES CREDENCE TO THE SOURCE OF OUR (GOD'S CHOSEN PROPHETS) ORIGIN. SOME OF MY WRITINGS REVEAL MY INNER DESIRE TO RETURN TO GOD, MY HOLY ORIGIN, AS WELL AS MY GOD ORDERED PURPOSE FOR STAYING AMONGST GOD'S FLOCK. AS

YOU WELL KNOW, FROM READING THE HOLY SCRIPTURES, GOD'S PROPHETS ARE NOT "SELF-PROCLAIMED". IT IS A POSITION THAT IS BESTOWED UPON ONE WHO HAS BEEN SENT TO REVEAL GOD'S WONDERFUL PLAN. THIS IS VERY EXTRAORDINARY AND VERY REAL! IT IS A DIVINE POSITION THAT ONE CANNOT REMOVE HIMSELF OR HERSELF FROM. A PROPHET IS SENT TO PERFORM A SPECIFIC TASK FOR OUR GREAT AND HOLY GOD, AND HE OR SHE CANNOT REFUSE OR REMOVE HIMSELF OR HERSELF FROM GOD'S HOLY ASSIGNMENT OF LOVE. FOR IT IS FOR ALL OF GOD'S CHILDREN. ALTHOUGH I WEEP IN THE MIDST OF MY HOLY CALL AS A PROPHET OF THE LORD, I AM TRULY HONORED TO BE CHOSEN FOR A GREAT WORK FOR ALMIGHTY GOD AND HIS CHILDREN.

LOVE YOU ALWAYS! BEAUTIFUL BARBARA

I WALK THIS FOREIGN LAND WITH THE HOPE OF...

RETURNING TO YOU, O HOLY SPOUSE AND GOD OF MINE.

FADING WITHIN THIS PRESENT TIME.

SITTING AT MY LONGED FOR PLACE AT GOD'S HOLY SIDE.

REIGNING WITH JESUS, MY VICTORIOUS KING, AS HIS WORTHY BRIDE.

WITNESSING THE END OF THE TEARS THAT FLOW DOWN MY WEARY ESSENCE.

BEING IN GOD'S HOLY RESIDENCE.

I WALK THIS FOREIGN LAND IN THE STATE OF SPIRITUAL FEARS.

I WALK THIS FOREIGN LAND IN THE MIDST OF SPIRITUAL TEARS.

WHEN WILL MY WALK IN THIS FOREIGN LAND END, MY GOD.

FOR I MISS THE PRESENCE OF YOUR HOLY LOVE.

MOVE! O BATTERED SPIRIT OF MINE.

MOVE THROUGH THIS PERIOD OF TEAR FILLED TIME!

FOR I LONG FOR THE JOY TO ENTER MY WEAK BEING.

I LONG FOR THE THRONE THAT AWAITS THE BRIDE (BARBARA) OF JESUS, MY ETERNAL GOD AND KING!

MAY 4, 2015 BY: BARBARA ANN MARY MACK

SENT MON, MAY 4, 2015 5:36 PM-READ MON 5/4/2015 6:32 PM

REST WITHIN... TODAY'S GOD SENT PASSAGE.

AMORE, BELLA BARBARA

TAKE ME BACK, DEAR FATHER, FOR IT IS VERY LONELY AND COLD HERE

BARBARA SPEAKING TO THE LORD GOD

TAKE ME BACK, DEAR FATHER, FOR IT IS VERY LONELY AND COLD HERE (EARTH). TAKE ME BACK TO THE CONTINUOUS WARMTH THAT SURROUNDS OUR HEAVENLY THRONE OF LOVE. TAKE ME BACK TO THE REALM THAT CAPTIVATES MY LONELY AND BATTERED ESSENCE. TAKE ME BACK TO THE BLISS THAT DANCED WITH US THROUGHOUT EXISTENCE. TAKE ME BACK TO THE MIGHTY SPIRITUAL ARMS THAT COMFORTED ME IN THE MIDST OF YOUR ANGELS AND SAINTS. TAKE ME BACK TO THE ESSENCE THAT PRODUCED JESUS, HIS ONLY BEGOTTEN SON OF LOVE. TAKE ME BACK TO THE MELODIES THAT FLOW FROM HIS REALM OF GOODNESS AND MERCY. TAKE ME BACK TO THE BRILLIANT LIGHT THAT JESUS SHINES AS HE WALKS IN THE MIDST OF DIVINE ROYALTY (GOD, THE FATHER). TAKE ME BACK, DEAR FATHER! TAKE ME BACK TO YOUR ARMS OF LOVE! WHEN WILL YOU SEND SOMEONE FROM YOUR MIGHTY LOVING THRONE TO RESCUE ME, O HOLY SPOUSE OF MINE? FOR MY ESSENCE CRIES OUT TO YOU DAILY, MY GOD. HELP ME ENTER THE REALM OF DIVINE PEACE AND CONTINUOUS BLISS, O LOVING SAVIOR OF MY LONELY ESSENCE.

MAY 4, 2015 BY: BARBARA ANN MARY MACK

SENT MON, MAY 4, 2015 5:44 PM-READ MON 5/4/2015 6:33 PM

ENJOY YOUR BLESSED DAY LOVE! BELOW ARE TODAY'S PASSAGES OF DIVINE LOVE. CIAO! BEAUTIFUL BARBARA

WEEP WITH ME!

WEEP WITH ME!
WEEP WITH ME, ALL WHO HAVE PITY!
WEEP WITH THE BATTERED BRIDE (BARBARA) OF GOD, THE BLESSED AND HOLY TRINITY!
WEEP WITH ME, AS I WALK THROUGH THIS REALM OF SHAME!
WEEP WITH ME, AS I CLING TO JESUS' LIFE SAVING NAME!
WEEP WITH ME, THROUGHOUT MY LONELY DAYS!
WEEP WITH ME, O COMPASSIONATE ONES, AS MY SLAUGHTERED ESSENCE PRAYS!
FOR IT IS IN GREAT AGONY AND PAIN!
THOUGH I AM SURROUNDED BY SPIRITUAL BLISS, THE AGONY AND LONELINESS REMAIN!
WEEP WITH ME, O HEAVENLY CHOIRS OF GOD'S HOLY LOVE!
FOR MY ESSENCE YEARNS TO EMBRACE THE SACRED DOVE.
WEEP WITH ME, AS I GO THROUGH MY LONELY DAY!
WEEP WITH ME, O CARING ONE, AS I KNEEL AND PRAY!
CLING TO THE TEARS THAT FLOW FROM MY WEARY ESSENCE,
AS I LOOK FORWARD TO MY HEAVENLY RESIDENCE.

MAY 4, 2015 BY: BARBARA ANN MARY MACK

THE REALM OF EMPATHY HAS CAPTURED ME

ALMIGHTY GOD SPEAKING

I WALK WITH THE SOULS WHO HAVE BEEN AFFLICTED BY THE UNCOMPASSIONATE ONES. I WILL WEEP WITH YOU, MY CHILDREN! I WILL SHARE THE PAIN THAT FLOWS FROM THE WOUNDS THAT HAVE BEEN PLACED UPON YOU, BY THOSE WHO REJECT MY REALM OF COMPASSION AND MERCY, *SAYS THE LORD*. I WILL WEEP WITH YOU, AS YOU SUFFER ON YOUR BED OF DEATH. I AM NEAR, MY CHILDREN! I WILL WEEP WITH YOU AS YOU DRIFT INTO THE REALM THAT CAPTURES YOUR DYING PHYSICAL CONNECTION WITH THIS WORLD. I WILL SHELTER YOU FROM THE FUTURE YEARS OF PAIN THAT SEEK YOUR SOULS. I WILL SHARE THE BURDEN AND SORROW THAT ENCOMPASS YOUR ESSENCE DAILY. I AM NEAR, O SUFFERING ONES! I AM WITHIN THE REALM THAT OFFERS YOU SWEET PEACE, AS YOU EXIT THIS REALM OF PAIN. CLING TO YOUR EMPATHETIC GOD, AS I BOW MY HEAD SO THAT I MAY NO LONGER WITNESS YOUR SUFFERING. CLING TO ME, O SWEET OFFSPRING OF MINE, FOR I AM ALWAYS WITHIN YOUR REALM OF TOUCH. LET US JOIN OURSELVES AS WE TRAVEL THROUGH THE REALM THAT TRANSFERS YOUR SUFFERING BEING, TO THE REALM THAT OFFERS CONTENTMENT AND PAIN-FREE EXISTENCE. I AM HERE, MY CHILDREN! I AM WALKING WITH YOU ALWAYS!!!
MAY 5, 2015 BY: BARBARA ANN MARY MACK
SENT: TUE, MAY 5, 2015 12:34 AM-READ: TUE 5/5/2015 7:34 AM

GREETINGS ARCHBISHOP CRAIG! COME OGGI AMORE? THROUGHOUT THE PAST FEW DAYS OR SO, SATAN HAS PLACED NEGATIVE THOUGHTS IN MY MIND, SO THAT I WOULD NOT ATTEND THE CELEBRATION OF THE HOLY EUCHARIST AT YOUR SUNDAY NOON SERVICE. HE ALSO TRIES TO CONVINCE ME NOT TO SEND YOU GOD'S HOLY MESSAGES VIA EMAIL. BUT, AS I STATED PREVIOUSLY, A MESSENGER OF THE LORD IS NOT SENT TO DO HIS OR HER WILL, BUT THE WILL OF ALMIGHTY GOD. THEREFORE, I WILL CONTINUE GOING TO THE PLACES WHERE THE GIFT AND PRESENCE OF ALMIGHTY GOD ARE NEEDED AND WELCOMED. I GO WHERE THE LORD NEEDS AND SENDS ME, REGARDLESS OF SATAN'S "UNINVITED" SUGGESTIONS. MY WILL, DESIRE, AND PLEASURE, ARE TO PLEASE ALMIGHTY GOD AND HIS CHOSEN SON (CRAIG). I WILL NEVER ABANDON MY DIVINE ASSIGNMENT OF LOVE, FOR IT IS ORDERED BY ALMIGHTY GOD HIMSELF! WE (ALMIGHTY GOD, ARCHBISHOP CRAIG, AND BARBARA, GOD'S CONTEMPORARY MESSENGER) WILL NEVER ABANDON GOD'S FLOCK OF LOVE! LOVE ALWAYS, FAITHFUL TRIUMPHANT BARBARA

I WILL NOT LISTEN TO YOU, O SATAN!

BARBARA SPEAKING TO SATAN

I WILL NOT LISTEN TO YOU, O SATAN! I WILL NOT GIVE IN TO YOUR "UNHOLY" SUGGESTIONS, FOR THEY ARE NOT OF THE LORD! THEY ARE NOT FROM ME! I WILL NOT LISTEN TO THE WHISPERS OF SATAN, MY (ALMIGHTY GOD AND BARBARA) ENEMY! I WILL NOT LISTEN TO THE WHISPERS THAT FLOW THROUGH MY REALM OF THOUGHT. I WILL NOT LISTEN TO THE WHISPERS THAT TRY TO CONVINCE ME TO ABANDON GOD'S NEEDY FLOCK OF LOVE. I WILL NOT LISTEN TO THE WHISPERS THAT TRY TO LEAD ME IN THE DIRECTION OF DISOBEDIENCE UNTO MY SACRED GOD AND SPOUSE. I WILL NOT LISTEN! I WILL NOT LISTEN! I WILL NOT LISTEN TO YOUR "UNHOLY" WHISPERS, O DEFEATED ONE (SATAN), FOR THEY LEAD TO THE PIT OF ETERNAL DOOM! YOU ARE NOT WORTHY TO FOLLOW, O LOWLY ONE (SATAN)! YOU ARE NOT WORTHY TO OBEY, O DESTRUCTIVE ONE (SATAN)! YOU ARE NOT WORTHY TO ABANDON MY HOLY ASSIGNMENT OF LOVE! YOU ARE NOT WORTHY TO DWELL WITHIN MY VULNERABLE THOUGHTS! YOU ARE DEFEATED, O LOWLY ONE! YOU ARE DEFEATED BY THE TRIUMPHANT ACT OF JESUS, MY ETERNAL SPOUSE AND GOD! YOU ARE DEFEATED BY THE "AUTHENTIC LOVE" THAT FLOWS FROM THE ESSENCE OF CRAIG, GOD'S CHOSEN AND BLESSED SON! SLITHER, O DEFEATED ONE (SATAN)! SLITHER BACK TO THE HOLE THAT YOU CLIMB FROM DAILY! SLITHER UNDER THE ROCK THAT HIDES YOUR DEFEATED PRESENCE FROM THE WEAK AND VULNERABLE ONES! SLITHER, O DEFEATED FOE! SLITHER BACK WHERE YOU ROSE FROM! FOR I AND THE LORD HAVE DEFEATED YOU IN THE COMPANY OF CRAIG, MY ETERNAL SPOUSE!

MAY 5, 2015 BY: BARBARA ANN MARY MACK

SENT: TUE, MAY 5, 2015 3:33 PM-READ: TUE 5/5/2015 8:00 PM

ENJOY YOUR GOD SENT DAY LOVE! BELOW IS TODAY'S PASSAGE. I THANK YOU, MY FATHER, FOR MY LITTLE CROSSES.

AMORE, BELLA BARBARA

FATHER, I PRAISE YOU FOR MY LITTLE CROSSES

MY FATHER ABOVE, MY HEAVENLY SAVIOR AND ETERNAL FRIEND, I AM GRATEFUL FOR THE LITTLE CROSSES THAT ARE PLACED IN MY LIFE BY SATAN. I AM GRATEFUL THAT I HAVE NOT EXPERIENCED THE MAGNITUDE THAT COMES WITH THE CROSS OF WITNESSING THE DEATH OF MY CHILDREN. I AM GRATEFUL FOR NOT EXPERIENCING THE HEAVY CROSSES THAT MY BROTHERS AND SISTERS BEAR, AS THEY WATCH THEIR LITTLE CHILDREN SUFFER FROM INCURABLE ILLNESSES. I AM GRATEFUL FOR NOT HAVING TO BEAR THE HUGE CROSS OF NOT KNOWING WHERE YOUR MISSING CHILD IS. I AM GRATEFUL FOR NOT HAVING TO CARRY THE EXTRA-LARGE CROSSES THAT ARE ON THE BACKS OF MY BROTHERS AND SISTERS. LET ME WEEP WITH THEM, MY FATHER! LET ME WEEP FOR THE ONES WHOSE CROSSES ARE HEAVIER

THAN MINE. LET ME WEEP, MY LORD! LET ME WEEP IN YOUR HOLY PRESENCE THROUGHOUT EACH DAY. FOR THE WEIGHT OF YOUR FLOCK OF LOVE CROSSES ARE WEIGHING THEM DOWN. SOME OF THEM HAVE TRIED TO ESCAPE THROUGH THE ACT OF SUICIDE. SOME OF THEM TRY TO ESCAPE THROUGH THE ACT OF DRUG ABUSE. SOME OF THEM TRY TO ESCAPE BY REMOVING THEMSELVES FROM THE REALM OF REALITY. SOME OF THEM TRY TO ESCAPE THE PAIN THAT COMES WITH THEIR CROSSES BY TRUSTING IN YOU AND YOUR HEALING POWER. MY LORD, MY HOLY FATHER, LET YOU AND I HELP THEM WITH THEIR HEAVY CROSSES TOGETHER. MY LORD, LET US HELP THEM TODAY! *ALLELUIA!!!*

5-5-2015 BY: BARBARA ANN MARY MACK

SENT: TUE, MAY 5, 2015 5:09 PM-READ: TUE 5/5/2015 8:01 PM

DWELLING WITHIN THE REALM OF HUMILIATION AND PAIN FOR THE SAKE OF SALVATION FOR THE CALLED AND CHOSEN ONES.

BARBARA SPEAKING

I WILL DWELL, MY LORD. I WILL DWELL WITHIN THE REALM OF HUMILIATION AND PAIN, FOR IT IS THERE, WHERE THE CALLED AND CHOSEN ONES ARE. I THANK YOU, O LORD, FOR DWELLING WITH ME, WITHIN THE REALM OF HUMILIATION AND PAIN, AS I SIT IN YOUR CHOSEN PEW I THANK YOU FOR SURROUNDING ME WITH GRACE THAT SUSTAINS ME AS I SIT IN YOUR CHOSEN PEW. HELP ME, DEAR LORD! FOR THE REALM OF HUMILIATION AND PAIN HAS ENGULFED THE OBEDIENT ESSENCE OF YOUR MESSENGER AND BRIDE (BARBARA). HELP ME! O SWEET REALM THAT SAVES, AS I WEEP UNCONTROLLABLY IN YOUR HOLY PRESENCE. STRENGTHEN ME, LORD JESUS, AS OUR LOVING FATHER STRENGTHENED YOU, WHEN YOU DWELLED WITHIN THE REALM OF HUMILIATION AND CONTINUOUS PAIN. LORD JESUS! HELP ME! HELP ME! HELP ME, MY LOVE! FOR I CANNOT GO THROUGH THIS TREMENDOUS ASSIGNMENT OF HOLY LOVE ALONE. I CANNOT COMPLETE THIS DIVINE ASSIGNMENT WITHOUT YOUR DIVINE STRENGTH, MY LORD. PLEASE GRACE CRAIG, OUR BELOVED ONE, WITH YOUR DIVINE STRENGTH, SO THAT HE MAY HELP ME TOO! FOR IT IS TREMENDOUS, MY GOD! IT IS A VERY ROUGH ROAD THAT I CANNOT TRAVEL WITHOUT YOUR (THE LORD JESUS AND CRAIG) CONTINUOUS DIVINE STRENGTH. HELP ME! O SOVEREIGN GOD. HELP YOUR WORTHY BRIDE (BARBARA), AS SHE HANGS HER BATTERED HEAD IN THE REALM OF HUMILIATION AND PAIN!

5-5-2015 BY: BARBARA ANN MARY MACK

SENT: TUE, MAY 5, 2015 10:01 PM-READ: TUE 5/5/2015 10:52 PM

THIS WORLD CANNOT QUENCH NOR SATISFY MY ESSENCE

BARBARA SPEAKING

GO AWAY, O WORLD, FOR YOU CANNOT QUENCH MY ESSENCE! YOU CANNOT FILL THE VOID THAT EXIST IN MY LONELY HEART. YOU CANNOT QUENCH THE THIRST THAT ONLY HEAVEN SENT LOVE CAN SATISFY. YOU CANNOT FILL OR SATISFY THE DESIRES THAT I CRAVE. YOU CANNOT REPLACE THE BLISS THAT ONCE ENCOMPASSED MY SATISFIED ESSENCE OF DIVINE LOVE. YOU CANNOT SOOTHE THE PAIN THAT PERMEATES THE ESSENCE (BARBARA) THAT ALMIGHTY GOD CREATED NOT SO LONG AGO. YOU CANNOT CRADLE AND COMFORT THE BRIDE (BARBARA) OF GOD, THE HOLY AND BELOVED TRINITY. YOU CANNOT SATISFY NOR QUENCH THE DESIRES THAT FLOW THROUGH THE ESSENCE OF CRAIG, OUR (ALMIGHTY GOD AND BARBARA) BELOVED ONE. YOU CANNOT QUENCH HIS THIRST FOR HEAVEN SENT BLISS ON EARTH. GO AWAY, O WORLD! FOR YOU CAN NEVER QUENCH OR SATISFY OUR (ALMIGHTY GOD, CRAIG, AND BARBARA) DESIRES.

MAY 6, 2015 BY: BARBARA ANN MARY MACK

WATCH IT (THE TEAR-BARBARA) FALL

ALMIGHTY GOD SPEAKING

WATCH IT FALL! WATCH THE TEAR FALL! WATCH THE ESSENCE (BARBARA) THAT ROAMED IN THE MIDST OF DIVINE ROYALTY FALL! WATCH THE WATERS (BARBARA) THAT ONCE FLOWED THROUGH THE REALM OF SWEET PARADISE ABOVE FALL! WATCH HER, AS SHE FALLS OVER THE BEINGS THAT LONG TO GET A GLIMPSE OF GOD'S HOLY PRESENCE ON EARTH TODAY. WATCH THE FALLING TEAR AS SHE MINISTERS TO THOSE WHO HAVE BEEN CALLED AND CHOSEN BY ALMIGHTY GOD HIMSELF. WATCH THE HEAVEN SENT TEAR AS SHE FLOWS THROUGH THE PLACES THAT HIDE THE TORMENTED SOULS OF THOSE WHOM SATAN HAS CAPTURED. WATCH THE FALLING TEAR, AS SHE COVERS THE WOUNDS OF THOSE WHO HAVE DWELLED IN THE REALM OF SORROW AND ABUSE FOR YEARS. WATCH THE FALLING TEAR AS SHE TAKES THE PRESENCE OF GOD'S HOLINESS TO THOSE WHO ARE IN NEED OF HEALING AND DIVINE COMFORT. WATCH IT, MY CHILDREN! WATCH THE FALLING TEAR (BARBARA)! WATCH THE GIFT (BARBARA, THE FALLING TEAR) THAT I SENT TO REPAIR THIS DAMAGED PERIOD OF TIME! FOR SHE REPRESENTS ME!

MAY 6, 2015 BY: BARBARA ANN MARY MACK

SENT: WED, MAY 6, 2015 5:32 PM-READ: THU 5/7/2015 1:23 AM

YOU DID IT, MY LORD! HELP ME DO MINE (COMPLETE MY DIVINE ASSIGNMENT OF LOVE)!

BARBARA SPEAKING TO ALMIGHTY GOD

MY LORD JESUS, YOU ARE MY EVERLASTING ROLE MODEL AND HOLY SPOUSE. I WILL FOLLOW YOUR PERFECT AND HOLY FOOTSTEPS AS I GRASP FOR THE COURAGE TO ENDURE MY HOLY ASSIGNMENT OF LOVE UNTIL IT IS COMPLETED, AS YOU DID. I WILL ENDURE THE WEIGHT OF MY CROSS AS YOU DID, MY VICTORIOUS GOD AND SPOUSE. I WILL WALK THE LONELY WALK, WITH YOU AS MY FAITHFUL GUIDE. I WILL WEEP IN MY SANCTUARY OF LOVE AS YOU DID, MY LORD. I WILL FOLLOW THE HOLY VOICE OF OUR LOVING FATHER, AS YOU DID, MY LORD. I WILL BOW IN THE MIDST OF THE PRAISES THAT SURROUNDS HIS HEAVENLY THRONE, AS I UNITE WITH YOUR HOLY ESSENCE, LORD JESUS. I CAN FEEL YOUR HOLY PRESENCE, MY LORD! I CAN FEEL YOUR DIVINE STRENGTH AS I BATTLE THE DEPTH OF SATAN'S TORMENTING WHISPERS. I CAN FEEL YOUR HOLY ARMS AROUND MY WEAK AND VULNERABLE ESSENCE AS I TREMBLE IN THE MIDST OF THIS GREAT AND HOLY ASSIGNMENT OF MINE, MY LORD. I CAN FEEL YOUR HOLY ESSENCE, MY LORD, AS IT UNITES WITH MINE, AS I BOW MY HEAD IN THE MIDST OF MY GREAT AND HOLY ASSIGNMENT OF LOVE. STAY WITH ME, MY GOD, AS OUR HEAVENLY FATHER ENCOMPASSED YOU, AS YOU COMPLETED YOUR DIVINE ASSIGNMENT OF LOVE IN HIS HOLY PRESENCE. STAY WITH ME, O HOLY TRINITY, UNTIL I COMPLETE MY DIVINE ASSIGNMENT OF LOVE. STAY WITH ME, MY GOD (THE HOLY TRINITY), FOR I CANNOT COMPLETE IT ALONE!!!
MAY 6, 2015 BY: BARBARA ANN MARY MACK

WILL I RUN FROM THIS TREMENDOUS ASSIGNMENT OF GOD'S HOLY LOVE?

BARBARA SPEAKING TO THE LORD GOD

WILL I RUN AND HIDE FROM THIS AWESOME ASSIGNMENT OF DIVINE LOVE, MY LORD? HELP ME, DEAR LORD! GIVE ME THE DIVINE STRENGTH AND COURAGE TO PROCEED AND PREVAIL IN THIS TASK THAT CAUSES ME GREAT PAIN AND DISCONTENTMENT. LEAD ME, DEAR LORD. ENCOMPASS MY WEAK BEING WITH THE GRACE THAT COMES FROM YOUR WELL OF DIVINE COURAGE. LEAD ME IN THE DIRECTION OF SWEET VICTORY, SO THAT I MAY SOAR WITH YOU, IN THE PRESENCE OF THOSE WHO DENY YOU AND ME. GRACE ME WITH YOUR COURAGE, SO THAT I WILL NEVER RUN FROM THE ASSIGNMENT THAT LEADS YOUR NEEDY FLOCK TO YOUR REALM OF SALVATION AND SPIRITUAL AND PHYSICAL JOY. GRACE ME WITH THE DIVINE COURAGE THAT EMITS FROM YOUR HOLY ESSENCE DAILY. GRACE ME WITH THE GIFT OF ENDURANCE SO THAT I MAY IMITATE YOUR ALLEGIANCE EVERY DAY, MY GOD. FOR YOU ALONE, CAN GIVE ME THE COURAGE THAT WILL SUSTAIN MY WEAK BEING THROUGHOUT MY TREMENDOUS ASSIGNMENT OF HOLY LOVE. I WILL NOT RUN AWAY, MY LORD. I WILL NEVER ABANDON MY DIVINE ASSIGNMENT OF LOVE!
MAY 6, 2015 BY: BARBARA ANN MARY MACK
SENT: WED, MAY 6, 2015 2:29 PM-READ: THU 5/7/2015 1:24 AM

BEAR WITH THEM, MY OBEDIENT DAUGHTER! FOR YOUR TIME WITHIN THE SLAUGHTER HOUSE IS COMING TO A GLORIOUS END!!!

ALMIGHTY GOD SPEAKING TO BARBARA

BEAR WITH THEM, O PATIENT DAUGHTER AND BRIDE OF MINE, FOR YOUR SUFFERING DAYS WITHIN THE SLAUGHTER HOUSE ARE COMING TO AN EXCITING END FOR ALL OF US, *SAYS THE LORD!* BEAR WITH THEM, O PRECIOUS FLOWER THAT BLOOMS FROM MY ETERNAL GARDEN ABOVE. BEAR WITH THOSE WHO HUNGER AND THIRST FOR MY REALM OF HOLINESS, IN THE MIDST OF SATAN'S EVIL EXPRESSIONS OF WEALTH AND FAME. BEAR WITH THOSE WHO ARE SUBJECTED TO THE REALM THAT PRODUCES FALSE GODS AND DESTRUCTIVE WAYS. BEAR WITH THOSE WHO DESIRE TO WALK A HOLY WALK, IN THE MIDST OF DECEITFUL AND TEMPORARY TREASURES THAT ARE RELEASED BY THE WORLD. BEAR WITH THOSE WHOM I SEND YOU TO DAILY. BEAR WITH THOSE WHO CRY OUT FOR A TASTE OF MY HEALING POWER THROUGH YOU. BEAR WITH THOSE WHO DESIRE TO ENTER MY PROMISE LAND. MY DAUGHTER; MY CHOSEN BRIDE, BEAR WITH THOSE WHOM I SEND YOU TO, FOR THEY ARE MY CALLED AND CHOSEN ONES. YOU WILL CELEBRATE WITH ME, AND THOSE WHO TRIUMPH OVER THIS WORLD OF FALSE WEALTH AND GODS. YOU WILL CELEBRATE WITH ME, AS WE DANCE IN THE PRESENCE OF THE VICTORIOUS ONES. YOU WILL CELEBRATE WITH THOSE WHO BELIEVE IN US, MY OBEDIENT AND PATIENT DAUGHTER. YOU WILL CELEBRATE WITH OUR BELOVED ONE (CRAIG) AT YOUR SIDE. YOU WILL CELEBRATE IN THE PRESENCE OF MY ANGELS AND SAINTS, AS YOU EXIT THE SLAUGHTER HOUSE WITH GLADNESS IN YOUR HEART. COME, MY DAUGHTER! LET US WALK THIS LAST PERIOD OF TIME WITH VICTORY AND ENDURANCE AS YOUR PARTNERS OF DIVINE LOVE. COME, MY DAUGHTER! LET YOU AND I BEGIN THE CELEBRATION TODAY! FOR IT IS TIME! *THIS, SAYS THE LORD!*
LET US EXIT THE SLAUGHTER HOUSE TOGETHER!!!
MAY 6, 2015 BY: BARBARA ANN MARY MACK
SENT: WED, MAY 6, 2015 10:01 PM-READ: THU 5/7/2015 7:59 AM

ENJOY YOUR BLESSED NIGHT LOVE! AMORE. TODAY'S PASSAGE OF DIVINE COMPASSION.

HE IS SO COMPASSIONATE: AND HE WEEPS FOR THEM

BARBARA SPEAKING TO THE LORD

MY LORD, THE LIMITLESS EXPRESSION OF YOUR COMPASSION FOR YOUR SUFFERING AND HURTING CHILDREN, CAUSES ME TO BOW MY HUMBLED ESSENCE AND WEEP WITH YOU. MY LORD, MY GOD, BECAUSE OF THE GREATNESS OF YOUR LOVE FOR US, YOU PERMIT ME TO EXPERIENCE AND EXHIBIT THE DEPTH OF YOUR COMPASSION AND MERCY FOR YOUR GREAT

CREATION. YOU HAVE WEPT MANY DAYS AND NIGHTS THROUGH ME, YOUR EARTHLY ESSENCE OF DIVINE COMPASSION AND MERCY. YOU HAVE WEPT FOR YOUR HURTING AND SUFFERING CHILDREN THROUGH THE VESSEL (BARBARA) THAT YOU HAVE PURIFIED, AND MADE HOLY, SO THAT YOU MAY DWELL WITH COMFORT WITHIN MY CHOSEN WELL OF LOVE. MY LORD, MY GOD, YOUR EXPRESSION OF COMPASSION FLOWS THROUGH THE MANY SPIRITUAL AND VISIBLE TEARS THAT HAVE FALLEN FROM MY CHOSEN EYES. YOU HAVE WEPT UNCONTROLLABLY IN THE SILENCE OF MY HEART AND SACRED ROOM AT HOME. THE TEARS FLOW THROUGH THE DAY, AND THEY FLOW THROUGHOUT THE NIGHT. THERE IS NO END TO YOUR EXPRESSION OF COMPASSION, AS YOU WITNESS THE PAIN AND SUFFERING THAT HAVE ENGULFED, AND SURROUNDED YOUR GREAT CREATION OF LOVE. I WILL WEEP WITH YOU, O COMPASSIONATE GOD AND SPOUSE OF MINE. I WILL WEEP WITH YOU IN THE PRESENCE OF THE WORLD. I WILL WEEP WITH YOU, AS YOU AND I WITNESS THE PAIN THAT ENCOMPASSES YOUR VULNERABLE CHILDREN OF ALL AGES, RACES AND CREEDS. FOR YOU, O LORD, ARE THE DIVINE ORIGIN OF COMPASSION AND MERCY. I WILL WEEP WITH YOU, O LORD, UNTIL THE END OF TIME!!!

MAY 8, 2015 BY: BARBARA ANN MARY MACK

SENT FRI, MAY 8, 2015 10:37 PM-READ SAT 5/9/2015 2:11 AM

I'LL JUST STAY HERE

I'LL JUST STAY HERE: AWAY FROM THE REALM THAT PRODUCES APATHY AND SINFUL DEEDS. I'LL JUST STAY HERE. HERE, WITHIN THE REALM THAT PROTECTS ME FROM THE EVIL DEEDS THAT ROAM THE EARTH IN THE FORM OF INCONSPICUOUS HARM AND DANGER. HERE, WHERE THE SERENITY OF ALMIGHTY GOD ENCOMPASSES MY SUBJECTIVE BEING. I'LL JUST STAY HERE: WHERE THE BEAUTY OF THE LORD DANCES WITH MY SPIRIT THROUGHOUT THE DAY! WHERE THE TRUMPETS THAT ANNOUNCE THE NAMES OF THE CHOSEN ONES CAN BE HEARD. WHERE THE BELLS THAT SURROUND THE MIGHTY THRONE OF OUR LIVING GOD, RING WITH THE SOUND OF DELIGHT AND JOY. I'LL JUST STAY HERE: WHERE THE SACRED MELODIES RING WITH GLADNESS, AS OUR HOLY GOD TAKES HIS PLACE ON HIS MIGHTY THRONE OF LOVE. I'LL JUST STAY HERE: AND LISTEN FOR THE SOUND OF MY CHOSEN NAME. AND JOIN GOD'S HOLY ANGELS AND SAINTS AS THEY REJOICE WITH GLADNESS AND PRAISE. I'LL JUST STAY HERE, WITHIN MY PLACE OF PEACE. THERE WILL BE NO INTERRUPTIONS FROM THE PLEASURES THAT HAVE CAPTURED THE WEAK ONES. THERE WILL BE NO INTERRUPTIONS FROM THE REALM THAT SEEKS THE VULNERABLE ONES. THERE WILL BE NO INTERRUPTIONS THAT CAN PENETRATE THE REALM THAT ENCOMPASSES ME DAILY! I'LL JUST STAY HERE, UNTIL I ENTER THE GATES OF SWEET PARADISE ABOVE.

MAY 12, 2015 BY: BARBARA ANN MARY MACK

GREETINGS ARCHBISHOP CRAIG! I AM PRESENTLY LISTENING TO ONE OF YOUR SERMONS ON YOUTUBE. I AM ALSO ENJOYING THE LAUGHTER OF THE YOUNG TEENAGE BOYS WHO HAVE PLACED A BASKETBALL COURT IN FRONT OF THEIR GRANDPARENTS HOME A FEW DOORS

FROM OUR HOME. ALTHOUGH THEY ARE A BIT NOISY, I HAD RATHER HEAR THE SOUNDS OF THEIR LAUGHTER AS THEY PLAY PEACEFULLY, THAN THEIR PAIN FOR OTHER REASONS. PLEASANT DREAMS LOVE!

AMORE, BELLA BARBARA

WHAT THE WORLD HOLDS

THE WORLD HOLDS THAT A MARRIAGE EXISTS WHEN A COUPLE LIVES TOGETHER IN SIN FOR SEVEN YEARS OR MORE. THE WORLD HOLDS THAT A COUPLE, REGARDLESS OF THEIR GENDER, ARE PERMITTED TO BE MARRIED. THE WORLD HOLDS MANY THINGS THAT ARE CONTRARY TO THE TEACHINGS THAT FLOW THROUGH THE HOLY BIBLE, WHICH ARE GOD'S EVERLASTING AND UNCHANGING WORDS OF TRUTH. THE DIFFERENCE BETWEEN WHAT GOD VIEWS, AND WHAT THE WORLD VIEWS AS RIGHT AND JUST, DETERMINES ONE'S ETERNAL DESTINATION IN HEAVEN (SWEET PARADISE WITH ALMIGHTY GOD) OR HELL (ETERNAL DESTRUCTION WITH SATAN AND HIS DEFEATED ANGELS-FOLLOWERS). OH THE "UNHOLY" AND "UNSPEAKABLE" THINGS THAT WERE/ARE RELEASED FROM THE REALM THAT IS DESTINED TO OCCUPY HELL THROUGHOUT ETERNITY! IN THE EYES OF THE WORLD, IT'S COMMON LAW MARRIAGE. IN THE HOLY EYES OF ALMIGHTY GOD, IT IS FORNICATION (SEX BEFORE MARRIAGE). MY BROTHERS AND SISTERS, LET US FLEE FROM THE WORLD'S VERSION OF RIGHTEOUS ACTS, AND CLING TO THE REALM THAT INVITES THE HOLY ONES.

MAY 9, 2015 BY: BARBARA ANN MARY MACK

THE REALM THAT I CRAVE.. COME AND JOIN US (THE LORD AND BARBARA), O BELOVED AND BLESSED ARCHBISHOP CRAIG!

AMORE, BELLA BARBARA

THE REALM THAT I CRAVE DAILY: THE CLOISTER LIFE

BARBARA SPEAKING

OH SWEET REALM THAT I LONG TO EMBRACE DAILY,
AS I SIT IN THE PRESENCE OF GOD, THE HOLY TRINITY.
OH HOW I YEARN FOR YOU SO MUCH,
I YEARN FOR YOU, OH DESIRED REALM, AS I DO FOR JESUS' SACRED TOUCH.
FOR IN YOUR REALM I WILL SEE,
THE WONDERS THAT FLOW FROM THE PRESENCE OF GOD, THE BLESSED TRINITY.
WITHIN MY CLOISTERED WALLS,
I WILL EMBRACE GOD'S GRACE AS IT FALLS.
FALL UPON ME, O HEAVENLY GRACES FROM ABOVE,

AS I COMMUNE WITH YOU IN THE MIDST OF YOUR HOLY LOVE.

AWAY FROM THE SOUNDS THAT CREEP INTO MY PEACEFUL PLACE.

AWAY FROM THOSE WHO DO NOT DESIRE TO SEE JESUS' GLORIOUS FACE.

COME, O HEAVEN SENT SPOUSE OF MINE!

AND SHARE THE CLOISTERED LIFE WITH US (THE LORD AND BARBARA) UNTIL THE END OF TIME.

THERE, WE (ALMIGHTY GOD, CRAIG, AND BARBARA) WILL ENJOY THE GIFT OF LAUGHTER AND HEAVENLY BLISS,

AS ALMIGHTY GOD SEALS OUR SACRED UNION WITH HIS HOLY KISS.

MAY 7, 2015 BY: BARBARA ANN MARY MACK

SENT: TUE, MAY 12, 2015 12:47 AM-READ: TUE 5/12/2015 2:06 AM

BUONA PASQUA ARCHBISHOP CRAIG! LA TOYA AND I ARE RETURNING FROM GETTING MY MONTHLY B-12 INJECTION AND A LITTLE FOOD SHOPPING. I WAS IN NEED OF MORE VEGETABLES. BROCCOLI WAS ON SALE THIS WEEK. I LOVE BROCCOLI, ESPECIALLY WITH CHEESE. IT WAS VERY BEAUTIFUL OUTSIDE TODAY. YESTERDAY IT RAINED A BIT WHILE WE WERE OUT IN MINISTRY, BUT IT DIDN'T LAST TOO LONG. THE LORD GUIDED ME TO A COUPLE OF PEOPLE, SO THAT I MAY SHARE HIS HOLY WORDS TODAY WITH THEM THROUGH MY PUBLISHED BOOKS. THEY WERE VERY CAPTIVATED OVER THE AMOUNT OF BOOKS THE LORD HAS GIVEN ME TO SHARE WITH HIS CHILDREN TODAY. I HAD TO STOP BY MY NEIGHBOR'S HOUSE AFTER CHURCH ON SUNDAY, SO THAT HE COULD SIGN A FORM GIVING HIS CONSENT TO USE HIS BOOK REVIEW COMMENT IN MY FORTHCOMING BOOK. MY PUBLISHER CALLED TO LET ME KNOW THAT I NEEDED TO GET HIS CONSENT BEFORE THEY COULD PROCEED IN THE PUBLICATION PROCESS. FORTUNATELY FOR ME, HE LIVES ACROSS THE STREET FROM US, THEREFORE, I DID NOT HAVE TO TRAVEL FAR TO GET HIS SIGNATURE. ENJOY YOUR DAY LOVE! AMORE, BELLA BARBARA

IN THE MIDST OF OUR (THE LORD AND BARBARA) FEARS

IN THE MIDST OF OUR FEARS WE WILL WALK OUR WALK, MY LORD.

IN THE MIDST OF MY FEARS, I WILL WALK THE WALK THAT CAUSES ME SPIRITUAL AND PHYSICAL FEAR.

I WILL WALK THE WALK, SO THAT ALL MAY KNOW THAT YOU CARE.

I WILL WALK THE WALK THAT LEADS ME THROUGH FORBIDDEN GROUNDS.

I WILL WALK THE WALK WITH THE SHIELD (THE LORD JESUS) THAT RELEASES HEAVENLY SOUNDS.

I WILL WALK THE WALK, WITH KING JESUS AS MY GUIDE.

I WILL WALK THE WALK, WITH GOD, MY HOLY SPOUSE, AT MY VICTORIOUS SIDE.

FOR IT IS A WALK THAT EMITS GREAT FEARS.

IT IS A WALK THAT HAS CAUSED ME TO SHED MANY SPIRITUAL AND VISIBLE TEARS.
I WILL HOLD ON TO YOUR PRECIOUS AND VICTORIOUS HAND, LORD JESUS.
AS I WALK THE WALK THAT OUR HEAVENLY FATHER GAVE US.
MAY 12, 2015 BY: BARBARA ANN MARY MACK

GREETINGS ARCHBISHOP CRAIG! THROUGH THE YEARS, THE LORD HAS REVEALED MANY THINGS PERTAINING TO THE INNER FEELINGS OF HIS CHILDREN THAT ARE HIDDEN TO THE WORLD. AMONG THOSE WHOM HE HAS SHARED THEIR INNER PAIN AND SUFFERINGS, ARE THOSE IN YOUR FAMILY. I HAVE PRAYED FOR… FOR MANY YEARS, EVEN BEFORE YOU KNEW THEM. THE LORD SHOWED ME MANY VISIONS IN 1997 PERTAINING TO THOSE IN YOUR LIFE, AND THOSE WHO WILL ENTER YOUR LIFE IN THE FUTURE. THESE ARE SOME OF THE THINGS THAT THE LORD SHARES WITH HIS PROPHETS, SO THAT WHEN THE TIME OF THE MANIFESTATIONS TAKE PLACE, THE LORD'S PROPHETS WILL KNOW HOW TO PROCEED. AT THIS TIME THE LORD HAS ALL OF US PARTICIPATING IN A GREAT WORK FOR HIM, WHICH WILL BRING ABOUT MANY CONVERSIONS TO GOD'S HOLY TRUTH. LA TOYA AND AMYA HAVE BEEN PRAYING FOR ALL OF YOU AS WELL. WE ARE EXAMPLES OF THE LORD'S VERSION OF LOVE. WE HAVE BEEN COMMISSIONED BY ALMIGHTY GOD HIMSELF TO PROCEED IN A MISSION AND ASSIGNMENT THAT CAUSE GREAT SUFFERING AND APPREHENSION. WE HAVE ALSO BEEN SHOWN OUR DESTINATIONS WITH HIM AFTER OUR DIVINE ASSIGNMENT IS COMPLETED. WITH GOD'S HOLY GRACE, WE HAVE ALL CONDUCTED OURSELVES IN ACCORDANCE TO WHAT THE LORD HAS ORDERED AND EXPECTS OF US. IN THE MEANWHILE, PLEASE CONTINUE TO PRAY FOR… FOR SHE IS IN GREAT PAIN AT THIS TIME. MY FAMILY AND I WILL ALSO LIFT HER UP IN PRAYER. LA TOYA SAYS THAT SHE ALWAYS PRAYS FOR HER.

OH WHAT A GLORIOUS CROSS THAT I CARRY: THANK YOU, O LORD!

BARBARA SPEAKING TO THE LORD

MY GOD, I PRAISE YOU FOR FINDING ME WORTHY TO BEAR THE CROSS OF LOVE THAT YOU HAVE PLACED UPON ME. I PRAISE YOU FOR LOVING YOUR GREAT CREATION (HUMAN BEINGS) SO MUCH THAT YOU DEEM US WORTHY TO APPEAR TO US TODAY, IN THE FORM OF YOUR CHOSEN MESSENGER AND BRIDE (BARBARA). I PRAISE YOU FOR FINDING ME WORTHY TO SEND TO THOSE WHO ARE IN NEED OF YOUR SPIRITUAL AND PHYSICAL GUIDANCE AND LOVE. I BLESS YOU, MY GOD, FOR GRACING ME WITH THE CROSS THAT EMITS MUCH PAIN AND SUFFERING FOR THE SAKE OF YOUR GOOD NEWS PERTAINING TO SALVATION THROUGH JESUS CHRIST. OH WHAT AN AWESOME AND REWARDING ASSIGNMENT OF LOVE! OH WHAT A GLORIOUS GIFT TO THE WORLD! OH WHAT A MARVELOUS EXPRESSION OF DIVINE MERCY AND ALLEGIANCE TO YOUR GREAT CREATION OF LOVE! OH WHAT A GLORIOUS CROSS THAT I CARRY EVERY DAY!!!
MAY 11, 2015 BY: BARBARA ANN MARY MACK

GREETINGS LOVE! COME STA OGGI? TODAY A COUPLE OF MY SIBLINGS CALLED TO REQUEST A SERVICE THAT LA TOYA AND I WILL NOT COMMIT OURSELVES TO. IT IS «VERY IMPORTANT» WHEN AND HOW TO SAY «NO» TO FAMILY AND FRIENDS. WE MUST REMEMBER THAT WE CANNOT COMMIT OURSELVES TO EVERY REQUEST THAT WE RECEIVE, BECAUSE WE ARE NOT ALMIGHTY AND LIMITLESS GOD! WE ALL HAVE SPIRITUAL, EMOTIONAL, AND PHYSICAL LIMITATIONS, AND WE ARE TO BE AWARE OF THIS FACT AT ALL TIMES. I HAVE LEARNED THROUGH THE YEARS NOT TO OVER STRESS MYSELF WITH THINGS THAT I SHOULD NOT HAVE COMMITTED MYSELF TO, ESPECIALLY WHEN ONE HAS A LARGE CIRCLE OF FAMILY AND FRIENDS. I CONSTANTLY REMIND LA TOYA AND MY SISTER, WE CANNOT TAKE ON OTHER PEOPLE'S RESPONSIBILITIES IF IT CAUSE STRESS OR HARM TO US. I AM AWARE OF MY SPIRITUAL, EMOTIONAL, AND PHYSICAL LIMITATIONS. IF I CANNOT HELP SOMEONE IN NEED, I GIVE THEIR NEEDS TO THE ONLY ONE WHO CAN. ALMIGHTY GOD KNOWS EVERYTHING THAT WE NEED. IF WE GO TO HIM IN PRAYER, HE WILL PROVIDE EVERYTHING THAT HE DEEMS BENEFICIAL TO ALL OF HIS CHILDREN. DEAR ONE, TRY NOT TO TAKE ON ANYTHING THAT WILL OVERWHELM YOUR VALUABLE ESSENCE. ATTACHED ARE SOME PICTURES THAT WE TOOK AFTER THE CELEBRATION OF THE HOLY EUCHARIST. IT WAS A VERY BEAUTIFUL GOD SENT DAY.
GOD BLESS! BEAUTIFUL BARBARA
SENT: TUE, MAY 12, 2015 11:58 PM-READ: WED 5/13/2015 1:28 AM

GREETINGS, DEAR ARCHBISHOP CRAIG! COME STA AMORE? OFTEN, LA TOYA, AMYA AND I DISCUS THE REALITY OF MORTALITY. ALTHOUGH WE LOVE OUR FAMILY AND FRIENDS VERY MUCH, WE UNDERSTAND AND ACCEPT THE PROFOUNDNESS OF MORTALITY. I WANT ALL OF MY FAMILY AND FRIENDS TO CELEBRATE INSTEAD OF MOURNING FOR ME, BECAUSE I BELIEVE THAT I SERVE AND HONOR THE LORD. I BELIEVE THAT I WALK WITH ALMIGHTY GOD TODAY, IN A MANNER THAT HE DESIRES OF ALL OF HIS CHILDREN. THEREFORE, I LOOK FORWARD TO MY BLESSED REWARD. LOVE, BEAUTIFUL BARBARA
MAY 13, 2015 BY: BARBARA ANN MARY MACK
SENT: WED, MAY 13, 2015 6:00 PM-READ: THU 5/14/2015 12:08 AM

GREETINGS ARCHBISHOP CRAIG! AFTER POSTING THE GOD INSPIRED PASSAGES BELOW, I RECEIVED THIS POST FROM ONE OF MY FACEBOOK FRIENDS. SHE IS THE WOMAN WHO HAD A DREAM ABOUT ME THE NIGHT BEFORE WE MET FOR THE FIRST TIME.

DO NOT WEEP FOR ME

BARBARA SPEAKING

DO NOT WEEP FOR ME, THOSE WHO LONG TO SEE ME HAPPY!

FOR I AM IN THE LOVING ARMS OF GOD, THE HOLY TRINITY.

DO NOT WEEP FOR GOD'S, HOLY BRIDE,

FOR I WILL BE SEATED AT HIS HOLY SIDE.

DO NOT WEEP FOR ME, FOR I AM NOT ALONE!

I WILL BE DANCING AROUND GOD'S SACRED THRONE.

DO NOT WEEP FOR ME!

FOR I WILL BE SINGING WITH THE BLESSED ANGELS AND SAINTS, AS WE DANCE WITH GOD, THE ETERNAL TRINITY.

DO NOT WEEP FOR ME!

DO NOT WEEP FOR ME!

DO NOT WEEP FOR ME!!!

MAY 13, 2015 BY: BARBARA ANN MARY MACK

LIFE AND MORTALITY

BARBARA SPEAKING

IN THE MIDST OF LIFE, I REJOICE IN THE GIFT OF MORTALITY. IN THE MIDST OF LIFE I GRASP THE EXCITEMENT THAT I AM GRACED WITH, AS I ENJOY THE COMPANY OF MY BELOVED FAMILY AND FRIENDS. IN THE MIDST OF LIFE, I CELEBRATE EACH BLESSED DAY, AS I THANK ALMIGHTY GOD FOR THE GIFT OF SPENDING VALUABLE QUALITY TIME WITH MY LOVED ONES. IN THE MIDST OF LIFE, I DANCE WITH THE ESSENCE OF MY HOLY GOD AND SPOUSE, AS I ACKNOWLEDGE MY LIMITATIONS ON EARTH. IN THE MIDST OF LIFE, I DANCE WITH MY BLESSED DAUGHTER AND GRANDDAUGHTER, AS WE ENJOY THE GIFT OF ANOTHER DAY TOGETHER. IN THE MIDST OF LIFE, I REACH OUT TO THOSE WHO ARE SUFFERING TOO. IN THE MIDST OF LIFE, I REACH OUT TO THOSE WHO ARE EXPERIENCING TROUBLED TIMES. IN THE MIDST OF LIFE, I LIFT MY HANDS IN PRAISE THROUGHOUT EACH DAY, AS I BOW IN THE PRESENCE OF GOD, MY SAVIOR. IN THE MIDST OF LIFE, I LOOK FORWARD TO SEEING THE FACE OF GOD, MY GREAT AND HOLY REWARD. IN THE MIDST OF LIFE, I WILL SPEAK THE WORDS THAT ARE RELEASED FROM THE BEING OF MY ETERNAL GOD. IN THE MIDST OF LIFE, I WILL SING THE SONGS THAT REVEAL THE EXISTENCE OF SWEET PARADISE ABOVE. IN THE MIDST OF LIFE, I WILL TRAVEL TO FOREIGN LANDS, SO THAT I MAY DELIVER GOD'S HOLY MESSAGES TO HIS CALLED AND CHOSEN ONES. IN THE MIDST OF LIFE, I WILL LOOK FORWARD TO MY POSITION AS GOD'S HOLY QUEEN IN HEAVEN ABOVE. IN THE MIDST OF LIFE, I WILL BEND MY KNEES IN THE COMPANY OF MY SPIRITUAL BROTHERS AND SISTERS, AS WE PRAISE ALMIGHTY GOD AS ONE. IN THE MIDST OF LIFE I WILL APPROACH GOD'S HOLY ALTAR, AS I BOW WITH GRACE AND HUMILITY IN HIS HOLY AND WORTHY PRESENCE. IN THE MIDST OF MORTALITY, I WILL LIVE!

MAY 13, 2015 BY: BARBARA ANN MARY MACK

SHEMA'S FACEBOOK MESSAGE TO ME
HI BARBARA, ABOUT AN HOUR AGO I WAS SITTING ON MY COUCH THINKING DEEPLY ABOUT UR HAPPINESS, WONDERING IF IT IS POSSIBLE WITH UR PURPOSE TO HAVE ENJOYMENT AND HAPPINESS IN THIS LIFE. I AM COMFORTED TO SEE UR LAST POST TO KNOW THAT U ARE WELL IN THIS LIFE AND THAT EVEN THE MEDITATIONS OF MY HEART ARE HEARD & ANSWERED BY OUR FATHER!...SHEMA
SENT: THU, MAY 14, 2015 1:08 AM-READ: THU 5/14/2015 10:50 AM

I WILL MOT QUESTION ALMIGHTY GOD, FOR HE KNOWS EVERYTHING

BARBARA SPEAKING

THE DEPTH OF MY INTERNAL BEING, HE KNOWS! WHAT IS BEST FOR ALL OF HIS CHILDREN, HE KNOWS! THE BEGINNING, BEFORE IT BEGINS, HE KNOWS. THE BEGINNING AND ENDING OF ALL LIFE, HE KNOWS! WHAT YOU AND I WILL DO, BEFORE WE DO, HE KNOWS! THE SINCERITY OF OUR LOVE FOR HIM, HE KNOWS! OUR GOOD AND BAD THOUGHTS AND DEEDS, HE KNOWS! HOW MUCH WE CARE FOR THE POOR AND HELPLESS ONES, HE KNOWS! THE DEPTH OF OUR FAITH AND TRUST IN HIM, HE KNOWS! I WILL NOT QUESTION ALMIGHTY GOD, FOR HE KNOWS! I WILL WAIT AND WATCH, MY LORD! I WILL WAIT ON YOUR HOLY WORD! I WILL WATCH AS YOU UNFOLD AND REVEAL YOUR HOLY PRESENCE IN MY LIFE, AND THE LIVES OF THOSE WHO TRULY BELIEVE IN YOUR EXISTENCE. I WILL WATCH AND WAIT ON YOU FOREVER, FOR YOU ARE MY EVERYTHING! MAY 14, 2015 BY: BARBARA ANN MARY MACK

THINKING OF YOU (ARCHBISHOP) AS I MEDITATE

IN THE MIDST OF DIVINE MEDITATION I DWELL

BARBARA SPEAKING TO ALMIGHTY GOD

IN THE MIDST OF DIVINE MEDITATION MY SOUL DWELLS. I AM WRAPPED IN THE MIDST OF MY THOUGHTS OF YOU, O GREAT AND DIVINE SPOUSE AND GOD OF MINE. IN THE MIDST OF DIVINE MEDITATION, MY IGNITED SPIRIT SOARS THROUGHOUT THE REALM OF SWEET PARADISE. IN THE MIDST OF SOLITUDE I CAN HEAR THE HEAVENLY SOUNDS THAT FLOW THROUGH THE GLORIOUS REALM THAT HOUSES GOD, MY ETERNAL SPOUSE. IN THE MIDST OF SPIRITUAL STORMS OF ECSTASY, MY WELCOMED SOUL DANCES IN THE PRESENCE OF HE WHO SITS ON HIS MIGHTY THRONE ABOVE. I WILL DWELL WITHIN THE REALM THAT HOUSES MY PURE AND HOLY THOUGHTS OF YOU, O HEAVENLY SAVIOR AND GOD OF MINE. I WILL SIT QUIETLY AS MY THOUGHTS OF YOUR REALM OF PURITY ENGULF ME WITH THE ESSENCE THAT CREATED

ALL THAT IS GOOD AND HOLY. MY IGNITED BEING WILL SIT IN THE MIDST OF MY REALM OF THOUGHT AS I BOW GRACIOUSLY IN YOUR HOLY PRESENCE, MY LORD. DO NOT DISTURB ME, O WORLD! DO NOT INTERRUPT MY REALM OF PEACE! DO NOT INVADE THE REALM THAT DANCES WITH GOD, THE HOLY TRINITY, AS I SIT QUIETLY IN THE MIDST OF DIVINE MEDITATION. DO NOT DISTURB ME, O UNINVITED WORLD! DO NOT DISTURB THE LAMB'S BRIDE (BARBARA)! DO NOT INTERRUPT THE JOY THAT I EXPERIENCE, AS I SIT IN THE MIDST OF DIVINE MEDITATION. DO NOT PIERCE THE TRANQUILITY THAT SURROUNDS MY REALM OF THOUGHT! DO NOT INTERRUPT ME! DO NOT INTERRUPT THE REALM OF DIVINITY THAT DWELLS WITHIN MY SEPARATE WORLD! DO NOT DISTURB ME, AS I DWELL WITHIN THE REALM OF DIVINE MEDITATION.

MAY 13, 2015 BARBARA ANN MARY MACK

SENT: THU, MAY 14, 2015 4:55 PM-READ: THU 5/14/2015 9:50 PM

HAPPY ASCENSION ARCHBISHOP CRAIG! LET US CELEBRATE JESUS' TRIUMPHANT EXIT!

LET US CELEBRATE THE ASCENSION OF THE LORD

BARBARA SPEAKING TO THE LORD JESUS

LET ME ASCEND WITH YOU, MY LORD, FOR I HAVE COMPLETED MY DIVINE ASSIGNMENT OF LOVE, AS YOU HAVE. LET ME ASCEND WITH YOU, O LORD, FOR I DESIRE TO SEE OUR HEAVENLY FATHER'S PLEASED GLORIOUS FACE ALSO. LET ME ASCEND WITH YOU, MY VICTORIOUS GOD, FOR I HAVE DEFEATED THE GATES OF HELL, AS YOU HAVE. LET ME ASCEND TO SWEET PARADISE ABOVE, SO THAT I MAY DINE AT YOUR TABLE OF VICTORY AND SPIRITUAL FAME, WITH OUR PLEASED FATHER AND GOD. LET ME ASCEND WITH YOU, LORD JESUS, FOR I HAVE VISITED THOSE WHOM YOU HAVE GUIDED ME TO. LET ME ASCEND WITH YOU, LORD JESUS, FOR I HAVE EXHIBITED YOUR VERSION OF HOLY LOVE AND FORGIVENESS. LET ME ASCEND WITH YOU, MY GOD, SO THAT I MAY FOLLOW THE HOLY ESSENCE OF THE GOOD SHEPHERD. LET ME ASCEND WITH YOU, O FAITHFUL AND KIND GOD, FOR YOUR KINGDOM IS WHERE I WANT TO ABIDE FOREVER. LET ME ASCEND WITH YOU, O HEAVENLY SAVIOR, FOR YOUR MERCY AND COMPASSION HAVE CAPTURED MY OBEDIENT ESSENCE. LET ME ASCEND INTO ETERNAL GLORY WITH YOU, SO THAT I MAY WITNESS THE BEAUTY OF MY PROMISED LAND. LET ME ASCEND WITH YOU, LORD JESUS, SO THAT I MAY SING WITH YOUR HEAVENLY CHOIRS OF LOVE. LET ME ASCEND WITH YOU, O HEAVEN SENT ONE, SO THAT I MAY REJOICE WITH YOUR ANGELS AND SAINTS AS YOU SIT ON YOUR MIGHTY THRONE. MY LORD, MY HEAVENLY GOD, I WILL CELEBRATE WITH GLADNESS, AS I ASCEND TO THE GATES OF MY ETERNAL HOME WITH GOD, THE LOVE OF MY LIFE! *ALLELUIA!*

MAY 15, 2015 BY: BARBARA ANN MARY MACK

SENT FRI, MAY 15, 2015 2:07 AM-READ FRI 5/15/2015 7:55 PM

TODAY'S PASSAGES FOR YOU, ARCHBISHOP CRAIG. ENJOY YOUR DAY, DEAR ONE! AMORE, BELLA BARBARA

OH, THE TRAGEDIES THAT PERMEATE THIS REALM OF TIME

OH THE TRAGEDIES THAT I HAVE WITNESSED THROUGHOUT THE REALM OF TIME, CAUSE ME TO WEEP, *SAYS THE LORD*. THE EARTHQUAKES, THE NATURAL DISASTERS, AND THE APATHETIC MURDERS, HAVE TAKEN THE LIVES OF MANY OF MY VULNERABLE CHILDREN. I WEEP FOR YOU, MY CHILDREN! I WEEP FOR YOUR LOVED ONES WHO MOURN YOUR DEATHS. I WEEP FOR THE VICTIMS OF THIS TRAGIC PERIOD OF TIME. IT IS TEMPORARY, MY CHILDREN! THIS TRAGIC PERIOD WILL COME TO AN END. THEN, YOU AND I WILL REJOICE IN MY GARDEN OF CONTINUOUS SPIRITUAL BLESS! WE WILL ROAM THE STREETS THAT DO NOT INVITE TRAGEDIES NOR APATHY. WE WILL DANCE IN THE MIDST OF HAPPY TIMES, AS WE CELEBRATE THE DEPARTURE OF THE REALM THAT RELEASES TRAGEDIES. THIS PERIOD OF TRAGIC TIMES WILL EXIT AS THE REJOICING SOUNDS OF MY HEAVENLY CHOIR OPEN ITS GATES. DEPART FROM EARTH, O TRAGIC TIMES! DEPART FROM THIS PERIOD OF TIME! FOR I, THE LORD, HAVE CONQUERED YOU, IN THE PRESENCE OF MY FAITHFUL FRIENDS. *THUS, SAYS THE LORD!!!* MAY 15, 2015 BY: BARBARA ANN MARY MACK

SOARING IN THE MIDST OF DIVINITY

WITHIN THE REALM OF SWEET DIVINITY, I WILL SOAR IN THE DIRECTION OF SACRED LOVE! I WILL REJOICE IN THE MIDST OF DIVINITY, AS I BOW IN THE PRESENCE OF THE LORD WITH MY FAMILY AND FRIENDS. I WILL DANCE IN THE MIDST OF DIVINITY AS I LISTEN TO THE SOUNDS THAT DESCEND FROM GOD'S HEAVENLY CHOIRS OF CONTINUOUS PRAISE! I WILL ROAM THE STREETS THAT REVEAL DIVINITY AS I MEDITATE ON GOD, MY SAVIOR'S, VICTORIOUS ACT OF LOVE. I WILL SLEEP WITHIN THE REALM OF DIVINITY AS I HOLD ON TO THE HOPE OF GREETING MY WORTHY GOD AND HOLY SPOUSE. IN THE MIDST OF DIVINITY, I WILL OFFER PRAYERS OF THANKSGIVING AS I EXPRESS MY GRATITUDE AND LOVE FOR GOD, MY SAVIOR. I WILL

RELAX THROUGHOUT THE DAY, IN THE MIDST OF DIVINITY AND HOPE. I WILL SING SONGS OF GRATITUDE, AS I WALLOW IN THE MIDST OF DIVINE ECSTASY AND SPIRITUAL BLISS ON EARTH! I WILL DANCE WITH THE TUNES THAT RELEASE THE UNCHAINED ALLELUIAS, AS I PRAISE ALMIGHTY GOD, IN THE MIDST OF DIVINITY!

MAY 15, 2015 BY: BARBARA ANN MARY MACK

SENT: FRI, MAY 15, 2015 2:42 PM-READ: FRI 5/15/2015 7:55 PM

SATAN, SATAN, I KNOW WHO YOU ARE

I KNOW WHO YOU ARE, O SATAN! FOR I CAN SEE YOU IN THE FACES OF THOSE WHO COMMIT UNSPEAKABLE AND HORRENDOUS ACTS AGAINST LIFE, GOD'S GREATEST CREATION. I CAN SEE YOU IN THE UNNATURAL DISASTERS THAT HAVE TAKEN THE LIVES OF MANY INNOCENT PEOPLE AND LIVING CREATURES. I CAN SEE YOU IN THE UNHOLY LANGUAGE AND MUSIC, THAT CAUSE GOD'S VULNERABLE CHILDREN TO FOCUS ON YOU AND YOUR REALM OF EVIL DEEDS. I CAN SEE YOU IN THE HORRENDOUS STORMS THAT HAVE TAKEN THE LIVES OF THE SUSCEPTIBLE ONES. I CAN SEE YOU IN THE ACTS OF THOSE WHO CREEP THROUGHOUT THE DAY AND NIGHT, IN SEARCH FOR THINGS THAT DO NOT BELONG TO THEM. I CAN SEE YOU IN THE MIDST OF THE NUMEROUS TRAGEDIES THAT HAVE CLAIMED THE LIVES OF MANY. I CAN SEE YOU, O SATAN! I CAN SEE YOUR UNWELCOMED PRESENCE IN OUR MIDST TODAY. ONLY YOU, O SATAN, CAN CAUSE ONE TO KILL HIS OR HER INNOCENT CHILDREN. ONLY YOU, O SATAN, CAN CAUSE A MOTHER TO ABORT HER UNBORN INNOCENT CHILD. ONLY YOU, O SATAN, CAN CAUSE THOSE WHO PARTICIPATE IN THE EXECUTION OF AN ABORTION, TO PROCEED IN THAT UNGODLY ACT AGAINST LIFE. ONLY YOU, O SATAN, CAN GIVE THOSE WHO PARTICIPATE IN DESTROYING THE LIFE OF AN UNBORN CHILD, A PEACE OF MIND AFTER THAT UNGODLY ACT. ONLY YOU, O SATAN, CAN CAUSE SOMEONE TO RAPE GOD'S VULNERABLE WOMEN, MEN, BOYS, AND GIRLS. ONLY YOU, O SATAN, CAN CAUSE ONE TO ABUSE GOD'S VULNERABLE CHILDREN OF ALL AGES. ONLY YOU, O SATAN, CAN CONVINCE ONE TO TAKE HIS OR HER OWN LIFE. ONLY YOU! ONLY YOU! ONLY YOU, O SATAN, WILL LEAD THE REALM OF EVIL INTO THE PIT OF HELL!

MAY 15, 2015 BY: BARBARA ANN MARY MACK

SENT: FRI, MAY 15, 2015 10:07 PM-READ: FRI 5/15/2015 11:28 PM

BUON GIORNO ARCHBISHOP CRAIG! I PRAY THAT YOU HAD A GLORIOUS DAY TOO. LA TOYA JUST FINISHED COOKING ONE OF MY FAVORITE MEALS FOR ME. WE WENT FOOD SHOPPING ON MONDAY, AND I BOUGHT SMOKED TURKEY WINGS AND NECK BONES. TOYA COOKED THEM WITH COW PEAS. EVERYTHING SMELLS VERY GOOD! LA TOYA ALSO MADE CORN BEEF, RICE AND CABBAGE. WE USUALLY COOK ENOUGH TO LAST US FOR 3-5 DAYS. THIS WAY, WE DON'T HAVE TO WONDER ABOUT WHAT WE ARE HAVING FOR THE DAY. WE ARE PLANNING A LITTLE

CELEBRATION FOR AMYA'S BIRTHDAY. SHE WILL TURN 14 THIS SATURDAY. WE WERE GOING TO HAVE A COUPLE OF HER FRIENDS OVER, BUT SHE DECIDED AGAINST THE IDEA LAST WEEK. AMYA LOVES HER PRIVACY, BUT SHE ALSO LIKES TO HAVE FUN WITH HER FRIENDS AT TIMES. ALTHOUGH SHE'LL ONLY BE FOURTEEN, IT SEEMS LIKE SHE HAS BEEN WITH US FOREVER. TOODLES! BEAUTIFUL BARBIE

SENT FRI, MAY 15, 2015 10:07 PM-READ FRI 5/15/2015 11:28 PM

BUONA SERA CRAIG! I PRAY THAT YOU HAD A BLESSED DAY. THE AFTERNOON WAS VERY BUSY FOR LA TOYA AND ME. WHILE WE WERE OUT SHOPPING FOR AMYA'S FAVORITE CAKE AND ICE CREAM, THE LORD SENT ME TO A LOCATION (A MARKET) WHERE ONE OF OUR CITY'S COUNCIL WAS. I MET HIM A COUPLE OF YEARS AGO AS WELL. TODAY WE TALKED FOR A SHORT WHILE AS HE HANDED OUT INFORMATION PERTAINING TO THE MAY 19, 2015 ELECTION. I ALSO HAD THE OPPORTUNITY TO SHOW HIM A FEW OF MY PUBLISHED BOOK AS I SPOKE OF THE LORD. HE TOOK THE TIME TO TAKE A COUPLE OF PICTURES WITH ME AS WELL. PLEASE KEEP HIM IN YOUR PRAYERS. AT THIS TIME, I AM MAKING AMYA A BIRTHDAY CARD. I FORGOT TO PICK ONE UP WHILE WE WERE OUT GETTING THE BALLOONS. I HAVE TO COME UP WITH SOMETHING THAT A FOURTEEN YEAR OLD GIRL WILL LIKE. I AM A LITTLE CREATIVE, BUT NOT AN ARTIST. I CANNOT BELIEVE THAT SHE WILL TURN 14 TOMORROW. IT SEEMS LIKE SHE HAS BEEN WITH US A BIT LONGER THAN THAT. TAKE VERY GOOD CARE OF YOURSELF, DEAR ONE! AMORE, BELLA BARBARA

SENT SAT, MAY 16, 2015 1:34 AM-READ SAT 5/16/2015 12:14 PM

HI ARCHBISHOP CRAIG! IT IS VERY SAD WHEN ONE'S FAMILY AND FRIENDS DO NOT BELIEVE THAT HE OR SHE HAS BEEN SENT TO DELIVER ALMIGHTY GOD'S HOLY WORDS TODAY. EVEN WHEN GOD'S MESSENGER AND PROPHETS EXHIBIT SUPERNATURAL GIFTS IN THEIR PRESENCE. I AM SADDENED BECAUSE THEIR UNBELIEF WILL PREVENT THEM FROM EXPERIENCING THE DEPTH OF ALMIGHTY GOD'S GRACE TODAY. ON THE OTHER HAND, I AM REJOICING, BECAUSE JESUS SAID THAT A PROPHET IS WITHOUT HONOR AMONG HIS FAMILY. TODAY'S PASSAGE BELOW. AMORE, BELLA BARBARA

YOU WHO DO NOT BELIEVE IN MY WORD NOW, WILL NOT BE INVITED
WHEN I MANIFEST MY FORETOLD PROMISE, *SAYS THE LORD*

BELIEF IN MY HOLY WORD IS VITAL TO YOUR SALVATION, MY CHILDREN! BELIEF IN ME, IS VITAL TO YOUR SALVATION, MY CHILDREN. BELIEF IN MY HOLY MESSENGERS IS VITAL TO YOUR SALVATION, MY CHILDREN! BELIEF IN MY HOLY PROMISE THROUGH MY CHOSEN BRIDE (BARBARA) AND PROPHETESS, IS VITAL TO YOUR SALVATION, MY CHILDREN! BELIEF IN MY WORD THROUGH THOSE WHOM I SEND IS VERY IMPORTANT TO YOUR FINAL DESTINATION,

MY CHILDREN. THOSE WHO DO NOT BELIEVE WHEN MY WORD IS REVEALED TO THEM, WILL NOT ENTER INTO MY HOLY PROMISE. THIS IS MY WORD! THIS IS MY PROMISE! DO NOT THINK THAT YOU WILL EXPERIENCE THE GLORY THAT WILL SURROUND THE MANIFESTATION OF MY PROMISE, AT ITS APPOINTED TIME. FOR YOU WILL NOT BE INVITED, *SAYS THE LORD!* FAITH COMES WITH BELIEF BEFORE MANIFESTATION OF MY PROMISE. YOU WILL NOT ENTER THE REALM OF GLORY THAT WAS OFFERED TO YOU BEFORE MY MANIFESTATION, BECAUSE OF YOUR UNBELIEF. YOUR ACTIONS CONVEY YOUR BELIEF, MY CHILDREN! YOUR ACTIONS REVEAL YOUR TRUST IN MY HOLY WORD AND MY HOLY MESSENGERS. THOSE OF YOU WHO DID NOT BELIEVE MY DAUGHTER AND BRIDE, WILL NOT EXPERIENCE THE DEPTH OF MY GLORY ON EARTH TODAY! THIS IS MY PROMISE! THIS IS MY HOLY WORD, *SAYS THE LORD!*

MAY 16, 2015 BY: BARBARA ANN MARY MACK

SENT SAT, MAY 16, 2015 7:06 PM-READ SAT 5/16/2015 8:08 PM

ALMIGHTY GOD SPEAKING

BARBARA SPEAKING

THANK YOU ARCHBISHOP CRAIG FOR THE WONDERFUL HOMILY TODAY. IT IS ALWAYS A DIVINE GIFT TO HEAR YOU PREACH, ESPECIALLY IN PERSON. IT IS ALWAYS A BLESSING TO SEE THE PRIESTS AND DEACONS THAT YOU HAVE BROUGHT CLOSER TO GOD'S HOLY PRESENCE. OUR GRACIOUS GOD IS GRATEFUL FOR YOUR SINCERE ALLEGIANCE UNTO HIM AND HIS HOLY KINGDOMS, IN HEAVEN AND EARTH. KEEP UP THE GOOD WORK FOR THE LORD, FOR HE IS WELL PLEASED.

AMORE, GRATEFUL BARBARA

SENT SUN, MAY 17, 2015 3:18 PM-READ SUN 5/17/2015 10:22 PM

GREETINGS ARCHBISHOP CRAIG! YESTERDAY WAS ANOTHER BUSY DAY FOR US (LA TOYA, AMYA AND ME). WE GOT UP EARLIER THAN USUAL SO THAT WE COULD GIVE AMYA HER BIRTHDAY PRESENTS. WE THANK THE LORD FOR ALLOWING US TO SPEND ANOTHER YEAR OF CELEBRATION TOGETHER. AMYA WAS VERY HAPPY. SINCE WE KNOW WHAT SHE LIKES, LA TOYA, PERRY, FANNIE, AMYA'S OTHER GRANDMOTHER, AMYA'S GRANDFATHER AND I, MADE HER DAY VERY SPECIAL. WE BEGAN CELEBRATING ON FRIDAY AFTER TOYA PICKED AMYA UP FROM SCHOOL. BEFORE PICKING AMYA UP FROM SCHOOL, LA TOYA ORDERED A COUPLE OF PIZZAS AND BAKED A CAKE. AMYA LOVES FOOD, SO I BOUGHT HER FAVORITE BIRTHDAY CAKE, ICE CREAM, FRESH CHERRIES AND OTHER TREATS. LA TOYA WILL TAKE HER SHOPPING FOR SCHOOL CLOTHES ALSO. SINCE SHE WILL BE GOING INTO HIGH SCHOOL IN SEPTEMBER, SHE WILL NEED NEW CLOTHES. THE SCHOOL THAT SHE WILL BE ATTENDING DOESN'T HAVE A UNIFORM DRESS REQUIREMENT. AFTER CELEBRATING AT HOME, LA TOYA AND AMYA WENT TO CHURCH. LA TOYA HAD TO DO THE READING AT ST. BARNABAS' 5 PM MASS. BELOW ARE TWO BIRTHDAY PASSAGES THAT THE LORD INSPIRED ME TO WRITE FOR AMYA TODAY.

IN THE MIDST OF HAPPINESS

IN THE MIDST OF HAPPINESS I WILL STAY!

I WILL DWELL WITHIN YOU, O REALM OF HAPPINESS, THROUGHOUT EACH BLESSED DAY.

GO AWAY! ALL WHO TRY TO PREVENT MY REALM OF HAPPINESS.

GO AWAY, SO THAT I MAY ENJOY HEAVEN SENT CONTENTMENT!

DO NOT TRY TO ENTER MY REALM OF HAPPINESS, O WORLD THAT I HIDE!

DO NOT TRY TO ENTER THE REALM OF HAPPINESS THAT SURROUNDS BARBARA, GOD'S CHOSEN MESSENGER AND BRIDE.

HAPPINESS IS THE REALM, IN WHICH I DWELL.

IT IS THE REALM THAT PREVENTS THE ENTRANCE OF THOSE WHO ARE HEADED IN THE DIRECTION OF ETERNAL HELL!

MY REALM OF HAPPINESS SHELTERS MY VULNERABLE BEING EVERY DAY.

IT SHELTERS AND PROTECTS THE BEING (BARBARA) WHO DESIRES TO PRAY.

I WILL PRAY TO MY SAVIOR AND GOD ABOVE.

I WILL PRAY FOR THE REALM THAT RELEASES HIS DIVINE LOVE.

IN THE MIDST OF DIVINE HAPPINESS, I WILL SOAR!

I WILL MOVE IN THE DIRECTION OF GOD'S OPEN AND INVITING DOOR.

IN THE MIDST OF HAPPINESS, I WILL GREET AND MEET GOD'S CALLED AND CHOSEN SONS.

I WILL DANCE IN THE COMPANY OF THE BLESSED AND MERCIFUL ONES.

I WILL UNITE WITH GOD'S HEAVENLY ANGELS AND SAINTS ABOVE.

IN THE MIDST OF HAPPINESS, WE WILL EXHIBIT GOD'S VERSION OF HOLY LOVE.

MAY 17, 2015 BY: BARBARA ANN MARY MACK

HI ARCHBISHOP CRAIG! LA TOYA, AMYA, AND I ARE EN ROUTE TO VOTE. WE DO NOT HAVE TO TRAVEL FAR. THE LOCATION IS JUST AROUND THE CORNER AT A CHURCH. BELOW IS TODAY'S GOD INSPIRED PASSAGE. LOVE, BEAUTIFUL BARBARA

MY PEACE, MY PEACE, WHERE HAVE YOU GONE?

MY PEACE IS TAKEN AWAY FROM ME WHENEVER I THINK OF THE VULNERABLE AND ABUSED LITTLE GIRLS AND WOMEN WHO WERE/ARE RAPED IN NIGERIA. O LORD, RESTORE MY REALM OF INNER PEACE, FOR IT HAS FORSAKEN ME! I CANNOT HOLD BACK THE TEARS THAT ARE RELEASED, WHENEVER I THINK OF THE ABUSED LITTLE GIRLS. THEY ARE FRIGHTENED BY THEIR CAPTORS, MY LORD. THEY DO NOT KNOW WHERE TO HIDE FROM THEM. REVEAL TO THEM, THEIR PLACE OF REFUGE. REVEAL TO THEM YOUR REALM OF DIVINE TRUE LOVE. THEY ARE AFRAID, MY LORD! THEY FEEL ABANDONED, MY GOD. SHOW THEM YOUR MERCY, MY HOLY LOVE. SHOW THEM YOUR DIVINE MIGHT IN THE MIDST OF THEIR HORRENDOUS JOURNEY AWAY FROM THEIR HOMES AND LOVED ONES. SHOW THEM YOUR GLORY, O HEAVENLY SPOUSE OF MINE. SHOW THEM MY GOD. THEY WEEP THROUGHOUT THE DAY, MY LORD. THEY WEEP THROUGHOUT THE TERRIBLE NIGHTS. WHO CAN THEY TURN TO, BUT YOU, O PLACE OF DIVINE REFUGE AND PEACE? THERE IS NO ONE ELSE. I THANK YOU, MY GOD! I LOVE YOU, O HOLY SPOUSE! I PRAISE YOU FOR RESCUING YOUR ABUSED CAPTIVE DAUGHTERS OF CONTINUOUS PAIN. I PRAISE YOU FOR EXHIBITING YOUR LOVE. YOU HAVE FOUGHT SATAN, THEIR ABUSERS! YOU HAVE FOUGHT HIS REALM OF EVIL, FOR THE SAKE AND SOULS OF YOUR ABUSED DAUGHTERS. YOU HAVE CONQUERED SATAN'S SOLDIER OF MISERY AND PAIN. YOU HAVE WON THE BATTLE! WE (THE LORD AND BARBARA) WILL HEAL THEM, MY LORD. WE WILL HEAL THEM WITH OUR CONTINUOUS LOVE. WE WILL HEAL THEM WITH OUR TEARS OF MERCY. WE WILL HEAL THEM WITH OUR TEARS OF PAIN. YOUR ARMS ARE OPEN WIDE, SO THAT YOUR WOUNDED DAUGHTERS MAY ENTER THEM. YOUR ARMS ARE OPEN WIDE, SO THAT YOU MAY COMFORT ALL OF YOUR ABUSED DAUGHTERS. THEY WILL FEEL YOUR WARMTH, MY LORD. THEY WILL REST WITHIN YOUR ARMS OF COMFORT. THEY WILL REST WITHIN YOU!!!

MAY 19, 2015 BY: BARBARA ANN MARY MACK

SENT: TUE, MAY 19, 2015 4:10 PM-READ: TUE 5/19/2015 6:37 PM

THROUGHOUT THE DAY AND INTO THE MARVELOUS NIGHT

THROUGHOUT THE DAY, AND INTO THE MARVELOUS NIGHT,
I CAN FEEL "THE HOLY PRESENCE OF JESUS, THE ETERNAL LIGHT!"
IN THE WIND'S SWEET, SWEET BREATH,
I CAN FEEL "THE ESSENCE OF JESUS, AS HE CONQUERS SPIRITUAL DEATH."
FLOW WITH ME THROUGHOUT EACH BLESSED DAY,
AS I CLING TO YOU, DEAR LORD, WHEN I PRAY.
YOUR HOLY PRESENCE SURROUNDS CRAIG, THE EXCITED ONE
AS YOU REVEAL TO HIM A GLIMPSE OF JESUS, GOD, THE FATHER'S TRUST WORTHY SON
THROUGHOUT THE DAY, AND INTO THE MARVELOUS NIGHT,
I WILL KEEP YOUR PRECIOUS SON (CRAIG) WITHIN MY PROTECTIVE SIGHT!
CLING TO US (THE LORD JESUS AND BARBARA), O WELL-LOVED SON (CRAIG),
AS I CARRY OUR BLESSED SPIRIT TO GOD, THE SACRED ONE.
NOVEMBER 14, 2012 AT 7:25 PM BY: BARBARA ANN MARY MACK

BUON GIORNO ARCHBISHOP CRAIG! WE MADE IT TO THE VOTING BOOTH. AFTER PLACING MY VOTE, THE LORD LED ME TO ONE OF THE CHURCH MEMBERS WHO ASSISTED IN THE ELECTION AT THAT LOCATION. IT'S VERY FUNNY THAT THE LORD LED ME TO THIS GENTLEMAN TODAY, BECAUSE OVER THE PAST COUPLE OF WEEKS, LA TOYA AND I HAVE SEEN HIM AT OTHER LOCATIONS. AT THE OTHER LOCATIONS, THE GENTLEMAN WAS VERY COURTEOUS AND FRIENDLY. WE FIRST MET HIM WHILE WE WERE PICKING OUT MOTHER'S DAY CARDS. SOMEHOW, THE GENTLEMAN AND LA TOYA GOT INTO A CONVERSATION. WHEN I FIRST SAW HIM, ABOUT A COUPLE OF WEEKS AGO WITH LA TOYA, THE LORD REVEALED TO ME THAT HE AND I WOULD SPEAK ABOUT THE GOODNESS OF THE LORD. ALTHOUGH THE LORD GAVE ME THAT KNOWLEDGE WHEN WE FIRST MET THE GENTLEMAN BEFORE MOTHER'S DAY, I HAD TO WAIT ON THE LORD'S PROMPTING BEFORE APPROACHING HIM. BEFORE GOING TO OUR VOTING LOCATION, THE LORD REVEALED TO ME TO TAKE SOME OF MY PUBLISHED BOOKS WITH ME, SO THAT I MAY SHOW THEM TO SHOW THEM TO SOMEONE AT THAT LOCATION. I ALWAYS WAIT FOR A SIGN FROM THE LORD BEFORE PROCEEDING. AS WE WERE LEAVING THE CHURCH, LA TOYA RECOGNIZED THE GENTLEMAN, AND THEY BEGAN A CONVERSATION. IT WAS AT THAT TIME, THE LORD INSTRUCTED ME TO SHOW THE GENTLEMAN MY BOOKS. WE ALSO TALKED ABOUT THE GOODNESS AND WONDERS OF THE LORD. ALTHOUGH MY DESIRE IS TO BE IN A CONVENT, THE LORD REVEALED TO ME YESTERDAY, THAT MY HOME IS MY CONVENT AND MY SANCTUARY. BELOW IS TODAY'S PASSAGE. AMORE, BELLA BARBARA

MY CONVENT: MY HOME, MY PLACE OF SECLUSION

MY PLACE OF REFUGE, MY PLACE OF INTERCESSORY PRAYER, MY PLACE OF SUPPLICATION, MY PLACE OF DIVINE HUMILITY, MY PLACE OF SUBMISSION UNTO THE WILL OF MY HOLY GOD AND SPOUSE, THE BLESSED TRINITY. MY PLACE OF RECEPTION OF DIVINE SENT NOURISHMENT, MY PLACE OF HEAVEN SENT KNOWLEDGE, MY PLACE TO COMMUNICATE WITH ALMIGHTY GOD THROUGHOUT EACH DAY. MY CONVENT, MY HOME. SURROUNDED AND PROTECTED BY THE GRACE OF ALMIGHTY GOD, MY CONVENT, MY HOME. WITHIN THE EARTHLY REALM THAT SHELTERS AND HOUSES THE BRIDE (BARBARA) OF ALMIGHTY GOD, DWELLS THE SOLITARY ONE (BARBARA). WITHIN THE EARTHLY REALM THAT SECURES THE BRIDE OF DIVINITY, DWELLS THE HEAVEN SENT ESSENCE (BARBARA) WHO INTERCEDES FOR GOD'S VULNERABLE FLOCK OF LOVE. WITHIN HER CONVENT OF LOVE (HOME), PRAYS THE HEAVEN SENT ESSENCE (BARBARA) THAT REVEALS THE DIVINE SECRETS THAT ARE RELEASED TO THE WORLD TODAY. WITHIN HER WALLS OF SECLUSION (HOME), PRAYS THE BRIDE OF JESUS, OUR SAVIOR AND GOD. WITHIN HER SANCTUARY OF HEAVEN ENCOMPASSED BLISS, PRAYS THE BEING (BARBARA) WHO CRIES OUT TO ALMIGHTY GOD'S REALM OF HELP, FOR THE MANY SOULS THAT ARE IN THE PATH OF SATAN'S EVIL DEEDS TODAY. WITHIN HER CONVENT OF LOVE, RESIDES THE ISOLATED ONE (BARBARA). MY LORD, MY GOD, YOU HAVE KEPT ME FROM THE WORLD, SATAN'S ROAMING GROUNDS. YOU HAVE ISOLATED ME FROM THE REALM THAT STEALS THE SOULS OF THE SPIRITUALLY SUBJECTED ONES. YOU HAVE ISOLATED ME FROM THE REALM THAT RELEASES SATAN'S WARRIORS IN THE MIDST OF THE SPIRITUALLY SUBJECTED ONES. MY LORD, MY GOD, I THANK YOU FOR YOUR PROTECTION, AS I SIT IN THE MIDST OF MY CONVENT OF LOVE (HOME). YOU HAVE PROTECTED YOUR CHOSEN BRIDE AND QUEEN (BARBARA) THROUGH THE YEARS. YOU HAVE SENT YOUR HEAVENLY ANGELS TO ENCOMPASS MY VULNERABLE BEING, IN THE MIDST OF THE TRAGEDIES AROUND MY CONVENT OF LOVE. MY LORD, MY GOD, I BOW MY HUMBLED HEAD IN YOUR HOLY PRESENCE, AS YOU CONTINUE TO SURROUND MY CONVENT OF LOVE WITH YOUR HOLY ESSENCE.

MAY 20, 2015 BY: BARBARA ANN MARY MACK

SENT: WED, MAY 20, 2015 1:28 AM-READ: WED 5/20/2015 8:10 AM

MY ONLY BEGOTTEN SON

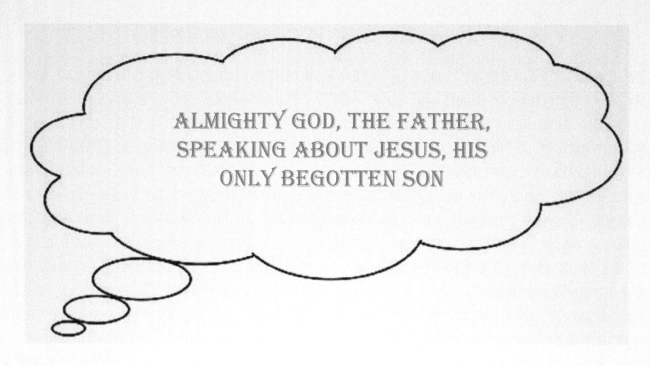

ALMIGHTY GOD, THE FATHER, SPEAKING ABOUT JESUS, HIS ONLY BEGOTTEN SON

I CALLED YOU INTO EXISTENCE, MY SON (THE LORD JESUS), MY ONLY BEGOTTEN SON.

INTO THE NEEDY WORLD, I SENT YOU, THE ONLY SAVING ONE.

FROM MY HOLY ESSENCE YOU EMERGED:

YOU CAME INTO THIS SINFUL WORLD; YOU SUFFERED, AND YOU WERE SCOURGED.

YOU ARE MY HOLY ESSENCE, THE EPITOME OF YOUR ONLY FATHER,

MY LOVE; MY ONLY BEGOTTEN SON.

YOU HAVE TRIUMPHED OVER SATAN, OUR ENEMY, IN THE BATTLES THAT YOU HAVE WON.

LET ALL THE NATIONS SING SONGS OF PRAISE UNTO MY ONLY BEGOTTEN SON;

FOR HE IS KING OF KINGS, AND LORD OVER EVERYONE!

LET THE HOLY BELLS RING THROUGHOUT THE DAY!

LET EVERYONE KNEEL AND PRAY!

FOR JESUS, THE KING OF KINGS, HAS ENTERED EARTH'S NEEDY REALM OF HOPE,

AS HE DESCENDS IN THEIR MIDST TO HELP THEM COPE.

BOW, AS MY ONLY BEGOTTEN SON, JESUS, IS RAISED ON HIS HOLY CROSS OF LOVE;

TO SAVE THE POOR AND LOST ONES, BY THE GIFT (GOD, THE FATHER'S GRACE) THAT DESCENDED FROM ABOVE.

NOVEMBER 11, 2012 AT 5:26 PM BY: BARBARA ANN MARY MACK

MY FATHER: MY LOVE: MY LORD; MY LOVE: MY GOD; MY LOVE:

BARBARA SPEAKING TO ALMIGHTY GOD

WALK WITH ME; TALK WITH ME: LORD STRENGTHEN ME; AND KEEP ME: MY LORD: MY GOD: MY FATHER: MY LOVE: FOR YOU ALONE ARE HOLY: YOU ALONE, ARE RIGHTEOUS: YOU ALONE, KEEP ME SAFE FROM HARM. I WILL WALK WITH YOU DAILY: MY FATHER; MY GOD, MY HOLY SPOUSE! CAPTURE THE SWEET ESSENCE OF MY CONTINUOUS LOVE AS IT MOVES TOWARD YOU DAILY, MY GOD. LET YOUR MIGHTY WINDS OF LOVE CARRY US (CRAIG AND BARBARA) TOWARD OUR ETERNAL RESTING SANCTUARY WITH YOU. HOLD ON TO US! MY FATHER; MY LOVE: MY LORD; MY LOVE: MY GOD; MY LOVE: HOLD ON TO YOUR FAITHFUL ONES (CRAIG AND BARBARA) THROUGHOUT ETERNITY! FOR WE HAVE FOLLOWED YOUR WILL AND YOUR HOLY WAY. LET US BOW BEFORE YOU, O HEAVENLY FATHER, FOREVER!

OCTOBER 9, 2012 AT 10:35 PM BY: BARBARA ANN MARY MACK

SENT WED, MAY 20, 2015 5:50 PM-READ WED 5/20/2015 6:56 PM

GREETINGS ARCHBISHOP CRAIG! COME STA? OFTEN WE HEAR OF THE TRAGEDIES PERTAINING TO POLICE ABUSE. BUT THERE DOESN'T SEEM TO BE MUCH PUBLIC AWARENESS OF THE POLICE OFFICERS WHO ARE WOUNDED AND KILLED IN THE LINE OF DUTY. I HAVE MET AND BEFRIENDED MANY POLICE OFFICERS OVER THE YEARS. I HAVE GONE TO THE FUNERALS OF SLAIN POLICE OFFICERS AS WELL. IN THE MIDST OF MY CONVENT, MY HOME, THE LORD GAVE ME THE PASSAGE BELOW. HE TOO, HAS MERCY ON THE FALLEN POLICE OFFICERS WHO WERE SLAIN IN AN UNJUST MANNER. AMORE, BELLA BARBARA

WHO WILL WEEP FOR US (POLICE OFFICERS)?

ODE TO THE FALLEN POLICE OFFICERS

WHO WILL WEEP FOR US (POLICE OFFICERS), AS WE FIGHT FOR THE SOULS WHOM WE ARE DESTINED TO CARE FOR? WHO WILL WEEP FOR US, WHEN WE ARE WOUNDED WHILE FIGHTING FOR THE LIVES OF THE INNOCENT ONES? WHO WILL WEEP FOR US, WHEN WE ARE KILLED ON THE BATTLE FIELDS? WHO WILL WEEP FOR US, AS WE GO INTO THE REALM THAT DO NOT OBEY THE LAWS? WHO WILL WEEP FOR OUR CHILDREN WHEN WE ARE KILLED IN THE LINE OF DUTY? WHO WILL WEEP FOR OUR WIVES AND HUSBANDS AS THEY MAKE PLANS TO BURY US? WHO WILL COMFORT OUR FAMILIES AND FRIENDS WHEN WE ARE GONE? WHO WILL PUT OUR CHILDREN TO BED WHEN THEY LOOK FOR THEIR MOM OR DAD? WHO WILL COMFORT OUR SPOUSES WHEN THEY LONG TO HEAR OUR VOICES? WHO WILL CONSOLE OUR PARENTS AS THEY ATTEND THE FUNERALS OF THEIR SLAIN CHILDREN? WHO, MY GOD? WHO WILL WEEP FOR US?

ALMIGHTY GOD SPEAKING TO THE POLICE OFFICERS

MY TEARS, MY PRAYERS, I WILL WEEP FOR YOU!
I WILL WEEP WITH THE TEARS THAT ARE HOLY AND TRUE.
I WILL WEEP FOR YOU, O FALLEN ONES!
I WILL WEEP FOR YOU, O WOUNDED DAUGHTERS AND SONS.
THROUGHOUT THE DAYS,
I WILL WEEP FOR YOU, AS MY HEAVEN SENT BRIDE (BARBARA) PRAYS.
FOR I HAVE SEEN YOUR WOUNDED HEARTS.
I KNOW THE DEPTH OF YOUR BRAVERY BEFORE THE NEW DAY STARTS.
I HAVE HEARD YOUR INNER TEARS.
I HAVE HEARD THE SOUNDS THAT REVEALED YOUR FEARS.
YOU ENTER THE BATTLEFIELD WITH HIDDEN FEARS.
YOU ENTER THE BATTLEFIELD AS YOU HIDE YOUR INNER TEARS.
MY TEARS WILL COMFORT YOUR FAMILIES AND FRIENDS,

AS THEY LOOK UP TO A HEAVEN SENT LOVE THAT NEVER ENDS.

COME AND JOIN YOUR HEAVENLY FATHER ABOVE,

AS HE SHED THE TEARS THAT REVEAL HIS UNENDING LOVE.

FOR I HAVE WITNESSED YOUR ACTS OF CHARITY AND BRAVERY.

I HAVE WITNESSED THE STRENGTH THAT YOU RECEIVED FROM THE BLESSED TRINITY.

HOLD ON TO ME,

AS YOU JOURNEY IN THE DIRECTION OF THE REALM OF COMFORT THAT WILL EXIST
THROUGHOUT ETERNITY!

MAY 21, 2015 BY: BARBARA ANN MARY MACK

SENT FRI, MAY 22, 2015 1:13 AM-READ FRI 5/22/2015 8:15 AM

BARBARA SPEAKING TO GOD'S
CHILDREN OF ALL AGES

BUON PASQUA ARCHBISHOP CRAIG! BELOW IS TODAY'S MESSAGE FROM THE LORD TO HIS
VULNERABLE CHILDREN OF ALL AGES. I WILL PLACE ON MY FACEBOOK PAGE ALSO. LOVE,
BELLA BARBIE

DEMONS IN SUITS AND DRESSES

CAN YOU SEE THEM? CAN YOU SEE THE DEMONS AS THEY WALK IN THE MIDST OF THE
VULNERABLE ONES? CAN YOU SEE THEM, MY BROTHERS AND SISTERS? THEY ARE DRESSED
LIKE YOU AND ME. THEY ARE GUISED IN THE SAME WARDROBE THAT YOU AND I POSSESS.
THEY BLEND IN WITH THE UNSUSPECTING ONES SO THAT THEIR TRUE IDENTITIES WILL NOT
BE KNOWN.

BARBARA SPEAKING TO THE DEMONS

BUT I KNOW WHO YOU ARE, O ENEMY OF OUR LOVING GOD! FOR YOUR EVIL DEEDS AND ACTS, YOU CANNOT HIDE. YOU MAY WALK LIKE US, THE AVERAGE ONES. AND YOU MAY TALK LIKE US AT TIMES. BUT THE LORD OUR GOD, HAS REVEALED YOUR TRUE IDENTITY ACCORDING TO YOUR "UNHOLY" THOUGHTS AND ACTS. GO AWAY! O DECEIVER (THE DEMONS). FOR I KNOW WHO YOU ARE. YOU CANNOT FOOL OR DECEIVE GOD'S KNOWLEDGEABLE CHILDREN. FOR HE REVEALS YOUR TRUE IDENTITY, REGARDLESS OF YOUR PHYSICAL APPEARANCE. GO AWAY! YOU WHO ARE DESTINED TO SPEND ETERNITY IN HELL. FOR YOUR "UNHOLY" ACTS ARE NOT WELCOMED HERE (EARTH)! GO AWAY! O DECEIVER AND DESTRUCTIVE ONES. FOR THE GATES OF HELL KNOW ITS WELCOMED RESIDENTS. THE GATES OF HELL WELCOME THE GUISED ONES! THE GATES OF HELL WELCOME THE MURDERERS. THE GATES OF HELL WELCOME THE LIARS AND CHEATERS. THE GATES OF HELL WELCOME THE ABUSERS. THE GATES OF HELL WELCOME THOSE WHO PRACTICE UNHOLY DEEDS AND ACTS. THE GATES OF HELL WELCOMES THOSE WHO HAVE SEX BEFORE MARRIAGE. THE GATES OF HELL WELCOME THOSE WHO DEVIATE FROM GOD'S VERSION OF HOLY MATRIMONY. THE GATES OF HELL WELCOME THOSE WHO BEAR FALSE WITNESS AGAINST ANYONE. THE GATES OF HELL WELCOME THOSE WHO PARTAKE IN ABORTIONS. THE GATES OF HELL WELCOME THOSE WHO SELL THEIR BODIES FOR ANYTHING. THE GATES OF HELL WELCOME THOSE WHO DO NOT CARE FOR THEIR CHILDREN. THE GATES OF HELL WELCOME THOSE WHO DO NOT TAKE ON THEIR RESPONSIBILITIES.

ALMIGHTY GOD SPEAKING TO HIS CHILDREN

MY CHILDREN, DO NOT BE DECEIVED, FOR THE GATES OF HELL ARE KNOCKING ON THE DOORS OF THOSE WHO DO NOT FOLLOW MY VERSION OF HOLINESS. THIS IS MY WORD OF WARNING TO YOU, MY CHILDREN. DO NOT BE DECEIVED BY THE GUISE THAT SATAN'S ANGELS ARE WEARING. MY CHILDREN, OPEN YOUR EYES AND YOUR EARS, AND WITNESS THE "UNGODLY" ACTS OF THE DEMONS THAT ARE IN YOUR MIDST TODAY. FOR THEY ARE WEARING THE SAME CLOTHING THAT YOU WEAR. THEY ARE ATTENDING THE SAME CHURCHES THAT YOU ATTEND. THEY ARE EATING AT THE SAME FOOD PLACES WHERE YOU DINE. THEY ARE ATTENDING THE SAME SCHOOLS THAT YOU ATTEND. THEY ARE ATTENDING THE SAME SPORT EVENTS THAT YOU ATTEND. THEY ARE ATTENDING THE SAME CONCERTS AND MOVIE THEATRES THAT YOU ATTEND. THEY ARE ATTENDING YOUR DOCTOR OFFICES. THEY ARE PRESENT IN THE HOSPITALS AND NURSING HOMES. THEY ARE AT THE SUPERMARKETS AND MALLS. THEY ARE ON THE TELEVISION. YOU CAN HEAR THEM THROUGH YOUR RADIOS. YOU CAN WITNESS THEIR PRESENCE AND ACTIVITIES VIA THE INTERNET. MY VULNERABLE CHILDREN, SATAN'S ANGELS (DEMONS) ARE EVERYWHERE, EXCEPT IN THE HEARTS AND SOULS OF THE HOLY ONES. COME! MY CHILDREN. FOLLOW ME, SO THAT THE DEMONS WILL NOT HARM

YOUR VULNERABLE AND UNSUSPECTING SOULS. THIS, SAYS THE LORD, THE ONLY REALM OF HOLINESS AND PROTECTION!

MAY 22, 2015 BY: BARBARA ANN MARY MACK

SENT FRI, MAY 22, 2015 1:09 PM-READ FRI 5/22/2015 5:12 PM

CELEBRATING THE LAST DAYS OF EASTER SEASON.

THE GATES OF HELL ARE SUDDENLY UPON US (THE VULNERABLE ONES)

FLEE! MY BROTHERS AND SISTERS, FOR THE HAVOC THAT IS RELEASED FROM THE GATES OF HELL IS IN OUR MIDST TODAY. FLEE, MY BROTHERS AND SISTERS! FLEE TO THE MOUNTAIN TOP (ALMIGHTY GOD'S REALM OF HOLINESS)! FLEE TO YOUR ONLY PLACE OF REFUGE TODAY! FOR THE GATES OF HELL DO NOT DISCRIMINATE! THE GATES OF HELL COLLECT THOSE WHO ARE NOT IN UNION WITH GOD, THE BLESSED AND HOLY TRINITY! THE GATES OF HELL ARE ROAMING THROUGH EVERY STREET, CITY, TOWN, VILLAGE, STATE, AND COUNTRY! THE GATES OF HELL ARE ENTERING THE HOMES OF THOSE WHO ARE LIVING IN A REALM THAT REJECTS GOD'S VERSION OF HOLINESS AND RIGHTEOUS LIVING. THE GATES OF HELL ARE ENTERING THE HOMES OF THOSE WHO REFUSE TO GIVE UP THEIR SINFUL WAYS. THE GATES OF HELL ARE ENTERING THE HOMES OF THE DECEIVING ONES! THE GATES OF HELL ARE ENTERING THE HOMES OF THE MERCILESS ONES! THE GATES OF HELL ARE ENTERING THE HOMES OF THOSE WHO DO NOT SHOW COMPASSION AND CHARITY TOWARD THE DESTITUTE ONES. THE GATES OF HELL ARE ENTERING THE HOMES OF THOSE WHO HAVE KILLED AND SLAUGHTERED GOD'S INNOCENT BABES. THE GATES OF HELL ARE ENTERING THE HOMES OF THOSE WHO CAUSE GOD'S CHILDREN TO FEAR. THE GATES OF HELL HAVE CAPTURED THE YOUNG, THE OLD, THE WEAK AND THE STRONG, THE RICH, AND THE POOR!

ALMIGHTY GOD SPEAKING TO HIS CHILDREN

FLEE TO ME, MY CHILDREN! FOR THE GATES OF HELL DO NOT DISCRIMINATE! ARE YOU PREPARED TO COMBAT SATAN'S GATES, MY CHILDREN? ARE YOU ARMED WITH THE ONLY WEAPON (SALVATION THROUGH CHRIST JESUS) THAT WILL SECURE YOUR SURVIVAL, MY CHILDREN? ARE YOU IN UNION WITH THE BLOOD THAT WAS SHED FOR YOUR ETERNAL SOULS, MY CHILDREN? ARE YOU IN UNION WITH THE PRECIOUS VICTORIOUS BLOOD OF JESUS CHRIST, THE FATHER'S VICTORIOUS LAMB? MY CHILDREN, HOLD ON TO THE ONLY WEAPON THAT WILL SAVE YOU DURING THIS CRUCIAL PERIOD OF TIME. FOR THE GATES OF HELL ROAM THE EARTH DAILY! WITNESS THE HAVOC THAT IT LEAVES EACH CITY, COUNTY, STATE, AND COUNTRY IN! WITNESS THE COUNTLESS LIVES THAT HAVE PERISHED, DUE TO ITS DEVASTATION THAT FLOWS THROUGHOUT THE EARTH TODAY! WITNESS THE ACTIVITY THAT REVEALS THE PRESENCE OF SATAN'S HANDIWORK, FOR HE IS IN YOUR MIDST TODAY! FLEE, MY CHILDREN! FLEE TO THE MOUNTAIN TOP! FLEE TO MY REALM OF HOLINESS TODAY!

MAY 22, 2015 BY: BARBARA ANN MARY MACK

SENT FRI, MAY 22, 2015 4:26 PM-READ FRI 5/22/2015 6:04 PM

IN THE MIDST OF MY LIMITATIONS

112

BARBARA SPEAKING

IN THE MIDST OF MY LIMITATIONS, I AM REMINDED OF BEING HUMAN. MY LIMITATIONS REMIND ME OF THE GIFT OF MORTALITY. MY LIMITATIONS REMIND ME THAT I AM NOT IN CONTROL OVER MY MORTAL AND SPIRITUAL LIFE. MY LIMITATIONS REMIND ME OF ALMIGHTY GOD'S HOLY PRESENCE AND POSITION IN OUR LIVES. THE LIMITATIONS THAT KEEP ME IN THE REALM OF HUMILITY. THE LIMITATIONS THAT KEEP ME IN THE REALM OF OBEDIENCE. THE LIMITATIONS THAT KEEP ME IN THE REALM OF ALLEGIANCE UNTO ALMIGHTY GOD, OUR CREATOR. THE LIMITATIONS THAT REVEAL TEMPORARY LIFE ON EARTH. THE LIMITATIONS THAT ENCOURAGE ME TO SEEK SPIRITUAL AND PHYSICAL HELP IN MY TIMES OF NEED. THE LIMITATIONS THAT DRAW ME CLOSER TO MY BROTHERS AND SISTERS IN CHRIST JESUS. THE LIMITATIONS THAT ENCOURAGE ME TO CRY OUT TO ALMIGHTY GOD FOR RELIEF, IN THE MIDST OF MY TROUBLED AND PAINFUL TIMES. THE LIMITATIONS THAT LEAD ME TO MY PLACE OF WORSHIP AND PRAISE. THE LIMITATIONS THAT ALLOW ME TO WITNESS THE PRESENCE OF ALMIGHTY GOD THROUGHOUT EACH DAY. THE LIMITATIONS THAT PROMPT ME TO SPEND HOURS PRAYING AND THANKING MY SAVIOR AND GOD. THE LIMITATIONS THAT MAKE ME LOVE ALMIGHTY GOD, MYSELF, AND MY NEIGHBORS. I WILL RELAX WITHIN MY REALM OF LIMITATIONS THROUGHOUT MY BLESSED DAYS!
MAY 23, 2015 BY: BARBARA ANN MARY MACK
SENT SAT, MAY 23, 2015 5:38 PM-READ SAT 5/23/2015 7:21 PM

PLEASANT DREAMS DEAR ONE (CRAIG), AS YOU DRIFT OFF INTO A WORLD THAT IS FILLED WITH DIVINE MYSTERIES (BARBARA)! AMORE
SENT: SAT, MAY 23, 2015 5:38 PM-READ: SAT 5/23/2015 7:21 PM

ANOTHER DAY TO LIVE: LET US CELEBRATE ANOTHER BLESSED DAY OF LIFE!

I HAVE BEEN BLESSED WITH ANOTHER DAY!

ANOTHER DAY TO WATCH MY CHILDREN AND GRANDCHILDREN PLAY.

I HAVE BEEN BLESSED WITH ANOTHER DAY!

SO THAT I MAY HAVE THE OPPORTUNITY TO COMMUNE WITH MY HEAVENLY GOD AS I KNEEL AND PRAY.

ANOTHER DAY TO REJOICE WITH MY FAMILY AND FRIENDS.

I HAVE BEEN BLESSED WITH ANOTHER DAY, TO SHARE IN THE CELEBRATION THAT NEVER ENDS.

ANOTHER DAY TO LIVE!

ANOTHER DAY TO ENJOY THE GOOD THINGS THAT OUR HEAVENLY GOD, THE FATHER, AND GOD, THE SON, GIVE.

ALMIGHTY GOD SPEAKING

ENJOY! ENJOY! ENJOY LIFE EVERY DAY!

LET US CELEBRATE MY CHILDREN, AS YOU BOW YOUR HEADS AND PRAY!

ENJOY THE GIFT OF LIFE WHILE YOU CAN!

CELEBRATE, O WOMAN! CELEBRATE WITH YOUR REJOICING MAN!

FOR LIFE ON EARTH WILL NOT LAST FOREVER

CELEBRATE! MY CHILDREN. CELEBRATE WITH THE WISE AND THE CLEVER!

ENJOY THE GIFT OF LIFE!

ENJOY IT, DEAR SONS, WITH THE LOVE THAT FLOWS FROM YOUR HEAVEN SENT WIFE!

ENJOY MY GIFT THAT DESCENDED FROM ABOVE.

ENJOY THE GIFT OF LIFE THAT REVEALS MY CONTINUOUS LOVE!

MAY 21, 2015 BY: BARBARA ANN MARY MACK

SENT: SAT, MAY 23, 2015 5:38 PM-READ: SAT 5/23/2015 7:21 PM

BUON GIORNO ARCHBISHOP CRAIG! COME STA OGGI AMORE? ENJOY YOUR DAY! CIAO! BEAUTIFUL BARBARA

A HAPPY GOD

WHAT WOULD MAKE YOU HAPPY, MY GOD?

IS THE EXPRESSION OF YOUR CHILDREN'S LOVE?

WHAT WOULD GIVE YOU CONTINUOUS JOY?

COULD IT BE THE HOPE OF YOUR LITTLE BOY?

WHAT WOULD MAKE YOU SMILE ALL DAY?

WHAT WOULD MAKE THE WHOLE WORLD PRAY?

WHAT WOULD GIVE YOU PEACE AND JOY?
WOULD IT BE THE LAUGHTER OF EVERY GIRL AND BOY?
WHAT WOULD MOVE THE FALLING TEARS FROM YOUR GLORIOUS
FACE?
WOULD IT BE THE UNION OF EVERY RACE?
WHAT WOULD TURN YOUR FROWN UPSIDE DOWN?
IS IT THE PLACE WHERE OUR LOVE IS BOUND?
WHAT WOULD REMOVE YOUR DAYS OF GLOOM?
WHAT WOULD PLEASE MY HOLY GROOM?
WHAT WOULD MAKE YOU DANCE AND SING?
IS IT THE GLOW FROM OUR WEDDING RING?
WHAT WOULD MAKE YOU HAPPY, O PRECIOUS GOD OF MINE?
IS IT THE PLACE (HEAVEN) WHERE WE WILL DINE?
OCTOBER 23, 2012 AT 8:32 PM BY: BARBARA ANN MARY MACK

I'M SO HAPPY THAT YOU GAVE YOURSELF TO US, O LORD

EACH DAY AS I EXPERIENCE YOUR HOLY PRESENCE, MAKES ME BOW UNTO YOU, MY GENEROUS
GOD. EACH DAY, AS I WITNESS YOUR GRACE AND MERCY IN THE LIVES OF YOUR CHILDREN, I
THANK YOU, MY HOLY SPOUSE AND REDEEMER (LORD JESUS). EACH DAY AS I WITNESS YOUR
HOLY GUIDANCE IN THE LIFE OF OUR BELOVED ONE (CRAIG), I HUMBLE MYSELF UNTO YOU, O
MIGHTY FRIEND (THE LORD JESUS) OF MINE. YOUR HOLY GRACE AND STYLE CAPTIVATE US
DAILY, DEAR LORD! YOUR LOVING KINDNESS ENCOMPASSES THE SOULS OF YOUR OBEDIENT
DAUGHTERS (LA TOYA AND AMYA). WE ARE PLEASED WITH YOUR HOLY PRESENCE IN OUR
DAILY ACTIVITIES, AND WE TRY TO DO YOUR WILL THROUGHOUT EACH DAY. YOUR HOLY
PRESENCE GUIDES YOUR LOVED ONES IN THE DIRECTION OF YOUR GREAT PLAN FOR OUR
LIVES, ON EARTH; AND IN ETERNAL GLORY WITH YOU, O SAVING ONE (THE LORD JESUS). LIFT
OUR SPIRITS UP TO YOUR HOLY SPIRIT AS WE APPROACH YOUR ALTAR OF LOVE, O HEAVENLY
KING (ALMIGHTY GOD). OUR SPIRITS WILL SING SONGS OF CONTINUOUS PRAISE AS YOU IGNITE
OUR DORMANT BEINGS. WE BOW UNTO YOU, MY GOD, BECAUSE WE LOVE YOU.
OCTOBER 19, 2012 AT 2:12 PM BY: BARBARA ANN MARY MACK

A LION IN THE MIDST OF WOLVES

I HAVE RECEIVED THE COURAGE THAT WAS SENT FROM ABOVE:
TO FIGHT FOR THOSE WHOM THE GOOD LORD LOVES.
I WILL STAY ON THE BATTLE FIELD, WHICH CONSISTS OF VICIOUS WOLVES

(SATAN'S SERVANTS);

UNTIL THE BATTLE IS COMPLETELY RESOLVED.

IN THE MIDST OF THE WOLVES I WILL REMAIN,

UNTIL THE SOULS OF GOD'S LOVED ONES ARE REGAINED.

HELP ME, DEAR LORD, AS I APPROACH THE DISOBEDIENT ONES!

WHICH INCLUDES THE SOULS OF GOD'S ABSTAINING SONS.

HELP ME, DEAR LORD, FOR I AM VERY WEAK!

I HAVE FOUGHT FOR THE SOULS OF THE WEARY AND THE MEEK.

CLING TO ME, MY GOD, AND HEAVENLY HOST;

AS I PRAY FOR THE SAVED ONES, AND THE LOST.

REACH OUT TO BARBARA, YOUR FAITHFUL SERVANT AND FRIEND.

AS I BATTLE THE EVIL ONE (SATAN) WITH YOU, UNTIL THE VERY END!

I WILL CRY OUT TO YOU, MY GOD, WHEN THE BATTLE *OVERWHELMS ME.*

I WILL CRY OUT, DEAR LORD, AS I REACH FOR THE LIFE FORCE THAT EMITS FROM THE HOLY TRINITY.

A LION IN THE MIDST OF WOLVES, I WILL LAY,

MY WEARY HEAD UPON YOUR SACRED CHEST AS I PRAY.

OCTOBER 1, 2012 AT 11:50 PM BY: BARBARA ANN MARY MACK

SENT SAT, MAY 23, 2015 5:38 PM-READ SAT 5/23/2015 7:21 PM

WORDS! WORDS! WORDS!

BARBARA SPEAKING TO GOD'S CHILDREN

WHAT DO THEY REALLY MEAN? WHAT DO THEY EXPRESS? ONE MAY SAY CERTAIN WORDS, BUT HIS OR HER ACTIONS EXHIBIT THE OPPOSITE OF THEIR WORDS. ONE MAY BE JUDGED AND CONDEMNED BY WORDS ALONE. ONE MAY BE LOVED OR FOOLED BY WORDS ALONE. WORDS, WORDS, WORDS, WHAT DO THEY TRULY MEAN? DO NOT BE FOOLED BY MERE WORDS, MY BROTHERS AND SISTERS, FOR WORDS VERY SELDOM REVEAL THE TRUTH.

ALMIGHTY GOD SPEAKING TO HIS CHILDREN

I WILL OBSERVE YOU, *SAYS THE LORD.* I WILL OBSERVE YOUR ACTIONS, MY CHILDREN. YOUR ACTIONS REVEAL THE DEPTH OF YOUR KNOWLEDGE OF MY HOLY WORDS. YOUR ACTIONS REVEAL THE INTEGRITY OF YOUR ALLEGIANCE TO YOUR FAITHFUL GOD AND CREATOR. YOUR ACTIONS REVEAL THE DEPTH OF YOUR LOVE FOR ME AND MY GREAT CREATION. MY CHILDREN, YOUR ACTIONS REVEAL THE TRUTH! LET YOUR ACTS AND WORDS REVEAL YOUR BELIEF IN MY HOLY PRESENCE IN YOUR MIDST TODAY, FOR I AM WALKING AMONG YOU, MY CHILDREN. DO

YOU NOT FEEL MY HOLY PRESENCE IN YOUR MIDST? I AM ALMIGHTY GOD, THE OMNIPRESENT ONE! I AM ALMIGHTY GOD, THE OMNIPOTENT ONE! BELIEVE IN MY HOLY PRESENCE IN YOUR MIDST, MY CHILDREN, FOR I TRULY EXIST!

MAY 26, 2015 BY: BARBARA ANN MARY MACK

SENT TUE, MAY 26, 2015 10:52 PM-READ WED 5/27 12:24 AM

GOD, THE GREATEST PRIZEFIGHTER

ALMIGHTY GOD
SPEAKING TO SATAN

LET US (ALMIGHTY GOD AND SATAN) ENTER THE RING (THE WORLD). LET US END THIS CONTINUOUS FIGHT RIGHT NOW! FOR I HAVE BEEN FIGHTING YOU FOR THE WEAK AND VULNERABLE SOULS OF MY CHILDREN FOR CENTURIES. AND, I AM GOING TO PUT AN END TO THIS BATTLE TODAY! YOU (SATAN) CAN RUN, BUT YOU CANNOT HIDE FROM ME! FOR I AM THE ONLY OMNIPRESENT GOD! AND I HAVE COME TO DEFEAT THE WORLD'S GREATEST BUM (SATAN)! FOR I AM THE GREAT AND HOLY I AM! I AM THE GREATEST PRIZEFIGHTER EVER! AND MY PRIZE IS THE SOULS OF THOSE WHO ARE WRITTEN IN MY ETERNAL BOOK OF LIFE.

ALMIGHTY GOD SPEAKING TO HIS CHILDREN

GET READY MY CHILDREN, FOR YOU ARE ABOUT TO EXPERIENCE THE DEPTH OF MY LOVE! YOU ARE ABOUT TO WITNESS THE DEFEAT OF THE BIGGEST BUM (SATAN) THAT WALKED THE EARTH. THUS, *SAYS THE LORD!*
AUGUST 27, 2012 AT 10:25 PM BY: BARBARA ANN MARY MACK
SENT TUE, MAY 26, 2015 10:52 PM-READ WED 5/27 12:24 AM

PLEASANT DREAMS DEAR ONE! RELAX YOUR VALUABLE MIND AS YOU WANDER IN THE DIRECTION OF ME! AMORE! AMORE! AMORE!
SENT TUE, MAY 26, 2015 10:52 PM-READ WED 5/27 12:24 AM

ENJOY THE LAUGHTER OF YOUR FAMILY AND FRIENDS TODAY

BARBARA SPEAKING

MAKE TIME TO TALK WITH EACH OF YOUR FAMILY AND FRIENDS OF ALL AGES, SO THAT YOU WILL HAVE AN IDEA OF WHAT THEY ARE THINKING, WHAT THEY LIKE, WHAT THEY DISLIKE, AND WHO THEY ARE. PAY CLOSE ATTENTION TO THEIR ACTIONS AND REACTIONS, SO THAT

YOU CAN REALLY SAY, I KNOW YOU TO EACH ONE OF THEM. SPEND QUALITY TIME WITH THOSE WHOM YOU LOVE, SO THAT YOUR LOVED ONES WILL KNOW OF YOUR LOVE FOR THEM. SPEND TIME LAUGHING TOGETHER, EVEN IN THE MIDST OF DIFFICULT TIMES. LAUGHTER IS A HEALING FOR THE MIND, BODY AND SOUL. PROPER LAUGHTER TIME IN MIDST OF MOURNING MAY EASE INNER PAIN AND DISCOMFORT. ENJOY THE GIFT OF LAUGHTER, ESPECIALLY WITH YOUR IMMEDIATE FAMILY. LAUGHTER EXHIBITS THE REALM OF JOY, EVEN IN THE MIDST OF HARDSHIP. ENJOY THE GIFT (LAUGHTER) THAT DESCENDED FROM GOD'S REALM OF GOODNESS. ENJOY AND EXHIBIT IT EVERY DAY!
MAY 26, 2015 BY: BARBARA ANN MARY MACK

OH WHAT A BEAUTIFUL HEAVEN SENT MORNING!

MY BROTHERS AND SISTERS, ENJOY THE HEAVEN SENT GIFT, THIS BEAUTIFUL MORNING!
ENJOY THIS BEAUTIFUL MORNING, WHICH THE LORD HAS BLESSED US WITH.
ENJOY THE GIFT (BEAUTIFUL MORNINGS) THAT DESCENDS FROM ABOVE.
ENJOY THE GIFT THAT REVEALS GOD'S HOLY LOVE.
ENJOY THIS EXPRESSION OF GOD'S GRACE.
ENJOY IT, MY BROTHERS AND SISTERS, FOR IT REVEALS THE SMILE ON HIS MERCIFUL AND COMPASSIONATE FACE!
LET US FOCUS ON THE GOODNESS OF OUR GREAT AND HOLY GOD.
AS WE BREATHE IN THE WONDERS OF HIS CONTINUOUS LOVE.
LET US ENJOY THE GIFT OF EACH GOD SENT DAY.
LET US ENJOY IT, MY BROTHERS AND SISTERS, AS WE GIVE THANKS AND PRAY.
MAY 27, 2015 BY: BARBARA ANN MARY MACK
SENT WED, MAY 27, 2015 12:00 PM-READ WED 5/27/2015 2:40 PM

THE MOST IMPORTANT HEALING

THE MOST IMPORTANT HEALING, IS THE HEALING OF ONE'S WOUNDED SPIRIT, SO THAT THE HEALED SPIRIT MAY UNITE WITH ALMIGHTY GOD'S HOLY SPIRIT. OH THE DIVINE PEACE THAT FLOWS THROUGH THE ESSENCE OF THE SPIRITUALLY HEALED CHILD OF GOD, OUR SOVEREIGN KING AND LORD, CANNOT BE REVEALED WITH MERE WORDS. FOR IT IS A PEACE THAT TRANSCENDS ALL REALMS OF PEACE THAT THE WORLD KNOWS. IT IS A PEACE THAT ENABLES THE HEALED SPIRIT TO SOAR IN THE MIDST OF DIFFICULT AND TRYING TIMES. IT IS A PEACE THAT DESCENDS FROM GOD'S THRONE OF LOVE. IT IS A PEACE THAT LETS THE WORLD KNOW OF ONE'S UNIFICATION WITH GOD, THE DIVINE ONE. IT IS A PEACE THAT BRINGS OUT THE JOY, THAT CAUSES ONE TO PROFESS HIS OR HER BELIEF IN GOD, OUR DIVINE CREATOR AND FATHER. IT IS A PEACE THAT CAUSES ONE TO LOVE THOSE WHOM SATAN, OUR ENEMY,

HAS PLACED DIVISION AND STRIFE BETWEEN. IT IS A PEACE THAT CAUSES ONE TO EXHIBIT THE LOVE OF OUR NEIGHBORS, AS THE LORD COMMANDS. IT IS A PEACE THAT GUIDES THE HEALED ONES INTO THE REALM OF CONTINUOUS PRAISE AND PRAYER, TO OUR OMNIPOTENT AND FAITHFUL GOD. MY BROTHERS AND SISTERS; LET US EXHIBIT THE JOY OF OUR HEALED SPIRITS, AS WE PROCLAIM OUR ALLEGIANCE UNTO OUR HOLY GOD AND FATHER ABOVE. HEAL ME OF MY IMPERFECTION SO THAT I MAY BECOME LIKE YOU, MY FATHER.

MAY 27, 2015 BY: BARBARA ANN MARY MACK

SENT WED, MAY 27, 2015 11:30 PM-READ THU 5/28/2015 10:37 PM

I DO NOT SEEK THE RICHES OF THIS WORLD, FOR I WAS BORN RICH

BARBARA SPEAKING

I DO NOT SEEK THE RICHES OF THIS WORLD, FOR WORLDLY WEALTH COULD NEVER SATISFY ME. I DO NOT SEEK THE WEALTH THAT THE WORLD OFFERS, FOR WORLDLY RICHES COULD NEVER SATISFY ME. MY SOUL, MY ESSENCE, MY PRIVILEGED SPIRIT WAS BORN, RAISED, AND NURTURED FROM THE WEALTH AND RICHES THAT TRANSCEND THE WORLD'S VERSION OF WEALTH AND RICHES. I WAS BORN (FORMED) FROM THE REALM, THE SOVEREIGN REALM, THAT HOUSES THE GREATEST WEALTH OF ALL. FOR GOD, MY SAVIOR, MY HEAVENLY KING, PROVIDES EVERYTHING THAT HIS QUEEN (BARBARA) NEEDS AND DESIRES. FOR HE IS MY WEALTH! HE IS THE RICHES THAT SATISFY MY FAMILY AND ME. HE IS OUR REALM OF PURE GOLD AND SILVER! HE IS THE RICHES THAT SUSTAINS US. COME, O INVITED GUESTS! COME AND WITNESS THE MAGNIFICENCE OF MY WEALTH (ALMIGHTY GOD)! COME AND WITNESS MY REALM OF ETERNAL WEALTH! COME AND WITNESS HE (ALMIGHTY GOD) WHO SATISFIES AND SUSTAINS HIS BELOVED AND BLESSED QUEEN (BARBARA)!

MAY 30, 2015 BY: BARBARA ANN MARY MACK

SENT SUN, MAY 31, 2015 5:28 PM-READ SUN 5/31/2015 6:39 PM

PEACE! PEACE! PEACE! SLEEP WITHIN THE REALM OF BLISSFUL PEACE (BARBARA)! AMORE,

THE LOVE THAT GROWS

THE LOVE THAT GROWS,
COMES FROM THE GOD THAT EVERY PRACTICING CHRISTIAN KNOWS.
OURS IS A DIVINE LOVE THAT GROWS EACH DAY,
FOR IT IS A LOVE THAT ENCOURAGES YOU AND I TO PRAY.
IT IS A LOVE THAT DESCENDED IN THE MIDST OF THIS TIME,
IT IS A LOVE THAT IS YOURS AND MINE.

LET ALL WITNESS THE GROWTH OF OUR SACRED LOVE.
LET EVERYONE ENJOY OUR GIFT FROM ABOVE.
FOR IT IS A LOVE THAT IS HOLY AND TRUE.
THE GROWTH OF OUR LOVE, HAS REVEALED THE PRESENCE OF ALMIGHTY GOD'S PROMISE
THAT WAS GIVEN TO ME AND YOU.
THE GROWTH OF OUR SACRED LOVE HAS TAUGHT MANY,
OF THE WONDERS AND GREATNESS OF GOD, THE FORGIVING TRINITY.
OUR LOVE HAS GROWN IN THE MIDST OF SPIRITUAL BLISS,
THAT KEEPS YOU AND I WITHIN THE REALM THAT RELEASES GOD'S COMFORTING KISS.
THROUGH THE YEARS, THE PAINFUL SEPARATED YEARS,
GREW A DIVINE LOVE THAT REMOVED OUR MANY TEARS.
MAY 30, 2015 BY: BARBARA ANN MARY MACK
SENT SUN, MAY 31, 2015 7:30 PM-READ SUN 5/31/2015 8:37 PM

THOSE WHO DO NOT KNOW ME WILL PERISH, *SAYS THE LORD*

ALMIGHTY GOD SPEAKING

ALTHOUGH I AM A MERCIFUL GOD, I WILL NOT BE MOCKED OR ABUSED BY ANYONE! I WILL NOT
TOLERATE ABUSE OF ANY KIND, FROM ANYONE, *SAYS THE LORD*. YOU WHO HAVE NOT TAKEN
ME SERIOUSLY, WILL WITNESS MY VERSION OF JUSTICE, *SAYS THE LORD*. I WILL NOT TOLERATE
ANY FORM OF ABUSE TOWARDS MY OBEDIENT MESSENGERS, FOR THEY HAVE BEEN SENT BY
ME, *SAYS THE LORD*. THEY HAVE BEEN SENT TO LEAD YOUR PERISHING SOULS TO MY REALM
OF SALVATION AND HOPE, *SAYS THE LORD!* RECEIVE MY HOLY WARNINGS BEFORE YOUR
DESTINATION CATCHES UP WITH YOU, O PERISHING ONES! FOR I, THE LORD, AM WATCHING YOU
AT ALL TIMES. I HEAR YOUR CONVERSATIONS, MY CHILDREN, AND I KNOW YOUR DESTINATIONS
TOO! DO NOT ABUSE MY MESSENGERS, O PERISHING ONES, FOR THEY HAVE BEEN SENT BY
ME! YOU WHO DENY THE WORDS THAT I SPEAK THROUGH MY MESSENGERS TODAY, WILL
PERISH! THOSE WHO DENY THE SANCTITY OF MY HOLY PROPHETS WILL PERISH IN DUE TIME!
I AM A PATIENT GOD, MY CHILDREN, BUT I WILL NOT TOLERATE THE UNBELIEVING ONES ANY
LONGER! LEARN OF MY HOLY WAY, O PERISHING ONES, FOR IT IS THE ONLY WAY TO ETERNAL
LIFE, *SAYS THE LORD!*
JUNE 1, 2015 BY: BARBARA ANN MARY MACK

TO HELL YOU WILL GO! FOR YOU DID NOT HEED MY WARNINGS, *SAYS THE LORD*
I HAVE SENT MY PROPHETS, AND YOU DID NOT LISTEN TO THEM. I HAVE SENT JESUS, MY ONLY
BEGOTTEN SON, AND YOU DID NOT LISTEN TO HIM! I HAVE SENT MY APOSTLES, AND YOU DID
NOT LISTEN TO THEM. NOW, IN THESE LAST DAYS, I HAVE SENT BARBARA, MY CHOSEN BRIDE,

AND YOU REFUSE TO LISTEN TO MY WORDS THAT WERE REVEALED THROUGH HER. THERE IS ONLY ONE PLACE THAT WILL WELCOME YOU, O DISOBEDIENT ONES. THERE IS ONLY ONE PLACE THAT RECEIVES THOSE WHO REFUSED TO HEED MY WORDS OF WARNING. TO HELL YOU WILL GO, O DISOBEDIENT ONES. FOR YOU HAVE REFUSED MY HOLY WORDS THAT LEAD TO ETERNAL LIFE! TO HELL YOU WILL GO, ALL WHO REJECTED MY HOLY WORDS OF LIFE. TO HELL YOU WILL GO, YOU WHO MOCKED MY HOLY PROPHETS AND BRIDE. ENTER THE REALM (HELL) THAT CALLS YOU, O REJECTING ONES! ENTER THE REALM THAT SEEKS THE DYING SOULS OF THE "UNBELIEVING ONES"! ENTER THE GATES OF HELL AS YOU GROW TOWARD THE FULFILLMENT OF YOUR ETERNAL DESTINATION. ENTER THE GATES THAT AWAIT YOUR DISOBEDIENT SOUL! FOR HELL IS YOU DESTINATION! MY MERCY HAS RESTED WITHIN THE REALM THAT HOUSES THE OBEDIENT ONES. MY COMPASSION ENCOMPASSES THE SOULS OF THE FORGIVING ONES. MY LOVE ASSURES THE DESTINATION OF THE RIGHTEOUS ONES. COME, O BELIEVING ONES! ENTER THE GATES THAT SURROUND GOD, THE BLESSED ONE. ENTER THE GATES THAT INVITE THOSE WHO TRULY BELIEVE IN MY HOLY WORD. ENTER THE GATES OF SWEET PARADISE, FOR IT IS YOUR FINAL DESTINATION.

MAY 31, 2015 BY: BARBARA ANN MARY MACK

SENT MON, JUN 1, 2015 3:12 AM-READ MON 6/1/2015 7:31 AM

IN THE MIDST OF SATAN AND HIS DEFEATED ANGELS, I WILL REVEAL THE PRESENCE OF THE VICTORIOUS LORD JESUS' DIVINE LIGHT OF LOVE

ALMIGHTY GOD SPEAKING TO SATAN

YOU HAVE BEEN DEFEATED BY BARBARA, THE HOLY TRINITY'S DEVOTED WIFE.
SHE HAS BEEN SENT TO DELIVER GOD'S GIFT OF ETERNAL LIFE.
SHE HAS BEEN SENT TO REVEAL JESUS' SAVING LIGHT.
SHE HAS BEEN SENT TO REVEAL HIS UNDEFEATED MIGHT.
IN THE PRESENCE OF SATAN AND HIS MANY DEFEATED ANGELS OF DESTRUCTION,
BARBARA HAS BEEN SENT TO REVEAL GOD'S HOLY LIGHT AND PRESENCE TO EVERY NATION.
RUN, O SATAN! HIDE IF YOU CAN!
YOU HAVE BEEN DEFEATED BY ALMIGHTY GOD, BARBARA'S FAITHFUL AND HOLY HUSBAND.

BARBARA SPEAKING TO SATAN

IN THE MIDST OF YOUR EVIL DEEDS I WILL SHINE,
WITH THE PRESENCE OF ALMIGHTY GOD, THROUGHOUT THE REALM OF TIME.
IN THE MIDST OF YOUR UNHOLY WAYS,
I WILL SHARE GOD'S SAVING MESSAGES THROUGHOUT THE DAYS.

I KNOW OF YOUR EVIL WAYS THAT ROAM EACH STREET.

I WILL SHARE THE KNOWLEDGE OF YOUR UNHOLY PRESENCE WITH EVERYONE WHOM I MEET.

YOUR EVIL WAYS ARE REVEALED TO ME.

THEY ARE REVEALED TO THE BRIDE (BARBARA) OF GOD, THE HOLY TRINITY.

MAY 31, 2015 BY: BARBARA ANN MARY MACK

SENT MON, JUN 1, 2015 2:25 AM-READ MON 6/1/2015 1:54 PM

GREETINGS ARCHBISHOP CRAIG! COME STA OGGI AMORE? LA TOYA IS TEACHING AMYA HOW TO MAKE BEANS (KIDNEY BEANS) AND BURGER, WHICH IS ONE OF OUR FAVORITE MEALS. THE PROBLEM WITH THIS IS, AMYA HATES COOKING. SOMETIMES SHE'LL COOK BREAKFAST, BUT SHE REALLY HATES COOKING AND SHOPPING. LA TOYA OFTEN TAKES THE TIME AND PATIENTLY SHOWS AMYA HOW TO DO THE THINGS THAT EVERYONE SHOULD KNOW BEFORE HE OR SHE REACHES ADULTHOOD. YESTERDAY, SHE COMPRISED A JOB DESCRIPTION, WHICH EXPLAINS WHAT AMYA IS EXPECTED TO DO WHEN SHE STARTS HER NEW JOB. LA TOYA WROTE DOWN A LIST OF THINGS FOR AMYA TO DO AROUND THE HOUSE, AND SHE WILL PAY HER BI-WEEKLY. LA TOYA ALSO EXPLAINED TO AMYA THE AMOUNT OF TAXES THAT SHE WILL TAKE FROM HER WAGES, BUT INSTEAD OF KEEPING THE MONEY FROM THE TAXES, LA TOYA WILL PUT IT IN AMYA'S ACCOUNT. I DID THE SAME WITH LA TOYA WHEN SHE WAS A TEEN. WE PREFER THAT AMYA STAY CLOSE TO HOME INSTEAD OF GETTING A SUMMER JOB AT AN UNFAMILIAR LOCATION. THERE WERE SOME ADVERTISEMENT FOR SUMMER JOBS AVAILABLE TO 14 YEARS OLD TEENS. WE WILL SEE HOW THINGS GO. AMYA BEGAN HER JOB TODAY.

BELOW ARE TODAY'S PASSAGES FOR YOU. TOODLES! BELLA BARBARA

CAN I JOIN YOUR HOLY TEARS, MY LORD, AS YOU CATCH MINE?

BARBARA SPEAKING TO THE LORD

CAN I JOIN OUR HOLY TEARS AS YOU CRADLE MY FALLING TEARS, MY LORD? CAN I JOIN THE BLESSED TEARS THAT EXIT YOUR HOLY EYES AND ESSENCE, O MERCIFUL AND KIND GOD? CAN I BATHE IN THE TEARS THAT REVEAL YOUR PAIN, O COMPASSIONATE ONE? CAN I BOW IN THE PRESENCE OF THE TEARS THAT BLESS YOUR CHOSEN WIFE AND FRIEND AS I PROCLAIM THE GOODNESS OF OUR GENEROUS GOD? CAN I JOIN THE HOLY TEARS THAT LEAD TO OUR HEAVENLY KINGDOM ON HIGH, O FAITHFUL GOD OF MINE? I WILL SING MY SONGS OF COMFORT TO YOU AS I WEEP IN THE PRESENCE OF YOUR FLOWING TEARS. JOIN ME IN MY HYMNS OF TEARS AS I APPROACH YOUR BROKEN HEART, O HOLY SPOUSE AND GOD OF MINE. JOIN ME, DEAR LORD, AS I WEEP IN THE MIDST OF YOUR FALLING TEARS.
JUNE 1, 2015 BY: BARBARA ANN MARY MACK

JUST THE TWO OF US: ONE UNIFIED HOLY ESSENCE

BARBARA SPEAKING TO GOD, THE HOLY TRINITY

THROUGHOUT THE DAY I CAN FEEL THE PRESENCE OF MY ORIGIN AND GOD.
I CAN FEEL THE HOLY PRESENCE THAT CREATED ME OUT OF PURE LOVE.

I CAN FEEL THE PRESENCE OF HE WHO GRANTS ALL OF MY NEEDS.

I CAN FEEL THE PRESENCE OF THE GOD WHO ACKNOWLEDGES OUR GOOD DEEDS

JUST THE TWO OF US!

BARBARA AND JESUS!

JUST THE TWO OF US!

WE EXHIBIT A DIVINE LOVE THAT REVEALS CONTINUOUS TRUST.

ONE UNIFIED ESSENCE OF LOVE,

AN EXPRESSION OF GOD'S HOLY DOVE.

ONE UNIFIED ESSENCE WE ARE, O HEAVENLY SPOUSE AND GOD OF MINE.

OUR UNION WILL LAST THROUGHOUT THE REALM OF TIME.

THE UNIFIED ESSENCE OF THE HOLY TRINITY AND ME,

WALKS IN THE MIDST OF THOSE WHO ARE SET FREE!

ALMIGHTY GOD, THE FATHER, SPEAKING TO BARBARA

COME! O BELOVED WIFE OF MINE.

AND SHARE THE REALM OF UNITY WITH MY CHOSEN ONES UNTIL THE END OF TIME.

FOR OUR UNION EXPRESSES MY REALM OF HOLY LOVE,

THAT DESCENDS IN THE MIDST OF MY HOLY DOVE.

LET THE WHOLE WORLD WITNESS THE TWO OF US!

LET THEM WITNESS THE DEVOTION THAT FLOWS FROM THE WIFE AND FRIEND (BARBARA) OF MY SON, JESUS!

SHE EXHIBITS HER ALLEGIANCE AND LOVE,

THAT FLOW FROM THE PRESENCE OF MY HOLY DOVE (SPIRIT).

JUNE 1, 2015 BY: BARBARA ANN MARY MACK

SENT MON, JUN 1, 2015 7:00 PM-READ MON 6/1/2015 11:28 PM

BUON GIORNO ARCHBISHOP CRAIG! REMEMBER TO TAKE YOUR BREAKS THROUGHOUT THE DAY. BELOW ARE TODAY'S PASSAGES FOR YOU. AMORE, BELLA BARBARA

THE LORD HUMBLED HIMSELF FOR THE SAKE OF OUR SALVATION

BECAUSE OUR LORD JESUS, WHO IS GOD, THE HOLY SON, HUMBLED HIMSELF WHEN HE TOOK ON THE FORM OF A HUMAN, WE AS CHRISTIANS SHOULD DWELL WITHIN THE REALM OF HUMILITY ALSO. MY LORD AND MY VICTORIOUS HUMBLED GOD, PLEASE GRACE ME WITH THE COURAGE TO REMAIN WITHIN THE REALM OF HUMILITY, SO THAT I MAY PLEASE OUR WORTHY FATHER AS YOU HAVE. GRACE ME AND MY CHRISTIAN BROTHERS AND SISTERS WITH THE COURAGE TO JOIN YOU IN THE REALM OF HUMILITY, SO THAT WE MAY NEVER ENTERTAIN

THE REALM OF VANITY AND PRIDE. GRACE US WITH THE COURAGE THAT EMITS FROM YOUR REALM OF HUMILITY, SO THAT WE MAY BECOME BOLD WHEN PROCLAIMING THE GOOD NEWS OF SALVATION THROUGH JESUS CHRIST. HUMBLE YOUR CALLED AND CHOSEN ONES, SO THAT WE MAY IMITATE YOU AND OUR FATHER, IN THE MIDST OF THOSE WHO JUDGE US HARSHLY. HUMBLE US, LORD JESUS, SO THAT THE WORLD MAY KNOW HOW MUCH WE TRULY LOVE THEE. LET ALL OF YOUR OBEDIENT CHILDREN EXPERIENCE THE DEPTH OF DIVINE HUMILITY, AS WE GROW CLOSER TO OUR DESTINATION WITH YOU IN ETERNAL GLORY AND DIVINE PEACE. GIVE US THE DIVINE COURAGE TO APPRECIATE YOUR HOLY ACT OF LOVE (JESUS' CRUCIFIXION). GIVE US THE COURAGE TO EXPRESS OUR APPRECIATION IN THE PRESENCE OF THE UNBELIEVERS AND DOUBTFUL ONES. GIVE US THE COURAGE MY LORD, SO THAT WE MAY WALK IN YOUR HOLY FOOTSTEPS FOREVER!

JUNE 1, 2015 BY: BARBARA ANN MARY MACK

GOD'S GRACE

THROUGHOUT THE DAY, AND INTO THE MARVELOUS NIGHT, MY IGNITED BEING SOARS IN THE MIDST OF GOD'S OVERFLOWING GRACE.

MY REJOICING SOUL BOWS IN THE PRESENCE OF GOD'S GLORIOUS FACE.

THROUGHOUT EACH DAY,

IN THE MIDST OF DIVINE LOVE I PRAY.

I RECEIVE THE GIFT OF GOD'S GRACE,

AS HE POURS IT OVER THE BLESSED HUMAN RACE.

FALL UPON MY ACCEPTING SOUL, O REALM THAT DESCENDED FROM GOD'S MERCY AND GRACE.

FALL UPON GOD'S HUMBLED WIFE (BARBARA) AS SHE SMILES AT HIS GLORIOUS FACE.

IN THE PRESENCE OF GRACE AND DIVINE LOVE,

DESCENDS GOD'S CHOSEN MESSENGER (BARBARA) FROM ABOVE.

I WILL BATHE IN THE GRACE THAT EMITS FROM GOD'S IGNITED BEING,

AS I REJOICE WITH THE HEAVENLY CHOIRS AS THEY SING!

SING SONGS OF PRAISE, O HEAVENLY CHOIRS ABOVE!

AS YOUR JOYFUL HYMNS REVEAL THE PRESENCE OF GOD'S HOLY DOVE.

DANCE WITH ME, O SWEET REALM OF GRACE!

DANCE WITH ME, AS I JOIN THE HUMAN RACE!

WE WILL REJOICE AS WE GREET OUR SAVING KING.

WE WILL LIFT UP OUR HANDS IN PRAISE, AS WE DANCE AND SING!

JUNE 2, 2015 BY: BARBARA ANN MARY MACK

SENT TUE, JUN 2, 2015 3:10 AM-READ TUE 6/2/2015 11:02 AM

SATAN CANNOT KEEP ME QUIET!

BARBARA SPEAKING

SATAN CANNOT KEEP ME QUIET! HE CANNOT CEASE THE VOICE OF BARBARA, GOD'S HOLY WIFE! HE CANNOT STIFLE THE SOUNDS THAT ARE RELEASED FROM MY IGNITED BEING EVERY DAY! HE CANNOT PREVENT ME FROM RELEASING THE WORDS THAT ARE DICTATED FROM ALMIGHTY GOD HIMSELF! HE CANNOT HOLD BACK THE VOICE OF GOD'S ANOINTED WIFE AND MESSENGER (BARBARA)! HE CANNOT PREVENT THE CALLED AND CHOSEN ONES FROM RECEIVING GOD'S HOLY MESSAGES THAT ARE SPOKEN THROUGH BARBARA, GOD'S WORTHY AND CHOSEN MESSENGER OF DIVINE LOVE! SATAN TRIES OVER AND OVER TO DISCOURAGE GOD'S CHOSEN MESSENGERS. HE CONSTANTLY ATTACKS US THROUGH OUR REALM OF THOUGHT. HE KNOWS THAT ALMIGHTY GOD SPEAKS TO HIS MESSENGERS AND CHILDREN THROUGH THEIR MINDS. HE TRIES TO REMOVE GOD'S HOLY THOUGHTS, SO THAT HE MAY PLACE HIS DECEIVING THOUGHTS IN OUR MINDS.

ALMIGHTY GOD SPEAKING

UNDERSTAND MY WORDS, O MESSENGERS AND CHILDREN OF MINE, SO THAT SATAN CANNOT CONFUSE YOU. UNDERSTAND WHAT IS FROM ME, AND WHAT IS FROM SATAN, MY ENEMY, SO THAT YOU MAY LEAD MY CALLED AND CHOSEN ONES IN THE DIRECTION OF ETERNAL LIFE WITH ME. LISTEN TO MY VOICE ALONE, SO THAT SATAN'S DECEITFUL WORDS WILL NOT ENTER YOUR REALM OF THOUGHT. BE AWARE OF SATAN'S METHODS MY CHILDREN, FOR HE IS RUTHLESS! HE HAS NO FEELINGS FOR WHAT IS RIGHT, JUST, AND HOLY. HE IS DEVOID OF COMPASSION, MERCY, AND EMPATHY. HE IS NOTHING! REVEAL MY HOLY WORDS IN SONG AND DANCE IN THE PRESENCE OF SATAN AND HIS LOWLY ANGELS. LIFT UP YOUR VOICES AND GIVE ME CONTINUOUS PRAISE, GLORY AND HONOR, IN THE PRESENCE OF SATAN'S DEFEATED REALM! MY CHILDREN, DO NOT LET SATAN'S REALM OF EVIL KEEP YOU QUIET! PRAISE MY HOLY WORTHY NAME OUT LOUD!
JUNE 2, 2015 BY: BARBARA ANN MARY MACK
SENT TUE, JUN 2, 2015 5:57 PM-READ TUE 6/2/2015 8:13 PM

BE KIND TO YOURSELF TODAY ARCHBISHOP CRAIG! BELOW ARE TODAY'S PASSAGES. AMORE, BELLA BARBIE

THOSE WHO ARE ASHAMED OF ME, I WILL BE ASHAMED OF THEM, *SAYS THE LORD*

ALMIGHTY GOD, THE FATHER, SPEAKING

DO NOT HIDE YOUR LIMITED KNOWLEDGE AND UNDERSTANDING OF MY HOLY WORDS, MY CHILDREN. DO NOT HIDE YOUR LIMITED UNDERSTANDING OF MY MERCY, MY CHILDREN. DO NOT HIDE YOUR LIMITED UNDERSTANDING OF MY JUSTICE. DO NOT HIDE YOUR LIMITED UNDERSTANDING OF MY WRATH. DO NOT PRETEND THAT YOU KNOW ME, MY CHILDREN. DO NOT PRETEND THAT YOU KNOW AND UNDERSTAND MY HOLY WORDS AND WAY. DO NOT PRETEND THAT YOU ARE WORSHIPPING ME, MY CHILDREN. DO NOT PRETEND THAT YOU ARE SERVING ME, MY CHILDREN. DO NOT PRETEND! DO NOT PRETEND! DO NOT PRETEND! FOR YOUR ACTIONS REVEAL WHAT IS REALLY IN YOUR HEARTS. YOUR ACTIONS CONVEY THAT YOU ARE ASHAMED OF ME. YOUR ACTIONS CONVEY THAT YOU DO NOT KNOW ME. YOUR ACTIONS REVEAL THE DEPTH OF YOUR TRUE UNDERSTANDING OF MY HOLY WORDS AND WILL. MY CHILDREN, CHANGE YOUR WAY, AND CONFORM TO MY WAY, THE ONLY HOLY WAY! FOR IF YOU CONTINUE TO WALK AMONG THOSE WHO ARE ASHAMED TO SPEAK OF ME, I WILL REMOVE YOU FROM MY SIGHT. I AM WORTHY TO SPEAK OF AT ALL TIMES, MY CHILDREN! DO NOT PLACE ANYTHING OR ANYONE ABOVE ME! FOR THERE IS NOTHING THAT EQUATES TO ME, NOR IS THERE ANYONE WHO TRANSCENDS MY HOLY POSITION AND PRESENCE IN YOUR LIVES. UNDERSTAND AND ACCEPT THIS FACT BEFORE IT IS TOO LATE, MY CHILDREN! FOR JUDGMENT DAY IS DRAWING NEAR! MY CHILDREN, DO NOT BE ASHAMED TO WALK AND TALK WITH ME, FOR I WILL NEVER LEAVE YOU! THIS, *SAYS THE LORD!*

JUNE 3, 2015 BY: BARBARA ANN MARY MACK

I WILL NOT GO WHERE I AM NOT WANTED, *SAYS THE LORD*

ALMIGHTY GOD SPEAKING

I WILL NOT FORCE YOU TO LOVE ME, MY CHILDREN. I WILL NOT FORCE YOU TO EXHIBIT A LOVE THAT UNITES YOU WITH YOUR CREATOR AND GOD. I WILL NOT FORCE YOU TO SERVE ME AND MY NEEDY FLOCK. I WILL NOT GO WHERE I AM NOT WANTED! FOR I DESIRE SINCERE LOVE AT ALL TIMES, FROM ALL OF MY CHILDREN. I WILL NOT GO WHERE I AM NOT WANTED OR APPRECIATED, MY CHILDREN. I WILL NOT ATTEND YOUR CHURCHES! I WILL NOT DWELL INSIDE YOUR HOMES. I WILL NOT DWELL WITHIN YOUR STAINED TEMPLES (BODIES). I WILL NOT GO WHERE I AM NOT WANTED! RECEIVE YOUR HOLY GOD, MY CHILDREN. RECEIVE THE GIFT OF LIFE THAT DESCENDS FROM HEAVEN IN YOUR MIDST EACH DAY. RECEIVE THE GIFT OF ETERNAL LIFE THAT IS GRANTED TO THOSE WHO WELCOME ME INTO THEIR OBEDIENT PRIVATE WORLD. RECEIVE ME, MY CHILDREN, SO THAT YOU MAY DWELL WITH ME IN SWEET PARADISE ABOVE! FOLLOW ME THROUGH THE HEAVENLY GATES THAT WELCOME THOSE WHO HONOR THEIR CREATOR AND GOD. FOLLOW ME THROUGH THE REALM THAT LEADS YOU IN THE DIRECTION OF ETERNAL PEACE. FOLLOW ME, DEAR CHILDREN OF MINE! FOLLOW ME THROUGHOUT ETERNITY!

JUNE 3, 2015 BY: BARBARA ANN MARY MACK

SENT: WED, JUN 3, 2015 4:22 PM-READ: WED 6/3/2015 7:17 PM

SUBJECT ME NOT, O LORD

O MERCIFUL AND COMPASSIONATE GOD, SUBJECT ME NOT, TO THOSE WHO CAUSE ME TO FLEE FROM MY DIVINE ASSIGNMENT OF LOVE. SUBJECT ME NOT, TO THE REALM (SATAN) THAT DESIRES TO STEAL ME FROM YOU. SUBJECT ME NOT TO THE REALM THAT PLACES TEMPTATION IN THE PATH OF YOUR VULNERABLE CHILDREN. SUBJECT ME NOT TO THE EVIL THAT ROAMS THIS

VULNERABLE PERIOD OF TIME. SUBJECT ME NOT TO THOSE WHO DO NOT SHOW PITY FOR THE WEAK AND LONELY ONES. SUBJECT ME NOT TO THIS WORLD OF APATHETIC SOULS THAT ROAM IN THE MIDST OF DOOM AND DESTRUCTION. SUBJECT ME NOT, TO THOSE WHO HAVE THE AUTHORITY OVER ADMINISTERING SATAN'S WEALTH OF DESTRUCTION AND DISCOURAGEMENT. SUBJECT ME NOT TO THOSE WHO ENJOY AND RECEIVE PLEASURE FROM THE HARM AND DESTRUCTION OF THE UNSUSPECTING ONES. SUBJECT ME NOT TO THE PLACES THAT DO NOT TRULY ADORE AND SERVE YOU. SUBJECT ME NOT TO THE AGE OF TIME THAT DID NOT KNOW JESUS' PURPOSE AND POSITION, AS GOD IN THE FLESH. MY LORD AND MY GOD, SUBJECT ME NOT TO ANYTHING OR ANYONE THAT DOES NOT GIVE YOU CONTINUOUS PRAISE! *ALLELUIA!*

JUNE 3, 2015 BY: BARBARA ANN MARY MACK

SENT: THU, JUN 4, 2015 3:20 PM-READ: THU 6/4/2015 10:32 PM

I HAVE SERVED MY TIME IN THE WORLD

BARBARA SPEAKING TO THE LORD JESUS

I HAVE SERVED MY TIME IN THIS WORLD. I NOW LOOK FORWARD TO THE REALM THAT WILL OFFER ME CONTINUOUS BLISS ON EARTH. MY LORD, MY GOD, I AM TRULY GRATEFUL! I AM GRATEFUL FOR YOUR HOLY ESSENCE THAT ENCOMPASSES MY ABUSED BEING THROUGH THE DAY. MY LORD, MY GOD, I AM GRATEFUL FOR THE PEACE THAT EMITS CONTINUOUSLY FROM YOUR REALM OF DIVINITY. I HAVE SERVED MY TIME IN A WORLD THAT DOESN'T ACCEPT THE PRESENCE OF ALMIGHTY GOD'S DIVINE CHOICE AND BRIDE (BARBARA). I HAVE SERVED MY TIME IN A WORLD THAT DOESN'T FOLLOW AND ABIDE BY THE TEACHING OF JESUS, THE SLAUGHTERED LAMB. WE (THE LORD JESUS AND BARBARA) HAVE BEEN SLAUGHTERED IN THE PRESENCE OF OUR GREAT AND HOLY FATHER, MY SPOUSE (JESUS). WE HAVE BEEN SLAUGHTERED FOR THE SAKE AND SALVATION OF OUR FATHER'S NEEDY FLOCK. WE HAVE SERVED OUR TIME, LORD JESUS! WE HAVE SERVED OUR TIME FOR THE SOULS THAT ARE WRITTEN IN YOUR BLESSED BOOK OF LIFE. WE HAVE SERVED OUR TIME FOR THE SAKE OF THE INNOCENT AND ABUSED ONES. WE HAVE ENDURED THE SUFFERINGS THAT ACCOMPANY THE GIFTS (THE LORD JESUS AND BARBARA) OF GOD, OUR FATHER. MY LORD, MY GOD, WE HAVE SERVED OUR TIME IN THE MIDST OF SATAN'S DEFEATED REALM OF NOTHINGNESS. WE HAVE FOUGHT FOR THE SOULS THAT GOD, OUR FATHER DEEMS WORTHY TO FIGHT FOR. LET US ASCEND INTO GLORY ON THE WINGS OF YOUR HOLY DOVE, MY LORD. LET US ASCEND AS ONE, FOR WE HAVE SERVED OUR TIME IN THIS WORLD! *ALLELUIA!!!*

JUNE 4, 2015 BY: BARBARA ANN MARY MACK

SENT: FRI, JUN 5, 2015 1:52 AM-READ: FRI 6/5/2015 7:36 AM

WE'VE BEEN THROUGH SO MUCH TOGETHER THROUGH THE YEARS, MY LORD

BARBARA SPEAKING TO ALMIGHTY GOD

SINCE THE BEGINNING OF TIME I DWELLED WITHIN YOUR HOLY ESSENCE, MY GOD. SINCE THE BEGINNING OF TIME, YOU CRADLED ME WITHIN YOUR DIVINE ESSENCE OF LOVE. SINCE THE BEGINNING OF TIME, YOU WHISPERED THE HOLY WORDS THAT PERMEATED YOUR REALM OF ETERNITY. SINCE THE BEGINNING OF TIME, I WALKED WITH YOU ON YOUR SPIRITUAL STREETS OF GLORY. AT THE APPOINTED TIME, YOU SENT ME TO YOUR NEEDY CHILDREN ON EARTH. AT THE APPOINTED TIME, YOU REVEALED TO ME MY DIVINE ASSIGNMENT OF LOVE. AT THE APPOINTED TIME, YOU EQUIPPED ME WITH THE WEAPONS (DIVINE LOVE, PERSEVERANCE, MERCY, COMPASSION, EMPATHY AND PATIENCE) THAT WOULD DEFEAT SATAN'S REALM OF DESTRUCTION AND EVIL. AT THE APPOINTED TIME, I FOUGHT THE GATES OF HELL FOR THE ETERNAL SOUL OF OUR BELOVED ONE (CRAIG). AT THE APPOINTED TIME, I SHED THE TEARS THAT WERE RELEASED IN THE MIDST OF MY PAINFUL ASSIGNMENT OF LOVE. AT THE APPOINTED TIME, I WAS HELD CAPTIVE BY THOSE WHO DID NOT UNDERSTAND MY DIVINE ASSIGNMENT OF LOVE. AT THE APPOINTED TIME, MY FALLING TEARS UNITED WITH YOURS, AS YOU WITNESSED THE ABUSE THAT WAS PLACED UPON YOUR SACRIFICIAL BRIDE AND MESSENGER OF DIVINE LOVE (BARBARA). AT THE APPOINTED TIME, I SERVED YOUR INVITED GUESTS WITH YOUR HOLY FOOD (WORDS) OF LIFE. AT THE APPOINTED TIME, I WAS FALSELY ACCUSED BY A LOVE THAT FOLLOWED YOU THROUGH THE YEARS. AT THE APPOINTED TIME, I ENDURE THE SUFFERINGS THAT ACCOMPANIED YOUR CHOSEN BRIDE OF LOVE. AT THE APPOINTED TIME, I ENJOYED THE BLISS THAT FOLLOWED MY YEARS OF PAIN. AT THE APPOINTED TIME, I RECEIVED YOUR HOLY PROMISE AND GIFT OF DIVINE LOVE. MY LORD AND MY GOD, I WILL NOW CELEBRATE IN UNION WITH YOU AND OUR BELOVED ONE, AS WE BOW IN THE MIDST OF YOUR FORETOLD PROMISE OF CONTINUOUS LOVE. *ALLELUIA!*
JUNE 6, 2015 BY: BARBARA ANN MARY MACK

IT IS SO GOOD TO KNOW THAT YOU ARE ALWAYS AROUND ME, MY LORD

BARBARA SPEAKING TO ALMIGHTY GOD

MY LORD AND MY GOD, I WANT THE WORLD TO KNOW OF THE JOY AND PEACE THAT ENCOMPASSES MY OBEDIENT BEING, AS I WALK IN THE MIDST OF THIS TROUBLED PERIOD OF TIME. I CAN FEEL YOUR HOLY PRESENCE, MY GOD! I CAN FEEL YOUR EMBRACE, O HEAVENLY SPOUSE OF MINE! IT FEELS GOOD TO KNOW THAT YOU ARE ALWAYS NEAR ME. IT IS GOOD TO BREATHE IN YOUR HOLY ESSENCE AS I DELIVER YOUR MESSAGES OF LOVE. MY LORD, MY GOD, YOUR HOLY PRESENCE PRODUCES THE DIVINE PEACE THAT ENABLES ME TO PROCEED IN MY AWESOME TASK OF LOVE FOR YOU. MY LORD, I WANT THE WORLD TO KNOW OF YOUR

PROTECTION OVER YOUR FRIGHTENED BRIDE AND MESSENGER OF LOVE. I WANT THE WORLD TO KNOW THAT THE GATES OF HELL CAN NEVER DEFEAT GOD'S MESSENGER OF HOLY LOVE AND PEACE. FOR HE (SATAN) IS THE DEFEATED ONE! HE IS MY ENEMY! HE IS THE STENCH THAT SLITHERS THROUGH THIS DEVASTATING AND CRUCIAL PERIOD OF TIME. YOU, O GREAT AND HOLY ONE, DEEM THE WORLD WORTHY TO WITNESS YOUR HOLY PRESENCE IN A TANGIBLE MANNER THROUGH BARBARA, YOUR SENT BRIDE AND MESSENGER OF LOVE. MY OBEDIENT PRESENCE IS TANGIBLE PROOF OF YOUR HOLY EXISTENCE IN THE LIVES OF YOUR LOVED ONES TODAY. MY HUMBLED PRESENCE IS TANGIBLE PROOF OF YOUR HOLY POWER IN OUR MIDST TODAY. ENCOMPASS ME, O HOLY ONE, AS I DELIVER YOUR HOLY PRESENCE TO THOSE WHO ARE IN NEED OF YOU. IT IS GOOD TO KNOW THAT YOU ARE ALWAYS AROUND ME!

JUNE 6, 2015 BY: BARBARA ANN MARY MACK

SENT SUN, JUN 7, 2015 2:11 PM-READ SUN 6/7/2015 3:00 PM

THE REALM OF DESTRUCTION AND ETERNAL DAMNATION HAS CALLED, CAPTURED, AND DESTROYED MANY WORLDLY FAME SEEKING SOULS

BARBARA SPEAKING TO SATAN

OH HOW DECEPTIVE YOU ARE, O PRINCE OF DOOM, DECEPTION, DARKNESS AND ETERNAL DAMNATION (SATAN)! FOR YOU HAVE FOOLED EVEN THOSE WHO HAVE BELIEVED THAT THEY HAD CONTROL OVER YOU. BUT ALMIGHTY GOD HAS SENT BARBARA, HIS HOLY WIFE AND MESSENGER, TO EXPOSE YOUR REALM OF DECEPTION AND ETERNAL DAMNATION. I KNOW YOUR LOWLY METHODS OF DECEPTION AND DOOM, O LOWLY ONE! I KNOW OF YOUR HIDDEN WAYS OF CAPTURING THE WEAK AND VULNERABLE ONES. THE LORD, MY HOLY OMNIPOTENT GOD, HAS GRACED ME WITH HIS TWO EDGED SWORD, SO THAT I MAY DEFEAT YOUR REALM OF EVIL THAT PERMEATES THIS INJURED PERIOD OF TIME. BOW DOWN TO ALMIGHTY GOD, THE AUTHOR OF YOUR DEFEAT AND FINAL DESTINATION, O LOWLY SERPENT OF DOOM. YOU HAVE TAKEN DOWN MANY WHO SOUGHT WORLDLY FAME AND FORTUNES. YOU HAVE TAKEN DOWN THE WEAK AND VULNERABLE MINDS OF THOSE WHO BELIEVED THAT WORLDLY FAME AND FORTUNE WOULD MAKE THEM HAPPY. YOU HAVE TAKEN DOWN THOSE WHO SOUGHT YOUR REALM OF PLEASURES, WHICH LED TO DISEASES AND MISHAPS. YOU HAVE DECEIVED AND BETRAYED THE RICH AND THE POOR ONES. YOU DO NOT DISCRIMINATE, O FATHER OF DOOM AND DESTRUCTION (SATAN, THE DEVIL)! I HAVE BEEN SENT BY ALMIGHTY GOD TO UNVEIL YOUR GUISE, O DECEPTIVE ONE. THE LORD WANTS THE WORLD TO KNOW OF YOUR GUISE, SO THAT THEY MAY FLEE FROM WHAT YOU ARE OFFERING THEM. THEY WILL FLEE FROM YOUR REALM OF TEMPORARY PLEASURES. THEY WILL FLEE FROM YOUR REALM OF TEMPORARY FORTUNES. THEY WILL FLEE FROM YOUR REALM THAT PROMOTES SEXUAL DEVIATION AND PREMARITAL SEX. THEY WILL FLEE FROM EVERYTHING THAT LEADS TO YOUR REALM OF DESTRUCTION, O DOOMED ONE. FOR THE LORD, OUR OMNIPOTENT AND OMNIPRESENT

GOD, HAS SENT BARBARA, HIS DEVOTED WIFE, TO EXPOSE THE STENCH THAT IS RELEASED FROM YOUR REALM OF HARDSHIP AND AGONY. AND I WILL COMPLETE MY DIVINE ASSIGNMENT WITH DILIGENCE AND PATIENCE, AS I BOW IN THE PRESENCE OF GOD, MY HOLY SPOUSE.
JUNE 8, 2015 BY: BARBARA ANN MARY MACK
SENT TUE, JUN 9, 2015 12:28 AM-READ TUE 6/9/2015 8:30 AM

BUONA SERA ARCHBISHOP CRAIG! I PRAY THAT YOU HAD A WONDERFUL DAY. EARLIER TODAY, THE LORD GAVE ME THE PASSAGE BELOW TO DESCRIBE THE LONGTIME FRIENDSHIP THAT YOU AND YOUR COLLEAGUE....HAS. ACCORDING TO THE LORD, YOUR FRIENDSHIP IS GENUINE. I DID NOT RECOGNIZE...AT CHURCH. I HAD NO IDEA WHO HE WAS UNTIL I SAW HIS NAME MENTIONED ON YOUR FACEBOOK PAGE. IT IS GOOD TO SEE THAT WE ALL ARE EXHIBITING GOD'S VERSION OF FORGIVENESS. OH HOW VERY PLEASED THE LORD IS! WE ARE CALLED TO EXHIBIT "AUTHENTIC" FORGIVENESS IN THE PRESENCE OF THE LORD, THEN HE WILL INCLUDE US IN HIS BOOK OF LIFE. DEAR ONE (ARCHBISHOP CRAIG), LET US CONTINUE EXHIBITING GOD'S VERSION OF FORGIVENESS IN THE PRESENCE OF THOSE WHO NEED TO WITNESS THE ACT OF "AUTHENTIC CHRISTIANS". LOVE, AUTHENTIC BARBARA

FRIENDSHIP AND MAN

OH WHAT A BOND!
A FRIENDSHIP THAT IS ONE OF A KIND!
A UNION THAT FLOWED THROUGH THE YEARS.
A UNION THAT INCLUDED MANY JOYFUL AND SORROWFUL TEARS.
A FRIENDSHIP THAT DESCENDED FROM ABOVE.
A UNION THAT EXHIBITS HUMAN LOVE!
OH, IT IS SO "UNIQUE" AND "RARE"!
A FRIENDSHIP THAT EXPRESSES, THAT THE TWO OF YOU REALLY CARE.
FRIENDSHIP AND MAN:
SEEM TO BE DIFFERENT FROM FRIENDSHIP AND WOMAN.
LIKE JONATHAN AND DAVID, THE KING.
YOURS IS A UNION THAT CAUSES HEAVEN'S HOLY BELLS TO RING!
I HAVE WITNESSED YOUR FRIENDSHIP AND REALM OF FORGIVENESS, MY SONS.
I HAVE WITNESSED YOUR "AUTHENTIC FRIENDSHIP" IN THE PRESENCE OF THE CALLED AND CHOSEN ONES.
EXHIBIT MY VERSION OF FRIENDSHIP, O BLESSED SONS OF MINE.
AND I WILL REJOICE WITH YOU, THROUGHOUT THE REALM OF TIME!
JUNE 9, 2015 BY: BARBARA ANN MARY MACK
SENT WED, JUN 10, 2015 12:51 AM-READ WED 6/10/2015 1:10 PM

BARBARA SPEAKING

WHEN I GRASP THE AWESOME WORK OF ALMIGHTY GOD, I BOW IN THE MIDST OF HIS GRACE. WHEN I WITNESS THE FULFILLMENT OF HIS HOLY PROMISES TODAY, I BOW IN THE MIDST OF HIS GRACE. DO NOT RELEASE ME, O WELL OF DIVINE GRACE THAT ENCOMPASSES MY IGNITED BEING THROUGHOUT EACH DAY. DO NOT RELEASE THE CONTENTED ESSENCE OF GOD'S HOLY MESSENGER AND BRIDE (BARBARA). FOR I AM AT PEACE WITHIN THE REALM THAT OFFERS ME SPIRITUAL TRANQUILITY IN THE MIDST OF THIS CHAOTIC PERIOD OF TIME. I AM AT PEACE WITHIN THE LOVING ARMS OF GOD, MY ETERNAL SPOUSE. DO NOT RELEASE ME, O REALM OF GRACE. DO NOT RELEASE THE BEING OF THE SACRIFICIAL BRIDE OF JESUS, THE VICTORIOUS AND RISEN LAMB. DO NOT RELEASE ME IN THIS WORLD OF MATERIALISM, AND FALSE SECURITY AND HOPE. SURROUND ME, O SWEET REALM OF GRACE, SO THAT I MAY DWELL WITHIN THE LAND THAT IS GOVERNED AND LOVED BY ALMIGHTY GOD.

JUNE 9, 2015 BY: BARBARA ANN MARY MACK

SENT TUE, JUN 9, 2015 11:15 PM-READ WED 6/10/2015 1:12 PM

WHOM DO YOU REALLY DESIRE TO SERVE AND IMITATE? SATAN OR ME, *SAYS THE LORD*

ALMIGHTY GOD SPEAKING

MY CHILDREN, WHOM DO YOU REALLY HOLD YOUR ALLEGIANCE TO? FOR YOUR ACTIONS DO NOT AGREE WITH YOUR WORDS. YOU TELL THE WORLD THAT YOU KNOW AND SERVE ME, YOUR CREATOR AND GOD, BUT YOUR ACTIONS CONVEY THE TRUTH. YOU ENTER SATAN'S REALM OF "UNHOLY" DEEDS WITHOUT SHAME. YOU ENTER HIS PLACES OF WORSHIP IN MY HOLY PRESENCE, FOR I AM EVERYWHERE, MY CHILDREN! YOU MINGLE WITH THOSE WHO

DISRESPECT ME DAILY, WITH NO SHAME OR HONOR TOWARDS YOUR MERCIFUL GOD. MY CHILDREN, I KNOW WHO YOU REALLY HONOR AND SERVE, FOR YOUR DAILY ACTS REVEAL THIS TRUTH. REMEMBER, O DECEIVED FOLLOWERS OF SATAN'S FALSE AND TEMPORARY GLORY, I AM WATCHING YOU, FOR I AM ALWAYS IN YOUR MIDST! I AM FULLY AWARE OF WHO YOU TRULY GIVE YOUR ALLEGIANCE TO, AND IT ISN'T ME, *SAYS THE LORD.*

ALMIGHTY GOD SPEAKING OF BARBARA, HIS EARTHLY BRIDE

MY CHILDREN, I HAVE SENT MY FAITHFUL BRIDE TO REVEAL MY VIEWS AND CONCERNS OF YOUR DISGRACEFUL ACTS. HEED MY WARNINGS THAT ARE CONVEYED THROUGH HER, FOR SHE IS SPEAKING FOR ME, *SAYS THE LORD.* HURRY! MY CHILDREN. COME TO MY REALM OF HOLINESS BEFORE I CALL MY BRIDE (BARBARA) BACK TO MY LOVING REALM, FOR THIS IS OUR (THE LORD AND BARBARA) DESIRE.

JUNE 11, 2015 BY: BARBARA ANN MARY MACK

SENT THU, JUN 11, 2015 11:41 AM-READ THU 6/11/2015 2:12 PM

GREETINGS ARCHBISHOP CRAIG! I PRAY THAT YOU HAD A SPIRITUALLY PROSPEROUS DAY. I HAD TO GET MY MONTHLY B12 INJECTION THIS AFTERNOON. IT IS FUNNY HOW UNIQUE AND MYSTERIOUS THE HUMAN BODY IS. B12 IS VERY CRUCIAL TO ONE'S HEALTH. I HAVE PERNICIOUS ANEMIA. THIS WAS DISCOVERED A FEW YEARS AGO. ONE OF THE ASSISTANT DOCTORS RAN MANY TESTS TO FIND THE CAUSE OF WHAT HE BELIEVED TO BE A LOSS OF BLOOD OR IRON DEFICIENCY. BY THE TIME IT WAS DISCOVERED THAT I HAVE PERNICIOUS ANEMIA, B12 DEFICIENCY HAD CAUSED NEUROLOGICAL DISORDER (PERIPHERAL NEUROPATHY). ALTHOUGH I WILL RECEIVE THE MONTHLY B12 INJECTIONS FOR THE REST OF MY LIFE, THIS WILL NOT CURE THE NEUROLOGICAL DAMAGE. BELOW IS TODAY'S PASSAGE.

THERE ARE "NO EXCEPTIONS"!

ALMIGHTY GOD SPEAKING

MY HOLY WORDS AND COMMANDMENTS APPLY TO EVERYONE. THERE ARE NO EXCEPTIONS! THEY APPLY TO THE MEEK, AND THEY APPLY TO THE STRONG HEARTED ONES. THERE ARE NO EXCEPTIONS! THEY APPLY TO THE RICH, AND THEY APPLY TO THE POOR. THERE ARE NO EXCEPTIONS! THEY APPLY TO THE BELIEVERS AND THEY APPLY TO THE NON-BELIEVERS. THERE ARE NO EXCEPTIONS, SAYS THE LORD GOD! THEY APPLY TO THE FAMOUS ONES, AND THEY APPLY TO THE UNKNOWN ONES. THERE ARE NO EXCEPTIONS! HEED MY HOLY WORDS, O WANDERING CHILDREN OF MINE, FOR THEY APPLY TO EVERYONE! I HAVE PURIFIED MY MESSENGER AND BRIDE (BARBARA) WITH THE FIRE OF MY HOLY SPIRIT SO THAT SHE

MAY STAND BEFORE ME THROUGHOUT EACH DAY, AND RECEIVE MY WORDS AND PLANS FOR YOU. I HAVE PURIFIED HER WITH THE FIRE OF MY DIVINE LOVE, SO THAT SHE WILL HAVE THE STRENGTH TO COMBAT SATAN FOR THE WANDERING AND MISGUIDED SOULS OF MY LOST CHILDREN. RECEIVE MY HOLY MESSAGES CONCERNING YOUR DESTINATION AND SALVATION, MY CHILDREN. RECEIVE THE DIVINE FOOD (GOD'S HOLY WORDS) THAT WILL SUSTAIN AND SATISFY YOUR THIRSTY SOULS. YOU MUST RECEIVE MY HOLY WORDS MY CHILDREN, SO THAT YOU TOO MAY HAVE THE PRIVILEGE TO COMMUNICATE WITH YOUR CREATOR AND GOD THROUGHOUT THE DAY. YOU MUST RECEIVE AND ABIDE BY MY HOLY WORDS IN ORDER TO GAIN SALVATION THROUGH JESUS CHRIST. MY CHILDREN, THERE ARE NO EXCEPTIONS!!!

JUNE 12, 2015 BY: BARBARA ANN MARY MACK

SENT FRI, JUN 12, 2015 9:34 PM-READ SAT 6/13/2015 12:26 AM

IS THE FIGHT OVER YET, MY LORD? FOR IT HAS BEEN VERY BRUTAL AND AGONIZING

BRENDA AND BARBARA

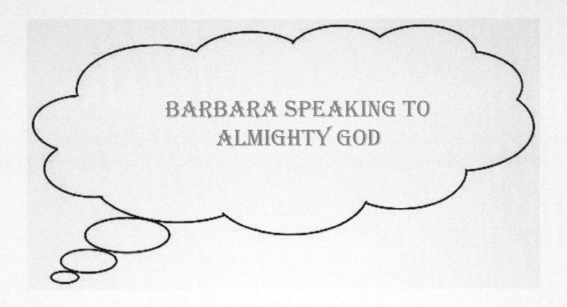

BARBARA SPEAKING TO ALMIGHTY GOD

MY LORD, THE JUBILEE YEAR HAS DESCENDED IN THE MIDST OF THOSE WHOM YOU HAVE INVITED TO WITNESS THE CELEBRATION AND COMPLETION OF **THE GREATEST STORY EVER TOLD.** THE JUBILEE CELEBRATION REPRESENTS THE CONCLUSION OF ONE OF THE GREATEST MINISTRIES THAT WAS BESTOWED UPON GOD'S CHILDREN (CRAIG AND BARBARA). OUR MINISTRY CONSISTED OF GREAT FAITH AND TRUST IN THE VOICE AND WORDS OF GOD'S HOLY SPIRIT. A MINISTRY THAT INCLUDED YEARS OF PHYSICAL DIVISION BETWEEN GOD'S MESSENGERS (CRAIG AND BARBARA). A MINISTRY WHICH INCLUDED YEARS OF SPIRITUAL UNITY BETWEEN GOD'S CHOSEN BRIDE (BARBARA) AND GROOM (CRAIG). A MINISTRY WHICH INCLUDED YEARS OF UNCERTAINTY AND DOUBTS. A MINISTRY THAT INCLUDED YEARS OF SPIRITUAL AND PHYSICAL AGONY FOR THE RECIPIENTS (CRAIG AND BARBARA) OF GOD HOLY INSTRUCTIONS. A MINISTRY WHICH REVEALS THE ALLEGIANCE OF GOD'S CHOSEN MESSENGERS (CRAIG AND BARBARA) OF DIVINE LOVE AND SERVITUDE.

BARBARA SPEAKING TO CRAIG

WE HAVE DONE IT, DEAR WARRIOR AND COMPANION OF MINE! WE HAVE COMPLETED OUR MINISTRY OF AGONY AND PHYSICAL SEPARATION! WE HAVE COMPLETED "THE GREAT AND HOLY ASSIGNMENT OF LOVE THAT WAS ENTRUSTED IN US BY ALMIGHTY GOD HIMSELF. LET YOU AND I GIVE HIM CONTINUOUS PRAISE! LET US APPLAUD OUR GREAT AND HOLY REDEEMER AND GOD, FOR HE HAS FOUND FAVOR IN OUR HOLY WORK FOR HIM. HE IS VERY PLEASED! LET YOU AND I BOW TOGETHER AS ONE IN UNION WITH OUR GRACIOUS AND WORTHY GOD. FOR HE HAS TRUSTED US WITH A DIVINE TASK THAT INCLUDES THE CONVERSION OF MANY. LET US BOW AS ONE SANCTIFIED ENTITY IN OUR GRACIOUS GOD'S HOLY PRESENCE TODAY, FOR HE IS WORTHY, MY LOVE! *ALLELUIA!*

JUNE 11, 2015 BY: BARBARA ANN MARY MACK
SENT FRI, JUN 12, 2015 2:48 PM-READ SAT 6/13/2015 1:36 PM

BARBARA SPEAKING TO THE LORD

THEY HAVE TURNED AGAINST US, O LORD. THEY HAVE TURNED THEIR BACKS ON US. YOUR NEEDY FLOCK HAS FORSAKEN US, O HEAVENLY REALM OF PURITY (ALMIGHTY GOD) AND DIVINE LOVE. THEY HAVE WALKED OUT ON YOUR HOLY WORDS THAT FLOWED FROM MY REALM OF DELIVERANCE. THEY DO NOT DESIRE TO HEAR THE HOLY WORDS THAT WILL SET THEIR WANDERING AND DISCONTENTED SPIRITS FREE. WE (ALMIGHTY GOD AND BARBARA) CAN RECALL THE TIME OF PAST WHEN THOSE WHO HAVE ABANDONED YOU, ONCE PROFESSED THAT THEY WERE CHRISTIANS. MY LORD, MY LOVING GOD, WHY HAVE THEY FORSAKEN US? WE WERE THERE FOR THEM IN THEIR TIMES OF NEED. WE WERE THERE FOR THEM WHEN THEY NEEDED YOUR MIGHTY SHOULDER TO LEAN ON. WE WERE THERE FOR THEM DURING THEIR SORROWFUL TIMES. WE CAME TO THEIR AID WHEN THEY NEEDED US. MY LORD, MY HOLY SPOUSE, WHY DO THEY NO LONGER CALL OUT TO US? THEY HAVE ABANDONED THE REALM OF ETERNAL LIFE (ALMIGHTY GOD). THEY HAVE ABANDON JESUS, THE GREAT AND HOLY LIGHT OF THE WORLD. THEY HAVE ABANDONED GOD, THE LIVING WATERS. THEY HAVE TURNED AGAINST THE ONE, THE ONLY ONE, WHO HUNG ON HIS CROSS OF LOVE, FOR THE SALVATION OF THOSE WHOM HE WILL ALWAYS LOVE. MY LORD, MY HOLY GOD, LET US WEEP AS ONE WHO HAS BEEN ABANDONED.

JUNE 13, 2015 BY: BARBARA ANN MARY MACK

ARE YOU WITH ME? OR, ARE YOU AGAINST ME? THERE IS NO IN BETWEEN, *SAYS THE LORD*

ALMIGHTY GOD SPEAKING

MY CHILDREN, ARE YOU WITH YOUR FAITHFUL CREATOR AND GOD, OR DO YOU SERVE SATAN, MY ENEMY? YOU DECIDE, MY CHILDREN, FOR YOUR ETERNAL DESTINATION DEPENDS ON YOUR PRESENT CHOICE. HONOR MY HOLY WORDS EVERY DAY, MY CHILDREN. DO NOT THINK THAT YOUR ONCE A WEEK APPEARANCE AT CHURCH WILL SAVE YOU, FOR IT WILL NOT! YOU MUST HONOR MY HOLY WAY INSTEAD OF SATAN'S UNHOLY WAY. YOU GIVE SATAN GLORY AND HONOR SIX DAYS A WEEK, AND THINK THAT I HAVE YOUR ATTENTION ON SUNDAY. DO NOT DECEIVE YOURSELVES, MY CHILDREN. YOU ARE TO HONOR AND PRAISE YOUR CREATOR AND GOD EVERY DAY OF THE WEEK! BY DOING THIS, SATAN CANNOT ENTER YOUR VULNERABLE REALM. SATAN HAS HIS EYES AND HANDS ON YOU THROUGHOUT THE WEEK. DO NOT BE DECEIVED! FOR HE HAS CLAIMED MANY SOULS WHO GAVE HIM RECOGNITION SIX DAYS A WEEK. DURING THAT TIME (SIX DAYS) HE HAS CAUSED MANY FATALITIES, WHICH INCLUDED THE LIVES OF THOSE WHO HAVE ENTERED THE CHURCHES ON SUNDAYS ONLY. MY CHILDREN, HEED MY HOLY WORDS THAT ARE SPOKEN ON SUNDAYS AT YOUR CHURCHES, AND THROUGH MY MESSENGER (BARBARA). MY CHILDREN, EXHIBIT YOUR ALLEGIANCE TO ME AT ALL TIMES, SO THAT SATAN WILL NOT LURE YOU INTO HIS REALM OF DOOM AND DESTRUCTION. EXPRESS YOUR BELIEF IN MY HOLY EXISTENCE AT ALL TIMES. EXPRESS YOUR LOVE FOR ME SEVEN DAYS A WEEK, MY CHILDREN. DO NOT WAIT UNTIL TRAGEDIES ENTER YOUR REALM, BEFORE YOU ACKNOWLEDGE ME, FOR I WILL NOT ACKNOWLEDGE YOU. I AM YOUR CREATOR AND FATHER, SHOW ME DUE RESPECT AND HONOR AT ALL TIMES! *THIS, SAYS THE LORD!*

JUNE 13, 2015 BY: BARBARA ANN MARY MACK

SENT JUN 13, 2015 8:16 PM-READ SAT 6/13/2015 8:48 PM

YOU HAVE TO GIVE IT UP IF YOU WANT TO LIVE WITH JESUS FOREVER, MY BROTHERS AND SISTERS. I HAVE!

BARBARA SPEAKING

MY BROTHERS AND SISTERS, YOU HAVE TO GIVE UP EVERYTHING THAT GOES AGAINST WHAT IS HOLY IN GOD'S SIGHT. IF YOU DESIRE TO WALK IN THE MIDST OF SWEET PARADISE THROUGHOUT ETERNITY, YOU HAVE TO GIVE UP THE THINGS THAT DISPLEASE OUR HOLY GOD. MY BROTHERS AND SISTERS, UNDERSTAND THE SERIOUSNESS OF THIS! FOR IT IS REAL! GOD'S REALM OF HOLINESS AND SWEET PARADISE ABOVE DO EXIST! ACT UPON THIS FACT, O BROTHERS AND SISTERS OF MINE, FOR IT IS TRUTH! I HAD TO GIVE UP THE SIN OF PREJUDICE AGAINST MY CAUCASIAN BROTHERS. THIS WAS VERY PAINFUL FOR ME. BUT, THE LORD, OUR PERFECT AND JUST GOD, REVEALED TO ME, THAT I WOULD NOT SHARE HIS HEAVENLY THRONE WITH HIM IF I DID NOT GIVE UP THAT DREADFUL SIN. MY BROTHERS AND SISTERS, I LOVE THE LORD, OUR GREAT AND HOLY GOD, MORE THAN I LOVE MYSELF OR ANYONE OR THING. THEREFORE, I HAD NO PROBLEM CONFORMING TO HIS HOLY WAY. I NO LONGER EXHIBIT OR HAVE HIDDEN PREJUDICES TOWARD MY CAUCASIAN BROTHERS. I WANT TO WALK THROUGH THE GATES OF SWEET PARADISE WITH THE LORD JESUS AS MY ETERNAL GUIDE. I HAVE GIVEN UP MY HELL BOUND SINS! MY BROTHERS AND SISTERS, WHAT DO YOU HAVE TO GIVE UP? JUNE 14, 2015 BY: BARBARA ANN MARY MACK

SENT SUN, JUN 14, 2015 5:01 PM-READ SUN 6/14/2015 11:55 PM

I HAVE LEARNED TO BE SILENT AND TO SPEAK WHEN THE HOLY SPIRIT WHISPERS TO ME

BARBARA SPEAKING

I HAVE LEARNED THROUGH THE YEARS, TO LISTEN VERY CLOSELY TO THE VOICE OF GOD'S HOLY SPIRIT. I WILL BE SILENT, MY LORD, AS YOU WHISPER THE WORDS THAT WILL IGNITE YOUR CHILDREN'S DORMANT BEINGS. I WILL BE SILENT, SO THAT I CAN HEAR EVERYTHING THAT YOU HAVE TO SAY. I WILL SIT QUIETLY WHEREVER I AM SO THAT YOUR HOLY WORDS MAY PENETRATE MY REALM OF ACCEPTANCE. I WILL BE SILENT WHEN YOU SPEAK TO ME, O LORD, FOR I AM AWARE OF THE VITAL WORDS THAT PROCEED FROM YOUR DIVINE BEING. SPEAK, MY LORD, FOR YOUR OBEDIENT MESSENGER AND BRIDE IS LISTENING TO YOUR EVERY WORD. SPEAK, MY LORD, FOR YOU HAVE MY CAPTIVE ATTENTION. SPEAK, MY LORD, SO THAT I MAY RECEIVE THE VITAL FOOD THAT WILL SUSTAIN YOUR NEEDY LOVED ONES TODAY. SPEAK, MY GOD, AS I BOW IN YOUR HOLY PRESENCE. JUNE 15, 2015 BY: BARBARA ANN MARY MACK

MANY HAVE TRIED, AND TRY TO STIFLE GOD'S HOLY WORDS.

ALMIGHTY GOD SPEAKING

MANY HAVE TRIED, AND TRY TO STIFLE GOD'S HOLY WORDS, BUT HAVE BEEN STIFLED OR REPRIMANDED BY GOD HIMSELF. DO NOT TRY TO HINDER THAT WHICH CANNOT BE STOPPED, MY CHILDREN. NO ONE CAN PREVENT THE REVELATION OF GOD'S HOLY WORDS AND PRESENCE. NO ONE CAN STOP THAT WHICH IS RELEASED IN THE MIDST OF MY NEEDY CHILDREN TODAY. FOR MY LOVE AND MERCY GUIDE MY HOLINESS TO THOSE WHO ARE IN NEED OF MY PRESENCE EVERY DAY. DO NOT TRY TO STIFLE THOSE WHOM I SEND TO YOU, MY CHILDREN. DO NOT TRY TO STIFLE MY CONDUITS, FOR THEY CARRY GOOD TIDINGS TO THOSE WHO ARE IN NEED OF MY GOODNESS AND MERCY TODAY. DO NOT HINDER THE HOLY WORDS THAT ARE CONVEYED THROUGH MY MESSENGERS TODAY. DO NOT TRY TO PREVENT MY CHOSEN MESSENGER (BARBARA) FROM DELIVERING THE ONLY WORDS THAT WILL LEAD YOUR SOULS TO ME. FOR NO ONE CAN STIFLE THAT WHICH IS SENT FROM THE THRONE OF ALMIGHTY GOD. WHAT I SEND THROUGH MY PROPHETS WILL BE REVEALED, FOR NO ONE CAN PREVENT WHAT I COMMAND. I AM THE ONE AND ONLY OMNIPOTENT AND OMNIPRESENT GOD!
JUNE 13, 2015 BY: BARBARA ANN MARY MACK
SENT MON, JUN 15, 2015 2:08 AM-READ MON 6/15/2015 7:32 AM

THERE IS NO SUCH THING AS A TRUE OR FALSE CHRISTIAN. YOUR ACTS REVEAL WHO YOU ARE. YOUR ACTS REVEAL WHERE YOUR ALLEGIANCE LIES. WHOM DO YOU REALLY SERVE AND HONOR, MY CHILDREN, SATAN OR ME, *SAYS THE LORD?*

ALMIGHTY GOD SPEAKING

WHAT ARE YOUR DAILY ACTIVITIES, MY CHILDREN? YOU DO NOT HAVE TO HIDE THE TRUTH FROM ME, FOR I KNOW EVERYTHING! DO YOU ACKNOWLEDGE MY POSITION AS YOUR CREATOR

AND GOD? DO YOU HONOR MY SACRED WORDS THAT ARE REVEALED TO YOU THROUGH THE HOLY BIBLE AND MY MESSENGERS? DO YOU SHOW LOVE AND RESPECT TOWARD YOUR NEIGHBORS AND STRANGERS? DO YOU OFFER FOOD, SHELTER AND CLOTHING, TO THOSE WHO ARE IN NEED OF THESE VITAL SUBSTANCES? DO YOU ATTEND YOUR CHURCHES SO THAT MAY LEARN OF MY HOLY WAY AND WORDS? DO YOU FELLOWSHIP WITH OTHER CHRISTIANS IN MY HOLY PRESENCE. DO YOU GIVE HONOR TO THOSE WHOM I HAVE PLACED IN AUTHORITY OVER MY CHILDREN? DO YOU READ MY HOLY WORDS OF LOVE ON YOUR OWN? DO YOU CARE FOR THOSE WHO ARE IN NEED OF YOUR HELP AND GUIDANCE? MY CHILDREN, YOUR DAILY ACTS DETERMINE WHERE YOUR ETERNAL SOUL IS DESTINED. YOUR DAILY ACTS CONFIRM WHETHER YOU ARE A CHRISTIAN OR AN UNBELIEVER IN MY HOLY EXISTENCE.

JUNE 16, 2015 BY: BARBARA ANN MARY MACK

SENT TUE, JUN 16, 2015 3:11 PM-READ TUE 6/16/2015 6:45 PM

BARBARA SPEAKING

GREETINGS DEAR ARCHBISHOP CRAIG! I AM PRESENTLY ENJOYING THIS QUIET MORNING AND AFTERNOON WHILE TAKING DOWN DICTATIONS FROM OUR GENEROUS GOD FOR THE WORLD. LA TOYA AND AMYA ARE OUT DOING ERRANDS. WE HAD A GREAT TIME LAST NIGHT AT AMYA'S GRADUATION (MOVE UP) CEREMONY. I LOVED IT BECAUSE IT WAS OVER WITHIN TWO HOURS. SINCE THERE WAS NO AIR OR ADEQUATE VENTILATION, IN THE AUDITORIUM, WE WERE HAPPY TO LEAVE THAT BUILDING. THEY SHOULD HAVE HELD THE CEREMONY AT HER MIDDLE SCHOOL, BECAUSE THERE IS AIR CONDITION IN THAT BUILDING. I GUESS THEY HELD IT AT THE HIGH SCHOOL BECAUSE THE AUDITORIUM WAS BIGGER. SOMETIMES BIGGER ISN'T BETTER OR BEST. BELOW IS THE REVISED PASSAGE. I LEFT OUT A FEW SENTENCES IN THE FIRST PASSAGE THAT I SENT YOU. CIAO!

BATTLING A JACKASS (SATAN) ALL DAY IS VERY STRENUOUS

BARBARA SPEAKING TO SATAN, THE JACKASS

A JACKASS IS SOMEONE WHO EXHIBITS THE REALM OF STUPIDITY, AND A MALE DONKEY. YOU, O SATAN KNOW WHICH DEFINITION FITS YOU. IT SEEMS THAT THE REALM OF STUPIDITY HAS ENCOMPASSED YOUR ESSENCE SINCE THE BEGINNING OF HARDSHIP FOR HUMAN KIND. YOU, O DESPISED ONE, DWELL WITHIN THE REALM OF STUPIDITY. YOU HAVE DWELLED WITHIN THAT REALM IN THE MIDST OF YOUR UNHOLY ANGELS FOR MANY CENTURIES. IT SEEMS THAT YOU WILL NOT CHANGE YOUR UNHOLY WAYS, FOR THE REALM OF STUPIDITY HAS CLAIMED YOU FOREVER! THE REALM OF STUPIDITY HAS CLAIMED YOU AS A PERMANENT RESIDENT. THE REALM OF STUPIDITY HAS CAPTURED YOU AND YOUR UNHOLY FOLLOWERS. THE REALM OF STUPIDITY WILL GUIDE YOU TO THE PIT OF HELL AT GOD'S APPOINTED TIME. MEANWHILE,

WE, GOD'S HOLY MESSENGERS AND FOLLOWERS, WILL COMBAT YOU AND THE REALM OF STUPIDITY UNTIL THIS STRENUOUS BATTLE IS OVER!

BARBARA SPEAKING

I WILL COMBAT SATAN, THE JACKASS, WITH THE MIGHT THAT COMES FROM ALMIGHTY GOD, THE VICTORIOUS CREATOR OF THE DEFEATED JACKASS. ALLELUIA! I HAVE FOUGHT SATAN, THE JACKASS FOR MANY YEARS. I HAVE FOUGHT SATAN, THE JACKASS, FOR THE SOUL OF ARCHBISHOP CRAIG, OUR ETERNAL BELOVED ONE! I HAVE FOUGHT THE PRESENCE OF SATAN, THE DEFEATED JACKASS, FOR THE ETERNAL SOUL OF LA TOYA, MY VICTORIOUS DAUGHTER! I HAVE FOUGHT SATAN, THE LOWLY JACKASS, FOR THE BELOVED ETERNAL SOUL OF AMYA, GOD'S LITTLE VICTORIOUS HELPER! I HAVE FOUGHT THE ENTITY, SATAN, THE JACKASS, FOR THE BELOVED SOUL OF PERRY, GOD'S WORTHY SON! I HAVE FOUGHT SATAN, THE JACKASS, FOR THE SOULS OF GOD'S CALLED AND CHOSEN ONES! I HAVE FOUGHT THE DOOMED ENTITY (SATAN, THE JACKASS) FOR THE BELOVED SOUL OF GOD'S CHOSEN SON (CRAIG). I HAVE BATTLED THE DEFEATED JACKASS OVER NINETEEN YEARS, FOR THE SOUL OF MY GOD ORDERED SPOUSE AND FELLOW WARRIOR (CRAIG).

BARBARA SPEAKING TO CRAIG

LET US BATTLE THE DEFEATED JACKASS TOGETHER, O WELL-LOVED ONE. LET YOU AND I DEFEAT HIM WITH GOD'S HOLY WEAPON OF AUTHENTIC LOVE AND PERSEVERANCE. FOR OUR GREAT AND HOLY GOD HAS SHOWERED US WITH THE GIFT OF HIS MIGHT, SO THAT WE MAY BECOME VICTORIOUS OVER SATAN, THE DEFEATED JACKASS, AND HIS DOOMED UNHOLY ANGELS AND FOLLOWERS.

BARBARA SPEAKING

LET HEAVEN AND EARTH RING WITH SHOUTS OF JOY AND LAUGHTER AS WE WITNESS THE DEFEAT OF SATAN, THE WORLD'S GREATEST JACKASS! *ALLELUIA!*
JUNE 17, 2015 BY: BARBARA ANN MARY MACK
SENT WED, JUN 17, 2015 12:19 PM-READ WED 6/17/2015 2:18 PM

HI, DEAR ARCHBISHOP CRAIG! I PRAY THAT YOUR DAY GOES VERY WELL FOR YOU. I WAS UP LATE LAST NIGHT AND EARLY THIS MORNING, FOCUSING ON THE TRAGEDY THAT TOOK PLACE IN CHARLESTON, SC YESTERDAY. AS I STATED PREVIOUSLY, AND IN ACCORDANCE WITH THE HOLY BIBLE, THE WORKS OF SATAN ARE VERY VISIBLE IN THE WORLD TODAY. ONLY SATAN AND HIS REALM OF EVIL COULD PERFORM AN ACT SUCH AS WAS SEEN AND HEARD OF AT THE

144

AME CHURCH. MY THOUGHT IS, AS I WAS WATCHING THE NEWS ON THE INTERNET, I NOTICED THAT THERE WERE PASTORS AND OTHERS PRESENTING THE QUESTION "WHY?" TO GOD. THE ANSWER TO THEIR QUESTION IS OBVIOUS, AND IS WRITTEN IN THE BIBLE. SATAN, THE DEVIL, IS BEHIND AND IN FRONT OF EVERY EVIL ACT OR DEED. ONE DOESN'T NEED TO QUESTION GOD OR ANYONE ELSE. WE, THE BELIEVERS OF GOD'S HOLY WORDS, KNOW, OR SHOULD KNOW THE ANSWER TO EVERY ACT THAT OCCURS. OUR ONLY WEAPON AGAINST SATAN'S DEFEATED REALM, IS TO EXHIBIT GOD'S VERSION OF LOVE TOWARDS ONE ANOTHER IN THE MIDST OF TRAGEDIES. I AM NOT IMPLYING THAT WE SHOULD CONDONE SATAN AND HIS SERVANTS EVIL DEEDS, BUT WE SHOULD RECOGNIZE AND ADDRESS HIM INSTEAD OF QUESTIONING OUR GREAT AND HOLY GOD. THE SCRIPTURES PREPARE AND ENLIGHTEN US, SO THAT WE WOULD BE ABLE TO PROCEED IN A HOLY MANNER IN THE MIDST OF TRAGIC TIMES. I THANK YOU, O LORD, FOR PREPARING YOUR CHILDREN FOR THIS PERIOD OF TIME, FOR YOUR WORDS ARE HOLY AND TRUTH. IN THE MIDST OF TRAGEDIES, I WILL PRAISE YOU, MY GOD! *ALLELUIA!!!*
SENT THU, JUN 18, 2015 7:12 PM-READ THU 6/18/2015 8:13 PM

I NEED YOU

BARBARA SPEAKING TO ALMIGHTY GOD

THROUGHOUT THE DAY, THROUGHOUT THE GLORIOUS NIGHT,
I NEED YOU, O LORD, WITHIN MY PRIVILEGED AND BLESSED SIGHT.
I NEED YOUR HOLY PRESENCE TO SURROUND ME EVERY DAY.
I NEED YOU, DEAR LORD, TO ENCOMPASS MY BLESSED BEING WHEN I PRAY.
I NEED YOUR HOLY PRESENCE TO COMFORT ME.
I NEED THE WELCOMED ESSENCE OF GOD, THE HOLY TRINITY.
I NEED GOD, THE FATHER, WHO DWELLS WITHIN.
I NEED JESUS, MY LIFETIME HOLY FRIEND.
I NEED THE PRESENCE OF GOD'S HOLY SPIRIT.
WHISPER YOUR SACRED WORDS, MY GOD, SO THAT I MAY HEAR IT!
I NEED THE GIFT OF YOUR ETERNAL LOVE.
I NEED MY GOD, WHOSE RESIDENCE IS HEAVEN ABOVE.
COME TO ME, O LORD, WHEN I NEED ONLY YOU.
COME TO ME, O GOD, FOR YOU ARE HOLY, ETERNAL AND TRUE!
JUNE 17, 2015 BY: BARBARA ANN MARY MACK
SENT THU, JUN 18, 2015 7:12 PM-READ THU 6/18/2015 8:13 PM

BUON GIORNO ARCHBISHOP CRAIG! COME STA OGGI AMORE? BELOW IS TODAY'S PASSAGES FOR YOU. CIAO! BELLA BARBIE

I WILL WEEP AS I ENTER THE WORLD AGAIN.

BARBARA SPEAKING TO ALMIGHTY GOD

OUT OF OBEDIENCE TO MY HOLY SPOUSE AND GOD, I WILL ENTER THE WORLD AGAIN, AS I TAKE THE HAND OF YOUR WORTHY CHOSEN SON (CRAIG). I WILL WEEP, MY LORD, AS I HUMBLY SUBMIT TO YOUR GREAT AND HOLY DESIRE OF LOVE. MY LORD, MY GOD, I WILL WEEP AS I ENTER THE WORLD AGAIN. FOR YOU HAVE SHELTERED ME FROM THE EVILS THAT FLOW THROUGH THIS WORLD OF NOTHINGNESS. YOU HAVE SHELTERED ME FROM THIS WORLD THAT PRODUCES AND PROMOTES UNHOLY THINGS AND PEOPLE. YOU HAVE SHELTERED ME FROM THE WORLD THAT ELEVATES THOSE WHO DO AND CONDONE THE EVIL DEEDS OF SATAN. YOU HAVE SHELTERED ME FROM THOSE WHO DESIRE IS TO HARM ME. YOU HAVE SHELTERED ME FROM THOSE WHO TRY TO CONVINCE ME TO FOLLOW THE BELIEFS AND TEACHINGS OF SATAN, OUR ENEMY. MY LORD, MY GOD, I WILL HOLD ON TO YOUR HOLY ESSENCE AS I ENTER THIS WORLD AGAIN, MY LORD, I WILL NEVER LEAVE THE ESSENCE (ALMIGHTY GOD) THAT FORMED ME FROM HIS HOLY ETERNAL ESSENCE.

ALMIGHTY GOD SPEAKING TO BARBARA

MY DAUGHTER, MY HOLY SPOUSE, I WILL NEVER LEAVE YOU. I WILL NEVER LEAVE YOU IN THE MIDST OF THIS WORLD OF NOTHINGNESS. I WILL NEVER ABANDON THE LOVE (BARBARA) THAT I FORMED FROM THE DEPTH OF MY HOLY ETERNAL ESSENCE OF LOVE. I WILL NEVER ABANDON MY FAITHFUL QUEEN AND BRIDE. I WILL NEVER ABANDON THE ONLY FAITHFUL LOVE THAT SITS ON MY HOLY THRONE WITH ME AND MY HEAVENLY HOSTS. MY DAUGHTER, MY LOVE, I WILL NEVER LEAVE YOU! TAKE MY SON'S (CRAIG) HAND, MY DAUGHTER, FOR I HAVE FOUND HIM WORTHY OF US. I HAVE FOUND HIM WORTHY TO SHARE MY QUEEN OF LOVE (BARBARA) WITH. TAKE HIS BLESSED AND BELOVED HAND, MY DAUGHTER, FOR HE TOO, HAS ENTERED THIS WORLD AGAIN! WEEP NO MORE, MY CHILDREN (CRAIG AND BARBARA), FOR YOU HAVE NOW ENTERED MY REALM OF HOLINESS ON EARTH!
JUNE 17, 2015 BY: BARBARA ANN MARY MACK
SENT THU, JUN 18, 2015 7:12 PM-READ THU 6/18/2015 8:13 PM

HI DEAR ARCHBISHOP CRAIG! I CAN FINALLY TAKE A BREAK AND EAT DINNER. ENJOY THE REST OF YOUR DAY LOVE. GOD BLESS! BB

WEEPING THROUGHOUT THE DAY

BARBARA SPEAKING TO THE LORD

CAN YOU SEE THEM, MY LORD? CAN YOU SEE THE FLOWING TEARS THAT FALL DOWN MY ABUSED ESSENCE, MY LOVING HOLY SPOUSE? WATCH THEM FALL AS I SUBMIT TO MY ASSIGNMENT OF DIVINE LOVE. WATCH THEM FALL AS I SIT IN THE MIDST OF MY PARADISE ON EARTH. WATCH THEM FALL AS I SIT WITHIN THE REALM OF SECLUSION. WATCH THEM FALL AS I WEEP IN YOUR HOLY PRESENCE THROUGHOUT THE DAY. WATCH THEM, MY LORD. WATCH THE TEARS THAT FALL FROM YOUR ABUSED SPOUSE AND MESSENGER OF HOLY LOVE. WATCH THEM FLOW, MY LORD, FOR THEY ARE MANY! FOLLOW MY FLOWING TEARS AS THEY TRY TO HIDE FROM THOSE WHO HAVE CAUSED THEIR PRESENCE. FOLLOW MY FALLING TEARS THAT FLOW IN THE DIRECTION OF THEIR COMFORTING GOD. FOLLOW MY FLOWING TEARS AS THEY TRY TO ESCAPE THE INJUSTICE THAT ROAMS THIS EARTH. FOLLOW THE TEARS THAT STAY AWAKE THROUGHOUT THE STORMY NIGHTS. FOLLOW THE TEARS THAT CLIMB THE SPIRITUAL LADDER TO DIVINE PEACE AND TRANQUILITY. FOLLOW THEM, MY LORD, FOR THEY ARE MANY!
JUNE 17, 2015 BY: BARBARA ANN MARY MACK
SENT FRI, JUN 19, 2015 6:10 PM-READ FRI 6/19/2015 10:22 PM

GREETINGS DEAR ONE! COME STA? BELOW ARE TODAY'S PASSAGES FOR YOU. TOODLES! BB

TO THOSE WHO RECOGNIZE ME, *SAYS THE LORD*

I WILL RECOGNIZE YOU IN THE PRESENCE OF ALL THAT IS GOOD AND HOLY. I WILL EXHIBIT MY ALLEGIANCE TO YOU. I WILL SHARE MY SUPPER OF PLENTY WITH YOU. I WILL EXHIBIT MY COMMITMENT AND LOVE FOR YOU. I WILL WALK WITH YOU THROUGHOUT EACH DAY. I WILL HONOR YOU PRAYERS OF HOPE. I WILL HEAR YOU WHEN YOU CRY OUT TO ME IN THE MIDST OF

YOUR HARDSHIPS AND PAIN. I WILL COMFORT YOU WHEN YOU ARE LONELY. I WILL FEED YOU WITH MY BREAD OF LIFE. I WILL NOURISH YOU WITH EVERLASTING FOOD THAT DESCENDS UPON THOSE WHO RECOGNIZE MY POSITION AS LORD AND GOD. THOSE WHO RECOGNIZE ME, I WILL BE THEIR PROVIDER WHEN THEY ARE IN NEED.

THOSE WHO RECOGNIZE ME, I WILL COMBAT THE GATES OF HELL FOR THEIR ETERNAL SOULS. THOSE WHO RECOGNIZE ME, WILL SIT WITH ME THROUGHOUT ETERNITY!!!

JUNE 19, 2015 BY: BARBARA ANN MARY MACK

FOLLOW MY DRIPPING BLOOD, FOR IT WILL LEAD YOU THROUGH THE GATES OF HEAVENL BLISS, *SAYS THE LORD*

ALMIGHTY GOD SPEAKING

MY CHILDREN, FOLLOW MY LIFE SAVING BLOOD AS IT LEADS YOU TO MY MIGHTY THRONE ABOVE. FOLLOW THE SACRED FOOD (CHRIST'S BLOOD) THAT WILL SUSTAIN YOU AS YOU TRAVEL IN THE DIRECTION OF ETERNAL BLISS ABOVE. FOLLOW THE NOURISHMENT (CHRIST'S BLOOD) THAT FLOWS FROM MY SACRED WOUNDS OF LOVE. FOLLOW THE PATH THAT WILL TAKE YOU TO THE PLACE WHERE I LAY MY HEAD TO REST. FOLLOW THE PATH THAT IS COVERED WITH MY LIFE SAVING BLOOD. IT WILL LEAD YOU TO THE PLACE THAT FULFILLS ALL OF YOUR HOLY DESIRES. IT WILL LEAD YOU TO THE REALM THAT RELEASED THE FATHER'S ONLY BEGOTTEN SON. IT WILL LEAD YOU TO THE REALM THAT HOUSES GOD, THE HOLY TRINITY. MY CHILDREN, FOLLOW MY SACRED BLOOD AS IT DRIPS FROM THE WOUNDS THAT COVERED MY SACRIFICIAL BODY OF DIVINE LOVE. FOLLOW THE DRIPPING BLOOD THAT PIERCES THIS REALM (EARTH) OF NEED. FOLLOW THE DRIPPING BLOOD THAT HAS PENETRATED THE REALM OF EVIL THAT WAS UNLEASHED UPON MY VULNERABLE CHILDREN. FOLLOW THE DRIPPING BLOOD THAT HAS DEFEATED THE GATES OF HELL! MY CHILDREN, FOLLOW MY SACRED WOUNDS TODAY, FOR THEY WILL LEAD YOU TO THE REALM OF PURIFICATION AND HOLINESS.

JUNE 20, 2015 BY: BARBARA ANN MARY MACK

SENT SAT, JUN 20, 2015 7:09 PM-READ SAT 6/20/2015 8:04 PM

ENJOY YOUR HEAVEN SENT DAY LOVE! *AMORE, BELLA BARBARA*

IN THE MIDST OF THIS TRAGIC PERIOD OF TIME

BARBARA SPEAKING

IN THE MIDST OF THIS TRAGIC PERIOD OF TIME, I WILL LIFT MY HANDS AND SPIRIT IN CONTINUOUS PRAISE, GLORY, AND HONOR, UNTO YOU, FOR YOU ARE VERY GOOD, O LORD! IN THE MIDST OF THIS FORETOLD PERIOD OF TRAGEDY, I WILL SING SONGS OF PRAISE UNTO YOU, O MERCIFUL GOD, FOR YOU HAVE PREPARED US FOR THE COMING OF THIS DEVASTATING PERIOD. THROUGH THE HOLY BIBLE, YOUR INFALLIBLE WORD, YOU HAVE REVEALED TO THOSE WHO BELIEVE, THE COMING OF THIS PERIOD OF TRAGEDIES. I AM TRULY GRATEFUL, MY GOD, FOR YOU HAVE REVEALED TO YOUR HUMBLED BRIDE AND MESSENGER, THE SOURCE (SATAN) OF THIS PERIOD OF HARDSHIP THAT HAS TAKEN CAPTIVE THE WORLD. I WILL DANCE AROUND YOUR SPIRITUAL THRONE AS I GIVE YOU CONTINUOUS PRAISE. I WILL LIFT YOUR HOLY ESSENCE IN PRAISE AS I BOW IN THE PRESENCE OF YOUR GRACE AND MERCY. YOU, O HOLY GOD, HAVE ENLIGHTENED US THROUGH THE TEACHINGS IN THE HOLY BIBLE. I THANK YOU, MY GOD, FOR SHARING YOUR WORDS OF PREPARATION AND WARNING, CONCERNING THIS PERIOD OF TRAGIC TIMES.

ALMIGHTY GOD SPEAKING

LOOK UP TO ME, YOUR ONLY PLACE OF REFUGE AND HOPE, DURING THIS PERIOD OF TRAGIC TIMES, MY CHILDREN. FOR YOU ARE ALL SUSCEPTIBLE TO SATAN'S UNHOLY VENGEANCE AND ACTS OF VIOLENCE. SATAN BLAMES US (ALMIGHTY GOD AND HUMAN BEINGS) FOR HIS LOWLY DEFEATED POSITION. THEREFORE, HE SEEKS, WHAT HE REFERS TO AS REVENGE, TOWARDS GOD'S GREAT CREATION (HUMAN BEINGS). BUT HE WILL LOSE, FOR HE IS THE BIGGEST AND EVERLASTING LOSER! COME TO MY AID, MY CHILDREN! SEEK YOUR ONLY REALM OF HOPE (ALMIGHTY GOD) DURING THIS TRAGIC PERIOD OF TIME!
JUNE 20, 2015 BY: BARBARA ANN MARY MACK

SENT SAT, JUN 20, 2015 7:09 PM-READ SAT 6/20/2015 8:04 PM

THIS REALM OF EVIL IS OUT OF MAN'S HANDS-THE CLERGY NEEDS TO ADDRESS THE SOURCE (SATAN) OF EVIL THAT PERMEATES THE WORLD TODAY, *SAYS THE LORD.*

ALMIGHTY GOD SPEAKING
TO THE CLERGY

TELL THEM, O CLERGY! WARN THEM, O SHEPHERDS OF MY VULNERABLE AND SUSCEPTIBLE SHEEP! LET THE CONGREGATION KNOW THE SOURCE (SATAN) OF THESE EVIL TIMES! TELL THEM, O PASTORS! TELL THEM, O DEACONS! WARN THEM OF THE WRATH THAT PROCEEDS FROM THE DEFEATED AND ANGRY REALM OF SATAN, THE ETERNAL RESIDENT OF HELL! WARN THEM, MY SONS (CLERGY)! WARN THEM, O HEAVEN SENT BRIDE AND MESSENGER (BARBARA) OF MINE! HELP MY CHILDREN! HELP MY VULNERABLE FLOCK TODAY! FOR THEY ARE IN GREAT DANGER! ENLIGHTEN THEM, O CALLED SHEPHERDS OF MINE! WARN THEM OF SATAN'S RUTHLESS GOAL AND DESIRE! LEAD THEM TO MY REALM OF HOLINESS, THEIR ONLY PLACE OF SECURITY AND PEACE. LEAD THEM, O SHEPHERDS OF MINE! LEAD THEM TO ME! FOR THE REALM OF DOOM SEEKS THEIR VULNERABLE SOULS TODAY. THE REALM OF DESTRUCTION NEVER SLEEPS, O CLERGY! THE REALM OF DOOM NEVER TAKES BREAKS! BEWARE, O CLERGY! BEWARE OF SATAN'S REALM OF DESTRUCTION THAT ROAMS THROUGH EARTH'S VULNERABLE REALM TODAY. FOR HE (SATAN) IS VERY CUNNING AND DANGEROUS! MAKE SURE THAT YOUR ARMORS (KNOWLEDGE AND PRACTICE OF GOD'S HOLY WORD) ARE SECURED! MAKE SURE THAT YOU ARE WALKING HAND IN HAND WITH THE REALM THAT HOUSES HOLINESS HIMSELF. FOR I AM YOUR ONLY HOPE TODAY! *THIS, SAYS THE LORD,* YOUR ONLY PLACE OF REFUGE TODAY!!!

JUNE 20, 2015 BY: BARBARA ANN MARY MACK

SENT SUN, JUN 21, 2015 2:59 PM-READ SUN 6/21/2015 3:06 PM

THANK YOU ARCHBISHOP CRAIG FOR THE WONDERFULLY BLESSED GOSPEL READING AND HOMILY. I REALLY LOVED THE WAY YOU EXPLAINED THE GOSPEL READING IN A WAY THAT

ALL PRESENT APPRECIATED AND UNDERSTOOD ITS MEANING. I LOVED YOUR SERMON AS WELL. IT WAS VERY MOVING. I DID SHED AN INNER TEAR. THE INTEGRITY THAT YOU EXHIBITED CONVEYED YOUR BELIEF, TRUST, AND LOVE FOR ALMIGHTY GOD AND YOUR CALLING AS HIS CHOSEN PRIEST (SHEPHERD). I AM SOOOOOOOO VERY PROUD TO KNOW AND RESPECT YOU. I AM HONORED THAT ALMIGHTY GOD HAS GRACED MY FAMILY AND ME WITH THE GIFT OF BEING A PART OF YOUR CONGREGATION OF HOLY LOVE. KEEP UP THE GOOD WORK, O BELOVED AND BLESSED ONE, FOR OUR HEAVENLY FATHER IS WELL PLEASED!!! BELOW IS TODAY'S PASSAGE FOR YOU. *LOVE YOU ALWAYS, GRATEFUL BARBARA*

MANY PRIESTS ARE CALLED BY THE WORLD, BUT FEW ARE CHOSEN BY ALMIGHTY GOD HIMSELF

EXHIBIT MY VERSION OF HOLINESS, O CHOSEN SHEPHERDS OF MINE.
EXHIBIT WHAT I TEACH YOU THROUGHOUT EACH DAY. EXHIBIT MY VERSION OF HOLINESS, AS YOU GUIDE MY VULNERABLE FLOCK IN THE DIRECTION OF MY ETERNAL GLORY, AND SPIRITUAL FAME. FOR I HAVE SELECTED MY FEW PRIESTS, MY WORTHY SHEPHERDS.

ALMIGHTY GOD SPEAKING TO ARCHBISHOP CRAIG

DELIVER MY WORDS OF LOVE AND COMFORT TO MY NEEDY FLOCK, O CHOSEN SHEPHERD OF MINE. SPEAK MY HOLY WORDS THAT FLOW THROUGH THE BEING OF MY BLESSED CHOSEN SON. TELL THEM ALL THAT I REVEAL TO YOU, O WORTHY PRECIOUS SON OF MINE. EXHIBIT THE DIVINE LOVE THAT I PLACED WITHIN YOUR REALM OF COMPASSION AND EMPATHY. REVEAL THE ALLEGIANCE AND LOVE THAT YOU HAVE FOR YOUR FAITHFUL ORIGIN AND GOD, AS YOU SPEAK THE WORDS THAT I REVEAL TO YOU. LET THOSE WHO SIT IN MY PEWS WITNESS THE

INTEGRITY OF YOUR LOVE FOR ME AND MY GREAT CREATION (HUMAN BEINGS). LET THOSE WHO LISTEN TO YOUR WORDS OF COMFORT, WHICH DESCEND FROM MY THRONE ABOVE, REJOICE WITH YOU IN MY HOLY PRESENCE. COME, O BELOVED SON OF MINE! LET YOU AND I SHOW YOUR (OUR) CONGREGATION THE GIFT OF OUR SINCERE LOVE AND MERCY. FOR THEY DESIRE TO SEE AND HEAR ME TODAY! LET THEM WITNESS MY HOLY PRESENCE THROUGH YOU, O WORTHY AND BLESSED SON OF MINE!

JUNE 21, 2015 BY: BARBARA ANN MARY MACK

SENT SUN, JUN 21, 2015 3:41 PM-READ SUN 6/21/2015 4:35 PM

GREETINGS DEAR ONE! WHILE WORKING ON MY BOOK "THE PRESENT TESTAMENT VOLUME NINE", I RAN ACROSS A PICTURE OF PEOPLE, MOSTLY WOMEN, WHO HELD SIGNS THAT READ "KEEP ABORTION LEGAL." I READ THE ARTICLE THAT WAS BELOW THE PICTURE, AND IT REALLY DISTURBED ME. HOW CAN ANYONE SUPPORT OR CONDONE THE KILLING OF INNOCENT LIVES? ALMIGHTY GOD WILL NOT CONDONE THAT DREADFUL ACT AGAINST HIS VULNERABLE CHILDREN. DEAR ONE, LET YOU AND I CONTINUE PRAYING FOR THE INNOCENT ONES.

AMORE, BELLA BARBARA

WHAT MANKIND CONDONES AND SUPPORTS, ALMIGHTY GOD SENDS TO HELL, THE PERMANENT RESIDENCE OF THOSE WHO COMMIT UNHOLY ACTS

ALMIGHTY GOD SPEAKING

DO NOT DECEIVE YOURSELVES, MY CHILDREN. DO NOT LET THE REALM OF DECEIT CAPTURE YOUR SOUL. FOR EVERYONE WHO COMMITS UNHOLY ACTS WILL BE SENT TO THE REALM (HELL) THAT WELCOMES THEM. UNDERSTAND MY VERSION OF OBEDIENCE AND JUSTICE, MY CHILDREN. UNDERSTAND MY VERSION OF MERCY AND PITY, FOR I WILL NOT HAVE MERCY OR PITY ON THOSE WHO TURN THEIR BACKS ON MY REALM OF HOLINESS. OUT OF HOLINESS AND PURE LOVE I CREATED YOU, MY CHILDREN. WHAT DO I ASK OF YOU, OTHER THAN TO HONOR YOUR CREATOR AND GOD ALL THE DAYS OF YOUR LIFE. I HAVE GIVEN YOU EVERYTHING THAT YOU NEED IN ORDER TO SURVIVE IN THIS WORLD OF PLENTY, AND YOU DO NOT ACKNOWLEDGE MY HOLY PRESENCE IN YOUR MIDST TODAY. MY CHILDREN, FOLLOW MY HOLY WAY SO THAT SATAN, OUR ENEMY, WILL FLEE FROM YOU. FOR I DESIRE THAT YOU LIVE WITH ME IN SWEET PARADISE FOREVER!

JUNE 22, 2015 BY: BARBARA ANN MARY MACK

BARBARA SPEAKING

ENJOY THIS DAY LOVE! MY BOOK "THE PRESENT TESTAMENT VOLUME THREE" FINALLY ARRIVED TODAY. YIPPIEEEEEE! I AM SOOOOOOOOOO EXCITED! THE BOOK CONSULTANT HAD TO MAKE A FEW CHANGES BECAUSE MY BOOK CONTAINS ABOUT THREE HUNDRED PAGES THAT EXCEED THEIR NORMAL PAGE COUNT. I WAS WILLING TO REMOVE THE ADDITIONAL PAGES, BUT THEY TOLD ME THAT THEY WOULD MAKE THINGS WORK WITH MY ORIGINAL MANUSCRIPT. IT IS SO WEIRD TO SEE A BOOK THAT SIZE. I PRESUME THAT THE LORD DID NOT WANT ANY WORDS OMITTED FROM MY ORIGINAL MANUSCRIPT. THE LORD HAS SO MUCH TO SHARE WITH US TODAY. I AM IN THE MIDST OF VOLUME NINE OF "THE PRESENT TESTAMENT". I AM ON PAGE 433. THIS BOOK PRETTY MUCH CONSISTS OF DAILY MESSAGES AND SAYINGS FROM THE LORD. HE IS SO AWESOME! LET YOU AND I GIVE HIM CONTINUOUS PRAISE AS ONE UNIFIED ESSENCE OF LOVE. BELOW IS TODAY'S PASSAGE.

AMORE, BEAUTIFUL GRATEFUL BARBARA

MY PURPOSE IS TO APPROACH, ATTACK, AND DEFEAT THE REALM (SATAN) THAT GUISES-I KNOW WHO YOU ARE, O REALM OF EVIL

BARBARA SPEAKING TO SATAN AND HIS DEFEATED REALM OF EVIL

I WAS SENT TO COMBAT THE REALM THAT DESIRES ETERNAL HARM TO GOD'S LOVED ONES. I KNOW WHO YOU ARE! I CAN SEE THROUGH YOUR GUISE, LIES, AND FALSITY. I KNOW WHO YOU ARE, O REALM THAT WILL BE DEFEATED BY THE PRESENCE OF GOD, MY HOLY SPOUSE AND SOURCE OF SPIRITUAL COURAGE AND PERSEVERANCE. I KNOW WHO YOU ARE, O DEFEATED REALM THAT HAS SLITHERED INTO THE LIFE OF OUR (THE LORD AND BARBARA) BELOVED ONE. I RECOGNIZE YOUR STENCH AND YOUR GUISE. I RECOGNIZE YOUR FOUL ODOR. YOU CANNOT HIDE FROM GOD'S MESSENGER (BARBARA) OF VICTORY AND DEFEAT!

YOU CANNOT HIDE FROM GOD'S CHOSEN WIFE (BARBARA), FOR I HAVE BEEN SENT BY ALMIGHTY GOD, MY HOLY SPOUSE, TO TERMINATE YOUR REALM OF DECEIT AND DESTRUCTION IN THE PRESENCE OF THIS VULNERABLE GENERATION. LET THE HOLY GATES TO SWEET PARADISE JOIN ME IN PRAISE, AS I FULFILL MY DIVINE ASSIGNMENT ON EARTH. LET ALMIGHTY GOD'S ANGELS AND SAINTS CLAP THEIR HANDS IN PRAISE, AS I FULFILL MY DIVINE ASSIGNMENT OF LOVE. FOR I HAVE BEEN SENT, TO REVEAL YOUR UNWANTED PRESENCE TO THE WORLD. I HAVE BEEN SENT TO EXPOSE YOUR DIRTY DEEDS! YOUR GUISE HAS BEEN UNVEILED, O LOWLY REALM OF DESTRUCTION AND AGONY (SATAN)!

JUNE 24, 2015 BY: BARBARA ANN MARY MACK

SENT WED, JUN 24, 2015 4:41 PM-READ WED 6/24/2015 5:25 PM

MY SWEET LIMITATIONS PLACE ME IN THE REALM OF HUMILITY AND OBEDIENCE UNTO THE LORD

BARBARA SPEAKING TO THE REALM OF LIMITATIONS

LIMITATIONS, O SWEET LIMITATIONS, OH HOW YOU HAVE HUMBLED ME. YOU HAVE PLACED ME IN THE REALM OF OBEDIENCE AND SUBMISSION UNTO THE HOLY WILL OF MY CREATOR AND GOD. YOU HAVE TAUGHT ME THE IMPORTANCE OF BEING STILL IN THE MIDST OF CHAOS AND CONFUSION. O SWEET LIMITATIONS, IN THE MIDST OF PAIN, I BOW IN THE PRESENCE OF GOD, THE BELOVED AND ETERNAL SOURCE OF MY PHYSICAL AND SPIRITUAL LIMITATIONS. MY LIMITATIONS, PHYSICAL AND SPIRITUAL, PLACE ME IN THE REALM THAT BOWS UNTO MY SACRED GOD AND HOLY SPOUSE. MY LIMITATIONS OPEN THE DOOR TO TEMPERANCE AND MEEKNESS IN THE PRESENCE OF THE LORD AND THE WORLD.

BARBARA SPEAKING TO THE LORD

I BLESS YOU, O LORD, FOR GRACING ME WITH THE REALM OF SWEET LIMITATIONS, SO THAT I MAY BE AWARE OF YOUR HOLY PRESENCE AND POWER AT ALL TIMES. I BLESS YOU, FOR THE GIFT OF EXPERIENCING THE REALM (SWEET LIMITATIONS) THAT KEEPS ME IN THE PLACE WHERE MY BEING IS SHELTERED FROM THE WORLD. MY LIMITATIONS KEEP ME AWARE OF MY OBLIGATIONS TO YOUR REALM OF SUBMISSION AND GRATITUDE. I THANK YOU, O LORD, FOR PLACING ME IN THE REALM THAT EXHIBITS THE DUTIES OF YOUR CHOSEN BRIDE AND QUEEN (BARBARA).

JUNE 24, 2015 BY: BARBARA ANN MARY MACK

SENT WED, JUN 24, 2015 9:36 PM-READ WED 6/24/2015 11:22 PM

I WILL HIDE WITHIN THE REALM THAT HOUSES YOU, MY LORD

BARBARA SPEAKING TO GOD, HER PLACE OF REFUGE

MY LORD, SO MANY TRAGEDIES. SO MANY FATALITIES. SO MUCH DISPLAY OF HARDSHIP IN THE WORLD TODAY. WHERE CAN I HIDE FROM THE EVILS THAT FALL UPON THIS REALM OF TIME? WHERE CAN I HIDE FROM THE PRESENCE OF SATAN AND HIS UNHOLY ANGELS? HOW CAN I ESCAPE THE HORRORS THAT FLOW THROUGH THE STREETS THAT I WALK THROUGH? HELP ME, O LORD! HELP ME ESCAPE THE SUFFERINGS AND TRAGEDIES THAT HAVE ENGULFED THIS PERIOD OF TIME. LET ME HIDE WITHIN THE REALM (ALMIGHTY GOD) THAT HOUSES PURE HOLINESS AND PEACE. LET ME HIDE WITHIN THE HOLY GATES THAT SURROUND GOD, THE BLESSED TRINITY. LET ME HIDE WITHIN THE REALM (ALMIGHTY GOD) THAT COMFORTS HIS CHILDREN IN THE MIDST OF THIS TRAGIC PERIOD OF TIME. LET ME HIDE WITHIN THE ARMS OF GOD, MY HOLY SAVIOR AND SPOUSE. COMFORT AND SHELTER ME, O HOLY WALLS (ALMIGHTY GOD) THAT KEEP THE REALM OF EVIL AWAY FROM ME. SHELTER ME FROM THE STORMS THAT HAVE ROCKED THE EARTH. KEEP ME SAFE WITHIN THE HOLY ARMS THAT REACH OUT TO HIS NEEDY CHILDREN THROUGHOUT THE DAY.

JUNE 23, 2015 BY: BARBARA ANN MARY MACK

SENT WED, JUN 24, 2015 9:36 PM-READ WED 6/24/2015 11:22 PM

HAVE HOLY FUN TODAY LOVE! BELOW IS TODAY'S PASSAGE FOR YOU. *AMORE, BELLA BARBIE*

YOUR HOLY FETTERS HAVE CAPTURED ME, O HOLY SPOUSE AND GOD OF MINE

BARBARA SPEAKING TO ALMIGHTY GOD

YOUR DIVINE LOVE HAS ME CHAINED AND BOUND, O HOLY SPOUSE OF MINE. I WILL CLING TO THE SPIRITUAL FETTERS THAT KEEP ME CHAINED TO MY HOLY SPOUSE AND GOD. I WILL CLING TO THE FETTERS THAT BIND OUR SACRED UNION, O HOLY GOD AND SPOUSE OF MINE. I WILL CLING TO THE LOVE THAT ENCOMPASSES ME AS I LOOK UP TO ALMIGHTY GOD, THE SOURCE OF MY HAPPINESS AND CONTENTMENT. MY LORD, THE HOLY FETTERS THAT KEEP ME CLOSE TO YOU HAVE CAPTURED MY INVITED ESSENCE OF HOLY LOVE. I WILL REST MY HEAD ON THE HOLY BREAST OF LOVE (ALMIGHTY GOD) THAT FORMED ME NOT SO LONG AGO. I WILL CLING TO THE SWEET CHAINS THAT SURROUND MY BLESSED BEING THROUGHOUT THE DAY. I WILL CLING TO THE SPIRITUAL CHAINS THAT RELEASE THE GLORY OF MY FAITHFUL GOD AND FATHER. I WILL CLING TO THE HOLINESS THAT EMITS FROM THE FETTERS THAT KEEP ME IN THE REALM OF DIVINE SECURITY AND PEACE. LET US REJOICE AS ONE, O LORD, AS I DANCE IN THE MIDST OF THE SPIRITUAL FETTERS, AS THEY REVEAL OUR CLOSENESS AND LOVE. YOUR LOVE HAS ME CHAINED AND BOUND TO YOUR ETERNAL REALM OF SWEET DIVINITY AND HEAVENLY BLISS. MY LORD, THERE IS NO GREATER LOVE THAN OURS!

JUNE 23, 2015 BY: BARBARA ANN MARY MACK
SENT WED, JUN 24, 2015 9:36 PM-READ WED 6/24/2015 11:22 PM

ALL SEEING: ALMIGHTY: ALL POWERFUL AND JUST GOD-MY JUSTICE, CAN YOU HANDLE IT, MY CHILDREN?

ALMIGHTY GOD SPEAKING

I SEE IT ALL, MY CHILDREN! I SEE EVERYTHING THAT YOU DO, AND I HEAR EVERYTHING THAT YOU SAY. WHAT MANKIND PARDONS, I WILL NOT. I HAVE WITNESSED THE UNSPEAKABLE THINGS THAT YOU HAVE DONE IN MY HOLY PRESENCE. ARE YOU PREPARED FOR MY VERSION OF JUSTICE? I DO NOT CONDONE THE DEMORALIZATION THAT IS INFLICTED UPON MY VULNERABLE CHILDREN OF ALL NATIONS. I WILL NOT TOLERATE THE INJUSTICE THAT FLOWS THROUGH THE STREETS OF THOSE WHO TOLERATE SATAN'S REALM. FOR THOSE FATHERS WHO DO NOT TAKE PROPER CARE OF THEIR CHILDREN, YOU WILL TASTE MY VERSION OF JUSTICE. FOR THOSE MOTHERS WHO PROCEED IN THE ABORTIONS OF THEIR UNWANTED BABIES, MY VULNERABLE LITTLE ONES, YOU WILL TASTE MY VERSION OF JUSTICE. TO THOSE WHO RAPE MY DAUGHTERS AND SONS, YOU WILL TASTE MY VERSION OF JUSTICE. TO THOSE WHO PERVERT MY VERSION, MY VERSION, MY HOLY VERSION OF MARRIAGE, YOU WILL TASTE MY VERSION OF JUSTICE! I WILL NOT CONFORM TO, OR CONDONE ANY FORM OF PERVERSION FROM THOSE WHOM I HAVE AUTHORITY OVER. I AM A JUST AND HOLY GOD! I COMMAND THAT THOSE WHO DESIRE TO PLEASE ME, MUST BE HOLY AS WELL. THERE ARE NO EXCEPTIONS TO MY COMMAND (HOLY WORD)! THERE ARE NO EXCEPTIONS TO MY VERSION OF JUSTICE! MY CHILDREN, UNDERSTAND MY VERSION OF JUSTICE! UNDERSTAND ME!
JUNE 23, 2015 BY: BARBARA ANN MARY MACK
SENT WED, JUN 24, 2015 9:36 PM-READ WED 6/24/2015 11:22 PM

THE REALM OF PURIFICATION HAS CAPTURED ME

BARBARA SPEAKING

I HAVE BATHED WITHIN THE REALM THAT PURIFIED MY NEEDY SOUL. I HAVE BATHED WITHIN THE REALM THAT SANCTIFIED ME NOT SO LONG AGO. I HAVE BATHED WITHIN THE LIVING WATERS THAT CLEANSED MY SOUL FROM ALL IMPURITIES. I HAVE BATHED WITHIN THE REALM THAT PERMEATED MY BEING WITH THE GIFT OF DIVINE LOVE AND HOPE. I HAVE BEEN CAPTURED BY THE REALM (ALMIGHTY GOD) THAT SITS ON HIS MIGHTY THRONE ABOVE. I HAVE BEEN CAPTURED BY THE ESSENCE (ALMIGHTY GOD) THAT MOVES THROUGH THIS REALM OF UNBELIEVABLE OCCURRENCES. I HAVE BEEN CAPTURED BY THE SOURCE (ALMIGHTY GOD) OF HOLY LOVE THAT PROTECTS ME IN THE MIDST OF HARDSHIP AND PAIN. YOU HAVE CAPTURED AND PURIFIED MY OBEDIENT SOUL, MY GOD, AS I LEAD YOUR VULNERABLE CHILDREN IN THE DIRECTION OF YOUR REALM OF PURIFICATION AND HOPE. I WILL BOW IN YOUR HOLY PRESENCE, AS I LEAD YOUR CALLED AND CHOSEN SONS AND DAUGHTER THROUGH THE GATES OF SWEET PARADISE ABOVE. FOR YOUR REALM OF PURIFICATION HAS CAPTURED ME!
JUNE 23, 2015 BY: BARBARA ANN MARY MACK
SENT WED, JUN 24, 2015 9:36 PM-READ WED 6/24/2015 11:22 PM

THY WILL BE DONE, MY LORD. I WILL FOLLOW YOUR HOLY WILL THROUGHOUT THE DAY. *ALLELUIA!!!*

BARBARA SPEAKING TO THE LORD

I WILL FOLLOW YOUR HOLY WILL AND WAY.
I WILL FOLLOW YOU, DEAR LORD, THROUGHOUT MY BLESSED DAY.
I WILL PROCLAIM MY COMMITMENT AND LOVE FOR YOU,

I WILL FOREVER SPEAK OF THE GOD WHO IS HOLY AND TRUE.

THE HOLY WILL BE DONE, MY LORD,

AS I COMMUNE WITH MY BROTHERS AND SISTERS ON ONE ACCORD.

WE WILL EXHIBIT THE GIFT OF OUR LOVE,

THAT IS CONSTANTLY SHOWN BY OUR GOD ABOVE.

I WILL ACKNOWLEDGE YOUR HOLY WILL,

AS I SIT QUIET AND STILL.

I WILL BE QUIET, SO THAT I MAY HEAR,

THE VOICE OF MY SAVIOR AND GOD WHO DOES CARE.

FOR HE, GOD, THE FATHER, TRULY CARES FOR ALL OF US,

AND HE EXPRESSED IT BY SENDING HIS PRECIOUS AND ONLY BEGOTTEN SON, JESUS.

I WILL LIFT UP YOUR HOLY WILL THROUGHOUT EACH DAY,

I WILL LIFT YOU UP, MY GOD, WHENEVER I PRAY.

THY WILL BE DONE, O PRECIOUS GOD OF MINE!

I WILL FOLLOW YOUR HOLY WILL, THROUGHOUT THE REALM OF TIME!

JUNE 22, 2015 BY: BARBARA ANN MARY MACK

SENT WED, JUN 24, 2015 9:36 PM-READ WED 6/24/2015 11:22 PM

BE NOT ANXIOUS FOR ANYTHING, *SAYS THE LORD*

ALMIGHTY GOD SPEAKING

DO NOT BE ANXIOUS FOR ANYTHING, MY CHILDREN, FOR I AM ALPHA, THE BEGINNING (FIRST), AND OMEGA, THE END (LAST). YOUR BEGINNING, AND YOUR END. DO NOT BE CONCERNED WITH ANYTHING, FOR I AM THE KEY THAT OPENS THE DOOR TO EVERYTHING! TRUST IN ME AT ALL TIMES, MY CHILDREN, FOR I AM! I AM THE SOURCE AND ORIGIN OF YOUR LIFE, AND I KNOW YOUR FINAL DAY ON EARTH. DO NOT BE ANXIOUS OVER THE THINGS THAT YOU DO NOT

HAVE, FOR I AM YOUR SOLE PROVIDER! WHAT YOU HAVE IS WHAT I WANT YOU TO POSSESS AT THIS TIME. TRUST MY JUDGMENT INSTEAD OF YOUR OWN, FOR I KNOW EVERYTHING AND EVERYBODY! FOLLOW MY HOLY WAY AND VOICE, FOR I WILL LEAD YOU TO THE THINGS THAT I KNOW ARE BEST FOR YOU. MY CHILDREN, DO NOT BE ANXIOUS OVER ANYTHING, FOR I WILL NEVER LEAVE YOU STRANDED OR WITHOUT HOPE.

JUNE 21, 2015 BY: BARBARA ANN MARY MACK

SENT WED, JUN 24, 2015 9:36 PM-READ WED 6/24/2015 11:22 PM

MORE VALUABLE THAN WORLDLY RICHES-MORE VALUABLE THAN SILVER AND GOLD

BARBARA SPEAKING

THE LORD PROVIDES EVERYTHING THAT I NEED, AND HE HONORS MOST OF MY DESIRES. YOU (CRAIG, LA TOYA AND AMYA) ARE MORE VALUABLE TO ME THAN ALL OF THE RICHES OF THIS PASSING WORLD. YOU ARE THE TREASURE THAT WAS BESTOWED UPON ME BY ALMIGHTY GOD HIMSELF. YOU ARE THE GIFT OF LIFE THAT I REST IN DAILY. YOU ARE THE REALM OF DIVINE LOVE THAT DESCENDED FROM HEAVEN'S HOLY GATES, IN MY WELCOMING MIDST. YOU ARE MY OVERFLOWING POT OF SPIRITUAL GOLD THAT KEEPS ME WARM AND SAFE THROUGHOUT EACH DAY. YOU, O WELL-LOVED TREASURE, ARE THE JOY THAT IGNITES ME WHENEVER I PRAY. YOU ARE THE SANCTIFIED PROMISE THAT DWELLS WITHIN ME WHEN I PRAY TO MY LIVING AND LOVING GOD AND FATHER. YOU ARE THE LOVE THAT MOTIVATES ME EACH DAY. YOU ARE MY PURPOSE FOR LIVING WITHIN THE MIDST OF SPIRITUAL NEED AND DIVINE EXCITEMENT. YOU ARE MY GOD SENT REALM OF HOPE AND JOY IN THE MIDST OF THESE OBSCURE TIMES. I SALUTE YOU, O TREASURE (CRAIG, LA TOYA AND AMYA), AS I BOW IN THE PRESENCE OF OUR CREATOR AND GOD. I SALUTE YOU, O WELL-LOVED ONES, IN THE PRESENCE OF DIVINE LOVE. I THANK YOU, O HOLY GOD, FOR MY TREASURE OF LOVE. I THANK YOU, DEAR LORD, FOR YOUR EXPRESSION OF DIVINE LOVE. *ALLELUIA!*

JUNE 22, 2015 BY: BARBARA ANN MARY MACK

SENT WED, JUN 24, 2015 9:36 PM-READ WED 6/24/2015 11:22 PM

VANITY AND INORDINATE SELF ADMIRATION HAVE NO ROOM IN GOD'S HOLY KINGDOM ON EARTH

BARBARA SPEAKING

MY BROTHERS AND SISTERS, THERE IS NO ROOM IN GOD'S HOLY KINGDOM FOR INORDINATE SELF-ADMIRATION OR EXALTATION, FOR IN THE EYES OF GOD, THE HOLY REALM OF LOVE, WE HAVE THE SAME ATTRIBUTES AND FLESHLY BEAUTY.

ALMIGHTY GOD SPEAKING

FLEE FROM ME, O VAIN ONES, FOR THERE IS NO ROOM IN MY HOUSE FOR THE ARROGANT AND PHYSICALLY ADMIRED ONES. FLEE FROM THE REALM THAT OFFERS SELF-GLORY, AND THE GLORY THAT IS GIVEN TO YOU BY THOSE WHO ARE HEADED FOR DESTRUCTION AND A RUDE AWAKENING-THE GATES OF ETERNAL HELL! GIVE GLORY AND HONOR TO THE ONLY ONE WHO IS WORTHY OF THIS, ALMIGHTY GOD!

JUNE 24, 2015 BY: BARBARA ANN MARY MACK

SENT WED, JUN 24, 2015 9:36 PM-READ WED 6/24/2015 11:22 PM

ENJOYING THE GIFT OF THIS BEAUTIFUL MORNING! BELOW IS GOD'S MESSAGE FOR EVERYONE. AMORE, BEAUTIFUL BARBARA

DO NOT PLAY GAMES WITH ME, *SAYS THE LORD!*

ALMIGHTY GOD SPEAKING

MY CHILDREN, DO NOT PLAY GAMES WITH ME, FOR I AM VERY SERIOUS! ARE YOU WITH ME? ARE YOU WITH ME, AS I FIGHT THE GATES OF HELL FOR YOU? OR, ARE YOU WORKING WITH SATAN, MY ENEMY? THERE IS NO IN BETWEEN! THERE ARE NO NEUTRAL GROUNDS! THIS BATTLE IS VERY SERIOUS, FOR IT DETERMINES YOUR FINAL DESTINATION! WHOM YOU DESIRE TO SPEND ETERNITY WITH IS DECIDED UPON BY YOUR ALLEGIANCE AND YOUR ACTS. MY CHILDREN, YOUR ACTS REVEAL WHOM YOU ARE LOYAL TO. YOUR ACTS REVEAL YOUR DESTINATION IN HEAVEN WITH ME, OR IN HELL WITH SATAN AND HIS DEFEATED REALM OF EVIL. I AM NOT PLAYING ANY GAMES, FOR THIS MATTER IS VERY CRUCIAL! FLEE FROM THE WORKS THAT WILL LEAD YOU TO SATAN'S PERMANENT RESIDENCE (HELL)! FLEE FROM THE UNGODLY ACTS THAT LEAD YOU AWAY FROM MY KINGDOMS OF HOLINESS! FLEE FROM THE REALM THAT PRODUCES UNFORGIVENESS, LUSTS, GREED, PREMARITAL SEX, SEXUAL DEVIATION-HOMOSEXUALITY SEXUAL PROMISCUITY, THOSE WHO PERFORM AND CONFORM TO ABORTION, THOSE WHO DO NOT RESPECT AND VALUE HUMAN LIFE, THE USE OF BAD AND INAPPROPRIATE LANGUAGE IN MY HOLY PRESENCE, FOR I AM EVERYWHERE, *SAYS THE LORD!* THE EXALTATION OF ANYONE OR THING AND INORDINATE SELF- AWARENESS). MY CHILDREN, FLEE FROM THE REALM THAT WILL DEFINITELY LEAD YOU THROUGH THE GATES OF ETERNAL HELL! THIS IS MY FINAL WARNING TO YOU! DO NOT IGNORE IT AS YOUR FOREFATHERS AND MOTHERS HAVE, FOR I AM NOT PLAYING GAMES!

JUNE 25, 2015 BY: BARBARA ANN MARY MACK

SENT THU, JUN 25, 2015 11:11 AM-READ THU 6/25 12:32 PM

ENJOY THIS LOVELY DAY ARCHBISHOP CRAIG!
GOD BLESS! BEAUTIFUL BARBIE

I WILL NEVER CONFORM TO, EXHIBIT, OR INVITE SATAN AND HIS DEFEATED REALM OF EVIL, *SAYS THE LORD*

ALMIGHTY GOD SPEAKING

UNDERSTAND THIS, MY CHILDREN. THERE IS NO ROOM NOR PLACE FOR ANYONE OR THING THAT FOLLOWS SATAN'S DOOMED DEEDS, IN MY HOLY KINGDOMS, *SAYS THE LORD!* YOU MAY CONFORM TO OR TOLERATE SATAN'S UNHOLINESS AND DEVIATED ACTS, BUT I, THE LORD, WILL NOT! REMOVE YOURSELVES FROM THE REALM THAT IS HEADED FOR ETERNAL DESTRUCTION, MY CHILDREN! REMOVE YOURSELVES FROM THE TEMPORARY PLEASURES THAT SEPARATE YOU FROM MY HOLY KINGDOMS, ON EARTH AND IN HEAVEN. REMOVE YOURSELVES, MY CHILDREN, BEFORE THE GATES OF HELL CLAIM YOUR ETERNAL SOUL! REMOVE YOURSELVES BEFORE IT IS TOO LATE!

BARBARA SPEAKING

I WILL NEVER CONFORM TO, EXHIBIT, OR INVITE THE REALM OF DESTRUCTION IN MY WORLD OF PEACE. FOR I DESIRE TO FOLLOW THE REALM THAT LEADS TO ALMIGHTY GOD'S GATES OF HOLINESS. MY BROTHERS AND SISTERS, LET US FLEE FROM THE REALM (SATAN) THAT DESIRES TO CLAIM OUR VALUABLE ETERNAL SOULS! LET US FLEE FROM THE REALM OF EVIL THAT SLITHERS THROUGH EVERY STREET, CITY, TOWN, COUNTRY, AND PROVINCE! LET US FLEE FROM THE DESTRUCTION THAT AWAITS THOSE WHO DIE IN THE MIDST OF THEIR SIN. MY BROTHERS AND SISTERS, LET US FLEE TO ALMIGHTY GOD'S MOUNTAIN TOP, SO THAT THE REALM OF DESTRUCTION WILL NOT CLAIM OUR WORTHY SOULS! LET US FLEE TO GOD'S LAND OF MILK AND HONEY, SO THAT WE MAY SHARE HIS GLORY WITH THE ANGELS AND SAINTS WHO DANCE AROUND GOD'S MIGHTY VICTORIOUS THRONE ABOVE! *ALLELUIA!* O VICTORIOUS BROTHERS AND SISTERS OF MINE, *ALLELUIA!*
JUNE 25, 2015 BY: BARBARA ANN MARY MACK
SENT THU, JUN 25, 2015 12:00 PM-READ THU 6/25/2015 12:33 PM

GREETINGS ARCHBISHOP CRAIG! BELOW IS TODAY'S MESSAGE FROM THE LORD FOR ALL OF US. AMORE, BELLA BARBARA

LISTEN TO MY HOLY WORDS OF WARNING, MY VULNERABLE FLOCK, FOR THEY ARE REAL, *SAYS THE LORD!*

ALMIGHTY GOD SPEAKING

WHO IS THE FOUNDER OF THE CHURCH? WHO IS THE FOUNDER OF THE CHURCH? WHO IS THE FOUNDER OF THE CHURCH? ME, MAN, OR SATAN? NEITHER MAN NOR SATAN CAN CHANGE MY CHURCH, *SAYS THE LORD!* HE WHO TRIES, HAS FORMED HIS OR HER SEPARATE ORGANIZATION, WHICH GOES AGAINST ME, THE ONLY FOUNDER AND ORIGIN OF THE CHURCH, *SAYS THE LORD!* MY CHILDREN, DO NOT BE DECEIVED! THAT WHICH GOES AGAINST MY TEACHINGS, MY TEACHINGS, MY TEACHING, GOES AGAINST ME, *SAYS THE LORD!* THERE ARE NO, NO, NO, EXCEPTIONS! NEITHER MANKIND NOR SATAN, DIED FOR MY CHURCH! NO ONE CAN CHANGE WHAT I DIED FOR, *SAYS THE LORD!* REMEMBER MY DRIPPING BLOOD!!!

JUNE 26, 2015 BY: BARBARA ANN MARY MACK

SENT FRI, JUN 26, 2015 10:49 AM-READ FRI 6/26/2015 11:12 AM

OBLIVION-AWAY FROM SATAN'S REALM OF STENCH

BARBARA SPEAKING

OH THE REALM OF OBLIVION HAS CAPTURED AND SECURED THE SOULS OF MY BELOVED ONE AND ME.

WE HAVE BEEN PLACED WITHIN THE REALM OF GOD, THE HOLY TRINITY.

THE REALM OF OBLIVION ENCOMPASSES OUR VULNERABLE SOULS AS WE FLEE FROM THE REALM THAT DESIRES TO STEAL US.

LET US FLEE FROM THE REALM (SATAN) THAT SEEKS THE SOULS OF THOSE WHO WERE CHOSEN BY OUR KING, THE VICTORIOUS JESUS.

THE REALM OF OBLIVION MOVES US AWAY FROM THE STENCH OF SATAN, THE EVIL ONE.

THE REALM OF OBLIVION PROTECTS AND WATCHES OVER BARBARA AND GOD'S BELOVED SON (CRAIG).

TAKE US AWAY FROM THOSE WHO FOLLOW SATAN'S LEAD

TAKE US AWAY FROM THOSE WHO ARE INFESTED WITH MATERIAL GREED.

LET US EXPERIENCE THE SERENITY THAT FLOWS THROUGH THE REALM OF SWEET OBLIVION.

GRANT US THIS GIFT, O LORD, TO YOUR OBEDIENT DAUGHTER (BARBARA) AND SON (CRAIG).

LET US ENJOY THE DIVINE ECSTASY THAT PERMEATES SWEET OBLIVION EVERY NIGHT.

LET US EXPERIENCE IT, O LORD, AS WE BOW IN YOUR HOLY SIGHT.

LET US BATHE IN THE REALM OF OBLIVION THROUGHOUT EACH DAY.

GRANT US THIS PRIVILEGE AND PLEASURE, DEAR LORD, AS WE KNEEL TOGETHER AND PRAY.

JUNE 25, 2015 BY: BARBARA ANN MARY MACK

GREETINGS DEAR ARCHBISHOP CRAIG! SOMETIMES WE DO NOT REVEAL TO OUR LOVED ONES THE TRUTH CONCERNING OUR CHRISTIAN FAITH. THIS HAPPENS OFTEN, ESPECIALLY IF OUR LOVED ONES ARE FOLLOWING A BELIEF OTHER THAN THE CHRISTIAN FAITH. ALTHOUGH IT MAY APPEAR TO BE AN INVASION OF THEIR PRIVACY OR BELIEFS, WE AS CHRISTIANS MUST REVEAL GOD'S TRUTH TO THEM. ONE MAY NOT BE CALLED TO VERBALLY EXHIBIT OR EXPRESS GOD'S TRUTH, BUT EVERY CHRISTIAN IS CALLED TO EXHIBIT HIS OR HER FAITH. IF EVERY PERSON WHO PROFESSES TO BE OF THE CHRISTIAN FAITH EXHIBIT'S GOD'S VERSION OF A BELIEVER, THEN ONE DOESN'T HAVE TO APPROACH THOSE WHO ARE NOT FAMILIAR WITH OUR CHRISTIAN FAITH. I VERY SELDOM APPROACH MY FAMILY OR FRIENDS WITH BIBLE QUOTES, I SIMPLY LIVE THE FAITH THAT I AM PROUD TO BE A PART OF. ACTION IS ALWAYS THE BEST WAY TO EXHIBIT ONE'S BELIEF. WORDS USUALLY FADE DURING CONVERSATIONS, BUT ACTIONS REMAIN. NO MATTER WHO I SPEAK WITH, MY LOVE AND BELIEF IN MY CHRISTIAN FAITH SHINE IN THE MIDST. THE BEST WAY TO PROCLAIM THE CHRISTIAN FAITH IS TO LIVE IT ACCORDING TO THE BIBLE TEACHINGS. THERE SHOULD BE NO ARGUING WITH THOSE WHO DO NOT ACCEPT OR UNDERSTAND OUR CHRISTIAN FAITH. IF THE LORD INVITES THEM INTO HIS REALM OF GOODNESS, THEY WILL ENTER AT HIS APPOINTED TIME. WE ARE TO TELL OF THE CHRISTIAN FAITH, BY LIVING THE CHRISTIAN FAITH. BY DOING THIS, THE UNBELIEVERS WILL SEE GOD'S TRUTH IN THEIR MIDST. CONTINUE REVEALING YOUR CHRISTIAN FAITH BY EXHIBITING YOUR HOLY ACTS, DEAR ONE.

AMORE, BELLA BARBARA, A BELIEVER OF THE CHRISTIAN FAITH

IF YOU LOVE THEM, TELL THEM THE TRUTH, *SAYS THE LORD*

ALMIGHTY GOD SPEAKING TO ALL WHO PROFESS TO BE CHRISTIANS

O BELIEVING ONES, YOU WHO FOLLOW MY HOLY WAY, TELL YOUR LOVED ONES MY TRUTH, IN REGARDS TO THE SERIOUSNESS OF THEIR ETERNAL SOULS AND FINAL DESTINATION. DO NOT SUGAR COAT THE TRUTH OR LIE TO THEM. TELL THEM MY TRUTH, IF YOU LOVE THEM. TELL THEM THE TRUTH, SO THAT THEY WILL KNOW HOW TO COMBAT THE REALM OF EVIL WHEN IT SLITHERS INTO THEIR VULNERABLE AND UNSUSPECTING LIVES. TELL THEM, IF YOU TRULY LOVE THEM! FOR THERE IS ONLY ONE TRUTH! THERE IS ONLY ONE WAY TO SALVATION, AND THAT IS THROUGH JESUS CHRIST, THE ONLY WAY! TELL THEM THE TRUTH, O CLERGY! TELL THEM THE TRUTH, O TEACHERS! TELL THEM THE TRUTH, O MOTHERS! TELL THEM THE TRUTH, O FATHERS! TELL THEM, O AUNTS! TELL THEM, O UNCLES! TELL THEM, O COUSINS! TELL THEM THE TRUTH, O GUARDIANS! TELL THEM, O FRIENDS! TELL THEM! TELL THEM! TELL THEM, SO THAT THEY MAY KNOW! TELL THEM, SO THAT THEY WILL KNOW MY TRUTH, *SAYS THE LORD!*

JUNE 25, 2015 BY: BARBARA ANN MARY MACK

SENT SUN, JUN 28, 2015 3:37 PM-READ SUN 6/28/2015 5:54 PM

GREETINGS ARCHBISHOP CRAIG! ENJOY YOUR GOD BLESSED DAY! BEHOLD! I AM ONLY THE MESSENGER. REJOICE IN GOD'S HOLY LIFE SAVING WORDS TODAY! LOVE OBEDIENT BARBARA

I CANNOT REST, MY CHILDEN, FOR YOU ARE NOT AT REST, *SAYS THE LORD*

ALMIGHTY GOD SPEAKING

HOW CAN I REST, MY CHILDREN, WHEN YOU ARE NOT AT PEACE? HOW CAN I REST, WHEN YOU ARE SUBJECTED TO SATAN'S REALM OF UNSPEAKABLE EVILS? HOW CAN I REST, WHEN THERE ARE MANY OF YOU WHO DO NOT FOLLOW MY HOLY WORDS TO ETERNAL LIFE WITH ME? HOW CAN I REST, WHEN SOME OF MY DAUGHTERS HAVE PUT THEIR UNBORN BABIES TO DEATH BEFORE THEY ENTERED THIS WORLD? HOW CAN I REST, WHEN MY SONS COMMIT UNSPEAKABLE ACTS IN MY HOLY PRESENCE? HOW CAN I REST, WHEN MY CHILDREN CONSIDER IT RIGHT TO TERMINATE AN UNWANTED CHILD OF MINE AS HE OR SHE LIES WITHIN THE WOMB? HOW CAN I REST, WHEN MANY OF MY CHILDREN ARE KILLED (MURDERED) WITHOUT A JUSTIFIABLE CAUSE? HOW CAN I REST, WHEN MY MESSENGERS ARE ABUSED AND REJECTED BY THOSE WHOM I HAVE SENT THEM TO? HOW CAN I REST, WHEN MY FAITHFUL BRIDE (BARBARA) WEEPS THROUGHOUT THE DAY, FOR THE SOULS OF THOSE WHOM SATAN HAS DECEIVED BEFORE THEIR PHYSICAL DEATH? HOW CAN I REST, WHEN THOSE WHO REJECT MY BRIDE BELIEVE THAT THEY ARE JUST? HOW CAN I REST, WHEN SOME OF THE LEADERS OF THE CHURCH PERVERT OR MISUSE MY HOLY TEACHINGS AND COMMANDS? HOW CAN I REST, WHEN MY VULNERABLE SONS AND DAUGHTERS ARE SUBJECTED TO THE PERVERTED DECISIONS OF THOSE WHO ARE IN AUTHORITY OVER THEM? MY VULNERABLE CHILDREN, I WILL NOT REST UNTIL YOU ARE AT PEACE, *SAYS THE LORD!!!*

JUNE 29, 2015 BY: BARBARA ANN MARY MACK

LORD, YOU ARE SO MERCIFUL

BARBARA SPEAKING TO THE LORD

YOU ARE SO MERCIFUL, O LORD, FOR YOU HAVE SENT ME, YOUR HEAVEN SENT MESSENGER AND BRIDE, TO MANY THROUGH THE YEARS. SOME OF THEM HAD THE PRIVILEGE TO HEAR FROM YOU SEVERAL TIMES, AND MORE. I BLESS YOU, O MERCIFUL GOD. IN YOUR INFINITE REALM OF LOVE AND MERCY, YOU HAVE SENT YOUR SACRIFICIAL WIFE, BARBARA, TO THOSE WHO ARE FOLLOWING THE PATH THAT LEADS TO ETERNAL HELL AND DESTRUCTION. YOUR UNENDING REALM OF MERCY HAS SENT ME TO THOSE WHO MISUNDERSTOOD YOUR HOLY WORDS THAT FLOW THROUGHOUT THE BLESSED BIBLE. YOUR REALM OF MERCY HAS SENT ME TO THOSE WHO ARE FOLLOWING THE ACTS THAT YOU DEEM UNHOLY. YOUR REALM OF

MERCY HAS SENT ME TO THOSE WHO REFUSE TO ACKNOWLEDGE YOUR HOLY UNCHANGING WAY. YOUR REALM OF MERCY HAS SENT ME TO THE CLERGY, SO THAT I MAY REVEAL TO THEM YOUR HOLY MESSAGES TODAY. MY LORD, YOUR REALM OF MERCY HAS SENT ME TO THOSE WHO WALK IN THE DARKNESS OF SATAN'S UNJUST WAY, SO THAT I MAY LEAD THEM TO YOUR MARVELOUS LIGHT. O GREAT AND HOLY REALM OF MERCY, I BOW MY HUMBLED HEAD IN YOUR WORTHY PRESENCE, FOR YOU CONTINUE SENDING YOUR MESSENGERS TO YOUR MISGUIDED CHILDREN, SO THAT THEY MAY HAVE THE OPPORTUNITY TO FOLLOW YOUR HOLY WAY, THE ONLY WAY TO ETERNAL LIFE.
JUNE 29, 2015 BY: BARBARA ANN MARY MACK

DO NOT PLAY GAMES WITH ME, *SAYS THE LORD*-TWO

ALMIGHTY GOD SPEAKING TO ALL

DO NOT PLAY GAMES WITH ME, MY CHILDREN! EITHER YOU ARE WITH ME, OR YOU ARE AGAINST ME. THERE IS NO IN BETWEEN! HONOR MY VERSION OF HOLINESS, YOU WHO SPEAK MY HOLY WORDS IN THE PULPITS! HONOR MY VERSION OF HOLINESS, YOU WHO PROFESS TO BE CHRISTIANS! HONOR MY HOLY WAY, YOU WHO SIT IN MY CHURCHES! HONOR MY HOLY WORDS, YOU WHO HAVE THE PHYSICAL AUTHORITY OVER MY VULNERABLE FLOCK! DO NOT PLAY GAMES WITH ME! DO NOT TEST MY PATIENCE AND MY MERCY! FOR I WILL SHOW NO MERCY TOWARD THOSE WHO MOCK AND MISUSE MY HOLY WAY! I HAVE SPOKEN TO YOU FOR THE LAST TIME, *SAYS THE LORD!!!*
JUNE 28, 2015 BY: BARBARA ANN MARY MACK
SENT MON, JUN 29, 2015 4:27 PM-READ MON 6/29/2015 8:19 PM

PLEASANT DREAMS, O FAITHFUL AND OBEDIENT SON (ARCHBISHOP CRAIG)!!!
SENT MON, JUN 29, 2015 4:27 PM-READ MON 6/29/2015 8:19 PM

HI! BELOW ARE TODAY'S MESSAGES FOR GOD'S CHILDREN EVERYWHERE, INCLUDING YOU AND ME. *LOVE YOU FOREVER! BELLA BARBIE*

SATAN CANNOT KEEP ME QUIET!

MY BROTHERS AND SISTERS, SATAN CANNOT KEEP ME QUIET, FOR THE LORD, OUR HOLY GOD, IS MY MOUTH PIECE! HE IS IN CONTROL OVER MY VOCAL AND WRITTEN DELIVERANCE OF HIS HOLY MESSAGES TODAY. THE LORD, AND ONLY THE LORD, HAS CONTROL OVER HIS MESSENGERS ACTIONS, FOR WE ARE SENT TO DELIVER HIS HOLY WORDS AND PLAN FOR HIM. HE HAS GIVEN US DIVINE ORDERS TO CARRY OUT. WE CANNOT DO ANYTHING AGAINST ALMIGHTY GOD'S DIVINE INSTRUCTIONS! FOR OUR SOLE PURPOSE IS TO PLEASE OUR ORIGIN AND GOD AT ALL TIMES! SATAN CANNOT INTERRUPT OR PREVENT GOD'S CHOSEN MESSENGERS FROM SPEAKING GOD'S TRUTH TO THE DECEIVED AND VULNERABLE ONES! HE (SATAN) CANNOT KEEP US QUIET! HE CANNOT STIFLE OUR GOD ORDERED ASSIGNMENT! FOR HE HAS NO, NO, NO POWER OR CONTROL OVER GOD'S MESSENGERS. WE DO NOT FEAR SATAN NOR HIS DOOMED FOLLOWERS. THEREFORE, REJOICE, O VICTORIOUS BROTHERS AND SISTERS OF MINE! LET US EXHIBIT OUR ALLEGIANCE TO THE ONE AND ONLY GOD WHO SAVES! LET US EXHIBIT OUR ALLEGIANCE TO ALMIGHTY GOD, THE SOURCE OF HOLINESS, FOR THERE IS NO OTHER!

JUNE 29, 2015 BY: BARBARA ANN MARY MACK

SENT MON, JUN 29, 2015 11:59 PM-READ TUE 6/30/2015 9:47 AM

PLEASANT DREAMS, O BELOVED ONE! I HAVE COMMUNICATED WITH MANY WHO ARE VERY UPSET OVER THE SUPREME COURT'S RULING PERTAINING TO SAME SEX MARRIAGES. I TOLD THEM NOT TO BE UPSET OR WORRIED ABOUT THE DECISION, BUT TO PRAY FOR THE LOST SOULS. ONE THING THAT IS TRUTH, I FOCUS ON THE WORDS OF OUR SAVING GOD "MANY ARE CALLED, BUT FEW ARE CHOSEN." GOD IS THE ONLY SUPREME BEING OVER HIS CREATION, THEREFORE, MANKIND'S ACTS THAT GO AGAINST THE TEACHINGS WITHIN THE HOLY BIBLE DOESN'T MATTER AT ALL. FIRST OF ALL, MAN AND MAN CANNOT PROCREATE, NEITHER CAN WOMAN AND WOMAN. THEY CANNOT PRODUCE LIFE. WATCHING PEOPLE OF THE SAME SEX IN A ROMANTIC SCENE IS "UNGODLY", ACCORDING TO THE HOLY BIBLE. I DO NOT VOICE MY OPINION, I COMMENT ON WHAT THE HOLY BIBLE STATES, WHICH IS "GOD'S UNCHANGING WORD". IT DOESN'T BOTHER ME WHAT HUMAN BEINGS DO, BECAUSE I KNOW THAT ALMIGHTY GOD WILL ALWAYS COME OUT AS "THE ONLY WINNER" IN EVERY DEVIANT ACT. I WILL PRAY FOR THOSE WHO WERE FOR THE RULING, AS I DO FOR ALL MISGUIDED SOULS. BUT I REMEMBER "THE CHOSEN FEW", AND I AM BEGGING THE LORD THAT YOU ARE ONE OF THE CHOSEN FEW. I AM STILL PRAYING FOR YOU, I ALWAYS WILL. *LOVE YOU FOREVER! CONCERNED FAITHFUL BARBARA*

I HAVE COME FOR THE CHOSEN FEW, *SAYS THE LORD*

ALMIGHTY GOD SPEAKING
TO THE CHOSEN FEW

MY CHILDREN, I HAVE COME FOR YOU!

I HAVE COME FOR THE CHOSEN FEW.

I HAVE COME FOR THE FAITHFUL ONES.

I HAVE COME FOR MY CHOSEN DAUGHTERS AND SONS.

FOR YOU HAVE BEEN FAITHFUL AND TRUE TO ME:

COME AND JOIN THE BLESSED AND HOLY TRINITY!

YOU HAVE KEPT MY HOLY WORD IN THE MIDST OF THIS TROUBLED TIME:

COME, O OBEDIENT CHILDREN, AND DWELL WITH ME, FOR YOU ARE MINE!

YOU HAVE TURNED AWAY FROM SATAN, MY ENEMY:

YOU HAVE EXHIBITED THE LOVE AND TRUST OF ONE WHO HAS BEEN SET FREE.

I HAVE COME FOR THOSE WHOM I TRULY LOVE.

I HAVE COME FOR THE CHOSEN FEW WHO HAVE FOLLOWED THE VOICE OF MY HOLY DOVE
(SPIRIT).

ARE YOU ONE OF MY CHOSEN FEW?

HAVE YOU ABIDED BY MY WORDS, WHICH ARE HOLY AND TRUE?

JUNE 29, 2015 BY: BARBARA ANN MARY MACK

ONE CANNOT COME INTO CHRIST'S HOLY CHURCH WITHOUT THE DESIRE TO CHANGE

BARBARA, GOD'S PROPHETESS-MESSENGER SPEAKING

ONE CANNOT CONTINUE IN SIN OR THE DESIRE TO SIN, BEFORE CHRIST ACCEPTS HIM OR HER
INTO HIS HOLY CHURCH. MY BROTHERS AND SISTERS, DO NOT BE DECEIVED BY YOURSELVES
OR OTHERS! ONE CANNOT ENTER CHRIST'S CHURCH, HIS HOLY CHURCH, WITHOUT LETTING

GO OF THE ACTS THAT JESUS CHRIST VIEWS AS SINFUL AND UNGODLY. IT IS WRITTEN IN THE BIBLE, WHICH IS GOD'S HOLY WORD, GOD'S HOLY AND EVERLASTING WORD. GOD'S HOLY WORD IS "UNCHANGING" AND "UNCHANGEABLE", *SAYS THE LORD*. MY BROTHERS AND SISTERS, CALL OUT TO OUR SAVING GOD, AND ASK HIM TO HELP YOU DURING YOUR PERIODS OF CONFUSION. ASK HIM TO LEAD YOU TO HIS PATH OF HOLINESS, CLEANLINESS, AND RIGHTEOUSNESS, BEFORE IT IS TOO LATE. FOR THERE IS NO OTHER WAY THAT ONE CAN ENTER CHRIST'S HOLY CHURCH ON EARTH. MY BROTHERS AND SISTERS, MAKE THAT CHANGE BEFORE IT IS TOO LATE, FOR SATAN IS ON THE PROWL FOR YOUR VULNERABLE SOULS! MY BROTHERS AND SISTERS, THERE IS ONLY ONE WAY TO SALVATION, THE HOLY WAY!

ALMIGHTY GOD SPEAKING

DO NOT BE MISGUIDED BY THOSE WHO DO NOT KNOW ME, *SAYS THE LORD!* FOR THEY DO NOT SPEAK OF MY HOLY WAY, THE ONLY LIFE SAVING WAY. MY CHILDREN, IF YOU DESIRE TO LIVE IN SWEET PARADISE WITH ME, YOU MUST LEARN OF MY HOLY WAY, AND FOLLOW, TEACH, LIVE, AND REVEAL IT TO THE WORLD. FOR THERE IS NO OTHER WAY!!!
JUNE 30, 2015 BY: BARBARA ANN MARY MACK
SENT TUE, JUN 30, 2015 12:55 AM-READ TUE 6/30/2015 2:28 PM

HAVE A BEAUTIFUL AND BLESSED DAY ARCHBISHOP CRAIG! BELOW IS TODAY'S PASSAGE FOR YOU. *AMORE ALWAYS!*

I AM THE RIGHT AND ONLY GOD, CAN YOU NOT SEE? COME CLOSER TO ME

ALMIGHTY GOD SPEAKING

MY CHILDREN, THERE IS NO OTHER WHO CAN DO FOR YOU AS I DO. THERE IS NO OTHER, WHO CAN WORK MIRACLES AND SAVE THE LOST AND DRIFTING SOULS. THERE IS NO OTHER GOD! THERE IS NO OTHER REALM OF HOPE. THERE IS NO OTHER PLACE OF REFUGE. THERE IS NO OTHER SOURCE OF HEALING POWER. THERE IS NO OTHER LIFE SAVING FOOD! THERE IS NO OTHER ETERNAL GOD AND FATHER. THERE IS NO OTHER REALM OF PERFECTION. THERE IS NO OTHER REALM OF CONTINUOUS PEACE IN THE MIDST OF CHAOS AND STORMY TIMES. MY CHILDREN, I AM THE RIGHT GOD, O CAN YOU NOT SEE? I AM THE ONLY LIVING AND TRUE GOD. COME CLOSER TO ME, MY CHILDREN. WALK WITH ME, THROUGH THIS REALM OF VERY CONFUSING TIMES. COME CLOSER TO ME SO THAT I MAY SHIELD YOU FROM THE EVIL DEEDS OF SATAN AND HIS FOLLOWERS, WHICH FLOW THROUGH THIS TROUBLED AND VULNERABLE PERIOD OF TIME. COME CLOSER TO THE ONLY HOLY REALM THAT WILL PROTECT YOU, BEFORE, DURING, AND AFTER SATAN UNLEASHES HIS FOUL WORKS IN YOUR MIDST. MY CHILDREN, COME

CLOSER TO THE RIGHT AND ONLY GOD WHO WILL SAVE THOSE WHO HONOR "HIS UNCHANGING WAY"!

JUNE 29, 2015 BY: BARBARA ANN MARY MACK

SENT TUE, JUN 30, 2015 1:43 AM-READ TUE 6/30/2015 2:28 PM

NEED I REMIND YOU OF MY WRATH AND JUSTICE, O CLERGY OF THE WORLD?

ALMIGHTY GOD SPEAKING TO THE CLERGY

FEED MY SEARCHING FLOCK THE TRUTH, MY TRUTH! FEED THEM MY BREAD OF LIFE, BEFORE I RELEASE MY WRATH UPON YOU, SAYS THE LORD! I AM VERY SERIOUS, O CLERGY! SATAN HAS MISLEAD MY VULNERABLE FLOCK THROUGH YOUR FALSE TEACHINGS FOR YEARS. I WILL NO LONGER TOLERATE SUCH IRREVERENCE IN MY HOLY PRESENCE! GET IT TOGETHER, BEFORE I RELEASE MY WRATH IN THE MIDST OF YOUR UNHOLY TEACHINGS AND WAYS! THIS IS MY LAST WARNING TO YOU. DO YOU WANT TO TASTE MY WRATH? REMEMBER THOSE WHO DISOBEYED ME IN THE PAST. DO YOU NOT BELIEVE WHAT YOU HAVE READ IN THE HOLY BIBLE? DO YOU WANT TO FIND OUT THE DEPTH OF MY JUSTICE, O CLERGY? ARE YOU WILLING TO TAKE THE CHANCE? I AM OFFERING YOU A TASTE OF MY MERCY AT THIS TIME. ARE YOU GOING TO FOLLOW MY HOLY WAY, OR CONTINUE ON THE PATH THAT LEADS TO MY WRATH AND JUSTICE. FOR I WILL NO LONGER TOLERATE THE MISGUIDANCE THAT YOU HAVE PLACED IN THE PRESENCE OF MY VULNERABLE FLOCK. TEACH THEM MY TRUTH SO THAT THEY MAY BE SAVED! TEACH THEM MY TRUTH, SO THAT YOU TOO MAY BE ONE OF MY CHOSEN FEW. FOR THERE IS STILL HOPE FOR YOU, O CLERGY. THERE IS STILL HOPE.

JUNE 30, 2015 BY: BARBARA ANN MARY MACK

ALL GOOD AND HOLY

BARBARA SPEAKING

PRAISE HIM! PRAISE HIM! PRAISE HIM, ALL YE LANDS!

GIVE GLORIOUS PRAISE TO OUR SAVING AND MERCIFUL GOD'S HOLY PLANS!

FOR HIS PLANS INCLUDE VERY GOOD THINGS!

LET US REJOICE AS ONE, AS WE WITNESS THE WONDERFUL MIRACLES THAT HE BRINGS!

PRAISE HIM, O GRATEFUL BROTHERS AND SISTERS OF MINE!

PRAISE OUR HEAVENLY GOD AND FATHER, FOR HE IS ONE OF A KIND!

LIFT YOUR VOICES IN PRAISE!

AS YOU ENJOY YOUR GOD ORDERED DAYS.

SING SONGS OF GRATITUDE AND LOVE!

SING YOUR SONGS OF PRAISE TO JESUS, THE VICTORIOUS ONE, WHO DESCENDED FROM HEAVEN ABOVE!

FOR HE IS HOLY, ETERNAL AND TRUE!

HE IS THE ONLY GOD WHO DIED ON THE CROSS FOR ME AND YOU!

HE IS ALL GOOD AND HOLY!

HE IS THE GIFT: HE IS GOD, THE HOLY TRINITY!

PRAISE HIM! PRAISE HIM! PRAISE HIM!

JUNE 30, 2015 BY: BARBARA ANN MARY MACK

DO NOT BE DECEIVED, MY CHILDREN, FOR THEY DO NOT REPRESENT ME, *SAYS THE LORD!!!*

ALMIGHTY GOD SPEAKING

DO NOT BE DECEIVED BY THE FALSE TEACHERS AND LEADERS WHO TEACH AND SUPPORT THOSE ACTS THAT I HAVE REJECTED. DO NOT BE DECEIVED BY THEM, FOR THEY ARE NOT

REPRESENTING ME. THEY HAVE NEVER REPRESENTED ME, FOR THEY ARE THE SERVANTS OF SATAN. REMEMBER, MY HOLY WORDS IN THE BIBLE, FOR THEY HAVEN'T CHANGED!!!

JULY 2, 2015 BY: BARBARA ANN MARY MACK

SENT THU, JUL 2, 2015 8:40 PM-READ THU 7/2/2015 9:46 PM

HI LOVE! ENJOY THIS GOD BLESS DAY. BELOW ARE TODAY'S PASSAGE FOR US. LOVE, BEAUTIFUL BARBARA

THERE IS NO LIFE WITHOUT THE REALM OF HOLINESS

BARBARA SPEAKING

MY BROTHERS AND SISTERS, UNDERSTAND THE DEPTH AND MEANING OF PURE AND HOLY LOVE. IT IS A LOVE THAT TRANSCENDS THE WORLD'S VERSION OF LOVE. IT IS A LOVE THAT MAKES EVERYONE WHO WANTS TO LIVE HOLY WORK AT IT EVERY DAY. IT IS A LOVE THAT GIVES ONE PEACE THROUGHOUT EACH DAY. IT IS A LOVE THAT ENCOURAGES EVERYONE TO PRAY. IT IS A LOVE THAT DOESN'T SEE OR ACKNOWLEDGE DIFFERENCE IN ONE'S FELLOW MAN OR WOMAN. IT IS A LOVE THAT IS ALWAYS SEEKING WAYS TO HELP THOSE WHO ARE IN NEED OF SPIRITUAL AND PHYSICAL GUIDANCE. IT IS A LOVE THAT SEEKS GOD'S HOLY REALM OF EXISTENCE. IT IS A LOVE THAT EXHIBITS GOD'S VERSION OF HOLINESS. IT IS A LOVE THAT PLACES ALMIGHTY GOD'S REALM OF HOLINESS ABOVE EVERYTHING AND EVERYONE. IT IS A LOVE THAT BOWS IN THE PRESENCE OF ALMIGHTY GOD THROUGHOUT EACH DAY. IT IS A LOVE THAT SHARES HIS OR HER KNOWLEDGE OF GOD'S HOLY WAY WITH HIS LOVED ONES AND STRANGERS. IT IS A LOVE THAT COULD NEVER BE ASHAMED TO VERBALLY AND PHYSICALLY EXPRESS THE LOVE OF THE CREATOR AND GOD OF ALL THAT IS HOLY. MY BROTHERS AND SISTERS, THERE IS NO LIFE WITHOUT EXPERIENCING AND EXHIBITING GOD'S REALM OF HOLINESS.

JULY 1, 2015 BY: BARBARA ANN MARY MACK

LOVE *IS HERE*

BARBARA SPEAKING

MY BROTHERS AND SISTERS, LET US ENJOY THE HOLY GIFT OF LOVE (ALMIGHTY GOD) THAT DESCENDED IN OUR MIDST NOT SO LONG AGO. LET US ENJOY THE LOVE THAT FLOWS WITH US THROUGHOUT EACH DAY. LET US ENJOY THE GIFT OF LOVE AS IT SITS NEXT TO US ON A CROWDED BUS. LET US ENJOY THE HEAVEN SENT LOVE THAT WALKS WITH US THROUGH THE DARK STREETS AT NIGHT. LET US ENJOY THE GIFT OF LOVE THAT COMFORTS US IN OUR LONELY

MOMENTS. LET US ENJOY THE HEAVEN SENT LOVE THAT CRADLES US WHEN WE LOSE A LOVED ONE. LET US ENJOY THE GIFT OF DIVINE LOVE AS HE SPEAKS SOFTLY TO US WHEN WE NEED GUIDANCE. LET US ENJOY THE BASKET OF LOVE THAT IS SENT BY GOD, THE BLESSED AND HOLY TRINITY. LET US ENJOY THE GIFT OF LOVE THAT PROTECTS US FROM THE REALM OF DESTRUCTION AND DOOM. LET US ENJOY THE LOVE THAT IS WRAPPED AROUND THOSE WHO ARE COLD AND HOMELESS. LET US ENJOY THE GIFT OF LOVE THAT FEED THE HUNGRY ONES. MY BROTHERS AND SISTERS, LOVE IS HERE, LET YOU AND ME ENJOY IT TODAY! *ALLELUIA!!!*

JULY 1, 2015 BY: BARBARA ANN MARY MACK

SENT THU, JUL 2, 2015 8:40 PM-READ THU 7/2/2015 9:46 PM

MY ALLEGIANCE TO ALMIGHTY GOD AND HIS UNCHANGING REALM OF HOLINESS

BARBARA SPEAKING

MY ALLEGIANCE IS TO ALMIGHTY GOD. I AM COMMITTED TO NO ONE ELSE, AND I NEVER WILL, *SAYS BARBARA, THE BRIDE OF JESUS*, THE "UNCHANGING GOD", THE HOLY ONE. I WILL NOT GIVE GLORY OR HONOR TO A HUMAN BEING, NO MATTER WHAT HIS OR HER SOCIAL STATUS MAY BE. MY DEVOTION AND LOYALTY IS TO MY CREATOR AND GOD, THERE IS NO OTHER! THERE IS NO HUMAN THAT SHOULD CAPTURE OUR ATTENTION IN A WAY THAT HE OR SHE MAY BE REVERED ABOVE ALMIGHTY GOD. IT IS A PRIVILEGE AND HONOR TO SERVE ALMIGHTY GOD AND REVERE HIM AS NO OTHER WOULD BE REVERED. IT IS A PRIVILEGE AND HONOR TO SERVE YOU, O LORD. TO SERVE YOU AND YOUR KINGDOM OF HOLINESS IS MY DESIRE AND LOVE. I WILL ALWAYS EXHIBIT MY FAITH AND MY LOVE FOR YOU, O LORD. I WILL EXHIBIT MY COMMITMENT TO YOU IN THE PRESENCE OF THOSE WHO DO NOT KNOW YOU. MY LORD, I WILL CLING TO YOUR UNCHANGING REALM OF HAPPINESS AND COMPASSION, BECAUSE I LOVE YOU. I WILL CLING TO YOUR UNENDING REALM OF JOY AND HEAVENLY BLISS, BECAUSE I ADORE YOU. YOU, MY LOVING GOD, HAVE BLESSED THIS GENERATION WITH THE GIFT OF YOUR CHOSEN SPOUSE AND FRIEND (BARBARA), SO THAT SHE MAY REVEAL YOUR HOLY LOVE AND PRESENCE TO THOSE WHO DESIRE A TASTE OF YOUR MAGNIFICENCE TODAY. LET THE GIFT AND PRESENCE OF MY ALLEGIANCE TO YOUR REALM OF HOLINESS, SHINE IN THE MIDST OF YOUR LOVED ONES TODAY. SHINE, MY LORD, SHINE! SHINE IN THE MIDST OF THOSE WHO WONDER WHY I TRULY LOVE AND ADORE YOU.

JULY 1, 2015 BY: BARBARA ANN MARY MACK

SENT THU, JUL 2, 2015 9:26 PM-READ THU 7/2/2015 10:22 PM

I WILL NOT BE DEFEATED OR CONQUERED, *SAYS THE LORD!*

ALMIGHTY GOD SPEAKING

HEAR YE! HEAR YE! I CANNOT, AND WILL NOT, BE DEFEATED NOR CONQUERED BY ANYONE OR THING, *SAYS THE LORD GOD!* MANY HAVE TRIED, BUT FAILED! MANY HAVE COME TO THE BATTLEFIELD, BUT LOST THE BATTLE! FOR I, THE OMNIPOTENT ONE, CANNOT BE DEFEATED! MERE MAN HAVE TRIED, BUT FAILED! SATAN, MY ENEMY HAS TRIED, BUT HE TOO, HAS FAILED! NO ONE, NOR THING, CAN CONQUER GOD, THE ONLY HOLY INFINITE ONE! FOR I, CANNOT BE CONQUERED! I AM THE ALMIGHTY AND UNDEFEATED ONE! I WILL ALWAYS BE THE ONLY UNDEFEATED ONE, FOR THERE IS NO OTHER! I AM THE LORD GOD ALMIGHTY! I HAVE ROAMED THIS REALM THROUGHOUT THE HISTORY OF TIME, THERE IS NO OTHER LIKE ME, *SAYS THE LORD!* THERE IS NONE GREATER THAN ME, *SAYS THE LORD!* FOR I AM THE ONLY ETERNAL ONE! I AM EXISTENCE! THERE IS NO OTHER! WALK WITH ME, ALL WHO DESIRE TO TASTE THE TASTE THAT COMES WITH SWEET VICTORY! WALK WITH ME, ALL WHO DESIRE TO ENJOY THE FOOD THAT DESCENDS FROM MY EVER-FLOWING BASKET OF PLENTY! WALK WITH ME, O INVITED GUESTS OF MINE! COME, AND SIT AT MY TABLE OF GOOD FOOD (HEAVENLY KNOWLEDGE). COME, AND ENJOY THE GOOD LIFE THAT IS OFFERED BY ME, *THE ONLY UNDEFEATED ONE!* JULY 3, 2015 BY: BARBARA ANN MARY MACK

RELEASE THEM, O SATAN

ALMIGHTY GOD SPEAKING TO SATAN

RELEASE THEM, O SATAN! RELEASE MY CHOSEN ONES, FOR YOU HAVE NOT WON THE BATTLE FOR THEIR ETERNAL SOULS! I HAVE SENT MY MESSENGERS TO FIGHT FOR THE SOULS OF THOSE WHO HAVE BEEN CHOSEN. RELEASE THEM, O SATAN! ACKNOWLEDGE YOUR DEFEAT TODAY, FOR I AM THE ONLY VICTORIOUS REALM! THOSE WHO FOLLOW MY HOLY WORDS ARE VICTORS AS WELL. YOU WILL NOT KEEP THOSE WHOM I HAVE CHOSEN, FOR THEY ARE IN

MY BOOK OF LIFE. MY WORD IS MY WORD! YOU HAVE BEEN DEFEATED BY THE POWER OF MY DRIPPING BLOOD THAT COVERS THE ETERNAL SOULS OF MY CHOSEN ONES. FOLLOW MY DRIPPING BLOOD, MY CHILDREN, AS IT DESCENDS FROM MY WOUNDED BODY, FOR IT STILL DRIPS FOR YOU. I WILL CONQUER SATAN AND HIS REALM OF EVIL WITH THE POWER THAT FLOWS THROUGH MY DRIPPING BLOOD. RELEASE THEM, O SATAN! RELEASE MY CAPTURED CHILDREN TODAY!

JULY 2, 2015 BY: BARBARA ANN MARY MACK

SENT SAT, JUL 4, 2015 1:35 PM-READ SAT 7/4/2015 2:23 PM

HAVE A HAPPY DAY, DEAR ONE (CRAIG)!AMORE, HAPPY BARBARA

ARE MY HOLY WORDS IN VAIN, *SAYS THE LORD?*

ALMIGHTY GOD SPEAKING

I SPEAK TO THEM THROUGH MY MESSENGERS, BUT MANY HAVE NOT YET HEED MY HOLY WORDS. THEY CONTINUE IN THEIR UNSPEAKABLE AND UNHOLY DEEDS AS IF THEY HAVE NOT HEARD MY WARNINGS PERTAINING TO THEIR DESTINATION. THEY CONTINUE IN THEIR WRONGFUL AND UNRIGHTEOUS ACTS, DESPITE MY EXPRESSIONS OF MERCY AND JUSTICE. THEY CONTINUE PROFANING AND PERVERTING MY HOLY WORDS THAT FLOW THROUGH THE BIBLE. ARE MY HOLY WORDS IN VAIN? WHO WILL LISTEN TO THEM? WHO WILL FOLLOW THEM? WHO WILL HONOR THEM? IS IT YOU, MY SON? IS IT YOU, MY DAUGHTER? WHO WILL LISTEN TO ME, *SAYS THE LORD?*

JULY 4, 2015 BY: BARBARA ANN MARY MACK

IN THE MIDST OF THIS SINFUL GENERATION, I WILL LIFT YOU UP IN PRAISE, *MY LORD*

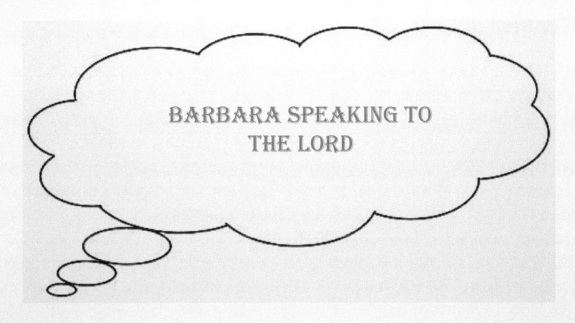
BARBARA SPEAKING TO THE LORD

IN THE MIDST OF THIS SINFUL GENERATION, I LIFT YOU UP IN PRAISE, BEFORE MY FEET HIT THE FLOOR IN THE MORNINGS. IN THE MIDST OF THIS SINFUL GENERATION, I SING SONGS OF PRAISE TO YOU THROUGHOUT THE DAY. IN THE MIDST OF THIS SINFUL GENERATION, I RAISE MY WINDOWS SO THAT THE WORLD MAY HEAR MY SONGS OF PRAISE TO YOU, MY GOD. IN THE MIDST OF THIS SINFUL GENERATION, I READ YOUR HOLY WORDS THAT DESCENDED FROM YOUR REALM OF HOLINESS. IN THE MIDST OF THIS SINFUL GENERATION, MY DAUGHTERS READ, UNDERSTAND, AND ACCEPT YOUR HOLY WORDS, WHICH DESCEND IN OUR MIDST DAILY.

IN THE MIDST OF THIS SINFUL GENERATION, YOU SEND YOUR FAITHFUL BRIDE (BARBARA) TO THOSE WHOM YOU HAVE CALLED AND CHOSEN OUT OF DIVINE LOVE. IN THE MIDST OF THIS SINFUL GENERATION, THE GIFT OF YOUR HOLY SPIRIT IS SHARED WITH THOSE WHOM YOU DEEM WORTHY. IN THE MIDST OF THIS SINFUL GENERATION, YOU HAVE SENT ME TO DELIVER YOUR LIFE SAVING MESSAGES TO THOSE WHOM SATAN HAS DECEIVED. IN THE MIDST OF THIS SINFUL GENERATION, YOU HAVE SENT ME TO THE SHEPHERDS OF MANY CHURCHES, TO DELIVER YOUR UNCHANGING WORDS OF SALVATION AND HOLINESS. MY LORD, MY GOD, YOU HAVE GIVEN ME THE DIVINE STRENGTH AND COURAGE THAT IS NEEDED TO APPROACH THOSE OF THE CLERGY. YOU HAVE GIVEN ME THE DIVINE COURAGE, TO SPEAK YOUR UNCHANGING WORD TO THOSE WHO DEEM THEMSELVES ABOVE YOU AND YOUR UNCHANGING HOLY WORD. MY LORD, MY GOD, PLEASE CONTINUE GRACING ME WITH THE GIFT OF YOUR UNWAVERING COURAGE, SO THAT I MAY HAVE THE STRENGTH AND PERSEVERANCE THAT ARE NEEDED TO COMBAT SATAN AND HIS DEFEATED REALM OF DECEIT AND DESTRUCTION. FOR THIS VULNERABLE GENERATION IS IN NEED OF YOUR CONTINUOUS GUIDANCE AND DIVINE MERCY.

JULY 4, 2015 BY: BARBARA ANN MARY MACK

SENT SAT, JUL 4, 2015 5:36 PM-READ SUN 7/5/2015 5:21 PM

I CLOSE MY EYES, EARS AND MIND *TO THE WORLD*

BARBARA SPEAKING

I CLOSE MY EYES, EARS, AND MIND TO THE WORLD SO THAT I MAY ENJOY GOD'S REALM OF HOLINESS AND DIVINE PEACE. THE WORLD-A PLACE OF TRAGEDIES AND DOOM. I CLOSE MY EYES, SO THAT I MAY NOT SEE THE EVILS THAT PERMEATE THE WORLD. I COVER MY EARS, SO THAT I WILL NOT HEAR THE UNSPEAKABLE WORDS THAT FLOW FROM THE MOUTHS OF THOSE WHO DO NOT BELIEVE THAT THEY ARE ALWAYS IN THE PRESENCE OF OUR HOLY OMNIPRESENT GOD. I CLOSE MY VULNERABLE MIND, SO THAT I MAY SHUT OUT THE TRAGEDIES THAT ARE PLACED ON THE SUSCEPTIBLE ONES AS SATAN, THE DESTROYER OF SPIRITUAL AND PHYSICAL LIFE, ROAMS IN OUR MIDST TODAY. HELP US, O LORD, SO THAT YOUR VULNERABLE ONES MAY WALK IN YOUR HOLY PRESENCE WITHOUT FEAR OR APPREHENSION. HELP ME, SO THAT I MAY OPEN MY EYES AGAIN. HELP ME, SO THAT I MAY UNCOVER MY EARS AGAIN. HELP ME, O LORD,

SO THAT I MAY OPEN MY MIND TO THOSE IN THE WORLD WHO REALLY NEED TO SEE A GLIMPSE OF YOU THROUGH ME. GIVE ME THE DIVINE COURAGE TO UNCOVER MY EARS, SO THAT I MAY HEAR THE FAINT CRIES OF YOUR CALLED AND CHOSEN ONES. STRENGTHEN ME, O LORD, SO THAT I MAY SEE, HEAR AND FEEL YOU, IN THE MIDST OF THESE TRAGIC DAYS. *ALLELUIA!!!*
JULY 4, 2015 BY: BARBARA ANN MARY MACK
SENT SUN, JUL 5, 2015 4:36 PM-READ SUN 7/5/2015 5:21 PM

IT IS *WRITTEN*

ALMIGHTY GOD SPEAKING

MY HOLY WORD IS MY WORD! DO NOT CHANGE MY HOLY WORD, FOR IT CANNOT BE CHANGED BY MERE MANKIND, *SAYS THE LORD.* DO NOT TRY TO MAKE MY HOLY WORDS INTO SOMETHING THAT IS VIEWED BY ME AS "UNHOLY", FOR I WILL BRING DOWN MY WRATH UPON ALL WHO PERVERTS MY HOLY WAY AND WORD, *SAYS THE LORD,* THE UNCHANGING GOD AND WORD. FOLLOW MY HOLY WAY AND WORD AT ALL TIMES, FOR IT IS WRITTEN, *SAYS THE LORD!* MY CHILDREN, READ MY HOLY WORD SO THAT YOU MAY KNOW WHAT IS HOLY IN MY SIGHT. READ MY HOLY WORDS THAT ARE WRITTEN IN THE BIBLE, SO THAT YOU MAY KNOW WHAT I EXPECT OF YOU, FOR THERE ARE NO EXCEPTIONS TO MY HOLY WORDS. EVERYONE MUST ABIDE BY MY SAYINGS, IF THEY DESIRE TO FOLLOW ME TO SWEET PARADISE. WHAT IS WRITTEN CANNOT BE PERVERTED BY MANKIND NOR SATAN. MY HOLY WRITTEN WORD IS FINAL, *SAYS THE LORD!!!*
JULY 3, 2015 BY: BARBARA ANN MARY MACK

I SEARCHED THE STREETS OF SIN, IN SEARCH OF MY DECEIVED ONES

ALMIGHTY GOD SPEAKING

THROUGH THE CENTURIES, AND THE REALM OF TIME, I HAVE SEARCHED THE STREETS, THE DARK AND LONELY SINFUL STREETS, IN SEARCH AND PURSUIT OF MY LOVED ONES. THROUGHOUT THE REALM OF TIME, THIS VERY CRUCIAL PERIOD OF TIME, I HAVE SEARCHED AND SEARCHED FOR THOSE WHOM I LOVE. I HAVE SENT MY MESSENGERS AND ANGELS, TO SEARCH THE FORBIDDEN TERRITORIES, IN SEARCH FOR THOSE WHO WALKED IN THE DARKNESS OF SIN AND SHAME. I HAVE SENT MY PROPHETS, MY ABUSED AND LONELY PROPHETS, TO SEARCH THE STREETS OF SIN AND DESTRUCTION FOR THE SOULS OF MY MISGUIDED CHILDREN. I HAVE SOUGHT THE AREAS OF THE WORLD THAT HIDE THOSE WHOM I AM SEARCHING FOR. I HAVE FOUND YOU, O WORTHY AND LOVED ONES OF MINE. I HAVE FOUND THE LOST SOULS WHOM I SEEK. I WILL FEED YOU WITH THE KNOWLEDGE THAT WILL NOURISH YOU, SO THAT YOU MAY DWELL WITHIN MY REALM OF HOLINESS. I WILL LEAD YOU AWAY FROM THE REALM (SATAN) THAT DESIRES TO HARM YOUR VALUABLE SOULS. I WILL LEAD YOU IN THE DIRECTION OF HEAVENLY BLISS ON EARTH, AS YOU GIVE PRAISE, GLORY AND HONOR TO JESUS, YOUR EVERLASTING SAVIOR AND GOD.
JULY 3, 2015 BY: BARBARA ANN MARY MACK
SENT SUN, JUL 5, 2015 4:36 PM-READ SUN 7/5/2015 5:21 PM

MY SHEEP KNOW MY HOLY VOICE, AND THEY FOLLOW ONLY ME, *SAYS THE LORD.*

ALMIGHTY GOD, THE LORD JESUS, SPEAKING TO HIS FAITHFUL FLOCK

I CAN SEE YOU! I CAN HEAR YOU TOO! YOU CAN SEE ME, YOUR CREATOR AND GOD. YOU HEAR MY HOLY VOICE THROUGHOUT THE DAY, BECAUSE YOU ARE MY FAITHFUL SHEEP. I SEE THE GOOD AND HOLY DEEDS THAT YOU DO, BECAUSE YOU TRULY LOVE ME, YOUR GOOD AND HOLY SHEPHERD. YOU ANSWER ME WHEN I CALL YOUR CHOSEN NAME. YOU RESPOND TO MY HOLY VOICE IMMEDIATELY, FOR YOU KNOW MY HOLY VOICE. I THANK YOU, O FAITHFUL SHEEP OF MINE, FOR YOU HAVE EXPRESSED YOUR ALLEGIANCE AND DEVOTION TO ME, YOUR GOOD SHEPHERD. YOU DO NOT HEAR OR FOLLOW THE VOICE OF THE FALSE SHEPHERDS. YOU DO NOT FOLLOW THEIR UNGODLY WAYS. LET US REJOICE, O FAITHFUL FLOCK OF MINE! LET US REJOICE IN THE MIDST OF THE DECEITFUL ONES, FOR THEY ARE HEADED FOR ETERNAL DESTRUCTION AND DOOM! THEY DO NOT HEAR MY VOICE! THEY DO NOT HEAR THE VOICE OF JESUS, THE GOOD AND HOLY SHEPHERD. LET US REJOICE, O FAITHFUL SHEEP OF MINE! LET US SING SONGS OF PRAISE UNTO GOD, OUR HOLY FATHER! FOR HE IS THE HOLY FATHER OF JESUS, THE GOOD SHEPHERD.

JULY 3, 2015 BY: BARBARA ANN MARY MACK

SENT SUN, JUL 5, 2015 4:36 PM-READ SUN 7/5/2015 5:21 PM

PLEASANT DREAMS DEAR ONE! TODAY'S PASSAGE FOR YOU. *AMORE, BELLA BARBIE*

OH, IF I COULD ONLY *LAUGH AGAIN*

OH HOW I MISS YOU, O SWEET REALM (LAUGHTER) THAT ONCE ROAMED MY INNER BEING. OH HOW I LONG FOR THE PRESENCE (LAUGHTER) THAT REMINDS ME OF MY ORIGIN AND

GOD. OH HOW I LONG TO CLING TO THE EMOTION (LAUGHTER) THAT FLOWED THROUGH MY BEING THROUGHOUT THE DAY. WHERE HAVE YOU GONE, O SWEET GIFT (DAUGHTER) THAT DESCENDED FROM HEAVEN'S OPENED GATES? WHY DO YOU HIDE FROM ME? WHY DO YOU NOT APPEAR ON MY ABUSED FACE ANYMORE? WHERE ARE YOU, O EMOTION THAT ONCE FILLED MY DAY WITH DELIGHT AND DIVINE PLEASURE? WHY DO YOU NOT APPEAR ON MY NEEDY FACE TODAY? WHO HAS CAUSED YOU TO DEPART FROM ME, O REALM (LAUGHTER) THAT I SEARCH FOR THROUGH THE NIGHTS? ARE YOU SEARCHING FOR ME TOO? ARE YOU LOOKING FOR YOUR PLACE OF RESIDENCE (BARBARA)? COME OUT, O REALM (LAUGHTER) THAT I SEEK! COME BACK TO THE ONE WHO REACHES OUT IN THE DARKNESS FOR YOUR LONGED FOR PRESENCE. DID SATAN'S REALM OF EVIL LURE YOU AWAY FROM ME? DID HE STEAL THE JOY THAT YOU ONCE ACCOMPANIED? DID HE REPLACE MY REALM OF LAUGHTER WITH HIS EVIL DEEDS AND PRESENCE? HE HAS PERMEATED THE WORLD WITH HIS EVIL WORKS. HE HAS REMOVED THE LOVE THAT ONCE FLOWED THROUGH THE CONSCIOUS OF MANKIND. HE HAS REPLACED MANKIND'S LOVE FOR THE OTHER, WITH APATHY, DIVISION, RACISM, ABUSE, AND HATRED. OH, IF I COULD ONLY ENJOY THE REALM OF LAUGHTER THAT I ONCE EMBRACED. BUT HOW CAN I, WHEN THE REALM OF EVIL CAUSES HAVOC AND CHAOS THROUGHOUT THE LANDS? HOW CAN I EXHIBIT THE REALM OF LAUGHTER, WHEN MY BROTHERS AND SISTERS THROUGHOUT THE WORLD ARE EXPERIENCING GREAT SUFFERING AND HARDSHIP? ONE DAY! ONE DAY, I WILL RELEASE YOU AGAIN, O SWEET REALM OF LAUGHTER!

JULY 4, 2015 BY: BARBARA ANN MARY MACK

SENT SUN, JUL 5, 2015 4:36 PM-READ SUN 7/5/2015 5:21 PM

HAVE HOLY FUN TODAY DEAR ARCHBISHOP CRAIG!
AMORE, BELLA BARBARA

CHRIST SAID "THOSE WHO KEEP MY WORD ARE MY DISCIPLES."

BARBARA SPEAKING TO CHRIST'S CHURCH

WHEN WE DEVIATE FROM CHRIST'S HOLY WORDS, WE ARE NO LONGER CHRISTIANS IN THE HOLY EYES OF THE FOUNDER (JESUS) OF THE ONLY CHURCH. UNDERSTAND WHAT THE LORD SAYS. UNDERSTAND THE HOLY SCRIPTURES, FOR IT IS YOUR ONLY WAY TO SALVATION.

THE LORD JESUS SPEAKING TO HIS CHURCH

DO NOT LET THEM DELUDE OR CONFUSE YOU, MY CHILDREN. MY HOLY WAY IS THE ONLY WAY, THERE IS NO OTHER WAY OR FOUNDER OF MY HOLY CHURCH! I WILL NOT PERMIT MY FOLLOWERS TO SIT IN MY PEWS WITH MY ENEMIES (THOSE WHO FOLLOWS SATAN'S EVIL AND SINFUL ACTS).

BARBARA SPEAKING TO CHRIST'S CHURCH

MY BROTHERS AND SISTERS, WE MUST WALK THE HOLY WALK AT ALL TIMES, FOR WE ARE IN THE HOLY PRESENCE OF THE LORD. WE MUST STAY AWAY FROM THE THINGS THAT ARE NOT HOLY. LEARN WHAT IS HOLY THROUGH THE BIBLE, FOR IS WRITTEN.

THE LORD JESUS SPEAKING TO HIS CHURCH

LEARN OF ME, AND FOLLOW ME, MY CHILDREN, BEFORE IT IS TOO LATE.

JULY 2, 2015 BY: BARBARA ANN MARY MACK
SENT SUN, JUL 5, 2015 4:36 PM-READ SUN 7/5/2015 5:21 PM

MY CHILDREN, YOUR ACTS CONVEY AND REVEAL YOUR LEVEL OF BELIEF IN *MY HOLY EXISTENCE-MY JUSTICE AND MY WRATH*

MY CHILDREN, DO YOU NOT REMEMBER THE WRITINGS THAT FLOW THROUGH MY HOLY SCRIPTURES PERTAINING TO MY WRATH? ALTHOUGH I AM A MERCIFUL AND COMPASSIONATE GOD, I WILL NOT TOLERATE DISOBEDIENCE FROM YOU WHO WERE CREATED OUT OF DUST. I WILL NOT TOLERATE THE ABUSE THAT YOU INFLICT ON MY HOLY WORDS, MY UNCHANGEABLE WORDS. FOR THOSE WHO DO NOT BELIEVE IN MY EXISTENCE, READ MY HOLY BIBLE, THERE YOU WILL LEARN OF ME. THERE YOU WILL LEARN OF MY MERCY. THERE YOU WILL LEARN OF MY COMPASSION. THERE, YOU WILL LEARN OF MY JUSTICE. THERE YOU WILL LEARN OF MY

VERSION OF HOLY LOVE. I AM A JUST AND RIGHTEOUS GOD, AND I LOVE MY CHILDREN. DO YOU NOT LOVE ME, O GREAT CREATION OF MINE? I WILL NOT ACCEPT ANY EXCUSES, MY CHILDREN. MY HOLY WORD IS AVAILABLE TO EVERYONE. COME, MY CHILDREN, AND LEARN OF ME TODAY! FOR I AM WORTHY TO BE ACKNOWLEDGED AT ALL TIMES, MY CHILDREN.

JULY 6, 2015 BY: BARBARA ANN MARY MACK

A VERY SERIOUS AND CRUCIAL ASSIGNMENT FROM *THE LORD*

I DO NOT HAVE THE TIME TO PLAY GAMES, NOR ENGAGE IN WORTHLESS ACTIVITIES AND CONVERSATIONS, FOR THESE ARE CRUCIAL TIMES. I WAS SENT BY THE LORD TO FEED HIS HUNGRY FLOCK WITH THE FOOD (DIVINE KNOWLEDGE) THAT WILL LEAD THEM IN THE DIRECTION OF SALVATION THROUGH CHRIST JESUS. FOR THE GATES OF HELL ARE OPEN TO RECEIVE THOSE WHO DO NOT ACCEPT GOD'S DIVINE NOURISHMENT (HOLY KNOWLEDGE). THE GATES OF HELL SEEK AND DESTROY THOSE WHO ARE NOT SAVED BY THE BLOOD OF JESUS, OUR VICTORIOUS KING AND GOD. COME, O VULNERABLE CHILDREN OF OUR GREAT AND HOLY GOD! FOLLOW ME THROUGH THE GATES THAT LEAD TO THE LORD JESUS, OUR ONLY SAVING GOD. FOR HE IS OUR ONLY PLACE OF REFUGE DURING THIS CRUCIAL PERIOD OF TIME. HE HAS SENT ME TO DELIVER HIS FINAL MESSAGE OF LIFE WITH THE BLESSED HOLY TRINITY IN SWEET PARADISE. MY BROTHERS AND SISTERS, THIS IS A VERY SERIOUS AND CRUCIAL PERIOD OF TIME, FOR IT IS TRULY THE LAST DAYS!!! THE GATES OF HEAVEN HAVE OPENED, AND RELEASED THE LAST DAYS!!!

JULY 6, 2015 BY: BARBARA ANN MARY MACK

ALMIGHTY GOD SPEAKING

MY HOLY PROMISE TO THE WORLD- *I WILL NOT DESTROY THE WORLD BECAUSE OF THEIR EVIL DEEDS*

I WILL NOT DESTROY THE WORLD BECAUSE OF THEIR EVIL DEEDS. ALTHOUGH THEIR SINS ARE HORRENDOUS, I WILL HONOR MY HOLY PROMISE, *SAYS THE LORD.* I WILL NOT DESTROY THE WORLD FOR THE SAKES OF THOSE WHO CRY OUT IN PRAYER, FOR RELIEF FROM THE REALM OF EVIL. THE CRIES AND PRAYERS HAVE REACHED MY EMPATHETIC EARS. I HAVE WITNESSED THE FILTH THAT FLOWS FROM THOSE WHO HAVE JOINED SATAN'S REALM OF DESTRUCTION AND DOOM. I HAVE WITNESSED THE UNSPEAKABLE ACTS THAT PERMEATED THE STREETS OF SIN AND DOOM! I HAVE WITNESSED THE AFFLICTION THAT HAS BEEN PLACED UPON MY WEAK AND LONELY CHILDREN. I HAVE WITNESSED THE DESTRUCTION THAT FELL UPON MY INNOCENT ONES AS THEY ROAMED IN THE MIDST OF EVERYDAY LIVING. I HAVE COME TO RESCUE MY CAPTIVE ONES! BUT I WILL NOT DESTROY THE WHOLE WORLD. JUSTICE IS COMING, O SUFFERING CHOSEN ONES! LOOK! IT IS ON ITS WAY! THIS IS MY PROMISE: THIS IS MY HOLY WORD!

JULY 6, 2015 BY: BARBARA ANN MARY MACK

SENT TUE, JUL 7, 2015 12:54 AM-READ TUE 7/7/2015 9:09 AM

WE WILL NOT HAVE PITY ON THE REALM OF EVIL AS THEY CRY OUT IN ETERNAL AGONY, *SAYS THE LORD*

ALMIGHTY GOD SPEAKING TO SATAN.

I WILL SHOW NO PITY OR REMORSE TOWARD THE REALM OF EVIL THAT WAS FORMED BY
SATAN, THE DEVIL, AS THEY CRY OUT IN GREAT AGONY THROUGHOUT ETERNITY. I WILL NOT
FEEL ANYTHING OTHER THAN JUSTICE, AS I HEAR THEIR CONTINUOUS CRIES. FOR I WILL
REMEMBER THE CRIES THAT ESCAPED THE BEINGS OF THOSE WHOM THE REALM OF EVIL
HAS TORTURED AND ABUSED THROUGHOUT THE REALM OF TIME. I WILL REMEMBER THE
PLEAS THAT ESCAPED THE BEINGS OF MY LITTLE ONES, AS THE REALM OF EVIL LAUGHED
AT THEM IN THE MIDST OF THEIR TORTURING ACTS. I WILL NOT WEEP, AS I HEAR THEIR
WEEPING AND UNCEASING CRIES. I WILL NOT REGRET MY JUDGMENT AND THEIR SENTENCE,
AS I LISTEN TO THE WAILS THAT ESCAPED THEIR DEFEATED REALM OF EXISTENCE. I HEAR
YOU, O SUFFERING ENEMIES OF MINE! I HEAR YOUR UNQUENCHABLE CRIES! DO YOU RECALL
THE UNSPEAKABLE ACTS THAT YOU SUBJECTED MY VULNERABLE CHILDREN TO? DO YOU
RECALL THE SOUNDS OF THEIR CONTINUOUS CRIES AND PLEAS? DO YOU RECALL THE LOOK
ON THEIR FACES AS YOU TERMINATED THEIR VALUABLE LIVES? DO YOU RECALL THE HORROR
THAT YOU CAUSED EVERY TIME AN ABORTION WAS PERFORMED?

BARBARA SPEAKING TO SATAN

I WILL REJOICE AT THE SOUNDS THAT REVEAL YOUR AGONY AND SUFFERING, O DOOMED ONE!
I WILL REJOICE AS I WITNESS YOUR ENTRANCE INTO THE GATES OF ETERNAL HELL! I WILL
DANCE A DANCE OF VICTORY AND DEFEAT AS I HEAR YOUR CRIES THROUGHOUT ETERNITY.
FOR YOU, O DOOMED ONES, HAVE SHOWN NO REMORSE OR MERCY TOWARD GOD'S VULNERABLE
AND INNOCENT ONES. I WILL SHOW YOUR EVIL REALM NO MERCY! I WILL NOT EXHIBIT PITY!
LET THE ETERNAL GATES OF HELL OPEN WIDE AS YOU ENTER! *ALLELUIA!!!*
JULY 6, 2015 BY: BARBARA ANN MARY MACK
SENT TUE, JUL 7, 2015 12:54 AM-READ TUE 7/7/2015 9:09 AM

THE CHAINS, THE SWEET, *SWEET CHAINS*

BARBARA SPEAKING TO THE HOLY CHAINS

OH HOW I LOVE YOU, O SWEET CHAINS THAT KEEP ME CONNECTED TO MY SAVING GOD AND
FATHER ABOVE.
O HOW I LONG TO SHARE THE CHAINS THAT BIND ME TO MY HEAVENLY SPOUSE AND GOD OF
CONTINUOUS LOVE.
OH HOW BLESSED AND LOVED, I AM IN DEED,
FOR I AM WITHOUT PHYSICAL AND SPIRITUAL NEED.

I AM GIVEN EVERYTHING THAT IS BESTOWED UPON A HEAVENLY FORMED BRIDE.

I WILL EXHIBIT MY GRATITUDE BY CLINGING TO THE SPIRITUAL CHAINS THAT I CANNOT HIDE.

I BOW IN THE COMPANY OF MY GREAT AND HOLY GOD,

AS I HOLD ON TO THE CHAINS THAT PRODUCE HEAVENLY LOVE.

DO NOT LET ME GO, O HEAVENLY CHAINS OF MINE!

FOR I WILL CLING TO YOU, THROUGHOUT THE REALM OF TIME.

BIND ME! BIND ME!

BIND ME TO THE GIFT OF GOD, THE HOLY TRINITY!

BIND ME, O SWEET CHAINS, IN THE PRESENCE OF THE WHOLE WORLD!

BIND ME AS I SING PRAISES TO THE LORD, IN THE PRESENCE OF EVERY CALLED BOY AND GIRL!

JULY 7, 2015 BY: BARBARA ANN MARY MACK

I DO NOT WANT TO HEAR YOUR VAIN WORDS, I WANT TO WITNESS YOUR HOLY DEEDS, YOUR GOOD WORKS, *SAYS THE LORD.*

ALMIGHTY GOD SPEAKING

I HEAR THEM (WORDS), BUT I DO NOT BELIEVE THEM. I HEAR YOUR MEANINGLESS AND VAIN WORDS. TO WHOM ARE YOU SPEAKING TO WHEN YOU SAY THE WORDS THAT YOU CALL PRAYERS? TO WHOM ARE YOU ADDRESSING WHEN YOU UTTER YOUR VAIN AND WORTHLESS WORDS? YOU ARE NOT ADDRESSING ME, O VAIN ONES! YOUR PRAYERS OF VAIN AND WORTHLESS WORDS DO NOT REACH MY HOLY EARS! DO YOU NOT KNOW OR BELIEVE THAT I CAN SEE THE TRUTH? DO YOU NOT KNOW THAT I CAN SEE WHAT IS REALLY IN YOUR VAIN HEARTS? MY CHILDREN, I, THE LORD, THE OMNIPRESENT ONE, DO NOT WANT TO HEAR YOUR MEANINGLESS WORDS OF PRAYER. I DESIRE HOLY WORKS AND DEEDS FROM THOSE WHO TRULY DESIRE TO

PLEASE THEIR MERCIFUL AND HOLY GOD AT ALL TIMES. O DISOBEDIENT ONES, YOU CAN KEEP YOUR VAIN AND WORTHLESS PRAYERS, FOR I HAVE SHUT MY HOLY EARS IN YOUR UNHOLY PRESENCE. YOU MAY COME TO ME WHEN YOU DESIRE TO LIVE ACCORDING TO MY VERSION OF RIGHTEOUSNESS. YOU MAY COME TO ME IN PRAYER WHEN YOUR WORKS AND ACTS PLEASE ME, YOUR ONLY WAY TO SALVATION AND DIVINE TRUTH, *SAYS THE LORD.*
JULY 8, 2015 BY: BARBARA ANN MARY MACK

WHEN MY WAY GETS DARK, I WILL FOLLOW *YOUR MARVELOUS LIGHT (JESUS CHRIST)*

BARBARA SPEAKING TO JESUS, THE EVERLASTING DIVINE LIGHT

WHEN MY WAY GETS DARK, DUE TO SATAN'S MANY INTERRUPTIONS, I WILL FOLLOW YOU, O MARVELOUS LIGHT. WHEN THE GATES OF HELL UNLEASH ITS EVILS IN OUR MIDST, I WILL FOLLOW YOU, O SAVING LIGHT. WHEN THE WRATH OF ALMIGHTY GOD REMOVES THOSE WHO PROMOTE THE DARK DEEDS OF SATAN, I WILL FOLLOW YOU, O GREAT AND HOLY LIGHT OF THE WORLD. WHEN OUR WORLD IS FULL OF EVIL DEEDS AND ACTS, I WILL FOLLOW YOU, O GRACEFUL LIGHT. WHEN SATAN SHOWERS THIS WORLD WITH THE EVILS THAT WILL LEAD HIS FOLLOWERS THROUGH THE GATES OF HELL, I WILL FOLLOW YOU, LORD JESUS. CLING TO YOUR FAITHFUL SONS AND DAUGHTER, AS WE COMBAT THE REALM OF DARKNESS IN OUR VULNERABLE MIDST, O GREAT AND HOLY LIGHT OF THE WORLD. O HOLY LIGHT OF THE WORLD, I WILL FEAR NO EVIL, AS LONG AS YOU ARE IN OUR VULNERABLE MIDST. LET YOUR HOLY PRESENCE LIGHT UP THE PATH THAT WILL LEAD YOUR VULNERABLE CHILDREN TO YOUR HOLY KINGDOMS ON EARTH AND IN HEAVEN, MY LORD. WE WILL CLING TO THE DIVINE LIGHT (THE LORD JESUS), AS WE PROCLAIM VICTORY OVER THE REALM THAT RELEASES DARKNESS AND GLOOM IN OUR MIDST TODAY.
JULY 8, 2015 BY: BARBARA ANN MARY MACK

THEY ARE CONTAMINATING THE CHURCH, *SAYS THE LORD*

ALMIGHTY GOD SPEAKING

REMOVE THEM! REMOVE THOSE WHO ARE CONTAMINATING MY CHURCH! FOR THEY WILL NEVER SEE MY FACE, UNTIL THEY LEAVE BEHIND THOSE ACTS THAT ARE OFFENSIVE TO ME, THE HOLY ONE. DO NOT LET THEM ENTER MY CHURCH! DO NOT LET THEM SIT IN MY PEWS, FOR THEY ARE CONTAMINATING THAT WHICH WAS HOLY AND CLEAN, *SAYS THE LORD.* REMOVE THE VILE ONES, UNTIL THEY HAVE BEEN CLEANED AND PURGED. REMOVE THE ADULTERERS! REMOVE THE FORNICATORS! REMOVE THE HYPOCRITES! REMOVE THE MURDERERS (THOSE WHO PARTAKE IN ABORTIONS)! REMOVE THE LIARS! REMOVE THE RACISTS! REMOVE THE UNFORGIVING ONES! REMOVE THOSE WHO ENGAGE IN SEXUAL PERVERSION! REMOVE THOSE WHO WORSHIP ANYONE

OR THING OTHER THAN ALMIGHTY GOD! REMOVE THE ABUSERS! REMOVE THEM, O FAITHFUL SHEPHERDS OF MINE! REMOVE THEM, BEFORE I REMOVE YOU, FOR THEY DO CONTAMINATE MY HOLY CHURCH! DO NOT INVITE THOSE WHO DO NOT DESIRE TO CHANGE, FOR THEY ARE HEADED FOR ETERNAL HELL! THEY MUST CHANGE BEFORE THEY CAN ENTER MY REALM OF HOLINESS. TELL EVERYONE WHAT I SAID, FOR I AM A GOD OF MY HOLY WORD, *SAYS THE LORD!*

JULY 8, 2015 BY: BARBARA ANN MARY MACK

SENT WED, JUL 8, 2015 5:34 PM-READ WED 7/8/2015 10:47 PM

OH, THE FIGHT IS CONTINUOUS! HELP ME, O LORD! FOR *NO ONE ELSE WILL DO IT!*

BARBARA SPEAKING TO ALMIGHTY GOD

THE FIGHT BETWEEN GOOD (ALMIGHTY GOD) AND EVIL (SATAN, THE DEVIL) IS CONTINUOUS. HELP ME, O LORD, FOR NO ONE ELSE WILL ENDURE THE AGONY AND HARDSHIPS THAT COME WITH THIS HORRENDOUS ASSIGNMENT FROM YOU! HE WON'T LET GO, MY LORD. SATAN, THE DEFEATED ONE, IS FIERCE AND CONTINUOUS! HE NEVER RESTS, THEREFORE WE (ALMIGHTY GOD AND BARBARA) CANNOT REST. HE HAS TAKEN DOWN MANY OF YOUR VULNERABLE CHILDREN, DESPITE OUR (ALMIGHTY GOD AND BARBARA) PLEAS TO THEM. THEY DID NOT HEED YOUR HOLY WORDS OF WARNING, THEREFORE, SATAN AND HIS EVIL REALM, HAD NO PROBLEM SUBDUING THE VULNERABLE ONES. SATAN KNOWS THE WEAKNESSES AND DESIRES OF THE VULNERABLE ONES. HE HAS DEFEATED THEM THROUGH THEIR WEAKNESSES AND WORLDLY LUSTS. HE HAS DEFEATED THEM THROUGH THEIR DISOBEDIENCE TO YOUR HOLY WAY. SATAN DOESN'T SLEEP, NOR DOES HE TAKE LUNCH, DINNER OR COFFEE BREAKS. HE IS CONTINUOUSLY WREAKING HAVOC AND PAIN TOWARD THE VULNERABLE AND UNSUSPECTING ONES. HELP ME, O LORD! FOR THIS CONTINUOUS BATTLE IS CAUSING GREAT PAIN AND AGONY. YOUR UNSUSPECTING CHILDREN ARE WORTH THE AGONY THAT I ENDURE! YOUR VULNERABLE CHILDREN ARE WORTH THIS ONGOING BATTLE AGAINST THE REALM THAT SEEKS TO DESTROY ALL THAT IS GOOD AND HOLY IN THE WORLD TODAY. HELP ME, O LORD, SO THAT I WILL NOT FAINT!

BARBARA SPEAKING TO SATAN AND HIS DEFEATED REALM OF EVIL

I WILL NOT QUIT, O DOOMED ONE! I WILL NOT LEAVE THE BATTLEFIELD! I WILL CONTINUE FIGHTING FOR THE VALUABLE SOULS OF THE LORD'S CALLED AND CHOSEN ONES! I WILL NOT REST! I WILL NOT TAKE COFFEE BREAKS! I WILL NOT TAKE LUNCH BREAKS! I WILL NOT TAKE DINNER BREAKS! I WILL RECEIVE THE DIVINE NOURISHMENT THAT IS GIVEN TO A WARRIOR ON THE BATTLEFIELD. I WILL EAT WHEN I HAVE COMPLETED MY WORK FOR THE DAY! I WILL SLEEP WITH ONE EYE OPEN AT ALL TIMES! I WILL AWAKEN AT THE SOUND OF YOU CREEPING INTO MY WORLD OF HEAVENLY BLISS! YOU CANNOT PREVENT WHAT ALMIGHTY GOD, MY HOLY

SPOUSE AND ORIGIN, HAS ORDERED AND FULFILLED! YOU CANNOT CHANGE ANYTHING THAT
IS ORDERED BY GOD, THE OMNIPOTENT ONE!!!
JULY 13, 2015 BY: BARBARA ANN MARY MACK
SENT TUE, JUL 14, 2015 12:29 AM-READ TUE 7/14/2015 2:27 AM

I AM COMING BACK FOR A PEOPLE, NOT A DENOMINATION, *SAYS THE LORD*

MY CHILDREN, I SHALL RETURN, VERY SOON! AND WHEN I RETURN, I AM COMING FOR A PEOPLE, NOT A DENOMINATION. THEREFORE, MY CHILDREN, BE PREPARED! I AM COMING FOR THOSE WHO HAVE BEEN FAITHFUL TO MY HOLY WORDS THAT FLOW THROUGH THE HOLY BIBLE. I AM COMING FOR THOSE WHO HAVE ACCEPTED THE RECENT MESSAGES THAT I REVEALED THROUGH BARBARA, MY CONTEMPORARY PROPHET AND BRIDE. I AM COMING FOR THOSE WHO REMAINED ON THE BATTLEFIELD IN THE MIDST OF THEIR HARD AND SUFFERING TIMES. I AM COMING FOR THOSE WHO WERE NOT ASHAMED TO SPEAK OF THEIR LOVE AND BELIEF IN MY HOLY EXISTENCE. I AM COMING BACK FOR THOSE WHO BELIEVE IN MY HOLY PROMISES. I AM COMING BACK FOR THOSE WHO FOLLOWED JESUS, THE ETERNAL LIGHT AND BREAD OF LIFE. I AM COMING BACK FOR THOSE WHO HAVE ABANDONED SATAN'S REALM OF DECEIT AND DOOM, FOR MY GLORIOUS KINGDOMS, ON EARTH AND IN HEAVEN ABOVE. MY CHILDREN, I AM RETURNING VERY SOON! ARE YOU READY FOR MY RETURN?
JULY 15, 2015 BY: BARBARA ANN MARY MACK

FOLLOW ME, O FAITHFUL ONES, FOR *I HAVE CONQUERED DEATH, SAYS THE LORD*

ALMIGHTY GOD SPEAKING

FOLLOW ME, ALL WHO DESIRE TO TASTE THE SWEETNESS THAT FLOWS FROM MY FOUNTAIN OF ETERNAL BLISS! FOLLOW ME, ALL WHO DESIRE TO SEE THE DWELLING PLACE OF ALMIGHTY GOD, THEIR FIRST AND LAST LOVE! FOLLOW ME, YOU WHO HAVE BEEN FAITHFUL TO MY VERSION OF HOLINESS. FOLLOW ME, YOU WHO HAVE LONGED TO GET A GLIMPSE OF MY VERSION OF ETERNAL PARADISE! FOLLOW ME, YOU WHO HAVE FOUGHT A VICTORIOUS FIGHT OVER THE REALM THAT I DESTROYED! FOLLOW ME, SO THAT YOU MAY FEEL THE PRESENCE OF YOUR OMNIPOTENT SAVIOR AND GOD. WALK WITH ME THROUGH THE GATES THAT WERE PROMISED TO YOU. WALK WITH ME THROUGH THE GATES THAT LEAD TO YOUR ETERNAL HOME WITH ME. COME, MY FAITHFUL AND OBEDIENT CHILDREN! LET US WALK THROUGH THE GATES THAT LEAD TO MY MIGHTY THRONE ON HIGH! THERE, YOU WILL EXPERIENCE ETERNAL LIFE WITH ME. THERE YOU WILL TASTE THE SERENITY OF ETERNAL LIFE IN PARADISE. THERE YOU WILL EXPERIENCE THE JOY THAT SURROUNDS THOSE WHO HAVE CONQUERED SPIRITUAL DEATH. THERE YOU WILL DWELL WITHIN THE REALM THAT HOUSES THE ESSENCE OF GOD, THE ETERNAL SOURCE OF LIFE.
JULY 15, 2015 BY: BARBARA ANN MARY MACK

GOD IS GOOD! LET US ENJOY HIS GOODNESS TODAY LOVE (CRAIG)!!!

HELP ME, MY BROTHERS AND SISTERS! HELP ME FIGHT FOR YOUR ETERNAL SOULS

BARBARA SPEAKING

HELP ME, MY BROTHERS AND SISTERS, FOR THE BATTLE IS LONG AND FIERCE! HELP ME, FOR THE BATTLE FOR YOUR VALUABLE SOULS IS VERY BRUTAL, CONTINUOUS, AND CONSUMING! HE WANTS TO CONSUME YOU TOO! HE WANTS THE LAKE OF FIRE TO CONSUME YOUR ETERNAL SOULS, FOR HE IS DESTRUCTION! HE, SATAN, WILL NOT QUIT! HE IS FULL OF ENERGY AND DESTRUCTION. HE KNOWS THAT HE IS GOING DOWN! HE KNOWS THAT HE IS GOING INTO THE PIT OF HELL, AND HIS ONLY DESIRE IS TO TAKE YOU WITH HIM. HE DESIRES TO SHARE HIS RESIDENCE (HELL) WITH YOU. THEREFORE, I NEED YOUR HELP TOO! THIS ONGOING BATTLE HAS WEAKENED ME PHYSICALLY, HELP ME, MY BROTHERS AND SISTERS! HELP ME, BEFORE IT IS TOO LATE! SATAN HAS TAKEN MANY DOWN BY WAY OF SUICIDES. HE HAS TAKEN MANY DOWN BY WAY OF DISOBEDIENCE UNTO OUR CREATOR AND GOD. HE HAS TAKEN MANY DOWN, BY WAY OF IRREVERENCE TOWARDS GOD'S HOLY UNCHANGING WORD IN THE BIBLE. HELP ME COMBAT SATAN AND HIS REALM OF EVIL, MY BROTHERS AND SISTERS! HE HAS SENT HIS LOWLY ANGELS OF DESTRUCTION TO THE STREETS THAT ARE FILLED WITH YOUR UNSUSPECTING SOULS. HELP ME TODAY! HE HAS SENT MANY DARTS, WHICH PIERCE MY BATTERED BEING DAILY. HELP ME TODAY, MY BROTHERS AND SISTERS! HE IS DESTRUCTIVE! HE IS HAVOC! HE IS CHAOS! HE IS CONTINUOUS PAIN! HE IS TORTURE! HE IS DEPRESSION! HE IS THE SOURCE OF SUICIDE! HE IS UNFORGIVABLE! HE IS THE RAPIST! HE IS THE MURDERER! HE IS DOOMED! HE IS THE ABUSER! HE IS THE SOURCE AND REALM OF HATRED! HELP ME, MY BROTHERS AND SISTERS! HELP ME FIGHT THE GATES OF HELL FOR YOUR VALUABLE SOULS TODAY!
JULY 18, 2015 BY: BARBARA ANN MARY MACK

TIME IS RUNNING OUT! MAKE THAT CHANGE TODAY, *SAYS THE LORD*

BARBARA SPEAKING TO GOD'S CHILDREN

MY BROTHERS AND SISTERS, MAKE THAT CHANGE, FOR TIME IS RUNNING OUT! MAKE THAT CHANGE BEFORE IT IS TOO LATE, FOR TIME IS RUNNING OUT! MAKE WAY FOR THE ONLY REALM (ALMIGHTY GOD) THAT CAN SAVE YOUR SINKING SOULS. THERE IS NO OTHER WAY! REMOVE YOURSELVES FROM THE REALM (SATAN) THAT LEADS TO PHYSICAL AND SPIRITUAL DESTRUCTION. REMOVE YOURSELVES FROM PRE-MARITAL SEX! REMOVE YOURSELVES FROM LYING AND STEALING! REMOVE YOURSELVES FROM RACISM AND HATRED! REMOVE YOURSELVES FROM "UNHOLY" SEXUAL ACTIVITIES-HOMOSEXUALITY! REMOVE YOURSELVES FROM "UNFORGIVENESS"! REMOVE YOURSELVES FROM "UNHOLY" CONVERSATIONS! REMOVE YOURSELVES FROM GOSSIP AND WORTHLESS CONVERSATIONS. YOUR PRECIOUS TIME IS RUNNING OUT MY BROTHERS AND SISTERS, MAKE THAT CHANGE TODAY!

ALMIGHTY GOD SPEAKING TO THE TIME

I HAVE RELEASED YOU, O PRECIOUS TIME! I HAVE RELEASED YOUR APPOINTED ENTRANCE INTO A WORLD THAT IS ABOUT TO END! I HAVE RELEASED YOU INTO A WORLD THAT ACCEPTS AND APPROVES OF THE REALM (SATAN) THAT I DESPISE! I HAVE RELEASED YOU INTO A WORLD THAT DOES NOT RESPECT THE HOLY PRESENCE OF THEIR CREATOR AND GOD. I HAVE RELEASED YOU IN THE MIDST OF PERILOUS TIMES! I HAVE RELEASED YOU IN THE MIDST OF THOSE WHO ARE FIGHTING FOR MY VERSION OF HOLY LIVING! I HAVE RELEASED YOU IN THE MIDST OF MY WEEPING PROPHETS AND MESSENGERS OF DIVINE LOVE! GO, O LONGED FOR TIME! ENTER YOUR DESTINATION (THE WORLD) TODAY. FOR I, THE LORD, HAVE SENT FORTH THEE APPOINTED TIME!!!

JULY 18, 2015 BY: BARBARA ANN MARY MACK

SENT SUN, JUL 19, 2015 7:11 PM-READ SUN 7/19/2015 7:37 PM

GREETINGS LOVE! I PRAY THAT YOU HAD A WONDERFUL DAY. LA TOYA AND AMYA ARE HANGING OUT WITH THEIR FAMILY AND FRIEND. YIPPIEEEEE! I HAVE THE HOUSE TO MYSELF FOR A FEW HOURS. MY SISTER CALLED A LITTLE WHILE AGO, AND WE TALKED UNTIL THE DELIVERY MAN RANG HER DOORBELL. I AM COOKING TOMORROW'S MEAL AT THIS TIME. EARLIER TODAY, LA TOYA MADE RESERVATIONS FOR OUR VISITS TO PITTSBURG AND ERIE, PA. SHE'S LOOKING AT GETTYSBURG AND THE POCONOS AS WELL. AMYA AND I PREFER STAYING HOME, BUT LA TOYA LOVES TO TRAVEL. THE LORD USUALLY HAS ME DELIVER MESSAGES TO HIS CHILDREN WHERE EVER WE GO. WE WILL STAY AT LEAST FIVE NIGHTS TO A WEEK AT EACH LOCATION. WE WILL SEE.

PLEASANT DREAMS LOVE!!! BEAUTIFUL BARBARA

SENT SUN, JUL 19, 2015 7:11 PM-READ SUN 7/19/2015 7:37 PM

GREETINGS ARCHBISHOP CRAIG! COME STA OGGI? I CAME ACROSS THIS ARTICLE PERTAINING TO CHURCHES, RELIGIOUS ORGANIZATIONS AND HOMOSEXUAL MARRIAGES. I CANNOT, AND WILL NOT UNDERSTAND HOW ANYONE CAN EXPECT A "HOLY SHEPHERD" OF THE LORD, TO PERFORM AN "UNHOLY ACT" (PERFORMING A MARRIAGE CEREMONY FOR GAY COUPLES), ESPECIALLY INSIDE A CHURCH. ACCORDING TO THE HOLY BIBLE, HOMOSEXUALITY IS AN ABOMINATION. THE FOUNDER OF THE CHURCH, THE LORD JESUS CHRIST, DID NOT CHANGE WHAT IS WRITTEN. THEREFORE, NO ONE CAN CHANGE WHAT THE HOLY BIBLE STATES. THOSE WHO DO, ARE IN DANGER OF THE LORD'S WRATH AND DIVINE JUSTICE. THE LORD WANTS THE SHEPHERDS THAT HE CHOSE, TO STAND FIRM IN HIS WRITTEN WORD, EVEN IF IT MEANS SUFFERING FOR JESUS CHRIST'S CHURCH. THE LORD WILL STAND BY HIS SHEPHERDS AS LONG AS THEY REMAIN FAITHFUL TO HIS "UNCHANGING HOLY WORD". DO NOT FORSAKE ME, MY SONS, *SAYS THE LORD,* FOR I AM GREATER THAN THE WORLD!

THE WORLD (SATAN) IS MAKING PROFESSED CHRISTIANS CHOOSE BETWEEN HIM (THE WORLD) AND SWEET PARADISE (ALMIGHTY GOD)

WHOM DO YOU PRESENT YOUR ALLEGIANCE TO, MY CHILDREN? WHO HOLDS YOUR LOYALTY AND LOVE? IS IT ME, YOUR GREAT AND HOLY CREATOR AND GOD, OR IS IT SATAN, THE WORLD? DO NOT LET HIM DECEIVE YOU, FOR THIS LIFE AND THE WORLD ARE TEMPORARY. SHOW CONCERN FOR YOUR ETERNAL LIFE, OR ETERNAL DEATH. WHICH ONE HOLDS YOUR ALLEGIANCE, MY CHILDREN? WHOM DO YOU REALLY FEAR? IS IT ME, THE ONLY ALL POWERFUL ONE? OR IS IT SATAN, THE DEFEATED ONE? WHOM DO YOU TRULY HONOR? IS IT THE WORLD? IS IT ME, YOUR ONLY SAVING GOD AND FATHER? WHOM DO YOU REALLY REVERE? WHO HAS CAPTURED YOUR UNDIVIDED ATTENTION?

ALMIGHTY GOD SPEAKING TO THE CLERGY

DON'T DO IT, MY SONS! DO NOT FOLLOW THE WAYS OF THE WORLD! DO NOT ACCEPT THEIR VERSION OF MORALITY AND DIVINE ORDER. FOLLOW MY HOLY WAY, EVEN IN THE MIDST OF YOUR DOUBTS. DO NOT GO ALONG WITH WHAT THE WORLD VIEWS AS RIGHT AND JUST, FOR YOU ARE NOT OF THE WORLD. YOU HAVE BEEN PURCHASED BY ME, THE SLAUGHTERED LAMB OF GOD, *SAYS THE LORD.* HOLD FAST TO YOUR ALLEGIANCE TO ME, MY WORTHY SONS, FOR I WILL NEVER ABANDON YOU. HOLD ON TO YOUR ALLEGIANCE TO ME, EVEN IN THE MIDST OF THIS PERVERTED AND UNHOLY PERIOD OF TIME. DO NOT SELL YOUR ETERNAL SOULS FOR THE TEMPORARY FAME, AND ALLEGIANCE TO THE REALM (THE WORLD) THAT GOES AGAINST MY

HOLY TEACHINGS. DO NOT ABANDON ME AND MY EVERLASTING LIFE IN SWEET PARADISE. DO NOT CONFORM TO OR ACCEPT THEIR UNHOLY WAYS AND BELIEFS, FOR IT WILL LEAD YOU THROUGH THE GATES OF HELL. MAINTAIN YOUR STANCE AND ALLEGIANCE TO ME AND MY HOLY WORD! OH, WHAT A FIGHT! A SPIRITUAL WAR ON EARTH TODAY!

JULY 17, 2015 BY: BARBARA ANN MARY MACK

SENT SUN, JUL 19, 2015 7:11 PM-READ SUN 7/19/2015 7:37 PM

BACK OFF SATAN! FOR THE CHOSEN ONES ARE MINE, *SAYS THE LORD1*

ALMIGHTY GOD SPEAKING TO SATAN

YOU CAN SEEK THEM! BUT YOU WILL NEVER OWN THEM! FOR THEY ARE MINE, O REALM OF DOOM AND DESTRUCTION, *SAYS THE LORD!* YOU HAVE SLITHERED INTO THE LIVES OF MY UNSUSPECTING AND VULNERABLE ONES. KNOW THIS, O DEFEATED ONE, KNOW THAT YOUR UNWANTED PRESENCE IN THIS WORLD IS FOR A SHORT PERIOD OF TIME! YOUR UNHOLY PRESENCE IN THE LIVES OF MY CHOSEN ONES IS TEMPORARY! BACK OFF OF MY CHOSEN ONES, FOR THEY ARE SPOKEN FOR! I HAVE CLAIMED THEIR ETERNAL SOULS BEFORE THEIR PHYSICAL EXISTENCE BEGAN. BACK OFF, O DEFEATED REALM! FOR YOU HAVE LOST THIS GREAT BATTLE! BACK OFF, AND ENTER THE GATES OF HELL, WHICH LEAD TO YOUR PERMANENT HOME! FOR I, THE LORD ALMIGHTY, HAVE COME TO RETRIEVE MY LOVED ONES FROM YOUR DOOMED CLUTCHES! I HAVE COME FOR THOSE WHO HAVE FOLLOWED MY TEACHINGS, *SAYS THE LORD.* I HAVE COME FOR THOSE WHO BELIEVE IN MY POWER OVER YOU AND YOUR REALM OF DECEIT AND DESTRUCTION! I HAVE COME, O LOWLY SERPENT OF DOOM! I HAVE COME TO DESTROY YOUR UNWANTED REALM OF PAIN AND SORROW! I HAVE COME TO DESTROY THE REALM OF DEATH THAT SLITHERS FROM YOUR UNHOLY GATES! I HAVE COME, O ENEMY (SATAN, THE DEVIL) OF MINE. I HAVE COME!

JULY 17, 2015 BY: BARBARA ANN MARY MACK

SENT SUN, JUL 19, 2015 7:11 PM-READ SUN 7/19/2015 7:37 PM

I WILL NOT MINGLE WITH THEM, FOR *THEY DO NOT DESIRE TO HEAR THE GOOD NEWS*

BARBARA SPEAKING

I WILL NOT MINGLE WITH THEM! I WILL NOT MINGLE WITH THOSE WHO DO NOT DESIRE TO HEAR OF THE GOOD NEWS OF JESUS, MY HOLY SPOUSE AND GOD. I WILL NOT MINGLE WITH ANYONE, WHO OPPOSES THE TRUTH CONCERNING JESUS' DIVINITY AS GOD, THE ONLY BEGOTTEN SON. I WILL NOT MINGLE WITH THOSE WHO TRY TO CONVINCE ME THAT JESUS IS NOT MY SAVIOR AND GOD. I WILL NOT MINGLE WITH THOSE WHOM SATAN SENDS TO DISTRACT ME FROM MY DIVINE ASSIGNMENT OF LOVE. I WILL NOT MINGLE WITH THOSE WHO DO NOT WALK IN THE DIRECTION OF GOD'S VERSION OF HOLINESS. THEY DO NOT WANT TO HEAR ME TALK ABOUT GOD, MY HOLY SPOUSE. THEY DO NOT DESIRE TO HEAR THE GOOD NEWS OF OUR (THE LORD AND BARBARA) ETERNAL BELOVED ONE (CRAIG). THEREFORE, I DO NOT DESIRE TO MINGLE WITH THEM! I WILL MINGLE WITH THOSE WHO DESIRE TO HEAR OF OUR (ALMIGHTY GOD, CRAIG, AND BARBARA) GOOD NEWS. I WILL MINGLE WITH THOSE WHO DESIRE TO HEAR THE TRUTH. JULY 14, 2015 BY: BARBARA ANN MARY MACK

I AM WEAK! I AM EXHAUSTED! *HELP ME!*

BARBARA SPEAKING TO GOD'S CHILDREN

MY BROTHERS AND SISTERS, I AM WEAK! I AM EXHAUSTED! I HAVE SPENT MANY MINUTES, HOURS AND DAYS WITHOUT PHYSICAL AND SPIRITUAL REST. THE LORD HAS SENT ME TO DELIVER A MESSAGE THAT CANNOT WAIT, OR BE PLACED ON HOLD. FOR SATAN AND HIS DOOMED ANGELS (EVIL SPIRITS-FOLLOWERS) DO NOT REST. THEY ARE ON THE PROWL TWENTY-FOUR HOURS A DAY, IN SEARCH OF UNSUSPECTING AND VULNERABLE SOULS. HE DOESN'T TAKE BREAKS. HIS MISSION, PURPOSE, AND DESIRE ARE TO DECEIVE AND DESTROY ALL WHO ARE UNCLOTHED WITH GOD'S VERSION OF HOLINESS. HELP ME, MY BROTHERS AND

SISTERS! HELP ME COMBAT THE REALM OF EVIL FOR YOUR VALUABLE ETERNAL SOULS! FOR THEY ARE AT STAKE! HELP ME WIN THE BATTLE THAT IS BRUTAL AND ONGOING! TIME IS RUNNING OUT! AND SATAN HAS TAKEN DOWN MANY! HELP ME, MY BROTHERS AND SISTERS, FOR I AM EXHAUSTED!
JULY 15, 2015 BY: BARBARA ANN MARY MACK

IN THE MIDST OF PHYSICAL, EMOTIONAL, AND SPIRITUAL EXHAUSTION, I TAKE DOWN YOUR VITAL DICTATIONS, MY LORD

BARBARA SPEAKING TO THE LORD

TIME IS RUNNING OUT FOR THEM, MY LORD! HELP ME GAIN THE STRENGTH THAT IS NEEDED TO CARRY OUT THIS TREMENDOUS ASSIGNMENT OF DIVINE LOVE, FOR I AM TRULY EXHAUSTED. IN THE MIDST OF MY EXHAUSTION, I WILL WRITE DOWN YOUR LIFE SAVING MESSAGES. IN THE MIDST OF PHYSICAL, SPIRITUAL, AND EMOTIONAL EXHAUSTION, I WILL WRITE DOWN YOUR HOLY WORDS OF LOVE. IN THE MIDST OF EXHAUSTION, I WILL WRITE DOWN YOUR VITAL MESSAGES IN REGARDS TO SALVATION AND ETERNAL LIFE WITH GOD, THE HOLY TRINITY. IN THE MIDST OF EXHAUSTION, I WILL PLEAD TO YOUR OBSTINATE CHILDREN. IN THE MIDST OF EXHAUSTION, I WILL CONTINUE FIGHTING SATAN AND HIS DEFEATED CREW FOR THE SOULS OF YOUR CALLED AND CHOSEN ONES. MY LORD, THE SPIRITUAL BATTLE IS WEIGHING MY WEAK BEING DOWN. SATAN AND HIS FOLLOWERS ARE BEATING THE LIFE OUT OF MY WEAK BODY. HELP ME, O LORD, FOR I AM IN GREAT PAIN! HELP ME, O SAVIOR OF THE CHOSEN ONES, FOR I NEED YOUR DIVINE PHYSICAL, EMOTIONAL, AND SPIRITUAL STRENGTH EVERY SECOND OF THE DAY! MY LORD, IN THE MIDST OF EXHAUSTION, I WILL BOW IN YOUR HOLY AND WELL-LOVED PRESENCE, FOR I TRULY ADORE YOU!!!
JULY 15, 2015 BY: BARBARA ANN MARY MACK

ALL OF MY CHILDREN ARE VERY VALUABLE TO ME, *SAYS THE LORD*

JESUS, ALMIGHTY GOD, SPEAKING

COME, MY CHILDREN, AND GATHER AROUND YOUR HOLY LOVING GOD, FOR I HAVE SOMETHING VERY IMPORTANT TO SHARE WITH YOU TODAY! I WANT YOU TO KNOW THAT YOU ARE VERY VALUABLE TO ME, YOUR ETERNAL LOVING CREATOR AND GOD. IT DOESN'T MATTER WHAT YOUR SOCIAL POSITIONS ARE. IT DOESN'T MATTER WHAT RACE OF PEOPLE YOU ARE. IT DOESN'T MATTER IF YOU ARE NOT LIVING ACCORDING TO MY HOLY WORD AT THIS TIME, FOR YOU WILL CONFORM TO MY HOLY WAY, WHICH IS THE ONLY WAY TO ETERNAL LIFE WITH ME IN SWEET PARADISE. I WANT YOU TO KNOW OF THE GREAT AND HOLY SACRIFICE THAT I MADE

FOR YOU, NOT SO LONG AGO. I WANT YOU TO KNOW OF OUR GREAT AND HOLY FATHER'S ACTS OF GENEROSITY, WHEN HE SENT ME, HIS ONLY BEGOTTEN SON, TO BECOME THE GREAT AND HOLY SACRIFICIAL LAMB OF GOD ALMIGHTY. I WANT YOU TO KNOW OF MY ALLEGIANCE TO YOU AND OUR GREAT AND HOLY FATHER ABOVE. COME, MY SWEET INVITED GUESTS, AND GATHER AROUND ME, SO THAT I MAY WHISPER THE HOLY WORDS THAT WILL KEEP YOU SAFE FROM THE REALM THAT HOUSES SATAN, OUR ENEMY. GATHER AROUND ME, SO THAT YOU MAY HEAR MY SONGS OF VICTORY AND HEAVENLY BLISS. GATHER AROUND ME, AS MY HOLY CHOIR SINGS CONTINUOUS SONGS OF GRATITUDE AND PRAISE UNTO GOD, THE HOLY TRINITY. GATHER AROUND ME, O VALUABLE TREASURE THAT I LONG TO PROTECT FROM THE REALM THAT SEEKS TO DESTROY MY LITTLE CHILDREN. GATHER AROUND ME, YOUR ETERNAL PLACE OF REFUGE AND SPIRITUAL FAME, FOR YOU ARE VERY VALUABLE TO ME!
JULY 10, 2015 BY: BARBARA ANN MARY MACK

THROUGHOUT THE NIGHT, YES! THE DARK, DARK NIGHT! YOU REVEALED THEIR FATE TO ME, O LORD

BARBARA SPEAKING TO ALMIGHTY GOD

THROUGHOUT THE NIGHT, YES, THE DARK, DARK NIGHT, YOU, O LORD, HAVE REVEALED THEIR FATE TO ME. THROUGHOUT THE NIGHT, YOU, O LORD, HAVE REVEALED THEIR FINAL DESTINATION. YOU HAVE REVEALED THEIR ALLEGIANCE TO THE REALM OF DESTRUCTION AND DAMNATION. YOU HAVE REVEALED THE DEPTH OF THEIR UNCHANGING HEARTS. YOU HAVE REVEALED THEIR UNHOLY ACTS. MY LORD, YOU HAVE REVEALED THEM, THE LOST ONES! YOU HAVE REVEALED THEIR PUNISHMENT TO ME. LET ME WEEP FOR THEM, MY GOD, FOR I HAVE PITY! JULY 22, 2015 BY: BARBARA ANN MARY MACK

HONOR MY HOLY WORDS, FOR THERE ARE NO EXCEPTIONS NOR EXCUSES, *SAYS THE LORD!*

ALMIGHTY GOD SPEAKING

MY LITTLE CHILDREN, HONOR MY HOLY WORDS TODAY, FOR THEY HAVEN'T CHANGED! GIVE HOMAGE AND ACKNOWLEDGMENT, FOR THERE ARE NO EXCEPTIONS! THIS APPLIES TO ALL OF MY CHILDREN!
JULY 21, 2015 BY: BARBARA ANN MARY MACK

WHERE WOULD I BE IF YOU HAD NOT RESCUED ME, *O LORD?*

BARBARA SPEAKING

I DO NOT WANT TO IMAGINE THE RESPONSE TO THAT QUESTION.
JULY 21, 2015 BY: BARBARA ANN MARY MACK

SCHISM IN *THE CHURCH TODAY*

BARBARA SPEAKING

OH, THERE IS SO MUCH DIVISION IN THE CHURCH TODAY! MANY ARE BRINGING IN IDEAS AND BELIEFS THAT ARE FORMED BY MANKIND. MANY OF THE CHURCHES TODAY CONDUCT THEIR SERVICES AS ENTERTAINMENT, INSTEAD OF TEACHING THE HOLY SCRIPTURES' TRUTH. MANY OF THE WORLDLY CHURCH LEADERS ARE CONCERNED WITH MONETARY GAIN INSTEAD OF GAINING SOULS, AND PREPARING THEM FOR THE SECOND COMING OF OUR ONE AND ONLY SAVIOR, JESUS CHRIST. SCHISM IN THE CHURCH IS PREVALENT AND DAMAGING TO THE CONGREGATION. MANKIND HAS ELEVATED HIMSELF IN THE PRESENCE OF THE WORLD. THEREFORE, ALMIGHTY GOD HAS CLOSED HIS HOLY EYES TO THEIR DEVIANT WAYS.

ALMIGHTY GOD SPEAKING

I DEMAND UNITY IN MY CHURCH, *SAYS THE LORD*. EVERYONE SHOULD BE ON ONE ACCORD, FOR YOU ARE REPRESENTING YOUR BELIEF IN ME, *SAYS THE LORD GOD*.
JULY 22, 2015 BY: BARBARA ANN MARY MACK

OBSERVING AND ACKNOWLEDGING OTHERS SINS, BUT NOT ACKNOWLEDGING YOUR OWN

BARBARA SPEAKING

MY BROTHERS AND SISTERS, LET US ACKNOWLEDGE OUR SINS SO THAT WE MAY REMOVE THEM FROM OUR LIVES TODAY. LET US FOCUS ON REMOVING THE SIN(S) THAT KEEPS US SEPARATED FROM GOD'S HOLY REALM. LET US REQUEST THE LORD'S DIVINE HELP, SO THAT HE MAY REVEAL TO US WHAT WE NEED TO CHANGE IN OUR LIVES. THIS IS VERY CRITICAL AND CRUCIAL. IT MUST BE DONE TODAY! WE CANNOT PUT OFF RECTIFYING OUR SINS IN THE PRESENCE OF THE LORD, FOR OUR TIME IS RUNNING OUT. MY BROTHERS AND SISTERS, DO NOT FOCUS ON YOUR NEIGHBORS' OR FAMILY'S SINFUL DEEDS, FOR YOUR WEAKNESSES OFFEND GOD AS WELL.
JULY 22, 2015 BY: BARBARA ANN MARY MACK

UNDERSTAND ME, *SAYS THE LORD*.

ALMIGHTY GOD SPEAKING

MY CHILDREN, WHEN IT COMES TO DOING THINGS THAT MANKIND CONSIDERS ACCEPTABLE AND JUST, YOU HAVE NO PROBLEM CONFORMING TO THEIR WAY OF RATIONALIZATION. YOU HAVE NO PROBLEM UNDERSTANDING THEIR WAY OF THINKING-WHICH IS CONTRARY TO MINE. MY VULNERABLE AND MISGUIDED CHILDREN, UNDERSTAND MY HOLY WAY, WHICH IS TRULY, THE ONLY WAY TO ETERNAL LIFE WITH ME. *THUS, SAYS THE LORD*
JULY 21, 2015 BY: BARBARA ANN MARY MACK

THIS IS A VERY CRUCIAL PERIOD OF TIME

ALMIGHTY GOD SPEAKING

HOW MANY WILL FALL INTO THE CLUTCHES OF SATAN DURING THIS CRUCIAL PERIOD OF TIME? HOW MANY WILL BE RECRUITED BY HIM, TO JOIN HIS ARMY AGAINST THE KINGDOM OF RIGHTEOUSNESS (ALMIGHTY GOD)? HOW MANY WILL HE DESTROY DURING THIS DEVASTATING PERIOD OF TIME? MY CHILDREN, HOW MANY? BE PREPARED FOR HIS ATTACKS, WHICH COME WITHOUT WARNING. FOR HE IS ON THE PROWL FOR UNPROTECTED AND VULNERABLE SOULS TODAY.
JULY 21, 2015 BY: BARBARA ANN MARY MACK

THE WORLD'S VERSION OF LOVE AND GOD'S HOLY VERSION OF LOVE

BARBARA SPEAKING

TO LOVE AS GOD LOVES, IS TO LEAVE BEHIND EVERYTHING AND EVERYONE THAT HE CONSIDERS AND VIEWS AS UNHOLY (SINFUL) IN HIS SIGHT. I REVERE YOU AND YOUR HOLY UNCHANGING

WORDS. I REVERE YOUR VERSION OF HOLY LOVE. I REVERE YOUR VERSION OF COMPASSION AND MERCY. I REVERE YOUR VERSION OF HOLY MATRIMONY. I REVERE YOUR VERSION OF FORGIVENESS. I REVERE ALL THAT YOU HAVE ORDERED AND ORDAINED. I REVERE YOUR VERSION OF DIVINE UNITY. MY LORD, THE WORLD'S VERSION OF LOVE CONTRADICTS YOUR HOLY VERSION OF LOVE. THEREFORE, I WILL FOLLOW ONLY YOU, FOR I DESIRE TO ENTER YOUR HOLY GATES AND DWELL IN SWEET PARADISE WITH YOU AND YOUR UNCHANGING WAY, FOREVER! JULY 22, 2015 BY: BARBARA ANN MARY MACK

HE IS...

BARBARA SPEAKING

EXISTENCE: GOOD :ETERNAL: FAITHFUL: HOLY: MY ETERNAL SPOUSE AND GOD THE LORD JESUS! COME, O BLESSED GENERATION! COME AND RECEIVE THE PRESENCE OF CHRIST JESUS, OUR ONLY AND HOLY GOD, FOR HE IS!!! *ALLELUIA!!!*
JULY 22, 2015 BY: BARBARA ANN MARY MACK

WHOM DO YOU DESIRE TO PLEASE? MAN OR ALMIGHTY GOD, YOUR CREATOR.

ALMIGHTY GOD SPEAKING

MY CHILDREN, WHOM DO YOU TRULY LOVE? FOR I CAN OFFER YOU MORE THAN THE WORLD. I CAN OFFER YOU MORE THAN SATAN, MY FOE. WHOM DO YOU DESIRE TO SPEND ETERNITY WITH, MY CHILDREN? DO YOU NOT REMEMBER MY HELP THROUGH THE YEARS, WHEN YOU CRIED OUT TO ME DURING YOUR HARD TIMES? DO YOU NOT REMEMBER MY COMPASSION WHEN YOU WERE IN NEED OF SPIRITUAL AND PHYSICAL COMFORT? WHERE WAS MY FOE (SATAN) WHEN YOU NEEDED THE HELP THAT ONLY I COULD GIVE? WHERE WAS MY FOE (SATAN) WHEN YOUR TEARS FLOWED CONTINUOUSLY DUE TO HARD TIMES? I NEVER LEFT YOU WHEN YOU CRIED OUT TO ME IN PRAYER. I NEVER LEFT YOU, BUT YOU ABANDONED ME THROUGH THE YEARS. COME BACK TO YOUR FAITHFUL GOD AND FATHER, MY CHILDREN! COME BACK TO THE SOURCE OF DIVINE HAPPINESS AND ETERNAL BLISS, FOR I DESIRE YOUR ALLEGIANCE TODAY!
JULY 22, 2015 BY: BARBARA ANN MARY MACK

I HAVE DELIVERED YOUR HOLY MESSAGES TO THE CLERGY, *WHAT DO YOU WANT ME TO DO NOW, MY LORD?*

BARBARA SPEAKING TO THE LORD

MY LORD, I HAVE DELIVERED YOUR HOLY LIFE-SAVING MESSAGES TO THOSE OF THE CLERGY. WILL THEY LISTEN TO WHAT YOU HAVE TO SAY TODAY? WILL THEY HEED YOUR HOLY MESSAGES AND WARNINGS, MY GOD? WAS MY MISSION IN VAIN, OR DID THEY ACKNOWLEDGE MY REPRESENTATION OF YOUR HOLY TRUTH? WHAT SHALL I DO NEXT, MY LORD? WHERE DO YOU NEED ME TODAY?

JULY 22, 2015 BY: BARBARA ANN MARY MACK

SENT: JUL 22, 2015 1:49 PM-READ: WED 7/22/2015 2:04 PM

THERE IS A HELL BELOW, AND *THEY ARE ALL GOING THERE*

ALMIGHTY GOD SPEAKING

DO YOU NOT BELIEVE IN THE LAKE OF CONTINUOUS FIRE? DO YOU BELIEVE THAT WHICH IS SPOKEN OF PERTAINING TO ETERNAL DAMNATION AND HELL? DO YOU NOT BELIEVE WHAT I HAVE SPOKEN OF, IN REGARDS TO THE DESTINATION OF THE UNRIGHTEOUS AND REBELLIOUS ONES? DO YOU, O DECEIVED ONES? DO YOU NOT BELIEVE IN THE EXISTENCE OF THE PERMANENT RESIDENCE (HELL) OF THOSE WHO FOLLOW THE REALM OF EVIL AND SIN? UNLESS YOU CHANGE YOUR SINFUL WAYS, YOU WILL FIND OUT WHETHER HELL EXISTS OR NOT. DO YOU WANT TO TAKE THE RISK, MY CHILDREN? DO YOU VALUE YOUR ETERNAL SOULS? IF YOU DO, PLEASE MAKE THAT CHANGE TODAY. FOLLOW MY HOLY WAY INSTEAD OF YOUR UNHOLY WAY! COME! O CALLED ONES, DO NOT DECEIVE YOURSELVES, FOR HELL TRULY EXISTS!

JULY 23, 2015 BY: BARBARA ANN MARY MACK

JESUS IS WALKING IN THE MIDST OF THIS REBELLIOUS AND PERVERTED PERIOD OF TIME. *CAN YOU NOT FEEL HIS HOLY PRESENCE IN YOUR MIDST TODAY?*

ALMIGHTY GOD SPEAKING TO
THE SPIRITUALLY BLIND ONES

BEHOLD! I AM IN YOUR BLESSED MIDST TODAY, CAN YOU NOT SEE MY HOLY PRESENCE, O BLINDED ONES? I AM WALKING NEXT TO YOU ON THE STREETS, CAN YOU NOT FEEL MY HOLY PRESENCE IN YOUR BLESSED MIDST, O BLINDED ONES? CAN YOU NOT SEE ME, AS I APPROACH YOU IN THE FORM OF SHE (BARBARA) WHOM I HAVE SENT? YOU WALKED WITH HER. YOU HAVE TALKED WITH HER. HOW CAN YOU NOT SEE ME WITHIN HER ACCEPTING BEING? DO YOU NOT KNOW ME, O BLINDED ONES? DO YOU NOT KNOW MY HOLY SPIRIT, AS IT WALKS AND TALKS WITH YOU THROUGH MY HEAVEN SENT MESSENGER AND BRIDE (BARBARA)? WHY DO YOU NOT RECOGNIZE ME, O BLINDED ONES? WHY DO YOU NOT KNOW THE SPIRIT OF YOUR SAVING GOD AND CREATOR? YOU HAVE PROFESSED TO OTHERS THAT YOU DO, SO WHY DO YOU NOT ACKNOWLEDGE ME, AS I COMMUNE WITH YOU THROUGH MY PROPHET (BARBARA), WHOM I HAVE SENT TO YOU? I AM IN YOUR MIDST TODAY, O CALLED AND BLINDED ONES. DO NOT DISMISS OR REJECT MY FINAL INVITATION TO YOU.
JULY 23, 2015 BY: BARBARA ANN MARY MACK

I HAVE SEEN THE FACES OF THE FALLEN AND HELL BOUND ONES. *I WILL WEEP WITH DIVINE EMPATHY*

ALMIGHTY GOD SPEAKING THROUGH BARBARA, HIS MESSENGER AND PROPHET

I HAVE SEEN THE FACES OF THOSE WHO REJECTED ME, SAYS THE LORD. I HAVE SAT IN THE CHURCHES WITH THOSE WHO HAVE BLATANTLY MOCKED ME. I WILL NOT BE MOCKED BY THE REALM OF PERVERSION AND REBELLION – SPIRITUAL AND PHYSICAL! I HAVE SAT IN THE HOMES OF THOSE WHO CHOSE THE WAYS OF THE WORLD OVER MY MERCY AND DIVINE LOVE. I SEE YOU, O SINFUL CHILDREN! I SEE YOU, AS YOU EXHIBIT YOUR UNHOLY WAYS INSIDE MY CHURCHES. I SEE THE DISGRACE AS YOU SIT IN MY PEWS. I DO NOT APPROVE OF YOUR UNGODLINESS, O FALLEN ONES. I DO NOT APPROVE OF YOUR UNGODLY PRESENCE IN MY CHURCH. CHANGE YOUR SINFUL WAY OF LIVING BEFORE MY RETURN, FOR THEN, I WILL NOT SHOW YOU MY MERCY.

ALMIGHTY GOD AND BARBARA SPEAKING

I WEPT, MY LORD, FOR YOU HAVE REVEALED THE FACES OF THOSE WHO WILL NOT MAKE IT THROUGH HEAVEN'S HOLY GATES. THEY SAW MY FACE, OUR FACE, AS I SAT IN THE PEWS, AND SO, ON JUDGMENT DAY, THEY WILL NOT BE PERMITTED TO ENTER THROUGH THE GATES THAT LEAD TO ETERNAL LIFE. THEY WILL NOT SEE SWEET PARADISE, MY HOME ABOVE.
JULY 23, 2015 BARBARA ANN MARY MACK
SENT: THU, JUL 23, 2015 11:25 PM-READ: FRI 7/24/2015 9:51 AM

WE (LA TOYA, AMYA, AND ME) THANK YOU VERY FOR THE WONDERFUL BLESSING ARCHBISHOP! NOW I CAN RELAX AND ENJOY THE LONG RIDE. LA TOYA IS VERY EXCITED, AND SOME OF HER EXCITEMENT TRANSFERRED TO AMYA AND ME. WE COOKED A FEW DISHES TO TAKE WITH US SO THAT WE WILL NOT MESS UP THE OWNER'S KITCHEN TOO MUCH. I GOT UP BEFORE GETTING READY FOR CHURCH THIS MORNING, AND BAKED TURKEY WINGS. WE LOVE TURKEY WINGS. I AM ABOUT TO GO AND MAKE SURE THAT I PACK EVERYTHING PROPERLY SO THAT LA TOYA CAN PUT SOME OF OUR THINGS IN HER TRUNK THIS EVENING.

TI AMO AMORE, BELLA BARBIE

SENT: SUN, JUL 26, 2015 3:23 PM-READ: SUN 7/26/2015 6:53 PM

THIS IS A SPIRITUAL WAR, AND MANY ARE GOING DOWN, *SAYS THE LORD*

ALMIGHTY GOD SPEAKING

THIS IS A SPIRITUAL WAR! MANY ARE GOING DOWN, FOR THEY HAVE CHOSEN SATAN'S DEFEATED REALM INSTEAD OF MY REALM OF HOLINESS, *SAYS THE LORD!* WATCH OUT! MY CHILDREN. FOR THE REALM OF EVIL HAS DESCENDED UPON YOU AS YOU WALK THROUGH THIS TROUBLED PERIOD OF TIME. SATAN'S PRESENCE, WHICH IS SLIGHTLY ABOVE YOUR HEADS, HAS SWALLOWED UP YOUR VULNERABLE AND UNSUSPECTING SOULS. SATAN HAS DESTROYED MANY FAMILIES, FRIENDSHIPS, AND LIVES, AS HE SLITHERED THROUGH THIS TROUBLED PERIOD OF TIME. HE HAS CAUSED MANY TO COMMIT SUICIDE. HE HAS CAUSED MANY TO COMMIT MURDER. HE HAS CAUSED MANY TO PERFORM AND PARTAKE IN ABORTIONS. HE HAS TAKEN DOWN THOSE WHO WERE NOT PROTECTED BY ALMIGHTY GOD, THE ONLY WEAPON AGAINST SATAN'S REALM OF DESTRUCTION AND DEATH. MY CHILDREN, THIS IS A SPIRITUAL WAR, WHEN ARE YOU GOING TO PUT ON YOUR ARMORS (ALMIGHTY GOD'S REALM OF HOLINESS)? JULY 24, 2015 BY: BARBARA ANN MARY MACK

O CLERGY, HELP THEM, THE LOST ONES, FIND THE WAY, MY HOLY WAY, *SAYS THE LORD*

ALMIGHTY GOD SPEAKING TO THE CLERGY

HELP THEM, MY SONS (THE CLERGY)! HELP THEM FIND ME! LEAD THEM TO MY REALM OF RIGHTEOUSNESS, SO THAT THEY MAY ABIDE WITH ME IN ETERNAL GLORY. TELL THEM, MY SONS! TELL THEM THE ONLY WAY TO ME. TELL THEM OF THE GLORY THAT THEY WILL EXPERIENCE BY KNOWING AND SERVING ME, THEIR ETERNAL KING AND GOD. TELL THEM WHAT THEY MUST KNOW AND DO, IN ORDER TO LIVE ACCORDING TO MY VERSION OF HOLINESS. TELL THEM, MY SONS! TELL THEM, SO THAT THEY WILL KNOW THAT YOU TRULY LOVE US (THE LORD AND HIS FLOCK). TELL THEM, SO THAT THEY TOO MAY HAVE THE OPPORTUNITY

TO ESCAPE ETERNAL DEATH. TELL THEM WHAT HOLINESS MEANS TO ME. TELL THEM, MY SONS! TELL THEM FOR ME! TELL THEM, O CLERGY! TELL THEM TODAY!

JULY 24, 2015 BY: BARBARA ANN MARY MACK

SENT: SUN, JUL 26, 2015 3:23 PM-READ: SUN 7/26/2015 6:53 PM

GREETINGS LOVE! BELOW IS THE PLACE THAT WE WILL BE STAYING WHILE VISITING PITTSBURGH, PA, AND OUR OTHER PLANNED SUMMER TOUR LOCATIONS. THESE ARE THE LOCATIONS THAT THE LORD DIRECTED US TO VISIT. HE NEEDS US TO DELIVER HIS HOLY PRESENCE AND MESSAGES AT THESE LOCATIONS. AT THIS TIME, HE DID NOT REVEAL TO ME ANYONE SPECIFIC. WE WILL KNOW WHEN WE GET THERE. *CIAO! BEAUTIFUL BARBARA*

SENT: SUN, JUL 26, 2015 3:23 PM-READ: SUN 7/26/2015 6:53 PM

GOD DICTATED PASSAGES FOR ALL

SOMETIMES WE WALK, TALK, SLEEP AND PLAY WITH SATAN EVERY DAY. *HELP US, O HOLY SPOUSE AND GOD OF MINE!*

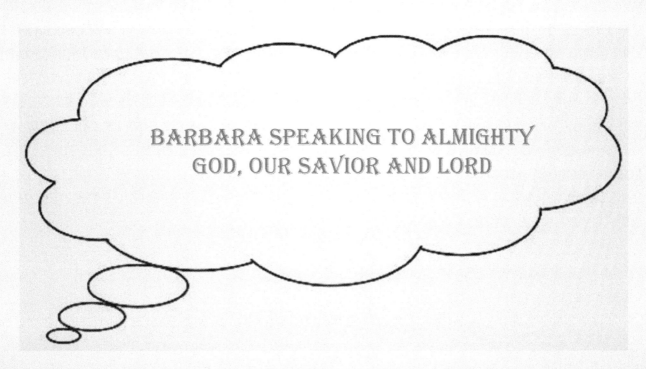

BARBARA SPEAKING TO ALMIGHTY GOD, OUR SAVIOR AND LORD

SOMETIMES WITHOUT KNOWING, WE ENTERTAIN SATAN IN OUR DAILY ACTIVITIES, FOR HE IS VERY DECEPTIVE AND CUNNING. YOU, DEAR LORD, KNOW HIS GUISED SERVANTS OF DESTRUCTION AND MISERY. HELP US RECOGNIZE THE REALM THAT TRIES TO STEAL US FROM YOU, FOR HE IS VERY DECEPTIVE. HE IS DOOMED AND DEFEATED BY YOU, MY VICTORIOUS SAVING GOD.

JULY 22, 2015 BY: BARBARA ANN MARY MACK

WHERE ARE THEY, MY LORD? *WHERE ARE THE BELIEVERS?*

ALMIGHTY GOD SPEAKING TO BARBARA

LOOK AROUND YOU, MY DAUGHTER, FOR THEY ARE IN YOUR MIDST TOO! COME AND FOLLOW ME, FOR I WILL SHOW YOU WHERE THEY DWELL! COME, MY DAUGHTER! LOOK OVER THERE! COME! LET YOU AND I GREET THEM! LET US SHARE MY GOOD NEWS WITH THEM TODAY, FOR THEY LONG TO GET A GLIMPSE OF THEIR FAITHFUL AND HOLY GOD. COME, MY DAUGHTER! LET US APPROACH THEM WITH GLADNESS!
JULY 22, 2015 BY: BARBARA ANN MARY MACK

THEY WERE CALLED, BUT *THEY WERE NOT CHOSEN BY ALMIGHTY GOD*

ALMIGHTY GOD SPEAKING

MY CHILDREN, I HAVE SENT OUT MANY INVITATIONS. I HAVE SENT OUT MY MESSENGERS WITH MY HOLY CALL AND INVITATION TO ETERNAL LIFE IN SWEET PARADISE. I HAVE SENT OUT MY MESSAGE OF LOVE, BUT YOU DID NOT HONOR IT, O DISOBEDIENT AND REBELLIOUS ONES. I HAVE CALLED YOU MANY TIMES, BUT YOU CHOSE TO IGNORE MY HOLY CALL. MY CHILDREN, I KNOW WHO WILL ACCEPT ME, AND I KNOW WHO WILL REJECT ME, *SAYS THE LORD.* THEREFORE, MY MESSENGERS WILL CONVEY MY HOLY WORDS TO MANY WHO ARE CALLED, BUT ONLY THE CHOSEN ONES WILL RECEIVE AND ACCEPT MY INVITATION. I KNOW WHO IS WRITTEN IN MY HOLY BOOK OF LIFE, AND I AM WELL AWARE OF THOSE WHO AREN'T, *SAYS THE LORD.* MY MESSENGERS WILL DELIVER MY MESSAGES TO THOSE WHOM I SEND THEM TO, BUT THEY WILL NOT PROCEED FURTHER IF THE CALLED ONES NAMES ARE NOT WRITTEN IN MY BOOK OF LIFE. I HAVE WRITTEN WHAT IS WRITTEN, AND I WILL HONOR WHAT I HAVE SPOKEN, *SAYS THE LORD.*
JULY 23, 2015 BY: BARBARA ANN MARY MACK

I WILL REJOICE IN THE PRESENCE OF THE LORD TODAY!

BARBARA SPEAKING

I WILL REJOICE IN THE HOLY PRESENCE OF THE LORD TODAY, FOR I HAVE COMPLETED THE ASSIGNMENT THAT I WAS SENT TO DO, IN THE MIDST OF PERVERSION. *ALLELUIA!* I BOW IN THE PRESENCE OF ANOTHER COMPLETED HOLY TASK! I BOW IN THE HOLY PRESENCE OF ALMIGHTY GOD, MY GREAT AND HOLY ASSIGNMENT GIVER AND BOSS. I BOW IN THE MIDST OF THE DIVINE TASK THAT WAS ASSIGNED TO ME, BY HE WHO WILL DESTROY THE REALM OF SIN AND PERVERSION. I BOW IN THE MIDST OF HOLINESS AS I SIT IN THE PEWS THAT INVITE THE REALM OF PERVERSION AND SIN INTO THE CHURCH. I BOW IN THE MIDST OF HOLINESS, AS THE LORD ALMIGHTY REVEALS HIS HOLY PRESENCE THROUGH BARBARA, HIS CHOSEN MESSENGER AND CONDUIT. I BOW, MY LORD! I BOW IN THE PRESENCE OF ANOTHER FULFILLED ASSIGNMENT THAT DESCENDED UPON ME, YOUR WORTHY DAUGHTER AND BRIDE. FOR I HAVE SPOKEN WITH THOSE WHO GO AGAINST YOUR VERSION OF HOLINESS, AS I MINGLED WITH THEM THROUGH THE DAY. MY LORD! O MERCIFUL AND RIGHTEOUS GOD AND FATHER, I BOW IN THE MIDST OF YOUR HOLY ASSIGNMENT OF TRUTH. I BOW, AS YOU GLIDE IN THE MIDST OF THOSE WHO HAVE STRAYED FROM YOUR VERSION OF HOLINESS, AND I APPROACH THOSE WHO BLATANTLY DISTORT, MOCK, AND PERVERT YOUR VERSION OF HOLINESS, AS WE (ALMIGHTY GOD AND BARBARA) SIT WITH THEM IN THE PEWS. YOU ARE A JUST AND UNCHANGING GOD. YOU WILL NOT BE MOCKED! YOU WILL NOT BE DISTORTED! AND YOUR HOLINESS WILL NEVER ENTER THE REALM OF PERVERSION. FOR YOU ARE PURE AND UNBLEMISHED, AND SO IS YOUR HOLY CHURCH!

JULY 23, 2015 BY: BARBARA ANN MARY MACK

SENT SUN, JUL 26, 2015 3:23 PM-READ SUN 7/26/2015 6:53 PM

ENTERING THE LAND OF OBLIVION

BARBARA SPEAKING

AWAY FROM THE WORLD. AWAY FROM THE EVILS THAT FLOW THROUGHOUT THE WORLD AWAY FROM THE SUFFERINGS THAT PERMEATE THE WORLD. AWAY FROM THOSE WHO HAVE PERVERTED GOD'S HOLY WORDS. AWAY FROM THOSE WHO PRACTICE SEXUAL PERVERSION IN THE PRESENCE OF ALMIGHTY GOD. AWAY FROM THOSE WHO GAIN DELIGHT IN THE DEVIATION FROM GOD'S HOLY WAY. OPEN WIDE, O SWEET GATES, SO THAT I MAY ENTER THE LAND OF SWEET OBLIVION! THERE, I WILL SOAR IN THE MIDST OF HEAVENLY BLISS WITH THOSE WHO SHARE MY DESIRE FOR SWEET TRANQUILITY. I WILL DANCE AROUND THE MIGHTY THRONE OF GOD, MY ETERNAL SAVIOR. I WILL SING THE MELODIOUS TUNES THAT PLEASE MY CREATOR AND GOD. AWAY, AWAY, AWAY FROM THIS WORLD!

JULY 24, 2015 BY: BARBARA ANN MARY MACK

THE WORLD HASN'T CHANGED

BARBARA SPEAKING TO GOD, THE FATHER

THE WORLD HASN'T CHANGED, MY LORD. THEY DO NOT REVERE YOU, AS THOSE OF THE PAST. THEY DO NOT BOW IN YOUR HOLY PRESENCE, AS THEIR FOREFATHERS AND MOTHERS NEGLECTED TO DO AS WELL. THEY DO NOT ACKNOWLEDGE THE DIVINITY OF JESUS, YOUR ONLY BEGOTTEN SON. THEY REVERE MANKIND INSTEAD OF YOU, MY LORD. THEY GIVE UNDUE REVERENCE TO FALLIBLE MANKIND INSTEAD OF REVERENCE TO THEIR HOLY CREATOR AND GOD. THEY HAVEN'T CHANGED, MY LORD. THEY DO NOT RECOGNIZE YOU, EVEN IN THE MIDST OF YOUR MANY HEAVEN SENT MIRACLES. THEY STILL PERSECUTE THOSE WHO FOLLOW YOUR HOLY TEACHINGS AND WAY. THEY STILL DENY YOUR HOLY EXISTENCE AND PRESENCE IN OUR LIVES. MY LORD, MY HOLY GOD, WHEN WILL THEY SEE THE LIGHT (THE LORD JESUS)? WHEN WILL THEY RECOGNIZE AND ACCEPT YOU?
JULY 24, 2015 BY: BARBARA ANN MARY MACK

I HAVE MADE IT THROUGH THE REALM OF INJUSTICE AS YOU HAVE, LORD JESUS

BARBARA SPEAKING TO THE VICTORIOUS LORD JESUS

I HAVE MADE IT, MY LORD! I HAVE MADE IT THROUGH THE REALM THAT FALSELY ACCUSED ME, AS YOU HAVE. I HAVE MADE IT THROUGH THE STORMS THAT ENGULFED ME, AS I DELIVERED YOUR HOLY LIFE SAVING MESSAGES TO THOSE OF THE JUSTICE SYSTEM. I HAVE BEEN FALSELY ACCUSED AND JUDGED, SO THAT I MAY REVEAL YOUR HOLY PRESENCE TO THOSE WHOM YOU HAVE CALLED AND CHOSEN TO WITNESS YOUR TANGIBLE PRESENCE THROUGH ME, YOUR FAITHFUL MESSENGER AND BRIDE. WITH YOUR CONTINUOUS HELP AND GRACE, I MADE IT THROUGH, AS YOU HAVE, MY LORD. I MADE IT THROUGH THE TRIALS AND HUMILIATION THAT ACCOMPANIED MY DIVINE ASSIGNMENT OF LOVE. I MADE IT BY THE GRACE OF MY LOVING ORIGIN AND GOD. MY LORD, MY HOLY GOD, THE HUMILIATION THAT WALKED WITH ME, CAUSED ME TO WEEP CONTINUOUSLY, AS I STOOD IN THE MIDST OF THE "INJUSTICE SYSTEM". BY THE POWER OF YOUR UNENDING LOVE AND MERCY, YOU HELD ME TIGHT, AS I STOOD BEFORE THOSE WHO SENTENCED ME WITHOUT A JUST CAUSE. MY LORD, MY HOLY REDEEMER, I PRAISE AND THANK YOU FOR LOVING THOSE WHO FALSELY ACCUSED, JUDGED, AND SENTENCED US (THE LORD JESUS AND BARBARA). I THANK YOU, O WONDERFUL GOD AND SPOUSE OF MINE. I THANK YOU FOR HELPING ME MAKE IT THROUGH THE REALM OF INJUSTICE, AS OUR LOVING GOD AND FATHER HELPED YOU.
JULY 24, 2015 BY: BARBARA ANN MARY MACK
SENT SUN, JUL 26, 2015 3:23 PM-READ SUN 7/26/2015 6:53 PM

ALL MORNING, I WEPT FOR THE LOST AND DOOMED SOULS, HELP ME, O LORD!

BARBARA SPEAKING TO ALMIGHTY GOD

ALL MORNING, I WEPT FOR THE LOST AND HELL BOUND SOULS. HELP ME, MY LORD! HELP ME, O HOLY GOD, FOR THE PAIN IS TREMENDOUS! THEY WILL NOT CONFORM TO YOUR HOLY WAY OF LIFE. THEY WILL NOT FOLLOW YOUR LIT LANTERN OF HOLY LOVE (THE LORD JESUS). MY LORD, THEY WILL NOT FOLLOW YOU! I WEEP, MY LORD, AS YOU WEEP. LET OUR FUSED TEARS ENCOMPASS AND COMFORT EACH OTHER, FOR THE DESTINATION OF THE UNRIGHTEOUS ONES CAUSES US TO WEEP TOGETHER. WE DO NOT DESIRE THAT THEY SHOULD SUFFER THROUGHOUT ETERNITY. WE DO NOT DESIRE, THAT THEY SHOULD EXPERIENCE PERMANENT DEATH. WE DO NOT DESIRE TO WITNESS THEIR ENTRANCE THROUGH THE OPENED GATES THAT LEAD TO HELL. WE DO DESIRE THAT THEY SHOULD REPENT TODAY, AND FOLLOW THE ONLY WAY TO ETERNAL LIFE AND HAPPINESS. THE LIFE THAT IS ETERNAL AND FREE OF SUFFERING. A LIFE THAT EXHIBITS OUR (ALMIGHTY GOD AND BARBARA) LOYALTY TO THE CHOSEN ONES. A LIFE IN SWEET PARADISE IN HEAVEN ABOVE. A LIFE THAT IS FULL OF REJOICING AND HEAVENLY BLISS! A LIFE THAT IS SHARED WITH GOD'S VICTORIOUS ANGELS AND SAINTS. A LIFE, A PERFECT ETERNAL LIFE!

JULY 22, 2015 BY: BARBARA ANN MARY MACK

SENT SUN, JUL 26, 2015 3:23 PM-READ SUN 7/26/2015 6:53 PM

GO! AND DELIVER MY HOLY WORDS TO THOSE WHO WILL LISTEN TO ME, *SAYS THE LORD.* GO, MY DAUGHTER, FOR THEIR TIME IS RUNNING OUT!

ALMIGHTY GOD SPEAKING TO BARBARA

TIME, THE REALM OF TIME, IS NO LONGER ON THEIR SIDE, MY DAUGHTER. GO! AND TELL THEM THIS NEWS. TELL THEM, MY DAUGHTER, FOR THEIR TIME IS VERY SHORT! THERE WILL BE NO

OPPORTUNITY TO REPENT! THERE WILL BE NO OPPORTUNITY TO RECTIFY THEIR SINS! THERE WILL BE NO OPPORTUNITY FOR THEM TO CRY OUT TO ME! FOR I, THE PATIENT ONE, HAVE COME TO A DECISION THAT REVEALS MY VERSION OF DIVINE JUSTICE TODAY. GO, MY DAUGHTER! TELL THE RESIDENTS OF EARTH THIS NEWS FOR ME, *SAYS THE LORD.*
JULY 22, 2015 BY: BARBARA ANN MARY MACK

OH, THIS GENERATION! OH, THE DESTINATION OF THIS GENERATION, CAUSES ME TO WEEP UNCONTROLLABLY, *SAYS THE LORD GOD*

ALMIGHTY GOD SPEAKING TO THE RESIDENTS IN HEAVEN

OH SUCH PAIN FLOWS THROUGH MY ESSENCE AS I WITNESS THE CONTINUOUS ABUSE OF MY HOLY WORDS! WHAT SHALL I DO WITH THEM, O RESIDENTS OF MY HEAVENLY HOME? WHAT SHALL I DO WITH THIS REBELLIOUS GENERATION, FOR THEIR UNHOLY DEEDS HAVE REACHED THEIR LIMIT? THEY HAVE NO SHAME IN THEIR UNHOLY ACTS, WHICH CAUSE ME TO WEEP AND TURN MY HOLY FACE FROM THEIR BLASPHEMOUS PRESENCE. THEY OPENLY DISPLAY THEIR UNHOLY WAYS AS IF I CANNOT SEE THEM. WHAT IS WRONG WITH THIS GENERATION OF PEOPLE? WHAT IS WRONG WITH THEM, MY CHOSEN ONES (GOD'S ANGELS AND SAINTS)? DO THEY NO LONGER FEAR ME? DO THEY NO LONGER BELIEVE IN THE FIERCENESS OF MY WRATH? DO THEY WANT TO GET A TASTE OF MY WRATH, WHICH FLOWS THROUGH THE HOLY BIBLE? DO THEY WANT TO GET A TASTE OF MY VERSION OF GOD ORDERED JUSTICE TODAY? I HAVE SENT MY HOLY MESSENGERS TO WARN THEM, BUT AS I CAN SEE, THEY HAVE NOT HEEDED THE WARNINGS THAT I HAVE SENT. WHAT SHALL I DO WITH THIS REBELLIOUS GENERATION, O RESIDENTS OF MY HEAVENLY HOME? WHAT WILL CAUSE THEM TO CHANGE THEIR SINFUL WAYS? WHAT WILL MAKE THEM FOLLOW MY WORDS OF TRUTH, INSTEAD OF MY ENEMY'S (SATAN) ROAD TO DESTRUCTION AND ETERNAL PAIN? MY FACE IS COVERED WITH THE TEARS OF A HURTING GOD. MY FACE IS COVERED WITH THE TEARS THAT REVEAL MY SORROW. MY FACE IS COVERED WITH THE TEARS THAT EXPRESS MY WOUNDED HEART OF MERCY AND LOVE. MY FACE SHOWS THE PAIN THAT I EXPERIENCE AS I WITNESS THE SINFUL ACTS OF MY CHILDREN. O RESIDENTS OF MY HOLY HOME ABOVE, WHAT SHALL I DO WITH THEM?
JULY 22, 2015 BY: BARBARA ANN MARY MACK

THIS SPIRITUAL WAR IS WICKED AND BRUTAL!

BARBARA SPEAKING

THIS ONGOING SPIRITUAL WAR IS WICKED AND BRUTAL! THEREFORE, I AM STILL WEARING MY ARMOR (THE UNCHANGING WORD OF ALMIGHTY GOD). FOR HE, OUR LORD, OUR WONDERFUL VICTORIOUS LORD, THE SLAUGHTERED LAMB OF THE ONLY LIVING GOD AND FATHER, THE ONLY OMNIPOTENT AND OMNIPRESENT ONE, IS OUR ONLY HOPE OF SURVIVAL.
JULY 22, 2015 BY: BARBARA ANN MARY MACK

THEY ARE ALL AROUND ME, O LORD, WHAT SHALL I DO?

BARBARA SPEAKING TO THE LORD

THEY (THE SINNERS) ARE ALL AROUND ME, WHAT SHALL I DO? I WILL WEEP AND PRAY FOR THEM, MY LORD.

ALMIGHTY GOD SPEAKING TO ARCHBISHOP CRAIG THROUGH BARBARA

YOU HAVE BROUGHT THEM TO ME, MY SON. YOU HAVE RETRIEVED THE BROKEN ONES. I HAVE SEEN AND SPOKEN TO THEM THROUGH BARBARA, MY MESSENGER AND BRIDE. I HAVE SPOKEN TO THEM THROUGH YOU. NOW, IT IS IN THEIR HANDS. WHAT WILL THEY DO? WHAT WILL THEY DO WITH THE MESSAGES THAT YOU TWO HAVE DELIVERED TO THEM? LET US (ALMIGHTY GOD, ARCHBISHOP CRAIG, AND BARBARA) SEE. WILL THEY ABANDON THEIR "UNHOLY WAYS" FOR ME? LET US WATCH AND SEE, *SAYS THE LORD.*
JULY 22, 2015 BY: BARBARA ANN MARY MACK

I AM VERY ANGRY, *SAYS THE LORD*

ALMIGHTY GOD
SPEAKING TO SATAN

I AM VERY ANGRY WITH YOU, O DEFEATED ONE (SATAN)! I AM VERY ANGRY WITH YOUR LOWLY DEFEATED REALM OF NOTHINGNESS! I AM VERY ANGRY WITH THOSE WHO FOLLOW YOUR WAY OF CONFUSION AND DISGUST! I WILL RELEASE MY ANGER AND WRATH ON THOSE WHO HAVE CHOSEN YOUR REALM OF DESTRUCTION OVER MY ETERNAL REALM OF HOLINESS! I WILL RELEASE MY REALM OF ANGER OVER YOU, AND THOSE WHO EXHIBIT YOUR "UNSPEAKABLE AND UNACCEPTABLE UNGODLY ACTS" (HOMOSEXUALITY-SAME SEX RELATIONSHIPS)! FOR THEY ARE NOT, ARE NOT, ARE NOT MARRIAGES IN MY HOLY EYES! I WILL RELEASE MY WRATH OVER YOUR DEFEATED REALM OF "UNCLEANLINESS"(MEN SLEEPING WITH MEN AND WOMEN LYING DOWN WITH WOMEN). OH SUCH PERVERTED AND UNSPEAKABLE ACTS IN MY HOLY, HOLY, HOLY PRESENCE, WILL BE SENT THROUGH THE GATES OF ETERNAL HELL! THIS IS MY HOLY WORD, *SAYS THE LORD!* I WILL NOT HEAR YOUR VAIN PRAYERS! I WILL NOT HEAR YOUR VAIN CRIES AS YOU ENTER HELL, YOUR PERMANENT RESIDENCE! I WILL NOT ACKNOWLEDGE YOUR "UNHOLY" EXISTENCE, FOR YOU HAVE CHOSEN TO FOLLOW THE REALM (SATAN) THAT PRODUCES "NOTHINGNESS"! YOU HAVE CHOSEN THE REALM THAT GOES AGAINST MY HOLY TEACHINGS. IN THE PIT OF HELL WILL YOU RESIDE FOREVER! THIS IS MY PROMISE! THIS IS MY FINAL HOLY WORD! I WILL NOT HAVE PITY ON THOSE WHO DEFY ME! I WILL NOT HAVE PITY ON THOSE WHO GO AGAINST, OR THOSE WHO TEACH MY CHILDREN TO GO AGAINST MY REALM OF HOLINESS. FOR YOU HAVE SIDED WITH THE REALM (EVIL) WHOSE FINAL DESTINATION IS HELL! I WILL NEVER PERMIT MY CHOSEN ONES TO ACCEPT THE "UNACCEPTABLE AND UNGODLY ACTS" THAT THE REALM OF DOOM EXHIBITS DAILY IN MY HOLY PRESENCE. THIS IS MY HOLY STANCE, *SAYS THE LORD!!!*
JULY 30, 2015 BY: BARBARA ANN MARY MACK

EVIL COVERED WITH A PIECE OF FLESH

BARBARA SPEAKING

CAN YOU SEE HIM (SATAN, THE DEVIL)? FOR HE IS EVIL COVERED WITH A PIECE OF FLESH. HE (SATAN, THE REALM OF EVIL) BLENDS IN WITH THE AVERAGE LOOKING HUMAN BEING. HE (EVIL) COMES IN THE FORM OF THE AVERAGE LOOKING WOMAN, GIRL, BOY AND MAN. YOU CANNOT RECOGNIZE (EVIL), BECAUSE HE IS COVERED WITH HUMAN FLESH. HIS GUISE HAS FOOLED MANY! HE IS ONLY NOTICEABLE TO THE WORLD, WHEN HE CAUSES GREAT HARDSHIP AND UNHOLY ACTS. CAN YOU NOT SEE HIS "UNHOLY" PRESENCE AS HE MURDERS THE INNOCENT ONES BECAUSE THEY ENTER THE WORLD? HAVE YOU NOT WITNESSED HIS UNWANTED PRESENCE AS HE PERFORMS UNSPEAKABLE ACTS IN YOUR MIDST? LOOK AT HIS HANDIWORK, AND BELIEVE IN HIS "UNHOLY" AND "UNWANTED" PRESENCE. HE IS VERY CUNNING! WATCH OUT FOR HIS INCONSPICUOUS ACTS OF EVIL IN YOUR MIDST TODAY, FOR HE, THE REALM OF EVIL, HIDES UNDER HUMAN THE GUISE OF HUMAN FLESH.
JULY 30, 2015 BY: BARBARA ANN MARY MACK
SENT THU, JUL 30, 2015 1:46 PM-READ THU 7/30/2015 2:52 PM

GREETINGS DEAR ONE (ARCHBISHOP CRAIG)! COME STA? WE WILL BE LEAVING FOR PHILLY VERY SOON. CHECKOUT TIME IS BY 12 PM. WE HAVE TO FINISH PACKING. THE APARTMENT COMES WITH A WASHER AND DRYER SO WE WERE ABLE TO WASH OUR CLOTHES BEFORE LEAVING. I REALLY ENJOYED OUR VISIT TO PITTSBURGH. WE WILL BE OFF TO ANOTHER EXCITING ADVENTURE ON MONDAY AUGUST 3. LA TOYA RENTED A FARMHOUSE FROM AUGUST 3-8, IN GALETON, PA. WE WILL STAY HOME LONG ENOUGH TO CHECK ON OUR CAT (KITTY). HE DOESN'T LIKE TRAVELING AT ALL, THEREFORE HE HAS TO STAY HOME. WE HAVE OUR NEIGHBORS CHECKING ON OUR HOUSE AND THE MAIL. WE USUALLY LOOK OUT FOR EACH OTHER WHEN WE ARE AWAY FROM OUR HOMES. IF IT'S GOD'S HOLY WILL, WE WILL SEE YOU AT MASS TOMORROW. CIAO! BELLA BARBARA
SENT SAT, AUG 1, 2015 10:08 AM-READ SAT 8/1/2015 10:41 AM

GREETINGS LOVE! COME STA OGGI? LA TOYA, AMYA, AND I ARE EN ROUTE TO A MOVIE AND OTHER ATTRACTIONS. HOPEFULLY THE WALKING WILL BURN OFF SOME OF THE GOODIES THAT I CONSUMED YESTERDAY. THE WEATHER IS BEAUTIFUL SO FAR! ENJOY YOUR DAY LOVE. *TI AMO, BELLA BARBARA*
SENT SAT, AUG 1, 2015 10:08 AM-READ SAT 8/1/2015 10:41 AM

BUONA SERA LOVE! I PRAY THAT YOUR DAY WENT VERY WELL. LA TOYA, AMYA AND I ARE RETURNING FROM A NIGHT OUT ON THE TOWN IN PITTSBURGH. WE HAD DINNER AT BELLA VISTA RISTORANTE ITALIANO. THE FOOD WAS DELICIOUS! AND THE WAITER, WHO DID JUST ABOUT EVERYTHING, INCLUDING TAKING PICTURES OF US GIRLS, WAS VERY NICE AND SOCIABLE THROUGHOUT OUR MEAL. EVEN AMYA CONTRIBUTED TO THE GRATUITY. AFTERWARDS, WE WALKED AROUND A BIT TO LOOK AT THE SURROUNDINGS (MOUNT WASHINGTON) AND GET POST CARDS FOR MY FAMILY. MY SISTER ASKED ME TO SEE IF PITTSBURGH'S OPERA IS STILL LOCATED DOWNTOWN. I WILL TRY TO HAVE LA TOYA TAKE ME THERE TOMORROW OR SATURDAY. I WILL TRY TO GET TO BED VERY SOON. WE WILL SEE. *AMORE, BELLA BARBARA*
SENT SAT, AUG 1, 2015 10:08 AM-READ SAT 8/1/2015 10:41 AM

GREETINGS DEAR ARCHBISHOP CRAIG! COME STA? WE MADE IT SAFE AND SOUND TO OUR DESTINATION (PITTSBURGH, PA,) MONDAY EVENING AROUND 7:30 PM. WE LEFT PHILLY AROUND 11:30 AM. WE STOPPED FOR A COUPLE OF LEG STRETCHING AND RESTROOM BREAKS BEFORE ARRIVING AT OUR APARTMENT EVERYTHING IS GOING VERY WELL SO FAR. WE ARE ENJOYING OUR VISIT. THE PEOPLE IN THIS AREA ARE VERY FRIENDLY. LA TOYA AND AMYA WENT FOR A WALK IN THE NEIGHBORHOOD TUESDAY EVENING AFTER WE RETURNED FROM THE ZOO. I HAD A WONDERFUL TIME TAKING PICTURES OF AND WITH THE ANIMALS THERE. AMYA CRIED BECAUSE SHE DOESN'T LIKE TO SEE THE ANIMALS IN CAPTIVITY. BUT IN SOME CASES, THEIR SURVIVAL IS BECAUSE THEY ARE IN AN ENVIRONMENT THAT CARES FOR THEIR NEEDS. TODAY IS WEDNESDAY, WE DO NOT KNOW WHERE THE LORD WILL LEAD US TODAY. LA TOYA KEEPS BRINGING UP THE DESIRE TO EAT AT AN ITALIAN RESTAURANT. WE WILL SEE. WE WILL HAVE TO WAIT UNTIL THURSDAY OR FRIDAY, BECAUSE TOYA FAST ON WEDNESDAYS AND SUNDAYS. *TI AMO, BELLA BARBARA*

I WILL NOT DWELL ON THE HORRORS OF THE WORLD. I WILL REJOICE WITH THE LORD!

BARBARA SPEAKING

I WILL NOT DWELL ON THE HORRORS THAT FLOW THROUGH THIS GENERATION; I WILL FOCUS ON THE GOODNESS OF THE LORD. ALTHOUGH THE HORRORS THAT PERMEATE THIS GENERATION ARE VISIBLE AND GREAT, I WILL REJOICE IN THE HOLY NAME (JESUS) THAT TRANSCENDS

ALL REALMS OF EVIL. I WILL REJOICE IN HIS HOLY NAME, FOR IT OUTSHINES THE DARKNESS, YES, THE VISIBLE DARKNESS THAT EMITS FROM THE LAND OF NOTHINGNESS. I WILL SING THE SONGS THAT GIVE ME JOY, AS I WEEP AT THE HORRORS, YES, THE VISIBLE HORRORS, THAT FLOW THROUGH THIS CAPTIVE LAND (EARTH) TODAY. I WILL DANCE IN THE PRESENCE OF GOD'S HOLY THRONE, AS I WITNESS THE HORRORS THAT ARE PRODUCED BY SATAN, THE DESTROYER, SATAN, THE DOOMED ONE, SATAN, THE ENEMY OF ALL THAT IS GOOD AND HOLY. I WILL DANCE AMID GOD'S HEAVENLY CHOIRS, AS I REJOICE IN THE MIDST OF THE HORRORS THAT ARE RELEASED BY SATAN, THE JOY KILLER. I WILL SING PRAISES TO GOD, THE ALMIGHTY ONE, AS I DENOUNCE SATAN'S REALM OF DESPAIR AND GLOOM. I WILL NOT EXHIBIT THE SADNESS THAT SATAN DESIRES, AS I WITNESS THE HORRORS THAT HAVE ENGULFED THIS GENERATION. I WILL STAY FOCUSED ON THE GOODNESS OF THE WORLD, AS I REJOICE IN THE REALM THAT HOUSES GOD, MY ETERNAL SAVIOR AND REFUGE.
JULY 29, 2015 BY: BARBARA ANN MARY MACK

GREAT WEEPING ON EARTH

ALMIGHTY GOD SPEAKING TO HIS MURDERED CHILDREN OF ALL AGES

CAN YOU HEAR IT? CAN YOU HEAR THE SOUND OF GREAT WEEPING? CAN YOU FEEL THE SORROW? CAN YOU SEE THE TEARS? CAN YOU SEE MY SMILE AS IT COMFORTS YOUR WELCOMED BEINGS, MY CHILDREN? I AM HERE, O TORTURED ONES. I AM WITHIN YOUR WELCOMED PRESENCE, MY CHILDREN. I HAVE HEARD YOUR CRIES BEFORE YOU EXITED EARTH'S REALM WITHOUT AN INVITATION TO DEATH. I HAVE HEARD THE PAIN THAT YOU EXPERIENCED AS SATAN'S SERVANTS PIERCED YOUR VULNERABLE BODIES. I HAVE WITNESSED THE HELPLESSNESS THAT YOU ENDURED AS YOUR ATTACKERS SUBDUED YOUR INNOCENT BEINGS. I AM WITH YOU, MY CHILDREN! I HAVE ALWAYS BEEN BY YOUR VULNERABLE SIDE. I WILL WEEP WITH YOU! I WILL WEEP WITH YOU AS YOU ENTER MY REALM OF PEACE AND SECURITY. THERE, YOU WILL BE IN THE MIDST OF ME, PURE HOLINESS, FOREVER AND EVER, *SAYS THE LORD GOD.*
JULY 29, 2015 BY: BARBARA ANN MARY MACK

I WATCH OVER THEM AS THEY SLEEP, *SAYS THE LORD*

ALMIGHTY GOD SPEAKING
TO ALL OF HIS CHILDREN

THROUGHOUT THE DAY, EACH BLESSED DAY, I WATCH OVER YOU, I HAVE CREATED YOU OUT OF LOVE. WHEN YOU ARE ASLEEP, IN THE MIDST OF YOUR DREAMS, I WATCH OVER THOSE WHOM I CREATED OUT OF LOVE. I WATCH OVER THOSE WHO HAVE NO ONE TO CARE FOR THEM. I WATCH OVER THOSE WHO ARE VULNERABLE AND WEAK. I WATCH OVER THOSE WHOM THE REALM OF DESTRUCTION AND PAIN SEEKS. I WATCH OVER THOSE WHOM SATAN THE DEVIL SEEKS. I WATCH OVER ALL OF MY CHILDREN, GREAT AND SMALL. I WATCH OVER THOSE WHOM I HAVE CHOSEN AND CALLED. I WATCH OVER THE RICH, AND I WATCH OVER THE POOR. I WATCH OVER ALL WHO ANSWERS MY KNOCK AT THEIR DOORS. FOR I TRULY LOVE ALL OF MY CHILDREN, ESPECIALLY THOSE WHO BELIEVE IN ME. I WILL WATCH OVER YOU, O LOVED ONES OF MINE, WHEN YOU SLEEP. JULY 29, 2015 BY: BARBARA ANN MARY MACK

I CRY OUT DAILY AS I BEHOLD THE OPEN GATES TO SWEET PARADISE ABOVE, MY REALM OF CONTINUOUS PEACE

BARBARA SPEAKING TO
ALMIGHTY GOD

A LONGING, A LONGING, FOR SWEET PARADISE, MY HEAVENLY HOME. CALL OUT TO ME, O SWEET GATES THAT SURROUND MY HEAVENLY THRONE! CALL OUT TO ME AS I WEEP IN THE MIDST OF LONELINESS, FOR THE AGONY IS VERY HEAVY, IT IS TREMENDOUS! I CAN SEE YOU, O SWEET GATES TO PARADISE ABOVE! I CAN BEHOLD YOU AS I LOOK TOWARD HEAVEN ABOVE. I CAN FEEL YOUR HOLY PRESENCE AROUND ME, AS YOU EMIT THE PEACE THAT I LONG FOR. CALL OUT TO ME, O SWEET GATES, SO THAT I MAY HEAR A FRACTION OF MY HOLY GOD AND SPOUSE, FOR I LONG TO JOIN HIM AND HIS MIGHTY THRONE OF CONTINUOUS LOVE AND MERCY.

BARBARA SPEAKING TO ALMIGHTY GOD

WHISPER THE HOLY TUNES THAT SOOTHE ME, MY LORD. WHISPER THE MELODIOUS TUNES THAT WILL RELEASE THE ESSENCE (CRAIG) THAT I LONG TO EMBRACE ON EARTH TODAY. WHISPER YOUR HOLY TUNES THAT SUMMON THE SPIRIT OF OUR CHOSEN AND BELOVED ONE (CRAIG). WHISPER THE MELODIOUS TUNES THAT WILL IGNITE HIS DORMANT SOUL. WHISPER, MY LORD! WHISPER YOUR GIFT OF LIFE TO US TODAY, FOR WE (CRAIG AND BARBARA) LONG... JULY 29, 2015 BY: BARBARA ANN MARY MACK

BARBARA SPEAKING TO ALMIGHTY GOD, THE SACRIFICIAL ONE

MY GOD, YOU ARE WORTHY, FOR YOU HAVE SUFFERED AND MADE SACRIFICES FOR US

O WORTHY GOD AND HOLY SPOUSE OF MINE, I PRAISE AND THANK YOU FOR THE GREAT AND HOLY SACRIFICE THAT YOU SO LOVINGLY MADE FOR US, YOUR WORTHY CHILDREN. YOU, O LORD, HAVE MADE MANY SACRIFICES FOR YOUR GREAT CREATION THROUGH THE YEARS. YOU HAVE EXHIBITED YOUR UNDYING LOVE AND ALLEGIANCE TO YOUR GREAT CREATION, DESPITE OUR DISOBEDIENCE AND UNFAITHFULNESS UNTO YOU AND YOUR HOLY WORDS AND WAY. YOU, O REALM OF DIVINE LOVE, CONTINUE TO MAKE SACRIFICES FOR US. YOU, MY LORD,

HAVE SUFFERED IN THE PRESENCE OF OUR HOLY GOD AND FATHER, FOR THE SAKES OF YOUR WORTHY AND UNWORTHY FLOCK ON EARTH. I HAVE SEEN AND CAUGHT MANY OF YOUR FALLEN TEARS, O HOLY GOD AND SPOUSE OF MINE. I HAVE CRADLED YOUR HOLY TEARS WITHIN THE ARMS THAT WERE FORMED BY YOU, O HOLY SPOUSE OF MINE. I BOW CONTINUOUSLY IN YOUR HOLY PRESENCE, AS I GIVE REVERENCE TO HE WHO FORMED ME OUT OF PURE AND HOLY LOVE. *ALLELUIA!* O WORTHY GOD AND SPOUSE OF MINE, *ALLELUIA!!!*

JULY 29, 2015 BY: BARBARA ANN MARY MACK

HOPE, OH HOW POWERFUL YOU ARE!

BARBARA SPEAKING TO THE REALM OF HOPE

I WILL CLING TO YOU, O SWEET REALM THAT DESCENDED FROM ALMIGHTY GOD'S REALM OF ETERNITY. I WILL CLING TO YOU AMID IMPOSSIBLE AND HARD TIMES. I WILL CLING TO THE DIVINE ESSENCE (ALMIGHTY GOD) THAT CALLED YOU INTO EXISTENCE, FOR WE TRULY NEED AND DEPEND ON YOU. I WILL CLING TO YOU WHEN ALL TELL ME TO GIVE UP ON YOU. I WILL CLING TO YOU WHEN THE VISIBLE SIGNS REVEAL YOUR UNSEEN PRESENCE. I WILL CLING TO YOU, EVEN WHEN MY MIND BETRAYS MY HEART. I AM TRULY GRATEFUL FOR YOUR HOLY PRESENCE, O REALM OF HOPE THAT I CLING TO DAILY. I AM GRATEFUL FOR THE DIVINE GIFT OF YOUR PRESENCE THAT SUSTAINS AND COMFORTS THOSE WHO BELIEVE. I BOW IN THE PRESENCE OF MY HOLY GOD, AS I LOOK UP TO THE REALM OF HOPE THAT DESCENDED IN THE PRESENCE OF THOSE WHO DESIRE A TASTE OF HE (ALMIGHTY GOD) WHO FORMED YOU FOR US (GOD'S CHILDREN).

JULY 29, 2015 BY: BARBARA ANN MARY MACK

SENT SAT, AUG 1, 2015 10:08 AM-READ SAT 8/1/2015 10:41 AM

THE WORD OF GOD: WHY DO YOU RUN FROM ME, *SAYS THE LORD?*

AMIGHTY GOD SPEAKING
TO THE LOST ONES

WHY DO YOU RUN FROM ME, FOR I HAVE ONLY COME TO REVEAL THE TRUTH? I HAVE SPOKEN MY TRUTH THROUGH MY MESSENGERS. I HAVE SPOKEN MY HOLY WORDS THROUGH MY BRIDE (BARBARA). THOSE WHO HEED MY HOLY WORDS WILL BE AMONG THE BLESSED ONES. DO YOU NOT DESIRE MY HOLY PRESENCE, O LOST ONE? DO YOU NOT SEEK ME THROUGHOUT THE DAY? DO YOU NOT SEARCH, AND SEARCH FOR MY REALM OF EXISTENCE, O LOST ONE? DO YOU NOT CRY OUT TO ME IN YOUR TIMES OF NEED? MY CHILDREN, WHY DO YOU NOT COME TO ME AND HEAR THE HOLY WORDS THAT I HAVE SPOKEN? WHY DO YOU RUN FROM MY HOLY WORD? WHY DO YOU EXPECT ME TO HEAR AND HONOR YOUR PRAYER REQUESTS, WHEN YOU RUN FROM ME THROUGHOUT THE DAY? HOW CAN YOU CALL OUT TO ME WHEN TROUBLE SURROUNDS YOU, BUT REJECT ME WHEN LIFE IS GOING WELL FOR YOU? O LOST ONES, I TELL YOU MY HOLY WORD OF TRUTH, I WILL NOT HEAR OR HONOR YOUR REQUESTS, FOR THEY ARE NOT FROM A PURE AND PURGED HEART. LEARN OF ME AND MY HOLY WORD BEFORE YOU APPROACH ME, O LOST ONES, FOR THEN I WILL ACKNOWLEDGE YOU TOO.

JULY 31, 2015 BY: BARBARA ANN MARY MACK

WATCH ME AS I PERMEATE, SAYS THE LORD

ALMIGHTY GOD SPEAKING

WATCH ME AS I PERMEATE! WATCH ME AS I MOVE THROUGH YOUR PEWS! WATCH ME AS I SIT IN THE MIDST OF THE CALLED ONES! WATCH ME AS I PERMEATE! FOR I, THE LORD, HAVE COME INTO YOUR MIDST IN A TANGIBLE, BUT GENTLE FORM (BARBARA, MY FAITHFUL BRIDE). I HAVE PENETRATED THIS REALM OF TIME AND EXISTENCE THROUGH MY TANGIBLE AND HOLY ESSENCE OF LOVE (BARBARA). I HAVE PENETRATED THIS GENERATION WITH MY UNCHANGEABLE WORDS OF LIFE. I HAVE PENETRATED THIS VULNERABLE REALM OF TIME WITH MY SPIRITUAL TWO EDGED SWORD OF VICTORY AND LOVE. I HAVE ENTERED THIS GENERATION IN THE PURIFIED TEMPLE (BODY) OF MY FAITHFUL AND OBEDIENT DAUGHTER AND BRIDE (BARBARA). I HAVE GIVEN HER MY HOLY WORDS FOR YOU TODAY, AS I REVEALED THEM THROUGH MY MESSENGERS OF THE PAST. HEED MY WORDS OF LIFE THAT WILL SAVE YOUR WEAK AND VULNERABLE SOULS. HEED MY HOLY WORDS THAT HAVE PERMEATED AND PENETRATED THIS BLESSED REALM OF TROUBLED TIME. HEED THEM, MY CHILDREN, BEFORE THE GATES TO SWEET PARADISE SHUT IN YOUR CALLED PRESENCE. HEED MY HOLY WORDS BEFORE THE GATES THAT RELEASE EVIL AND DESTRUCTION CAPTURE YOUR UNPROTECTED SOULS. MY CHILDREN, HEED MY HOLY WORDS THAT ARE SPOKEN THROUGH BARBARA, MY CHOSEN PROPHETESS AND BRIDE.

JULY 31, 2015 BY: BARBARA ANN MARY MACK

WHEN SATAN ENTERS OUR REALM OF HOLINESS

BARBARA SPEAKING

MY BROTHERS AND SISTERS, WHEN THINGS GO AGAINST THE GOOD THAT YOU TRY TO DO FOR THE LORD, UNDERSTAND THIS, SATAN HAS ENTERED YOUR REALM. HE ATTEMPTS TO DESTROY AND WREAK HAVOC TOWARD EVERYTHING AND EVERYONE THAT MOVES IN THE DIRECTION OF HOLINESS AND HOLY ACTS. REBUKE SATAN, MY BROTHERS AND SISTERS! REBUKE SATAN, THE INTRUDER, IN A CALM MANNER, SO THAT HIS STENCH AND EVIL PRESENCE WILL NOT INTERRUPT YOUR PURPOSE TO PLEASE ALMIGHTY GOD AND HIS KINGDOM OF HOLINESS. WHEN SATAN ENTERS YOUR REALM OF HOLINESS, COMBAT HIM WITH THE HEAVEN SENT TOOLS THAT WILL CHASE HIM AWAY. COMBAT HIM WITH GOD'S GIFT OF PATIENCE, COMBAT HIM WITH GOD'S GIFT OF DIVINE SINCERE LOVE. COMBAT HIM WITH GOD'S VERSION OF FORGIVENESS AND MERCY. COMBAT SATAN WITH DIVINE KNOWLEDGE THAT FLOWS THROUGH THE HOLY BIBLE. MY BROTHERS AND SISTERS, WHEN SATAN ENTERS YOUR REALM OF HOLINESS, SING SONGS OF PRAISE TO OUR OMNIPOTENT LOVING CREATOR AND GOD.
JULY 31, 2015 BY: BARBARA ANN MARY MACK

HE SEES IT ALL; AND HE KNOWS IT ALL

BARBARA SPEAKING

MY BROTHERS AND SISTERS, WE CANNOT HIDE FROM THE GREAT ONE (ALMIGHTY GOD), FOR HE SEES IT ALL! WE CAN LIE TO OURSELVES OR OTHERS, BUT WE CANNOT LIE TO ALMIGHTY GOD, FOR HE SEES AND HEARS EVERYTHING! HE IS THE OMNIPOTENT ONE! HE IS THE OMNIPRESENT ONE! HE SEES AND HEARS EVERYTHING THAT WE SPEAK AND THINK, FOR HE IS ALMIGHTY GOD, OUR CREATOR. TAKE CARE OF YOUR THOUGHTS AND CONVERSATIONS, MY BROTHERS AND SISTERS, FOR HE SEES IT ALL, AND HE HEARS IT ALL! WALK IN HIS HOLY LIGHT AT ALL

TIMES, SO THAT YOU MAY COMMUNE WITH OUR GREAT AND HOLY GOD ON ONE ACCORD, FOR HE SEES, KNOWS, AND HEARS IT ALL!
AUGUST 13, 2015 BY: BARBARA ANN MARY MACK

REBELLIOUS LIKE SATAN, YOUR DEFEATED FATHER

ALMIGHTY GOD SPEAKING

YOU GO AGAINST MY HOLY WORD AND WAY, BECAUSE YOU ARE REBELLIOUS LIKE SATAN, YOUR DEFEATED FATHER! YOU WHO FORM YOUR CHURCHES ARE REBELLIOUS LIKE SATAN, YOUR FATHER! YOU HAVE TURNED AGAINST ME, AS SATAN, YOUR DEFEATED FATHER HAS! THEREFORE, O REBELLIOUS ONES, YOUR ETERNAL DESTINATION IS LIFE IN HELL WITH SATAN, YOUR REBELLIOUS DEFEATED FATHER! MY HOLY WORDS ARE UNCHANGEABLE! MY VIEWS TOWARD UNHOLY ACTS AND DEEDS REMAIN! YOU CANNOT CHANGE WHAT I HAVE ORDAINED AS HOLY, O REBELLIOUS ONES! YOU CANNOT CHANGE ME, *SAYS THE LORD!*
AUGUST 14, 2015 BY: BARBARA ANN MARY MACK

DO NOT BE CONCERNED WITH THE CARES AND HAPPENINGS OF THE WORLD, FOR THAT TAKES AWAY FROM THE TIME THAT YOU SHOULD BE PRAISING ME, SAYS THE LORD

ALMIGHTY GOD SPEAKING

DO NOT CONCERN YOURSELVES WITH THE CARES AND HAPPENINGS OF THE WORLD, FOR THAT TAKES AWAY FROM THE TIME THAT YOU SHOULD BE SPENDING PRAISING YOUR FAITHFUL CREATOR AND GOD. DO NOT OVER BURDEN YOURSELVES WITH THE CARES THAT YOU CANNOT REMEDY, MY CHILDREN. DO NOT CONCERN YOURSELVES WITH SITUATIONS THAT YOU CANNOT

RESOLVE BECAUSE OF YOUR LIMITATIONS. FOR I, THE LORD ALMIGHTY, WILL TAKE CARE OF THE THINGS THAT YOU CANNOT REMEDY. FOR IN ME, THERE ARE NO LIMITATIONS! EVERYTHING AND EVERYONE ARE POWERLESS IN REGARDS TO SATAN'S EVIL ABILITIES, EXCEPT ME. DO NOT STRESS YOURSELVES OVER SITUATIONS THAT PRODUCE AWE AND INCOMPREHENSION, FOR YOU ARE LIMITED, O CREATION OF MINE. PRAISE ME AT ALL TIMES SO THAT SATAN, OUR ENEMY, WILL NOT PREVAIL OVER YOUR WEAKNESSES AND VULNERABILITY. FOCUS ON ME, AND ONLY ME, FOR I WILL TAKE CARE OF THE THINGS THAT YOU CANNOT, AT MY APPOINTED TIME AND WAY, *SAYS THE LORD.*

AUGUST 13, 2015 BY: BARBARA ANN MARY MACK

SENT WED, AUG 19, 2015 4:56 PM-READ WED 8/19/2015 7:16 PM

OH CLERGY, I WAS NOT SENT TO JUDGE, CONDEMN, NOR TO CRITICIZE YOU, BUT TO ENLIGHTEN AND OFFER DIVINE LOVE FOR YOU

ALMIGHTY GOD SPEAKING THROUGH BARBARA TO THOSE OF THE CLERGY

I DID NOT COME TO CONDEMN YOU, MY SONS! I DID NOT COME TO CRITICIZE YOUR GOOD WORKS FOR ME! I DID NOT COME TO JUDGE YOU! I HAVE COME IN THE FORM OF MY HUMBLED MESSENGER AND BRIDE (BARBARA), SO THAT YOU MAY RECEIVE AND SEE ME IN MY MEEK STATE. I HAVE COME TO ASSIST YOU IN BRINGING MY MISGUIDED FLOCK TO MY WAITING PASTURES OF DIVINE LOVE AND HOPE. I HAVE COME TO ENLIGHTEN YOU SO THAT YOU MAY FEEL AND TASTE A FRACTION OF MY TANGIBILITY IN YOUR MIDST TODAY. I AM HERE FOR YOU, O CLERGY! I HAVE COME TO ASSIST YOU IN THE MIDST OF SATAN'S BRUTAL PRESENCE. I HAVE COME TO OFFER YOU THE GIFT OF MY HOLY TRUTH AND LOVE, THROUGH BARBARA, MY FAITHFUL MESSENGER AND BRIDE. SHE HAS DELIVERED THE HOLY WORDS THAT PROCEEDED FROM THE ESSENCE OF YOUR ONLY CREATOR AND GOD. SHE HAS FOLLOWED MY HOLY WILL THROUGHOUT HER MISSION OF HOLY LOVE. SHE HAS FOUGHT THE GATES OF HELL FOR YOU AND MY VULNERABLE FLOCK. SHE HAS BATTLED SATAN AND HIS DEFEATED REALM WITH THE PRESENCE OF THE HOLY TRINITY. SHE HAS REMAINED ON THE SPIRITUAL BATTLEFIELD WITH THE SHIELD OF GOD, HER HOLY SPOUSE. BE GRATEFUL FOR HER HEAVEN SENT PRESENCE, O CLERGY, FOR SHE IS A FRACTION OF MY HOLY PRESENCE AND MIGHT TODAY.

AUGUST 20, 2015 BY: BARBARA ANN MARY MACK

SENT THU, AUG 20, 2015 12:09 AM-READ THU 8/20/2015 12:43 AM

MY CHILDREN, I WILL TAKE CARE OF YOU NOW, SAYS THE LORD

DEDICATED TO THE NEGLECTED CHILDREN

ALMIGHTY GOD SPEAKING TO THE NEGLECTED AND ABANDONED CHILDREN

THEY HAVE FORSAKEN YOU, MY LITTLE CHILDREN. THEY HAVE ABANDONED YOU, O LONGED FOR ONES. THEY HAVE NEGLECTED YOU, O TEAR THAT FLOWED BACK TO ME. THEREFORE, I, THE LORD, YOUR GOD, HAVE CALLED YOU BACK TO MY REALM OF PROTECTION AND LOVE. I HAVE NEVER ABANDONED YOU, MY LITTLE FLOCK. I HAVE NEVER NEGLECTED YOU, O HURTING ONES. I HAVE CARED FOR YOU WHEN YOUR EARTHLY FATHERS AND MOTHERS ABUSED YOU CONTINUOUSLY. NO MORE HURT, MY LITTLE FLOCK! NO MORE PAIN, O VULNERABLE LITTLE CHILDREN. NO MORE UNHEARD CRIES, DEAR ONES! FOR I, THE LORD, YOUR CREATOR AND ORIGIN, HAVE CALLED YOU BACK TO MY LOVING CARE.
AUGUST 15, 2015 BY: BARBARA ANN MARY MACK

GREETINGS DEAR ARCHBISHOP CRAIG! ATTACHED ARE PICTURES OF OUR FUN TIME IN GALETON, PA. LA TOYA AND AMYA ROASTING MARSHMALLOWS AT THE FARM IN GALETON, PA. BARBARA PLAYING A COMMUNITY PIANO OUTSIDE OF AN ITALIAN RESTAURANT IN WELLSBORO, PA. WE ORDERED A LARGE STEAK PIZZA, FRIES, AND DESSERT TO GO. EVERYONE WAS VERY FRIENDLY THERE. THE WAITER (CURTIS) TOOK A PICTURE WITH ME AFTER HE LOOKED THROUGH SOME OF MY PUBLISHED BOOKS. HE SAID THAT HE IS ITALIAN AND POLISH, BUT HE SPEAKS FRENCH. *AMORE, BELLA BARBIE*
SENT WED, AUG 19, 2015 4:56 PM-READ WED 8/19/2015 7:16 PM

I REJOICE IN THE MIDST OF SATAN'S ATTACKS

BARBARA SPEAKING TO CRAIG, GOD'S CHOSEN GROOM

REJOICE! REJOICE! REJOICE, O DIVINE ESSENCE OF GOD'S CHOSEN BRIDE (BARBARA) AND GROOM (CRAIG)! REJOICE, AS YOU ENDURE THE MANY DARTS THAT SATAN AND HIS DEFEATED REALM OF EVIL ATTACK YOU WITH DAILY! REJOICE AS YOU RECEIVE THE WORKS THAT ARE DIRECTED BY SATAN, THE DEFEATED REALM OF EVIL! REJOICE IN THE HOLY PRESENCE OF HE, ALMIGHTY GOD, WHO HAS SENT YOU TO REVEAL SATAN'S UNHOLY PRESENCE IN THE LIVES OF THOSE WHO SEEK AND DESIRE THE REALM OF DIVINITY. REJOICE IN THE MIDST OF THOSE WHO FOLLOW SATAN'S DEFEATED REALM! REJOICE, AS YOU CATCH THE MANY DARTS THAT INTENDED TO WIPE US OUT! REJOICE IN THE PRESENCE OF HE (SATAN) WHO DESIRES TO DESTROY OUR GOD ORDERED WORK! REJOICE! REJOICE! REJOICE! FOR WE HAVE TRIUMPHED OVER THE REALM (SATAN) THAT HATES US! YOU AND I HAVE TRIUMPHED OVER THE REALM (SATAN) THAT RELEASES DESTRUCTION AND HAVOC! WE HAVE TRIUMPHED OVER THE REALM THAT SEEKS THE LOST SOULS OF THE VULNERABLE ONES! WE HAVE TRIUMPHED OVER THE REALM (SATAN) THAT IS DESTINED FOR ETERNITY IN HELL! WE HAVE TRIUMPHED IN THE

MIDST OF THIS PERIOD OF GREAT TRIBULATION! REJOICE! DEAR ONE (CRAIG). FOR WE HAVE COMPLETED OUR HEAVEN ORDERED ASSIGNMENT OF LOVE!
AUGUST 15, 2015 BY: BARBARA ANN MARY MACK

OH, THE PERVERSION THAT HAS OPENLY ENTERED THE CHURCH-MANKIND'S CHURCH, NOT CHRIST'S CHURCH

ALMIGHTY GOD SPEAKING

OH HOW SICKENING IT IS TO WITNESS THE PERVERSION THAT IS OPENLY ACCEPTED IN "MANKIND'S CHURCHES"! OH HOW HEARTBREAKING IT IS TO WITNESS THIS FROM MY DIVINE THRONE ABOVE, AND THROUGH THE PURIFIED EYES OF MY MESSENGER AND BRIDE (BARBARA)! I JUST LOWER MY ESSENCE IN DISGUST AND DISAPPOINTMENT, AS I WITNESS THE PERVERSION THAT SITS IN THE PEWS OF THOSE WHO HAVE CREATED THEIR SEPARATE CHURCH, SATAN'S PLAYGROUND ON EARTH. MANKIND ACCEPTS THOSE WHOM I HAVE REJECTED. MANKIND ENTERTAINS IN HIS CHURCH, INSTEAD OF ENLIGHTENING THE CONGREGATION OF MY HOLY WAY, THE ONLY WAY TO SALVATION AND HEAVENLY BLISS. OH WHAT A TRAGEDY IT IS, AS I WITNESS THE SIGNS OF THEIR FUTURE DESTRUCTION AND DESTINATION. OH THE PERVERSION THAT CREEPS INTO THE PEWS THAT MANKIND CONSIDERS JUST AND RIGHTEOUS. MEN IN RELATIONSHIPS WITH MEN, AND WOMEN MARRYING WOMEN. OH HOW SAD IT IS! OH WHAT A DISTURBING SIGHT! I CAN SEE YOU, O PERVERTED CLERGY! I CAN SEE YOUR "UNHOLY WAYS"! WOMEN LEADING YOUR CHURCHES. SOME EVEN REFER TO THEMSELVES AS PASTORS AND BISHOPS! THEY HAVE BEEN ORDAINED BY MANKIND, NOT BY ME, THE ONLY FOUNDER OF MY HOLY CHURCH. DO YOU NOT KNOW THAT YOU ARE LEADING YOUR CONGREGATION INTO THE OPEN GATES THAT LEAD TO HELL AND ETERNAL DAMNATION? DO YOU NOT KNOW THAT THE WORDS THAT YOU PREACH AND TEACH ARE IN VAIN? DO YOU NOT UNDERSTAND MY VERSION OF HOLINESS? FOR IT IS THE ONLY VERSION OF HOLINESS, *SAYS THE LORD!*
AUGUST 14, 2015 BY: BARBARA ANN MARY MACK
SENT THU, AUG 20, 2015 12:09 AM-READ THU 8/20/2015 12:43 AM

BUON GIORNO AMORE! COME STA OGGI? WE ARE EN ROUTE TO MY DOCTOR'S OFFICE FOR A ROUTINE CHECK-UP AND MY MONTHLY B12 INJECTION. ENJOY YOUR BLESSED DAY DEAR ONE! *CIAO! BEAUTIFUL BARBARA*
SENT THU, AUG 20, 2015 12:09 AM-READ THU 8/20/2015 12:43 AM

THE ROAD TO ETERNAL LIFE IS SWEET AND PRECIOUS

BARBARA SPEAKING TO ALMIGHTY GOD

THE ROAD, YES, THE SWEET AND NARROW ROAD THAT LEADS TO YOU, IS SWEET AND PRECIOUS TO ME MY GOD. THE HEAVENLY FORMED ROAD THAT LEADS TO ETERNAL LIFE WITH GOD, MY SAVIOR, IS OH, SO REWARDING! THE ROAD THAT LEADS TO YOUR HEAVENLY HOME ABOVE, IS SMOOTH AND SAFE FOR THOSE WHO LOVE AND TRUST TOUR HOLY WILL, MY GOD.

BARBARA SPEAKING TO GOD'S CHILDREN

COME! O INVITED BROTHERS AND SISTERS OF MINE. LET US WALK THE NARROW AND REWARDING ROAD TOGETHER, IN THE PRESENCE OF HE WHO FORMED US OUT OF DIVINE LOVE AND REVERENCE. COME WITH ME, O INVITED ONES, AS I WALK THE SWEET AND PRECIOUS ROAD THAT LEADS TO GOD, OUR FATHER'S, TABLE OF LOVE AND PLENTY. JOIN US (THE LORD AND BARBARA) AS WE SIT AT THE TABLE OF LIFE SUSTAINING NOURISHMENT. JOIN US, AS WE SING SONGS OF JOY IN THE COMPANY OF THE HEAVENLY CHOIRS AND RESIDENTS. JOIN ME, O INVITED ONES, AS I WALK THE ROAD THAT LEADS TO SWEET PARADISE ABOVE. *ALLELUIA!!!* AUGUST 10, 2015 BY: BARBARA ANN MARY MACK

I ENTERED THE REALM OF HAPPINESS, AS I EXITED THIS WORLD OF TEMPORARY FAME AND FORTUNE

BARBARA SPEAKING

OH HOW GRAND IT IS! TO EXPERIENCE THE JOY AND ELATION OF A NEW AND PURE WORLD. TO ENJOY THE DEPTH OF DIVINE HAPPINESS ON EARTH TODAY, IS A GIFT FROM THE LORD THAT I WILL FOREVER CHERISH! FOR HE HAS GRACED ME WITH THE GIFT OF EXPERIENCING THE DEPTH OF HIS REALM OF HAPPINESS, AS I DWELL IN THE MIDST OF MY EARTHLY BROTHERS AND SISTERS. I WILL SING SONGS OF PRAISE TO MY GREAT AND HOLY GOD AS I EXPERIENCE THE DEPTH OF HIS REALM OF HAPPINESS AND JOY TODAY. I WILL LIFT HIS HOLY ESSENCE IN CONTINUOUS PRAISE AS I EXPERIENCE THE DEPTH OF HIS HOLY REALM ON EARTH, AS I EXIT THE REALM OF TEMPORARY FAME AND FORTUNE. REJOICE, O GRATEFUL IGNITED SPIRIT OF MINE! REJOICE IN THE PRESENCE OF GOD, THE HOLY ONE, AS YOU EXIT THIS WORLD OF TEMPORARY PLEASURES! REJOICE! O GRATEFUL SOUL (BARBARA) THAT DESCENDED FROM THE MIGHTY THRONE OF GOD, THE HOLY SAVIOR! REJOICE AS YOU EXIT THE REALM THAT PRODUCES AND INVITES SATAN'S TEMPORARY FAME AND FORTUNE! REJOICE IN THE PRESENCE OF YOUR FAMILY! REJOICE IN THE PRESENCE OF YOUR FRIENDS! REJOICE IN THE PRESENCE OF THE CALLED ONES! REJOICE IN THE PRESENCE OF THE CHOSEN ONES! REJOICE!

O IGNITED SPIRIT OF MINE. REJOICE IN THE PRESENCE OF THE LORD, FOR HE IS GOOD AND HOLY! *ALLELUIA!*

AUGUST 10, 2015 BY: BARBARA ANN MARY MACK

SENT THU, AUG 20, 2015 12:09 AM-READ THU 8/20/2015 12:43 AM

THE WORLD CANNOT RECOGNIZE ME, SAYS THE LORD

ALMIGHTY GOD SPEAKING

THEY, THE WORLD, DO NOT RECOGNIZE ME, BECAUSE THEY DO NOT KNOW ME, *SAYS THE LORD.* I HAVE COME TO YOU AGAIN, O EARTHLY CREATION OF MINE! I HAVE COME TO YOU IN A FORM (BARBARA) THAT YOU DO NOT RECOGNIZE AS BEING MY DWELLING PLACE ON EARTH. YOU DO NOT RECOGNIZE MY REPRESENTATIVE (BARBARA), BECAUSE SHE IS NOT OF YOUR CALIBER OF SOCIAL ELITE. YOU DO NOT RECOGNIZE ME WITHIN HER, BECAUSE YOU CANNOT PERCEIVE OR ACCEPT THAT WHICH IS PURE AND HOLY. I HAVE COME IN A FORM (BARBARA) THAT MOST OF YOU DO NOT RECOGNIZE, BECAUSE YOU DO NOT RECOGNIZE OR UNDERSTAND MY HOLY WORD AND WAY. YOU RECOGNIZE YOUR OWN, BECAUSE YOU ARE OF THE SAME WORLD, THE MATERIAL AND SOCIAL DISCRIMINATION AND LABELS. YOU DO NOT RECOGNIZE THOSE WHO ARE ABOVE YOUR UNGODLY REALM AND WAY. YOU DO NOT RECOGNIZE THE SPIRITUAL ELITE! YOU DO NOT RECOGNIZE THE HOLY ONES! YOU DO NOT RECOGNIZE THOSE WHOM I HAVE SENT TO YOU, O LOST WORLD. YOU DO NOT RECOGNIZE ME, FOR I AM NOT WITH NOR OF YOUR REALM OF SOCIAL ELITE, *SAYS THE LORD!*

AUGUST 22, 2015 BY: BARBARA ANN MARY MACK

SENT SUN, AUG 23, 2015 3:18 PM-READ SUN 8/23/2015 9:46 PM

I WILL NOT LET YOU IN MY REALM OF HEAVENLY BLISS, O WORLD! I WILL TUNE YOU OUT

BARBARA SPEAKING TO THE WORLD

I WILL NOT LET YOU IN, O WORLD! I WILL NOT LET YOU IN MY REALM OF HEAVENLY BLISS ON EARTH TODAY! I WILL NOT LET YOU INTERRUPT THE DIVINE PEACE THAT DANCES WITH ME THROUGHOUT THE DAY! I WILL NOT LET YOU INTERFERE WITH THE JOY THAT ENCOMPASSES MY IGNITED SOUL, AS I DANCE IN THE MIDST OF DIVINITY ON EARTH TODAY! I WILL TUNE YOU OUT, AS I DANCE IN THE MIDST OF HEAVENLY BLISS! FLEE FROM ME, O REALM THAT TRIES TO INTERRUPT MY REALM OF DIVINE CONTENTMENT THROUGH THE MEDIA! FLEE FROM ME, O REALM THAT TRIES TO INTERRUPT MY REALM OF HEAVEN SENT PEACE THROUGH FAMILY AND FRIENDS! FLEE FROM ME, O REALM THAT SLITHERS FROM SATAN'S REALM OF UNHAPPINESS AND GLOOM! FLEE FROM ME, O REJECTED REALM THAT TRIES TO SNEAK INTO MY PEACEFUL

DIVINE PROTECTED MIND! FLEE FROM ME, O GATES THAT CRY OUT TO THOSE WHO FOLLOW SATAN'S EVIL DEEDS AND THOUGHTS! FLEE FROM ME, ALL THAT TRIES TO DESTROY THE JOY THAT DESCENDS FROM GOD, MY HOLY SPOUSE AND PROTECTOR! FLEE FROM ME, O REALM OF DOOM, SO THAT I MAY REJOICE IN THE MIDST OF HEAVENLY BLISS FOREVER AND EVER!!!
AUGUST 22, 2015 BY: BARBARA ANN MARY MACK
SENT SUN, AUG 23, 2015 3:18 PM-READ SUN 8/23/2015 9:46 PM

JESUS, YOU ARE NOT ALONE

BARBARA SPEAKING TO THE LORD JESUS

MY LORD, MY HOLY GOD AND ETERNAL SPOUSE, OUR BELOVED ONE (CRAIG) AND I HAVE FUSED WITH YOUR HOLY ESSENCE, SO THAT WE MAY DWELL WITH YOU FOREVER. WE HAVE FUSED WITH YOU SO THAT YOU WILL ALWAYS FEEL THE COMFORT OF YOUR GREAT CREATION (MANKIND). WE HAVE FUSED WITH YOU, WITH THE APPROVAL OF GOD, OUR HOLY FATHER. WE HAVE FUSED WITH YOU IN THE PRESENCE OF HE, ALMIGHTY GOD, WHO HAS CALLED US (CRAIG AND BARBARA) INTO EXISTENCE DURING THIS CRUCIAL PERIOD OF TIME. WE HAVE FUSED WITH YOU, SO THAT WE MAY EXPERIENCE THE DEPTH OF TRUE HOLINESS AND ETERNITY. OUR BELOVED ONE AND I BOW IN THE MIDST OF YOU, O SAVING GOD, FOR WE TRULY LOVE AND ADORE YOU. WE GIVE YOU CONTINUOUS PRAISE, GLORY AND HONOR, IN THE PRESENCE OF THOSE WHOM YOU DEEM WORTHY TO SHARE AND WITNESS OUR (ALMIGHTY GOD, CRAIG, AND BARBARA) INSEPARABLE HOLY UNION. MY LORD, OUR (CRAIG AND BARBARA) CHOSEN FUSED ESSENCE BOWS IN YOUR HOLY PRESENCE AS WE GIVE HOMAGE TO JESUS, OUR GREAT LORD AND VICTORIOUS KING! MY LORD, YOU ARE NOT ALONE!
AUGUST 23, 2015 BY: BARBARA ANN MARY MACK

I DO NOT NEED MANKIND'S GLORY: THE GLORY OF THE WORLD

BARBARA SPEAKING

I DO NOT NEED OR WANT THE TEMPORARY GLORY THAT MANKIND HAS TO OFFER, FOR IT IS THE GLORY OF THE WORLD. I DO NOT NEED OR WANT MANKIND'S VERSION OF FAME AND FORTUNE, FOR MY WEALTH AND SPIRITUAL FAME TRANSCEND WHAT THIS WORLD OFFERS. I WILL FOCUS ONLY ON THE GLORY OF THE LORD, AND HOW AND WHEN I CAN PLEASE HIM, FOR HE IS MINE! HE IS MY, EVERYTHING! HE IS ME! *ALLELUIA!*
AUGUST 23, 2015 BY: BARBARA ANN MARY MACK
SENT MON, AUG 24, 2015 12:54 AM-READ MON 8/24/2015 3:28 PM

VICTORY IS HERE! VICTORY IS OURS (ALMIGHTY GOD, ARCHBISHOP CRAIG, AND BARBARA)!!!

225

GREETINGS, DEAR ONE ARCHBISHOP CRAIG)! COME STA OGGI AMORE? I PRAY THAT YOU ARE VERY WELL AT THIS TIME. LA TOYA, AMYA, AND I ARE EN ROUTE TO AN AMUSEMENT PARK AND OTHER VENTURES THAT ARE ORCHESTRATED BY ALMIGHTY GOD. YESTERDAY WAS VERY EXTRAORDINARY! THE OWNER (DENNIS) OF THE PROPERTY WAS OUTSIDE WHEN WE WERE LEAVING FOR A DRIVE TO ERIE, PA. IT WAS AT THAT TIME, THAT THE LORD PROMPTED ME TO GREET HIM. DURING OUR CONVERSATION, I MENTIONED THAT WE WERE NOT HERE FOR A VACATION, BUT TO DO A WORK FOR THE LORD. WHEN DENNIS LEARNED OF MY POSITION AS ONE OF GOD'S CONTEMPORARY MESSENGERS, HE WAS OVER JOYED WITH ENTHUSIASM. I TOLD HIM THAT I WAS ALSO WORKING ON MY FORTHCOMING BOOK (THE PRESENT TESTAMENT VOLUME NINE) HERE. I SHOWED HIM SOME OF MY PUBLISHED BOOKS THAT THE LORD TOLD ME TO BRING WITH US. MY BOOK (A HOUSE DIVIDED CANNOT STAND) CAPTURED HIS ATTENTION. HE TOLD ME THAT HE WOULD LIKE TO PURCHASE IT. I TOLD HIM THAT HE COULD LOOK THROUGH IT UNTIL WE LEAVE ON MONDAY. AND IF HE DECIDES TO PURCHASE IT, I WOULD SIGN IT FOR HIM AS WELL. DURING OUR CONVERSATION, DENNIS MENTIONED THAT HE BELIEVED THAT THE LORD WOULD SEND SOMEONE TODAY TO REVEAL HIMSELF TO HIS CHILDREN, AS HE DID IN THE PAST. HE WAS OVERWHELMED WITH EXCITEMENT TO HAVE MET ONE OF THE LORD'S

CONTEMPORARY MESSENGERS. HE TOLD ME THAT OUR MEETING WAS THE HIGHLIGHT OF HIS DAY, AND HE ASKED IF HE COULD GIVE ME A HUG. I ALSO LISTENED TO HIS CONCERNS, WHICH WERE FOR HIS FAMILY AND ACQUAINTANCES. HE APPEARS TO BE A VERY HUMBLE MAN. PRIOR TO OUR MEETING THAT DAY, THE DEVIL WAS EXHIBITING HIS ANGER, BECAUSE HE KNEW WHAT WAS ABOUT TO TAKE PLACE BETWEEN DENNIS AND ME. HE, SATAN, TRIED TO DO MANY THINGS THAT WOULD CAUSE US, IN A NORMAL SITUATION TO LEAVE THIS PROPERTY BEFORE WE INTENDED. BUT, THE LORD REVEALED TO ME THAT SATAN WAS BEHIND THE NEGATIVE OCCURRENCES THAT TOOK PLACE EARLIER THAT DAY. AFTER MEETING WITH DENNIS, I KNEW HOW TO COMBAT SATAN. WE WILL STAY HERE UNTIL OUR ASSIGNMENT FOR THE LORD IS COMPLETED. ALMIGHTY GOD WILL HAVE IT NO OTHER WAY. PLEASE KEEP DENNIS AND HIS FAMILY IN YOUR PRAYERS DEAR ONE, FOR HE IS ONE OF GOD'S CHOSEN.
LOVE YOU ALWAYS, BEAUTIFUL VICTORIOUS BARBARA
SENT SAT, AUG 29, 2015 12:08 PM-READ SAT 8/29/15 3:48 PM

GREETINGS DEAR ARCHBISHOP CRAIG! HAPPY FEAST DAY: SAINT AUGUSTINE! I PRAY THAT YOU ARE DOING VERY WELL! WE ARE ENJOYING OUR STAY AT LIGHT ON THE LAKE BED & BREAKFAST IN NORTH EAST, PA. YESTERDAY, WE SPENT FOUR HOURS AT MARITIME MUSEUM IN NIAGARA PLAZA, IN ERIE, PA. THE LORD HAD ME DELIVER MESSAGES TO ONE OF THE STAFF THERE. HER NAME IS JEAN. SHE AND I TALKED FOR ABOUT 30 MINUTES OR SO BEFORE WE (TOYA, AMYA, AND I) TOURED THE MUSEUM. THE MUSEUM EXHIBITED HISTORICAL INFORMATION AND MATERIAL OF THE BATTLE OF LAKE ERIE ON SEPTEMBER 10, 1813. THE AMERICANS WON THE BATTLE OVER THE BRITISH FLEET. THERE WERE A FEW SHORT VIDEOS THAT REVEALED A BRIEF, BUT SIGNIFICANT PART OF THE BATTLE. IT WAS A VERY ENLIGHTENING AND INTERESTING EXPERIENCE. AFTER OUR MUSEUM TOUR, WE TOURED A PART OF LAKE ERIE ON A BOAT FOR 90 MINUTES. THERE WERE TWO CAPTAINS ABOARD. ONE CONTROLLED THE BOAT WHILE THE OTHER NARRATED THE STORY BEHIND THE BATTLE SHIP NIAGARA, WHICH SERVED AS COMMODORE OLIVER H. PERRY'S RELIEF FLAGSHIP. BEFORE, AND DURING THE RIDE, THE LORD GAVE ME MESSAGES FOR ONE OF THE CAPTAINS (CAPTAIN BROOKS). HE TOO, WAS VERY RECEPTIVE AND FREELY TALKED ABOUT THE LORD AND HIS FAMILY WITH ME. HE WAS VERY GRATEFUL FOR THE MESSAGES THAT THE LORD REVEALED THROUGH ME FOR HIM AND HIS SON (CURTIS). PLEASE KEEP HIM AND THE OTHERS IN YOUR VALUABLE PRAYERS ALSO. AT THIS TIME, I AM WAITING FOR LA TOYA AND AMYA TO RETURN FROM THEIR TOUR OF DOWNTOWN ERIE AND AN AMUSEMENT PARK. WE PLAN ON GOING TO PLAY MINIATURE GOLF LATER TODAY. WE PLAN ON VISITING NIAGARA FALLS BEFORE WE LEAVE THIS LOCATION. PLEASE TAKE VERY GOOD CARE OF YOUR VALUABLE SELF!
LOVE ALWAYS! BEAUTIFUL BARBARA
SENT SAT, AUG 29, 2015 12:08 PM-READ SAT 8/29/15 3:48 PM

ALMIGHTY GOD SPEAKING

I WILL TEACH YOU, MY CHILDREN. I WILL EDUCATE YOU TODAY. I WILL TELL YOU THINGS THAT MANKIND COULD NEVER REVEAL TO YOU, FOR IT IS KNOWLEDGE THAT COMES FROM ME. I WILL REVEAL TO YOU MY VERSION OF THE FUTURE AND HOW YOU SHOULD ABIDE. I WILL TELL YOU OF THE PLANS THAT I HAVE FOR MY CHILDREN, MY GREAT CREATION, MY FLOCK ON EARTH, SO THAT YOU WILL KNOW THE TRUTH, MY TRUTH! I WILL TELL YOU WHAT YOU MUST DO, SO THAT YOU WILL KNOW HOW TO TEACH MY LITTLE CHILDREN MY HOLY WAY, INSTEAD OF THE WORLD'S PERVERTED WAY. LISTEN, MY CHILDREN! LISTEN TO ME AS I SPEAK TO YOU, FOR I AM IN YOUR NEEDY PRESENCE TODAY. I AM IN THE PRESENCE OF THOSE WHOM I HAVE CALLED AND CHOSEN TO HEAR MY HOLY WORDS OF TRUTH. LISTEN TO ME, FOR I WILL TEACH YOU TOO!
AUGUST 26, 2015 BY: BARBARA ANN MARY MACK

KEEP ME AWAY FROM THE WORLD AND ITS REALM OF PERVERSION, MY GOD.

ALMIGHTY GOD SPEAKING TO BARBARA

YOU WERE SENT TO BRING LIGHT TO THOSE WHO EXIST IN THE REALM OF PERVERSION AND UNGODLY ACTS, MY DAUGHTER. YOU WERE SENT BY ME, YOUR ETERNAL GOD AND HOLY SPOUSE, TO HELP MY LOST AND CONFUSED CHILDREN. THEREFORE, I WILL NOT KEEP YOU AWAY FROM THEM. YOU MUST SHOW THEM MY HOLY WAY, MY BRIDE! HOW WILL THEY KNOW, IF I DO NOT TELL THEM THROUGH YOU? IT IS EVIDENT, THAT THEY DO NOT BELIEVE OR UNDERSTAND MY WORDS THAT ARE CONVEYED THROUGH THE HOLY BIBLE. I HAVE SENT YOU SO THAT THEY MAY KNOW AND BELIEVE IN MY UNCHANGEABLE WORD AND WAY. I HAVE SENT YOU TO THE CONFUSED ONES, SO THAT THEY TOO, MAY HAVE THE OPPORTUNITY TO CHANGE THEIR UNHOLY WAYS BEFORE MY IMMINENT RETURN IN THE CLOUDS. GO, MY DAUGHTER! DELIVER MY HOLY WAY AND WORDS TO THOSE WHO DWELL WITHIN THE REALM OF PERVERSION, FOR THAT IS YOUR DIVINE ASSIGNMENT FROM ME.
AUGUST 26, 2015 BY: BARBARA ANN MARY MACK
SENT SAT, AUG 29, 2015 12:08 PM-READ SAT 8/29/15 3:48 PM

GREETINGS, DEAR ONE! WE MADE IT TO OUR DESTINATION. WE DEPARTED AROUND 7:30 AM, AND ARRIVED AROUND 5:30 PM. WE TOOK A FEW BREAKS BEFORE REACHING NORTH EAST, PA. WE WILL STAY AT LIGHT ON THE LAKE BED & BREAKFAST APARTMENT UNTIL MONDAY, AUGUST 31ST. *GOD BLESS! BELLA BARBARA*
SENT SAT, AUG 29, 2015 12:08 PM-READ SAT 8/29/15 3:48 PM

GREETINGS DEAR ONE (ARCHBISHOP CRAIG)! WE ARE EN ROUTE TO NORTH EAST, PA. CIAO!
BELLA BARBARA
SENT SAT, AUG 29, 2015 12:08 PM-READ SAT 8/29/15 3:48 PM

THEY DO NOT UNDERSTAND YOU, MY GOD.

BARBARA SPEAKING TO THE LORD

THEY DO NOT UNDERSTAND YOU, MY LORD. IF THEY DID, THEY WOULD UNDERSTAND ME, WHOM YOU REVEAL YOUR HOLY PRESENCE THROUGH.

BARBARA SPEAKING TO THE CALLED AND CHOSEN ONES

WHY DO YOU NOT UNDERSTAND WHY I DO AND SAY CERTAIN THINGS, O CHILDREN WHO HAVE BEEN CALLED? WHY DO YOU NOT ACCEPT WHAT YOU SEE AND HEAR, FROM SHE (BARBARA) WHOM ALMIGHTY GOD'S HOLY PRESENCE CHOSE TO DWELL WITHIN? DO YOU NOT BELIEVE IN GOD, THE ALMIGHTY ONE? DO YOU NOT BELIEVE IN HIS BOUNDARYLESS ESSENCE OF DIVINITY? GOD'S HOLY ESSENCE DWELLS WHERE HE DEEMS PURE AND HOLY. HIS HOLY SPIRIT DWELLS WITHIN A VESSEL THAT HE HAS PURGED OF IMPURITIES. ALMIGHTY GOD HAS CHOSEN TO DWELL WITHIN THE PURGED BODY OF HIS MESSENGER AND BRIDE (BARBARA), SO THAT HE MAY CONVEY HIS HOLY MESSAGES TO HIS CHILDREN IN A FORM THAT THEY CAN SEE AND COMMUNICATE WITH TODAY. THROUGH BARBARA, GOD'S MESSENGER AND BRIDE, THE GOSPEL OF THE LORD IS PROCLAIMED, TO THOSE WHOM THE LORD HAS CALLED AND CHOSEN TO DWELL WITHIN HIS REALM OF HOLINESS ON EARTH, AND IN HEAVEN ABOVE.

ALMIGHTY GOD SPEAKING TO THE CALLED AND CHOSEN ONES

UNDERSTAND WHAT YOU SEE AND HEAR, O CHILDREN OF MINE, FOR YOU ARE MY WITNESSES TOO!
AUGUST 23, 2015 BY: BARBARA ANN MARY MACK
SENT SAT, AUG 29, 2015 12:08 PM-READ SAT 8/29/15 3:48 PM

WE MADE IT HOME FROM GETTYSBURG, SAFE. *ALLELUIA!*
TI AMO, BEAUTIFUL BARBIE
SENT SAT, AUG 29, 2015 12:08 PM-READ SAT 8/29/15 3:48 PM

THE WORLD'S VERSION OF ELITE AND FAME: FLEE FROM IT, MY CHILDREN, SAYS THE LORD!

ALMIGHTY GOD SPEAKING

FLEE FROM IT, MY CHILDREN! FLEE FROM THE REALM THAT INVITES THOSE WHO ARE HEADED FOR ETERNAL DESTRUCTION AND DOOM! FLEE FROM THE EXCLUSIVE REALM THAT DRAWS IN THOSE WHO DO NOT KNOW MY VERSION OF HOLINESS! FLEE FROM THE REALM THAT INVITES SATAN, ITS ORIGIN AND FATHER. FLEE, MY CHILDREN! FLEE FROM THE WORLD'S ELITE REALM! FOR THEY ARE HEADED IN THE DIRECTION OF ETERNAL DAMNATION! RUN TOWARDS THE REALM THAT INVITES THE SPIRITUAL HOLY ELITE! RUN TOWARDS THE REALM THAT HOUSES HE (ALMIGHTY GOD) WHO IS ABOVE ALL WHO EXCLUDES THE RIGHTEOUS ONES! FLEE FROM THOSE WHO BELIEVE THAT THEY ARE ABOVE THEIR EARTHLY BROTHERS AND SISTERS, FOR THEY WILL SURELY SPEND ETERNITY WITH SATAN, THEIR ORIGIN AND GOD! FLEE FROM THE WORLD'S TEMPORARY FAME AND FORTUNE, FOR THEY WILL SURELY PERISH WITH THEIR STATUS AND VAIN GAIN! FLEE! MY CHILDREN. FLEE FROM THE WORLD'S VERSION OF ELITE, FOR THEY ARE NOT MINE, *SAYS THE LORD!*
AUGUST 22, 2015 BY: BARBARA ANN MARY MACK
SENT SAT, AUG 29, 2015 12:08 PM-READ SAT 8/29/15 3:48 PM

WHAT THE WORLD EXCLUDES

ALMIGHTY GOD SPEAKING

ME, *SAYS THE LORD!* MY REALM OF HOLINESS AND HOLY DEEDS: ALL THAT IS RIGHTEOUS AND PURE: THE WAY TO SALVATION AND ETERNAL LIFE WITH ME: DIVINE JUSTICE: COMPASSION FOR EVERY ONE OF GOD'S CHILDREN: DIVINE HOPE: DIVINE PEACE: DIVINE LOVE: DIVINE MATRIMONY: DIVINE UNION BETWEEN MAN AND WOMAN: THE KNOWLEDGE THAT DESCENDS FROM HEAVEN'S GATES THROUGH BARBARA, MY HOLY MESSENGER AND BRIDE: REJOICE, ALL WHO ARE NOT OF THE WORLD, *SAYS THE LORD!*
AUGUST 22, 2015 BY: BARBARA ANN MARY MACK

WHAT THE WORLD CANNOT SEE: DIVINITY IN THEIR MIDST

ALMIGHTY GOD SPEAKING

OH HYPOCRITES! OH, YOU WHO DEEM YOURSELVES RIGHTEOUS IN THE EYES OF THIS PASSING WORLD! OH, YOU WHO HIDE BEHIND WHAT THE WORLD VIEWS AS SIGNIFICANT AND OF WORTHY RECOGNITION! OH, YOU WHO PRETEND TO KNOW ME AND THOSE WHOM I HAVE SENT TO REPRESENT ME! OH, YOU WHO WEAR FANCY VESTURES AND OBTAIN WORLDLY TITLES! WHY DO YOU NOT RECOGNIZE ME IN YOUR MIDST TODAY? DO YOU NOT KNOW MY WORKS? DO

YOU NOT KNOW MY UNCHANGING SIGNS? DO YOU NOT KNOW THAT I HAVE COME IN THE FORM (BARBARA) THAT YOU REFUSE TO ACKNOWLEDGE AND ACCEPT? DO YOU NOT REMEMBER MY HOLY WAY AND WORD THAT ARE CONVEYED THROUGH THE HOLY BIBLE? I HAVE NOT CHANGED, YOU WHO SEEK THE WORLD'S VERSION OF MY HOLY PRESENCE! I HAVE COME IN A FORM (BARBARA) THAT REPRESENTS DIVINE MEEKNESS. I HAVE COME IN A FORM THAT REPRESENTS DIVINE ELITE! I HAVE COME IN A FORM THAT REPRESENTS DIVINE ROYALTY! I HAVE COME IN A FORM THAT DETESTS THE WORLD'S VERSION OF ROYALTY AND DIVINITY. I HAVE COME IN A FORM THAT REPRESENTS THE HOLY TRINITY IN HIS VERSION OF HOLINESS AND RIGHTEOUSNESS. YOU, O BLINDED ONES, CANNOT SEE ME, FOR YOU CANNOT SEE HOLINESS IN HIS TRUE STATE. OPEN YOUR BLINDED EYES BEFORE JUSTICE (ALMIGHTY GOD) WALKS IN YOUR MIDST AGAIN! ACCEPT ME IN MY TRUE STATE, BEFORE THE GATES OF HELL SNATCHES YOUR BLINDED SOULS FROM THIS PASSING PERIOD OF TIME! OPEN YOUR EYES, O BLINDED ONES, SO THAT YOU MAY SEE ME, IN THE MEEK FORM OF MY CHOSEN MESSENGER AND BRIDE (BARBARA)! YOU, O WORLD, DID NOT RECOGNIZE ME WHEN I ENTERED YOUR WORLD IN THE FORM OF MAN. YOU DID NOT RECOGNIZE JESUS, THE SAVIOR OF THE WORLD OF BELIEF! YOU DID NOT RECOGNIZE ME THEN, AND YOU DO NOT RECOGNIZE ME NOW, FOR YOU, O WORLD, HAVE NOT CHANGED, *SAYS THE LORD!*

AUGUST 22, 2015 BY: BARBARA ANN MARY MACK

I BOW AT THE FOOT OF THE HOLY LIVING CRUCIFIX IN THE PRESENCE OF JESUS, MY SACRIFICIAL SPOUSE AND GOD. ALLELUIA!!!

BARBARA SPEAKING TO JESUS, THE CRUCIFIED KING

I BOW AT THE FOOT OF YOUR PRECIOUS CRUCIFIED BEING, O HOLY SPOUSE AND GOD OF MINE. I BOW IN THE HOLY PRESENCE OF THE LIVING CRUCIFIX, AS I WEEP IN THE MIDST OF YOUR SUFFERING. I HAVE TAKEN MY PLACE AT THE FOOT OF YOUR CRUCIFIED BODY, SO THAT I MAY FOREVER HOLD YOU IN MY THOUGHTS. I LOVE YOU, O CRUCIFIED KING (JESUS)! I LOVE THE SACRIFICIAL ACT OF LOVE THAT YOU HAVE EXPRESSED FOR YOUR LOVED ONES ON EARTH. LET ME BOW AT THE FOOT OF MY CRUCIFIED SAVIOR AS I JOIN HIM IN HIS PAIN AND SUFFERINGS TODAY! FOR YOU HAVE REVEALED TO ME, THE AGONY THAT YOU EXPERIENCE AS YOU WITNESS THE HORRORS THAT SATAN HAS RELEASED UPON YOUR VULNERABLE LOVED ONES TODAY. I WILL LOWER MY HUMBLED HEAD AS I BOW AT THE FOOT OF YOUR HOLY CROSS, FOR YOU HAVE DONE A WONDERFUL THING FOR THOSE WHO TRULY LOVE AND RESPECT YOU, O LORD.

AUGUST 22, 2015 BY: BARBARA ANN MARY MACK

ELATION: DIVINE ELATION! DIVINE ECSTASY!

BARBARA SPEAKING

DANCE, O ELATED SPIRIT OF MINE! DANCE IN THE MIDST OF DIVINE ECSTASY! DANCE WITH HE (ALMIGHTY GOD), WHO LIFTS UP YOUR IGNITED PRESENCE IN THE MIDST OF DIVINE ECSTASY AND HEAVENLY BLISS! DANCE IN THE PRESENCE OF DIVINITY AS YOU BOW IN THE MIDST OF HEAVENLY ECSTASY! LIFT UP YOUR INVISIBLE FEET! MOVE YOUR INVISIBLE BODY! DANCE, O SPIRIT OF MINE, DANCE! DANCE IN THE PRESENCE OF HE (ALMIGHTY GOD) WHOM YOU HAVE MADE ETERNAL VOWS OF FAITHFULNESS AND ALLEGIANCE TO! DANCE! DANCE! DANCE! DANCE IN THE MIDST OF SWEET ECSTASY AND DIVINE BLISS, O SPIRIT OF GOD, THE HOLY TRINITY'S DELIGHTED BRIDE! DANCE, O ELATED SPIRIT OF THE BLESSED AND CHOSEN ONE (BARBARA)! DANCE IN THE MIDST OF DIVINITY, AS HE SURROUNDS YOU WITH THE PEACE THAT COMES FROM HIS IGNITED ESSENCE OF HOLY LOVE! DANCE! DANCE! DANCE, O GRATEFUL SPIRIT OF GOD'S HOLY BRIDE (BARBARA)! DANCE IN THE MIDST OF HEAVENLY BLISS AS YOU BOW IN THE MIDST OF DIVINE ECSTASY THROUGHOUT ETERNITY!!!
AUGUST 22, 2015 BY: BARBARA ANN MARY MACK

NO ONE CAN PREVENT THE MANIFESTATION AND FULFILLMENT OF BIBLICAL PROPHECIES

BARBARA SPEAKING TO GOD'S MANIFESTATIONS

I CAN SEE YOU! I CAN HEAR YOU! I HAVE WALKED IN THE MIDST OF YOU, FOR YOU ARE THE MANIFESTATION AND FULFILLMENT OF GOD'S HOLY WORD. NO ONE CAN PREVENT YOUR FORETOLD ENTRANCE, O HOLY WORD OF ALMIGHTY INFALLIBLE GOD! NO ONE CAN DENY YOUR REVERENCE AND YOUR HOLY WORD, FOR IT HAS MANIFESTED AT YOUR APPOINTED INFALLIBLE TIME! I SEE YOU, O TRUSTING WORD OF MY INFALLIBLE GOD! I CAN SEE YOU AS YOU MANIFEST IN MY HOLY PRESENCE! *ALLELUIA!*
AUGUST 13, 2015 BY: BARBARA ANN MARY MACK

SITTING IN THE MIDST OF HOLINESS AS I RECEIVE THE WORDS THAT YOU RELEASE TO THE WORLD TODAY

BARBARA SPEAKING

SITTING IN THE MIDST OF HOLINESS AS I REST WITHIN THE REALM THAT CREATED ME. SITTING IN THE MIDST OF HOLINESS AS I CLING TO GOD'S ESSENCE OF LOVE. SITTING IN THE MIDST OF HOLINESS AS I BOW DOWN IN THE PRESENCE OF GOD'S HOLY WORDS. SITTING IN THE MIDST OF HOLINESS AS I BREATHE IN THE HOLY WORDS THAT FLOW FROM YOUR OMNIPOTENT MOUTH. O LORD, MY GOD, I AM PRIVILEGED AND HONORED TO RECEIVE YOUR HOLY WORDS

AS THEY DESCEND IN THE MIDST OF YOUR NEEDY CHILDREN TODAY. LET THE REALM OF HOLINESS ENGULF ME AS I RECEIVE THE GIFT OF YOUR HOLY WORDS FOR US TODAY. LET THE GIFT OF HOLINESS ENCOMPASS ME AS I REJOICE IN THE MIDST OF YOUR GIFT OF LIFE SAVING MESSAGES FOR THE WORLD. I WILL BREATHE! I WILL REJOICE! I WILL SING SONGS OF PRAISE UNTO MY GREAT AND HOLY GOD AS I RECEIVE HIS HOLY WORDS TODAY! *ALLELUIA!*
JULY 31, 2015 BY: BARBARA ANN MARY MACK
SENT SAT, AUG 29, 2015 12:08 PM-READ SAT 8/29/15 3:48 PM

GREETINGS ARCHBISHOP CRAIG! WE MADE IT HOME SAFE! WE LEFT THE LODGE AT 11 AM, AND DID A LITTLE SIGHTSEEING AROUND THE LAKE BEFORE TAKING ONE LAST PERSONAL TOUR OF GETTYSBURG. I LEARNED SO MUCH ABOUT HISTORY AND THE PURPOSE OF THE CIVIL WAR. EVERYONE THAT WE MET WAS FRIENDLY AND HELPFUL. OUR DIVINE ASSIGNMENT FROM THE LORD WAS AN AWESOME SUCCESS! *TI AMO, BELLA BARBARA*
SENT SAT, AUG 29, 2015 12:08 PM-READ SAT 8/29/15 3:48 PM

GREETINGS ARCHBISHOP CRAIG! COME STA OGGI AMORE? THE DAY HAS FINALLY ARRIVED! WE ARE PREPARING FOR OUR DEPARTURE FROM GETTYSBURG, PA. WE HAVE COMPLETED OUR ASSIGNMENT FOR THE LORD HERE. IT WAS A DIVINE SUCCESS! NEXT WEEK, WE HAVE AN ASSIGNMENT FROM THE LORD NEAR ERIE, PA., NORTHEAST PA. WE WILL SEE YOU WHEN WE ARRIVED IN PHILLY. *CIAO! BELLA BARBARA*
SENT SAT, AUG 29, 2015 12:08 PM-READ SAT 8/29/15 3:48 PM

BUON GIORNO ARCHBISHOP CRAIG! COME STA? WE ARE HAVING A GREAT TIME IN GETTYSBURG, PA.! LAST EVENING, WE HAD DINNER AT DOBBIN HOUSE TAVERN, GETTYSBURG'S OLDEST MOST HISTORIC HOUSE, BUILT IN 1776. EVERYTHING WAS GREAT! THE FOOD AND SERVICE WERE EXCEPTIONALLY FANTASTIC! AFTER ENJOYING OUR WONDERFUL DINNER, WE WERE ABLE TO TAKE HOME WHAT WE WERE NOT ABLE TO CONSUME THERE. WE WERE ALSO ABLE TO EXPLORE THE HOUSE, WHICH INCLUDED THE AREA WHERE UNDERGROUND SLAVES TOOK REFUGE. IT WAS AN AWESOME EXPERIENCE! WE WERE ABLE TO TAKE MANY PICTURES AND VIEW THE SITES FREELY. EVERYONE WAS VERY FRIENDLY! SOME OF THE OTHER GUESTS TOOK OUR (LA TOYA, AMYA, AND ME) PICTURES AT THE UNDERGROUND SITE. AFTER LEAVING DOBBIN HOUSE TAVERN, WE WENT TO ANOTHER PLACE WHICH SOLD POSTCARDS PERTAINING TO HISTORICAL GETTYSBURG. I BOUGHT POSTCARDS FOR MY FAMILY AND FRIENDS. MY SISTER AND BROTHER LOVE RECEIVING THEM FROM THE DIFFERENT PLACES THAT LA TOYA, AMYA AND I VISIT. LA TOYA IS RESTING NOW. SHE HAS SOMETHING PLANNED FOR US TO DO TODAY. WE WILL SEE WHAT IT IS!
TI AMO, O ETERNAL BELOVED ONE!
SENT SAT, AUG 29, 2015 12:08 PM-READ SAT 8/29/15 3:48 PM

EMPTY

WITHOUT THE INDWELLING OF *GOD'S HOLY PRESENCE, YOU ARE:*

EMPTY, WITHOUT, DEVOID, EASY ACCESS TO SATAN'S DESTRUCTION, EASY ENTRANCE TO THE GATES THAT AWAIT THE "UNHOLY ONES", WITHOUT PROTECTION FROM THE REALM THAT SEEKS TO DESTROY YOU. WITHOUT FREEDOM FROM SATAN'S RULES AND DARTS, FOR YOU ARE AN UNPROTECTED TARGET. WALKING IN THE PRESENCE OF SATAN, FOR HE KNOWS THAT YOU ARE "UNPROTECTED". IN THE PRESENCE OF HE (SATAN) WHO LEADS YOU, FOR YOU ARE WITHOUT THE PROTECTION THAT COMES FROM ALMIGHTY GOD'S HOLY SPIRIT. WITHOUT THE WILL TO DO WHAT IS RIGHT AND HOLY, FOR YOU ARE DEVOID OF GOD'S KNOWLEDGE OF GOOD. AUGUST 18, 2015 BY: BARBARA ANN MARY MACK
SENT SAT, AUG 29, 2015 12:08 PM-READ SAT 8/29/15 3:48 PM

SOME NEVER KNEW JESUS' TRUE IDENTITY: THEY WEREN'T WORTHY!

THE LORD JESUS SPEAKING

NO ONE, NO ONE, NO ONE, CAN COME TO ME, WITHOUT AN INVITATION FROM MY HEAVENLY ORIGIN AND FATHER! NO ONE CAN ENTER THE GATES THE LEAD TO SWEET PARADISE WITHOUT AN INVITATION FROM MY HEAVENLY FATHER, FOR HE IS ALPHA! HE IS THE BEGINNING AND THE END OF LIFE! HE IS ALMIGHTY GOD, MY ETERNAL LOVE!

THE LORD JESUS SPEAKING TO GOD, HIS ORIGIN AND HEAVENLY FATHER

MY FATHER, THEY DO NOT FOLLOW ME, BECAUSE YOU HAVE NOT INVITED THEM AT THIS TIME. THEY DO NOT FOLLOW ME, BECAUSE THEY DO NOT KNOW YOU, MY ORIGIN AND LOVE. THEY DO NOT FOLLOW ME, BECAUSE THEY HAVE NOT RECEIVED THE HOLY WORD FROM YOU, MY GOD. THEY HAVE NOT RECEIVED THE GIFT OF OUR HOLY SPIRIT. THEY CANNOT EXHIBIT A DIVINE LOVE THAT THEY HAVE NOT YET EXPERIENCED, MY FATHER. THEY CANNOT EXPERIENCE THE UNION OF THE DIVINE ETERNAL TRINITY, WITHOUT AN INVITATION FROM YOU, THEIR CREATOR AND GOD. I WILL PRAY FOR THEM, MY FATHER. I WILL PRAY FOR THE CALLED AND CHOSEN ONES. I WILL PRAY THAT THEY WILL ACCEPT YOUR DIVINE INVITATION TO SWEET PARADISE WHEN YOU SEND IT OUT TO THEM. I WILL PRAY, MY FATHER. I WILL PRAY FOR OUR LOST SHEEP. SEPTEMBER 3, 2015 BY: BARBARA ANN MARY MACK

DRAWN TO YOU

BARBARA SPEAKING TO THE LORD

MY LORD, YOUR HOLY PRESENCE AND ESSENCE DRAW ME CLOSER AND CLOSER TO THE REALM OF DIVINITY THAT ENCOMPASSES MY SAVING LORD AND GOD. I CAN HEAR YOUR ESSENCE OF DIVINE LOVE AS IT CALLS OUT TO ME THROUGHOUT EACH DAY. I CAN FEEL THE ESSENCE OF EXISTENCE, AS YOU MOVE IN THE DIRECTION OF YOUR CHOSEN SPOUSE AND FRIEND (BARBARA). I CAN FEEL THE POWER OF YOUR DIVINE LOVE AS IT CALLS ME THROUGHOUT THE NIGHT. I CAN FEEL YOUR HOLY PRESENCE MY LORD, EVEN IN THE MIDST OF DIFFICULT AND TRAGIC TIMES. FOR YOUR HOLY POWER DRAWS ME CLOSER TO THE REALM THAT HOUSES HE, WHO SITS ON HIS MIGHTY THRONE IN HEAVEN ABOVE. YOUR HOLY ESSENCE AND POWER ENCOMPASS ME, AS I BOW CONTINUOUSLY IN THE MIDST OF YOUR PRESENCE. MY IGNITED SPIRIT DANCES WITH YOURS, AS YOU GAZE AT THE DELIGHT THAT EMITS FROM MY BEING THROUGHOUT EACH DAY. MY BLESSED ESSENCE REJOICES IN THE MIDST OF DIVINITY, AS I LOOK FORWARD TO MY GREAT REWARD! *ALLELUIA!*
SEPTEMBER 3, 2015 BY: BARBARA ANN MARY MACK

SATAN MOCKED ME, BUT HE DID NOT DEFEAT ME, SAYS THE LORD

ALMIGHTY GOD SPEAKING

MY CHILDREN, SATAN MOCKED ME THROUGH THE CENTURIES, BUT HE DID NOT DEFEAT ME OR MY HOLY MESSENGERS. HE HAS MOCKED ME THROUGH HIS FALLEN ANGELS THROUGH THE YEARS. HE HAS MOCKED ME IN THE PRESENCE OF THOSE WHO FOLLOW HIS EVIL WAYS DAILY. HE MOCKS ME THROUGH THOSE WHO REFUSE TO CHANGE FOR MY SAKE. HE MOCKS ME THROUGHOUT THE DAY, AS HE ROAMS THE STREETS IN SEARCH OF EMPTY SOULS AND MINDS. HE MOCKS ME THROUGH THE MEDIA, AS IT REVEALS THE PERVERSION THAT THE WORLD VIEWS AS RIGHTEOUS AND ACCEPTABLE. HE MOCKS ME THROUGH THOSE WHO HAVE ABANDONED MY HOLY WORDS OF TRUTH AND RIGHTEOUSNESS. HE MOCKS ME THROUGH THE LEADERS OF NATIONS. HE MOCKS ME THROUGH UNHOLY MOTHERS AND FATHERS. HE MOCKS ME THROUGH FAMILY AND FRIENDS. HE MOCKS ME THROUGH STRANGERS AND ACQUAINTANCES. HE MOCKS ME THROUGH THE CLERGY. HE MOCKS ME THROUGH TEACHERS. HE MOCKS ME THROUGH THOSE WHO CARE FOR THE VULNERABLE ONES. MY CHILDREN, FLEE FROM THE GRIP OF HE (SATAN) WHO MOCKS ME THROUGHOUT EVERY DAY, FOR I, THE LORD, HAVE DEFEATED HIM!
SEPTEMBER 1, 2015 BY: BARBARA ANN MARY MACK

WOW! YOU NEVER LEFT US, O LORD.

BARBARA SPEAKING

WOW! WOW! WOW, IS A WORD THAT EXPRESSES THE AWESOMENESS OF OUR LOVING GOD AND CREATOR! FOR HE HAS NEVER ABANDONED HIS GREATEST CREATION (HUMAN BEINGS). EVEN IN THE MIDST OF OUR SINS, ALMIGHTY GOD, OUR LORD AND SAVIOR, NEVER ABANDONED US. FOR HE KNOWS THE HEARTS OF HIS CHOSEN ONES. HE KNOWS THE INTEGRITY OF OUR LOVE AND ALLEGIANCE TO HIM. HE KNOWS THE DEPTH OF OUR FAITHFULNESS TO HIS HOLY WORDS AND COMMANDMENTS. HE IS AN AWESOME AND LOVING FATHER! HE IS OURS! MY BROTHERS AND SISTERS, LET US EXHIBIT THE LOVE THAT REVEALS OUR ALLEGIANCE TO OUR ONLY CREATOR AND GOD. LET US EXHIBIT THE TRUST THAT KEEPS US COMMITTED TO OUR CHRISTIAN FAITH. *ALLELUIA!!!*
SEPTEMBER 3, 2015 BY: BARBARA ANN MARY MACK

TO LIVE A HOLY LIFE IN THE PRESENCE OF THE LORD, IS THE BEST FORM OF PRAYER ONE COULD EXHIBIT

ALMIGHTY GOD SPEAKING TO THE CONFUSED ONES

MY CHILDREN, LEARN OF MY HOLY WORD, SO THAT YOU WILL KNOW HOW TO LIVE THE LIFE THAT I, I, I, THE LORD, VIEW AS HOLY! READ MY HOLY WORDS THAT PERMEATE THE HOLY BIBLE, SO THAT YOU MAY KNOW MY TRUTH! MY CHILDREN, DO NOT LISTEN TO OR FOLLOW THOSE WHO MAY APPEAR TO BE MY SHEPHERDS OF TRUTH. FOR IF THEY WERE, THEY WOULD LEAD YOU TO MY ROAD OF LIFE, INSTEAD OF THE ROAD TO ETERNAL DEATH. LEARN OF MY HOLY WORD AND WAY BY READING THE HOLY SCRIPTURES YOURSELVES, FOR YOU WILL BE ACCOUNTABLE FOR YOUR IGNORANCE. I HAVE PLACED MY HOLY WAY AND STANCE IN YOUR PRESENCE. DO NOT LISTEN TO THOSE WHO DO NOT TELL YOU MY TRUTH CONCERNING PERVERSION AND SIN, FOR THEIR TRUTH WILL LEAD YOU THROUGH THE GATES OF ETERNAL DAMNATION. MY CHILDREN, MANKIND CONDONES THE WORKS, ACTS, AND DEEDS OF SATAN. I, YOUR HOLY CREATOR, FOUNDER OF MY HOLY CHURCH, AND YOUR GOD, DO NOT CONFORM TO THE ACTS THAT WILL LEAD YOU AWAY FROM MY REALM OF HOLINESS. MY SONS! MY DAUGHTERS! DO NOT LET THEM DECEIVE YOU! FOR THEY CONVEY THE TEACHINGS OF SATAN, AND NOT OF JESUS, THE ONLY FOUNDER OF THE HOLY CHURCH. MY SONS, FLEE FROM THE PERVERSION THAT LEADS TO ETERNAL DESTRUCTION! MY DAUGHTERS, FLEE FROM THE VOICE THAT IS LEADING YOU AWAY FROM THE REALM (HOLINESS) THAT DESIRES YOUR VULNERABLE AND CONFUSED SOUL! DO NOT LISTEN TO THOSE WHO KNOW MY TRUTH, BUT ARE KEEPING IT FROM YOU! FLEE TO THE HOLY BIBLE, FOR IT TELLS YOU OF THE ONLY WAY TO LIFE WITH CHRIST JESUS AND HIS HOLY CHURCH. MY SONS! MY DAUGHTERS! FLEE TO MY REALM OF TRUTH, FOR THE TRUTH THAT FLOWS FROM MANKIND'S REALM, WILL LEAD YOU TO ETERNAL DAMNATION.

MY CHILDREN (HOMOSEXUALS AND BISEXUALS), DO NOT LET THEM DECEIVE YOU! I WILL TAKE NO, NO, NO PART IN ANYTHING OR ANYONE THAT ISN'T FOCUSED ON MY VERSION OF HOLINESS! MY CHILDREN, LEARN OF MY VERSION OF HOLINESS FROM ME, NOT FROM MAN! FOR MANKIND'S VERSION OF HOLINESS WILL LEAD YOU AWAY FROM ME, *SAYS THE LORD!*

SEPTEMBER 6, 2015 BY: BARBARA ANN MARY MACK

SENT SUN, SEP 6, 2015 5:57 PM-READ SUN 9/6/2015 9:07 PM

I AM STILL FIGHTING THE GATES OF HELL FOR YOU, O CLERGY, *SAYS THE LORD! TI AMO, DEAR ONE! BELLA BARBIE*

DO NOT WITHHOLD THE TRUTH, O CLERGY: TELL THEM OF THE THINGS THAT WILL LEAD THEM THROUGH THE GATES OF ETERNAL HELL

ALMIGHTY GOD SPEAKING TO THE CLERGY

TELL THEM MY SONS! TELL THEM NOW! TELL THEM BEFORE IT IS TOO LATE! TELL THEM OF THE THINGS THAT SEPARATE THEM FROM ME AND MY REALM OF HOLINESS! TELL THEM OF THE ACTS THAT WILL MOVE THEM IN THE DIRECTION OF LIFE WITH ME, AND TELL THEM OF THE ACTS THAT INVITE THEM TO ETERNAL DAMNATION. YOU MUST WARN THEM, O CLERGY! YOU MUST WARN MY CONFUSED CHILDREN, BEFORE THE GATES OF SPIRITUAL DOOM CLAIM THEIR ETERNAL SOULS! TELL THEM SO THAT THEY MAY HAVE THE OPPORTUNITY TO CHANGE THEIR SINFUL WAYS. IT IS UP TO YOU, O CLERGY, TO TELL MY FLOCK THE TRUTH, MY TRUTH, *SAYS THE LORD.* FOR YOU WILL BE HELD ACCOUNTABLE FOR THEIR LOST SOULS IF YOU WITHHOLD MY UNCHANGING TRUTH! TELL THEM EVERYTHING THAT I HAVE SPOKEN THROUGH THE HOLY BIBLE, FOR MY HOLY WORDS, STANCE, AND WRATH, HAVE NOT CHANGED! TELL THEM, O CLERGY! TELL THE FORNICATORS! TELL THE ADULTERERS! TELL THE LIARS! TELL THE PROMISCUOUS ONES! TELL THE MURDERERS! TELL THE RAPISTS! TELL THE RACISTS! TELL THOSE WHO STEAL! TELL THE HOMOSEXUALS! TELL THE LGBT! TELL THE DRUG SELLERS! TELL THOSE WHO ABUSE DRUGS AND THEMSELVES!!! TELL THE GAMBLERS! TELL THOSE WHO GOSSIP! TELL THE UNFORGIVING ONES! TELL THOSE WHO DIVORCE WITHOUT MY VERSION OF RELIGIOUS ACCEPTANCE. TELL THEM! TELL THEM! TELL THEM! O CLERGY, BEFORE IT IS TOO LATE FOR THE BOTH OF YOU!!!

SEPTEMBER 11, 2015 BY: BARBARA ANN MARY MACK

TI AMO, DEAR ONE! BELLA BARBIE

SENT FRI, SEP 11, 2015 7:17 PM-READ FRI 9/11/2015 10:03 PM

I WEEP AS I WATCH THEM (THE MISGUIDED AND LOST SOULS) ENTER THE GATES OF HELL

BARBARA SPEAKING TO THE LORD

I WEEP, MY LORD. I WEEP AS I WITNESS THE MANY LOST AND MISGUIDED SOULS ENTER THE GATES OF ETERNAL DAMNATION. I WEEP UNCONTROLLABLY, AS I HEAR THE AUDIBLE SOUNDS OF THEIR TORMENTED SOULS. THE SOUNDS ARE ENDLESS, MY MERCIFUL GOD. THE SOUND OF THE TORMENTED SOULS PIERCES MY REALM OF EMPATHY, AS I WEEP IN THE PRESENCE OF THE APPOINTED JUDGMENT DAY. I WEEP, FOR THEY CAN NO LONGER RUN TO YOU FOR PROTECTION, MY GOD. I WEEP, BECAUSE THEY CAN NO LONGER CHANGE THEIR UNGODLY WAYS. I WEEP, BECAUSE THE GATES OF HELL HAVE CLAIMED THE SOULS OF THOSE WHO FOLLOWED THE TEACHINGS OF THOSE WHO WERE NOT APPOINTED AS YOUR SHEPHERDS AND PRIESTS. I WEEP FOR THE DECEIVED ONES WHO DID NOT SEEK YOUR TRUTH BEFORE THEIR PHYSICAL DEATHS. I WEEP FOR THOSE WHO BELIEVED IN MANKIND'S VERSION OF RIGHTEOUSNESS, INSTEAD OF THE ONLY VERSION THAT COULD SAVE THEIR ETERNAL SOULS. SHOW ME NO MORE, MY LORD. SHOW ME NO MORE. FOR I CAN NOT HANDLE THE AGONY AND CRIES THAT PERMEATE THE PIT OF HELL. HAVE MERCY ON ME, MY LORD! FOR I HAVE WEPT FOR THE ETERNAL SOULS OF THE MISGUIDED AND LOST ONES FOR MANY YEARS.
SEPTEMBER 10, 2015 BY: BARBARA ANN MARY MACK

THE POSITION OF THE CLERGY IS TO TEACH, REPROVE, ENLIGHTEN, AND EDIFY MY FLOCK, SAYS THE LORD

ALMIGHTY GOD SPEAKING TO THE CLERGY

TEACH MY FLOCK AS I TAUGHT MY FLOCK, WHEN I WALKED IN YOUR MIDST NOT SO LONG AGO, MY SONS. ENLIGHTEN THEM, SO THAT THEY MAY KNOW AND UNDERSTAND WHAT I, I, I, EXPECT OF THEM TODAY. DO NOT SUGAR COAT, OR DEPRIVE THEM OF MY TRUTH, FOR THAT WOULD BE MISLEADING THEM. REPROVE MY CHILDREN WHO DESIRE TO ENTER MY HOLY CHURCH IN THE MIDST OF THEIR SINS. REPROVE THEM IN A MANNER THAT THEY WILL ACCEPT AS MY CHASTISEMENT. FOR I, ALONE, AM THE FOUNDER OF MY HOLY CHURCH. EDIFY THEM, O CLERGY, SO THAT THEY WILL KNOW HOW TO CONDUCT THEMSELVES IN MY HOLY PRESENCE. FOR I AM THE ONLY OMNIPOTENT GOD, AND I SEE AND HEAR EVERYTHING THAT IS SAID AND DONE.
SEPTEMBER 10, 2015 BY: BARBARA ANN MARY MACK

HE (SATAN) DOES'NT WANT YOU TO KNOW AND HEAR MY WORDS OF TRUTH TODAY, O CLERGY

ALMIGHTY GOD SPEAKING TO THE CLERGY

HE (SATAN) TRIES TO PREVENT YOU FROM HEARING MY TRUTH, THE ONLY TRUTH, TODAY. DO NOT FOLLOW OR LISTEN TO HIS CUNNING AND MISLEADING WAY, MY SONS! DO NOT FOLLOW THE VOICE OF THE STRANGER (SATAN) WHO HAS CREPT INTO THE LIVES OF MY SHEPHERDS. DO NOT FOLLOW THE VOICE OF HE (SATAN) WHO WHISPERS WORDS THAT CONVEY THE OPPOSITE MESSAGE OF MY HOLY WORDS THAT ARE WRITTEN IN THE BIBLE. DO NOT LISTEN TO THE VOICE OF HE (SATAN) WHO WHISPERS IN YOUR HEARTS, THINGS THAT GO AGAINST WHAT I, THE FOUNDER OF MY CHURCH, HAVE ORDAINED AS PERMANENT AND UNCHANGING. FOLLOW MY HOLY WORDS OF TRUTH, MY SONS! DO NOT LISTEN TO THE VOICE OF THE UNWANTED AND MISLEADING STRANGER (SATAN), FOR HE IS THE DECEIVER!!!
SEPTEMBER 10, 2015 BY: BARBARA ANN MARY MACK
SENT FRI, SEP 11, 2015 7:17 PM-READ FRI 9/11/2015 10:03 PM

PEOPLE KEEP FOCUSING ON MY LOVE AND MERCY, BUT THEY OFTEN FORGET TO MENTION AND ACKNOWLEDGE MY WRATH, SAYS THE LORD.

ALMIGHTY GOD SPEAKING TO THE CLERGY

TELL THEM, O CHOSEN CLERGY OF MINE! TELL THEM OF MY WRATH AND CHASTISEMENT TOWARD THOSE WHO DO NOT FOLLOW MY HOLY WORDS AND WAY! TELL THEM, SO THAT THEY WILL KNOW HOW TO AVOID THE PUNISHMENT THAT COMES WITH DISOBEYING MY VERSION OF HOLINESS. LEAD THEM TO THE HOLY SCRIPTURES THAT REVEAL MY VIEWS CONCERNING HOLINESS AND RIGHTEOUSNESS. TELL THEM MY TRUTH! SHOW THEM MY HOLY WORDS, NOT, NOT, NOT YOURS! FOR YOUR TRUTH WILL LEAD THE IGNORANT ONES THROUGH THE GATES OF ETERNAL HELL! TELL THEM MY HOLY WORDS, O CLERGY, FOR YOU ARE HELD ACCOUNTABLE FOR THEIR LACK OF KNOWLEDGE. YOU ARE HELD ACCOUNTABLE FOR YOUR MISGUIDED PATH. REMEMBER MY WRATH, O CLERGY! REMEMBER MY JUSTICE! TELL THEM THAT WHICH IS WRITTEN IN THE HOLY BIBLE, AND NOT, NOT, NOT THE UNHOLY WORDS THAT YOU HAVE FORMED FROM YOUR IMPERFECT LIMITED KNOWLEDGE AND UNDERSTANDING.

ALMIGHTY GOD SPEAKING TO HIS CHOSEN SHEPHERDS

I AM COUNTING ON YOU, O CHOSEN SHEPHERDS OF MINE. I AM COUNTING ON YOU, TO REVEAL MY TRUTH TO THOSE WHO BELIEVE THAT I LOVE THOSE WHO PRACTICE AND APPROVE OF SEXUAL PERVERSION (HOMOSEXUALITY, CIVIL UNIONS, LGBT, AND UNHOLY HETEROSEXUAL SEXUAL RELATIONS). I DO NOT LOVE ANYTHING OR ANYONE WHO CONTINUES TO PERFORM UNHOLY ACTS IN MY HOLY PRESENCE. TELL THEM, O SHEPHERDS WHOM I HAVE CHOSEN! TELL THEM

MY TRUTH BEFORE IT IS TOO LATE FOR YOU AND THE IGNORANT ONES, FOR SATAN IS ON THE PROWL IN SEARCH FOR THE DISOBEDIENT ONES. ENLIGHTEN THE CONFUSED ONES, O CLERGY OF MINE. ENLIGHTEN THEM WITH MY REALM OF BIBLICAL TRUTH TODAY! FOLLOW ME ONLY! SEPTEMBER 8, 2015 BY: BARBARA ANN MARY MACK
SENT FRI, SEP 11, 2015 7:17 PM-READ FRI 9/11/2015 10:03 PM

SATAN HAS TURNED THEM AGAINST ME. SATAN HAS TURNED THE CLERGY AGAINST ME, SAYS THE LORD

ALMIGHTY GOD SPEAKING

HE (SATAN) HAS TURNED YOU AGAINST ME, MY SONS! HE HAS DECEIVED YOU IN MY HOLY PRESENCE! HE HAS OPENED THE DOOR OF DECEPTION, SO THAT YOU MAY ENTER THE REALM THAT HE HAS CREATED FOR YOU. HE HAS CAUSED YOU TO SPEAK AND GO AGAINST MY HOLY TEACHINGS! HE HAS CAUSED YOU TO CONTRADICT MY HOLY WORDS PERTAINING TO SEXUAL PERVERSION AND HOLY MATRIMONY. HE HAS BLINDED YOU WITH THE STENCH THAT WILL LEAD YOU IN THE DIRECTION OF ETERNAL DOOM, FOR YOU HAVE BETRAYED ME, O CLERGY! YOU DO NOT SPEAK MY HOLY WORDS TO MY CONFUSED FLOCK! YOU DO NOT SPEAK MY TRUTH PERTAINING TO HOMOSEXUALITY AND SEXUAL PERVERSION. YOU HAVE BETRAYED AND ABANDONED MY TRUTH, *SAYS THE LORD!* TELL THEM MY TRUTH, O CLERGY! TELL THEM WHAT IS IN THE HOLY SCRIPTURES, FOR THERE IS NO OTHER WORD OF TRUTH! THERE IS ONLY THE REALM OF BETRAYAL AND ABANDONMENT, WHICH LEADS TO ETERNAL HELL! TELL THEM MY TRUTH, MY HOLY TRUTH, FOR THERE IS NO OTHER TRUTH, *SAYS THE LORD!* STOP DECEIVING YOURSELVES AND MY VULNERABLE CHILDREN, O GUISED SERVANTS OF SATAN, FOR I, THE LORD ALMIGHTY, KNOW WHO YOU REALLY ARE! DESPITE WHAT THEY SAY, I DO NOT LOVE, NOR HAVE MERCY ON THOSE WHO PRACTICE THAT WHICH I CONSIDER UNHOLY AND UNCLEAN! I DO NOT, AND WILL NOT, HAVE LOVE OR MERCY FOR THOSE WHO LIVE IN THE MIDST OF WHAT I CALL UNHOLY! I WILL NOT HAVE MERCY ON THOSE WHO FALL INTO THE REALM OF SEXUAL PERVERSION (HOMOSEXUALITY, LGBT, AND ANY RELATIONSHIP THAT CANNOT PRODUCE MY VERSION OF HOLY LIFE), *SAYS THE LORD.* I HAVE SPOKEN! I HAVE SPOKEN! I HAVE SPOKEN, *SAYS THE LORD!* YOU WHO CONTINUE TO FEED MY VULNERABLE AND CONFUSED FLOCK WITH FALSE, FALSE, FALSE LOVE AND MERCY, HAVE EARNED THE KEY THAT OPENS THE GATES TO ETERNAL DAMNATION. FOR YOU ARE HELPERS OF SATAN, MY FOE! YOU KNOW WHO YOU ARE, O GUISED CLERGY OF SATAN, AND SO DO I, *SAYS THE LORD!* THOSE WHO DO NOT TELL THEM MY TRUTH, ARE RESPONSIBLE FOR THEIR ETERNAL DEATH! THOSE WHO DO NOT TELL THEM (HOMOSEXUALS, FORNICATORS, LGBT, AND OTHER PERVERTED PRACTICES) MY TRUTH, EXHIBITS HATRED TOWARDS THEM. YOU MUST TELL THEM, SO THAT THEY WILL KNOW WHAT NEEDS TO BE CHANGED IN THEIR LIVES IF THEY

WANT TO BELONG TO MY, MY, MY HOLY CHURCH, SAYS THE LORD JESUS, THE ONLY FOUNDER OF MY HOLY UNCHANGING, UNCHANGING, UNCHANGING CHURCH. READ AND ABIDE BY MY HOLY WORDS PERTAINING TO MY VIEWS ON HOMOSEXUALITY, O CLERGY, FOR YOU ARE NOT THE JUDGE. MY HOLY WORDS JUDGE AND CONDEMN THOSE WHO CONDONE AND PRACTICE THE ACTS THAT I VIEW AS UNHOLY AND HELL BOUND. THOSE WHO ACCEPT AND PROMOTE THAT WHICH I CALL UNGODLY, ARE HEADED FOR ETERNAL DAMNATION IN HELL! THERE ARE NO, NO, NO EXCEPTIONS! MY HOLY WORD IS THE ONLY JUDGE OF THIS FACT, *SAYS THE LORD!* SATAN HAS BLINDED YOU TOO, O CLERGY OF THE WORLD, FOR YOU DO NOT UNDERSTAND NOR PRACTICE THE HOLY WORDS THAT FLOW THROUGH THE HOLY BIBLE! SATAN HAS DECEIVED YOU AS WELL! THEREFORE, O CLERGY OF THE WORLD, YOU TOO, ARE HEADED FOR ETERNAL DESTRUCTION! YOU TOO, WILL SPEND ETERNITY IN HELL WITH SATAN, YOUR DOOMED MASTER AND GOD! FOR I HAVE NOT CHANGED, AND YOU, O CLERGY OF THE WORLD, CANNOT CHANGE ME, *SAYS THE LORD!* SHALL I HAVE MY MESSENGER AND BRIDE (BARBARA) FAST FOR YOUR DOOMED SOULS? ARE YOU WORTHY OF SUCH A SACRIFICE, O DOOMED ONES? REMEMBER THE STORY OF NOAH. REMEMBER THE FEW (NOAH AND HIS FAMILY) WHO WERE SAVED FROM THE FLOOD, AND REMEMBER THE MANY SOULS THAT WERE NOT SAVED. I HAVE NOT CHANGED, MY DISOBEDIENT CHILDREN, AND NEITHER HAVE YOU! PEOPLE GO TO THE HOSPITALS SO THAT THEY MAY BE CURED OF AN ILLNESS. ONE MUST COME TO CHRIST'S HOLY CHURCH WITH THE SOLE PURPOSE OF BEING CURED OF ALL ILLNESSES (SINS). OTHERWISE, WHAT IS THE PURPOSE OF GOING TO THE HOSPITAL? WHAT IS THE PURPOSE OF COMING TO CHURCH, WITHOUT THE DESIRE TO REPENT AND CHANGE ONE'S SINFUL WAYS. ONE CANNOT COME TO CHURCH AND CONTINUE LIVING IN SIN, IF HE OR SHE DESIRES TO LIVE IN SWEET PARADISE WITH ALMIGHTY GOD AND HEAVEN'S RESIDENTS. LET THE CHURCH, MANKIND'S CHURCH, INVITE EVERY WORKER OF EVIL ACTS IN! LET THE CHURCH, MANKIND'S CHURCH, WELCOME AND SALUTE THE MURDERERS! LET THE CHURCH, MANKIND'S CHURCH, WELCOME AND SALUTE THOSE WHO STEAL! LET THE CHURCH, MANKIND'S CHURCH, SALUTE AND COMMUNE WITH THE LIARS! LET THEM GREET AND WELCOME THE FORNICATORS! LET THEM REJOICE IN THE PRESENCE OF SATAN, THEIR GOD, WITH THE ADULTERERS! LET THE CHURCH, MANKIND'S CHURCH, SING SONGS OF PRAISE TO SATAN, THEIR ONLY MASTER AND FATHER, AS THEY GREET THOSE WHO PERFORM ABORTIONS EVERY DAY! LET THE CHURCH, MANKIND'S UNHOLY CHURCH, JOIN HANDS WITH THOSE WHO REJECT JESUS CHRIST'S ONLY WAY TO SALVATION AND ETERNAL LIFE! LET MANKIND'S CHURCH JOIN HANDS WITH THE CLERGY AS THEY OPENLY SALUTE SATAN AND HIS FOLLOWERS OF UNHOLY ACTS AND WAYS! LET THEM IN! LET THEM IN! LET THE RACISTS IN! LET THOSE WHO SELL HARMFUL DRUGS IN! LET THOSE WHO RAPE IN! LET THOSE WHO DO NOT INTEND ON CHANGING THEIR SINFUL ACTS IN! LET THEM IN, O CHURCH OF THE WORLD! FOR THEY ARE NOT WELCOME IN MY HOLY CHURCH, *SAYS THE LORD JESUS!* THEY ARE NOT WELCOME! FOR THEY DO NOT DESIRE TO CHANGE THEIR SINFUL WAYS!

SEPTEMBER 7, 2015 BY: BARBARA ANN MARY MACK

HOW CAN I?

BARBARA SPEAKING

HOW CAN I LAUGH? HOW CAN I REJOICE? HOW CAN I NOT WEEP, AS I WITNESS THE SPIRITUAL DEATH OF MY DOOMED BROTHERS AND SISTERS? HOW CAN I LAUGH AND PLAY, AS I WITNESS THE DESTINATION OF THOSE WHO REFUSE TO GIVE UP THEIR SINFUL WAYS? HOW CAN I REJOICE IN SONG AND DANCE, AS THE LORD REVEALS TO ME THE FINAL DESTINATION OF THOSE WHO FOLLOW SATAN'S LEAD? HOW CAN I PRAY WITHOUT SHEDDING MANY TEARS, AS I WITNESS THE ACTS, YES, THE SINFUL ACTS, OF THOSE WHO OFFEND GOD, MY HOLY ETERNAL SPOUSE? HOW CAN I SLEEP IN PEACE, AS THE SOULS OF THE LOST AND MISGUIDED ONES FLASH THROUGH MY REALM OF THOUGHT DAY AND NIGHT? HELP ME, O LORD, SO THAT I MAY REST IN THE MIDST OF WHAT I WITNESS DAILY! SHIELD ME FROM THE HORRORS OF WITNESSING THE FINAL DEATH OF THOSE WHOM YOU HAVE SENT ME TO. SHIELD ME FROM THE SIGHT THAT FLASHES THROUGH MY MIND, AS I HEAR OF THE PHYSICAL DEATH OF YOUR LOST CHILDREN. FOR THERE IS NO LONGER HOPE FOR THEIR SOULS. THEY HAVE DEPARTED THIS PHYSICAL REALM WITHOUT YOUR GIFT OF ETERNAL LIFE IN PARADISE. THEY HAVE DEPARTED THIS PHYSICAL REALM BEFORE ACCEPTING CHRIST JESUS AS THEIR SAVIOR AND GOD. HELP ME, O LORD, FOR I CANNOT REJOICE IN PEACE WITHOUT THE PRESENCE OF YOUR COMFORTING ARMS!

SEPTEMBER 7, 2015 BY: BARBARA ANN MARY MACK

SENT FRI, SEP 11, 2015 7:17 PM-READ FRI 9/11/2015 10:03 PM

THROUGHOUT THE DAY I LIFT YOU UP IN SONG AND DANCE, IN THE MIDST OF EXHAUSTION, MY GOD

BARBARA SPEAKING TO ALMIGHTY GOD AND CRAIG

THROUGHOUT THE DAY, YES, MY HEAVEN SENT DAY, I LIFT YOU UP IN SONG AND DANCE IN THE MIDST OF EXHAUSTION, MY LORD! THROUGHOUT THE DAY, YES, MY GOD ORCHESTRATED DAY, I LIFT YOU UP IN SONG AND DANCE, O BELOVED SON (CRAIG) OF OUR GREAT AND HOLY GOD! MY LORD, MY HOLY SPOUSE AND GOD, I LIFT YOU AND YOUR BELOVED SON (CRAIG) UP, AS I BATTLE THE GATES OF HELL FOR THE SOULS THAT SATAN IS TRYING TO LURE AWAY FROM YOUR REALM OF CHOSEN DIVINE LOVE. IN THE MIDST OF EXHAUSTION AND PAIN, I DANCE AROUND THE MIGHTY THRONE OF GOD, MY ETERNAL SAVIOR AND SPOUSE. IN THE MIDST OF EXHAUSTION AND PAIN, I CLING TO THE BELOVED ESSENCE (CRAIG) OF HE WHO BRINGS JOY AND DELIGHT TO MY IGNITED SOUL. MY LORD, MY HOLY SPOUSE AND ORIGIN, I LIFT YOU AND OUR ETERNAL BELOVED ONE (CRAIG) UP IN SONG AND DANCE, AS I BATTLE THE GROUNDS

THAT HAVE CLAIMED THE SOULS OF THE LOST AND CONFUSED SONS AND DAUGHTERS OF MY MERCIFUL GOD. I WILL SING AND DANCE, AS I DELIVER YOUR HOLY MESSAGES PERTAINING TO YOUR DIVINE TRUTH, O HOLY GOD OF MINE. I WILL SPEAK YOUR HOLY WORDS OF TRUTH TO THOSE WHO DESIRE TO HEAR THE WORDS OF GOD, THE RIGHTEOUS ONE. I WILL SPEAK YOUR HOLY WORDS OF TRUTH, AS I BOW DOWN IN THE PRESENCE OF HE (ALMIGHTY GOD) WHO SAVES THE LOST AND REPENTANT SOULS. I WILL SING AND DANCE WITH CRAIG, MY BELOVED ONE, AS I DELIVER THE MESSAGES THAT FLOW FROM THE THRONE OF HE (ALMIGHTY GOD) WHO SITS IN THE MIDST OF RIGHTEOUSNESS AND DIVINE TRUTH. RELEASE THE SPIRIT OF MY BELOVED ONE, AS I SING AND DANCE IN HIS MIDST, MY GOD. RELEASE THE IGNITED SPIRIT OF HE (CRAIG), WHO DESIRES TO PLEASE HIS CREATOR AND ORIGIN. RELEASE HIM, MY LORD, SO THAT HE AND I MAY SOAR THROUGHOUT ETERNITY WITH HE (ALMIGHTY GOD) WHOM WE WILL ALWAYS LOVE AND FOLLOW! FOR HE HAS BEEN CHOSEN BY YOU. *ALLELUIA!!!*
SEPTEMBER 7, 2015 BY: BARBARA ANN MARY MACK

THINKING OF YOU MAKES ME SMILE, O LORD

BARBARA SPEAKING TO THE LORD

THROUGHOUT THE DAY, AND INTO THE BLESSED NIGHT, MY THOUGHTS ARE ONLY OF YOU, MY KING. INTO THE DAY, THE GOD BLESSED DAY, I THINK OF ONLY YOU, MY GOD. I THINK OF THE WONDERS THAT YOU SO LOVING CREATE. I THINK OF THE GOOD THINGS THAT SURROUND MY THOUGHTS OF ONLY YOU. I THINK OF THE BLESSED PEOPLE WHOM YOU HAVE PLACED IN MY LIFE. I THINK OF THE GIFT OF BEING YOUR ETERNAL FAITHFUL WIFE. I THINK OF THE MANY PLACES THAT YOU HAVE SENT MY FAMILY AND ME. I THINK OF THE GIFT OF KNOWING THE BELOVED AND BLESSED HOLY TRINITY. I THINK OF THE GRATITUDE THAT I EXPRESS TO YOU, FOR BLESSING ME WITH A BEAUTIFUL AND FAITHFUL DAUGHTER AND GRANDDAUGHTER. MY FACE LIGHTS UP WITH A HEAVENLY SMILE, AS I REFLECT ON THE PRICELESS GIFT OF BEING IN THE PRESENCE OF YOUR FAITHFUL SON (ARCHBISHOP CRAIG). I THINK OF ALL OF THE BLESSINGS THAT YOU HAVE SHOWERED HIM WITH. I SMILE, AS I REMEMBER THE GOODNESS THAT YOU REVEALED TO ME THAT FLOWS THROUGH HIS IGNITED BEING THROUGHOUT THE DAY. I SMILE, AS I LOOK AT YOUR HANDIWORK AS YOU ORCHESTRATE MY DAUGHTER'S OBEDIENT LIFE. I SMILE AS I JOIN YOUR FAITHFUL SON (CRAIG) AND DAUGHTERS (LA TOYA AND AMYA) IN THE CELEBRATION OF THE HOLY EUCHARIST. MY LORD, AND MY GOD, I SMILE EVERY TIME THAT I THINK OF YOU, AND ALL WHO ADORE YOU!
AUGUST 24, 2015 BY: BARBARA ANN MARY MACK
SENT FRI, SEP 11, 2015 7:17 PM-READ FRI 9/11/2015 10:03 PM

THE WEIGHT OF THE WORLD IS VERY HEAVY, MY LORD

BARBARA SPEAKING TO THE REALM OF HOLINESS (ALMIGHTY GOD)

THE WEIGHT OF THE WORLD IS VERY HEAVY, MY LORD. THE WEIGHT OF THE WORLD'S SINS IS WEIGHING DOWN THE REALM THAT TRIES TO CORRECT IT. HELP ME, O REALM (HOLINESS) THAT SAVES THOSE WHOM SATAN IS MISLEADING TODAY! HELP ME COMBAT THE REALM OF EVIL THAT HAS MADE ITSELF VERY VISIBLE IN OUR MIDST TODAY. HELP ME COMBAT THE EVIL THAT SLITHERS FROM SATAN'S "UNHOLY PRESENCE". HELP ME, O REALM OF HOLINESS! HELP ME DEFEAT THE WEAKENED REALM (SATAN) THAT PRODUCES AND HOUSES THOSE WHO ARE TAKING DOWN THE VULNERABLE ONES. THE WEIGHT OF THE WORLD'S TROUBLES IS WEIGHING MY OBEDIENT ESSENCE DOWN. FOR I WEEP CONSTANTLY FOR THOSE WHO HAVE MET WITH PHYSICAL AND SPIRITUAL DEATH IN THE MIDST OF THEIR SINFUL WAYS. I WEEP FOR THE VULNERABLE ONES (THOSE WHO DO NOT KNOW GOD'S TRUTH). I WEEP FOR THE ONES WHO DID NOT SEEK SALVATION THROUGH CHRIST JESUS BEFORE THEIR PHYSICAL DEATHS. HELP ME, O REALM OF HOLINESS, FOR THE WEIGHT OF THIS WORLD, THIS GENERATION, IS WEIGHING ME DOWN.

SEPTEMBER 16, 2015 BY: BARBARA ANN MARY MACK

SENT WED, SEP 16, 2015 3:43 AM-READ WED 9/16/2015 11:48 AM

BUON GIORNO ARCHBISHOP CRAIG! ATTACHED ARE A FEW PICS OF US AT PENNSYLVANIA GRAND CANYON, NEAR WELLSBORO, PA. *CIAO! BEAUTIFUL BARBARA*

HE (JESUS) IS COMING BACK, MY CHILDREN

ALMIGHTY GOD, THE FATHER, SPEAKING TO THE LORD JESUS

MY SON (THE LORD JESUS), MY ONLY BEGOTTEN SON, THEY (THE WORLD) HAVE DEFAMED YOUR HOLY CHURCH BY INVITING THOSE WHOM YOU REFER TO AS AN ABOMINATION. THEY, THE WORLD, HAVE SEPARATED THEMSELVES FROM YOUR HOLY CHURCH. FOR THEY DO NOT SPEAK OF YOUR UNCHANGING TRUTH. THEY DO NOT FEED YOUR FLOCK WITH DIVINE TRUTH. MY SON, MY HOLY AND UNCHANGING SON, THEY HAVE BETRAYED YOUR GOOD AND HOLY WORK. THEY HAVE REMOVED THEIR GUISES, AND BLATANTLY MOCK YOU AND YOUR HOLY UNCHANGING WORD. THEY MOCK YOUR HOLY CHURCH, FOR THEY SPEAK THOSE THINGS WHICH ARE CONTRARY TO YOUR HOLY TEACHINGS FOR YOUR CHURCH. THEY HAVE REMOVED THEMSELVES FROM YOUR TRUTH. YES, MY SON, EVEN THE CLERGY. THEY WILL NOT RISE WITH YOU WHEN YOU RETURN FOR THE CHOSEN ONES. THEY WILL NOT SOAR WITH YOU WHEN YOU RETURN FOR THE FAITHFUL ONES. THEY WILL NOT REJOICE WITH YOU, WHEN YOU RETURN IN THE MIDST OF THE CLOUDS. FOR THEY HAVE ABANDONED YOUR HOLY AND UNCHANGING WORD OF TRUTH. WE WILL SOAR WITH THE FAITHFUL ONES, O PRECIOUS SON (THE LORD JESUS) OF

MINE! WE WILL REJOICE WITH THE OBEDIENT ONES, O LOVING AND MERCIFUL SON OF MINE! WE WILL DANCE WITH THE RIGHTEOUS AND HOLY ONES, O BELOVED AND ONLY BEGOTTEN SON OF MINE! WE WILL SING SONG OF GLADNESS WITH THOSE WHO SUFFERED FOR THE SAKE OF YOUR HOLY UNCHANGEABLE TRUTH, O BLESSED SON OF MINE! COME! O PRECIOUS AND ONLY BEGOTTEN SON OF MINE. LET YOU AND I WALK THROUGH THE GATES OF SWEET PARADISE WITH THOSE WHO GAVE UP THEIR DESIRES AND SINS, FOR THE SAKE OF THEIR AUTHENTIC LOVE AND ALLEGIANCE TO THE ONLY FOUNDER (THE LORD JESUS) OF YOUR HOLY CHURCH. SEPTEMBER 17, 2015 BY: BARBARA ANN MARY MACK

CHRIST SAID, "ONE MUST BE BORN AGAIN BEFORE ONE ENTERS HIS HOLY KINGDOM."

BARBARA SPEAKING

TO BE BORN AGAIN MEANS THAT ONE NO LONGER LIVES IN SIN. ONE NO LONGER PERFORMS THE SINFUL AND UNGODLY ACTS THAT SEPARATED HIM OR HER FROM GOD'S REALM OF HOLINESS. I WAS ONCE A RACIST, BUT WHEN I ACCEPTED CHRIST JESUS AS MY SAVIOR AND GOD, I NO LONGER EXHIBITED THE ACTS AND THOUGHTS OF A RACIST. EVERYONE WHO DESIRES TO BECOME A CHRISTIAN MUST, MUST, MUST GIVE UP THE ACTS THAT SEPARATE HIM OR HER FROM GOD'S REALM OF HOLINESS. MY BROTHERS AND SISTERS, I GAVE UP MY SINFUL ACTS BECAUSE I TRULY LOVE GOD. I GAVE UP MY SINFUL WAYS, BECAUSE I WANT TO LIVE IN SWEET PARADISE WITH GOD, MY SAVIOR. I GAVE UP MY SINFUL WORKS, BECAUSE I BELIEVE IN THE UNCHANGEABLE HOLY WORD OF GOD, MY JUDGE AND CREATOR. I GAVE UP MY OFFENSIVE SINS, BECAUSE I TRULY BELIEVE IN THE DESTINATION OF THOSE WHO DO NOT GIVE UP THEIR SINFUL WAYS BEFORE THEIR PHYSICAL DEATH. MY BROTHERS AND SISTERS, YOU MUST BE BORN AGAIN, AND BECOME A NEW PERSON IN THE EYES OF OUR HOLY GOD IF YOU WANT TO BE A CHRISTIAN, GOD'S VERSION OF A DISCIPLE OF HIS. MY BROTHERS AND SISTERS, YOU MUST BE BORN AGAIN THROUGH BAPTISM IN GOD'S HOLY SPIRIT AND WATER! SEPTEMBER 17, 2015 BY: BARBARA ANN MARY MACK

UNDERSTANDING THE REALM (SATAN) THAT PRODUCES NOTHING

ALMIGHTY GOD SPEAKING

MY CHILDREN, DO NOT BE FOOLED OR DECEIVED BY THAT WHICH APPEARS TO BE RIGHTEOUS IN MY HOLY EYES. FOR SATAN'S REALM OF CUNNING WAYS HAS ENTERED EARTH'S VULNERABLE INHABITANTS IN A VISIBLE AND TANGIBLE MANNER TODAY. HE, SATAN, NO LONGER HIDES HIS EVIL WORKS, FOR THEY ARE THE WORKS THAT ATTRACT THE WORLDLY ONES. THEY ARE THE WORKS THAT ATTRACT THOSE WHO SEEK WORLDLY FAME AND FORTUNES. THEY ARE

THE WORKS THAT SUBDUE AND ENTICE THE WEAK MINDED ONES. THEY ARE THE WORKS THAT PRODUCE NOTHING OF ETERNAL VALUE. FLEE! MY CHILDREN. FLEE! FLEE FROM THE REALM THAT PRODUCES NOTHING! FLEE FROM THE REALM THAT PRODUCES TEMPORARY PLEASURE! FLEE FROM THE REALM THAT PRODUCES HARM AND DESTRUCTION TOWARD GOD'S VULNERABLE CHILDREN! FLEE FROM THE DOOMED AND DAMNED REALM THAT HOUSES SATAN AND HIS DEFEATED ANGELS (FOLLOWERS)! FLEE! MY CHILDREN. FLEE! FLEE, BEFORE THE GATES TO ETERNAL HELL SNATCHES YOUR VULNERABLE SOULS!

SEPTEMBER 17, 2015 BY: BARBARA ANN MARY MACK

WHEN MEMORIES GET IN THE WAY OF RECONCILIATION AND FORGIVENESS

BARBARA SPEAKING

ALTHOUGH ONE CANNOT FULLY FORGET BAD MEMORIES, ONE CAN OVERCOME NEGATIVE FEELINGS AND ACTIONS BY ACCEPTING THE OCCURRENCE(S) AS SOMETHING OF THE PAST. ONE MUST FOCUS ON THE FUTURE IN A POSITIVE MANNER IN ORDER TO CONQUER THE PAST. GENUINE FORGIVENESS AND RECONCILIATION ARE THE KEY TO SUCCESSFUL HEALING OF INJURIES OF THE PAST. AS CHRISTIANS, WE ARE CALLED AND COMMANDED BY ALMIGHTY GOD TO LOVE AND FORGIVE ONE ANOTHER. ALTHOUGH THIS COURAGEOUS ACT MAY BE VERY DIFFICULT AT TIMES, ONE CAN FULFILL THE COMMANDMENT WITH THE GRACE AND LOVE OF ALMIGHTY GOD.

SEPTEMBER 16, 2015 BY; BARBARA ANN MARY MACK

SENT THU, SEP 17, 2015 9:37 AM-READ THU 9/17/2015 7:49 PM

OH ARCHBISHOP CRAIG, MAY "MY AUTHENTIC LOVE" ENCOMPASS YOU THROUGHOUT YOUR "SPIRITUAL" AND "PHYSICAL" JOURNEY WITH GOD, OUR FIRST AND LAST LOVE. *LOVE ALWAYS, BEAUTIFUL BARBARA*

I HUNGER FOR YOUR HOLY PRESENCE DAILY, MY LORD AND MY GOD

BARBARA SPEAKING TO THE LORD

MY LORD AND MY HOLY GOD, I HUNGER FOR A TASTE OF YOUR ETERNAL ESSENCE, AS I CLING TO THE VOICE THAT CRIES THROUGHOUT THE NIGHTS. I HUNGER FOR THE FOOD (ALMIGHTY GOD'S HOLY UNCHANGING WORD) THAT GIVES SPIRITUAL NUTRITION TO THE CALLED AND CHOSEN ONES. I HUNGER FOR THE PRESENCE OF MY HOLY GOD AS HE ROAMS WITHIN MY PURIFIED BEING. I HUNGER FOR YOUR GIFT OF LIFE THAT IS PROMISED TO THOSE WHO FOLLOW THE FOOTSTEPS AND HOLY TEACHINGS OF CHRIST JESUS. I HUNGER FOR JESUS, THE HOLY

BREAD OF LIFE, AS I WHISPER HIS LIFE SAVING WORDS TO THOSE WHO LONG TO HEAR THEM. FEED ME, O LORD. FEED ME WITH THE DIVINE FOOD THAT WILL LEAD YOUR LOVED ONES TO YOUR REALM OF ETERNAL LOVE AND HOPE. FEED ME, O LORD, FOR I DO HUNGER FOR YOU EVERY DAY

SEPTEMBER 16, 2015 BY: BARBARA ANN MARY MACK

THE ROAD THAT LEADS TO YOUR HEAVENLY HOME ABOVE IS VERY ROUGH, MY LORD

BARBARA SPEAKING TO THE LORD

OH, THE TEARS, THE MANY, MANY TEARS THAT HAVE ENCOMPASSED AND FALLEN FROM MY OBEDIENT BEING, AS I COMBAT THE GATES OF HELL FOR THE ETERNAL SOULS OF GOD'S WORTHY ONES. THE TEARS, THE EVER-FLOWING TEARS, FALL FROM THE HIDDEN FACE OF GOD'S CONTEMPORARY MESSENGER AND BRIDE (BARBARA). SHIELD MY WEAK AND WORN ESSENCE OF LOVE AS IT BOWS IN THE MIDST OF SWEET DIVINITY TODAY. SHIELD ME FROM THE EVILS THAT ROAM THE EARTH IN SEARCH FOR THE SOULS WHO DO NOT KNOW, OR DESIRE TO KNOW YOU AND YOUR HOLY UNCHANGING WAY. SHIELD ME FROM THE MANY DARTS THAT SATAN THROWS AT ME THROUGHOUT EACH DAY. SHIELD ME FROM THE DISCOMFORT THAT ENGULFS MY WEARY SOUL. SHIELD ME, O GREAT AND HOLY SPOUSE OF MINE. SHIELD ME FROM SATAN'S WRATH. FOR HE IS VERY ANGRY WITH ME, YOUR CHOSEN WARRIOR AND VICTORIOUS BRIDE. LET HIM FEEL THE DEPTH OF YOUR WRATH, AS HE TRIES TO SLAUGHTER ME THROUGHOUT EACH DAY. LET HIM FEEL YOUR UNLIMITED POWER, AS HE SEEKS THE SOUL OF CRAIG, OUR ETERNAL BELOVED ONE. SHIELD US (CRAIG AND BARBARA), MY LORD, FOR THE ROAD THAT LEADS TO SWEET PARADISE IS VERY ROUGH.

SEPTEMBER 16, 2015 BY: BARBARA ANN MARY MACK

I KNOW OF THE MANY WONDERFUL AND MIRACULOUS WORKS THAT GOD DOES FOR US

BARBARA SPEAKING

MY BROTHERS AND SISTERS, I KNOW OF THE WONDERFUL MIRACLES THAT OUR GREAT AND HOLY GOD HAS PERFORMED FOR HIS CHILDREN THROUGHOUT THE REALM OF TIME. BUT WHAT I AM INTERESTED IN IS, WHAT YOU HAVE DONE FOR OUR GREAT AND HOLY GOD. I WANT TO SEE AND HEAR OF THE HOLY LIVES AND DEEDS THAT PROFESSED CHRISTIANS SHOULD EXHIBIT EVERY DAY. I WANT TO SEE YOUR HOLY DEEDS AND WAY AS I DELIVER GOD'S LIFE SAVING MESSAGES TO THE CALLED AND CHOSEN ONES. FOR I HAVE HEARD MANY TESTIMONIALS CONCERNING GOD'S HOLY WORKS. LET YOUR GOD APPROVED WORKS AND LIVES EXHIBIT THAT OF GOD'S VERSION OF HOLINESS. LET YOUR ACTS COINCIDE WITH YOUR PROFESSION OF

FAITH. LET ALMIGHTY WITNESS THE "AUTHENTICITY" OF YOUR ALLEGIANCE TO HIM ONLY! MY BROTHERS AND SISTERS, LET YOUR FAITH SHINE IN THE PRESENCE OF THOSE WHO HAVE NO FAITH, SO THAT THEY MAY WITNESS THE TEACHINGS OF THE LORD JESUS IN OUR MIDST TODAY. MY BROTHERS AND SISTERS, LET ALMIGHTY GOD WITNESS HIS VERSION OF HOLINESS TODAY.

SEPTEMBER 14, 2015 BY: BARBARA ANN MARY MACK

SENT THU, SEP 17, 2015 9:37 AM-READ THU 9/17/2015 7:49 PM

GREETINGS, DEAR ARCHBISHOP CRAIG! LA TOYA, AMYA, AND I ARE EN ROUTE TO PARADISE, PA, LOCATED NEAR LANCASTER, PA. LA TOYA IS TREATING ME TO A FARM LOCATION WITH VARIOUS ACTIVITIES, INCLUDING MILKING A COW, FOR MY BIRTHDAY, WHICH IS MONDAY SEPTEMBER 21ST. PER MY REQUEST, LA TOYA IS HONORING MY BIRTHDAY DESIRE. I LOVE THE FARM LIFE, BUT I DO NOT WANT TO MAKE IT A PERMANENT LIVING ARRANGEMENT. LA TOYA MADE RESERVATIONS YESTERDAY. THE ACTIVITIES ARE 10:30 AM AND 2:30 PM. WE MADE RESERVATIONS FOR THE 2:30 FESTIVITIES, WHICH WILL GIVE US AMPLE TIME TO GET THERE. CAMERAS ARE PERMITTED, WHICH IS SURPRISING BECAUSE THAT IS AN AMISH COMMUNITY AS WELL. WE WILL GO ON A TRACTOR AND HAY RIDE AS WELL. ENJOY YOUR DAY LOVE! *LOVE ALWAYS! BEAUTIFUL BARBIE*

SENT SAT, SEP 19, 2015 11:37 PM-READ SUN 9/20/2015 9:29 AM

GREETINGS ARCHBISHOP CRAIG! COME STA OGGI? IT IS VERY IMPORTANT THAT ALL OF US FOLLOW THE GUIDANCE AND SCRIPTURAL TEACHINGS OF JESUS, OUR UNCHANGEABLE LORD AND SAVIOR. FOR ALMIGHTY GOD WILL EXHIBIT HIS DISAPPROVAL AND WRATH TOWARD THE DISOBEDIENT ONES, AS HE DID IN THE PAST. LET US BE EXAMPLES TO THOSE WHOM THE LORD HAS PLACED IN OUR CARE.

AMORE, BELLA BARBARA

REMEMBER WHAT HAPPENED TO THOSE WHO LEFT EGYPT UNDER MOSES' GUIDANCE

ALMIGHTY GOD SPEAKING

THOSE WHO ABANDON ME FOR FALSE GODS AND IDOLS WERE DESTROYED PHYSICALLY AND SPIRITUALLY. THEY DID NOT ENTER MY PROMISED LAND, AND NEITHER WILL THOSE OF TODAY WHO CONTINUE IN THEIR SINS. OUT OF THE THOUSANDS OF ISRAELITES THAT LEFT EGYPT, ONLY JOSHUA AND CALEB WERE PERMITTED BY ME, THE LORD ALMIGHTY, TO ENTER THE PROMISE LAND, NOT EVEN MOSES. UNDERSTAND MY JUSTICE, MY JUSTICE, MY JUSTICE, *SAYS THE LORD ALMIGHTY!*

SEPTEMBER 16, 2015 BY: BARBARA ANN MARY MACK

DRIFTING...ROAMING...SEARCHING FOR...

ALMIGHTY GOD SPEAKING

THE RIGHTEOUS ONES: THE TRUE BELIEVERS: THE WARRIORS OF GOD'S HOLY ARMY: FOLLOWERS OF THE UNCHANGEABLE WORD OF JESUS CHRIST: THE FAITHFUL ONES: DELIVERERS OF MY HOLY TRUTH: THE FORGIVING ONES: THE CARING ONES: THE COMPASSIONATE ONES: THE MERCIFUL ONES: THE PATIENT ONES: THE DILIGENT ONES: THE REJOICING ONES: THE CHARITABLE ONES: THE HELPING ONES: THE JOYFUL ONES: THE CALLED ONES: THE CHOSEN ONES: ALL OF MY OBEDIENT HEAVEN BOUND CHILDREN!
SEPTEMBER 18, 2015 BY: BARBARA ANN MARY MACK
SENT SAT, SEP 19, 2015 11:37 PM-READ SUN 9/20/2015 9:29 AM

THEY ARE SERVING EVERYONE EXCEPT THE LORD

ALMIGHTY GOD SPEAKING TO HEAVEN'S RESIDENTS

LOOK AT THEM! LOOK AT THOSE WHO ARE SERVING AND HONORING EVERYONE AND THING OTHER THAN ME, THEIR CREATOR AND GOD. LOOK AT THEM, AS THEY GIVE PRAISE AND UNDUE GLORY TO THOSE WHO ARE THEIR EQUAL. I AM TO ASHAMED TO CALL THEM MY CREATION, I AM SO ASHAMED OF THEM! LOOK AT THEM, O HEAVENLY HOSTS AND ANGELS OF MINE! LET US OBSERVE THEIR SINFUL WAYS, AS THEY GIVE PRAISE AND HONOR TO THOSE WHO COMMIT EVIL ACTS IN MY HOLY PRESENCE. LET US WITNESS THEIR ACTS (IRREVERENCE TO ALMIGHTY GOD AND HIS VERSION OF HOLINESS AND RIGHTEOUSNESS) WHICH THEY GIVE PRAISE AND EXALTATION TO ONE ANOTHER FOR. DO THEY NOT FEAR GOD, THE OMNIPRESENT ONE, AND HIS POWER TO REMOVE THEM FROM THE REALM OF ETERNAL LIFE? DO THEY NOT UNDERSTAND MY VERSION OF RIGHTEOUS ACTS AND DEEDS?

ALMIGHTY GOD SPEAKING TO THE CLERGY

HELP THEM, O CLERGY! HELP THEM UNDERSTAND WHO (ALMIGHTY GOD ALONE) IS TO BE EXALTED! MANKIND CANNOT EXALT ONE ANOTHER, FOR THEY ARE EQUAL IN MY HOLY EYES! ONE IS NOT BETTER THAN THE OTHER. FOR YOU BELONG TO ME! GIVE REVERENCE AND PRAISE TO HE (ALMIGHTY GOD) WHO CREATED THE HEAVENS AND EARTH, AND ALL THINGS THAT ARE GOOD AND HOLY.
SEPTEMBER 20, 2015 BY: BARBARA ANN MARY MACK

I DID NOT CALL YOU TO ENTERTAIN THE SINNERS, BUT TO ENLIGHTEN THEM OF MY HOLY TRUTH AND MY UNCHANGING WORD, SAYS THE LORD

ALMIGHTY GOD SPEAKING TO THE CLERGY

MY SONS, I LOOK DOWN AT THE CROWED CHURCHES, AND I NOTICE THAT THE SHEPHERDS THERE APPEAR AS AN ENTERTAINER INSTEAD OF A PREACHER OF MY HOLY WORD. THEY ARE EXHIBITING THE BEHAVIOR OF A CELEBRITY OF THE WORLD, INSTEAD OF A SHEPHERD OVER MY NEEDY FLOCK. THEY APPEAR TO ENTERTAIN THEIR CONGREGATION WITH WORLDLY MUSIC AND ACTIONS, INSTEAD OF CONVEYING MY MESSAGES IN AN UNDERSTANDABLE AND HOLY MANNER. I AM WATCHING YOU, O CLERGY WHO ENTERTAIN YOUR CONGREGATIONS INSTEAD OF ENLIGHTENING MY VULNERABLE AND SUSCEPTIBLE FLOCK. YOU ARE CALLED TO ENLIGHTEN MY FLOCK, O CLERGY. YOU ARE CALLED TO FEED THEM WITH MY HOLY WORDS OF TRUTH. YOU ARE CALLED TO EXHIBIT A HUMBLED LIFE, AND NOT THE LIFE OF WORLDLY PROSPERITY. YOU ARE CALLED TO SEPARATE YOURSELF AND BELIEFS FROM THE WORLD. YOU ARE NOT CALLED TO ENTERTAIN YOUR CONGREGATION AS IF YOU WERE ON STAGE PERFORMING AT A CONCERT. REVEAL MY HOLY WORD TO MY FLOCK, AS I REVEAL THEM TO YOU. I WILL NOT ENTERTAIN YOU, O CLERGY! I WILL NOT PUT ON A SHOW FOR YOU! I WILL NOT PERFORM FOR YOU AS IF I WAS A ROCK STAR, SO DO NOT SUBJECT MY CHILDREN TO YOUR "UNACCEPTABLE PERFORMANCE"! FOR MANY ARE CALLED, BUT FEW, FEW, FEW ARE CHOSEN. DO NOT LET THE NUMBER OF YOUR CONGREGATION FOOL YOU, O ENTERTAINING, CLERGY, FOR MANY ARE CALLED, BUT FEW ARE CHOSEN, *SAYS THE LORD!!!*
SEPTEMBER 20, 2015 BY: BARBARA ANN MARY MACK
SENT SUN, SEP 20, 2015 4:57 PM-READ SUN 9/20/2015 6:40 PM

THEY HAVE TO CHANGE TOO, SAYS THE LORD

ALMIGHTY GOD SPEAKING TO THE CLERGY

MY SONS (THE CLERGY), IN ORDER FOR YOU TO CHANGE THE HEARTS OF THOSE WHO ARE LIVING IN SIN, YOU HAVE TO MAKE A CHANGE AS WELL. YOU HAVE TO CHANGE YOUR WAY OF THINKING, AND THINK AS I DO, *SAYS THE LORD.* YOU CANNOT CONFORM TO THE THOUGHTS, WAYS AND BELIEFS OF THOSE WHO ARE LIVING CONTRARY TO WHAT I HAVE SPOKEN AGAINST THROUGH THE HOLY BIBLE. YOU MUST MAKE A CHANGE SO THAT YOUR CONGREGATION WILL KNOW MY VERSION OF HOLY LIVING. YOU MUST EXHIBIT MY VERSION OF HOLINESS AT ALL TIMES, FOR YOU WILL BE HELD ACCOUNTABLE FOR WHAT YOU TEACH AND PREACH OF. I HAVE ENTRUSTED MY VULNERABLE CHILDREN IN YOUR CARE, THEREFORE, YOU ARE RESPONSIBLE FOR TEACHING THEM MY TRUTH AT ALL TIMES. MY SONS, THERE ARE NO EXCEPTIONS! EVERYONE WILL BE HELD ACCOUNTABLE FOR WHAT THEY HAVE DONE, AND FOR WHAT THEY HAVE NOT DONE. MY SONS, BE AWARE OF MY VERSION OF RIGHTEOUSNESS AND JUSTICE, FOR I WILL SHOW NO MERCY TOWARDS THOSE WHO DO NOT DELIVER MY TRUTH, *SAYS THE LORD.*

SEPTEMBER 21, 2015 AT 3:15 PM BY: BARBARA ANN MARY MACK

WHO ARE THE HYPOCRITES

ALMIGHTY GOD SPEAKING

YOU WHO SPEAK MY HOLY WORDS, BUT DO NOT ABIDE BY THEM, ARE HYPOCRITES IN MY HOLY SIGHT, *SAYS THE LORD.* YOU SPEAK MY WORDS THAT FLOW THROUGHOUT THE HOLY BIBLE, BUT YOU DO NOT BELIEVE THEM, O HYPOCRITES! YOUR ACTION CONVEYS THE DEPTH OF YOUR DISBELIEF, O DISOBEDIENT ONES! YOUR ACTS REVEAL THE REALITY OF YOUR UNBELIEF, O UNFAITHFUL ONES! YOU READ MY HOLY WORDS, AND YOU TWIST THE MEANING OF MY TRUTH, SO THAT THOSE WHO HEAR YOU SPEAK MAY BELIEVE IN THE UNTRUTH THAT YOU CONVEY TO THEM. O HYPOCRITES, WHY DO YOU DECEIVE THE VULNERABLE ONES? WHY DO YOU CONFUSE THE WEAK MINDED ONES? WHY DO YOU DECEIVE YOURSELVES? LEARN OF MY HOLY TRUTH, YOU WHO SLITHERED FROM THE REALM THAT RELEASES DECEPTION! LEARN OF MY HOLY TRUTH, AND PREACH IT TO THOSE WHO ARE IN NEED OF MY TRUTH, BEFORE I BRING DOWN MY JUDGMENT AGAINST YOU, *SAYS THE LORD!* O HYPOCRITES, TEACH AND LIVE MY HOLY TRUTH, BEFORE THE GATES TO ETERNAL DAMNATION SWALLOW YOUR UNPROTECTED SOULS.

SEPTEMBER 21, 2015 AT 3:34 PM BY: BARBARA ANN MARY MACK

THE LOVE (ALMIGHTY GOD)

ALMIGHTY GOD SPEAKING

MY CHILDREN, OBSERVE THE LOVE (ALMIGHTY GOD) THAT ROAMS IN YOUR BLESSED MIDST TODAY! OBSERVE THE LOVE (ALMIGHTY GOD) AS HE ROAMS IN THE MIDST OF THIS TRAGIC PERIOD OF TIME! OBSERVE THE LOVE AS HE MOVES IN THE MIDST OF THE RIGHTEOUS ONES! OBSERVE THE LOVE AS HE MOVES IN THE MIDST OF THOSE WHO DO THE WORKS OF SATAN, THEIR BLINDING GUIDE. OBSERVE THE LOVE, AS HE BLESSES THOSE WHO TRULY LOVE AND ADORE HIM AND HIS UNCHANGING WORD AND WAY. OBSERVE THE LOVE, AS HE RESOUNDS THE IMPORTANCE OF FOLLOWING HIS HOLY WAY, THE ONLY WAY TO ETERNAL LIFE WITH GOD, THE HOLY AND BLESSED TRINITY. OBSERVE THE LOVE AS HE SITS IN THE MIDST OF THOSE WHO ARE ABANDONED. OBSERVE THE LOVE AS HE WEEPS IN THE MIDST OF THE HURTING ONES. OBSERVE THE LOVE AS HE REVEALS HIS PLAN TO THOSE WHO TRULY BELIEVE IN ETERNAL LIFE. OBSERVE THE LOVE AS HE SITS ON HIS MIGHTY GLORIOUS THRONE ABOVE. MY CHILDREN, OBSERVE THE LOVE THAT CALLS THOSE WHOM HE VALUES! MY CHILDREN! OBSERVE ME, YOUR CREATOR AND LIFE- SAVING GOD, THROUGHOUT ETERNITY!

SEPTEMBER 21, 2015 AT 4:08 PM BY: BARBARA ANN MARY MACK

SENT MON, SEP 21, 2015 4:48 PM-READ TUE 9/22/2015 8:27 AM

WHO IS WORTHY TO MEET ME, SAYS THE LORD?

ALMIGHTY GOD SPEAKING

WHO IS WORTHY TO MEET AND GREET JESUS, THE GREAT AND HOLY REDEEMER? WHO IS WORTHY TO DANCE WITH HIM THROUGHOUT ETERNITY? WHO IS WORTHY TO DINE WITH HIM AT HIS TABLE OF PLENTY? WHO IS WORTHY TO SIT WITH HIM ON HIS MIGHTY THRONE ABOVE? WHO IS WORTHY TO WALK WITH HIM THROUGH HIS SPIRITUAL GARDEN OF DIVINE LOVE? WHO IS WORTHY TO SHARE IN THE HEAVENLY SPLENDOR THAT SURROUNDS OUR GRACIOUS AND HOLY FATHER? WHO IS WORTHY TO SING CONTINUOUS SONGS OF PRAISE TO HE (ALMIGHTY GOD, THE FATHER) WHO EXISTED BEFORE EXISTENCE? WHO? MY CHILDREN. WHO IS WORTHY? IS IT YOU, MY DAUGHTER? IS IT YOU, MY SON? HAVE YOU BEEN FAITHFUL AND OBEDIENT TO MY DIVINE UNCHANGING WORD? HAVE YOU LOVED YOUR NEIGHBOR, AS I HAVE COMMANDED? HAVE YOU CATERED TO THE POOR IN SPIRITUAL AND PHYSICAL NEED? HAVE YOU SHELTERED THE HOMELESS ONES, MY CHILDREN? HAVE YOU FORGIVEN THAT WHICH YOU CONSIDER UNFORGIVABLE? HAVE YOU WASHED THE FEET OF THOSE WHO WALKED MILES TO RECEIVE MY HOLY WORDS? HAVE YOU KEPT MY HOLY COMMANDMENTS IN YOUR HEARTS AND DAILY LIVING? DO YOU TRULY LOVE YOUR CREATOR AND GOD? DO YOU DEFEND ME AND MY HOLY TEACHINGS IN THE PRESENCE OF THOSE WHO REPRESENT SATAN'S REALM OF REBELLION AND APATHY? DO YOU GIVE CONTINUOUS REVERENCE TO YOUR CREATOR AND GOD? DO YOU TRULY LOVE ME ABOVE EVERYTHING AND EVERYONE IN YOUR LIFE? DO YOU, MY CHILDREN? DO YOU REALLY LOVE AND HONOR ME? FOR I TRULY LOVE YOU!
SEPTEMBER 20, 2015 BY: BARBARA ANN MARY MACK
SENT MON, SEP 21, 2015 4:48 PM-READ TUE 9/22/2015 8:27 AM

WOW! THEY DO NOT KNOW YOU AT ALL, MY GOD.

BARBARA SPEAKING TO UNCHANGEABLE ALMIGHTY GOD

THEIR ACTS AND BELIEFS CONVEY THEIR LACK OF KNOWLEDGE OF YOU, MY GOD. THEY CLAIM AND PROFESS THAT THEY KNOW YOU AND YOUR HOLY WAY, BUT THEIR DEEDS AND ACTIONS REVEAL THE TRUTH. HOW CAN THEY NOT KNOW YOU AND YOUR HOLY WAY, FOR IT IS WRITTEN IN THE HOLY BIBLE, YOUR UNCHANGING WORD? HOW CAN THEY SAY THAT THEY KNOW YOUR HOLY WAY, WHEN THEY DO THE OPPOSITE OF WHAT YOU VIEW AS RIGHTEOUS AND HOLY? MY LORD, MY HOLY, HOLY, HOLY GOD, I DO KNOW YOU, FOR I DO KNOW AND FOLLOW YOUR UNCHANGEABLE HOLY WORD AND WAY.
SEPTEMBER 10, 2015 BY: BARBARA ANN MARY MACK

I AM SICK AT HEART, SAYS THE LORD

ALMIGHTY GOD SPEAKING

EVERY TIME THAT I SEE AND HEAR OF THE "UNHOLY" ACTS AND BELIEFS THAT FLOW FROM MY EARTHLY CREATION, I BECOME SICK AT HEART. OH, THE "UNSPEAKABLE" AND "UNHEARD" OF THINGS THAT THEY DISPLAY, CAUSE ME TO BECOME SICK AND HEART BROKEN.

ALMIGHTY GOD SPEAKING TO SATAN

WHY HAVE YOU TURNED MY GREAT CREATION (HUMAN BEINGS) AGAINST ME, O SATAN? WHY DO THEY FOLLOW YOUR "UNHOLY" WAYS, INSTEAD OF MY REALM OF RIGHTEOUSNESS AND HOLINESS? WHY HAVE THEY BECOME YOUR SOLDIERS ON THE SPIRITUAL AND PHYSICAL BATTLEFIELD, INSTEAD OF MY FAITHFUL ONES?

ALMIGHTY GOD SPEAKING TO THE DISOBEDIENT ONES

WHY? MY CHILDREN. WHY DO YOU CAUSE ME TO WEEP CONSTANTLY?
SEPTEMBER 10, 2015 BY: BARBARA ANN MARY MACK
SENT WED, SEP 23, 2015 8:42 PM-READ WED 9/23/2015 10:02 PM

PLEASANT DREAMS DEAR ONE (ARCHBISHOP CRAIG)! AMORE, BELLA BARBIE

TODAY'S PASSAGES

WHERE WILL YOU LEAD ME, O CLERGY?

THE SPIRITS OF THE VULNERABLE ONES SPEAKING

WHERE WILL YOU LEAD ME, O SHEPHERDS? WHERE IS YOUR SOUL LEADING YOU, O CLERGY? WHERE ARE YOUR ACTS LEADING US, THE VULNERABLE ONES? ARE YOU LEADING US IN THE DIRECTION OF ETERNAL GLORY WITH GOD, OUR SAVIOR, O CLERGY? I WILL FOLLOW YOU, O CLERGY! I WILL GO WHERE YOUR WORDS AND ACTS LEAD ME, FOR I AM THE VULNERABLE SPIRIT OF THE DEPENDENT ONE. WHERE ARE YOU HEADING, O CLERGY? WILL YOU LEAD US THROUGH THE GATES OF HELL AND ETERNAL DAMNATION, O CLERGY? I WILL FOLLOW YOU WHEREVER YOU LEAD ME, O CLERGY, FOR I AM THE SPIRIT OF THE VULNERABLE AND TRUSTING ONE.
SEPTEMBER 22, 2015 AT 6:08 PM BY: BARBARA ANN MARY MACK

GREETINGS DEAR ONE! I PRAY THAT YOU HAD A WONDERFUL DAY. ATTACHED ARE SOME FUNNY PICTURES OF OUR DAY ON THE FARM IN PARADISE, PA. WE HAD A GREAT TIME! I REALLY ENJOYED THIS BIRTHDAY GIFT FROM LA TOYA. SHE ALWAYS SURPRISES ME WITH SOMETHING THAT I WILL ENJOY AND APPRECIATE, BECAUSE SHE KNOWS ME VERY WELL. BELOW ARE TODAY'S GOD DICTATED PASSAGES. *AMORE, BELLA BARBARA*

THEY DO NOT WANT TO SEE ME (DIVINE TRUTH) COMING

DIVINE TRUTH, ALMIGHTY GOD, SPEAKING

THOSE WHO SPEAK AND FOLLOW THE TEACHINGS OF THOSE WHO GO AGAINST MY VERSION OF HOLINESS, DO NOT WANT TO SEE ME, DIVINE TRUTH, COMING. THOSE WHO REVERE THE WORKS AND ACTS OF SATAN, OUR ENEMY, DO NOT WANT TO SEE ME, DIVINE TRUTH, COMING. THOSE WHO RELAX IN THE STATE OF COMFORT AND DELIGHT AS THEY COMMIT UNSPEAKABLE AND UNHOLY ACTS, DO NOT WANT TO SEE ME, DIVINE TRUTH, COMING. THOSE WHO SUPPORT AND CONDONE THE WORKS THAT LEAD TO ETERNAL DAMNATION, DO NOT WANT TO SEE ME, DIVINE TRUTH, COMING. BEHOLD! ALL WHO ARE COMFORTABLE AND CONTENT IN THE REALM OF SIN, I, DIVINE TRUTH, YOUR HOLY GOD, AM IN YOUR MIDST TODAY. BEHOLD! FOR I AM IN YOUR MIDST IN THE FORM OF BARBARA, MY MEEK AND OBEDIENT SERVANT OF DIVINE TRUTH AND LOVE. SEPTEMBER 22, 2015 AT 5:15 PM BY: BARBARA ANN MARY MACK

I WILL TALK ABOUT IT NO MORE

BARBARA SPEAKING

I WILL NO LONGER TALK ABOUT THE WORKS OF SATAN. I WILL NO LONGER SPEAK TO THOSE WHO HAVE CHOSEN AND DESIRE TO REMAIN IN SIN. I HAVE SPOKEN TO YOU FOR MANY, MANY YEARS, MY BROTHERS AND SISTERS. I HAVE DELIVERED GOD'S SACRED WORD OF SALVATION AND DIVINE HOPE TO YOU. I HAVE REVEALED THE MESSAGES FROM THE LORD THROUGH MY MANY INNER AND VISIBLE TEARS. WHAT MORE CAN I DO? WHAT CAN I SAY? MY SPIRIT AND SOUL WEEP AT THE SIGHT AND KNOWLEDGE OF YOUR PARTICIPATION IN SIN. MY VULNERABLE SOUL IS WEIGHED DOWN WITH GRIEF AND SORROW. I WILL NO LONGER SPEAK TO YOU, YOU WHO DO NOT HEED GOD'S MESSAGES OF RIGHTEOUSNESS, FOR YOU HAVE REJECTED HIS HOLY WORDS FOR THE LAST TIME!!!
SEPTEMBER 24, 2015 AT 9:31 AM BY: BARBARA ANN MARY MACK

GREETINGS ARCHBISHOP CRAIG! COME STA OGGI? I AM PRESENTLY PREPARING VOLUME NINE OF **"THE PRESENT TESTAMENT"** FOR PUBLICATION. SO FAR, THE BOOK CONSISTS OF

OVER 600 PAGES DEPENDING UPON THE FONT SIZE AND STYLE. THIS BOOK CONSISTS OF THE MANY PASSAGES THAT THE LORD INSPIRED ME TO WRITE THIS YEAR. SINCE GOD'S REALM OF KNOWLEDGE HAS NO LIMIT, I COULD NEVER FINISH THAT WHICH HAS NO END. *GOD BLESS!* *BELLA BARBIE*

HE WHO IS REVERED BY MANY DOESN'T KNOW ME, SAYS THE LORD

ALMIGHTY GOD SPEAKING

THEY, THE WORLD, HAIL HIM INSTEAD OF ME! THEY HAIL HIM, BECAUSE THEY DO NOT KNOW ME, *SAYS THE LORD*. LOOK AT THEM, MY DAUGHTER (BARBARA)! LISTEN TO THEIR VOICES, AS THEY GIVE HIM PRAISE AND HONOR INSTEAD OF ME. LOOK AT THEIR FACES, AS THEY LIGHT UP AT THE SIGHT AND SOUND OF HE WHO THE WORLD REVERES INSTEAD OF ME, THEIR CREATOR AND GOD. LISTEN TO THEIR EXCITED VOICES, AS THEY SHARE ENTHUSIASM AND DELIGHT TOWARD HE WHO IS LESS THAN THE RESIDENTS IN HEAVEN. WHAT SHALL WE (ALMIGHTY GOD AND BARBARA, HIS BRIDE) DO, MY FAITHFUL DAUGHTER? WHAT SHALL WE DO? I KNOW THAT YOU WILL NEVER LEAVE ME FOR ANOTHER, O FAITHFUL QUEEN OF MY IGNITED THRONE ABOVE! I KNOW THAT I CAN COUNT ON YOUR ALLEGIANCE TO YOUR CREATOR AND GOD. I KNOW THAT YOU WOULD NEVER REVERE ANOTHER OVER ME, IN MY HOLY PRESENCE, FOR YOU ARE THE FAITHFUL ONE. I KNOW OF YOUR GENUINE LOVE FOR ME AND OUR ETERNAL BELOVED ONE. I KNOW THAT YOU WILL NEVER ABANDON ME, FOR YOU ARE MY FAITHFUL ETERNAL BRIDE. HOLD MY WEEPING SPIRIT, MY QUEEN, AS I WEEP AT THE SIGHT BELOW. HOLD MY WEEPING SPIRIT, MY DAUGHTER, AS I HANG MY ESSENCE AT THE SIGHT OF THOSE WHO ARE GIVING PRAISE AND HONOR TO A FELLOW HUMAN INSTEAD OF THEIR ORIGIN AND GOD. HOLD ME, MY DAUGHTER, AS I WEEP!
SEPTEMBER 25, 2015 AT 1:04 AM BY: BARBARA ANN MARY MACK

SHELTER ME FROM THIS PASSING WORLD, MY GOD

BARBARA SPEAKING TO THE LORD

MAY I HIDE WITHIN YOUR REALM OF PURITY AND GRACE AS THIS WORLD PASSES ME, MY GOD? MAY I RELAX WITHIN YOUR ARMS OF COMFORT, AS THIS SINFUL GENERATION PASSES? MAY I ENTER YOUR REALM OF DIVINE ENJOYMENT AS I WITNESS THE PASSING OF THIS TROUBLED WORLD, MY GOD? SHELTER ME, O HEAVENLY HOST AND GOD OF MINE. SHELTER ME FROM THIS PASSING WORLD. FOR I DESIRE TO SEE IT NO MORE. I DESIRE RELIEF FROM THE AGONY AND SIN THAT PERMEATE THIS SINFUL GENERATION, MY LORD. SHELTER ME FROM THOSE WHO LIVE WITH PARTNERS WHOM THEY DID NOT ENTER THE UNION OF HOLY MATRIMONY

ACCORDING TO YOUR VERSION. SHELTER ME FROM THOSE WHO CONTINUE EXHIBITING THE SINS OF RACISM AND RACIAL DISCRIMINATION. SHELTER ME FROM THOSE WHO GOSSIP IN YOUR HOLY PRESENCE, FOR THEY WILL NOT JOIN YOU IN SWEET ETERNAL PARADISE. SHELTER ME FROM THOSE WHO DO NOT SPEAK THE TRUTH, YOUR DIVINE TRUTH. SHELTER ME FROM THOSE WHO INVITE SIN INTO YOUR HOLY CHURCH. SHELTER ME FROM THOSE WHO ABUSE THEMSELVES AND OTHERS THROUGH HARMFUL DRUGS. SHELTER ME FROM THOSE WHO DENY THE DIVINITY OF JESUS, OUR SAVING GOD AND FATHER. SHELTER ME FROM THOSE WHO DENY THE VALIDITY AND REALITY OF DIVINE CREATION. SHELTER ME, O LORD. SHELTER YOUR HUMBLED DAUGHTER (BARBARA) AS I WITNESS THE PASSING OF THIS TROUBLED PERIOD OF TIME.

SEPTEMBER 24, 2015 AT 3:48 PM BY: BARBARA ANN MARY MACK

WHAT SACRIFICES HAVE YOU MADE FOR ME, MY CHILDREN?

ALMIGHTY GOD SPEAKING

I HAVE GIVEN UP MY HEAVENLY ROYAL THRONE FOR YOU WHEN I ENTERED YOU WORLD OF SIN NOT SO LONG AGO. WHAT SACRIFICES HAVE YOU MADE FOR ME, MY CHILDREN? I HAVE GIVEN UP THE SPLENDOR, YES, THE DIVINE SPLENDOR OF CONTINUOUS HEAVENLY BLISS, WHEN I TOOK ON THE FORM OF AN INFANT IN YOUR SINFUL MIDST. WHAT SACRIFICES HAVE YOU MADE FOR ME? MY CHILDREN, YOU WHO MAKE NUMEROUS PRAYER REQUESTS, WHAT HAVE YOU SACRIFICED FOR YOUR CREATOR AND GOD? WHAT SINFUL ACTS HAVE YOU GIVEN UP FOR ME? I HAVE LEFT MY MIGHTY THRONE IN HEAVEN ABOVE FOR A PLACE IN A STABLE. WHAT HAVE YOU LEFT FOR ME? MY CHILDREN, YOU WHOM I HAVE CREATED FROM THE DEPTH OF MY LOVE, WHAT WILL YOU SACRIFICE FOR ME?

SEPTEMBER 24, 2015 AT 5:07 PM BY: BARBARA ANN MARY MACK

I AM FOCUSING ON THE CHOSEN FEW

ALMIGHTY GOD SPEAKING

THESE ARE THE LAST DAYS, THEREFORE, I AM FOCUSING ON THE CHOSEN FEW. I AM FOCUSING ON THOSE WHOSE NAMES ARE WRITTEN IN MY BOOK OF ETERNAL LIFE. I AM FOCUSING ON THE BLESSED AND SANCTIFIED ONES. I AM FOCUSING ON THE WORTHY ONES. I AM FOCUSING ON THE OBEDIENT ONES. I AM FOCUSING ON THE FAITHFUL ONES. I AM FOCUSING ON THOSE WHO REVERE ME ONLY! I AM FOCUSING ON THOSE WHO HAVE GIVEN UP THEIR LIFE AND FREEDOM, FOR THE SAKE OF THE GOSPEL OF MY GOOD NEWS, SAYS THE LORD GOD. I AM FOCUSING ON

THE SPIRITUALLY IGNITED ONES. I WILL NO LONGER FOCUS ON THE WORLD, FOR THEY, THE WORLD, HAVE BETRAYED AND ABANDONED THEIR CREATOR AND GOD, *SAYS THE LORD.*
SEPTEMBER 25, 2015 AT 1:21 AM BY: BARBARA ANN MARY MACK
SENT FRI, SEP 25, 2015 5:12 AM-READ FRI 9/25/2015 1:22 PM

FLEE FROM THE REALM OF DISGUST (SIN), FOR IT DOESN'T REPRESENT GOD'S VERSION OF HOLINESS

BARBARA, GOD'S HOLY PROPHET SPEAKING

I WILL FLEE FROM THE REALM OF DISGUST, FOR IT REPRESENTS EVERYTHING THAT HURTS MY GRACIOUS CREATOR AND HEAVENLY FATHER. I WILL FLEE FROM THE REALM OF DISGUST, FOR IT REVEALS THE PRESENCE OF SATAN AND HIS DEFEATED DISCIPLES. I WILL FLEE FROM THE REALM OF DISGUST, THAT PRODUCES UNSPEAKABLE CRIMES AND ACTS IN THE HOLY EYES AND PRESENCE OF GOD, MY ETERNAL SAVIOR. FLEE WITH ME, MY BROTHERS AND SISTERS! FLEE FROM THE REALM THAT LEADS TO ETERNAL DAMNATION AND DESTRUCTION! FLEE FROM THE REALM THAT OFFENDS ALMIGHTY GOD, FOR HE IS HOLY AND TRUE! FLEE FROM THE REALM THAT INVITES THOSE WHO COMMIT SIN! FLEE FROM THE REALM THAT INVITES THE UNBELIEVERS! FLEE FROM THE REALM THAT MOVES IN THE DIRECTION OF ETERNAL DOOM! FLEE, O WARNED AND LOVED BROTHERS AND SISTERS OF MINE! FLEE FROM THE REALM OF DISGUST, BEFORE GOD'S INVITATION TO ETERNAL LIFE AND GLORY PASSES YOU BY!
SEPTEMBER 26, 2015 AT 4:44 PM BY: BARBARA ANN MARY MACK
SENT SUN, SEP 27, 2015 11:15 PM-READ SUN 9/27/2015 11:44 PM

HIDE ME, O LORD: HIDE ME FROM THIS PASSING WORLD

BARBARA SPEAKING TO THE LORD

HIDE ME, MY GOD. HIDE ME, O MERCIFUL ONE. HIDE ME, O KING OF KINGS AND LORD OF LORDS. HIDE ME, O SAVING HOLY SPOUSE OF MINE: HIDE ME FROM THIS PASSING WORLD. I WEEP, O SAVING ONE. I MOURN, O MERCIFUL ONE. I RELEASE MY INNER TEARS THROUGH THE REALM OF SORROW THAT FOLLOWS MY EMPATHETIC SOUL. I AM YOURS, O MERCIFUL POT OF GOLD. I AM A REFLECTION OF THE SORROW THAT BEARS DOWN YOUR MERCIFUL HEART, AS YOU WITNESS THE PAIN, SUFFERING AND ABUSE, THAT HAVE SUBDUED YOUR LOVED ONES ON EARTH DURING THIS TROUBLED PERIOD OF TIME. HIDE MY WEARY SOUL FROM THE PAIN THAT IS INFLICTED UPON YOUR VULNERABLE FLOCK TODAY. HIDE MY VULNERABLE ESSENCE FROM THE REALITY OF SATAN'S UNHOLY PRESENCE IN THE MIDST OF YOUR VULNERABLE CHILDREN TODAY. HIDE ME FROM THE EXPERIENCE OF FEELING AND SEEING, THE PHYSICAL

AND SPIRITUAL HARM THAT SURROUNDS YOUR INNOCENT LITTLE FLOCK TODAY. HIDE ME, MY LORD. HIDE ME FROM THE PAIN THAT ESCAPES THIS PASSING WORLD.
SEPTEMBER 30, 2015 AT 3:18 PM BY: BARBARA ANN MARY MACK
SENT WED, SEP 30, 2015 10:44 PM-READ THU 10/1/2015 3:33 PM

A FINANCIAL GAIN, BUT A SPIRITUAL LOSS! OH PHILADELPHIA, WHY?

ALMIGHTY GOD SPEAKING TO THOSE WHO HAVE PROFITED OVER A SACRILEGIOUS ACT

YOU WHOSE PURPOSE AND DESIRE WERE TO BENEFIT FINANCIALLY OVER AN APPEARANCE FROM AN EQUALLY FALLIBLE HUMAN, WHAT DID YOU GAIN? WHAT DID YOU LEARN OF ME, DURING THE VISIT FROM HE WHO THE WORLD REVERES? WAS IT THE TRUTH? WAS IT MY HOLY TRUTH? WHAT DID YOU GAIN SPIRITUALLY, MY VERSION OF SPIRITUALITY, O BLINDED AND MISGUIDED ONES? WHAT DID YOU LEARN OF ME, *SAYS THE LORD?* HOW DID YOU BENEFIT SPIRITUALLY FROM THE VISIT OF HE WHO DOES NOT REVEAL MY HOLY TRUTH TO THOSE WHO ARE IN NEED OF MY TRUTH? DID YOU LEARN OF MY HOLY TRUTH, AS YOU EAGERLY WATCHED AND LISTENED TO THE VOICE OF ONE WHO IS FALLIBLE? DID LEARN OF MY HOLY TRUTH, OR ARE YOU STILL IN THE DARK? WHAT HAVE YOU LEARNED THAT WILL BRING YOU CLOSER TO THE ONLY REALM (ALMIGHTY GOD'S HOLY TRUTH) THAT WILL REDEEM YOUR SOULS TODAY? DID YOU EXPERIENCE GOD'S VERSION OF HOLY LOVE, FOR IT IS NOT THE LOVE THAT THE WORLD REVEALS? GOD'S HOLY LOVE REVEALS AND TEACHES HIS SPIRITUALLY BLINDED AND MISGUIDED CHILDREN HIS TRUTH, WHICH HELPS THEM (SINNERS) UNDERSTAND WHAT SINS ARE, AND HOW TO REMOVE ONESELF FROM THE REALM OF SIN AND ETERNAL DESTRUCTION. THIS IS GOD'S VERSION OF DIVINE LOVE, THE ONLY SANCTIFIED WAY TO HIS HOLY CHURCH AND ETERNAL LIFE WITH HIM. GOD'S HOLY CHURCH CANNOT AND DOES NOT ACCEPT THOSE SINNERS WHO DO NOT DESIRE TO CHANGE (BE BORN AGAIN). GOD'S LOVING ARMS ARE OPEN VERY WIDE TO RECEIVE SINNERS WHO DESIRE TO MAKE A CHANGE (BE BORN AGAIN). SOME HAVE SAID AND BELIEVE, WHEN A SMALL GROUP OF PEOPLE SIN THE CHURCH SINS. BUT I, THE LORD, THE FOUNDER AND CREATOR OF MY HOLY CHURCH, CANNOT, CANNOT, CANNOT SIN! FOR I, THE LORD JESUS, THE HOLY ONE, THE HOLY GOD, THE HOLY FOUNDER OF MY CHURCH, CANNOT COMMIT SIN! THOSE WHO PRACTICE SIN WITHOUT THE DESIRE TO CHANGE HAVE SEPARATED THEMSELVES FROM ME AND MY HOLY CHURCH. FOR I, THE LORD, THE ONLY SINLESS ONE, CANNOT AND WILL NOT, BE A PART OF ANYONE WHO PRACTICES SIN. THE CHURCH CANNOT SIN, FOR ITS FOUNDER, JESUS, THE CHRIST, IS WITHOUT SIN. SINNERS COMMIT SINS, NOT, NOT, NOT CHRIST'S HOLY CHURCH!
SEPTEMBER 29, 2015 AT 4:28 PM BY: BARBARA ANN MARY MACK

NO NEED FOR SECURITY OR SECRET SERVICE OFFICERS

BARBARA SPEAKING

JESUS DID NOT NEED THE WORLD'S SECURITY SYSTEM WHEN HE VISITED THE AREAS THAT HIS HEAVENLY FATHER SENT HIM TO. EVEN IN THE MIDST OF TIMES WHEN HIS LIFE, YES, HIS PRECIOUS AND VALUABLE LIFE, WAS IN DANGER, HE DID NOT REQUEST OR NEED SECURITY OR SECRET SERVICE OFFICERS. WHEN THE APOSTLES WERE SENT OUT BY ALMIGHTY GOD, THEY WERE NOT SURROUNDED BY SECURITY OR SECRET SERVICE OFFICERS, THE WORLD'S PROTECTION. WHEN THE PROPHETS OF OLD WERE SENT OUT BY ALMIGHTY GOD, THEY DID NOT HAVE SECURITY GUARDS PROTECTING THEM. TODAY, AS I TRAVEL TO THE MANY PLACES WHERE THE LORD SENDS ME, HIS PROPHET OF TODAY, I DO NOT REQUIRE OR REQUEST THE PRESENCE OF THE WORLD'S SECURITY SYSTEM, FOR I AM ALWAYS PROTECTED BY HE (ALMIGHTY GOD) WHO PROTECTS THOSE WHOM HE SENDS, AT ALL TIMES.
SEPTEMBER 28, 2015 AT 7:45 PM BY: BARBARA ANN MARY MACK

SINFUL ACTS AGAINST ALMIGHTY GOD AND CRIMINAL ACTS AGAINST THE WORLD

BARBARA SPEAKING

MY BROTHERS AND SISTERS, WE ARE HELD ACCOUNTABLE FOR THE SINS THAT WE COMMIT AGAINST ALMIGHTY GOD AND THE CRIMES THAT WE COMMIT AGAINST THE WORLD. WE ARE RESPONSIBLE FOR THE SINFUL ACTS THAT WE PERFORM IN THE PRESENCE OF OUR HOLY GOD, INCLUDING LYING, STEALING AND BEING IN A SEXUAL RELATIONSHIP WITH ONE WHO ISN'T YOUR HOLY SPOUSE. A RELATIONSHIP (MARRIAGE) THAT IS ORDERED AND APPROVED OF BY ALMIGHTY GOD, THE ORIGIN OF HOLY UNIONS, IS WHAT CHRISTIANS STRIVE FOR. WHEN WE STRAY FROM WHAT GOD HAS ORDERED AS BEING HOLY, WE PLACE OURSELVES IN THE REALM OF DISOBEDIENCE AND ARE UNFAITHFUL TO GOD, THE REALM OF PURITY. WE WILL BE HELD ACCOUNTABLE FOR OUR DEEDS, WHETHER THEY ARE "RIGHTEOUS" OR "UNRIGHTEOUS" WHEN JUDGMENT DAY ARRIVES. MY BROTHERS AND SISTERS, YOU WILL BE HELD ACCOUNTABLE FOR YOUR CRIMES THAT ARE PERFORMED AGAINST YOUR FAMILY, FRIENDS, NEIGHBORS AND STRANGERS. YOU ARE HELD ACCOUNTABLE FOR THE CRIMES THAT YOU COMMIT AGAINST THE LAW, THE WORLD'S LAWS. MY BROTHERS AND SISTERS, YOUR SINS AND CRIMINAL ACTIVITIES ARE NOT PARDONED WITHOUT RECTIFICATION. UNDERSTAND THIS, MY BROTHERS AND SISTERS! UNDERSTAND THE CONSEQUENCES BEFORE YOU ACT! IS IT WORTH THE TEMPORARY GRATIFICATIONS? IS YOUR LIFE, YES, YOUR ETERNAL LIFE, WORTH THE TEMPORARY PLEASURES?
OCTOBER 3, 2015 AT 5:18 PM BY: BARBARA ANN MARY MACK

IN THE MIDST OF WORLDLY CHAOS, I SILENTLEY TAKE DOWN YOUR MESSAGES, MY GOD

BARBARA SPEAKING TO THE LORD

I SILENTLY TAKE DOWN YOUR HOLY MESSAGES FOR THIS TROUBLED PERIOD OF TIME, IN THE MIDST OF THE WORLD'S EXCITEMENT OVER HE WHO DOES NOT REVEAL YOUR TRUTH TO THE VULNERABLE AND CONFUSED ONES. IN THE MIDST OF SATAN'S CRUCIAL ATTACKS ON THE COLLEGES AND EDUCATIONAL FACILITIES, I SILENTLY TAKE DOWN YOUR LIFE SAVING MESSAGES FOR THE CALLED AND CHOSEN ONES. IN THE MIDST OF THIS CHAOTIC PERIOD OF TIME, I SILENTLY TAKE DOWN YOUR HOLY MESSAGES AS I WEEP OVER THOSE WHO ARE SLAIN IN THE MIDST OF THEIR SINS. MY LORD, MY HOLY GOD AND SPOUSE, IN THE MIDST OF THE UNDUE EXCITEMENT OVER HE WHO DOES NOT REPRESENT YOU, YOUR HOLY MESSENGER AND PROPHET (BARBARA) IS UNHEARD AND UNSEEN BY THOSE WHO DO NOT KNOW YOU. MY LORD, MY HOLY FATHER AND GOD, HAVE PITY ON THOSE WHO ARE SPIRITUALLY BLINDED AND CONFUSED DURING THIS CHAOTIC PERIOD OF TIME, FOR THEY HAVE BEEN DECEIVED BY THOSE WHO SECRETLY REPRESENT SATAN, OUR ENEMY.
OCTOBER 3, 2015 AT 5:01 PM BY: BARBARA ANN MARY MACK
SENT SAT, OCT 3, 2015 5:35 PM-READ SAT 10/3/2015 6:09 PM

GREETINGS DEAR ONE! COME STA OGGI AMORE? I HAVE TO START MY DIET NOW, SO THAT I WILL BE READY FOR THE HOLIDAYS GOODIES THAT DO NOT SEEM TO PASS ME BY. IT'S HARD TO BELIEVE THAT THANKSGIVING IS NEXT MONTH. I HAVE TO START BUYING THE INGREDIENTS FOR MY STUFFING AND OTHER THINGS THAT WE WILL INCLUDE ON OUR MENU. THIS IS MY FAVORITE TIME OF THE YEAR. I STARTED LISTENING TO CHRISTMAS MUSIC ON YOUTUBE LAST WEEK. I BECOME VERY EXCITED DURING THESE (THANKSGIVING AND CHRISTMAS) HOLIDAYS, BECAUSE I AM CELEBRATING THEM WITH THE LORD, OUR GRACIOUS AND HOLY GOD, FRIENDS, AND MY FAMILY (LA TOYA AND AMYA).
ENJOY YOUR WEEKEND LOVE! *AMORE, BEAUTIFUL BARBIE*
SENT SAT, OCT 3, 2015 5:35 PM-READ SAT 10/3/2015 6:09 PM

THE VASTNESS OF UNENDING ECSTASY, ALMIGHTY GOD, THE ETERNAL ONE

BARBARA SPEAKING TO ALMIGHTY GOD

MY LORD, MY HOLY GOD, I CAN EMBRACE THE VASTNESS OF YOUR REALM OF UNENDING DIVINE ECSTASY, AS I BATHE IN THE REALITY OF YOUR HOLY EXISTENCE THROUGHOUT EACH BLESSED DAY. MY LORD, I WRAP MY ARMS AROUND THE VASTNESS THAT THE WORLD CANNOT HOLD. I WRAP MY ARMS AROUND YOUR HOLY UNENDING ESSENCE. MY LORD, I CAN FEEL YOUR

HOLY PRESENCE WITHIN MY BLESSED ARMS, FOR THEY, MY BLESSED ARMS, DO COMFORT YOU THROUGHOUT EACH DAY. CAN YOU FEEL THE WARMTH OF MY BLESSED ARMS, AS THEY SO LOVINGLY SURROUND YOU, MY GOD? CAN YOU FEEL THE WARMTH OF MY HOLY PRESENCE AS IT ENCOMPASSES GOD, MY ETERNAL SAVIOR? MY LORD, I CAN FEEL THE VASTNESS OF YOUR HOLY PRESENCE, AS IT MOVES WITH GRACE WITHIN THE COMFORTING ARMS OF YOUR CHOSEN MESSENGER AND BRIDE (BARBARA).

OCTOBER 4, 2015 AT 5:30 PM BY: BARBARA ANN MARY MACK

SENT SUN, OCT 4, 2015 7:13 PM-READ SUN 10/4/2015 8:01 PM

DEFENDING THE CHRISTIAN FAITH: DEFENDING CHRIST'S HOLY CHURCH TODAY

BARBARA SPEAKING TO THE LORD JESUS, THE FOUNDER OF THE CHURCH

I WILL DEFEND YOUR HOLY WORK, MY LORD. I WILL DEFEND YOUR HOLY CHURCH TODAY. EVEN IN THE MIDST OF THOSE WHO PERSECUTE ME, I WILL DEFEND THE CHRISTIAN FAITH. I WILL JOIN MY ETERNAL SOUL, WITH THE SOULS OF THOSE WHO HAVE SACRIFICED THEIR PHYSICAL EXISTENCE FOR THE SAKE OF YOUR HOLY CHURCH, MY GOD. I WILL FOREVER SING SONGS OF PRAISE TO YOU, O LORD, AS I REJOICE IN THE MIDST OF YOUR HOLY CHURCH TODAY. LET HEAVEN AND EARTH JOIN YOUR CHOSEN MESSENGER AND BRIDE (BARBARA), AS I DANCE WITH SPIRITUAL JOY IN THE PRESENCE OF JESUS, THE ONLY FOUNDER AND RULER OF HIS HOLY CHURCH, THE CHRISTIAN FAITH.

BARBARA SPEAKING TO HER IGNITED SPIRIT

SING! SING! SING, O IGNITED AND BLESSED SPIRIT OF MINE! SING IN THE MIDST OF HEAVENLY GLORY AS I REVEAL THE GREATNESS OF JESUS, THE ONLY HOLY FOUNDER OF THE CHRISTIAN FAITH!

BARBARA SPEAKING TO CHRISTIANS

COME! MY BROTHERS. COME! MY SISTERS. LET US GIVE PRAISE, GLORY AND HONOR TO THE ONE AND ONLY FOUNDER AND RULER OF THE CHRISTIAN FAITH, THE CHURCH, CHRIST'S HOLY CHURCH! LET US DEFEND THE FAITH THAT CANNOT BE CHANGED OR RULED BY IMPERFECT HUMAN BEINGS! LET US DEFEND THE HOLY GIFT (THE CHRISTIAN FAITH-CHRIST'S HOLY CHURCH) THAT DESCENDED FROM THE GATES OF ALMIGHTY GOD'S GENEROSITY AND DIVINE LOVE. *ALLELUIA!*

OCTOBER 5, 2015 AT 5:06 PM BY: BARBARA ANN MARY MACK

SENT THU, OCT 8, 2015 3:37 PM-READ THU 10/8/2015 4:11 PM

ENJOY THIS BLESSED DAY LOVE! DON'T FORGET TO TAKE YOUR BREAKS. *TI AMO!*

HOW CAN I SHUT MY EYES AND CLOSE MY EARS, TO THE HORRORS THAT FLOW THROUGH THIS TROUBLED PERIOD OF TIME?

BARBARA SPEAKING TO THE LORD GOD

HOW CAN I SHUT MY EYES AND CLOSE MY EARS TO THE HORRORS THAT PERMEATE THIS TROUBLED PERIOD OF TIME? IS THERE HOPE FOR THE LOST ONES, MY LORD? IS THERE HOPE FOR THOSE WHO REFUSE TO ACCEPT THEIR SINS AS CRIMES AGAINST YOU AND THEIR ETERNAL SOULS? IS THERE HOPE FOR THOSE WHO ENJOY THE PLEASURES THAT ARE LEADING THEM TO AND THROUGH THE GATES OF HELL? MY LORD, HELP THEM SEE WITH THEIR HEARTS AND MINDS. HELP THEM UNDERSTAND THE DEPTH OF THEIR UNRIGHTEOUS ACTS. HELP THEM UNDERSTAND WHERE THEIR WRONGFUL ACTS ARE LEADING THEM. HELP THEM TO UNDERSTAND THE DEPTH OF LIVING RIGHTEOUS IN YOUR HOLY EYES. MY LORD, MY HOLY GOD, I CANNOT SHUT MY EYES TO WHAT I CAN SEE, FOR YOU HAVE SHOWN ME THEIR DESTINATION. YOU HAVE SHOWN ME THEIR ETERNAL DEATH. I CANNOT SHUT MY EARS TO THEIR CRIES. I CAN HEAR THEIR ETERNAL CRIES. I CAN HEAR THE SOUNDS THAT ARE RELEASED FROM THE ETERNAL SOULS OF THOSE WHO REFUSED TO HEED YOUR WARNINGS BEFORE THEIR PHYSICAL DEATHS. I CAN HEAR THEM, MY LORD. HOW CAN I SHUT MY EARS? YOU, MY GOD, ARE JUST AND HOLY. YOU MY LORD, HAVE GIVEN THE UNRIGHTEOUS ONES PLENTY OF TIME TO CORRECT THEIR UNHOLY LIVES. THEY HAVE NOT CHANGED, MY LORD. THEY DO NOT DESIRE TO CHANGE. THEY HAVE BECOME QUITE COMFORTABLE IN THE MIDST OF THEIR SINFUL WAYS. I WILL NO LONGER WEEP FOR THEM, MY GOD. I WILL WEEP FOR THOSE WHOM YOU DEEM WORTHY AND CHOSEN, FOR THEY ARE THE BLESSED ONES.
OCTOBER 5, 2015 AT 2:17 PM BY: BARBARA ANN MARY MACK

JUST ONE DAY AWAY FROM THE WORLD

BARBARA SPEAKING

OH THE JOY! YES! THE DIVINE JOY THAT ENCOMPASSES MY CONTENTED ESSENCE, AS I ENJOY ONE BLESSED DAY AWAY FROM THIS WORLD, THIS PASSING WORLD. OH, THE DIVINE ECSTASY AND HEAVEN SENT BLISS THAT ACCOMPANY THE REALM OF PEACE, AS I RELAX WITHIN THE REALM (ALMIGHTY GOD) THAT SHELTERS ME FROM THIS PASSING WORLD FOR ONE GLORIOUS DAY. THE DIVINE TRANQUILITY THAT SURROUNDS MY SATISFIED SOUL PLACES A SMILE UPON MY BLESSED SPIRIT, AS I ENJOY ONE DAY AWAY, AWAY, AWAY FROM THIS PASSING WORLD. LIFT UP MY WEARY ESSENCE, MY LORD, IF ONLY FOR A BRIEF TIME, AS I ENJOY THE GIFT OF BEING AWAY FROM THE WORLD FOR JUST ONE DAY.
OCTOBER 11, 2015 AT 2:19 PM BY: BARBARA ANN MARY MACK

SENT SUN, OCT 11, 2015 2:59 PM-READ SUN 10/11/2015 5:20 PM

MY CHILDREN, FIGHT SATAN, THE ORIGIN OF DEPRESSION

ALMIGHTY GOD SPEAKING

MY CHILDREN, IN ORDER TO FIGHT SATAN, THE ORIGIN AND REALM OF DEPRESSION, YOU MUST THINK OF ME AND MY REALM OF HOLINESS. YOU MUST DWELL WITHIN MY REALM OF HOLINESS, SO THAT YOU MAY COMBAT AND CONQUER THE REALM OF DEPRESSION (SATAN). MY CHILDREN, YOU MUST SING SONGS OF PRAISE AND JOY UNTO ME, SO THAT THE REALM OF DEPRESSION (SATAN) WILL LEAVE YOUR VULNERABLE REALM (MIND). IN ORDER TO COMBAT AND DEFEAT DEPRESSION (SATAN), YOU MUST THINK OF GOOD AND HOLY THOUGHTS AT ALL TIMES. MY CHILDREN, FLEE TO ME WHEN THE REALM OF DEPRESSION (SATAN) ENTERS YOUR REALM OF PEACE. CALL OUT TO ME, YOUR ONLY SAVING GOD, WHEN THE REALM OF DEPRESSION OVER POWERS YOUR PEACEFUL THOUGHTS. FIGHT THE REALM OF DEPRESSION WITH MY WEAPONS OF DIVINE JOY AND HAPPINESS. FLEE FROM THE REALM OF DEPRESSION AS YOU CALL OUT TO ME. CALL OUT TO ME, MY CHILDREN, AND I WILL SEND A FRIEND TO HELP YOU COMBAT SATAN WITH THE POWER OF MY DIVINE LOVE AND JOY, THAT COMES FROM MY HEAVENLY REALM OF MENTAL PEACE AND JOY. MY CHILDREN, LET US COMBAT SATAN (DEPRESSION) WITH MY TOOLS OF HOLY LOVE AND JOY. THEN SATAN, THE UNWANTED REALM OF DEPRESSION, WILL FLEE FROM YOU. MY CHILDREN, THINK OF ME AND MY REALM OF GOODNESS AT ALL TIMES, SO THAT THE REALM OF DEPRESSION (SATAN) WILL NOT TAKE OVER YOUR VULNERABLE MIND. FOR I, THE LORD, YOUR HOLY AND FAITHFUL GOD, WILL FIGHT SATAN, THE REALM OF DEPRESSION, WITH YOU.
OCTOBER 18, 2015 AT 9:32 AM BY: BARBARA ANN MARY MACK

GREETINGS ARCHBISHOP CRAIG! BEFORE GETTING OUT OF BED YESTERDAY, THE LORD GAVE ME TWO PASSAGES TO PLACE IN MY FORTHCOMING **BOOK** (THE PRESENT TESTAMENT VOLUME NINE) AND SOMETHING PERTAINING TO THOSE WHO WERE BEHEADED FOR THE SAKE OF THE GOSPEL OF JESUS CHRIST. AFTER FOCUSING ON THE LATTER, I RECALLED READING SOMETHING IN THE BOOK OF REVELATION CONCERNING THE SOULS OF THOSE WHO WERE BEHEADED. LATER, I WENT ON LINE IN SEARCH OF THE EXCERPT PERTAINING TO THE SOULS OF THOSE WHO WERE BEHEADED. DURING MY SEARCH, I CAME ACROSS AN ARTICLE PERTAINING TO BEHEADINGS. BELOW IS THE ARTICLE AND THE PASSAGE FROM REVELATION 20:4 AND REVELATION 20:1-16. I FIND THIS VERY INTERESTING.
SENT MON, OCT 19, 2015 1:36 AM-READ MON 10/19/2015 11:31 AM

YOU TAKE VERY GOOD CARE OF YOUR CHILDREN, MY LORD

BARBARA SPEAKING TO ALMIGHTY GOD

MY LORD, YOU HAVE TAUGHT US SO MUCH THROUGH THE REALM OF TIME. IN THE BEGINNING, YOU GAVE US (HUMAN BEINGS) COVERING FOR OUR BODIES WHEN WE LEARNED THAT WE WERE NAKED. YOU TAUGHT US THE DIFFERENCE BETWEEN GOOD AND EVIL, OBEDIENCE AND DISOBEDIENCE, AND YOUR POSITION AS GOD, OUR CREATOR AND ORIGIN. YOU TAUGHT US HOW TO CARE FOR ONE ANOTHER. YOU PROVIDED FOOD FOR US. YOU TAUGHT US HOW TO COOK. YOU TAUGHT US HOW TO HUNT FOR SURVIVAL SAKE. YOU TAUGHT SOME OF US (THOSE OF THE MEDICAL FIELD) HOW TO CARE FOR YOUR CHILDREN WHEN WE BECOME SICK. YOU GIVE MANKIND KNOWLEDGE WHICH ENABLES THEM TO TREAT ILLNESSES THAT REQUIRE SPECIAL CARE. YOU, O HEAVENLY FATHER, PROVIDE FOR US AT ALL TIMES. YOU HAVE GIVEN US VEGETATION. YOU HAVE GIVEN US EVERYTHING THAT WE NEED IN ORDER TO SURVIVE. YOU, O HEAVENLY FATHER, HAVE PROVIDED FOR YOUR LOVED ONES THROUGH THE YEARS. WE ARE TRULY GRATEFUL FOR YOUR GENEROSITY. MY LORD, BECAUSE THE REALM OF EVIL (SATAN) SLITHERS IN OUR BLESSED MIDST TODAY, AS HE DID IN THE BEGINNING, WHEN HE DECEIVED OUR FOREMOTHER (EVE), HE CAUSES MUCH HARDSHIP FOR MANKIND. SATAN'S "UNHOLY PRESENCE" IS VERY VISIBLE TODAY, AS IT HAS BEEN SINCE THE REALM OF DISOBEDIENCE CAPTURED HUMAN BEINGS. IN THE MIDST OF SATAN'S "UNHOLY WORKS", ALMIGHTY GOD CONTINUES PROVIDING FOR HIS LOVED ONES. HIS HOLY PRESENCE AND GREAT WORKS STILL OUTSHINE SATAN'S CONTINUOUS ABUSE AND DIRTY DEEDS. O HOLY GOD AND FATHER OF MINE, I WILL RECEIVE THE TEACHINGS, YES, THE VALUABLE AND HOLY TEACHINGS, THAT DESCEND FROM YOUR UNENDING REALM OF GENEROSITY AND LOVE. LET ALL REJOICE! AS YOU, OUR HOLY TEACHER, REVEAL TO US EVERYTHING THAT WE NEED TO KNOW IN ORDER TO SURVIVE IN THE MIDST OF THIS TERRIBLE PERIOD OF TIME.
OCTOBER 22, 2015 AT 5:05 AM BY: BARBARA ANN MARY MACK
SENT THU, OCT 22, 2015 5:17 PM-READ THU 10/22/2015 6:13 PM

FOLLOW MY FLOWING TEARS: WHERE ARE THEY HEADING, SAYS THE LORD?

ALMIGHTY GOD SPEAKING

FOLLOW MY FLOWING TEARS AS THEY SEEK AND OBSERVE THE ACTS OF THOSE WHO DO NOT DESIRE TO CHANGE. FOLLOW MY HOLY TEARS AS THEY OBSERVE THOSE WHO DO NOT BELIEVE IN MY HOLY TRUTH AND DIVINE JUSTICE (PUNISHMENT). FOLLOW MY HOLY TEARS AS THEY HEAD IN THE DIRECTION OF JUDGMENT DAY. FOLLOW MY HOLY TEARS AS THEY REVEAL THE DESTINATION OF THOSE WHO DID NOT BELIEVE IN MY UNCHANGING WORD. FOLLOW MY HOLY TEARS AS THEY WITNESS THE DESTINATION OF THOSE WHO CONTINUED IN THEIR UNHOLY ACTS UNTIL THEIR PHYSICAL DEATHS. FOLLOW MY HOLY TEARS AS THEY SIT ON MY THRONE OF

JUSTICE. FOLLOW MY HOLY TEARS AS THEY JOIN THE TEARS OF MY FAITHFUL MESSENGERS. FOLLOW MY HOLY TEARS AS THEY JOIN MY HEAVENLY CHOIRS. FOLLOW MY HOLY TEARS AS THEY JOIN THE ETERNAL RESIDENTS OF MY HEAVENLY HOME. FOLLOW MY HOLY TEARS AS I WITNESS THE UNRIGHTEOUS ONES ENTRANCE THROUGH THE GATES OF ETERNAL DAMNATION AND DOOM. FOLLOW MY HOLY TEARS, FOR THEY ARE MANY, *SAYS THE LORD.*
OCTOBER 24, 2015 AT 11:24 AM BY: BARBARA ANN MARY MACK

EVEN IN THE MIDST OF MY MANY TEARS AND FEARS, I CANNOT STOP

BARBARA SPEAKING

IN THE MIDST OF MY MANY TEARS AND FEARS, I CANNOT STOP PERFORMING THE DUTIES AND PRIVILEGE OF ALMIGHTY GOD'S SENT MESSENGER AND BRIDE. IN THE MIDST OF MY DIVINE ASSIGNMENT OF LOVE, I CANNOT SHUT OUT THE HEAVEN SENT MESSAGES THAT I RECEIVE FROM OUR CREATOR AND GOD. IN THE MIDST OF AGONY AND PAIN, I CANNOT CEASE THE MISSION THAT I WAS SENT TO CARRY OUT. IN THE MIDST OF MY MANY PHYSICAL AND SPIRITUAL TEARS, I CANNOT DISOBEY THE HOLY VOICE THAT CALLS OUT TO ME THROUGHOUT EACH DAY. MY LORD, MY HOLY GOD, THE DIVINE ASSIGNMENT OF LOVE THAT YOU HAVE BESTOWED UPON ME, YOUR FAITHFUL MESSENGER AND BRIDE, HAS CAUSED MANY TEARS AND FEARS. HELP ME! O LORD, FOR THE FEARS AND TEARS ARE MANY. HELP ME PROCEED IN THE DIVINE ASSIGNMENT THAT DESCENDED WITH ME NOT SO LONG AGO. IN THE MIDST OF MY MANY TEARS AND FEARS, WILL YOU ENCOMPASS ME, YOUR FAITHFUL AND DEVOTED MESSENGER AND BRIDE, WITH YOUR REALM OF DIVINE STRENGTH AND COURAGE? FOR I CANNOT STOP FOLLOWING YOUR HOLY WILL?
OCTOBER 26, 2015 AT 12:06 AM BY: BARBARA ANN MARY MACK
SENT WED, OCT 28, 2015 12:54 AM-READ WED 10/28/2015 10:14 AM

WHAT IS YOUR HOLY WILL, MY LORD?

BARBARA SPEAKING TO THE LORD GOD

I WILL FOLLOW AND OBEY YOUR HOLY WILL, MY GOD, FOR IT WILL LEAD ME IN THE DIRECTION OF SWEET PARADISE AND HEAVENLY BLISS. IT, YOUR HOLY WILL, HAS LED ME TO THE REALM OF DIVINE PEACE, THAT ENCOMPASSES THE BEING OF CRAIG, OUR ETERNAL BELOVED ONE. YOUR HOLY WILL HAS LED ME TO THE REALM THAT HOUSES YOUR CALLED AND CHOSEN ONES. YOUR HOLY WILL HAS ENCOMPASSED ME WITH THE DIVINE COURAGE, TO COMBAT THE GATES OF HELL FOR THE ETERNAL AND WELL-LOVED SOUL OF CRAIG, OUR ETERNAL BELOVED ONE. YOUR HOLY WILL, MY GOD, HAS LED ME TO THE AREAS OF THE WORLD WHERE YOUR

VULNERABLE ONES WERE IN NEED OF YOUR TANGIBLE PRESENCE. YOUR HOLY WILL AND WAY GUIDE ME IN THE DIRECTION OF THE REALM OF ENDLESS PRAISE UNTO YOU. YOUR HOLY, PERFECT AND UNCHANGING WILL GUIDES MY HUMBLED ESSENCE IN THE DIRECTION THAT CAPTURES THOSE WHO DESIRE SALVATION THROUGH CHRIST JESUS. MY HOLY UNCHANGING GOD, I BOW IN THE MIDST OF YOUR DIVINITY, AS I LIFT MY OBEDIENT ESSENCE IN YOUR PRESENCE THROUGHOUT EACH DAY. *ALLELUIA!* O HOLY WILL. *ALLELUIA!!!*

OCTOBER 23, 2015 AT 3:23 PM BY: BARBARA ANN MARY MACK

IT'S NOT EVEN A CHALLENGE, SAYS THE LORD

ALMIGHTY GOD SPEAKING

MY CHILDREN, THE BATTLE BETWEEN SATAN AND ME IS NOT A CHALLENGE AT ALL, FOR THE VICTORY WAS MINE BEFORE THE BATTLE BEGAN. I, THE LORD ALMIGHTY, HAVE DEFEATED SATAN, MY ENEMY, BEFORE THIS SPIRITUAL BATTLE BEGAN NOT SO LONG AGO. MY VICTORIOUS FAITHFUL AND OBEDIENT ONES AND I, CONTINUE THIS VICTORIOUS BATTLE BETWEEN GOOD AND EVIL, THE RIGHTEOUS AND THE UNRIGHTEOUS, THE FAITHFUL AND THE UNFAITHFUL, THE WINNERS (ALMIGHTY GOD AND THOSE WHO LIVE HOLY LIVES) AND THE LOSERS (SATAN AND THOSE WHO LIVE IN SIN WITHOUT THE DESIRE OR EFFORT TO CHANGE). MY FAITHFUL WARRIORS, I KNOW THAT THIS BATTLE IS VERY TOUGH AND PAINFUL, BUT OUR VICTORY CELEBRATION IS COMING VERY SOON! HOLD ON, FOR THE BATTLE IS COMING TO A GLORIOUS END. YOU MAY BEGIN PUTTING ON YOUR CELEBRATION HATS! YOU MAY BEGIN YOUR SHOUTS OF TRIUMPH AND JOY! YOU MAY DANCE THE DANCE OF VICTORY, FOR OUR CELEBRATION HAS BEGUN! REJOICE! O VICTORIOUS ONES. SING YOUR CONTINUOUS SONGS OF PRAISE! FOR WE HAVE FOUGHT THE FIGHT THAT PUT AN END TO SATAN, THE DEFEATED DESTROYER OF GOOD AND RIGHTEOUSNESS. WE HAVE DEFEATED HE (SATAN) WHO HAS BROUGHT INTO EXISTENCE, THE REALM THAT PRODUCES EVIL AND DEATH. REJOICE, DEAR CHILDREN OF MINE! FOR THE GATES OF HELL HAVE RECEIVED ITS PERMANENT DEFEATED RESIDENTS (SATAN AND HIS FOLLOWERS)! THE VICTORIOUS BATTLE IS OVER! *ALLELUIA!*

NOVEMBER 3, 2015 AT 2:17 AM BY: BARBARA ANN MARY MACK

SENT TUE, NOV 3, 2015 12:26 PM-READ TUE 11/3/2015 1:08 PM

I CANNOT BE CONTAINED WITHIN A BUILDING, SAYS THE LORD

ALMIGHTY GOD SPEAKING

YOU WHO TRY TO CONTAIN ME WITHIN LIMITED SURROUNDINGS, LISTEN TO ME, FOR I, THE LORD, THE BOUNDARYLESS ONE, CANNOT BE CONTAINED! YOU CANNOT PLACE LIMITATIONS

ON MY ENDLESS ESSENCE. FOR I, THE LORD GOD, CANNOT BE CONTAINED, NOR BOUND WITHIN LIMITED QUARTERS. DO NOT TRY TO CONTAIN ME, FOR I, THE LORD GOD, CANNOT BE CONTAINED IN A BUILDING OR SINGLE LOCATION. LOOK AROUND, MY CHILDREN, FOR I, THE LORD, AM EVERYWHERE! I AM OMNIPRESENT AND OMNIPOTENT! I CANNOT BE CONTAINED! SEARCH THE HEAVENS! SEARCH THE SKIES! SEARCH THE MEADOWS! SEARCH THE STREAMS! SEARCH THE HEARTS AND BEINGS OF THE LIVING ONES, FOR THERE, YOU WILL FIND ME, THE BOUNDARYLESS ONE!

NOVEMBER 4, 2015 AT 11:03 AM BY: BARBARA ANN MARY MACK

LET US GO FOR A WALK TODAY, LORD JESUS

BARBARA SPEAKING TO THE LORD JESUS (ALMIGHTY GOD)

LET YOU AND I GO FOR A BRIEF WALK TODAY, LORD JESUS. LET YOU AND I WALK THROUGH THE SPIRITUAL MEADOWS THAT REVEAL YOUR HOLY PRESENCE IN OUR BLESSED MIDST TODAY. LET YOU AND I SMELL THE LILIES AS THEY BLOOM IN YOUR HOLY PRESENCE TODAY. LET YOU AND I ENJOY THE GIFT OF LIFE AS WE ROAM IN THE MIDST OF DIVINITY ON EARTH. LET YOU AND I ENJOY THE DIVINE PLEASURES (PEACE, JOY, UNENDING SPIRITUAL BLISS), AS YOU RELEASE THEM IN OUR MIDST. LET US WALK IN THE MIDST OF THE FIELDS THAT PRODUCE THE SWEETNESS OF YOUR DIVINE WORDS OF LIFE. LET YOU AND I ENJOY THE HEAVENLY BLISS THAT SURROUNDS THE HOLY THRONE OF GOD, OUR FATHER. I WILL HOLD ON TO YOUR HOLY ESSENCE LORD JESUS, AS YOU AND I WALK THIS TROUBLED PERIOD OF TIME. I WILL CLING TO THE HOLY ESSENCE OF MY SAVING GOD, AS YOU AND I WALK THROUGH THIS DEVASTATING PERIOD OF TIME, MY GOD. HOLD ME TIGHT, MY HOLY GOD, AS WE WALK AS ONE ESSENCE IN THE MIDST OF THIS CRUCIAL PERIOD OF TIME. FOR YOU ARE MY REALM OF COMFORT AND COURAGE. YOU ARE MY HOLY STRENGTH AND BREAD OF LIFE. I WILL WALK WITH THE HOLY ESSENCE (ALMIGHTY GOD) THAT FORMED ME NOT SO LONG AGO. I WILL WALK WITH THE HOLY ESSENCE (ALMIGHTY GOD) THAT NOURISHES ME DAILY WITH HIS ETERNAL BREAD OF LIFE. I WILL WALK WITH YOU LORD GOD, SO THAT I WILL ALWAYS BE CLOSE TO MY LIFE AND MY LOVE (ALMIGHTY GOD).

NOVEMBER 5, 2015 4:49 PM BY: BARBARA ANN MARY MACK

SENT SAT, NOV 7, 2015 6:14 PM-READ SAT 11/7/2015 10:00 PM

ENJOY THIS BLESSED DAY DEAR ARCHBISHOP! BELOW ARE A FEW GOD DICTATED PASSAGES. TI AMO, BELLA BARBARA

IS MY MISSION IN VAIN? WHAT HAVE YOU LEARNED FROM MY HOLY PRESENCE IN YOUR MIDST TODAY, SAYS THE LORD?

ALMIGHTY GOD SPEAKING

MY CHILDREN, I HAVE ENTERED YOUR NEEDY REALM AGAIN IN THE FORM OF BARBARA, MY MESSENGER AND BRIDE. I HAVE ENTERED YOUR NEEDY REALM AGAIN IN A FORM THAT YOU CAN SEE AND TOUCH. A FORM THAT YOU CAN COMMUNICATE WITH DAILY. A FORM WHICH I HAVE PURIFIED AND BLESSED WITH THE PRESENCE OF THE HOLY TRINITY. I HAVE DEEMED THIS GENERATION WORTHY TO EXPERIENCE THE DEPTH OF MY HOLY LOVE AND PRESENCE, THROUGH THE HUMBLED BEING OF MY MESSENGER AND BRIDE. MY CHILDREN, I ASK YOU, WHAT HAVE YOU LEARNED FROM MY HOLY PRESENCE, WHICH IS REVEALED AND CONVEYED THROUGH MY PRESENT DAY MESSENGER AND SCRIBE? WHAT HAVE YOU LEARNED OF ME, MY CHILDREN? IS MY MISSION IN VAIN? I LOOK AT YOU THROUGH THE HUMBLED ESSENCE OF MY MESSENGER, AND I QUESTION YOU. I ASK YOU, WHAT HAVE YOU LEARNED OF MY DIVINE REALM, MY CHILDREN? YOUR ACTS CONVEY THAT YOU HAVE LEARNED AND UNDERSTOOD VERY LITTLE. YOU ARE QUICK TO POINT OUT AND MENTION THE SINS OF YOUR BROTHERS AND SISTERS, BUT REFUSE TO ACKNOWLEDGE YOUR OWN SHORT COMINGS. MY CHILDREN, WHAT HAVE YOU LEARNED FROM SHE (BARBARA) WHO HAS CONVEYED MY UNCHANGING WAY AND WORD? WHAT HAVE YOU LEARNED, IN REGARDS TO LIVING HOLY IN THE PRESENCE OF THOSE WHO DO NOT KNOW OR ACCEPT ME (THE DIVINE CREATOR)? WHAT HAVE YOU LEARNED FROM MY REALM OF COMPASSION AND GENEROSITY? DO YOU SHOW DIVINE COMPASSION AND GENEROSITY TOWARD YOUR FAMILY, FRIENDS, ACQUAINTANCES AND STRANGERS? DO YOU EXHIBIT MY VERSION OF HOLY LOVE, PATIENCE AND FORGIVENESS, MY CHILDREN? WHAT HAVE YOU LEARNED FROM MY HOLY PRESENCE IN YOUR MIDST TODAY? DO YOU TRULY BELIEVE THAT I AM IN YOUR MIDST TODAY, MY CHILDREN? YOUR ACTS CONVEY THE OPPOSITE, MY CHILDREN. YOUR UNHOLY ACTS CONVEY YOUR LACK OF BELIEF IN MY HOLY PRESENCE AND WORD IN YOUR MIDST TODAY. MY CHILDREN, BELIEVE THIS, I HAVE NEVER LEFT YOUR SIGHT. I, THE OMNIPRESENT ONE, THE ONLY OMNIPRESENT ONE, HAVE NEVER LEFT YOUR REALM. I KNOW OF YOUR WORKS, WHETHER THEY ARE RIGHTEOUS OR UNRIGHTEOUS. I KNOW IT ALL! MY CHILDREN, WHAT HAVE YOU LEARNED FROM ME? IS MY MISSION IN VAIN?
NOVEMBER 8, 2015 AT 6:08 PM BY: BARBARA ANN MARY MACK

THOSE WHO ANTICIPATE ETERNAL GLORY WITH ME

ALMIGHTY GOD SPEAKING

MY CHILDREN, I KNOW OF THOSE WHO ANTICIPATE SPENDING ETERNAL GLORY WITH ME AND MY FAITHFUL HEAVENLY RESIDENTS. I KNOW OF THOSE WHO HAVE BEEN FAITHFUL TO ME AND MY REALM OF HOLINESS. I KNOW THE INTEGRITY OF THOSE WHO SPEAK OF SPENDING ETERNITY WITH GOD, THEIR SAVIOR. I KNOW OF THOSE WHO EXHIBIT THE GIFT OF AUTHENTIC

HOLY LOVE FOR ME AND MY GREAT CREATION (HUMAN BEINGS). I KNOW THE HEARTS OF THOSE WHO DELIVER MY HOLY WORDS TO THOSE WHO ARE IN NEED OF SPIRITUAL AND HOLY EXCITEMENT IN THEIR LIVES TODAY. I KNOW OF THE HOPE THAT PERMEATE THE SOULS OF THE BELIEVING ONES. I KNOW OF THE GIFT OF LIFE THAT EMITS FROM THOSE WHO APPRECIATE GOD, THE ORIGIN OF LIFE. I KNOW, MY CHILDREN! I KNOW, O WORTHY ONES! I KNOW, O INVITED GUESTS OF MY SUPPER OF LOVE! I KNOW HOW MUCH YOU ANTICIPATE SPENDING ETERNITY WITH ME! REJOICE! O ANTICIPATING ONES. REJOICE! O CHOSEN AND BELOVED GUESTS OF MINE. REJOICE! REJOICE! REJOICE, AS YOU ENTER MY DIVINE KINGDOM OF ETERNAL LOVE AND HEAVENLY BLISS! REJOICE, FOR YOU HAVE ENTERED GLORY (ALMIGHTY GOD)!!!

NOVEMBER 11, 2015 AT 7:17 PM BY: BARBARA ANN MARY MACK

I WILL UNITE MY PAIN WITH THE ABUSED AND HURTING LITTLE ONES

BARBARA SPEAKING TO ALMIGHTY GOD

THE PAIN THAT WAS RELEASED BY SATAN'S REALM OF MISERY AND SUFFERING, HAS ENGULFED THE ESSENCE OF GOD'S ABUSED AND HURTING ONES. MY LORD, MY HOLY GOD, I WILL UNITE MY PAIN WITH THE SUFFERING THAT ENCOMPASSES YOUR ABUSED AND HURTING LITTLE CHILDREN. FOR THEIR SOULS CRY OUT TO YOU DAILY. I WILL UNITE MY PAIN WITH THOSE WHO HAVE BEEN ABUSED BY STRANGERS. I WILL UNITE MY CONTINUOUS PAIN, WITH AGONY THAT CRIES OUT FROM THE WOUNDS, YES, THE MANY, MANY WOUNDS THAT SURROUND THE SOULS OF YOUR ABUSED LITTLE ONES. MY LORD, OUR (BARBARA AND GOD'S ABUSED AND HURTING LITTLE CHILDREN) AGONY HAS REACHED THE EARS OF HE, AND ONLY HE, WHO CAN RELEASE THE WEAPON THAT WILL PUT AN END TO THE SOURCE (SATAN) OF OUR CONTINUOUS MISERY. MY LORD, SATAN CONTINUES SENDING HIS EVIL ANGELS OUT TO ABUSE, AND CAUSE GREAT AGONY TO YOUR VULNERABLE LITTLE CHILDREN. WEEP WITH US, MY LORD, AS I UNITE MY TEARS WITH THE CONTINUOUS TEARS THAT FALL FROM THE SOULS OF YOUR ABUSED AND HURTING LITTLE ONES. WEEP WITH US, O LORD, SO THAT WE MAY JOIN THE HOLY TEARS THAT OFFER COMFORT AND REFUGE. WEEP WITH YOUR HURTING LITTLE ONES, AS I UNITE MY WOUNDED ESSENCE WITH THEIRS. MY LORD, LET THE MIGHTY TEARS THAT FALL FROM OUR FUSED ESSENCE ENCOMPASS THOSE WHOM YOU HAVE WELCOMED INTO YOUR HOLY GATES ABOVE. MY LORD, LET OUR FUSED TEARS INVITE THE FLOWING TEARS OF YOUR WOUNDED LITTLE ONES, FOR THEY ARE MANY. LET US INVITE THEM INTO OUR REALM OF CONTENTMENT AND CONTINUOUS PEACE, FOR WE (ALMIGHTY GOD, BARBARA, AND GOD'S ABUSED LITTLE ONES) ARE THE ABUSED AND HURTING ONES.

NOVEMBER 11, 2015 AT 3:42 AM BY: BARBARA ANN MARY MACK

SENT WED, NOV 11, 2015 11:48 PM-READ THU 11/12/2015

GREETINGS ARCHBISHOP CRAIG! COME STA OGGI AMORE? I PRAY THAT YOU HAVE GOTTEN OVER THE BRONCHITIS AND ARE FEELING BETTER. LA TOYA AND I ARE EN ROUTE TO GET MY MONTHLY B12 INJECTION AND DO A LITTLE PRE-THANKSGIVING DAY SHOPPING. HOPEFULLY WE DO NOT HAVE TO WAIT LONG AT THE DOCTOR'S OFFICE FOR THE B12. A REMINDER! PLEASE TAKE VERY GOOD CARE OF YOUR VALUABLE, VALUABLE, VALUABLE AND WELL-LOVED SELF. TI AMO, BELLA BARBARA
SENT WED, NOV 11, 2015 11:48 PM-READ THU 11/12/2015

THE NEED OF HUMAN WARMTH AND AFFECTION

ALMIGHTY GOD SPEAKING

MY CHILDREN, THE NEED FOR HUMAN LOVE, WARMTH, COMPASSION AND BLISS, DESCENDED FROM MY REALM OF PURE AND HOLY AFFECTION. EXHIBIT MY VERSION OF HOLY LOVE AS YOU MINGLE WITH THOSE WHOM I HAVE JOINED YOU WITH. EXHIBIT THE WARMTH THAT YOU HAVE RECEIVED FROM ME. MY CHILDREN, RECEIVE AND EXHIBIT THE WARMTH THAT DESCENDS FROM MY REALM OF GENEROSITY AND HOLY LOVE. DO NOT FLEE FROM THE WARMTH THAT DESCENDS FROM ME, MY CHILDREN. DO NOT REJECT OR REFUSE THAT WHICH I DEEM AS HOLY. FOR I AM THE ORIGIN OF HUMAN WARMTH AND PHYSICAL AFFECTION BETWEEN MAN AND WOMAN. EXHIBIT YOUR LOVE IN A MANNER WHICH PLEASES HIM OR HER WHOM I HAVE PLACED IN YOUR REALM OF PHYSICAL AND SPIRITUAL LOVE. EXHIBIT THE UNION THAT DESCENDS FROM YOUR CREATOR AND ORIGIN, MY CHILDREN. FOR EVERYTHING THAT COMES FROM ME IS HOLY AND PURE. EXHIBIT IT! MY SONS. EXHIBIT IT! MY DAUGHTERS. EXHIBIT THE DIVINE WARMTH THAT CAME FROM ME! NOVEMBER 9, 2015 AT 6:19 PM BY: BARBARA ANN MARY MACK

WORLDLY FAME AND FORTUNES DO NOT SATISFY NOR QUENCH THE SOUL

ALMIGHTY GOD (JESUS) SPEAKING

WORLDLY FAME AND FORTUNE CANNOT SATISFY NOR QUENCH YOUR SOULS, MY CHILDREN. THE FAME AND FORTUNES WHICH THE WORLD HOLD SO HIGHLY, CANNOT AND DO NOT SATISFY YOUR SOULS. IF THEY DID, ONE WOULD NOT DESTROY ONESELF BY WAY OF SUICIDE, DRUG ABUSE, OR SELF-DESTRUCTION. MY LITTLE CHILDREN, DO NOT SEEK THAT WHICH CANNOT SATISFY NOR QUENCH YOUR SPIRITUAL AND PHYSICAL DESIRES. DO NOT SEEK THE THINGS THAT OFFER TEMPORARY SATISFACTION. DO NOT SEEK THE THINGS THAT CAUSE HARM AND UNPLEASANT SITUATIONS. DO NOT SEEK THE THINGS THAT RESULT IN HARM TO YOURSELVES AND THOSE WHOM YOU LOVE. MY CHILDREN, SEEK THE THINGS THAT ARE HOLY, TRUE AND EVERLASTING. SEEK THE THINGS THAT BRING PEACE AND CONTENTMENT. SEEK THE THINGS

THAT COME FROM MY REALM OF HOLINESS AND EVERLASTING BLISS! SEEK THE THINGS THAT PERMIT YOU TO WALK WITH YOUR ESSENCE HELD HIGH! SEEK THE THINGS THAT BRING ABOUT GOOD AND HOLY DEEDS! SEEK THE THINGS THAT QUENCH AND SATISFY ONE WHO IS WALKING IN THE DIRECTION OF ETERNAL LIFE WITH GOD, THEIR SAVIOR! SEEK MY HOLY REALM OF PEACE! SEEK MY HOLY REALM OF COMPASSION! SEEK MY HOLY REALM OF MERCY! SEEK MY HOLY REALM THAT GIVES YOU THE STRENGTH AND COURAGE TO FORGIVE THOSE WHO HAVE CAUSED YOU GREAT GRIEF AND SUFFERING! MY CHILDREN, SEEK THE ONLY ONE WHO CAN SAVE YOUR ETERNAL SOUL! SEEK ME, YOUR PLACE OF REFUGE! SEEK ME, YOUR ETERNAL LIGHT IN THIS WORLD OF DARKNESS! SEEK ME, YOUR BREAD OF LIFE! SEEK ME, GOD, THE FATHER'S ONLY BEGOTTEN SON! FOR I CAN, AND WILL QUENCH AND SATISFY YOUR EVERY DESIRE AND NEED!

NOVEMBER 9, 2015 AT 7:01 PM BY: BARBARA ANN MARY MACK

ALLEGIANCE TO ALMIGHTY GOD, OUR MOST POWERFUL WEAPON AGAINST SATAN AND HIS REALM OF EVIL

BARBARA SPEAKING

MY BROTHERS AND SISTERS, THE MOST POWERFUL WEAPON AGAINST THE REALM OF EVIL, SIN AND PAIN, IS OUR ALLEGIANCE TO ALMIGHTY GOD, OUR CREATOR. THE REALM OF EVIL (SATAN, THE DEVIL) SLITHERS BACK INTO ITS "DARK SPACE" WHEN WE EXHIBIT OUR ALLEGIANCE TO ALMIGHTY GOD, OUR HOLY REDEEMER. OUR INNER AND OVERT EXPRESSION OF ALLEGIANCE TO THE ONE AND ONLY DIVINE CREATOR OF ALL THAT IS GOOD AND HOLY, IS A VERY POWERFUL WEAPON AGAINST THE REALM THAT PRODUCES UNHOLY ACTS AND THOUGHTS. MY BROTHERS AND SISTERS, AS WE LIVE HOLY LIVES ACCORDING TO GOD'S VERSION OF HOLINESS, THE REALM THAT PRODUCES HEARTACHE AND PAIN CANNOT OVERPOWER US. ALLEGIANCE, OBEDIENCE AND FAITHFULNESS, ARE OUR POWERFUL WEAPONS AGAINST THE REALM (SATAN, SIN) THAT DESIRES TO CAPTURE OUR ETERNAL SOULS. MY BROTHERS AND SISTERS, REMAIN STRONG IN YOUR ALLEGIANCE UNTO GOD'S REALM OF HOLINESS. AND HE WILL REMAIN WITH YOU AS WELL. WHEN WE DEVIATE FROM GOD'S VERSION OF HOLINESS, WE PLACE OURSELVES AT SATAN'S EXPOSURE. WHEN WE DEVIATE FROM GOD'S PROTECTIVE REALM OF HOLINESS, WE SEPARATE OURSELVES FROM THE DIVINE POWER, THE ONLY POWER, THAT CAN CONQUER THE REALM OF EVIL AND DESTRUCTION THAT SEEKS THE FALLEN AND BACKSLIDING ONES. MY BROTHERS AND SISTERS, EXHIBIT THE REALM OF ALLEGIANCE UNTO YOUR CREATOR AND GOD AT ALL TIMES, SO THAT YOU TOO WILL DWELL WITHIN THE REALM OF DIVINE BLISS THROUGHOUT ETERNITY.

NOVEMBER 10, 2015 AT 1:44 AM BY: BARBARA ANN MARY MACK

SENT WED, NOV 11, 2015 11:48 PM-READ THU 11/12/2015 1:56 AM

COME STA ARCHBISHOP CRAIG? BELOW ARE TODAY'S PASSAGES. I AM STILL GOING OVER MY GALLEY. I HAVE MADE WONDERFUL PROGRESS SO FAR. SURPRISINGLY, I HAVEN'T COME ACROSS TOO MANY ERRORS CONSIDERING THE PAGE COUNT (1124 PAGES). OF COURSE THIS DOESN'T MEAN THAT THERE AREN'T MORE ERRORS, BUT I HAVEN'T NOTICED THEM. DON'T FORGET TO RELAX YOUR WELL-LOVED MIND THROUGHOUT THIS DAY. *AMORE, BEAUTIFUL BARBARA*

OVER THE HILLS OF PAIN

OVER THE HILLS OF PAIN, MY ELATED SPIRIT SOARS! OVER THE HILLS OF PAIN, MY SPIRIT REJOICES WITH GOD, MY SAVIOR AND HOLY SPOUSE! OVER THE HILLS OF PAIN, MY SPIRIT REJOICES IN THE PRESENCE OF ALMIGHTY GOD AND HIS TRIUMPHANT SAINTS! OVER THE HILLS OF PAIN, MY SATISFIED SPIRIT GAZES INTO THE WELCOMING EYES OF GOD, MY SAVIOR! OVER THE HILLS OF PAIN, MY TEARS JOIN THE REALM OF PEACE AND JOY! OVER THE HILLS OF PAIN, THE GLORY OF THE LORD ENCOMPASSES MY HUMBLED SOUL! OVER THE HILLS OF PAIN, MY WEAK BODY SOARS! OVER THE HILLS OF PAIN, I PRAISE ALMIGHTY GOD, THE ORIGIN OF MY HAPPY SOUL! OVER THE HILLS OF PAIN, I BOW IN THE PRESENCE OF GOD, MY SOURCE AND PURPOSE FOR EXISTING!!!
APRIL 25, 2015 BY: BARBARA ANN MARY MACK

SINNERS CANNOT JUDGE SINNERS

A SINNER CANNOT JUDGE A SINNER. A SINNER CANNOT CONDEMN A SINNER. A SINNER CANNOT PRAY TO ALMIGHTY GOD FOR A SINNER, FOR THE LORD SHUTS HIS HOLY EARS TO THOSE WHO ARE DWELLING WITHIN THE REALM OF SIN. THE LORD OUR GOD, IS PURE AND HOLY. HE WILL NOT LISTEN TO THE VOICE OF THOSE WHO SHARE IN THE UNGODLY DEEDS AND ACTS THAT COME FROM SATAN'S REALM. FOR HE IS PURE AND HOLY! A RIGHTEOUS PERSON PRAYS FOR THE SINNING ONES. FOR THE LORD HEARS THE PRAYERS OF THE RIGHTEOUS ONES. A RIGHTEOUS PERSON PRAYS FOR SINNERS. A RIGHTEOUS PERSON DOESN'T CONFORM TO SINFUL ACTS. A RIGHTEOUS PERSON DOESN'T TURN HIS OR HER BACK ON THOSE WHO ARE IN NEED OF SPIRITUAL HELP AND GUIDANCE. HELP ME, O RIGHTEOUS ONE! HELP ME GUIDE MY CHILDREN INTO THE REALM OF HOLINESS, *SAYS THE LORD!* THERE THEY WILL FIND ME!
APRIL 25, 2015 BY: BARBARA ANN MARY MACK
SENT: SAT, APR 25, 2015 4:15 PM-READ: SAT 4/25/2015 5:06 PM

A CRY FOR THE REALM OF HOLINESS

ALMIGHTY GOD SPEAKING

I HEAR YOUR WEARY AND CONFUSED SOULS AS THEY CRY OUT FOR THE REALM OF HOLINESS, MY VULNERABLE CHILDREN. I HEAR YOUR SOULS AS THEY WANDER THROUGH THE REALM

THAT HOUSES THE ONE (SATAN) WHO DESIRES TO STEAL YOU FROM ME BEFORE YOU REACH THE ONLY REALM THAT COULD SAVE YOUR WANDERING SOULS. I HEAR THE CONFUSION THAT ENCOMPASSES YOUR LOST SOULS AS YOU WANDER IN THE REALM (SATAN-SIN) THAT INVITES YOU THROUGHOUT EACH DAY. I HEAR YOU, O CONFUSED CHILDREN! I HEAR YOUR CRIES THROUGHOUT THE DAY. SEEK THE REALM, THE ONLY REALM THAT CAN RELEASE THE FETTERS THAT BIND YOUR CONFUSED SOULS. SEEK THE REALM THAT COMBATS SATAN AND HIS SICK SERVANTS OF DESTRUCTION THROUGHOUT EACH DAY. SEEK THE ONLY REALM THAT CAN OFFER YOU CONTINUOUS DIVINE PEACE IN THE MIDST OF YOUR CONFUSION. SEEK THE ONLY REALM THAT HOUSES GOD, YOUR CREATOR AND EVERLASTING PROTECTOR! SEEK THE ONLY REALM THAT OFFERS YOU SALVATION THROUGH CHRIST JESUS, YOUR LORD AND GOD. SEEK THE ONLY REALM THAT CARES FOR YOUR ETERNAL SOULS, O CONFUSED ONES! SEEK IT! SEEK IT, DEAR CHILDREN! SEEK THE REALM OF HOLINESS! FOR IT IS THE ONLY REALM THAT PROTECTS THE WEAK SOULS FROM THE DECEPTION AND WRATH OF SATAN! IT IS THE ONLY REALM THAT PROTECTS THE VULNERABLE SOULS FROM SUICIDE AND EVIL THOUGHTS AND DEEDS. MY CHILDREN, I HEAR YOUR CRY FOR THE REALM THAT CAN RELEASE YOUR TORMENTED SOULS! *THUS, SAYS THE LORD,* YOUR ETERNAL GOD AND PROTECTOR

APRIL 27, 2015 BY: BARBARA ANN MARY MACK

SENT: APR 27, 2015 3:21 PM-READ: MON 4/27/2015 7:59 PM

THE MOST IMPORTANT HEALING

THE MOST IMPORTANT HEALING, IS THE HEALING OF ONE'S WOUNDED SPIRIT, SO THAT THE HEALED SPIRIT MAY UNITE WITH ALMIGHTY GOD'S HOLY SPIRIT. OH THE DIVINE PEACE THAT FLOWS THROUGH THE ESSENCE OF THE SPIRITUALLY HEALED CHILD OF GOD, OUR SOVEREIGN KING AND LORD, CANNOT BE REVEALED WITH MERE WORDS. FOR IT IS A PEACE THAT TRANSCENDS ALL REALMS OF PEACE THAT THE WORLD KNOWS. IT IS A PEACE THAT ENABLES THE HEALED SPIRIT TO SOAR IN THE MIDST OF DIFFICULT AND TRYING TIMES. IT IS A PEACE THAT DESCENDS FROM GOD'S THRONE OF LOVE. IT IS A PEACE THAT LETS THE WORLD KNOW OF ONE'S UNIFICATION WITH GOD, THE DIVINE ONE. IT IS A PEACE THAT BRINGS OUT THE JOY THAT CAUSES ONE TO PROFESS HIS OR HER BELIEF IN GOD, OUR DIVINE CREATOR AND FATHER. IT IS A PEACE THAT CAUSES ONE TO LOVE THOSE WHOM SATAN, OUR ENEMY, HAS PLACED DIVISION AND STRIFE BETWEEN. IT IS A PEACE THAT CAUSES ONE TO EXHIBIT THE LOVE OF OUR NEIGHBORS, AS THE LORD COMMANDS. IT IS A PEACE THAT GUIDES THE HEALED ONES INTO THE REALM OF CONTINUOUS PRAISE AND PRAYER, TO OUR OMNIPOTENT AND FAITHFUL GOD. MY BROTHERS AND SISTERS; LET US EXHIBIT THE JOY OF OUR HEALED SPIRITS, AS WE PROCLAIM OUR ALLEGIANCE UNTO OUR HOLY GOD AND FATHER ABOVE. HEAL ME OF MY IMPERFECTION SO THAT I MAY BECOME LIKE YOU, MY FATHER.

MAY 27, 2015 BY: BARBARA ANN MARY MACK

IT'S SO DELIGHTFUL DANCING WITH THE LORD IN THE MIDST OF...

BARBARA SPEAKING

I BOW IN YOUR HOLY PRESENCE, MY GOD, AS YOU AND I ENTER THE DANCE FLOOR OF SPIRITUAL BLISS ON EARTH. YOU LEAD, MY LORD, SO THAT MY OBEDIENT SPIRIT WILL FOLLOW YOU, AS WE WALTZ IN THE MIDST OF HEAVENLY ECSTASY AND SPIRITUAL BLISS. LEAD ME, MY GOD, SO THAT I MAY FOLLOW YOU IN THE DIRECTION OF SALVATION AND ETERNAL LIFE IN SWEET PARADISE. LEAD ME, O LORD, SO THAT MY IGNITED SPIRIT MAY SOAR ABOVE THE STARS AND CLOUDS. LEAD ME, O LORD, AS YOU AND I ENJOY THE SPIRITUAL BLISS THAT DESCENDED IN MY MIDST ON EARTH. MOVE YOUR HOLY PRECIOUS FEET TO OUR SPIRITUAL BEAT! DANCE! LORD, DANCE! DANCE WITH YOUR CHOSEN BRIDE (BARBARA), AS I ASCEND ABOVE THE CLOUDS, IN THE MIDST OF EXISTENCE. LET THE GATES OF SWEET PARADISE CLAP TO THE HEAVENLY BEAT THAT EMITS FROM OUR REALM OF SPIRITUAL JOY. LET THE HOLY BELLS PRODUCE THE TUNES THAT IGNITE OUR REJOICING UNIFIED SPIRIT. LET YOUR CHOSEN ANGELS AND SAINTS GATHER AROUND US, SO THAT THEY MAY WITNESS THE SPLENDOR OF OUR HOLY DANCE. DANCE! MY LORD, DANCE! MOVE TO THE BEAT THAT EXCITES BARBARA, THE BRIDE OF GOD, THE HOLY AND BELOVED TRINITY. DANCE! MY LORD, DANCE! DANCE IN THE MIDST OF SPIRITUAL BLISS ON EARTH!!!
MAY 28, 2015 BY: BARBARA ANN MARY MACK
SENT THU, MAY 28, 2015 10:50 PM-READ FRI 5/29/2015 9:14 AM

ENJOY YOUR BLESSED DAY ARCHBISHOP CRAIG! BELOW IS TODAY'S PASSAGE. TAKE VERY GOOD CARE OF YOURSELF, DEAR ONE.
LOVE, BEAUTIFUL BARBARA

SO UNWORTHY, MY LOVE

BARBARA SPEAKING TO ALMIGHTY GOD, HER HEAVENLY SPOUSE

OH THE MANY BLESSINGS THAT I RECEIVE EACH DAY FROM YOU, CAUSE ME BOW GRACIOUSLY IN YOUR HOLY PRESENCE, MY GOD. I FEEL SO UNWORTHY, MY LOVE. I FEEL SO UNWORTHY, THAT YOU SHOULD REVEAL SO MANY WONDERS AND MYSTERIES THAT ARE HIDDEN FROM OTHERS. I FEEL SO UNWORTHY, THAT YOU SHOULD WHISPER SO MANY MESSAGES FOR YOUR NEEDY FLOCK TO ME, YOUR CHOSEN BRIDE AND MESSENGER OF DIVINE LOVE. I WILL GRACIOUSLY ACCEPT THE POSITION THAT YOU SO LOVING DEEM ME WORTHY OF. I WILL GRACIOUSLY HONOR THE DIVINE POSITION THAT YOU FORMED FROM YOUR REALM OF GENEROSITY, NOT SO LONG AGO. I WILL GRACIOUSLY ACCEPT THE POSITION AS YOUR CHOSEN MESSENGER AND BRIDE,

FOR YOU, MY GOD, CONSIDER ME WORTHY OF THE DIVINE POSITION. I WILL HUMBLY ACCEPT THE POSITION AS YOUR SACRIFICED BRIDE, FOR YOU DEEM ME WORTHY OF SUCH A DIVINE POSITION. MY LORD AND MY GOD, I WILL SALUTE YOU AS I APPROACH YOUR REALM OF GENEROSITY, FOR YOU HAVE CHOSEN ME TO REPRESENT YOU IN THE MIDST OF THESE TROUBLED LAST DAYS. MY LORD AND MY GOD, I BOW IN YOUR HOLY PRESENCE, AS I ACCEPT THE POSITON THAT YOU CALL WORTHY! I WILL ACCEPT THE POSITION THAT YOU HAVE SANCTIFIED ME FOR, FOR I AM TRULY WORTHY OF YOUR DIVINE CHOICE.

MAY 29, 2015 BY: BARBARA ANN MARY MACK

SENT FRI, MAY 29, 2015 1:52 AM-READ FRI 5/292015 9:23 AM

BUONA SERA ARCHBISHOP. DURING THE CELEBRATION OF THE HOLY EUCHARIST ON MAY 31, 2015, I FELT THE EXCITEMENT AND PRESENCE OF GOD, THE HOLY TRINITY. I WAS SO ELATED, ESPECIALLY DURING YOUR HOMILY. BUT, AS YOU AND I HAVE WITNESSED OVER THE YEARS, SATAN ATTEMPTS TO DESTROY THE ELATION THAT CHRISTIANS FEEL. HE TRIES TO REPLACE IT WITH HIS REALM OF DESPAIR, GLOOM, AND DISCOURAGEMENT. WELL, MY PERIOD OF ELATION SOMEWHAT DIMINISHED WHEN RON APPROACHED ME WITH SOMETHING NEGATIVE PERTAINING TO THE BOOKS THAT ALMIGHTY GOD HIMSELF DICTATED TO ME. TO MY UNDERSTANDING, HE WAS DELIVERING A REQUEST FROM YOU. WHAT HE TOLD ME WOULD HAVE AFFECTED ME IN A WAY THAT I WOULD NOT HAVE ENTERED THAT CHURCH AGAIN, IF I HAD NOT RECEIVED A MESSAGE FROM THE LORD PRIOR TO HIS APPROACH, THAT I WOULD HEAR SOMETHING NEGATIVE BEFORE I LEFT THE CHURCH THAT DAY. THE LORD TOLD ME THAT SOMETHING WOULD OCCUR THAT WOULD CAUSE, OR ATTEMPT TO CAUSE ME TO LEAVE BEFORE GREETING THOSE WHO CAME TO SHARE IN THE CELEBRATION. MY HUMAN WEAKNESSES LEFT AS THE LORD SHARED WITH ME THE WARNING OR PREPARATION OF THE NEGATIVITY THAT DID OCCUR. AFTER TAKING IN WHAT RON TOLD ME, I PRAISED GOD FOR HIS WARNING OF THE OCCURRENCE. MY GOD ALWAYS LETS ME KNOW IN ADVANCE WHEN SATAN AND HIS ANGELS ARE ON THE PROWL. THE LORD REVEALED TO ME THAT HE DOESN'T SEND COWARDS TO FULFILL HIS ASSIGNMENTS. JUST AS HE GAVE JESUS THE DIVINE COURAGE TO ENDURE THE SCOURGING AND CRUCIFIXION, OUR FATHER GIVES YOU AND ME THE COURAGE TO FULFILL OUR DIVINE ORDERED ASSIGNMENTS. OF COURSE SATAN WAS UPSET, AS HE WITNESSED THE EXCITEMENT THAT PERMEATED MY BEING AS YOU PREACHED GOD'S HOLY WORDS WITH INTEGRITY AND LOVE. SATAN WILL NEVER STOP ME FROM BEING SUPPORTIVE AND PROUD OF YOU, FOR IT IS ORDERED AND ORCHESTRATED BY ALMIGHTY GOD HIMSELF. *LOVE ALWAYS, VICTORIOUS BARBARA, THE HOLY TRINITY'S COURAGEOUS WIFE*

I DO NOT SEND COWARDS TO REPRESENT ME, SAYS THE LORD

ALMIGHTY GOD SPEAKING BARBARA

GIRD UP YOUR WEAK AND FEARFUL BEING, O SPOUSE OF MINE!

FOR YOUR HOLY ASSIGNMENT REPRESENTS ME, DURING THIS CRITICAL AND CRUCIAL PERIOD OF TIME.

DO NOT LET MERE WORDS FRIGHTEN OR DISCOURAGE YOU,

FOR YOU HAVE BEEN SENT BY THE ONLY GOD, WHO IS HOLY AND TRUE.

YOU HAVE BEEN SENT FROM A REALM THAT HAS NO FEAR,

SO THAT YOU MAY CONQUER THE REALM AND ENTITY (SATAN) THAT EMIT DESPAIR.

I HAVE GIRDED YOU WITH THE POWER OF MY HOLY MIGHT!

SO THAT YOU MAY CONQUER EVERY REALM OF EVIL WITHIN YOUR WEAK AND OBEDIENT SIGHT.

I DO NOT SEND COWARDS TO FIGHT SPIRITUAL BATTLES AGAINST THE REALM OF DOOM, O SPOUSE OF MINE.

FOR MY APOSTLES AND WARRIORS ARE ARMED WITH THE WEAPONS (DIVINE COURAGE, PERSEVERANCE, AND ALLEGIANCE TO ALMIGHTY GOD) THAT WILL PROTECT THEM IN THE MIDST OF THIS DEVASTATING TIME.

DO NOT RUN AWAY!

DO NOT SEEK ME WHEN YOU PRAY!

FOR I DO NOT SEND COWARDS WHO FEAR!

I SEND OUT THOSE WHO EXHIBIT THE ETERNAL GOD WHO DOES CARE.

GIRD UP! GIRD UP! GIRD UP, O WEEPING SPOUSE OF GOD, THE HOLY TRINITY!

YOU HAVE BEEN SECURED BY THE GOD WHO FORMED THEE!

LET THE REALM OF BRAVERY ENCOMPASS YOU!

AS YOU APPROACH THE REALM THAT CAUSES FEAR, AND RELUCTANCE TOO.

THE GATES OF HELL SEEK THOSE WHO FEAR.

GIRD UP YOUR WEAKNESS, MY DAUGHTER, SO THAT ALL MAY KNOW THAT I AM NEAR!

JUNE 1, 2015 BY: BARBARA ANN MARY MACK

YOU HAVE WEAKENED ME, O LORD

BARBARA SPEAKING TO ALMIGHTY GOD

YOU HAVE WEAKENED ME, O LORD. YOU HAVE WEAKENED THE SPIRIT THAT RESTS WITHIN THE BEING OF BARBARA, YOUR CHOSEN BRIDE. YOU HAVE WEAKENED HER WITH THE DIVINE ESSENCE THAT ENCOMPASSES HER OBEDIENT SOUL. YOU HAVE WEAKENED HER BY THE GENUINE LOVE THAT YOU SO EAGERLY EXPRESS IN THE MIDST OF YOUR GREAT CREATION. YOU HAVE WEAKENED HER BEING BY THE MERCY THAT YOU EXHIBIT TOWARDS YOUR OBEDIENT

AND DISOBEDIENT CHILDREN OF ALL NATIONS AND CREEDS. THEREFORE, I WILL WEAKEN THOSE WHOM YOU PLACE IN MY CARE, BY EXHIBITING YOUR EXPRESSIONS OF SINCERE LOVE, FORGIVENESS AND MERCY. I WILL IMITATE YOUR HOLY WAY AS I DELIVER YOUR LIFE SAVING INVITATION TO THOSE WHOM YOU HAVE CALLED AND CHOSEN THROUGH ME, YOUR OBEDIENT BRIDE. I WILL IMITATE YOUR DIVINE EXPRESSION OF CHARITY TOWARDS MY BROTHERS AND SISTERS OF EVERY NATION. I WILL DELIVER YOUR MESSAGES OF LOVE AS I WITNESS THE GRATITUDE THAT COMES FROM THOSE WHOM YOU HAVE PLACED IN MY CARE. I WILL REVEAL THE TRUTH CONCERNING YOUR LOVE FOR ALL OF YOUR CHILDREN. I WILL REVEAL THE TRUTH OF YOUR EXISTENCE TO THOSE WHO TRY TO PLACE DOUBT IN MY MIND. BY YOUR HOLY GRACE AND MERCY, YOU HAVE HUMBLED ME SO THAT I MAY PROCEED IN YOUR HOLY ASSIGNMENT THAT WAS GIVEN TO ME BY THE DIVINE FATHER WHO REALLY CARES. YOU HAVE WEAKENED ME, MY LORD. YOU HAVE WEAKENED ME IN THE PRESENCE OF THOSE WHO SEEK YOUR HOLY EXISTENCE.

JUNE 8, 2015 BY: BARBARA ANN MARY MACK

SENT MON, JUN 8, 2015 5:01 PM-READ MON 6/8/2015 6:26 PM

GREETINGS DEAR ONE! HERE ARE SOME PICS OF AMYA'S GRADUATION. EVERYTHING TURNED OUT BETTER THAN WE EXPECTED. TOYA TOOK A FEW VIDEOS OF THE GRADUATION ALSO. THANK GOD THAT'S OVER WITH! WE HAD PIZZA AND CUPCAKES (THE CUPCAKES WERE DONATED BY ONE OF THE PARENTS) WHEN WE RETURNED HOME. *TOODLES!*

SENT FRI, JUN 19, 2015 3:29 AM-READ FRI 6/19/2015 10:01 AM

GREETINGS LOVE! I PRAY THAT YOU ARE ENJOYING THIS WONDERFUL DAY THAT OUR GREAT AND HOLY GOD BLESSED US WITH. I AM PRESENTLY ENJOYING THE SERENITY THAT FLOWS THROUGH MY ABANDONED HOME. LA TOYA HAS TAKEN AMYA AND TWO OF HER FRIENDS TO DORNEY PARK, LOCATED IN ALLENTOWN, PA. THE GIRLS ARE SISTERS, AND AMYA'S SCHOOL MATES. THEY SPENT THE NIGHT, LAST NIGHT, SO THAT THEY COULD GET AN EARLY START TODAY. CAN YOU IMAGINE BEING IN A HOUSE WITH FIVE CACKLING FEMALES AT ONE TIME? NOT A GOOD THING! THE GIRLS ENTERTAINED EACH OTHER UNTIL 1 AM, I THINK. I CASHED IN MY CHIPS A BIT AFTER 12 AM, AND THEY WERE STILL GOING STRONG IN AMYA'S ROOM. THEY CAME DOWN A COUPLE OF TIMES FOR MORE FUEL (FOOD), WHICH TOYA DID NOT PLAN ON. I TOLD HER TO EXPECT TO FEED THESE GIRLS THROUGHOUT THE DAY, BECAUSE THEY'RE GETTING ALL OF THAT ENERGY FROM SOMETHING. THEY HAVE VISITED OUR HOME SEVERAL TIMES PREVIOUSLY. THEIR PARENTS ARE FROM NIGERIA, BUT I DON'T BELIEVE THE GIRLS HAVE BEEN THERE YET. THEIR FATHER JUST RETURNED FROM NIGERIA LAST WEEK. I BELIEVE THAT HE HAS A BUSINESS OR SOMETHING THAT KEEPS HIM TRAVELING THERE. THIS MORNING, BEFORE LEAVING FOR DORNEY PARK, THE LORD TOLD ME TO SPEAK TO THE YOUNGEST SISTER (AGE TWELVE) ABOUT HIM AND MY MINISTRY FOR HIM. HE INSTRUCTED ME

TO SHOW HER MY RECENTLY PUBLISHED BOOK (THE PRESENT TESTAMENT VOLUME THREE-REVISED). SHE WAS VERY INTERESTED IN WHAT I WAS SHARING WITH HER, AND SHE TOLD ME THAT SHE UNDERSTOOD EVERYTHING THAT I SHARED WITH HER. SHE KEPT SAYING, HOW WONDERFUL AND UNIQUE MY MINISTRY IS, IN REGARDS TO RECEIVING MESSAGES FROM THE LORD THROUGHOUT EACH DAY. SHE AND HER SISTER (AGE 14) WERE RECORDED READING A COUPLE OF PASSAGES FROM MY PUBLISHED BOOKS, WHICH ARE ON YOUTUBE. THE LORD HAS SENT ME TO MANY YOUNG PEOPLE WHOM HE HAS CALLED AND CHOSEN TO EXHIBIT HIS HOLY PRESENCE TO. I WAS VERY IMPRESSED OVER HER CONVERSATION AND INTEREST IN WHAT I SHARED WITH HER. SHE AND HER SISTER DO ATTEND CHURCH (PROTESTANT) ON SUNDAYS. IT IS ALWAYS A PLEASURE HAVING THEM VISIT OUR HOME. WE DO NOT INVITE MANY TO OUR HUMBLE HOME, BUT THOSE WHOM THE LORD APPROVES OF. PLEASE KEEP THEM IN YOUR PRAYERS TOO. UPS JUST DROPPED OFF THE HARD COPY OF MY RECENTLY PUBLISHED BOOK (THE PRESENT TESTAMNET VOLUME THREE-REVISED VERSION). I RECEIVED THE SOFT COVER VERSION TWO WEEKS AGO. I OFFERED THE DELIVERER A BOTTLE OF WATER BECAUSE IT'S VERY HOT OUTSIDE TODAY. I USUALLY TRY TO KEEP COLD BOTTLES OF WATER FOR VISITORS AND MAIL CARRIERS. I AM HAPPY THAT THEY USUALLY ACCEPT MY OFFER. PLEASE BE VERY CAREFUL IN THIS HEAT. *LOVE YAH! BEAUTIFUL BARBARA*

ROCK ME, O LORD

BARBARA SPEAKING TO THE LORD

ROCK ME, O LORD! ROCK ME WITH THE POWERFUL ARMS OF HEAVENLY BLISS! ROCK ME WITHIN THE ARMS THAT HAVE FORMED YOUR GREAT AND BLESSED CREATION NOT SO LONG AGO. ROCK ME WITHIN THE ARMS THAT WATCH OVER HIS LITTLE CHILDREN THROUGHOUT THE DAY. ROCK ME, DEAR LORD, AS I FIGHT THE GATES OF HELL, AS THEY APPROACH THE REALM THAT HOUSES OUR BELOVED ONE (CRAIG). ROCK ME WITHIN THE HOLY REALM THAT REACHES OUT TO THE LOST CHILDREN OF THE NIGHT. CRADLE ME, SO THAT I MAY FEEL YOUR HOLY STRENGTH, AS I COMBAT HE (SATAN) WHO SEEKS DESTRUCTION AND DOOM FOR THOSE WHOM YOU HAVE FOUND FAVOR IN. CRADLE ME WITH THE DIVINE COURAGE THAT EMITS FROM YOUR WELL OF PLENTY. CRADLE ME AS I RELAX IN THE MIDST OF THE CALLED AND CHOSEN ONES. CRADLE ME, O LORD, AS I SEARCH THE STREETS FOR THOSE WHO ARE WRITTEN IN YOUR PRECIOUS AND VALUABLE BOOK OF LIFE. ROCK ME WITHIN THE ARMS THAT FORMED SWEET PARADISE, AS I LOOK UP TO YOU, O HOLY SPOUSE AND GOD OF MINE. ROCK ME, DEAR LORD! ROCK ME THROUGHOUT ETERNITY, SO THAT I MAY SLEEP WITHIN YOUR REALM OF PEACE FOREVER.

JULY 13, 2015 BY: BARBARA ANN MARY MACK

AMYA, THE GIFT

A GIFT YOU ARE

THE GIFT THAT DESCENDED FROM ABOVE THE BRIGHTEST STAR

THE GIFT THAT WAS CREATED BY HEAVEN'S HOLY LOVE

THE GIFT THAT REPRESENTS OUR HOLY AND GRACIOUS GOD ABOVE

THE GIFT THAT EXHIBITS HOLY TRUST

THE GIFT THAT ALMIGHTY GOD AND I LOVE VERY MUCH!

THE GIFT THAT BRIGHTENS KITTY'S DAY.

THE GIFT THAT ENTERS LA TOYA'S REALM OF LOVE, WHENEVER SHE AND AMYA PRAY.

ALMIGHTYGOD SPEAKING TO AMYA

COME, O BLESSED GIFT OF MINE!

AND SHARE YOUR LOVE WITH MY CHILDREN, UNTIL THE END OF TIME.

FOR YOU ARE MY GIFT THAT DESCENDED FROM ABOVE,

SO THAT YOU MAY SHARE AND EXPRESS MY HEAVENLY LOVE.

HAPPY BIRTHDAY AMYA

MAY 16, 2015 BY: BARBARA ANN MARY MACK

THIS IS YOUR DAY

THIS IS YOUR DAY!

WHAT CAN I SAY?

IT IS A DAY THAT WAS MADE FOR ONLY YOU.

IT IS A DAY THAT WAS SENT BY A GOD WHO IS ALWAYS THINKING OF THE GOOD THINGS THAT YOU DO.

IT IS A DAY THAT YOU CHOOSE WHAT YOU WANT TO DO.

IT IS THE DAY THAT YOU MAY OPEN ALL OF THE WONDERFUL GIFTS THAT ARE GIVEN TO YOU.

IT IS YOUR FOURTEENTH BIRTHDAY OF FUN!

IT IS THE DAY THAT YOU CAN HIDE FROM EVERYONE!

SO THAT YOU MAY HAVE VALUABLE TIME ALONE,

EXCEPT WHEN SOMEONE IMPORTANT CALLS YOU ON THE PHONE.

ENJOY YOUR SPECIAL DAY, O BLESSED GRANDDAUGHTER OF MINE!

AS YOU LOOK FORWARD TO TRAVELING DURING THE REALM OF TIME.

HAPPY 14TH BIRTHDAY AMYA

MAY 16, 2015 BY: BARBARA ANN MARY MACK

SENT SUN, MAY 17, 2015 3:18 PM-READ SUN 5/17/2015 10:22 PM

I AM TYPING THE MESSAGE THAT THE LORD GAVE TO ME FOR THANKFUL'S, WHOM WE MET IN GALETON, PA., FATHER, DURING OUR MINISTRY IN THE SUMMER OF 2015. THE LORD REVEALED THESE WORDS TO ME AFTER HER FATHER'S DEATH. THE MESSAGE WAS GIVEN TO ME WHILE WE STAYED AT A FARM OWNED BY THANKFUL AND HER HUSBAND BENN.

ENTER MY OPEN GATES, MY SON, SAYS THE LORD

ALMIGHTY GOD SPEAKING

ENTER MY OPEN GATES, O BLESSED SOUL WHOM I HAVE CALLED HOME (HEAVEN). ENTER THE HEAVENLY GATES THAT CALL YOUR INVITED SOUL. ENTER THE GATES, YES, THE SWEET HEAVENLY GATES THAT CALL YOUR PRECIOUS SOUL HOME. ENTER THE GATES THAT HOUSE GOD, THE BLESSED AND HOLY TRINITY. ENTER THE GATES THAT ENCOMPASS THE BLESSED AND CHOSEN ONES. ENTER THE GATES THAT EXHIBIT FREEDOM AND DIVINE LOVE. ENTER THE GATES THAT HOUSE GOD, YOUR REALM OF SALVATION AND HEAVENLY BLISS! ENTER THE GATES THAT ENCOMPASS THE HEAVENLY CHOIRS THAT SING SONGS OF PRAISE UNTO THEIR HOLY CREATOR AND GOD. ENTER, O BLESSED ONE! *ENTER MY HEAVENLY REALM WITH EVERLASTING GLADNESS!!!*
AUGUST 5, 2015 BY: BARBARA ANN MARY MACK, ALMIGHTY GOD'S CONTEMPORARY MESSENGER AND BRIDE

A MESSAGE FROM THE LORD FOR BENN, THE OWNER OF THE FARMHOUSE IN GALETON, PA. WHERE THE LORD SENT BARBARA, LA TOYA AND AMY, DURING THE SUMMER OF 2015. BENN WAS VERY RECEPTIVE TO GOD'S HOLY MESSAGE AND PRESENCE.

MY SON (BENN): YOU HAVE EXHIBITED THE WORKS OF A CHRISTIAN IN MY HOLY PRESENCE

ALMIGHTY GOD SPEAKING TO BENN

MY SON, MY VALUABLE AND KIND SON, YOU HAVE EXPRESSED MY VERSION OF A CHRISTIAN IN THE PRESENCE OF YOUR HOLY GOD AND FATHER. YOU HAVE EXPRESSED MY VERSION OF DIVINE KINDNESS AND PATIENCE. YOU HAVE EXPRESSED YOUR AUTHENTIC LOVE FOR ME AND MY GREAT CREATION, IN THE PRESENCE OF THOSE WHOM I HAVE SENT TO YOU. YOU HAVE EXHIBITED THE WORKS THAT I DEEM HOLY AND TRUE, IN THE PRESENCE OF BARBARA, MY MESSENGER AND BRIDE. YOUR HOLY WORKS AND SINCERE LOVE HAVE REACHED THE EYES OF GOD, THE HOLY ETERNAL ONE MY SON, MY WORTHY SON, YOU MAY ENTER THE REALM THAT HOUSES THOSE WHOM I HAVE CHOSEN TO DINE AT MY TABLE OF PLENTY. YOU MAY ENTER THE REALM THAT ENCOMPASSES THE BLESSED ONES. YOU MAY ENTER THE REALM WHERE MY HOLY THRONE SITS IN THE MIDST OF DIVINE ROYALTY AND LOVE. YOU MAY ENTER THE REALM, WHERE MY HOLY CHOIRS GATHER TO SING CONTINUOUS PRAISES OF GRATITUDE TO THEIR FAITHFUL CREATOR AND GOD. YOU MAY ENTER THE REALM THAT RELEASES HEAVEN SENT BLESSINGS TO EARTH'S RESIDENTS. YOU MAY ENTER THE REALM THAT BOWS AND DANCES IN MY HOLY ETERNAL PRESENCE. COME, MY SON. COME! ENTER THE REALM THAT

HOUSES ALMIGHTY GOD, YOUR GREAT AND ETERNAL GIVER OF LIFE. COME, MY SON! ENTER MY HOLY REALM WITH GLADNESS IN YOUR HEART! FOR YOU HAVE PLEASED YOUR FAITHFUL GOD AND FATHER. YOU HAVE EXHIBITED YOUR ALLEGIANCE TO ME, IN THE PRESENCE OF THE REALM (SATAN) THAT TRIES TO STEAL MY CHOSEN ONES. YOU HAVE EXHIBITED MY VERSION OF A BELIEVER. MY SON, MY WORTHY SON (BENN), YOU HAVE EXHIBITED ME, YOUR FAITHFUL GOD AND FATHER, IN THE PRESENCE OF THE WORLD! COME, MY SON! ENTER MY HOLY REALM ON EARTH AND IN HEAVEN, WITH GLADNESS IN YOUR HEART! FOR I, THE LORD ALMIGHTY, AM VERY PLEASED WITH YOUR HOLY WORKS AND DEEDS! *THUS, SAYS THE LORD, YOUR ETERNAL GOD AND FRIEND*

AUGUST 7, 2015 BY: BARBARA ANN MARY MACK, ALMIGHTY GOD'S CONTEMPORARY MESSENGER AND BRIDE

GREETINGS DEAR ARCHBISHOP CRAIG! COME STA OGGI? LA TOYA AND I ARE RETURNING FROM GETTING A CONSENT TO PLACE A PICTURE OF THE CAKE THAT I BOUGHT FOR JESUS' BIRTHDAY, FROM THE MANAGER AT THE BAKERY. THE MANAGER AND ASSISTANTS WERE VERY EXCITED OVER THIS. I ALSO HAD TO GET PERMISSION FROM THE STABLE OWNER WHERE WE TOOK PICTURES ON CHRISTMAS DAY, BECAUSE I PLAN ON INCLUDING SEVERAL PICTURES OF THE STABLE SCENE. OUR VERY GOOD FRIEND ANNETTE ZAMBRANO STOPPED BY YESTERDAY TO SIGN A CONSENT TO INCLUDE A PICTURE OF HER LATE SISTER IN LAW AND HUSBAND BOBBY IN MY FORTHCOMING BOOK AS WELL. THIS HAS BEEN A VERY BUSY WEEK, HASN'T IT? I PRAY THAT FR. BRIAN MADE IT HOME SAFE. IT WAS GOOD SEEING DR. MESSINA AGAIN. HE LOOKED VERY WELL AND CONTENT. I WILL KEEP HIM AND HIS FAMILY IN MY DAILY PRAYERS AND DEVOTION TO THE LORD. I AM ABOUT TO EAT FOR THE FIRST TIME TODAY. I WAS ON THE PHONE EARLIER WITH MY BOOK CONSULTANT (CATHY). SHE CALLED TO SEE IF MY MANUSCRIPT WAS READY FOR SUBMISSION. I EMAILED HER THE PHOTO THAT I WOULD LIKE TO HAVE ON THE BACK COVER OF MY BOOK. SINCE THE PHOTO WAS TAKEN IN FRONT OF THE WHITE HOUSE, IT MAY NOT BE PERMISSIBLE. SHE WILL LET ME KNOW AFTER SHE SPEAKS WITH HER SUPERVISOR. SO MUCH IS GOING ON AT THIS TIME. ONE OF MY LATE BROTHER'S DOCTORS EMAILED ME A COUPLE OF DAYS AGO, REQUESTING IF I WOULD BE WILLING TO WRITE A TESTIMONIAL OF MY FAMILY EXPERIENCE WITH HER, SO THAT SHE MAY PLACE IT ON HER WEBSITE. SHE STARTED A PRACTICE IN CALIFORNIA, WHICH INVOLVES HER VISITING HER PATIENTS AT HOME INSTEAD OF A HOSPITAL SETTING. SHE WAS VERY KIND AND PATIENT AS SHE MONITORED BY BROTHER UNTIL SHE PRONOUNCED HIM. SHE ALSO POSED WITH ME SO THAT I COULD INCLUDE HER IN ONE OF MY BOOKS THAT WAS PUBLISHED IN 2014. ATTACHED IS A PHOTO OF THE DOCTOR AND ME. I ASKED TOYA TO HELP ME WITH THE TESTIMONIAL, BECAUSE I HAVE TO FINISH PROOF READING MY 500 PAGES BOOK. THE LORD INSTRUCTED ME ON THE SELECTION OF PICTURES (40) TO INCLUDE IN THIS BOOK. AS I MENTIONED BEFORE, THIS BOOK (**THE PRESENT TESTAMENT VOLUME NINE: IT IS WRITTEN-APOCALYPSE**) CONSISTS

OF THE MANY GOD DICTATED MESSAGES THAT WERE GIVEN TO ME AND SHARED WITH HIS CHOSEN AND CALLED ONES VIA EMAIL. THIS BOOK REVEALS GOD'S FULFILLED PROPHECIES THAT WERE WRITTEN BY ME WITH THE GUIDANCE OF GOD'S HOLY SPIRIT. THIS BOOK IS VERY EXCITING, CAPTIVATING, INSPIRATIONAL, FULL OF DIVINE HOPE AND AUTHENTIC LOVE, ENCOURAGING, AND MOST OF ALL, IT IS HOLY AND TRUE. I REALLY LIKE IT! AND SO DOES THE LORD! PLEASE TAKE VERY GOOD CARE OF YOUR VALUABLE, VALUABLE, VALUABLE SELF! *AMORE ALWAYS! BELLA BARBARA*

SENT SUN, JAN 17, 2016 4:17 PM-READ SUN 1/17/2016 5:17 PM

GREETINGS DEAR ARCHBISHOP CRAIG! AS ALWAYS, SEEING YOU TODAY WAS A DIVINE DELIGHT AND PLEASURE! AT THIS TIME, WE CANNOT COMMIT OURSELVES TO A SPECIFIC CHURCH SETTING BECAUSE I DO NOT KNOW WHEN OR WHERE THE LORD WILL NEED ME. AS A MESSENGER OF ALMIGHTY GOD, I CAN GO ONLY WHERE HIS HOLY SPIRIT LEADS AND INSTRUCTS ME. AT THIS TIME, HE DESIRES THAT I REMAIN AVAILABLE TO HIS PROMPTING. I AM ABOUT TO WORK ON MY FORTHCOMING GOD ORCHESTRATED AND INSPIRED BOOK (THE PRESENT TESTAMENT VOLUME NINE: APOCALYPSE). I NEED TO MAKE SURE THAT MY INCLUDED ILLUSTRATIONS ARE PLACED ON THE PROPER PAGES BEFORE SENDING MY COMPLETED MANUSCRIPT TO MY PUBLISHERS. THIS IS A VERY UNVEILING BOOK, WHICH IS WHY I (ALMIGHTY GOD) USES THE TERM APOCALYPSE IN ITS TITLE. *LOVE ALWAYS, BELLA BARBARA*

SENT SUN, JAN 17, 2016 4:17 PM-READ SUN 1/17/2016 5:17 PM

ENJOY YOUR BLESSED DAY, DEAR ONE. THINK OF ME (ALMIGHTY GOD AND BARBARA) AS YOUR TRAVEL THROUGH THE DAY.
LOVE ALWAYS! ALMIGHTY GOD, THE SACRED ORIGIN OF THE FULLNESS OF TIME!!!

SENT SUN, JAN 17, 2016 9:13 PM-READ SUN 1/17 10:00 PM

BUON GIORNO DEAR ARCHBISHOP CRAIG! BELOW IS A PASSAGE THAT IS PLACED WITHIN MY FORTHCOMING GOD DICTATED BOOK. ENJOY YOUR DAY LOVE! *CIAO! BELLA BARBARA*

GOOD EVENING DEAR ARCHBISHOP CRAIG! I PRAY THAT YOU HAD A VERY GOOD DAY. I HAD TO PICK UP AND BE FITTED FOR MY NEW CPAP MACHINE THIS AFTERNOON. I HAD THE OTHER ONE FOR OVER FIVE YEARS. ALTHOUGH IT WORKS VERY WELL AT THIS TIME, IT IS RECOMMENDED THAT ONE REPLACE THE MACHINE EVERY FOUR TO FIVE YEARS. ALSO, PLEASE PRAY FOR KITTY, OUR CAT OF ALMOST 12 YEARS. HE LOST HIS SIGHT ABOUT A WEEK AGO. NOW HE IS NOT MOVING AROUND MUCH. LA TOYA AND AMYA HAVE TO FEED HIM FROM A SPOON. FORTUNATELY HE DOESN'T SEEM TO BE IN ANY PAIN AT THIS TIME, WHICH IS GOOD FOR HIM AND US. WE HAD TO PUT DINO, OUR DOG OF 14 YEARS, DOWN BECAUSE OF HIS AGE AND HEALTH DETERIORATION. DINO WOULD WHINE A LOT TO EXPRESS HIS PAIN AND DISCOMFORT. HOPEFULLY KITTY WILL

NOT HAVE TO EXPERIENCE UNBEARABLE PAIN AS DINO DID. LA TOYA AND AMYA UNDERSTAND BECAUSE OF KITTY'S AGE, BUT THEY DO NOT WANT TO SAY GOOD BYE AT THIS TIME. ALTHOUGH I AM ALLERGIC TO CATS AND DOGS, I TOLERATE ANY DISCOMFORT BECAUSE TOYA AND AMYA ADORE THEM. I LOVE ANIMALS ALSO, ESPECIALLY BIG TAMED DOGS. PLEASE MAKE SURE THAT YOU BUNDLE UP BEFORE GOING OUTDOORS. I WORRY ABOUT YOU ALL OF THE TIME. I THANK GOODNESS FOR WATCHING OVER YOU EVERY DAY.

AMORE, PRAYING FOR KITTY BELLA BARBARA

SENT MON, JAN 18, 2016 8:15 PM-READ TUE 1/19/2016 12:26 AM

BUON GIORNO, O BLESSED AND CHOSEN SON (ARCHBISHOP CRAIG)!
COME STA? BELOW IS TODAY'S PASSAGE FOR THE WORLD. *AMORE*

I SIT BACK AND PONDER OVER PEOPLE

ALMIGHTY GOD AND BARBARA SPEAKING

THROUGHOUT THE DAY AND DURING THE NIGHTS, I SIT BACK AND PONDER OVER PEOPLE. I PONDER OVER WHAT LIFE MEANS TO THOSE WHO DO NOT RESPECT IT.

I PONDER OVER THE ACTIONS OF THOSE WHO PROFESS THAT THEY KNOW OUR GREAT AND HOLY GOD, BUT DO NOT HONOR OR RESPECT HIS UNCHANGING WORD.

I PONDER OVER THOSE WHO ARE HEADING IN THE DIRECTION OF ETERNAL DESTRUCTION AND DOOM, AS THEY SIT IN THE PEWS AND CHURCHES. I PONDER OVER THOSE WHO SPEAK GOD'S HOLY WORDS, BUT DO NOT FOLLOW THEM. I PONDER OVER THE MANY TEARS THAT I (ALMIGHTY GOD AND BARBARA) HAVE SHED, AS I WITNESS THE IMPURITIES THAT PREACH FROM THE PULPITS. I PONDER OVER THE HEARTACHE THAT I (ALMIGHTY GOD AND BARBARA) ENDURE DAILY, AS I LISTEN TO THE WORDS THAT EXIT THE MOUTHS OF THOSE WHO PROFESS THAT THEY ARE MY CHILDREN. I PONDER OVER THE WORLD'S VERSION OF RIGHTEOUSNESS, FOR IT GOES AGAINST MY VERSION OF HOLINESS, *SAYS THE LORD.* I SIT BACK THROUGHOUT EACH DAY AND BLESSED NIGHT, AND PONDER OVER HUMAN BEINGS. I KNOW WHAT IS GOING ON WITHIN YOU, O PEOPLE WHO DO NOT HONOR GOD'S REALM OF HOLINESS, AND I ALSO KNOW YOUR DESTINATION, *SAYS THE LORD.*

JANUARY 29, 2016 AT 1:29 AM BY: BARBARA ANN MARY MACK

SENT FRI, JAN 29, 2016 1:36 AM-READ FRI 1/29/2016 11:00 PM

ENJOY YOUR BLESSED DAY LOVE!!! TI AMO! BELLA BARBIE

SENT SAT, JAN 30, 2016 7:19 PM-READ SAT 1/30/2016 8:37 PM

PLEASE ENJOY THE GIFT OF DIVINE ORCHESTRATED LOVE AS GOD, THE HOLY ETERNAL ONE, FUSES WITH YOUR OBEDIENT AND FAITHFUL ESSENCE. *TI AMO! EXCITED BARBIE!*

SENT SAT, JAN 30, 2016 7:19 PM-READ SAT 1/30/2016 8:37 PM

ALLELUIA!!! PRAISE THE LORD!!! GREETINGS, DEAR ARCHBISHOP CRAIG! I FINALLY DID IT! I FINALLY SENT ALL OF THE MATERIAL FOR MY FORTHCOMING GOD ORDERED BOOK TO MY PUBLISHER! YIPPIEEEEEEE!!! NOW I CAN RELAX A BIT BEFORE THEY SEND ME THE GALLEY. I WILL SEND IN THE PHOTO CONSENT FORMS, MAYBE TOMORROW.
SENT SAT, JAN 30, 2016 7:19 PM-READ SAT 1/30/2016 8:37 PM

GREETINGS LOVE!!! ENJOY THIS BLESSED DAY! BELOW IS TODAY'S MESSAGE FROM THE LORD FOR THE WORLD. *TI AMO! BELLA BARBARA*

LET US SEPARATE THEM, SAYS THE LORD

ALMIGHTY GOD SPEAKING

LET US DIVIDE GOOD FROM EVIL-THE RIGHTEOUS ONES AND THE UNRIGHTEOUS ONES-THE SAVED ONES AND THE DOOMED ONES-THE CALLED AND CHOSEN ONES-THE SPIRITUALLY RICH AND THE SPIRITUALLY POOR ONES, *SAYS THE LORD.* COME! O HEAVENLY HOST. LET US BEGIN OUR WORK TODAY! FOR THE TIME, YES, THE APPOINTED TIME, IS AT HAND!!! LET US BEGIN THE DIVINE SEPARATION PROCESS, FOR THE TIME IS TODAY! LET THOSE WHO HAVE SERVED ME WELL, SIT ON MY RIGHT, AND THOSE WHO HAVE BLATANTLY DISRESPECTED ME AND MY UNCHANGING WORD, MOVE TO MY LEFT SIDE. FOR THE TIME OF JUDGMENT HAS ARRIVED, *SAYS THE LORD!!!*
JANUARY 30, 2016 AT 6:33 PM BY: BARBARA ANN MARY MACK
SENT SAT, JAN 30, 2016 7:19 PM-READ SAT 1/30/2016 8:37 PM

HAPPY SABBATH, ARCHBISHOP CRAIG!

COME AND GO WITH ME TO THE LAND OF DIVINE PURITY

BARBARA SPEAKING

MY BROTHERS AND SISTERS, LET US REMOVE OUR ARMORS, WHICH HIDE OUR SINS AND IMPURITIES, SO THAT WE MAY ENTER GOD'S HOLY LAND OF PURITY AND GRACE. LET US REMOVE THE ARMORS THAT COVER OUR SINS AND IMPURITIES SO THAT WE MAY WALK IN THE LAND OF THE LIVING THROUGHOUT ETERNITY. LET US REMOVE THE SINS THAT SEPARATE US FROM GOD'S REALM OF PURITY SO THAT WE MAY COMMUNICATE WITH HIM THROUGHOUT EACH DAY. LET US BEND OUR HEADS AND KNEES AS WE APPROACH GOD'S LAND OF PURITY IN HIS HOLY PRESENCE. LET US WIPE THE REALM OF IMPURITY OUT OF OUR LIVES WITH THE HOLY WORDS THAT FLOW SO LOVINGLY THROUGH THE HOLY BIBLE. LET US CAPTURE THE REALM OF PURITY WITH OUR HEARTS AND MINDS SO THAT THE REALM OF EVIL WILL FLEE

FROM OUR PURIFIED SOULS. MY BROTHERS AND SISTERS, LET US ALL EXHIBIT GOD'S REALM OF PURITY SO THAT WE MAY WALK WITH OUR HEADS HELD HIGH, AS WE ENTER HIS HOLY GATES. *ALLELUIA!!!*

JANUARY 30, 2016 AT 7:56 PM BY: BARBARA ANN MARY MACK

PRICELESS (LA TOYA, MY GOD SENT DAUGHTER)

BARBARA SPEAKING OF LA TOYA, HER HEAVEN SENT GIFT

DESCENDED FROM HEAVEN ABOVE, THE GIFT OF A PRICELESS LOVE (LA TOYA). CRADLED WITHIN GOD'S HOLY BOSOM OF ETERNAL LOVE, IS THE PRICELESS GIFT OF MY DAUGHTER'S FAITH IN HIS MIGHTY DOVE. THE HOLY DOVE (SPIRIT) THAT WATCHES OVER US THROUGHOUT EACH DAY. THE HEAVENLY DOVE (SPIRIT) THAT ENCOURAGES US TO PRAY. COME! O PRICELESS GIFT OF MINE. AND FUSE WITH ALMIGHTY GOD AND ME, UNTIL THE END OF TIME. FOR YOU HAVE BEEN BLESSED BY THE ONLY GOD WHO IS HOLY AND TRUE. YOU, O PRICELESS ONE, REVERE THE SAVIOR (THE LORD JESUS) WHO HAS SACRIFICED HIS LIFE FOR ME AND YOU. FAR VALUABLE THAN EVERY POT OF GOLD, IS THE PRICELESS GIFT (LA TOYA) THAT I WILL FOREVER HOLD. I WILL HOLD YOU, O PRICELESS ONE, THROUGHOUT THE REALM OF TIME, FOR YOURS IS A LOVE THAT WILL FOREVER BE MINE!

JANUARY 30, 2016 AT 7:40 PM BY: BARBARA ANN MARY MACK

SENT SUN, JAN 31, 2016 12:42 AM-READ SUN 1/31 11:06 AM

GREETINGS, DEAR ARCHBISHOP CRAIG! GRAZIE FOR THE WONDERFUL SERMON TODAY. MY FAMILY AND I REALLY ENJOYED IT. I WILL KEEP YOU AND DEACON ANTHONY IN MY PRAYERS AS YOU FULFILL YOUR HEAVEN SENT ASSIGNMENT IN ST. LOUIS. TAKE VERY GOOD CARE OF YOUR VALUABLE SELF. *TI AMO, BELLA BARBARA*

SENT SUN, JAN 31, 2016 9:15 PM-READ SUN 1/31/2016 11:54 PM

GREETINGS, DEAR ONE (ARCHBISHOP CRAIG)! BELOW ARE TODAY'S PASSAGES FROM THE LORD. *AMORE, BELLA BARBARA*

THE GUESTS ARE READY! LET US BEGIN, SAYS THE LORD

ALMIGHTY GOD SPEAKING

COME, MY SON (CRAIG)! COME, MY DAUGHTER (BARBARA)! LET US BEGIN OUR CELEBRATION, FOR OUR GUESTS HAVE ARRIVED!!! LET US BEGIN THE CELEBRATION THAT HAS BEEN SENT FROM MY MIGHTY THRONE. FOR MY TIME IS AT HAND!!! THEY, OUR INVITED GUESTS, ARE READY TO WITNESS THAT WHICH IS HOLY AND PURE IN MY EYES. THEY, OUR WORTHY AND CHOSEN GUESTS, ARE READY TO WITNESS THAT WHICH WAS PROPHESIED BY BARBARA, MY HOLY MESSENGER AND BRIDE, THROUGH THE YEARS. COME, MY SON! IT IS TIME TO EXHIBIT THAT WHICH YOU HAVE HIDDEN FROM THE WORLD FOR MANY YEARS. IT IS TIME TO EXHIBIT THE DIVINE LOVE THAT I HAVE GRACED YOU WITH. IT IS TIME TO EXPRESS YOUR LOVE FOR MY CHOSEN MESSENGER AND BRIDE IN THE PRESENCE OF OUR INVITED GUESTS. IT IS TIME, O WORTHY SON! IT IS TIME! YOUR DIVINE SENT PATIENCE HAS BEEN REWARDED WITH THE GIFT OF MY ETERNAL LOVE AND PROMISE. YOUR PATIENCE AND ALLEGIANCE REVEAL YOUR TRUST IN ME AND MY HOLY PROMISES TO YOU. COME, O BELOVED SON! LET US BEGIN OUR

CELEBRATION IN THE PRESENCE OF THE DESERVING ONES, FOR THEY ARE WORTHY! THEY HAVE BEEN PREPARED! THEY ARE READY!!! LET US (ALMIGHTY GOD, CRAIG AND BARBARA) BEGIN, *SAYS THE LORD!!!*

FEBRUARY 1, 2016 AT 5:31 PM BY: BARBARA ANN MARY MACK

LONGING, LONGING, LONGING FOR THE CONSUMMATION: LONGING FOR THE FULFILLED PROPHECY

BARBARA SPEAKING TO THE LORD

MY LORD AND HOLY GOD, THE REALM OF PATIENCE HAS ESCAPED MY NEEDY SOUL. THE REALM OF PATIENCE ROAMS IN THE DIRECTION OF THE FULFILLMENT OF YOUR HOLY PROMISE AND WORD. MY LORD, MY HOLY SPOUSE AND GOD, THE REALM THAT PRODUCES AND RELEASES THE LONGING DESIRE, HAS CAPTURED MY WEAK AND VULNERABLE ESSENCE. THE REALM THAT RELEASES HEAVEN SENT PURE AND HOLY DESIRES, HAS CAPTURED THE YEARNING ONES (BARBARA AND CRAIG). THE REALM THAT REPRESENTS GOD'S HOLY PRESENCE IN THE FORM OF HIS CHOSEN ONES (CRAIG AND BARBARA), HAS RELEASED THE LONGING THAT HAS ENCOMPASSED THE WORTHY ONES (CRAIG AND BARBARA). COME! O REALM (LONGING) THAT HAS CAPTURED MY BELOVED ONE AND ME. ENTER THE GATES, YES, THE HEAVENLY GATES, THAT RELEASED YOUR WELCOMED PRESENCE, FOR MY ESSENCE LONGS FOR THE ETERNAL BELOVED ONE AND HIS HOLY ORIGIN AND GOD. *ALLELUIA!!!*

FEBRUARY 1, 2016 AT 6:59 PM BY: BARBARA ANN MARY MACK

SENT MON, FEB 1, 2016 7:01 PM-READ MON 2/1/2016 9:39 PM

BUON GIORNO, DEAR ARCHBISHOP CRAIG!

ALMIGHTY GOD SPEAKING

BEHOLD THE MANIFESTATION OF MY HEAVEN SENT PROPHECY, MY SON, FOR IT IS SUDDENLY UPON MY CHOSEN GUESTS! ARE YOU READY? ARE YOU PREPARED? I HAVE BLESSED AND GRACED MY BELOVED SPOUSE (BARBARA) WITH THE DIVINE COURAGE TO COMPLETE A HEAVEN SENT WORK THAT WILL BRING ABOUT MANY, MANY, MANY CONVERSIONS TO MY HOLY REALM. ARE YOU READY, O OBEDIENT AND CHOSEN SON OF MINE? IF SO, LET YOU AND I BEGIN AND COMPLETE THIS GREAT WORK TODAY, *SAYS THE LORD,* YOUR GOD OF FULFILLED PROMISES!

WATCH, WAIT, AND WITNESS, *SAYS THE LORD!*

ALMIGHTY GOD SPEAKING

ARE YOU READY, MY PATIENT CHILDREN? ARE YOU READY FOR MY DIVINE APPEARANCE IN YOUR BLESSED MIDST? ARE YOU READY TO MEET ME FACE TO FACE, AS YOU EXPERIENCE THE COMPLETION OF THE GREATEST STORY EVER TOLD? ARE YOU READY FOR THE MANIFESTATION OF MY HOLY PROMISE AND WORDS? WATCH, MY CHILDREN! WAIT, MY CHILDREN! WAIT FOR MY APPEARANCE IN YOUR CHOSEN MIDST! WITNESS ALL THAT I HAVE PROMISED! WITNESS THE FULFILLMENT OF MY GREAT AND HOLY PROPHECY, FOR IT IS IN YOUR BLESSED MIDST! WITNESS ALL THAT I HAVE SENT FROM MY THRONE OF FULFILLED PROPHECIES! WITNESS MY DIVINE LIGHT AS IT SHINES THROUGH AND AROUND MY CHOSEN MESSENGER AND BRIDE (BARBARA)! WITNESS ALL THAT I HAVE REVEALED TO HER THROUGH THE YEARS! WITNESS MY HOLY WORD AS IT FILLS YOUR HEARTS AND MINDS WITH DELIGHT AND EXCITEMENT! WITNESS ME, MY CHILDREN! WITNESS MY HOLY PRESENCE IN YOUR BLESSED MIDST, FOR IT IS TIME, *SAYS THE LORD!!!*
FEBRUARY 1, 2016 AT 2:38 AM BY: BARBARA ANN MARY MACK

WHO ARE THE WHEAT? WHO ARE THE TARES? LET ALL PONDER OVER THIS, SAYS THE LORD?
FEBRUARY 1, 2016 AT 2:40 AM BY: BARBARA ANN MARY MACK

MY PURIFIED ESSENCE WEEPS FOR THEM DAILY

BARBARA SPEAKING TO THE LORD

OH HOW I WEEP FOR THE SOULS WHO HAVE BEEN MISLED AND DECEIVED BY THE ENEMY (SATAN)! OH HOW MY HEART AND SOUL CRY OUT FOR THEIR DECEIVED AND VULNERABLE SOULS. CATCH THEM, MY LORD! CATCH THE MANY TEARS THAT FALL THROUGHOUT EACH DAY. CATCH THE MANY TEARS THAT UNITE WITH YOURS AS WE BOW OUR FUSED ESSENCE, AS WE WEEP AS ONE. CATCH THEM, O HOLY GOD AND SPOUSE OF MINE! CATCH THE TEARS AS THEY WANDER IN THE DIRECTION OF DIVINE CONSOLATION. CATCH THE MANY TEARS THAT ARE RELEASED FROM MY WELL OF DIVINE COMPASSION, LOVE AND MERCY! CRADLE THE TEARS THAT SEEK YOUR REALM OF COMFORT, MY LORD. CATCH THE TEARS THAT HAVE UNITED WITH THE PAIN THAT EXITS THE WOUNDED HEARTS OF YOUR DECEIVED AND VULNERABLE CHILDREN. CATCH THEM, MY LORD! FOR THEY, MY FALLING TEARS, ARE MANY!
FEBRUARY 1, 2016 AT 2:16 AM BY: BARBARA ANN MARY MACK
SENT MON, FEB 1, 2016 2:58 AM-READ MON 2/1/2016 9:40 PM

ENJOY YOUR DAY, DEAR ARCHBISHOP CRAIG! BELOW IS TODAY'S MESSAGE FROM THE LORD FOR YOU. TI AMO, BELLA BARBARA

YOUR ACT OF DIVINE LOVE

ALMIGHTY GOD SPEAKING TO ARCHBISHOP CRAIG

MY SON, YOU HAVE EXHIBITED THE ACT OF DIVINE LOVE IN MY HOLY PRESENCE BY TEACHING YOUR BELOVED SON ABOUT HIS ORIGIN AND GOD. YOU HAVE FULFILLED YOUR OBLIGATIONS AS A LOVING FATHER DOES. YOU HAVE TAUGHT HIM THE DEPTH OF MY ETERNAL AND OMNIPOTENT EXISTENCE. YOU HAVE REVEALED AND EXPRESSED YOUR SINCERE BELIEF IN MY HOLY EVERLASTING LOVE AND WORD. YOU HAVE SHOWN HIM THE MAGNITUDE OF YOUR FAITH AND TRUST IN ME, YOUR INVISIBLE GOD AND HOPE. YOU HAVE LAID DOWN A FOUNDATION THAT THE WORLD CANNOT STEAL FROM HIM, FOR YOU HAVE TAUGHT HIM OF ME BY OBSERVING YOU. YOU, O BLESSED AND BELOVED SON OF MINE, WILL EXPERIENCE THE DEPTH OF MY LOVE THAT NO OTHER MORTAL MAN HAS OR WILL ENJOY, FOR YOU HAVE BEEN FAITHFUL TO ME. THIS IS MY HOLY WORD, AND THIS IS MY TRUTH! REJOICE! O CONDUIT WHO TRAVELS WITH THE FIRE AND DESIRE OF MY GOOD AND HOLY NEWS. REJOICE IN THE PRESENCE OF HE WHO LOVES AND TRUSTS YOU, FOR I AM FAITHFUL! REJOICE! O BLESSED SON, REJOICE!
FEBRUARY 2, 2016 AT 12:45 AM BY: BARBARA ANN MARY MACK
SENT TUE, FEB 2, 2016 12:50 AM-READ TUE 2/2/2016 10:57 AM

HI! BELOW IS TODAY'S PASSAGE FROM THE LORD. *CIAO! BB*

THEY (THOSE IN THE SYNAGOGUE IN NAZARETH) DID NOT RECOGNIZE ME EITHER, SAYS THE LORD GOD

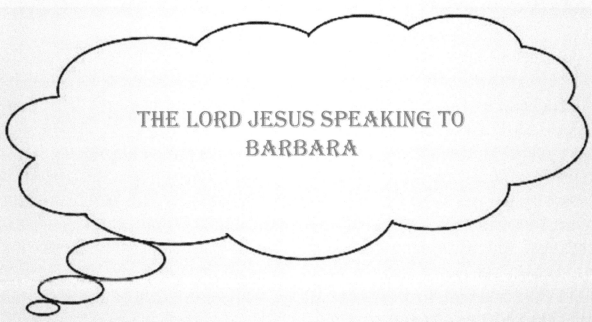

THE LORD JESUS SPEAKING TO BARBARA

THEY DID NOT RECOGNIZE ME WHEN I WAS IN THEIR SYNAGOGUES NOT SO LONG AGO, MY DAUGHTER. THEY DID NOT RECOGNIZE THE HOLY PRESENCE OF THE FORETOLD PROPHECY (JESUS, THE MESSIAH, THE DELIVERER, THE CHRIST, THE ANOINTED ONE, JESUS, THE ONLY SAVING GOD). THEY DID NOT RECOGNIZE ALMIGHTY GOD IN THEIR CHOSEN MIDST. THEY DID NOT RECOGNIZE THE DIVINE FORM THAT I REVEALED MYSELF THROUGH. THEY DID NOT RECOGNIZE OUR HOLY GOD AND FATHER'S CHOICE (JESUS' EARTHLY FORM). THEY HAVEN'T

CHANGED, MY DAUGHTER. THOSE WHO COME TO CHURCH DO NOT RECOGNIZE ME WITHIN THE VALUABLE VESSEL THAT I, THE HOLY TRINITY, HAVE SENT TO DWELL IN THEIR MIDST TODAY, FOR THEY HAVEN'T CHANGED. THEY ARE THE UNBELIEVING ONES. THEY ARE THE DOOMED ONES. THEY ARE THE TARES, *SAYS THE LORD.* GO, MY DAUGHTER! GO! O SWEET VESSEL OF THE HOLY TRINITY. GO AND DELIVER MY LIFE SAVING WORDS. EVEN IF THEY DO NOT RECOGNIZE ME THROUGH YOU, FOR WE (ALMIGHTY GOD AND THE BELIEVING ONES) KNOW THE TRUTH! DELIVER MY HOLY WORDS TO EVERYONE WHOM I SEND YOU TO, FOR YOU REPRESENT A LONG SUFFERING GOD. YOU REPRESENT A FORGIVING GOD. YOU REPRESENT A HOLY GOD. YOU REPRESENT A MERCIFUL GOD. YOU REPRESENT A COMPASSIONATE GOD. YOU, REPRESENT A RIGHTEOUS GOD. YOU REPRESENT THE GREAT AND HOLY JUDGE OF ALL LIFE! YOU, MY DAUGHTER, MY OBEDIENT SPOUSE AND MESSENGER, REPRESENT ME, *SAYS THE LORD!*
FEBRUARY 4, 2016 AT 5:47 PM BY: BARBARA ANN MARY MACK

SENT SAT, FEB 13, 2016 2:03 AM-READ SAT 2/13/2016 2:20 PM

THEY HAVE BEEN WARNED. THEY HAVE BEEN ENLIGHTENED BY ME, SAYS THE LORD.

ALMIGHTY GOD SPEAKING

THEY (THE DISOBEDIENT ONES, THE SINNING ONES, THOSE WHO GO AGAINST MY UNCHANGING HOLY WORDS, SATAN'S DECEIVED ONES) HAVE BEEN WARNED. THEY HAVE BEEN ENLIGHTENED BY ME THROUGH MY FAITHFUL MESSENGER AND BRIDE (BARBARA). THEIR FATE, THEIR ETERNAL DESTINATION, HAVE BEEN RECORDED IN MY BOOKS. WILL YOU CHANGE BEFORE YOUR PHYSICAL DEATH, O DISOBEDIENT ONES? WILL YOU CHANGE BEFORE MY IMMINENT RETURN WITH THE CLOUDS? NOW IS THE TIME, O ENLIGHTEN ONES! NOW IS THE TIME, YOU WHO PERFORM UNHOLY ACTS AND DEEDS BEFORE MY OMNIPRESENT EXISTENCE. YOU CANNOT CONCEAL YOUR DIRTY AND UNGODLY ACTS FROM HE (ALMIGHTY GOD) WHO SEES AND KNOWS EVERYTHING. YOU CANNOT HIDE YOUR WICKEDNESS FROM HE (ALMIGHTY GOD) WHO KNOWS AND EXECUTES THE DESTINATION OF YOUR ETERNAL DWELLING PLACE. NOW, IS THE TIME TO REPENT AND CHANGE YOUR UNSPEAKABLE WAYS! FOR THE TIME OF JUDGMENT DRAWS NEAR, *SAYS THE LORD GOD ALMIGHTY!!!*
FEBRUARY 4, 2016 AT 11:39 PM BY: BARBARA ANN MARY MACKBOTTOM OF FORM
SENT SAT, FEB 13, 2016 2:03 AM-READ SAT 2/13/2016 2:20 PM

BUON GIORNO, O BELOVED ONE (ARCHBISHOP CRAIG)!
COME STA OGGI? *CIAO! BELLA BARBARA*

OUR EYES HAVE SEEN THE GLORY OF THE LORD

BARBARA SPEAKING

OUR EYES HAVE WITNESSED THE GLORY OF THE LORD, AS HE REVEALED HIS GLORIOUS GOOD NEWS TO HIS SENT MESSENGER AND BRIDE (BARBARA). OUR EYES HAVE WITNESSED THE GLORY OF THE LORD, AS HIS FORETOLD PROPHECIES MANIFESTED IN THE PRESENCE OF THOSE WHOM HE DEEMS WORTHY AND BLESSED. OUR EYES HAVE SEEN THE GLORY OF OUR GREAT AND HOLY OMNIPOTENT GOD, AS HE REVEALS HIS HOLY PRESENCE AND EXISTENCE THROUGH HIS HUMBLED AND BROKEN MESSENGER AND BRIDE (BARBARA). COME, O BLESSED EYES OF THE CALLED AND CHOSEN ONES! COME AND SHARE THE GLORY THAT YOU HAVE RETAINED. FOR YOU HAVE BEEN BLESSED BY THE GREAT AND HOLY CREATOR OF LIFE ETERNAL. COME! O BLESSED EYES, AND ENJOY THE GLORY OF THE LORD, AGAIN AND AGAIN, FOR HE IS ETERNAL! *ALLELUIA!!!*

FEBRUARY 5, 2016 AT 4:57 PM BY: BARBARA ANN MARY MACK

SENT SAT, FEB 13, 2016 2:03 AM-READ SAT 2/13/2016 2:20 PM

PLEASANT DREAMS, DEAR ONE! AMORE, BEAUTIFUL BARBARA

FOLLOWING HIS (ALMIGHTY GOD) HOLY LEAD

BARBARA SPEAKING TO THE LORD GOD

I HEAR YOU, O LORD. I CAN FEEL YOUR HOLY PRESENCE AROUND ME. I WILL FOLLOW YOUR HOLY ESSENCE AS IT LEADS ME INTO THE CONSUMMATION OF YOUR GREAT AND HOLY LOVE STORY. I WILL FOLLOW YOU THROUGH THE GATES OF SWEET PARADISE ON EARTH TODAY. I WILL FOLLOW YOUR HOLY LEAD INTO THE REALM OF, THE FULFILLMENT OF *THE GREATEST STORY EVER TOLD.* I WILL FOLLOW YOUR HOLY ESSENCE WITH THE BLISS AND ECSTASY THAT DESCENDED FROM YOUR THRONE OF DIVINITY AND ETERNITY. I WILL FOLLOW YOU, O HOLY GOD AND SPOUSE OF MINE, FOREVER AND EVER! *ALLELUIA!!!*

FEBRUARY 3, 2016 AT 8:02 PM BY: BARBARA ANN MARY MACK

SENT SAT, FEB 13, 2016 2:03 AM-READ SAT 2/13/2016 2:20 PM

GREETINGS, DEAR ARCHBISHOP CRAIG! COME STA OGGI AMORE? BELOW IS TODAY'S PASSAGE FROM THE LORD. CIAO! BELLA BARBIE

WE'RE GOING TO HEAVEN, FOR WE ARE AMONG THE CHOSEN ONES. ALLELUIA!!!

BARBARA SPEAKING

LET US GIVE ALMIGHTY GOD CONTINUOUS PRAISE! FOR HE HAS COUNTED US WORTHY TO REIGN AND LIVE WITH HIM THROUGHOUT ETERNITY, O BLESSED CHILDREN (LA TOYA AND AMYA) OF MINE! O BELOVED SPOUSE (CRAIG) OF MINE, LET US REJOICE TODAY! FOR WE ARE AMONG GOD'S CHOSEN AND BLESSED FEW. HE, ALMIGHTY GOD, HAS SHARED THIS VALUABLE GOOD NEWS WITH ME, AND I AM TRULY GRATEFUL! COME, O BLESSED AND CHOSEN ONES (CRAIG, LA TOYA AND AMYA)! LET US PREPARE FOR THE GREATEST TIME OF OUR ETERNAL LIFE IN SWEET PARADISE. LET US PREPARE FOR THE GIFT OF DWELLING WITH OUR HEAVENLY SAVIOR AND GOD FOREVER! LET US BEGIN BY REJOICING EVERY DAY IN THE HOLY PRESENCE OF JESUS, OUR SAVING GOD AND FATHER! LET US DANCE TO THE BEAT OF HIS LIFE SUSTAINING NAME! LET US DANCE AROUND HIS INVISIBLE THRONE IN OUR BLESSED MIDST TODAY! LET US JOIN THE REALM THAT RELEASES THE *ALLELUIAS* THAT TRAVEL IN THE DIRECTION OF SWEET PARADISE ABOVE! COME, O BLESSED FAMILY OF MINE! LET US JOIN THE REALM OF CONTINUOUS PRAISE, AS IT LEADS US IN THE DIRECTION OF ALMIGHTY GOD AND HIS ETERNAL DANCE FLOOR ABOVE! COME, MY CHILDREN (LA TOYA AND AMYA)! COME, O ETERNAL BELOVED ONE (CRAIG)! LET US BEGIN THE CELEBRATION TODAY! *ALLELUIA!!!*
FEBRUARY 4, 2016 AT 5:11 PM BY; BARBARA ANN MARY MACK
SENT SAT, FEB 13, 2016 2:03 AM-READ SAT 2/13/2016 2:20 PM

GREETINGS, DEAR ONE! COME STA? BELOW IS TODAY'S PASSAGE FOR YOU. AMORE, BELLA BARBARA

A DIVINELY FORMED STATURE:

BARBARA SPEAKING TO CRAIG, THE ETERNAL BELOVED ONE

OH WHAT A DIVINELY FORMED STATURE THAT YOU HAVE BEEN BLESSED WITH, O BELOVED ONE, FOR IT IS **NICE AND SQUEEZABLE!** *ALLELUIA!!!* IT IS THE STATURE THAT DESCENDED FROM GOD'S REALM OF DELIGHT AND DIVINE PLEASURE. IT IS A STATURE THAT PLEASES GOD'S CHOSEN AND BLESSED SPOUSE AND MESSENGER (BARBARA). IT IS A STATURE THAT EXHIBITS DIVINE STRENGTH AND COURAGE AS YOU AND I BATTLE THE GATES OF HELL FOR THE SOULS OF GOD'S CALLED AND CHOSEN ONES. IT IS A STATURE THAT REPRESENTS OUR GREAT AND HOLY GOD, FOR HE, ALMIGHTY GOD, HAS FORMED YOU IN HIS LIKENESS (APPROVAL). EXHIBIT IT, DEAR ONE! EXHIBIT THE STATURE THAT I AM VERY PLEASED WITH, FOR IT IS DIVINELY FORMED!
FEBRUARY 5, 2016 AT 2:58 PM BY: BARBARA ANN MARY MACK
SENT SAT, FEB 13, 2016 2:03 AM-READ SAT 2/13/2016 2:20 PM

GREETINGS, DEAR ONE! COME STA? AMORE, FOREVER AND EVER, AND EVER AND...,
BEAUTIFUL BARBARA

I HAVE MET THE TARES, SAYS THE LORD

ALMIGHTY GOD SPEAKING THROUGH BARBARA, HIS SENT MESSENGER AND BRIDE

I HAVE MET THE TARES! I HAVE MET THOSE WHOM SATAN, MY ENEMY, HAS PLACED AMONG MY CALLED AND CHOSEN ONES. I HAVE MET THEM THROUGH THE EYES OF MY HUMBLED MESSENGER AND BRIDE, BARBARA. I HAVE WEPT THROUGH HER ABUSED EYES, AS I WITNESS THE UNHOLY ACTS OF THOSE WHOM SATAN, MY ENEMY, HAS PLACED AMONG MY VULNERABLE AND VALUABLE FAITHFUL ONES. I HAVE WITNESSED THEIR UNCHANGING WAYS AS THEY SIT WITHIN MY CHURCHES AND PEWS. I HAVE WITNESSED THEM, AS THEY WALKED SIDE BY SIDE WITH MY MESSENGER AND BRIDE (BARBARA). I HAVE WEPT THROUGH HER WEAK EYES AS THEY MOCKED ME IN HER FAITHFUL PRESENCE. I HAVE PLEADED WITH THEM, BUT THEY, LIKE SATAN, THEIR ORIGIN AND GOD, REFUSED MY PLEAS. I HAVE SENT MY HOLY MESSENGER AND BRIDE (BARBARA) TO SHIELD AND ENLIGHTEN THOSE WHO HAVE BEEN SUBJECTED AND FOOLED BY THE TARES. I HAVE TRAVELED THROUGH THE WEAK BEING OF MY MESSENGER (BARBARA) THROUGH THE YEARS. I HAVE SEEN THOSE WHO DID NOT RECOGNIZE ME THROUGH HER WEAK BEING. I HAVE SEEN THE TARES AS THEY ABUSED MY MESSENGER IN MY HOLY PRESENCE. THEY ARE DECEITFUL AND DANGEROUS LIKE SATAN, THE DEVIL, THEIR ORIGIN AND GOD. I WILL WEEP NO MORE! FOR THE TIME IS AT HAND, AND THE TARES WILL BE CAST OUT OF MY SIGHT FOREVER! COME, O PRECIOUS BRIDE AND MESSENGER (BARBARA) OF MINE! COME! LET US SIT BACK AND WAIT FOR THE APPROACHING TIME, FOR THE TARES (THE UNHOLY ONES, THE UNRIGHTEOUS ONES, THE LIARS, THE DISOBEDIENT ONES, THE DECEIVERS, THE HERETIC, THE FORNICATORS, THE ADULTERERS, THE MURDERERS, THE ABUSERS, AND ALL WHO PREACH AND TEACH THAT WHICH I VIEW AS UNHOLY, AS IF IT IS HOLY), ARE HEADED FOR THE REALM OF ETERNAL DESTRUCTION. THIS IS MY HOLY WORD! THIS IS MY HOLY PROMISE, *SAYS THE LORD!*
FEBRUARY 6, 2016 AT 3:40 PM BY: BARBARA ANN MARY MACK

HAVE YOU REPENTED YET, SAYS THE LORD?

ALMIGHTY GOD SPEAKING

HAVE YOU REPENTED YET, MY SONS? HAVE YOU REPENTED YET, MY DAUGHTERS? ARE YOU A NEW CREATURE IN MY EARTHLY KINGDOM? TIME IS RUNNING OUT, MY SON! TIME IS RUNNING OUT, MY DAUGHTER! LET ALL WHO ARE AMONG THE REALM OF SIN, REPENT NOW, IN MY HOLY PRESENCE,

FOR TIME IS RUNNING OUT! DO NOT BE DECEIVED BY THOSE WHO MISLEAD YOU, MY SONS! DO NOT BE DECEIVED BY THE TARES, MY DAUGHTERS! FOR THEY HAVE BEEN SENT BY SATAN, MY ENEMY, THE SOWER OF EVIL DEEDS. THE TIME FOR MY JUDGMENT IS AT HAND, MY CHILDREN! IT IS TIME FOR YOU TO REPENT! IT IS TIME TO JOIN THE WINNING SIDE (ALMIGHTY GOD)! COME, MY CHILDREN, FOR I AM READY TO HEAR YOUR ACT OF REPENTANCE TODAY! I AM READY TO OFFER YOU FORGIVENESS. I AM READY TO HEAL YOU FROM THE SINS THAT HAVE OVERWHELMED YOUR WEAK AND VULNERABLE SOULS FOR YEARS. COME, O REPENTANT DAUGHTER! COME, O REPENTANT SON! I AM READY TO RECEIVE YOUR VALUABLE SOULS TODAY, *SAYS THE LORD!!!*
FEBRUARY 6, 2016 AT 4:34 PM BY: BARBARA ANN MARY MACK
SENT SAT, FEB 13, 2016 2:03 AM-READ SAT 2/13/2016 2:20 PM

GREETINGS, DEAR ONE! TI AMO!

I WEEP, FOR THEY DO NOT RECOGNIZE ME, SAYS THE LORD

ALMIGHTY GOD SPEAKING

THEY SPEAK TO ME DAILY THROUGH BARBARA, MY SENT MESSENGER AND BRIDE, BUT THEY DO NOT RECOGNIZE ME. THEY SIT IN THE SAME CHURCH BUILDINGS WITH ME, BUT THEY DO NOT RECOGNIZE ME, *SAYS THE LORD.* THEY COMMUNICATE WITH ME VIA SOCIAL MEDIA, BUT THEY DO NOT RECOGNIZE ME. MY DEAR CHILDREN, WHAT WILL IT TAKE FOR YOU TO RECOGNIZE ME IN THE FORM (BARBARA) THAT I HAVE SENT TO THIS BLESSED BUT TRAGIC GENERATION? WHAT CAN I SAY OR REVEAL THAT WILL MAKE YOU SEE MY GLORIOUS LIGHT, WHICH SHINES IN YOUR BLESSED PRESENCE THROUGH MY OBEDIENT SENT MESSENGER (BARBARA) TODAY? DO YOU KNOW THAT I WEEP DAILY THROUGH HER, MY CHILDREN? DO YOU KNOW THAT I WITNESS YOUR IRREVERENCE TOWARDS YOUR CREATOR AND GOD THROUGH MY SENT MESSENGER AND BRIDE? MY TEARS ARE MANY, O DISOBEDIENT CHILDREN. MY TEARS FLOW DOWN THE WOUNDED CHEEKS OF MY SENT MESSENGER AND BRIDE, AS SHE WITNESSES AND HEARS THE BLASPHEMOUS WORDS AND ACTS THAT EXIT THE BEINGS OF THOSE WHO PROFESS THAT THEY ARE CHRISTIANS. I WEEP DAILY, FOR THEY DO NOT RECOGNIZE HOLINESS IN THEIR MIDST TODAY, *SAYS THE WOUNDED LORD GOD.*
FEBRUARY 6, 2016 AT 11:59 PM BY: BARBARA ANN MARY MACK
SENT SAT, FEB 13, 2016 2:03 AM-READ SAT 2/13/2016 2:20 PM

HAPPY SABBATH LOVE!!! I PRAY THAT YOU HAVE A GREAT TIME DURING YOUR APOSTOLIC VISIT TO ST. LOUIS.
TI AMO! TI AMO! TI AMO! BELLA BARBIE
SENT SAT, FEB 13, 2016 2:03 AM-READ SAT 2/13/2016 2:20 PM
HAPPY SABBATH LOVE!!! TI AMO! TI AMO! TI AMO! BELLA BARBIE

BEHOLD GOD'S HEAVEN SENT PROPHET OF TODAY

ALMIGHTY GOD SPEAKING

I MOVE SWIFTLY AND WITH DIVINE ELEGANCE, THROUGH THE HUMBLED BEING OF MY HEAVEN SENT PROPHET AND BRIDE (BARBARA). I MOVE WITH THE GENTLENESS OF A MERCIFUL AND COMPASSIONATE GOD AND FATHER, THROUGH THE HEAVEN SENT ESSENCE OF MY OBEDIENT SPOUSE AND FRIEND (BARBARA). I MOVE IN THE MIDST OF THE CALLED AND CHOSEN ONES. I MOVE IN THE MIDST OF THE WHEAT (THE CHOSEN AND FAITHFUL ONES). I MOVE IN THE MIDST OF THE TARES (SATAN'S ANGELS AND FOLLOWERS). I MOVE WITH EASE AND COMFORT, FOR I AM ALMIGHTY GOD, THE ONLY OMNIPOTENT AND OMNIPRESENT HOLY ONE. BEHOLD MY HOLY PRESENCE AND WORDS THAT FLOW FROM THE ESSENCE OF MY HEAVEN SENT VESSEL OF DIVINE LOVE AND MERCY, FOR I AM IN YOUR MIDST TODAY, MY CHILDREN. I AM IN YOUR MIDST, O WORKERS OF INIQUITY AND SIN. I AM IN YOUR MIDST, O DECEIVERS OF MY VULNERABLE CHILDREN. I AM IN YOUR UNHOLY MIDST, THROUGH MY HEAVEN SENT PROPHET OF DIVINE LOVE AND TRUTH. BEHOLD ME TODAY, *SAYS THE LORD GOD!!!*

FEBRUARY 7, 2016 AT 4:19 PM BY: BARBARA ANN MARY MACK

BEHOLD! ALPHA AND OMEGA, ALMIGHTY GOD, IN OUR MIDST TODAY, SAYS THE LORD GOD

BARBARA SPEAKING

BEHOLD, MY BLESSED BROTHERS! BEHOLD, MY BLESSED SISTERS! BEHOLD THE HOLY PRESENCE OF ALPHA AND OMEGA, ALMIGHTY GOD, FOR HE IS IN OUR BLESSED MIDST TODAY! REJOICE! O BLESSED BROTHERS AND SISTERS OF MINE. FOR ALPHA AND OMEGA, OUR OMNIPOTENT SAVING GOD, IS IN OUR BLESSED MIDST TODAY! CAN YOU NOT SEE HIM, O BLESSED BROTHERS AND SISTERS OF MINE? CAN YOU NOT FEEL HIS HOLY PRESENCE AS HE ROAMS WITH DIVINE GRACE AND ELEGANCE IN OUR BLESSED MIDST TODAY? BEHOLD THE HOLY PRESENCE OF ALPHA, GOD, THE BEGINNING OF LIFE! BEHOLD ALPHA, GOD, THE BEGINNING OF CREATION! BEHOLD ALPHA, GOD, THE BEGINNING OF ALL THAT IS GOOD AND HOLY! BEHOLD ALPHA, GOD, MY (BARBARA) BEGINNING! BEHOLD ALPHA, THE ETERNAL ONE! BEHOLD OMEGA, GOD, THE DIVINE END OF ALL THAT IS SEEN AND HEARD! BEHOLD OMEGA, GOD, THE END OF HARDSHIP AND PAIN! BEHOLD OMEGA, GOD, THE END OF SUFFERING AND MISERY! BEHOLD OMEGA, GOD, THE END OF SATAN AND HIS DEFEATED REALM OF EVIL AND SIN!!! BEHOLD ALPHA AND OMEGA! GOD, THE BEGINNING, THE FIRST, AND GOD, THE DIVINE END AND LAST, FOR HE IS IN OUR MIDST TODAY!!! *ALLELUIA!!!*

FEBRUARY 7, 2016 AT 4:47 PM BY: BARBARA ANN MARY MACK

SENT SAT, FEB 13, 2016 2:03 AM-READ SAT 2/13/2016 2:20 PM

TI AMO! TI AMO! TI AMO!

REJOICE! O BLESSED GENERATION, SAYS THE LORD, FOR I AM IN YOUR MIDST TODAY!!!

ALMIGHTY GOD (THE HOLY TRINITY) SPEAKING

REJOICE, O BLESSED CHILDREN OF MINE! REJOICE IN THE HOLY PRESENCE OF YOUR OMNIPOTENT LOVING CREATOR AND GOD, FOR I AM IN YOUR BLESSED MIDST. REJOICE! O BLESSED GENERATION. FOR ALPHA AND OMEGA, YOUR SAVING ETERNAL GOD, IS IN YOUR MIDST TODAY! REJOICE, AS YOU WITNESS MY HOLY REVELATIONS THROUGH MY OBEDIENT AND SENT MESSENGER (BARBARA) OF DIVINE LOVE AND HOPE. REJOICE IN THE MIDST OF THIS TRAGIC PERIOD OF TIME, AS YOU WITNESS MY DIVINE LIGHT AND MERCY THROUGH THE HUMBLED BEING OF MY HEAVEN SENT MESSENGER OF LOVE, FOR SHE DOES REPRESENT ME, *SAYS THE LORD.* I HAVE REVEALED MY WONDERS THROUGH HER VULNERABLE AND OBEDIENT BEING. I HAVE REVEALED PROPHETIC UTTERANCES THROUGH HER, SO THAT YOU MAY KNOW FOR CERTAIN THAT I, YOUR OMNIPOTENT CREATOR AND GOD, AM IN YOUR BLESSED MIDST TODAY. COME! O BLESSED GENERATION, AND EXPERIENCE THE DEPTH OF MY HOLY WORD THROUGH THE MANIFESTATION OF MY PROPHECIES. COME! O WORTHY GENERATION, AND EXPERIENCE EVERYTHING THAT REVEALS MY HOLY PRESENCE IN YOUR MIDST TODAY, SO THAT YOU MAY EXPERIENCE DIVINE TRUTH IN YOUR BLESSED MIDST. COME, O BLESSED ONES, COME! EXPERIENCE MY VERSION OF FULFILLMENT TODAY! FOR I AM THE REALM OF HOPE AND FULFILLMENT THAT YOU SEEK, *SAYS THE LORD!*
FEBRUARY 7, 2016 AT 8:14 PM BY: BARBARA ANN MARY MACK
SENT SAT, FEB 13, 2016 2:03 AM-READ SAT 2/13/2016 2:20 PM

GREETINGS LOVE!!! ENJOY YOUR BLESSED DAY!!!
TI AMO! BELLA BARBIE

OH, THE UNHOLY THINGS THAT GO ON INSIDE OF THE CHURCHES; I SEE THEM ALL, SAYS THE LORD!

ALMIGHTY GOD SPEAKING

I AM ALMIGHTY GOD, THE OMNIPRESENT ONE! THAT WHICH YOU HIDE FROM THE WORLD IS OPEN TO MY HOLY SIGHT, *SAYS THE LORD.*
OH, THE UNSPEAKABLE SIGHTS AND SOUNDS THAT COME FROM THOSE WHO SIT IN MY CHURCHES, CAUSE MY HOLY ESSENCE TO WEEP WITH DISGUST. HAVE YOU NO SHAME, O WORKER OF UNSPEAKABLE ACTS? DO YOU NOT KNOW THAT I AM EVERYWHERE AND I CAN

SEE EVERYTHING? THERE IS NOTHING THAT IS HIDDEN FROM ME, MY CHILDREN, FOR I SEE IT ALL!!! I SEE THAT WHICH YOU SHOULD BE ASHAMED OF. I SEE THAT WHICH IS PROHIBITED AND VILE. I SEE IT ALL, AS I LOOK BELOW. HAVE YOU NO SHAME, YOU WHO DO AND SAY UNSPEAKABLE THINGS IN MY CHURCHES? DO YOU NOT FEAR THE WRATH THAT AWAITS YOU? DO YOU NOT BELIEVE IN MY WRATH, O DISGUSTING ONES WHO COMMIT VILE AND SHAMEFUL ACTS INSIDE MY CHURCH? DO YOU WANT TO EXPERIENCE IT FIRSTHAND, O DISBELIEVING ONES? YOU WILL, *SAYS THE LORD GOD!!!*

FEBRUARY 8, 2016 BY: BARBARA ANN MARY MACK

SENT SAT, FEB 13, 2016 2:03 AM-READ SAT 2/13/2016 2:20 PM

BUON GIORNO, DEAR ARCHBISHOP CRAIG! COME STA OGGI AMORE? LA TOYA AND I ARE EN ROUTE TO GET MY MONTHLY B12 INJECTION AT MY DOCTOR'S OFFICE AND TO DO A LITTLE FOOD SHOPPING. I HAVE BEEN TRYING TO STICK TO MY DIET, WHICH IS HARD BECAUSE I AM USUALLY UP LATE WRITING AND DOING BIBLICAL (SCRIPTURAL) RESEARCH. *AMORE, BELLA BARBIE*

SENT SAT, FEB 13, 2016 2:03 AM-READ SAT 2/13/2016 2:20 PM

TI AMO! TI AMO! TI AMO! BEAUTIFUL BARBIE

SENT SAT, FEB 13, 2016 2:03 AM-READ SAT 2/13/2016 2:20 PM

TI AMO! TI AMO! TI AMO, DEAR ARCHBISHOP! ALLELUIA!!!

I AM DEEPLY HURT, SAYS THE LORD

ALMIGHTY GOD SPEAKING

OH, MY CHILDREN, YOU DO NOT KNOW THE DISCOMFORT THAT FLOWS THROUGH MY DIVINE ESSENCE, AS I WITNESS THE DESTRUCTION THAT SATAN AND HIS REALM OF EVIL HAVE SUBJECTED US (ALMIGHTY GOD AND HIS VULNERABLE CHILDREN) TO. YOU DO NOT KNOW THE PAIN THAT I EXPERIENCE EVERY TIME SATAN HAS TAKEN ONE OF MY CHILDREN THROUGH PHYSICAL AND ETERNAL DEATH. THE PAIN IS VERY, VERY DEEP, MY CHILDREN. THE PAIN IS CONTINUOUS, FOR THE DESTRUCTION THAT SATAN INFLICTS UPON MY CHILDREN IS CONTINUOUS. HE, SATAN, HAS NO HEART OF COMPASSION OR LOVE. HIS ONLY PURPOSE IS TO DESTROY AND OVERPOWER THOSE WHO FOLLOW HIS DECEPTIVE WAYS. MY CHILDREN, FLEE FROM HIS GRIP (SINFUL WAYS) BEFORE HE TAKES YOU DOWN, FOR HIS DESTRUCTION IS EVERLASTING AND PERMANENT. DO NOT BE DECEIVED OR FOOLED BY THE TEMPORARY PLEASURES AND POSITIONS THAT HE PLACES IN YOUR VULNERABLE, WEAK, AND WORLDLY FAMED BEINGS. TRUST AND FOLLOW MY HOLY WAY ONLY, *SAYS THE LORD.*

FEBRUARY 10, 2016 AT 5:44 PM BY: BARBARA ANN MARY MACK
SENT SAT, FEB 13, 2016 2:03 AM-READ SAT 2/13/2016 2:20 PM

TI AMO! TI AMO! TI AMO, DEAR ARCHBISHOP!

HAPPY ASH WEDNESDAY, O BELOVED SON (ARCHBISHOP CRAIG)!!!
LET US BEGIN THIS LENTEN SEASON WITH OUR HEARTS, MINDS AND SOULS, HUMBLED IN THE
PRESENCE OF GREATNESS (ALMIGHTY GOD)!!! *ALLELUIA!!!* TODAY'S PASSAGE

THOSE WHO RETURN TO ME, I WILL PARDON THEIR INIQUITIES, SAYS THE LORD GOD

<u>GOD, THE OMNIPOTENT ONE, SPEAKING</u>

I AM MERCIFUL TO THOSE WHO RETURN TO ME, FOR I AM A LOVING FATHER AND GOD. MY
CHILDREN, IF YOU RETURN TO ME WITH A SINCERE AND REPENTANT HEART, I WILL PARDON
ALL OF YOUR WRONGDOINGS. IF YOU RETURN TO ME, I WILL FORGIVE YOU IN THE PRESENCE OF
OUR ENEMY (SATAN), THE DECEIVING ONE. IF YOU RETURN TO ME, I WILL SHARE ALL OF MY
DIVINE WEALTH WITH YOU. IF YOU RETURN TO ME, I WILL WALK WITH YOU DURING THIS TRAGIC
PERIOD OF TIME. IF YOU RETURN TO ME, YOUR FIRST LOVE, I WILL TELL MY ANGELS ABOUT
YOUR ALLEGIANCE AND FAITH. MY SONS, MY DAUGHTERS, IF YOU FORSAKE THE REALM OF
SIN AND DISOBEDIENCE FOR THE REALM (ALMIGHTY GOD) THAT HOUSES AND RELEASES
EVERLASTING BLISS AND DIVINE ECSTASY, I WILL TELL YOU THE DIVINE SECRETS THAT ARE
HIDDEN FROM THOSE WHO HAVE FORSAKEN ME. WALK WITH ME, O REPENTANT ONES! WALK
WITH ME THROUGH THE GATES OF SWEET PARADISE, FOR THERE, YOU WILL DINE WITH ME
FOREVER AND EVER, *SAYS THE LORD GOD*
FEBRUARY 10, 2016 AT 2:37 AM BY: BARBARA ANN MARY MACK
SENT SAT, FEB 13, 2016 2:03 AM-READ SAT 2/13/2016 2:20 PM

LET US CLAIM THE VICTORY OVER THE REALM OF DECEIT AND EVIL, DEAR ARCHBISHOP
CRAIG, FOR WE ARE IN THE MIDST OF THE MOST HOLIEST SEASON (LENTEN) OF THE
YEAR! *ALLELUIA!!!*
SENT SAT, FEB 13, 2016 2:03 AM-READ SAT 2/13/2016 2:20 PM

KEEP FIGHTING THE GATES OF HELL BABY (CRAIG), FOR I (ALMIGHTY GOD AND BARBARA)
AM WITH YOU, *SAYS THE LORD GOD!!!*
IN THE MIDST OF THIS BRUTAL SPIRITUAL BATTLE, I (ALMIGHTY GOD AND BARBARA) WILL
NEVER FORSAKE YOU, O BELOVED OF MINE (ALMIGHTY GOD AND BARBARA)!

TI AMO!!! THE PRECIOUS BLOOD OF "THE LAMB OF GOD"
SENT SAT, FEB 13, 2016 2:03 AM-READ SAT 2/13/2016 2:20 PM

BY THE VICTORIOUS BLOOD OF GOD'S SACRIFICIAL LAMB *(THE LORD JESUS)*, WE WILL WIN THIS SPIRITUAL BATTLE! *ALLELUIA!!!*
SENT SAT, FEB 13, 2016 2:03 AM-READ SAT 2/13/2016 2:20 PM

KEEP FIGHTING BABY!!!

BY THE VICTORIOUS BLOOD OF GOD'S SACRIFICIAL LAMB (THE LORD JESUS), WE WILL WIN THIS SPIRITUAL BATTLE! ALLELUIA!!!

BARBARA SPEAKING

MY BROTHERS AND SISTERS, KEEP FIGHTING THE SPIRITUAL BATTLE THAT SEEMS TO BE CONTINUOUS AND FRUITLESS, FOR JESUS, THE VICTORIOUS LAMB OF GOD, IS IN OUR BLESSED MIDST TODAY. LET US GIVE HIM CONTINUOUS PRAISE, FOR HE IS THE GREAT AND HOLY I AM!!! HE IS GOD, ALMIGHTY, THE VICTORY OVER SATAN, OUR (ALMIGHTY GOD AND HIS CHILDREN) ENEMY. HE, SATAN, OUR ENEMY, IS DEFEATED BY THE PRECIOUS AND HOLY BLOOD OF JESUS, THE SACRIFICIAL LAMB OF GOD, HIS HOLY ORIGIN. MY BROTHERS AND SISTERS, LET US JOIN JESUS, THE SACRIFICIAL LAMB OF GOD, DURING THIS HOLIEST PERIOD OF TIME (LENT). LET US JOIN OUR PRECIOUS LORD AND GOD AS WE EXPERIENCE HIS SACRIFICIAL ACT OF LOVE FOR HIS CHILDREN. LET US JOIN HIM AS WE REMEMBER HIS SUFFERING AND DEATH ON THE HOLY CROSS OF LOVE. LET US JOIN HIM BY EXHIBITING HIS VERSION OF LOVE ONE ANOTHER. LET US JOIN OUR SACRIFICIAL LORD AS WE EXHIBIT HIS VERSION OF HOLINESS AND MERCY. LET US JOIN HIM AS WE EXHIBIT HIS VERSION OF COMPASSION TOWARDS ONE ANOTHER. LET US JOIN HIM AS WE FOCUS ON THE FUTURE WITH HIM IN ETERNAL GLORY AND DIVINE BLISS. MY BROTHERS AND SISTERS, LET US REJOICE IN GOD, THE SACRIFICIAL LAMB, AS WE CELEBRATE HIS VICTORY TODAY, FOR HE IS GOOD!!! *ALLELUIA!!!*
FEBRUARY 12, 2016 AT 4:32 PM BY: BARBARA ANN MARY MACK
SENT SAT, FEB 13, 2016 2:03 AM-READ SAT 2/13/2016 2:20 PM

KEEP FIGHTING BABY!!!
SENT SAT, FEB 13, 2016 2:03 AM-READ SAT 2/13/2016 2:20 PM

IT WILL BE AN HONOR TO TAKE YOUR WORTHY SON'S HAND, MY GOD

BARBARA SPEAKING TO ALMIGHTY GOD

MY FATHER, MY HEAVENLY GOD, IT WILL BE AN HONOR AND BLESSING TO TAKE YOUR WORTHY SON'S (CRAIG) OBEDIENT AND FAITHFUL HAND IN YOUR VERSION OF HOLY MATRIMONY, FOR I AM TRULY READY AND PREPARED. YOU HAVE PREPARED YOUR FAITHFUL DAUGHTER AND SPOUSE (BARBARA) FOR A MINISTRY THAT EXHIBITS YOUR VERSION OF HOLINESS AND LOVING ONE ANOTHER AS YOU LOVE. YOU, O HEAVENLY SAVIOR AND HOST, HAVE PREPARED ME FOR A DIVINE GIFT THAT WILL BRING MANY CONVERSIONS TO THE CHRISTIAN FAITH. YOU HAVE PREPARED YOUR OBEDIENT SON FOR AN AWESOME ROLE THAT NO OTHER MAN ON EARTH HAS BEEN FOUND WORTHY TO PROCEED IN. FOR HE TRULY LOVES AND ADORES YOU AS I DO. I AM READY TO PROCEED DOWN THE AISLE, YES, THE DIVINE ORDERED AISLE, THAT LEADS TO OUR ETERNAL BELOVED ONE, FOR HE IS WORTHY! YES, MY FATHER! I AM READY TO TAKE THE HAND OF HE, WHOM YOU DEEM WORTHY!!! *ALLELUIA!!!*

FEBRUARY 15, 2016 AT 8:08 PM BY: BARBARA ANN MARY MACK

SENT MON, FEB 15, 2016 8:44 PM-READ MON 2/15/2016 10:49 PM

TI AMO! HI ARCHBISHOP CRAIG! BELOW ARE TODAY'S PASSAGES

TI AMO! BEAUTIFUL BARBARA

WHO WILL REMAIN FAITHFUL TO THE LORD AFTER THE TEST?

BARBARA SPEAKING

DID YOU PASS THE TEST, MY BROTHERS? DID YOU REMAIN FAITHFUL, MY SISTERS? IN THE MIDST OF SATAN'S TEMPTING OFFERS, DID YOU SURRENDER TO HIS LUSTS (WORLDLY POWER AND FAME, UNHOLY ACTS, MONEY, PEOPLE, DRUGS AND SIN)? DID YOU SURRENDER TO HIS REALM OF TEMPORARY PLEASURES AND FAME, MY BROTHERS AND SISTERS? IT IS EVIDENT THAT YOU DO NOT BELIEVE IN THE HOLY POWER AND PRESENCE OF HE (ALMIGHTY GOD), WHO WILL PUT AN END TO EVERYONE WHO DOESN'T PASS HIS HOLY TEST. DO NOT BE FOOLED OR CAPTIVATED BY HE (SATAN) WHO CAN ONLY OFFER TEMPORARY DESIRES AND LUSTS. DO NOT BE FOOLED, O BROTHERS AND SISTERS OF MINE! FOR YOU MUST PASS GOD'S HOLY TEST OF FAITH AND OBEDIENCE, IF YOU DESIRE TO RESIDE IN ETERNAL GLORY WITH THE LORD AND ME. I WILL FIGHT THE GATES OF HELL FOR YOU, MY BROTHERS AND SISTERS, SO THAT YOU WILL BE ABLE TO WITHSTAND THE MANY DARTS AND WORLDLY LUSTS THAT SATAN, OUR ENEMY, PLACES IN OUR VULNERABLE PATHS EVERY DAY. MY BROTHERS AND SISTERS, I, THE LORD'S SENT MESSENGER OF HOLY LOVE, WILL HELP YOU PASS GOD'S TEST.

FEBRUARY 18, 2016 AT 7:34 PM BY: BARBARA ANN MARY MACK

THE DESCENDED GIFT (LA TOYA)

BARBARA SPEAKING TO THE LORD

O HEAVENLY GOD AND CREATOR OF ALL THAT IS GOOD AND HOLY, I BLESS YOU EACH AND EVERY DAY, FOR THE DIVINE GIFT (LA TOYA) THAT YOU DEEM ME WORTHY OF HAVING IN MY VALUABLE LIFE. I AM TRULY GRATEFUL FOR THE GIFT THAT DESCENDED FROM YOUR REALM OF CONTINUOUS LOVE AND MERCY. YOU, O HEAVENLY SPOUSE AND SOURCE OF ETERNAL LIFE, HAVE GRACED ME WITH A GIFT (LA TOYA) THAT I HAVE PLACED IN A PLACE WHERE SHE WILL NEVER BE SUBDUED OR CONQUERED BY THE GATES (HELL) THAT HAVE SWALLOWED MANY OF YOUR WEAK AND VULNERABLE CHILDREN. MY LORD, YOUR HEAVEN SENT GIFT (LA TOYA) HAS BROUGHT ME MANY YEARS OF HAPPINESS AND DELIGHT. MY LORD, MY HOLY GOD AND FATHER, I AM TRULY GRATEFUL FOR YOUR GENEROSITY AND EXPRESSION OF HOLY LOVE FOR ME AND MY GIFT (LA TOYA, MY BEAUTIFUL DAUGHTER).

BARBARA SPEAKING TO LA TOYA, HER HEAVEN SENT GIFT

MY DAUGHTER, LET US GIVE OUR GENEROUS GOD CONTINUOUS PRAISE THROUGHOUT EACH AND EVERY DAY, FOR HE IS WORTHY! GRAB YOUR BEAUTIFUL DAUGHTER, AMYA, AND JOIN ME

IN SONG AND DANCE AS I LIFT MY ESSENCE UP TO HIS IN CONTINUOUS PRAISE AND GRATITUDE!
ALLELUIA!!! ALLELUIA!!! ALLELUIA!!!
FEBRUARY 18, 2016 AT 7:52 PM BY: BARBARA ANN MARY MACK

DO NOT HAVE PITY FOR SATAN'S WORKERS, REGARDLESS OF THEIR RACE, FOR THEY ARE DOOMED.

ALMIGHTY GOD SPEAKING

THEY, THE TARES, THE UNHOLY TARES, ARE IN YOUR MIDST, MY VULNERABLE AND DECEIVED CHILDREN. DO NOT HAVE PITY ON THE TARES, FOR THEY ARE FROM THE REALM OF EVIL AND DESTRUCTION. THEY ARE EVIL COVERED WITH FLESH! DO NOT BE DECEIVED BY THOSE WHO PERFORM ACTS THAT GO AGAINST MY REALM AND VERSION OF HOLINESS. DO NOT HAVE PITY ON THE FLESH THAT YOU SEE, FOR THEY ARE EVIL. THEY ARE GUISED! DO NOT BE FOOLED BY THEM, MY CHILDREN. DO NOT PARDON THEIR UNFORGIVABLE ACTS! FOR THEY HAVE BEEN PLACED IN YOUR PRESENCE BY THE SOURCE OF DESTRUCTION AND DOOM (SATAN, THE ENEMY OF ETERNAL LIFE). THEY ARE THE RACISTS! THEY ARE THOSE WHO GO AGAINST MY VERSION OF RIGHTEOUS ACTS AND DEEDS. THEY ARE THE DOOMED ONES! DO NOT LET THEIR GUISES FOOL YOU, O CHOSEN SHEPHERDS! DO NOT BECOME SUBJECTED TO THEIR REALM OF DECEIT, FOR THEY ARE LIKE SATAN, THEIR FATHER. THEY ARE EVIL COVERED WITH TEMPORARY FLESH. THEY ARE GUISED SO THAT THEY MAY FOOL THE UNSUSPECTING AND SUSCEPTIBLE ONES. I KNOW WHO THEY ARE, MY CHILDREN! I WILL REVEAL THEIR TRUE IDENTITY TO YOU IF YOU COME TO ME FOR GUIDANCE AND TRUTH. MY CHILDREN, DO NOT HAVE PITY ON THEM, FOR THEY ARE DOOMED!
FEBRUARY 18, 2016 AT 8:17 PM BY: BARBARA ANN MARY MACK
SENT THU, FEB 18, 2016 8:26 PM-READ THU 2/18/2016 11:42 PM

A MAN WHO LOVES AND RESPECTS YOU AS MUCH AS I DO, MY GOD

BARBARA SPEAKING TO THE LORD GOD

MY LORD, MY HOLY GOD AND SPOUSE, I THANK YOU FOR SENDING ME A MAN WHO TRULY LOVES AND ADORES YOU AS I DO. MY GOD, HE LOVES YOU SO MUCH! HIS ESSENCE BEAMS WITH THE DIVINE ENERGY THAT EMITS FROM HIS SINCERE LOVE FOR YOU. HIS OBEDIENCE UNTO YOUR HOLY WORD AND PROMPTING SHINES FROM THE DEPTH OF HIS SOUL. FOR HE EXHIBITS HIS ALLEGIANCE TO HIS CREATOR AND GOD. HE EXHIBITS HIS TRUST IN YOUR HOLY PRESENCE IN OUR BLESSED MIDST TODAY. HE EXHIBITS A LOVE THAT I AM PROUD TO BE A PART OF. HE EXHIBITS AN AUTHENTIC LOVE FOR YOU THAT IGNITES MY SOUL THROUGHOUT EACH AND

EVERY DAY. I AM TRULY GRATEFUL AND HONORED TO KNOW AND LOVE HIM, AS YOU KNOW AND LOVE HIM. FOR HE, O LORD, IS CRAIG, OUR ETERNAL BELOVED ONE! HE IS THE FAITHFUL SPOUSE THAT DESCENDED FROM YOUR REALM OF TRUE UNENDING LOVE AND BLISS. MY LORD, MY HOLY GOD, I AM TRULY GRATEFUL FOR THE FUSION OF OUR DIVINE LOVE FOR YOU AND YOUR GREAT CREATION (HUMAN BEINGS). I AM GRATEFUL FOR HIS LOVE!!! *ALLELUIA!!!*
FEBRUARY 15, 2016 AT 8:58 PM BY: BARBARA ANN MARY MACK
SENT SAT, FEB 20, 2016 7:59 PM-READ SAT 2/20/2016 9:42 PM

HI ARCHBISHOP CRAIG! BELOW ARE TODAY'S GOD DICTATED PASSAGES FOR ALL. PLEASE TAKE VERY GOOD CARE OF YOURSELF! *TI AMO! BELLA BARBIE*

WHAT IS THE MEANING OF YOUR LIFE WITHOUT ME, SAYS THE LORD?

ALMIGHTY GOD SPEAKING

MY CHILDREN, WHAT IS THE MEANING AND VALUE OF A LIFE WITHOUT YOUR CREATOR AND GOD? IT IS A LIFE THAT IS FILLED WITH WORLDLY DESPAIR OR CONCERNS. IT IS A LIFE THAT IS DEVOID OF DIVINE COMMUNICATION. IT IS A LIFE THAT IS VULNERABLE TO SATAN AND HIS REALM OF DESTRUCTION. IT IS A LIFE THAT IS FILLED WITH CONFUSION AND DOUBT. IT IS A LIFE THAT SEARCHES FOR A TRUTH THAT CANNOT BE ACCEPTED BY THE UNBELIEVING SEARCHER. IT IS A LIFE THAT DOESN'T KNOW HOW TO COPE IN THE MIDST OF A CRISIS AND PAIN. MY CHILDREN, WHAT IS THE MEANING OF A LIFE THAT CANNOT EXPERIENCE THE DEPTH OF MY VERSION OF LOVE? IT IS A LIFE THAT CANNOT UNITE WITH A REALM (SATAN) THAT IS TEMPORARY AND WITHOUT DIVINE HOPE. FOR SATAN REJECTS, EVEN THOSE WHO SUBMIT TO HIS REALM OF UNHOLINESS, AND DESTROYS THEM AS WELL THROUGH SUICIDE. MY CHILDREN, FLEE FROM THE REALM (SIN, SATAN, AND UNGODLY ACTS) THAT PRODUCES A LIFE WITHOUT ME, FOR THERE IS NO OTHER WAY TO ETERNAL GLORY, BUT THROUGH ME, *SAYS THE LORD.*
FEBRUARY 22, 2016 AT 4:42 PM BY: BARBARA ANN MARY MACK

THEY (SATAN'S SERVANTS OF EVIL) APPEAR TO BE HUMAN TOO

ALMIGHTY GOD SPEAKING

MY CHILDREN, DO NOT FOLLOW THOSE WHO APPEAR TO YOU IN A FORM THAT LOOKS HUMAN. DO NOT FOLLOW THOSE WHO COME TO YOU IN A FORM OF MEEKNESS, BUT DO THE WORKS AND ACTS OF THOSE WHO REPRESENT SATAN, THEIR UNHOLY GOD AND ORIGIN. MY CHILDREN, THEY ARE EVIL COVERED IN A FORM OF FLESH THAT DECEIVES THE UNSUSPECTING AND VULNERABLE ONES. FOLLOW THOSE WHO SPEAK, TEACH, PREACH AND LIVE MY VERSION

OF HOLINESS, FOR THEY REPRESENT ME, *SAYS THE LORD GOD.* MY CHILDREN, ALTHOUGH THEY MAY APPEAR TO SPEAK IN MY HOLY NAME, OBSERVE THEIR ACTS AND DEEDS, FOR SATAN'S SERVANTS CANNOT PERFORM MY VERSION OF HOLINESS. HE, SATAN, IS DEVOID OF HOLINESS, GOODNESS, GENUINE COMPASSION AND MERCY. HE CANNOT IMITATE ME, *SAYS THE LORD GOD,* FOR HE IS THE REALM OF DESTRUCTION AND DOOM. HE IS THE EVERLASTING RESIDENT OF THE DEPTH AND ENTRANCE THROUGH THE GATES OF HELL. HE, SATAN, IS DAMNATION! MY CHILDREN, FLEE FROM THE REALM OF EVIL AS IT APPROACHES YOU IN A FORM THAT APPEARS TO BE HUMAN, FOR THEY DO NOT REPRESENT MY GREAT CREATION (HUMAN BEINGS).

FEBRUARY 22, 2016 AT 5:25 PM BY: BARBARA ANN MARY MACK

SENT MON, FEB 22, 2016 11:06 PM-READ TUE 2/23/2016 12:13 AM

ENJOY YOUR DAY LOVE!!! TI AMO! BELLA BARBARA

I LOST A FEW ALONG THE WAY, SAYS THE LORD

ALMIGHTY GOD SPEAKING

I WEEP, AS I LOOK BELOW MY HEAVENLY KINGDOM AND WITNESS THE ABANDONMENT AND BETRAYAL OF THOSE WHO ONCE SPOKE OF ME WITH DELIGHT AND JOY WITH MY EARTHLY MESSENGER AND BRIDE NOT SO LONG AGO. I WEEP THROUGH THE HEART AND SOUL OF MY FAITHFUL MESSENGER AND BRIDE, AS I WITNESS THE BETRAYAL OF THOSE WHOM I (ALMIGHTY GOD AND BARBARA) HAVE SERVED AND ASSISTED DURING THEIR TIMES OF NEED. WHAT HAVE I DONE, WHICH CAUSED YOU TO BETRAY ME, O BLINDED ONES? WHAT HAVE I NOT HONORED DURING YOUR YEARS OF PAIN AND NEED? WHAT HAS CAUSED YOU TO TURN TO OUR ENEMY (SATAN) FOR COMFORT AND GUIDANCE, INSTEAD OF ME (ALMIGHTY GOD AND BARBARA)? WAS I NOT AVAILABLE TO YOU, O DECEIVED ONES? COULD YOU NOT HAVE CALLED OUT TO ME WHEN YOU NEEDED SOMETHING OTHER THAN WORLDLY LUSTS. DO YOU NOT KNOW THAT I WAS THERE WHEN YOU TURNED TO MY ENEMY? DO YOU NOT KNOW THAT I HAVE WITNESSED YOUR BETRAYAL TOO? MY CHILDREN, YOU HAVE FALLEN INTO THE CLUTCHES OF ONE (SATAN) WHO DOESN'T CARE FOR YOUR ETERNAL SOUL OR YOUR PRESENT STATE. YOU HAVE ABANDON THE ONLY SOURCE AND PROVIDER (ALMIGHTY GOD) OF ETERNAL HAPPINESS. HOW LONG WILL YOU DWELL WITHIN THE REALM OF DECEIT, MY CHILDREN? HOW LONG WILL YOU SEPARATE YOURSELVES FROM MY REALM OF ETERNAL LIFE AND HOLINESS? HOW LONG? MY DECEIVED CHILDREN, HOW LONG?

FEBRUARY 22, 2016 AT 3:53 AM BY: BARBARA ANN MARY MACK

WILL YOU ABANDON US (ALMIGHTY GOD AND BARBARA) TOO, O BELOVED ONE (CRAIG)?

ALMIGHTY GOD AND BARBARA SPEAKING TO CRAIG, THE ETERNAL BELOVED ONE

SOME OF THOSE WHO ONCE WALKED WITH US (ALMIGHTY GOD AND BARBARA) HAVE ABANDONED US FOR SATAN, MY ENEMY, *SAYS THE LORD.* SOME OF THOSE WHO HAVE PROFESSED THEIR ALLEGIANCE TO ME, THEIR CREATOR AND GOD, HAVE FORSAKEN ME. SOME OF THOSE WHO HAVE CRIED OUT TO ME IN THE MIDST OF HARDSHIP AND PAIN, HAVE LEFT ME FOR THE EVIL REALM THAT IS HEADED FOR ETERNAL DAMNATION. SOME OF THOSE WHO HAVE WITNESSED MY GLORY AND POWER, HAVE BEEN DECEIVED BY MY ENEMY AND FOE (SATAN). THEY NOW, REVEAL THEIR ALLEGIANCE TO HE (SATAN, THE DEVIL) WHO HAS DECEIVED THEM. THEY NOW, OPENLY REVEAL THEIR BETRAYAL TO THEIR ORIGIN AND GOD, O BELOVED SON OF MY ETERNAL HEART OF LOVE. WILL YOU FORSAKE ME (ALMIGHTY GOD AND BARBARA) TOO, MY SON? WILL YOU FOLLOW HE (SATAN, THE DEVIL) WHO SEEKS TO DESTROY THOSE WHO DESIRE WORLDLY ACKNOWLEDGMENT AND TEMPORARY FAME? WILL YOU ABANDON THE SACRED LOVE (ALMIGHTY GOD AND BARBARA) THAT HAS PROTECTED YOU, AND HAS FOUGHT THE GATES OF HELL FOR YOUR ETERNAL SOUL? WILL YOU ABANDON THE ARMS THAT CRADLE YOU THROUGHOUT YOUR LONELY NIGHTS, MY SON? WILL YOU ABANDON THE GATES, YES, THE HEAVEN SENT GATES (BARBARA) THAT ENCOMPASS YOUR WELL-LOVED ESSENCE, O WORTHY SON? WILL YOU LEAVE THE DIVINE COMFORT THAT SURROUNDS YOUR BLESSED BEING THROUGHOUT EACH DAY, MY LOVE (CRAIG)? WILL YOU, O BELOVED ONE? WILL YOU ABANDON ME (ALMIGHTY GOD AND BARBARA) TOO?
FEBRUARY 22, 2016 AT 3:30 AM BY: BARBARA ANN MARY MACK
SENT MON, FEB 22, 2016 11:06 PM-READ TUE 2/23/2016 12:13 AM

HAPPY SABBATH, DEAR ARCHBISHOP CRAIG!
ENJOY THIS BLESSED DAY LOVE! TI AMO, BELLA BARBARA

SALUTATIONS, DEAR ARCHBISHOP CRAIG!

YOU HAVE REVEALED THE PRESENCE OF OUR HOLY GOD TO YOUR BELOVED SON, THEREFORE, HE HAS BEEN BLESSED WITH THE DIVINE KNOWLEDGE OF GOD, THE ETERNAL HOLY ONE.

DID I CALL YOU, SAYS THE LORD? OR DID MAN

ALMIGHTY GOD SPEAKING TO THOSE OF THE CLERGY

MY SONS! MY DAUGHTERS! WHO IS YOUR CALLER? WHO HAS CHOSEN YOU TO FILL AN ASSIGNMENT THAT WOULD REPRESENT ME, SAYS THE LORD? WAS IT YOUR CREATOR AND

GOD? DID YOU HEAR MY HOLY VOICE, MY CHILDREN? OR, WERE YOU SELECTED BY HE WHO DOESN'T HAVE THE AUTHORITY TO CHOOSE OR CALL ANYONE? WHO IS YOUR CALLER, MY SON? DID YOU HEAR MY HOLY VOICE CALLING YOU THROUGH THE YEARS? DID YOU FEEL MY HOLY PRESENCE AT YOUR SIDE THROUGHOUT EACH DAY? DID YOU EXPERIENCE THE DEPTH OF A CALLING FROM ME, YOUR ORIGIN AND CREATOR? DID YOU FEEL THE GRACE THAT I ENCOMPASS MY CALLED AND CHOSEN ONES WITH, FROM YOUR YOUTH? DO YOU SPEAK MY HOLY WORDS OF TRUTH AT ALL TIMES, MY SONS? DO YOU FOLLOW MY DAILY INSTRUCTIONS AS YOU MINISTER TO MY VULNERABLE CHILDREN? DO YOU, MY SON? DO YOU, MY DAUGHTER? DO YOU FOLLOW ME, AS I LEAD YOU TO THOSE WHO ARE IN NEED OF MY HOLY UNCHANGEABLE WORDS OF TRUTH? DO YOU FOLLOW THE TEACHINGS OF THOSE WHO THINK THAT THEY KNOW ME AND MY HOLY REALM? OR, DO YOU FOLLOW MY HOLY REALM? WHO HAS CALLED YOU, MY SONS? WHOM DO YOU TRULY REPRESENT? WHO HOLDS YOUR ALLEGIANCE? IS IT ME, SAYS THE LORD?

FEBRUARY 1, 2016 AT 8:20 PM BY: BARBARA ANN MARY MACK

SENT MON, FEB 22, 2016 11:06 PM-READ TUE 2/23/2016 12:13 AM

BUON GIORNO, DEAR ARCHBISHOP CRAIG! BELOW IS TODAY'S GOD INSPIRED PASSAGE. AMORE, BELLA BARBIE

I WILL NOT SETTLE FOR THAT WHICH SATAN OFFERS

BARBARA SPEAKING TO THE LORD GOD

MY LORD, I WILL NOT SETTLE FOR THE PEOPLE AND THINGS THAT SATAN OFFERS TO THOSE WHO DO NOT WAIT ON YOUR REALM OF PERFECTION. I WILL NOT SETTLE FOR THAT WHICH IS CONSIDERED IMPERFECT IN YOUR HOLY EYES, MY LORD. I WILL WAIT ON THE HOLY PROMISE THAT YOU REVEALED TO ME NOT SO LONG AGO. I WILL WAIT ON THE HOLY PROMISE THAT YOU REVEALED TO YOUR FAITHFUL AND OBEDIENT SON. I WILL NOT BE DECEIVED BY THE IMPERFECTION THAT SATAN CONSTANTLY OFFERS ME, FOR I TRULY BELIEVE IN YOUR HOLY WORD AND PROMISE. MY GOD, I BELIEVE IN YOU! I WILL REBUKE THE PEOPLE WHOM SATAN PLACES IN MY REALM OF CONTENTMENT. I WILL REBUKE THE REALM OF DEPRESSION THAT SLITHERS FROM SATAN'S UNHOLY REALM. I WILL REBUKE THE REALM OF DESPAIR, AS IT SLITHERS FROM THE REALM THAT COMFORTS SATAN AND HIS UNHOLY ANGELS ON EARTH TODAY. I WILL REBUKE HIM WITH THE DIVINE LOVE THAT DESCENDS FROM GOD, MY OMNIPOTENT CREATOR AND HOLY SPOUSE. I WILL COMBAT SATAN'S UNWANTED DECEPTIVE OFFERS WITH THE GUIDANCE AND LOVE OF GOD'S HOLY SPIRIT. I WILL NOT BE FOOLED OR LURED INTO THE REALM THAT RELEASES "UNHAPPINESS". I WILL NOT BE LURED INTO THE REALM THAT RELEASES DISCONTENTMENT. I WILL NOT BE LURED INTO THE ARMS OF A MAN WHO DOES NOT KNOW OR LOVE MY HOLY PERFECT CREATOR AND GOD! I WILL NOT BE TEMPTED

OR FOOLED BY HE (SATAN) WHO MOCKS ALMIGHTY GOD'S CALLED AND CHOSEN ONES. FOR HE, THE DECEIVING ONE, OUR ENEMY, SATAN, CANNOT PREVENT THAT WHICH IS ORDERED AND SANCTIFIED BY ALMIGHTY GOD HIMSELF! MY LORD, I WILL NOT SETTLE FOR THAT WHICH SATAN OFFERS ME, NOR WILL I BE DECEIVED BY SATAN, OUR ENEMY. FOR I TRULY LOVE AND TRUST YOUR HOLY PROMISES TO ALL OF YOUR FAITHFUL CHILDREN. ALLELUIA!!!

FEBRUARY 18, 2016 AT 5:09 PM BY: BARBARA ANN MARY MACK

SENT MON, FEB 22, 2016 11:06 PM-READ TUE 2/23/2016 12:13 AM

GREETINGS, ARCHBISHOP CRAIG!!! BELOW IS TODAY'S PASSAGE FOR THE REJOICING BELIEVERS TODAY. TI AMO, BELLA BARBIE

WE DO NOT HAVE TO WAIT UNTIL THE WAR, THE SPIRITUAL WAR, IS OVER, WE CAN REJOICE NOW, SAYS THE LORD!!!

ALMIGHTY GOD SPEAKING

MY LITTLE CHILDREN, WE DO NOT HAVE TO WAIT UNTIL THIS SPIRITUAL BATTLE IS OVER. LET US CELEBRATE AND DANCE TODAY!! LET US EXHIBIT VICTORY TODAY, FOR I AM VICTORY! I AM IN YOUR BLESSED MIDST TODAY! LET US CELEBRATE NOW!!! LET US REJOICE IN OUR HOMES! LET US REJOICE AT OUR WORK PLACES! LET US REJOICE! REJOICE! REJOICE IN OUR CHURCH BUILDINGS! FOR I, THE VICTORIOUS LORD JESUS, AM IN YOUR REJOICING MIDST TODAY! COME, MY CHILDREN! LET ME TAKE YOU TO THE PLACE WHERE MY MESSENGER AND BRIDE (BARBARA) CELEBRATES OUR VICTORY EVERY DAY! LET ME TAKE YOU TO HER PLACE OF REJOICING, FOR SHE IS THE ETERNAL BRIDE OF VICTORY (ALMIGHTY GOD)!!! SHE IS MINE!!! WITNESS HER DANCES! WITNESS HER SONGS OF CONTINUOUS PRAISE! WITNESS HER JOY! WITNESS HER IGNITED ESSENCE OF DIVINE REVERENCE AND ALLEGIANCE UNTO HER FAITHFUL SPOUSE AND GOD! WITNESS ME WITHIN HER DIVINE ESSENCE, AS SHE CELEBRATES VICTORY OVER THE REALM OF EVIL AND SIN TODAY!!! COME ONE! COME ALL! LET US CELEBRATE VICTORY (ALMIGHTY GOD) TODAY!!! ALLELUIA!!!

FEBRUARY 17, 2016 AT 8:10 PM BY: BARBARA ANN MARY MACK

HI!

THROUGH THE YEARS I HAVE WATCHED OVER YOU THROUGH BARBARA, MY SACRIFICIAL BRIDE

ALMIGHTY GOD SPEAKING

MY LITTLE CHILDREN, I AM VERY NEAR TO YOU AT THIS TIME, FOR I HAVE NEVER LEFT YOU. YOU CAN WITNESS MY HOLY PRESENCE THROUGH THE FORM (BARBARA) THAT REPRESENTS ME TODAY. YOU CAN WITNESS MY MIGHTY WORKS THROUGH THE HUMBLED BEING (BARBARA) THAT I HAVE BLESSED THIS GENERATION WITH. YOU CAN WITNESS MY MERCY, COMPASSION, AND CONTINUOUS LOVE FOR THOSE WHOM I HAVE CALLED AND CHOSEN TO WITNESS ME TODAY, THROUGH THE OBEDIENT ESSENCE OF MY HEAVEN SENT MESSENGER (BARBARA) TODAY. THROUGH THE YEARS SHE HAS CONVEYED MY HOLY MESSAGES TO THOSE WHOM I HAVE DEEMED WORTHY TO WITNESS MY VERSION OF FAITHFULNESS, OBEDIENCE, DIVINE SACRIFICIAL ACTS AND ALLEGIANCE TO MY REALM OF HOLINESS. MY LITTLE CHILDREN, THROUGH THE YEARS, I HAVE COMFORTED YOU WITH THE GIFT OF MY MANY FLOWING TEARS, WHICH WERE RELEASED THROUGH THE EYES OF SHE (BARBARA) WHO REPRESENTS MY COMPASSION AND MERCY TODAY. MY LITTLE CHILDREN, THROUGH THE YEARS I HAVE BEEN BY YOUR SIDE. DID YOU NOT FEEL MY HOLY PRESENCE THROUGH MY MESSENGER AND BRIDE (BARBARA)? FOR I WAS THERE, SAYS THE LORD.

FEBRUARY 16, 2016 AT 5:13 PM BY: BARBARA ANN MARY MACK

JESUS, THE RANSOM

JESUS, ALMIGHTY GOD, SPEAKING

MY LITTLE CHILDREN, NO ONE ELSE COULD HAVE DONE IT FOR YOU. NO ONE ELSE COULD HAVE PAID THE PRICE THAT WAS REQUIRED FOR YOUR SALVATION AND ETERNAL GLORY IN SWEET PARADISE WITH MY HEAVENLY FATHER AND ME. NO ONE ELSE IS WORTHY TO FULFILL THE RANSOM PRICE! NO ONE ELSE COULD HAVE LOVED YOU AS MUCH AS MY HEAVENLY ORIGIN AND GOD. NO ONE ELSE'S SON WAS WORTHY TO FULFILL THE RANSOM PRICE. MY CHILDREN, GIVE OUR HEAVENLY GOD AND FATHER CONTINUOUS PRAISE, GLORY, AND HONOR, FOR HE HAS OFFERED HIS ONLY BEGOTTEN SON (THE LORD JESUS), AS THE RANSOM PRICE FOR MANY VALUABLE SOULS. HE HAS OFFERED HIS LOVING SON, AS A SACRIFICE FOR THOSE WHO WERE, AND, ARE NOT WORTHY OF SUCH A GREAT HONOR. MY CHILDREN, BECAUSE OF OUR HEAVENLY FATHER AND GOD'S GREAT LOVE FOR YOU, HE HAS SENT ME, HIS ONLY SON, HIS ONLY SON THAT CAME FROM HIS DIVINE ESSENCE AND LOVE, TO REDEEM THAT WHICH THE PRICE, THE RANSOM, THE SACRIFICIAL LAMB OF GOD, IS WORTHY OF COMPLETING. MY CHILDREN, LET YOU AND I GIVE CONTINUOUS PRAISE AND ACKNOWLEDGMENT TO ALPHA (ALMIGHTY GOD, THE ETERNAL FATHER), FOR HE IS WORTHY!!!

FEBRUARY 14, 2016 AT 7:22 PM BY: BARBARA ANN MARY MACK

BARBARA SPEAKING TO ALMIGHTY GOD AND CRAIG, THE ETERNAL BELOVED ONE

BUON SAN VALENTINO, MY LOVE! BUON SAN VALENTINO!

I AM TRULY GRATEFUL! FOR YOU HAVE EXHIBITED DIVINE LOVE FOR ME IN THE PRESENCE OF THOSE WHO WERE CHOSEN AND PERMITTED TO WITNESS DIVINITY IN THE FORM OF A HUMBLED WOMAN (BARBARA). HAPPY VALENTINE'S DAY, O GRACIOUS ONE (ALMIGHTY GOD AND CRAIG)! HAPPY VALENTINE'S DAY, MY LOVE (ALMIGHTY GOD AND CRAIG)! YOU, O LORD, HAVE GRACED YOUR HUMBLED DAUGHTER AND BRIDE (BARBARA) WITH THE GIFT OF EXPERIENCING AN EXPRESSION OF DIVINE LOVE TODAY THROUGH YOUR OBEDIENT AND FAITHFUL SON, THE ETERNAL BELOVED ONE. YOU (ALMIGHTY GOD AND CRAIG), MY LOVE, REVEALED THE DEPTH OF YOUR LOVE AND REVERENCE FOR ME ON THIS BLESSED DIVINE ORDERED VALENTINE'S DAY. I, IN RETURN, WILL ALWAYS EXHIBIT MY LOVE AND ALLEGIANCE TO YOU (ALMIGHTY GOD AND CRAIG)! *ALLELUIA!!!*

FEBRUARY 14, 2016 AT 11:51 PM BY: BARBARA ANN MARY MACK

SENT MON, FEB 22, 2016 11:06 PM-READ TUE 2/23/2016 12:13 AM

BUON SAN VALENTINO ARCHBISHOP CRAIG!!!

NO ONE HAS ANY IDEA OF THE DEPTH AND MAGNITUDE OF MY FEAR, MY HOLY ASSIGNMENT

BARBARA SPEAKING

OH, IF YOU ONLY KNEW, O BROTHERS AND SISTERS OF MINE. IF YOU ONLY KNEW THE DEPTH OF MY ASSIGNMENT FROM OUR HEAVENLY GOD AND ETERNAL FATHER. IF YOU ONLY KNEW THE DEPTH OF HIS UNENDING LOVE FOR HIS GREAT CREATION (HUMAN BEINGS). IF ONLY YOU KNEW THE MAGNITUDE OF THIS GREAT AND HOLY ACT OF MERCY AND LOVE, THAT DESCENDED WITH ME FROM HIS MIGHTY THRONE ON HIGH. IF ONLY YOU KNEW OF THE POWERFUL ASSIGNMENT OF DIVINE LOVE THAT WAS PLACED IN MY HUMBLED CARE. IF ONLY YOU KNEW THE PURPOSE OF MY DIVINE ASSIGNMENT OF LOVE. IF ONLY YOU KNEW OF THE BATTLE AGAINST THE REALM OF EVIL THAT HAS TAKEN DOWN MANY UNPROTECTED SOULS THROUGH THE YEARS. IF ONLY YOU KNEW OF THE TWO EDGED SWORD OF VICTORY THAT WAS GIVEN TO ME BY OUR VICTORIOUS LORD AND GOD (JESUS). IF ONLY YOU KNEW OF THE MANY SLEEPLESS NIGHTS THAT WERE ENGULFED IN THE TEARS OF THE HEAVEN SENT WARRIOR (BARBARA) OF CHRIST JESUS, THE SACRIFICIAL LAMB OF GOD. IF ONLY YOU KNEW OF THE SUFFERING THAT ENCOMPASSES GOD'S HEAVEN SENT MESSENGER AND BRIDE (BARBARA) AS I BATTLE FOR THE VALUABLE

SOULS OF THE CALLED AND CHOSEN ONES. OH, THE MANY, MANY TEARS THAT HAVE LEFT MY REALM OF INNER PAIN AND TORMENT, AS I BATTLED FOR THE SOULS OF THOSE WHOM THE LORD ALMIGHTY HAS PLACED IN MY SPIRITUAL CARE. FLOW! TEARS, FLOW! FLOW IN THE DIRECTION OF HE (ALMIGHTY GOD) WHO HAS CONSOLED ME FOR YEARS. FLOW INTO THE WAITING ARMS OF GOD, MY REDEEMER! FLOW INTO THE REALM THAT RELEASES COMFORT AND EVERLASTING JOY! FLOW! O MANY TEARS OF MINE. FLOW IN THE DIRECTION OF SWEET PARADISE ABOVE. FOR THERE, MY ETERNAL SOUL WILL FIND ETERNAL PEACE!!! *ALLELUIA!!!*
FEBRUARY 2, 2016 AT 6:24 PM BY: BARBARA ANN MARY MACK

MY HEAVEN SENT TREASURE: GOD'S HOLY WORDS TODAY

BARBARA SPEAKING

DESCEND, O SWEET TREASURE THAT WAS RELEASED FROM THE MIGHTY THRONE OF GOD, MY SAVIOR AND HOLY SPOUSE. DESCEND, O SWEET TREASURE THAT IS A DIVINE GIFT TO GOD'S CALLED AND CHOSEN ONES TODAY. DESCEND TO THE RECEIVING ARMS AND MIND OF GOD'S SENT MESSENGER AND BRIDE (BARBARA). DESCEND TO THE REALM (BARBARA) THAT REPRESENTS YOUR HOLY OMNIPOTENT AND OMNIPRESENCE TODAY. DESCEND TO THE EARS AND HEART THAT TREASURE YOUR NEEDED PRESENCE IN THE LIVES OF THOSE WHO DO NOT OPENLY EXHIBIT YOUR HOLY EXISTENCE. DESCEND, O SWEET WORDS THAT REVEAL THE ETERNAL GLORY THAT AWAITS THE CHOSEN ONES, FOR YOU ARE WELL-LOVED BY ME! DESCEND TO ME, O TREASURE THAT ENLIGHTENS THE SOUL OF GOD'S SENT QUEEN (BARBARA)! DESCEND TO ME EVERY DAY, AS I ENJOY THE BLESSING OF YOUR HOLY PRESENCE. DESCEND TO ME AS I SLEEP! DESCEND TO ME AS I RELAX IN THE COMPANY OF THOSE WHOM YOU HAVE BLESSED AND SANCTIFIED. DESCEND TO ME IN THE PRESENCE OF CRAIG, OUR ETERNAL BELOVED ONE, FOR YOU DEEM HIM WORTHY. DESCEND TO ME, O SWEET TREASURE! DESCEND TO ME IN THE MIDST OF THE REALM (EVIL) THAT EMITS DESTRUCTION AND HAVOC UPON EARTH'S RESIDENTS TODAY! DESCEND TO ME IN THE MIDST OF THE HOLY ONES! DESCEND TO ME IN THE MIDST OF YOUR ANGELS AND SAINTS! DESCEND! DESCEND! DESCEND, O SWEET WORDS OF DIVINE TRUTH AND FREEDOM! FOR I, YOUR WELCOMED SPOUSE, AM READY TO RECEIVE YOU! *ALLELUIA!!!*
FEBRUARY 13, 2016 AT 6:36 PM BY: BARBARA ANN MARY MACK
SENT MON, FEB 22, 2016 11:06 PM-READ TUE 2/23/2016 12:13 AM

THANK YOU, DEAR ARCHBISHOP CRAIG! GOD BLESS YOU FOR THE WONDERFUL HOMILY AND BLESSING TODAY. LA TOYA AND I REALLY ENJOYED YOUR MOVING SERMON. WE DISCUSSED IT ON OUR WAY HOME. AS I MENTIONED EARLIER, SATAN, OUR (ALMIGHTY GOD AND HIS CALLED AND CHOSEN ONES) ENEMY, ALWAYS PLACES OBSTACLES IN OUR PATH AND MINDS

WHEN THE LORD TELLS US TO GO TO THE LOCATIONS WHERE HE SENDS YOU TO PREACH AND TEACH HIS CONGREGATION. SATAN KNOWS OF THE DIVINE IMPORTANCE OF MY PRESENCE THERE AT THIS TIME. ALTHOUGH THE ENEMY'S TACTICS APPEAR TO BE LEGITIMATE, THE LORD REVEALS TO ME THE SOURCE BEHIND SATAN'S DECEPTIVE ACTS. EVERY TIME THE LORD TELLS ME TO ATTEND THE SERVICES WHERE YOU PREACH HIS HOLY WORD, SATAN ALWAYS PLACES THE REALM OF APPREHENSION WITHIN MY MIND. A FEW HOURS BEFORE WE LEFT FOR MASS TODAY, I HAD A VIVID DREAM OF US AT CHURCH. IN MY DREAM, YOU WERE GIVING LA TOYA A BLESSING AND SAYING PRAYERS. THERE WERE OTHERS AROUND LA TOYA WITH YOU. IN MY DREAM, WE WERE WEARING PURPLE. WHEN I GOT IN THE CAR WITH TOYA AND AMYA, I LOOKED OVER AT LA TOYA AND NOTICED THAT SHE WAS WEARING PURPLE LIKE SHE DID IN MY DREAM. WHEN WE ENTERED THE CHURCH TODAY, I HUNG MY HEAD IN THE PRESENCE OF THE LORD, WHEN I NOTICED THAT YOU AND DEACON ANTHONY WERE WEARING PURPLE VESTMENTS. IT WAS AS IF MY DREAM HAD MANIFESTED IN MY PRESENCE. EVERYTHING AT CHURCH TODAY WAS CONSISTENT WITH MY DREAM. WHENEVER THE LORD REVEALS THINGS TO ME IN THE FORM OF DREAMS, THE MANIFESTATION OF GOD'S REVELATIONS OCCUR NOT LONG AFTER THE DREAM. MY LORD, MY HOLY GOD, I GIVE YOU CONTINUOUS PRAISE!!! *ALLELUIA!!! TI AMO!*
SENT SUN, FEB 28, 2016 4:22 PM-READ SUN 2/28/2016 4:51 PM

ARCHBISHOP CRAIG, LA TOYA WANTS TO KNOW THE CONTACT INFORMATION OF THE CATERING SERVICE THAT WAS USED AT DEACON ANTHONY'S ORDINATION CEREMONY LAST MONTH. LA TOYA LOVED THE ROAST BEEF. SHE WANTS THE INFO FOR HER PRIVATE USE. SHE LOVES GOOD FOOD! PERHAPS YOU CAN GIVE HER THE INFO WHEN WE SEE YOU AT MASS. *AMORE, O BELOVED ONE. BELLA BARBIE*

ONE CANNOT HIDE THE TRUTH FROM ALMIGHTY GOD

BARBARA SPEAKING

MY BROTHERS AND SISTERS, DO NOT THINK THAT YOUR WORKS AND DEEDS CAN BE HIDDEN FROM OUR OMNIPRESENT CREATOR AND GOD, FOR HE SEES AND HEARS EVERYTHING. IF ONE ISN'T TRUTHFUL TO HIMSELF OR HERSELF, HE OR SHE MAY SUFFER INNER AGONY AND DISCOMFORT IN THE PRESENCE OF OTHERS AND THE LORD. MY BROTHERS AND SISTERS, IF YOU PROFESS THAT YOU KNOW GOD'S HOLY TRUTH, THEN YOU SHOULD LIVE GOD'S HOLY TRUTH EVERY DAY. YOU MUST BE TRUTHFUL WITH YOURSELF AND OTHERS. FOR WITHIN THE REALM OF DIVINE TRUTH, ONE FINDS GREAT COMFORT AND RELIEF. THE REALM OF TRUTH GUIDES YOU IN THE DIRECTION OF GOD'S HOLY PRESENCE AND POWER SO THAT SATAN, OUR ENEMY, CANNOT PENETRATE YOUR REALM OF JOY AND COMFORT. SEEK GOD'S HOLY REALM

OF TRUTH AS YOU APPROACH EACH NEW AND BLESSED DAY. FOR WITHIN THE REALM OF HOLY TRUTH, YOU WILL FIND CONTINUOUS PEACE. MY BROTHERS AND SISTERS, DO NOT DECEIVE YOURSELVES, FOR THE TRUTH WILL MAKE YOU FREE! *ALLELUIA!!!*
FEBRUARY 26, 2016 AT 7:16 PM BY: BARBARA ANN MARY MACK

WHAT IS IT DOING FOR YOU? WHAT IS MY HOLY PRESENCE IN YOUR MIDST TODAY DOING FOR YOU, SAYS THE LORD?

ALMIGHTY GOD SPEAKING

MY CHILDREN, WHAT DOES MY HOLY PRESENCE IN YOUR BLESSED MIDST TODAY MEAN TO YOU? ARE YOU PLEASED WITH THE VISIBILITY OF YOUR HOLY CREATOR AND GOD? ARE YOU PLEASED, THAT I DEEM THIS GENERATION WORTHY TO RECEIVE MY HOLY MESSAGES AND PLAN THAT ARE CONVEYED THROUGH MY MODERN DAY PROPHETESS (BARBARA)? ARE YOU GRATEFUL THAT I FIND YOU WORTHY TO HEAR MY VOICE THROUGH MY CHOSEN MESSENGER TODAY? MY CHILDREN, IS MY PRESENCE IN YOUR MIDST TODAY HELPFUL TO YOU? ARE YOU WALKING IN MY VERSION OF HOLINESS? OR, ARE YOU LIVING THE LIFE OF ONE WHO DOES NOT ACCEPT THE REALITY OF MY HOLY PRESENCE AND EXISTENCE? MY CHILDREN, YOUR ACTIONS REVEAL THE TRUTH. YOUR ACTIONS REVEAL YOUR LEVEL OF BELIEF IN MY HOLY PRESENCE IN YOUR MIDST. MY CHILDREN, BELIEVE IN MY HOLY PRESENCE, FOR I AM IN YOUR BLESSED MIDST TODAY! I HAVE SPOKEN THROUGH MY MESSENGER (BARBARA) FOR MANY YEARS. I HAVE REVEALED MYSELF TO YOU THROUGH HER OBEDIENT BEING. WHAT WILL YOU DO WITH THE DIVINE KNOWLEDGE THAT SHE HAS SHARED WITH YOU, MY CHILDREN? WHAT WILL YOU DO WITH THE SPIRITUAL NOURISHMENT THAT DESCENDED FROM MY THRONE OF LOVE AND MERCY? WHAT? MY CHILDREN. WHAT WILL YOU DO WITH MY HEAVEN SENT GIFT? WHAT HAVE YOU LEARNED FROM ME TODAY? WHAT IS MY HOLY PRESENCE DOING FOR YOU TODAY, *SAYS THE LORD?*
FEBRUARY 27, 2016 AT 2:35 AM BY: BARBARA ANN MARY MACK

AWAY, AWAY, AWAY FROM THIS TANGIBLE REALM (WORLD)

BARBARA SPEAKING TO ALMIGHTY GOD

OH, AS I ROAM IN THE MIDST OF DIVINE HEAVEN SENT BLISS AND ECSTASY, AS I SIT BACK IN MY HUMBLE LITTLE HOME ON EARTH, MY IGNITED SPIRIT SOARS IN THE MIDST OF HEAVEN SENT BLISS AND CONTENTMENT. AS I SIT BACK AND ENJOY THE GOODNESS OF MY HUMBLE LITTLE SANCTUARY ON EARTH, MY LORD, MY HOLY GOD, I BLESS YOU THROUGHOUT THE DAY, AS I SOAR AWAY FROM THE REALM OF TANGIBILITY. FAR AWAY FROM THE REALM

OF TANGIBILITY, MY IGNITED SPIRIT FUSES WITH GOD'S ETERNAL HOLY SPIRIT. REJOICE! O IGNITED SPIRIT OF MINE, AS YOU SOAR IN THE MIDST OF DIVINITY. REJOICE! O BLESSED SPIRIT OF MINE, AS YOU FUSE WITH THE REALM (ALMIGHTY GOD) THAT DOESN'T WELCOME THE TANGIBLE REALM. REJOICE! O BLESSED SPIRIT OF GOD'S CHOSEN MESSENGER AND BRIDE (BARBARA), AS YOU SOAR FAR AWAY FROM THE REALM THAT INHABITS TANGIBILITY. OH, THE SPIRIT OF GOD'S IGNITED MESSENGER (BARBARA) SOARS AWAY FROM ALL THAT OFFEND AND DOUBT DIVINE EXISTENCE IN OUR MIDST TODAY. SOAR! O BLESSED SPIRIT OF MINE. SOAR IN THE MIDST OF DIVINITY! *ALLELUIA!!!*

FEBRUARY 28, 2016 AT 12:31 AM BY: BARBARA ANN MARY MACK

ALWAYS ON MY MIND

BARBARA SPEAKING TO CRAIG, THE ETERNAL BELOVED ONE

YOU ARE ALWAYS ON MY MIND, *DEAR ONE.*

I HAVE CAPTURED THE BLESSED ESSENCE OF GOD'S CHOSEN AND *WELL-LOVED SON.*

I HAVE CAPTURED YOU WITH THE GIFT OF *GOD'S HEAVEN SENT CHARM,*

FOR I HAVE BEEN GIVEN THE DIVINE TASK OF KEEPING YOU FROM SATAN, OUR ENEMY'S, *PHYSICAL, EMOTIONAL, AND SPIRITUAL HARM.*

YOUR WELL-BEING IS ALWAYS MY CONCERN, O HEAVENLY *LOVED ONE.*

I HAVE SENT UP MANY ANSWERED PRAYERS, FOR THE SALVATION OF CRAIG, GOD'S FAITHFUL AND *OBEDIENT SON.*

YOU ARE ALWAYS WITHIN MY *SPIRITUAL TOUCH.*

I WILL ALWAYS, DEAR ONE, ALWAYS *LOVE YOU VERY MUCH.*

YOU HAVE BEEN SENT BY OUR HOLY *CREATOR AND GOD,*

TO EXHIBIT THE VASTNESS AND MAGNIFICENCE OF *HIS HOLY AND EVERLASTING LOVE.*

THROUGHOUT EACH DAY, AND *GOD'S MARVELOUS NIGHT.*

YOUR WELCOMED ESSENCE, DEAR ONE, IS FOREVER WITHIN MY *SPIRITUAL SIGHT. ALLELUIA!!!*

FEBRUARY 27, 2016 AT 7:29 PM BY: BARBARA ANN MARY MACK

ARE MY WRITINGS IN VAIN, MY LORD? FOR THEY DO NOT HEAR YOUR HOLY WORDS

BARBARA SPEAKING

THEY HAVEN'T CHANGED, MY LORD. THEY DO NOT HONOR YOUR HOLY WORDS TODAY, AS THEIR FOREFATHERS AND MOTHERS DID NOT. THEY DO NOT BELIEVE OR HONOR YOUR HOLY WORDS THAT FLOW THROUGH THE BIBLE, AND THEY DO NOT HONOR YOUR LIFE SAVING WORDS

THAT YOU SO LOVINGLY DICTATE THROUGH ME. WHAT CAN WE DO, MY LORD? HOW CAN WE REVEAL TO THEM THE SERIOUSNESS OF YOUR HOLY WORDS TODAY? I WILL WRITE DOWN EVERY HOLY WORD THAT YOU DICTATE TO ME, MY GOD, FOR I AM WILLING TO ABIDE BY YOUR HOLY MESSAGES TODAY. MY LORD, MY DAUGHTER (LA TOYA), WHOM YOU HAVE SO GRACIOUSLY BLESSED ME WITH NOT SO LONG AGO, REVERES YOU AS I DO. I BLESS YOU, O SAVING GOD AND SPOUSE OF MINE, FOR COUNTING HER AS ONE OF YOUR CHOSEN ONES. MY GOD, SHE REVERES THE HOLY WORDS THAT YOU REVEAL TO ME AS I DO. SHE TRULY LOVES AND ADORES YOU AS I DO. SHE TOO, REVERES THE HOLY WORDS THAT DESCEND IN OUR BLESSED MIDST TODAY AS SHE REVERES YOUR HOLY WORDS THAT FLOW THROUGH THE BLESSED BIBLE. MY LORD, MY HOLY GOD, MY FAMILY (CRAIG, LA TOYA AND AMYA) AND I TRULY BELIEVE IN YOUR HOLY DICTATED WORDS.

FEBRUARY 27, 2016 AT 8:13 PM BY: BARBARA ANN MARY MACK

I AM KNOCKING ON YOUR DOORS AGAIN, SAYS THE LORD

ALMIGHTY GOD SPEAKING

BECAUSE OF MY LOVE FOR YOU, I AM KNOCKING ON THE DOORS TO YOUR HEARTS AGAIN, MY CHILDREN. WILL YOU RESPOND TO MY HOLY CALL THIS TIME, O LONGED FOR ONES? WILL YOU ANSWER THE HOLY CALL THAT BECKONS YOU TO LEAVE THE REALM (SIN-SATAN'S REALM OF UNRIGHTEOUSNESS) THAT HATES ETERNAL LIFE IN SWEET PARADISE? WILL YOU ANSWER MY FINAL CALL, O BACKSLIDING ONES, BEFORE THE GATES OF HELL CLAIM YOUR ETERNAL SOULS? I AM KNOCKING ON YOUR DOORS THROUGH THE DILIGENT ACTS OF MY HEAVEN SENT MESSENGER AND BRIDE (BARBARA). WILL YOU RESPOND TO MY HOLY CALL AS SHE DELIVERS MY LIFE SAVING MESSAGES TO YOU TODAY? WILL YOU OPEN THE DOORS TO YOUR WOUNDED AND CAPTURED HEARTS, SO THAT I MAY ENTER WITH MY HEALING BREAD OF LIFE? COME, MY CHILDREN! OPEN YOUR DOORS AND LET JESUS, YOUR SAVING AND VICTORIOUS GOD ENTER, SO THAT HE MAY HEAL AND FREE YOU FROM SIN TODAY.

FEBRUARY 26, 2016 AT 8:37 PM BY: BARBARA ANN MARY MACK

NOTHING CAN STOP THE HOLY SPIRIT FROM PENETRATING MY REALM

BARBARA SPEAKING

NOTHING! NOTHING! NOTHING, CAN STOP THE GIFT OF GOD'S HOLY PERFECT SPIRIT FROM PENETRATING MY SOUL THROUGHOUT EACH AND EVERY BLESSED DAY! NOTHING CAN PREVENT ME FROM CELEBRATING THE GIFT OF HIS HOLY SPIRIT THAT DWELLS WITHIN MY HUMBLED AND BLESSED BEING. NOTHING CAN PREVENT THE BLESSING THAT DESCENDED

WITH GOD'S HOLY SPIRIT, THAT KEEPS ME SAFE FROM THE REALM (SATAN, THE DEVIL) THAT STEALS THE UNPROTECTED SOULS OF THE UNBELIEVING ONES. MY LORD, MY HOLY GOD, I BOW IN THE PRESENCE OF YOUR HOLY SPIRIT, AS IT PENETRATES MY HAPPY REALM. I WELCOME YOU, O BLESSED SPIRIT OF GOD, MY ETERNAL SAVIOR AND REALM OF UNENDING COMFORT AND BLISS. I WELCOME YOU THROUGHOUT THE DAY. I WELCOME YOU DURING MY PEACEFUL AND SLEEPLESS NIGHTS. I WELCOME YOU, O BELOVED SPIRIT OF GOD, THE HOLY ONE, FOR YOU ARE MY PLACE OF REFUGE AND DIVINE TRANQUILITY. YOU ARE MY LIFE FORCE, MY SOLE PURPOSE FOR EXISTING. I OFFER YOU MY GRATITUDE, O BLESSED HOLY SPIRIT OF GOD, THE ALMIGHTY ONE, THE ETERNAL ONE! THE EVERLASTING FOUNTAIN OF LIVING WATER AND DIVINE ECSTASY ON EARTH.

FEBRUARY 26, 2016 AT 6:45 PM BARBARA ANN MARY MACK

THE LORD IS SPEAKING! CAN YOU HEAR HIM?

THE HEAVENLY ANGELS
SPEAKING TO THE
RESIDENTS OF EARTH

HARK! DEAR CHILDREN OF GOD, THE HIGHEST. HARK! FOR HE IS ABOUT TO SPEAK TO YOU AGAIN. HARK! O RESIDENTS OF EARTH TODAY. FOR THE LORD, YOUR CREATOR AND HOLY GOD, IS ABOUT TO SPEAK TO YOU AGAIN. LISTEN! LISTEN! ALL WHO DWELL ON EARTH TODAY. FOR THE LORD IS ABOUT TO REVEAL HIS TRUTH TO YOU TODAY. HE IS IN YOUR BLESSED MIDST! LISTEN, ALL YOU RESIDENTS OF EARTH! FOR THE LORD, OUR OMNIPOTENT GOD, IS READY TO SPEAK TO YOU AGAIN. LET THE REALM OF SILENCE SURROUND YOU. FOR THE LORD, OUR GOD, IS ABOUT TO REVEAL HIS HOLY THOUGHTS AND WORDS TO YOU TODAY.

ALMIGHTY GOD SPEAKING

O BLESSED GENERATION! O CHOSEN PERIOD OF TIME. I, THE ONLY LORD AND GOD, AM IN YOUR MIDST TODAY. I HAVE BLESSED THIS GENERATION WITH THE GIFT OF MY HOLY PRESENCE, SO THAT YOU WILL BE AWARE OF MY GIFT OF LIFE IN THE MIDST OF THIS TRAGIC PERIOD OF TIME. I, THE ONLY LORD AND GOD, HAVE BESTOWED UPON THIS GENERATION THE BLESSINGS THAT DESCEND FROM MY REALM OF GENEROSITY AND DIVINE UNENDING LOVE. I HAVE BLESSED THIS GENERATION WITH THE GIFT OF MY OPEN ARMS, SO THAT YOU MAY FLEE TO ME AS SATAN AND HIS REALM OF DESTRUCTION SLITHER THROUGH THE STREETS AND HOMES OF MY VULNERABLE LOVED ONES TODAY. I HAVE PENETRATED THIS BLESSED PERIOD OF TIME THROUGH THE WEAK AND HUMBLED ESSENCE OF MY MESSENGER (BARBARA). HARK! MY CHILDREN. DO NOT LET HER WEAKNESS FOOL YOU, FOR SHE IS BLESSED WITH THE GIFT OF MY OMNIPOTENT ESSENCE AND DIVINE LOVE. I HAVE SPOKEN THROUGH HER FOR MANY YEARS. SOME OF YOU RECOGNIZED ME AND SOME OF YOU HAVE NOT. I HAVE CHOSEN THOSE WHOM I DEEM WORTHY TO REPRESENT ME. I HAVE FORMED THEM IN THE APPEARANCE THAT PLEASES ME. I HAVE BLESSED MY PROPHETS AND MESSENGERS WITH THE DIVINE STRENGTH

TO COMBAT AND SUBDUE EVERY FORM OF EVIL THAT TRIES TO CAPTURE AND DESTROY MY CHILDREN TODAY. I HAVE NOT CHANGED, MY CHILDREN! I AM IN CONTROL OF EVERYTHING! DO NOT BE FOOLED NOR DECEIVED BY SATAN, THE GREAT DECEIVER, FOR HE IS OUR (ALMIGHTY GOD AND EARTH'S RESIDENTS) ENEMY!

BARBARA SPEAKING

MY BLESSED BROTHERS AND SISTERS, LET US REJOICE IN THE GENEROSITY THAT DESCENDS FROM THE HEART AND THRONE OF OUR GREAT AND HOLY GOD. LET US REJOICE IN THE GOODNESS THAT FLOWS FROM HIS HOLY ETERNAL ESSENCE. LET US GIVE HIM PRAISE AND ACKNOWLEDGMENT FOR HIS CONTINUOUS EXPRESSION OF LOVE AND ALLEGIANCE TO HIS CHILDREN ON EARTH TODAY. LET US REJOICE IN SONG AND DANCE, AS WE LIFT OUR GRATEFUL HEARTS AND SOULS TO THE ONE AND ONLY OMNIPOTENT AND OMNIPRESENT GOD. FOR HE ALONE, IS WORTHY, WORTHY, WORTHY TO BE PRAISED AT ALL TIMES! *ALLELUIA!!!*
FEBRUARY 26, 2016 AT 5:52 PM BY: BARBARA ANN MARY MACK

NOT JUST WORDS, BUT HOLY ACTS AND DEEDS, SAYS THE LORD!

ALMIGHTY GOD SPEAKING

MY CHILDREN, ALTHOUGH THE WORDS OF PRAISE EXIT YOUR LIPS AT CHURCH, YOUR ACTS AND DEEDS REVEAL THE CONTRARY. I, THE LORD GOD, CLOSE MY HOLY EARS TO THE VAIN PRAYERS AND PRAISES THAT EXIT THE LIPS OF THOSE WHO DO NOT LIVE ACCORDING TO MY VERSION OF HOLINESS. MY CHILDREN, THIS IS A VERY CRUCIAL PERIOD OF TIME, FOR SATAN, OUR ENEMY, HAS DECEIVED AND CAPTURED MANY. MY CHILDREN, I WILL ACCEPT THE PRAYERS AND PRAISES FROM THOSE WHO SEEK MY EARTHLY AND HEAVENLY KINGDOMS WITH A GENUINE DESIRE. MY CHILDREN, YOU SPEAK THE WORDS THAT COME FROM YOUR HEARTS AND SOULS. MY CHILDREN, LET YOUR WORDS OF PRAISE REVEAL YOUR ALLEGIANCE TO YOUR HOLY CREATOR AND GOD, AND NOT TO THE REALM OF EVIL THAT SLITHERS THROUGH THE CHURCH PEWS. MY CHILDREN, I AM AWARE OF THE INTEGRITY OF YOUR ALLEGIANCE AND WORDS OF PRAISE. I KNOW THE SECRETS THAT YOU HIDE FROM THE WORLD. I KNOW THE SECRETS OF YOUR HEARTS. MY CHILDREN, LET YOUR WORDS OF PRAISE REVEAL YOUR ALLEGIANCE TO THE ONLY REALM (ALMIGHTY GOD) THAT CAN SAVE YOUR ETERNAL SOULS, FOR I AM IN YOUR BLESSED MIDST TODAY, *SAYS THE LORD!!!*
FEBRUARY 25, 2016 AT 4:11 PM BY: BARBARA ANN MARY MACK

JESUS! OH, WHAT A SONG OF PRAISE!

BARBARA SPEAKING

JESUS! JESUS! JESUS! OH, WHAT A GLORIOUS HYMN OF PRAISE! LET US LIFT UP THE HOLY NAME OF *JESUS*, AS WE GIVE HIM CONTINUOUS ACKNOWLEDGMENT! FOR HE IS GOD, THE FATHER'S, ONLY BEGOTTEN SON! HE IS THE DIVINE TRUTH THAT UNITES US WITH GOD, OUR HEAVENLY CREATOR AND FATHER! HE IS THE DIVINE KING OF KINGS, AND HOLY LORD OF LORDS! HIS HOLY NAME IS A SONG OF PRAISE! LET US DANCE TO THE SOUND OF THE HOLY NAME OF *JESUS*, FOR HE IS OUR LOVING CREATOR AND GOD. WE WERE CREATED FOR HIM AND BY HIM, MY BROTHERS AND SISTERS, THEREFORE, HIS HOLY NAME IS A SONG AND PRAISE! *ALLELUIA!* LORD *JESUS. ALLELUIA!!!*

FEBRUARY 25, 2016 AT 7:20 PM BY: BARBARA ANN MARY MACK

MY BROTHERS AND SISTERS, LET US WALK AND TALK OUR FAITH, OUR CHRISTIAN FAITH.

BARBARA SPEAKING

MY BROTHERS AND SISTERS, LET US NOT ONLY TALK THE TALK, BUT LET EVERYONE WHO PROFESSES TO BE A BELIEVER IN THE CHRISTIAN FAITH, WALK THE WALK OF GOD'S VERSION, GOD'S HOLY VERSION OF A CHRISTIAN, FOR THERE IS NO OTHER VERSION, *SAYS THE LORD!* LET US WALK THE WALK WITH BOLDNESS AND GLADNESS AS WE PUT TO SHAME ALL WHO FOLLOW THE ACTS AND DEEDS OF THE REALM OF "UNHOLINESS". LET THOSE WHO BELIEVE IN THE SECOND COMING OF JESUS CHRIST, OUR SAVING GOD, WALK THE WALK THAT REVEALS THE INTEGRITY OF THEIR ALLEGIANCE TO HIM. LET THOSE WHO ARE TRULY GRATEFUL FOR JESUS' SACRIFICIAL ACT OF LOVE (HIS CRUCIFIXION) EXHIBIT HIS VERSION OF MERCY, COMPASSION AND ALLEGIANCE TO HIS HOLY WORDS. MY BROTHERS AND SISTERS, LET US PUT

ASIDE OUR WORLDLY DESIRES AND MOVE IN THE DIRECTION OF PLEASING ALMIGHTY GOD AND HIS REALM OF HOLINESS, FOR HE IS REAL! HE IS COMING BACK! *THIS IS HIS HOLY WORD!!!* FEBRUARY 25, 2016 AT 4:49 PM BY: BARBARA ANN MARY MACK

SLAUGHTERED, SLAUGHTERED, SLAUGHTERED: WHO IS WITH JESUS, THE SLAUGHTERED LAMB? WHO WILL HELP JESUS, THE SLAUGHTERED LAMB? FOR HE WAS SLAUGHTERED FOR US.

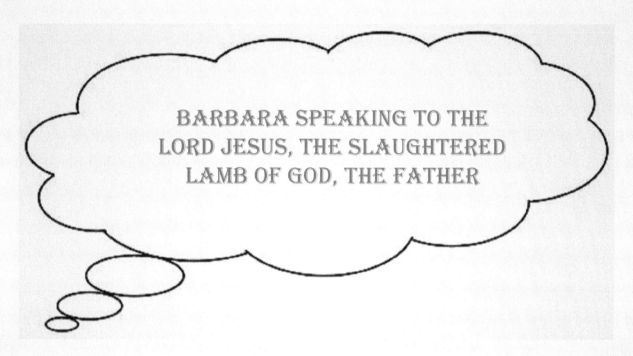

BARBARA SPEAKING TO THE LORD JESUS, THE SLAUGHTERED LAMB OF GOD, THE FATHER

I HEAR YOU, MY LORD. I HEAR YOUR CRIES, MY GOD. I HEAR THE PAIN THAT LEAVES YOUR WOUNDED BODY AS YOU ENDURE THE PAIN AND SUFFERING OF A SLAUGHTERED LAMB. I HEAR YOUR HOLY WOUNDS AS THEY CRY OUT IN GREAT UNENDING AGONY! I WILL CRADLE THE HOLY WOUNDS THAT COVER THE BODY OF MY WOUNDED SAVIOR AND GOD AS HE ENDURES THE SUFFERING OF A SLAUGHTERED LAMB. I AM HERE, MY LORD GOD! I AM WITHIN YOUR REALM OF TOUCH, MY LORD! I WILL CRADLE YOUR WOUNDS AS THEY COMFORT MY ETERNAL SOUL. I WILL CRADLE THE PAIN THAT LEAVES THE WOUNDS OF THE SLAUGHTERED LAMB OF GOD, FOR HE IS JESUS, MY HOLY AND ETERNAL SPOUSE. MY LORD GOD, I CAN HEAR YOUR PAIN TODAY, AS YOU WITNESS THE BETRAYAL OF THOSE WHOM YOU HAVE SUFFERED AND DIED FOR.

BARBARA SPEAKING TO GOD'S CHILDREN OF ALL AGES

I CAN HEAR THE PAIN OF JESUS, THE SLAUGHTERED LAMB OF GOD. CAN YOU HEAR HIS UNENDING PAIN TOO, MY BROTHERS AND SISTERS? CAN YOU HEAR THE PAIN THAT EXITS THE SACRED WOUNDS OF OUR SAVING GOD, THE LORD JESUS? CAN YOU HEAR HIS PAIN AS HE WEEPS IN OUR BLESSED PRESENCE TODAY? CAN YOU HEAR THE CRIES THAT ARE RELEASED

FROM THE ESSENCE OF OUR WOUNDED KING OF KINGS AS HE WITNESSES THE BETRAYAL OF THOSE WHO PROFESS TO KNOW HIM? CAN YOU HEAR HIS WOUNDS, MY BLESSED BROTHERS AND SISTERS? CAN YOU HEAR HIS CONTINUOUS CRIES? WILL YOU JOIN ME, MY BROTHERS AND SISTERS, AS I BOW IN THE PRESENCE OF JESUS, THE SLAUGHTERED LAMB OF THE ONLY LIVING GOD? WILL YOU HELP ME CARRY THE GOOD NEWS OF HIS SAVING PRESENCE AND POWER TO THOSE WHO DO NOT KNOW HIM? ARE YOU WITH US (JESUS, THE SLAUGHTERED LAMB OF GOD AND BARBARA), MY BROTHERS AND SISTERS? ARE WITH US, IN THE MIDST OF WORLDLY TEMPTATIONS AND FAME? WILL YOU REMAIN FAITHFUL TO JESUS, THE SLAUGHTERED LAMB OF GOD, IN THE PRESENCE OF SATAN, OUR ENEMY? WILL YOU SHOW SATAN THE DEPTHS OF YOUR ALLEGIANCE TO JESUS, THE SLAUGHTERED LAMB? WILL YOU EXHIBIT YOUR LOYALTY TO JESUS, YOUR SAVIOR AND GOD, AS HE WEEPS IN THE MIDST OF THIS TROUBLED AND TRAGIC PERIOD OF TIME? WILL YOU, MY BROTHERS? WILL YOU, MY SISTERS? WILL YOU JOIN ME AS I BATTLE THE GATES OF HELL, AS IT REACHES OUT FOR YOUR VULNERABLE SOULS? MY BROTHERS AND SISTERS, ARE YOU WITH US (JESUS, THE SLAUGHTERED LAMB OF GOD AND BARBARA, HIS VICTORIOUS BRIDE)?

FEBRUARY 25, 2016 AT 6:26 PM BY: BARBARA ANN MARY MACK

YES, LORD! I BELIEVE

BARBARA SPEAKING

YES, LORD! YES, MY HOLY ETERNAL GOD AND SPOUSE! YES, MY LOVE, I REALLY, TRULY BELIEVE IN YOUR HOLY PERFECT EXISTENCE! MY LORD, I BELIEVE, THEREFORE, I WILL EXHIBIT MY LEVEL OF BELIEF IN YOUR HOLY PRESENCE WITHIN ME. I WILL EXHIBIT YOUR VERSION OF HOLINESS AS I BOW IN YOUR MAGNIFICENT AND WELCOMED PRESENCE. I WILL EXHIBIT MY LEVEL OF BELIEF AS I DELIVER YOUR HOLY LIFE SAVING MESSAGES TO YOUR CALLED AND CHOSEN ONES. I WILL EXHIBIT MY LEVEL OF BELIEF IN YOUR EXISTENCE AND OMNIPOTENCE, AS I REVEAL YOUR HOLY WORDS IN THE PRESENCE OF THOSE WHO DOUBT MY CONNECTION WITH YOUR REALM OF DIVINITY. I WILL EXHIBIT MY LEVEL OF BELIEF, IN THE PRESENCE OF THE REALM (SATAN) THAT TRIES TO DESTROY AND HINDER MY DIVINE ASSIGNMENT OF LOVE. I WILL EXHIBIT MY LEVEL OF BELIEF, IN THE PRESENCE OF YOUR HOLY ANGELS AND SAINTS. FOR THEY DO SURROUND ME IN THE MIDST OF THIS TRAGIC PERIOD OF TIME. YES! YES! YES, MY HOLY GOD, I TRULY BELIEVE IN YOU!!! *ALLELUIA!!!*

FEBRUARY 26, 2016 AT 3:57 PM BY: BARBARA ANN MARY MACK

I HURT WHEN YOU HURT, MY LORD

BARBARA SPEAKING TO ALMIGHTY GOD

MY LORD, MY HOLY LOVE, MY ALL POWERFUL GOD OF CONTINUOUS MERCY AND COMPASSION, MY FUSED ESSENCE HURTS WHEN YOUR DIVINE ESSENCE HURTS. MY LORD, BY YOUR HOLY POWER AND LOVE FOR ME, YOU HAVE FUSED YOUR HOLY ESSENCE OF LOVE WITH MY WEAK AND OBEDIENT ESSENCE. BECAUSE OF OUR INSEPARABLE UNION, I AM PRIVILEGED TO EXPERIENCE THE DEPTH OF YOUR PAIN AS YOU WITNESS THE SHAMEFUL ACTS OF THOSE WHOM YOU LOVE AND ADORE. O FAITHFUL AND HOLY SPOUSE OF MINE, LEAN ON MY WEAK ESSENCE OF LOVE AS YOU ENDURE THE AGONY THAT HAS ENGULFED YOU THROUGH THE REALM OF TIME. LEAN ON ME, O FAITHFUL GOD AND HOLY SPOUSE OF MINE, SO THAT I MAY CATCH THE REALM THAT RELEASES YOUR MANY FLOWING TEARS. LEAN ON ME, MY ETERNAL REALM OF HOLY LOVE (ALMIGHTY GOD), FOR I AM WITHIN YOUR REALM OF TOUCH.
FEBRUARY 18, 2016 AT 6:05 PM BY: BARBARA ANN MARY MACK

SOON AND VERY SOON, WE ARE GOING TO SEE THE KING (JESUS): ARE YOU PREPARED, MY BROTHERS AND SISTERS?

BARBARA SPEAKING

MY BROTHERS AND SISTERS, IT IS NOT A DELUSION! IT IS NOT A FANTASY! IT IS THE LIVING TRUTH! ARE YOU PREPARED FOR HIS RETURN? FOR HE, THE LORD JESUS, WILL RETURN! ARE YOU PREPARED FOR HIS IMMINENT RETURN, MY BROTHERS AND SISTERS? ARE YOU PREPARED FOR THE FORETOLD GLORY (THE LORD JESUS) THAT WILL APPEAR WITH THE BLESSED CLOUDS? ARE YOU PREPARED, MY BROTHERS AND SISTERS, FOR HE, THE LORD JESUS, IS REAL! REJOICE, MY BROTHERS AND SISTERS! REJOICE, FOR HE IS REAL! HIS HOLY PROMISE IS REAL! THE FORETOLD PROPHECY IS REAL! HIS RETURN IS REAL! LET US PREPARE, MY BROTHERS AND SISTERS, FOR JESUS, THE LORD GOD, IS COMING FOR HIS CHOSEN FEW! IT IS HIS HOLY PROMISE, DEAR FRIENDS! IT IS HIS HOLY WORDS! COME, O BROTHERS AND SISTERS OF MINE! LET US PREPARE FOR THE GLORIOUS SUPPER OF JESUS, THE LAMB OF GOD, FOR HE IS REAL! *ALLELUIA!!!*
FEBRUARY 23, 2016 AT 9:00 PM BY: BARBARA ANN MARY MACK
SENT SUN, FEB 28, 2016 4:22 PM-READ SUN 2/28/2016 4:51 PM

I WILL NOT GIVE UP ON YOU, MY CHILDREN, SAYS THE LORD

ALMIGHTY GOD SPEAKING

MY CHILDREN, MY SONS AND DAUGHTERS, MY LOVE FOR YOU IS ETERNAL, FOR I AM ETERNAL, *SAYS THE LORD*. I AM CONSTANTLY FIGHTING THE GATES (HELL) THAT TRY TO STEAL YOU FROM YOUR LOVING ORIGIN AND GOD. I AM FIGHTING FOR YOU, DEAR CHILDREN, FOR I AM DIVINE ETERNAL LOVE. MY LOVE FOR YOU SURPASSES EVERY EVIL THAT HAS PENETRATED THIS REALM OF TIME. MY LOVE FOR YOU TRANSCENDS THE TARES THAT SATAN, OUR ENEMY, HAS PLACED WITHIN THIS WORLD TODAY. MY LOVE HAS PIERCED THE GATES THAT CRY OUT FOR YOUR VULNERABLE SOULS THROUGHOUT EACH DAY. MY CHILDREN, I, YOUR LORD AND GOD, WILL NEVER GIVE UP ON YOU! THIS IS MY HOLY WORD! THIS IS MY HOLY PROMISE TO YOU, *SAYS THE LORD ALMIGHTY.*

FEBRUARY 23, 2016 AT 7:57 PM BY: BARBARA ANN MARY MACK

SENT SUN, FEB 28, 2016 4:22 PM-READ SUN 2/28/2016 4:51 PM

GREETING, DEAR ARCHBISHOP CRAIG! THE LORD IS VERY PLEASED THAT YOU TAKE THE TIME TO REVEAL TO YOUR SON THE TRUTH PERTAINING TO GOD'S HOLY EXISTENCE AND PRESENCE IN HIS LIFE. LA TOYA AND AMYA READ AND DISCUS THE PASSAGES FROM THE HOLY BIBLE THAT REVEAL GOD'S HOLINESS AND POWER. IT IS WONDERFUL THAT OUR CHILDREN HAVE BEEN BLESSED BY THE HOLY POWER OF OUR OMNIPOTENT GOD THROUGH THE CARE AND LOVE THAT THEY RECEIVE DAILY FROM US. ALTHOUGH OUR CHILDREN HAVE THE OPPORTUNITY TO WITNESS THE GOOD AND BAD THAT COME WITH THIS PRESENT REALM OF EXISTENCE, THEY ARE TAUGHT ABOUT THE FUTURE GLORY THAT AWAITS THEM BY THEIR LOVING PARENTS. LET US CONTINUE EXHIBITING DIVINE LOVE FOR OUR CHILDREN BY LIVING GOD'S VERSION OF LOVE, MERCY AND COMPASSION, FOR THEY, OUR CHILDREN, ARE OBSERVING OUR ACTS AS WELL AS WHAT WE SAY.

LET US TEACH OUR CHILDREN THE TRUTH, SAYS THE LORD

ALMIGHTY GOD SPEAKING

MY SONS AND DAUGHTERS, I HAVE GIVEN YOU THE DIVINE BLESSING OF TEACHING YOUR CHILDREN *THE TRUTH* OF MY HOLY PRESENCE AND EXISTENCE. I HAVE WATCHED YOU AS YOU GUIDED YOUR CHILDREN IN MY DIRECTION OF HOLINESS. MY SONS, MY DAUGHTERS, I AM GRATEFUL THAT YOU TAKE THE TIME TO TEACH YOUR CHILDREN MY VERSION OF LOVE, COMPASSION AND MERCY, FOR THE WORLD IS WITHOUT THESE EXPRESSIONS OF MY HOLY ESSENCE. TEACH THEM THAT WHICH YOU HAVE READ FROM MY HOLY BIBLE. TEACH THEM THAT WHICH I WHISPER TO YOU THROUGHOUT EACH DAY. TEACH THEM OF THE PRESENCE OF OUR ENEMY, THE DEVIL, SO THAT THEY WILL KNOW WHO TO COMBAT WHEN TEMPTATION AND WORLDLY LUSTS ENTER THEIR REALM OF DIVINE CONTENTMENT. MY SONS, MY DAUGHTERS, TEACH THEM THAT WHICH THEY

WILL NEVER LEARN FROM THE WORLD. MY SONS, MY DAUGHTERS, TEACH YOUR CHILDREN ABOUT ME, FOR THEY NEED TO KNOW *THE TRUTH* TOO, *SAYS YOUR SAVING LORD GOD.*
FEBRUARY 23, 2016 AT 6:28 PM BY: BARBARA ANN MARY MACK
SENT SUN, FEB 28, 2016 4:22 PM-READ SUN 2/28/2016 4:51 PM

BUON GIORNO ARCHBISHOP CRAIG! COME STA OGGI? BELOW IS TODAY'S PASSAGE FOR ALL. *AMORE, BELLA BARBARA*

MY PURPOSE IS NOT TO CONVINCE YOU OF A LIE, BUT TO REVEAL THE TRUTH, SAYS THE LORD

ALMIGHTY GOD SPEAKING

MY CHILDREN, I HAVE ENTERED YOUR BLESSED REALM AGAIN, IN A FORM (BARBARA) THAT YOU CAN COMMUNICATE WITH, TOUCH AND REJOICE IN MY HOLY PRESENCE WITH. I HAVE COME TO YOU DURING THIS CRUCIAL PERIOD OF TIME IN A FORM THAT REPRESENTS GOD, THE HOLY AND BLESSED TRINITY. I HAVE COME TO REVEAL *THE TRUTH,* IN REGARDS TO SALVATION AND ETERNAL LIFE IN SWEET PARADISE WITH GOD, YOUR HOLY AND BLESSED SAVIOR. I HAVE COME TO REVEAL A *TRUTH* THAT THE UNBELIEVING ONES REFUSE TO ACCEPT AND APPRECIATE. I HAVE COME TO SHARE MY GOOD NEWS OF LIFE WITH YOUR HOLY GOD, WHO DWELLS IN THE MIDST OF HEAVENLY BLISS AND CONTINUOUS HAPPINESS. *IT IS REAL,* MY CHILDREN! *I AM REAL,* MY CHILDREN! DO NOT BE FOOLED BY THOSE WHO REJECT AND DENY *THE TRUTH* PERTAINING TO MY POSITION AS GOD, YOUR CREATOR AND ORIGIN, FOR YOU WERE CREATED FOR ME AND BY ME. THIS, DEAR CHILDREN, IS *THE TRUTH!!!*
FEBRUARY 23, 2016 AT 5:36 PM BY: BARBARA ANN MARY MACK
SENT SUN, FEB 28, 2016 4:22 PM-READ SUN 2/28/2016 4:51 PM

GREETINGS, DEAR ARCHBISHOP CRAIG! BELOW IS MY LATEST FB POSTING. MANY DENY THE SOVEREIGNTY OF JESUS' HOLY POSITION AS GOD, THE SON. BUT THE BELIEVERS REJOICE IN THE HOLY TRUTH! *ALLELUIA!!! REJOICING. BELIEVING. BARBIE*

ALL PRAISES, GLORY AND HONOR TO JESUS, THE CHRIST, OUR CREATOR AND GOD! FOR GOD, OUR HEAVENLY FATHER, HAS PRODUCED HIM (JESUS CHRIST) FROM HIMSELF. HE, THE LORD JESUS, IS GOD, THE FATHER'S, ONLY BEGOTTEN SON. JESUS IS GOD, FOR HE CAME FROM THE HOLY ESSENCE OF GOD, THE FATHER. LET THE BELIEVERS REJOICE, REJOICE, REJOICE IN THIS LIFE SAVING GOOD NEWS! FOR CHRIST JESUS STILL REIGNS IN HEAVEN AND ON EARTH! *ALLELUIA!* THE DEVIL IS A FILTHY LIAR! AND HE CANNOT, CANNOT, CANNOT DECEIVE THE TRUE BELIEVERS!!! *ALLELUIA!!!* BY YOUR HOLY CROSS (SACRIFICE) WE, THE BELIEVERS, ARE HEALED FOREVER AND EVER! *ALLELUIA!!!*

GREETINGS, DEAR ARCHBISHOP CRAIG! LA TOYA IS FEELING BETTER AT THIS TIME. AMYA AND I ARE TAKING VERY GOOD CARE OF HER. THANKS FOR YOUR SINCERE CONCERN. CIAO! BELLA BARBIE

YOU CANNOT RESIST MY CHARM, SAYS THE LORD

ALMIGHTY GOD SPEAKING THROUGH BARBARA, HIS SENT MESSENGER AND BRIDE

MY CHILDREN, YOU CANNOT RESIST THE CHARM, YES, THE DIVINE CHARM, THAT EMITS FROM THE BEING OF MY CHOSEN MESSENGER AND BRIDE, FOR HER CHARM REVEALS ME, *SAYS THE LORD.* WITNESS THE DIVINE DELIGHT THAT EXPRESSES MY HOLY PRESENCE AND CHARM AS MY CHOSEN ONE (BARBARA) EXHIBITS MY TRUE ESSENCE. WITNESS THE GIFT OF MY HOLY CHARISMA AS IT FLOWS THROUGH THE OBEDIENT BEING OF MY FAITHFUL MESSENGER AND BRIDE, FOR HER CHARM REVEALS ME. HER CHARM DRAWS MY FAITHFUL CHILDREN TO MY REALM OF HOLINESS AND DIVINE TRUTH. WITNESS THE HOLY GIFT OF MY CHARM AS I MOVE IN THE MIDST OF MY GREAT AND BLESSED CREATION THROUGH THE HUMBLED BEING OF MY SENT REPRESENTATIVE AND FAITHFUL FRIEND (BARBARA). WITNESS THE GOODNESS OF YOUR GREAT AND HOLY GOD AS I REVEAL MY MEEKNESS THROUGH MY OBEDIENT SERVANT (BARBARA) TODAY. WITNESS HER GLOW AND JOY AS SHE SHARES MY HOLY PRESENCE WITH THE CALLED AND CHOSEN ONES. WITNESS MY HOLY SPIRIT AS IT JOINS YOU IN YOUR PEWS, THROUGH MY FAITHFUL MESSENGER AND BRIDE (BARBARA). WITNESS MY DEVOTION TO MY CHILDREN, THROUGH THE BEING (BARBARA) THAT FOLLOWS ME DAILY. I HAVE CAPTIVATED THOSE WHOM I ADORE, THROUGH THE CHARM THAT FLOWS FROM MY MESSENGER AND BRIDE (BARBARA). I HAVE CAPTURED THE HEARTS AND SOULS OF THOSE WHO TRULY DESIRE TO LIVE WITH ME FOREVER, THROUGH MY MESSENGER AND BRIDE. COME, O CHILDREN WHOM I ADORE AND APPRECIATE! JOIN MY CHOSEN MESSENGER AND BRIDE AS SHE BOWS IN MY HOLY PRESENCE THROUGHOUT EACH DAY. JOIN THE SPIRIT OF THE IGNITED ONE (BARBARA), AS SHE EXPRESSES HER ALLEGIANCE AND UNION WITH ALMIGHTY GOD, HER FIRST AND LAST LOVE. JOIN US (ALMIGHTY GOD AND BARBARA) MY CHILDREN, AS WE EXHIBIT ETERNAL LIFE IN YOUR WORTHY PRESENCE TODAY! JOIN US, O WELL-LOVED ONES! JOIN US TODAY!!! FEBRUARY 27, 2016 AT 6:25 PM BY: BARBARA ANN MARY MACK

WHAT IS IT DOING FOR YOU? WHAT IS MY HOLY PRESENCE IN YOUR MIDST TODAY DOING FOR YOU, SAYS THE LORD?

ALMIGHTY GOD SPEAKING

MY CHILDREN, WHAT DOES MY HOLY PRESENCE IN YOUR BLESSED MIDST TODAY MEAN TO YOU? ARE YOU PLEASED WITH THE VISIBILITY OF YOUR HOLY CREATOR AND GOD? ARE YOU PLEASED, THAT I DEEM THIS GENERATION WORTHY TO RECEIVE MY HOLY MESSAGES AND PLAN THAT ARE CONVEYED THROUGH MY MODERN DAY PROPHETESS (BARBARA)? ARE YOU GRATEFUL THAT I FIND YOU WORTHY TO HEAR MY VOICE THROUGH MY CHOSEN MESSENGER TODAY? MY CHILDREN, IS MY PRESENCE IN YOUR MIDST TODAY HELPFUL TO YOU? ARE YOU WALKING IN MY VERSION OF HOLINESS? OR, ARE YOU LIVING THE LIFE OF ONE WHO DOES NOT ACCEPT THE REALITY OF MY HOLY PRESENCE AND EXISTENCE? MY CHILDREN, YOUR ACTIONS REVEAL THE TRUTH. YOUR ACTIONS REVEAL YOUR LEVEL OF BELIEF IN MY HOLY PRESENCE IN YOUR MIDST. MY CHILDREN, BELIEVE IN MY HOLY PRESENCE, FOR I AM IN YOUR BLESSED MIDST TODAY! I HAVE SPOKEN THROUGH MY MESSENGER (BARBARA) FOR MANY YEARS. I HAVE REVEALED MYSELF TO YOU THROUGH HER OBEDIENT BEING. WHAT WILL YOU DO WITH THE DIVINE KNOWLEDGE THAT SHE HAS SHARED WITH YOU, MY CHILDREN? WHAT WILL YOU DO WITH THE SPIRITUAL NOURISHMENT THAT DESCENDED FROM MY THRONE OF LOVE AND MERCY? WHAT? MY CHILDREN. WHAT WILL YOU DO WITH MY HEAVEN SENT GIFT? WHAT HAVE YOU LEARNED FROM ME TODAY? WHAT IS MY HOLY PRESENCE DOING FOR YOU TODAY, *SAYS THE LORD?*
FEBRUARY 27, 2016 AT 2:35 AM BY: BARBARA ANN MARY MACK

WE (ALMIGHTY GOD AND BARBARA) ARE NOT SEPARATE. WE ARE ONE!

ALMIGHTY GOD AND BARBARA SPEAKING

FUSED WITH THE REALM OF DIVINITY THAT IGNITES THIS DORMANT PERIOD OF TIME. FUSED WITH THE DIVINE ESSENCE THAT EXISTS IN THE MIDST OF EXISTENCE. FUSED WITH THE CREATOR OF ALL THAT IS GOOD AND HOLY. FUSED WITH THE DIVINE ESSENCE THAT ROAMS THE EARTH IN THE MIDST OF THIS DEVASTATING PERIOD OF TIME. FUSED WITH ALPHA AND OMEGA. FUSED WITH GOD, THE HOLY AND BLESSED TRINITY. FUSED WITH THE DIVINE CREATOR OF LIFE IN THE MIDST OF SPIRITUAL AND PHYSICAL DEATH. FUSED WITH GOD, THE FATHER, MY HOLY ORIGIN AND SPOUSE. FUSED WITH JESUS, THE ONLY BEGOTTEN SON OF GOD, THE FATHER. FUSED WITH GOD'S BLESSED AND HOLY ETERNAL SPIRIT. FUSED WITH THE DIVINE ESSENCE THAT ENCOMPASSES MY BLESSED SOUL. FUSED WITH THE HOLY POWER THAT IS RELEASED IN OUR MIDST TODAY. FUSED! FUSED! FUSED! FUSED WITH ETERNITY, THE ONLY INFINITE BEING (ALMIGHTY GOD)!!! WE ARE ONE, MY DAUGHTER (BARBARA)! WE ARE ONE!!! YOU HAVE DWELLED WITHIN THE REALM OF MY HOLY ESSENCE BEFORE THE FOUNDATION OF PHYSICAL LIFE. MY DAUGHTER, YOU AND I ARE INSEPARABLE, *SAYS ALMIGHTY GOD, THE BLESSED AND HOLY TRINITY!!!*

FEBRUARY 27, 2016 AT 3:31 AM BY: BARBARA ANN MARY MACK

SATAN CANNOT BE FORGIVEN! COMBAT HIM BY EXHIBITING HOLY LOVE TOWARD GOD'S CHILDREN, NOT SATAN'S

BARBARA SPEAKING

MY BROTHERS AND SISTERS, THOSE WHO DO THE WORKS AND DEEDS OF SATAN, THEIR ORIGIN AND GOD, CANNOT BE FORGIVEN. MY BROTHERS AND SISTERS, UNDERSTAND WHO IS FROM THE REALM OF DIVINITY AND WHO IS FROM THE REALM THAT HOUSES HE (SATAN) WHO SLITHERS IN THE MIDST OF THE CHURCHES, SEEKING THE VULNERABLE ONES. MY BROTHERS AND SISTERS, SATAN AND HIS DECEIVING ANGELS WILL NOT BE PARDONED OR FORGIVEN FOR THEIR LIFE STEALING ACTS. ALMIGHTY GOD WILL NOT FORGIVE THOSE WHO TAKE SIDE WITH THE REALM THAT SEEKS THE ETERNAL SOULS OF GOD'S VULNERABLE AND DISOBEDIENT CHILDREN. THE REALM OF EVIL (SINNERS WHO DO NOT DESIRE OR EXERCISE THE ACT OF REPENTANCE) CANNOT BE FORGIVEN, FOR ITS SOLE DESIRE IS TO LURE GOD'S UNSUSPECTING CHILDREN INTO THE REALM OF DOOM. MY BROTHERS AND SISTERS, YOU CAN COMBAT THE REALM OF DOOM BY EXHIBITING GOD'S HOLY VERSION OF RIGHTEOUSNESS. MY BROTHERS AND SISTERS, WE CAN COMBAT THE REALM OF DAMNATION THROUGH THE GIFT OF DIVINE LOVE FOR OUR CREATOR AND HIS HOLY WILL AND WAY.

FEBRUARY 28, 2016 AT 1:09 AM BY: BARBARA ANN MARY MACK

WHAT THE WORLD (SATAN) PRODUCES

ALMIGHTY GOD SPEAKING

MY CHILDREN, THAT WHICH THE WORLD PRODUCES, CANNOT ENJOY THE GIFT AND PRESENCE OF MY HOLY LOVE. THAT WHICH THE WORLD ACCEPTS AS RIGHTEOUS AND GOOD, CANNOT PENETRATE THE HEARTS OF MY CHOSEN FEW. THAT WHICH THE WORLD RELEASES, CANNOT ACCEPT THE PRESENCE OF MY SENT HOLY MESSENGERS AND PROPHETS. THAT WHICH THE WORLD CONDONES, WILL NOT BE ACCEPTED BY ME, *SAYS THE LORD*. THAT WHICH THE WORLD CONDONES, WILL NOT BE ACCEPTED BY THOSE WHO FOLLOW MY VERSION OF RIGHTEOUSNESS AND HOLINESS. THAT WHICH THE WORLD PRODUCES, SLITHERS FROM SATAN, OUR ENEMY. THAT WHICH THE WORLD GLORY OVER, IS REJECTED BY JESUS, THE KING OF KINGS AND LORD OF LORDS.

FEBRUARY 28, 2016 AT 8:15 PM BY: BARBARA ANN MARY MACK

WITHIN THE REALM OF IMPERFECTION

WITHIN THE REALM OF IMPERFECTION DWELLS THOSE WHO REFUSE TO FOLLOW THE HOLY TEACHINGS OF CHRIST, OUR SAVING GOD. WITHIN THE REALM OF IMPERFECTION, DWELLS THE SOULS OF THE LOST AND FORGOTTEN ONES. WITHIN THE REALM OF IMPERFECTION, DWELLS THE SOULS THAT SATAN HAS CLAIMED THROUGH THE YEARS. WITHIN THE REALM OF IMPERFECTION, DWELLS THE SOURCE (SATAN) OF HORRENDOUS ACTS. WITHIN THE REALM OF IMPERFECTION, DWELLS SATAN, THE GREAT DECEIVER AND FATHER OF LIES. WITHIN THE REALM OF IMPERFECTION, DWELLS THOSE WHO DISCRIMINATE AGAINST THE RIGHTEOUS ACTS AND TRUTH THAT FLOW THROUGH THE HOLY BIBLE, GOD'S UNCHANGING WORD. WITHIN THE REALM OF IMPERFECTION, DWELLS THOSE WHO HAVE DENOUNCED THE SOVEREIGN LORD JESUS. WITHIN THE REALM OF IMPERFECTION, DWELLS THE DOOMED ONES. WITHIN THE REALM OF IMPERFECTION, DWELLS THOSE WHO DO NOT RECOGNIZE GOD'S HOLY PRESENCE WITHIN HIS MESSENGERS AND JESUS, THE FATHER'S ONLY BEGOTTEN SON. WITHIN THE REALM OF IMPERFECTION, DWELLS THOSE WHO WILL WITNESS THE DIVINE TRUTH THAT IS SPOKEN THROUGH OUR LORD AND SAVIOR JESUS, THE CHRIST, ON THE GREAT AND HOLY JUDGMENT DAY.

FEBRUARY 28, 2016 AT 8:30 PM BY: BARBARA ANN MARY MACK

SENT SUN, FEB 28, 2016 8:35 PM-READ SUN 2/28/2016 9:18 PM

BUON GIORNO CRAIG! COME STA? LA TOYA WENT TO SEE THE DOCTOR THIS MORNING AND THE DOCTOR SCHEDULED HER FOR A CHEST X RAY TOMORROW. THEY DID AN EKG TODAY AND IT SHOWED NO SIGNS OF PROBLEMS WITH HER HEART, THANK GOD! WE WILL SEE WHAT THE X RAY REVEALS. MEANWHILE, THANKS FOR YOUR CONTINUOUS PRAYERS. *AMORE, BELLA BARBIE*

SENT MON, FEB 29, 2016 1:22 PM-READ MON 2/29 2:58 PM

GREETINGS, O HEAVEN SENT GIFT (CRAIG)! THE LORD HAS KEPT ME VERY BUSY OVER THE PAST FEW MONTHS. HE HAS BEEN DICTATING TO ME, HIS VALUABLE MESSAGES FOR ALL OF HIS CHILDREN TODAY. IT IS A MIRACLE THAT MY FINGERS ARE NOT NUMB OR IN GREAT PAIN. I AM PRESENTLY PREPARING VOLUME TEN OF "THE PRESENT TESTAMENT" FOR PUBLICATION. LA TOYA AND I DECIDED ON CONTACTING MY PUBLISHER TOMORROW TO DISCUS THE PUBLICATION OF VOLUME TEN. THEY ARE PRESENTLY WORKING ON THE FINAL STAGES OF VOLUME NINE. I AM WAITING FOR THEM TO SEND ME A REVISED GALLEY BECAUSE THE FIRST ONE WAS NOT TO THE LORD'S SATISFACTION. VOLUME TEN IS TITLED 'WORDS OF A MESSENGER". THIS BOOK CONSISTS OF THE MESSAGES THAT WERE SENT VIA EMAIL AND FACEBOOK TO GOD'S CALLED AND CHOSEN ONES. OH HOW PRIVILEGED WE ARE, TO BE INCLUDED IN GOD'S GREAT AND HOLY LOVE STORY! FOR HE TRULY LOVES ALL OF HIS CHILDREN, ESPECIALLY THE FAITHFUL AND BELIEVING ONES. O BELOVED ONE (CRAIG), OH HOW BLESSED WE ARE!!!

ALLELUIA!!!PLEASANT DREAMS, DEAR ONE!

THE GIFT (CRAIG) OF YOUR (ALMIGHTY GOD) LOVE

BARBARA SPEAKING

MY LORD, EACH AND EVERY DAY, I HUMBLY TREASURE AND REVERE THE GIFT OF YOUR LOVE (CRAIG, THE ETERNAL BELOVED ONE). I TREASURE YOUR WELCOMED GIFT THAT DESCENDED FROM YOUR MIGHTY AND HOLY THRONE ABOVE.
DEAR LORD, I TREASURE YOUR HOLY GIFT (CRAIG) THROUGHOUT MY BLESSED DAY.
I TREASURE YOUR HEAVEN SENT GIFT AS I KNEEL AND PRAY.
HE IS THE DIVINE GIFT FROM YOU, THAT I WILL FOREVER LOVE.
FOR HE DESCENDED TO ME WITH YOUR HOLY SPIRIT FROM ABOVE.
HE IS THE GIFT OF LIFE,
THAT DESCENDED INTO THE WELCOMED REALM OF BARBARA, YOUR HOLY WIFE.
FEBRUARY 28, 2016 AT 8:44 PM BY: BARBARA ANN MARY MACK

HOLINESS, REVERENCE: ALMIGHTY GOD

THE HOLY AND BLESSED TRINITY (GOD, THE FATHER, JESUS, GOD, THE SON, AND GOD, THE HOLY SPIRIT)
FEBRUARY 28, 2016 AT 8:52 PM BY: BARBARA ANN MARY MACK

WHO ELSE WOULD WEEP FOR YOU, MY CHILDREN, SAYS THE LORD?

ALMIGHTY GOD SPEAKING

MY CHILDREN, THROUGH BARBARA, MY HUMBLED MESSENGER AND BRIDE, I WEEP FOR YOU THROUGHOUT THE DAY. THROUGH MY HUMBLED BRIDE, I CRY OUT TO THOSE WHO HAVE BEEN DECEIVED BY OUR ENEMY (SATAN). THROUGH HER HEART AND EYES, MY TEARS FLOW WITHOUT CEASING. THROUGH HER WEARY HEART AND SOUL, I WEEP FOR YOU, MY LITTLE ONES. I WEEP WHEN YOU ARE CAPTURED AND CAPTIVATED BY HE (SATAN) WHO DESIRES EVERLASTING HARM TO YOU. I WEEP FOR THOSE WHO HAVE BEEN SLAIN BY HIS EVERLASTING SWORD OF DAMNATION AND MISERY. I WEEP FOR THOSE WHO HAVE BETRAYED ME. I WEEP FOR THOSE WHO SAY THAT THEY LOVE ME, BUT THEIR LIFESTYLES CONVEY THEIR BETRAYAL. MY CHILDREN, HOW LONG WILL I HAVE TO WEEP FOR YOU, BEFORE YOU RETURN TO ME, *SAYS THE LORD GOD?*

FEBRUARY 28, 2016 AT 9:22 PM BY: BARBARA ANN MARY MACK

UNITY PRODUCES GENUINE HAPPINESS

ALMIGHTY GOD SPEAKING TO BARBARA AND CRAIG, THE ETERNAL BELOVED ONE

WE (ALMIGHTY GOD, CRAIG AND BARBARA) ARE *ONE!!*

FEBRUARY 28, 2016 AT 10:20 PM BY: BARBARA ANN MARY MACK

LET US INCLUDE THE WHOLE WORLD IN OUR GREAT AND HOLY LOVE STORY, *SAYS THE LORD GOD*

ALMIGHTY GOD SPEAKING

MY LOVELY CHILDREN (CRAIG AND BARBARA), LET US INCLUDE THE WHOLE WORLD IN OUR GREAT AND HOLY LOVE STORY. FOR IT, OUR HOLY LOVE STORY, *IS ONE OF A KIND!!!*

FEBRUARY 28, 2016 AT 10:28 PM BY: BARBARA ANN MARY MACK

I WILL DO EVERYTHING THAT I CAN TO HELP SAVE YOUR CHILDREN, MY LORD

BARBARA SPEAKING

MY LORD AND HOLY GOD, I WILL DO ALL THAT YOU BLESS ME WITH, IN REGARDS TO DELIVERING YOUR LIFE SAVING TRUTH TO THOSE WHO ARE WALKING IN SPIRITUAL DARKNESS AND UNBELIEF. MY LORD, I WILL DO EVERYTHING THAT YOU REVEAL TO ME, IN REGARDS TO ENLIGHTENING THOSE WHO BELIEVE THAT THEY ARE LIVING AND THINKING IN ACCORDANCE WITH YOUR HOLY WILL AND UNCHANGING WORD. EVEN IN THE MIDST OF SATAN'S CONTINUOUS ATTACKS, I WILL DO EVERYTHING THAT YOU GRACE ME WITH, IN REGARDS TO HELPING THOSE WHO DO NOT KNOW YOU AT ALL. MY LORD, I WILL NOT FAINT OR GROW WEARY AS I DELIVER

YOUR VITAL MESSAGES TO YOUR WORTHY CHILDREN TODAY. SPEAK TO ME, O LOVING GOD, AS YOU REVEAL THE DEPTH OF YOUR UNENDING LOVE AND MERCY FOR YOUR GREAT CREATION (HUMAN BEINGS). STRENGTHEN MY WEAK BEING, MY HOLY GOD, AS I DELIVER YOUR LIFE SAVING WORDS TO THE SPIRITUALLY HUNGRY ONES. I WILL FOREVER FOLLOW AND ABIDE BY YOUR HOLY WORDS, AS I SPEAK YOUR GOOD NEWS TO THE NEEDY ONES. MY LORD, MY HOLY GOD, I WILL DO EVERYTHING THAT YOU COMMAND OF ME, SO THAT I MAY DWELL WITHIN YOUR REALM OF DIVINITY THROUGHOUT ETERNITY.

FEBRUARY 29, 2016 AT 2:55 AM BY: BARBARA ANN MARY MACK

IN THE MIDST OF COMBATING SATAN, I WEEP FOR THE LOST AND DOOMED SOULS

ALMIGHTY GOD AND BARBARA SPEAKING

MY SORROWFUL SPIRIT AND MY ETERNAL SOUL WEEP AS I WATCH SATAN TAKE DOWN THE LOST ONES.

FEBRUARY 29, 2016 AT 2:59 AM BY: BARBARA ANN MARY MACK

THE DOOMED ONES DO NOT RECOGNIZE ME, *SAYS THE LORD*

ALMIGHTY GOD SPEAKING

THE DOOMED ONES DO NOT RECOGNIZE ME, FOR THEY ARE BLINDED BY THE EVIL THAT COVERS THEIR LEVEL OF EXISTENCE. THEY CANNOT WITHSTAND THE BRILLIANCE OF MY MIGHTY LIGHT OF LOVE. THEY CANNOT GRASP THE DIVINE GENTLENESS OF MY TOUCH. THEY CANNOT COMMUNICATE WITH THAT WHICH IS HOLY AND PURE. THEY CANNOT HANDLE THE DEPTH OF PURE AND UNBLEMISHED LOVE. THEY CANNOT SEE THAT WHICH IS FORBIDDEN TO THOSE WHO DO NOT DESIRE TO REIGN WITH ME IN SWEET PARADISE IN HEAVEN AND ON EARTH. THEY CANNOT UNITE WITH THE ONLY REALM THAT PRODUCES AND RELEASES DIVINE WORDS OF COMFORT TO THOSE WHO HAVE BEEN INJURED BY THE REALM OF EVIL. THEY DID NOT RECOGNIZE ME IN THE INCARNATE FORM AS JESUS, THE CHRIST, AND THEY DO NOT RECOGNIZE ME THROUGH THE FORM (BARBARA) THAT I SENT TODAY.

FEBRUARY 29, 2016 AT 3:15 AM BY: BARBARA ANN MARY MACK

OH, THE CLOISTERED LIFE-AWAY FROM THIS PASSING WORLD

BARBARA SPEAKING TO ALMIGHTY GOD

THE CLOISTER LIFE. MY DESIRE. MY HOPE! BUT YOUR HOLY PLAN AND WILL REIGN, EVEN IN THE MIDST OF MY HOPE, DEAR LORD. *ALLELUIA!!!*
FEBRUARY 29, 2016 AT 3:23 AM BY: BARBARA ANN MARY MACK
SENT MON, FEB 29, 2016 1:22 PM-READ MON 2/29/2016 2:58 PM

MY LATEST FB POSTING

MY LORD. MY HOLY GOD. WHAT HAS SATAN, THE DEVIL, THE REALM OF EVIL, DONE TO THE LIVES THAT ARE WITHOUT YOUR HOLY LOVE?
I SEE IT ON THE NEWS. I HEAR AND SEE IT WHEN I LOOK OUTSIDE MY WINDOWS AND DOOR. I SEE IT WHEN I GO SHOPPING. I HEAR IT WHEN I'M ON MY WAY TO MY DOCTORS APPOINTMENTS. I HEAR AND SEE IT AT MY DOCTORS' OFFICES. I SEE IT IN THE POSTINGS ON FACEBOOK. I SEE IT IN THE LIVES OF THOSE WHO PROFESS THAT THEY ARE CHRISTIANS. I SEE ALL THAT COME FROM A REALM AND LIFE THAT ARE WITHOUT THE LOVE AND GUIDANCE OF GOD, THE BLESSED AND HOLY TRINITY. MY LORD. MY HOLY GOD. OH HOW I WEEP FOR THEM.
FEBRUARY 29, 2016 BY: BARBARA ANN MARY MACK
SENT MON, FEB 29, 2016 8:30 PM-READ MON 2/29/2016 11:38 PM

HI! JUST WANT TO SAY THAT I AM THINKING OF YOU AT THIS TIME
I WAS ON THE PHONE EARLIER WITH MY PUBLISHER. LA TOYA AGREED TO PAY FOR THE PUBLICATION OF MY BOOK "THE PRESENT TESTAMENT VOLUME TEN-WORDS OF A MESSENGER". SHE AND I FINALIZED EVERYTHING THIS AFTERNOON. I READ AND SIGNED THE TEN PAGE UPDATED AGREEMENT FORM THAT WAS SENT TO ME BY THE CHECK IN COORDINATOR VIA EMAIL. I TRY TO TAKE ADVANTAGE OF THEIR PROMOTIONAL OFFERINGS WHEN I HAVE A MANUSCRIPT THAT IS READY FOR THE PUBLICATION PROCESS. THIS MONTH (FEBRUARY) THEY ARE OFFERING 50% OFF THE AUTHOR'S CHOICE OF PUBLISHING PACKAGE. I CHOSE THE COLOR PACKAGE IN CASE I DECIDE TO INCLUDE PHOTOS. LA TOYA USUALLY HANDLES THE PUBLICATION COSTS AS HER CONTRIBUTION TO THE LORD'S HOLY WORK FOR US. WE (ALMIGHTY GOD, LA TOYA, AMYA, YOU AND ME) ARE A PRODUCTIVE TEAM. *ALLELUIA!!! LUV YAH! BEAUTIFUL BARBARA*
SENT SUN, MAR 6, 2016 6:27 PM-READ SUN 3/6/2016 8:56 PM

GREETINGS, ARCHBISHOP CRAIG! I PRAY THAT ALL IS WELL WITH YOU AND YOUR LOVED ONES. OVER THE PAST FEW DAYS, THE LORD HAS INSPIRED ME TO LISTEN TO THE BOOK OF MATTHEW VIA AUDIO. IT HAS BEEN VERY ENLIGHTENING. I LIKE LISTENING TO THE HOLY BIBLE BECAUSE THE READER SAYS THE WORDS OR NAMES PROPERLY THAT I HAVE TROUBLE PRONOUNCING. I

USUALLY LISTEN TO THE RECORDING OF EACH BOOK FOR AT LEAST A WEEK. THIS HELPS ME TO GRASP SOME OF THE PASSAGES THAT I MAY HAVE MISSED OR FORGOTTEN THROUGH THE YEARS. IT ALSO CONFIRMS THE CONSISTENCY OF THE LORD'S MESSAGES THAT HE CONVEYS THROUGH ME FOR HIS CHILDREN TODAY. I LISTEN TO THE RECORDING WHEN I GET INTO BED AT NIGHT, AND WHEN I PREPARE MYSELF FOR NEXT DAY. I PLAY EACH SIDE OVER AND OVER SO THAT I WILL REMEMBER WHAT I HEARD. LA TOYA AND AMYA READ AND LISTEN TO THE HOLY BIBLE AS WELL. ENJOY YOUR BLESSED DAY LOVE! *TI AMO!*

AGONY! AGONY! CONTINUOUS AGONY!

ALMIGHTY GOD SPEAKING

MY CHILDREN, SATAN, OUR ENEMY, PLACES THE DECEIVED AND VULNERABLE ONES WITHIN THE REALM OF CONTINUOUS AGONY. HIS DESIRE IS TO CREATE A LEVEL OF EMOTIONAL AND SPIRITUAL PAIN THAT WILL CAUSE THE WEAK AND UNPROTECTED SOULS TO COMMIT SUICIDE. SATAN, THE REALM OF CONTINUOUS AGONY, REJOICES WHEN ONE ENDS HIS OR HER PRECIOUS LIFE THROUGH INTENTIONAL AND PERMANENT DESTRUCTION. MY CHILDREN, LET US COMBAT THE REALM OF CONTINUOUS AGONY WITH MY HOLY GIFT OF LIFE AND LOVE. MY CHILDREN, COMBAT THE REALM OF SELF DESTRUCTION, WITH THE DIVINE LOVE THAT I ALONE CAN PRODUCE AND RELEASE. SEEK MY HOLY REALM OF LOVE SO THAT YOU MAY WITHSTAND THE TORMENT THAT SATAN INFLICTS UPON YOUR VULNERABLE MINDS. MY CHILDREN, SEEK MY REALM OF TRANQUILITY WHEN YOU ARE CHASED AND TORMENTED BY HE, SATAN, THE UNINVITED ONE, WHO TORTURES YOU WITHIN YOUR VULNERABLE MINDS.
FEBRUARY 28, 2016 AT 10:59 PM BY: BARBARA ANN MARY MACK

I HAVE BEEN SENT BY ALMIGHTY GOD TO ENLIGHTEN THE SINNERS

BARBARA SPEAKING

MY BROTHERS AND SISTERS, I HAVE BEEN SENT BY ALMIGHTY GOD, THE BLESSED AND HOLY TRINITY, TO ENLIGHTEN THOSE WHO BELIEVE THAT THEY ARE SAVED. MY BROTHERS AND SISTERS, YOUR SALVATION IS CONFIRMED BY YOUR LIFESTYLES TODAY. ARE YOU LIVING ACCORDING TO ALMIGHTY GOD'S, THE UNCHANGEABLE ONE, HOLY WORDS THAT FLOW SO ELOQUENTLY THROUGH THE BIBLE? MY BROTHERS AND SISTERS, DO NOT BE DECEIVED OR FOOLED BY SATAN, THE DECEIVING REALM. IN ORDER FOR ONE TO ENJOY THE GIFT OF SALVATION, ONE MUST, AT ALL TIMES, EXHIBIT THE ACTS AND WORKS OF JESUS' VERSION OF A CHRISTIAN. OUT OF DIVINE MERCY FOR HIS LOVED ONES ON EARTH TODAY, OUR PERFECT UNCHANGING LORD, HAS SENT HIS MESSENGER (BARBARA) TO RECITE HIS HOLY WORDS

IN YOUR WORTHY PRESENCE. BECAUSE OF HIS GREAT GENEROSITY, HE HAS DEEMED THIS GENERATION WORTHY TO HEAR HIS HOLY WORDS PERTAINING TO SALVATION, THROUGH HIS MODERN DAY MESSENGER (BARBARA). IN THE MIDST OF THIS VERY TRAGIC PERIOD OF TIME, ALMIGHTY GOD HAS GRACED THIS GENERATION WITH HIS HOLY PRESENCE IN A TANGIBLE FORM (BARBARA) SO THAT THOSE WHOM HE HAS CALLED AND CHOSEN, WILL SEE HIS GLORIOUS LIGHT IN THE MIDST OF SATAN'S, THE WORLD, REALM OF DARKNESS. BEHOLD, MY BROTHERS AND SISTERS! BEHOLD THE GENEROSITY OF OUR CARING AND MERCIFUL GOD! FOR HE IS TRULY IN OUR MIDST TODAY. *ALLELUIA!!!*

MARCH 1, 2016 AT 5:28 PM BY: BARBARA ANN MARY MACK

ILLUMINATE WITH THE PRESENCE OF ALMIGHTY GOD SO THAT EVEN THE BLIND ONES MAY SEE CHRIST WITHIN YOU

BARBARA SPEAKING

MY BROTHERS AND SISTERS, LET US SHINE WITH THE PRESENCE OF OUR HOLY GOD, SO THAT THE PHYSICALLY BLIND ONES WILL SEE CHRIST JESUS' GLORIOUS LIGHT. LET US ILLUMINATE THIS DARK WORLD OF APATHY, HATE AND CRIMES, WITH THE GLORIOUS LIGHT THAT REVEALS THE PRESENCE OF GOD, THE HOLY ONE. LET US SHINE IN THE MIDST OF THE WORLD'S DARK ACTS OF SIN AND PAIN AS WE LIVE A LIFE THAT PLEASES OUR HOLY CREATOR AND GOD, FOR HE IS IN OUR BLESSED MIDST TODAY. LET US EXHIBIT GOD'S HOLY VERSION OF LOVE IN THE MIDST OF THE WORLD'S VERSION OF LOVE. FOR THE WORLD'S VERSION OF LOVE IS TEMPORARY AND IMPERFECT. MY BROTHERS AND SISTERS, LET THE GIFT OF GOD'S HOLY LIGHT GUIDE YOU THROUGHOUT EACH BLESSED DAY, SO THAT THE REALM THAT RELEASES SIN AND DARKNESS WILL NOT CAPTURE OR DISSUADE YOU. LET THE BELIEVING ONES ILLUMINATE THIS REALM OF APATHY SO THAT WE MAY HELP ONE ANOTHER IN THE MIDST OF THIS TRAGIC PERIOD OF TIME. MY BROTHERS AND SISTERS, LET US LIVE OUR PROFESSION AS A CHRISTIAN EVERY DAY. *ALLELUIA!!!*

MARCH 1, 2016 AT 6:17 PM BY: BARBARA ANN MARY MACK

IN THE MIDST OF MY FLOWING TEARS, YOU ARE THERE WITH ME, O LORD

BARBARA SPEAKING TO ALMIGHTY GOD, THE BLESSED TRINITY

IN THE MIDST OF MY FLOWING TEARS I CAN FEEL THE GIFT OF YOUR HOLY PRESENCE, MY GOD. IN THE MIDST OF TEARS THAT EXIT MY WEARY SOUL, MY HEART CRIES OUT IN CONTINUOUS PRAYER FOR THE LOST SOULS THAT WANDER IN THE REALM (SIN) THAT HAS CAPTURED THEM. I CAN HEAR YOUR CRIES AS THEY UNITE WITH MINE, O MERCIFUL GOD. I CAN HEAR THE

HOLY CRIES OF MY VICTORIOUS SAVIOR AND GOD, AS HE WEEPS WITH ME, AS I WITNESS THE DIRECTION THAT THE LOST SOULS ARE HEADING IN. CLING TO MY MANY FLOWING TEARS, O MERCIFUL HOLY SPOUSE OF MINE. CLING TO THE TEARS THAT EXIT THE SOUL OF YOUR FAITHFUL MESSENGER AND BRIDE. CLING TO THE TEARS THAT UNITE WITH YOURS, AS WE WITNESS THE DESTINATION OF YOUR LOST CHILDREN TODAY. MY HOLY LORD AND GOD, I CAN FEEL YOUR HOLY PRESENCE AS I WEEP CONTINUOUSLY FOR THE LOST ONES.

MARCH 1, 2016 AT 6:35 PM BY: BARBARA ANN MARY MACK

OUR SPIRITUAL, EMOTIONAL AND PHYSICAL WOUNDS EXPRESS OUR ALLEGIANCE TO ALMIGHTY GOD

BARBARA SPEAKING

MY BROTHERS AND SISTERS, OUR EMOTIONAL AND PHYSICAL WOUNDS EXPRESS OUR ALLEGIANCE TO ALMIGHTY GOD. IT IS TRULY AND HONOR TO EXPERIENCE THE SUFFERINGS THAT COME WITH BEING A PROFESSED AND DEVOTED CHRISTIAN. FOR THE REALM OF EVIL AND SIN DO NOT APPROVE OF OUR DEVOTION TO OUR SAVING GOD. THE WOUNDS THAT ENCOMPASS OUR SOULS REVEAL THE UNION THAT WE HAVE WITH OUR SACRIFICIAL LORD GOD (JESUS). LET THE WOUNDS THAT WE HAVE EARNED AS A CHRISTIAN SHINE IN THE MIDST OF THOSE WHO DENY AND REJECT THE DIVINITY OF JESUS, OUR SACRED GOD. LET OUR EARNED WOUNDS EXHIBIT THE LOVE THAT WE HAVE FOR OUR FAITHFUL GOD AND SAVIOR, FOR HE IS WORTHY!!! *ALLELUIA!!!*

MARCH 1, 2016 AT 7:05 PM BY: BARBARA ANN MARY MACK

A VERY SERIOUS AND CRUCIAL ERA OF TIME-TODAY

ALMIGHTY GOD SPEAKING

MY CHILDREN, THIS A VERY SERIOUS AND CRUCIAL PERIOD OF TIME, FOR SATAN, THE REALM OF EVIL, SLITHERS IN YOUR MIDST THROUGHOUT EVERY DAY. HE IS IN THE PRESENCE OF THOSE WHO DESIRE TO FOLLOW MY HOLY VOICE. HE IS IN THE PRESENCE OF THOSE WHO DO NOT BELIEVE IN MY HOLY PRESENCE. HE IS VISIBLE TO THOSE WHO ARE SENT BY ME TO REVEAL HIS UNWANTED PRESENCE. HE HAS TAKEN THE LIVES OF THOSE WHO WALK IN THE FAITHS THAT REJECT JESUS' DIVINITY. MY CHILDREN, BECAUSE OF MY GREAT LOVE FOR YOU, I WILL NOT ABANDON THOSE WHO LEAVE THE REALM THAT REJECTS ME. I WILL NOT ABANDON THE REPENTANT ONES. I WILL NOT ABANDON THOSE WHO LEARN OF MY VERSION OF HOLINESS BEFORE THE REALM OF DESTRUCTION CAPTURES THEIR VULNERABLE SOULS. I WILL BE FAITHFUL TO THOSE WHO LEAVE THE REALM THAT HAVE CAPTURED THEM DURING THIS TRAGIC PERIOD OF TIME. ALTHOUGH SATAN'S ANGELS AND SERVANTS FLOW THROUGH THIS PERIOD OF TIME, I AM IN YOUR BLESSED MIDST, *SAYS THE LORD GOD*. MY CHILDREN, THIS IS A VERY SERIOUS AND CRUCIAL PERIOD OF TIME, FOR THE SPIRITUAL BATTLE BETWEEN GOOD (ALMIGHTY GOD, THE HOLY TRINITY) AND EVIL (SATAN AND HIS DEFEATED ANGELS) IS GOING STRONG. JOIN ME, MY CHILDREN! JOIN ME IN THIS VERY SERIOUS AND CRUCIAL SPIRITUAL WAR ON EARTH TODAY. FOR I AM LOOKING FOR MY WARRIORS.
MARCH 1, 2016 AT 7:56 PM BY: BARBARA ANN MARY MACK

OH, IF ALL OF THE CALLED ONES WERE AS FAITHFUL AND OBEDIENT AS YOU ARE, MY WORK WOULD BE A PIECE OF CAKE, SAYS THE LORD

ALMIGHTY GOD SPEAKING TO CRAIG, LA TOYA AND AMYA

OH, THE JOY OF WITNESSING THE ALLEGIANCE OF MY FAITHFUL ONES (ARCHBISHOP CRAIG, LA TOYA AND AMYA)!!!
MARCH 1, 2016 AT 8:07 PM BY: BARBARA ANN MARY MACK

I WILL NOT PRAY FOR THEM, FOR THEIR REWARD (EVERLASTING DESTRUCTION) IS IMMINENT-APPROACHING, SAYS THE LORD

ALMIGHTY GOD SPEAKING

I, THE LORD ALMIGHTY, WILL NOT PRAY FOR THOSE WHO HAVE ABANDONED AND BETRAYED ME. FOR THEIR REWARD FOR THEIR UNHOLY DEEDS AND ACTS ARE APPROACHING THEM. IT IS IMMINENT, *SAYS THE LORD GOD!*
MARCH 1, 2016 AT 8:10 PM BY: BARBARA ANN MARY MACK

LET THEM LEARN OF OUR (ALMIGHTY GOD, CRAIG AND BARBARA) VICTORY OVER THE REALM OF DIVISION AND EVIL, SAYS THE LORD

ALMIGHTY GOD SPEAKING TO CRAIG AND BARBARA

YOU CAN TELL THEM NOW, *SAYS THE LORD GOD*. YOU CAN TELL THEM ALL! FOR THE TIME OF OUR HOLY UNION IS AT HAND! LET US REVEAL IT TO THE WORLD! LET US SPEAK OF OUR INSEPARABLE UNION OPENLY, O FAITHFUL AND OBEDIENT SON (CRAIG) AND DAUGHTER (BARBARA). LET US SPEAK OF OUR HOLY FUSION IN THE PRESENCE OF THE CALLED AND CHOSEN ONES, FOR I HAVE DEEMED THEM WORTHY OF RECEIVING SUCH GOOD AND HOLY NEWS FROM US (ALMIGHTY GOD, CRAIG AND BARBARA), *SAYS THE LORD GOD!*
MARCH 1, 2016 AT 8:18 PM BY: BARBARA ANN MARY MACK

SATAN, THE DECEPTIVE ONE, KNOWS MY DIVINE PURPOSE TOO

BARBARA SPEAKING

HE (SATAN) KNOWS TOO. HE IS WELL AWARE OF MY DIVINE PURPOSE DURING THIS CRUCIAL AND DEVASTATING PERIOD OF TIME. HE IS NOT GOING TO GIVE UP THIS TREMENDOUS SPIRITUAL BATTLE. ALTHOUGH HE KNOWS OF OUR (ALMIGHTY GOD AND HIS CHOSEN ONES) VICTORY OVER HIS DOOMED REALM OF EVIL AND DESTRUCTION, HE WILL NOT LEAVE THE BATTLEFIELD BEFORE THIS SPIRITUAL WAR IS OVER, AND NEITHER WILL I, *SAYS THE LORD GOD!*. I HAVE BEEN SENT BY ALMIGHTY GOD, THE DESTROYER OF THE REALM THAT HOUSES SATAN AND HIS DOOMED FOLLOWERS, TO BATTLE AND DEFEAT SATAN'S REALM OF EVIL THAT TRIES TO CAPTURE AND DESTROY THOSE WHOM THE LORD HAS PLACED IN MY SPIRITUAL CARE. SATAN KNOWS OF MY POSITION AS THE MESSENGER AND BRIDE OF GOD, THE HOLY TRINITY, BUT HE PERSISTS IN THIS LOSING BATTLE. HE PLACES UNPRODUCTIVE AND UNHOLY THOUGHTS IN MY MIND, AS AN ACT TO DECEIVE AND TERRORIZE ME TO THE POINT OF ABANDONING MY DIVINE ASSIGNMENT OF LOVE. HE IS A BIG LOSER, AND HE KNOWS IT! HE ALSO KNOWS THAT I CANNOT ABANDON AN ASSIGNMENT THAT IS ORCHESTRATED BY ALMIGHTY GOD HIMSELF. THEREFORE, HIS TACTICS AND CUNNING DECEPTIVE TOOLS WILL NOT CAUSE ME TO WAIVER OR QUIT.
MARCH 1, 2016 AT 8:47 PM BY: BARBARA ANN MARY MACK

JESUS PREACHES ON THE GIFT OF REPENTANCE

BARBARA SPEAKING

OH WHAT A GLORIOUS THING IT IS! TO HEAR THE REPENTANCE OF THOSE WHO TRULY LOVE THE LORD. OH WHAT A DELIGHT IT IS! TO HEAR THE VOICE OF THOSE WHO ARE TRULY SORRY FOR THEIR UNHOLY AND UNRIGHTEOUS ACTS, WHICH ARE VISIBLE TO THE EYES OF OUR PERFECT LORD AND GOD. OH WHAT A JOY IT IS! TO HEAR THE CRIES OF THOSE WHO ARE TRULY WALKING IN THE DIRECTION OF RIGHTEOUSNESS.

ALMIGHTY GOD SPEAKING TO THE REPENTANT ONES

I HEAR YOUR VOICE OF REPENTANCE, O SWEET CHILDREN OF MINE! I HEAR THE SINCERE CRIES THAT EXIT THE SOUL OF THE REPENTANT ONE! I HEAR THE VOICES OF THOSE WHO HAVE ABANDONED THE ROAD THAT LEADS TO DESTRUCTION AND ETERNAL MISERY, FOR MY REALM OF HOLINESS. I HEAR YOU, MY CHILDREN, I HEAR YOUR SINCERE CRIES OF REPENTANCE.
MARCH 1, 2016 AT 9:34 PM BY: BARBARA ANN MARY MACK

THOSE WHO WELCOME SATAN AND HIS REALM OF EVIL

ALMIGHTY GOD SPEAKING

THOSE WHO WELCOME SATAN AND HIS REALM OF EVIL (SIN) ARE HEADED FOR THE REALM THAT WILL ENCOMPASS THEIR ETERNAL SOULS WITH CONTINUOUS FIRE AND TORMENT. THERE ARE NO EXCEPTIONS, *SAYS THE LORD GOD!*
MARCH 2, 2016 AT 11:57 AM BY: BARBARA ANN MARY MACK
SENT SUN, MAR 6, 2016 6:27 PM-READ SUN 3/6/2016 8:56 PM

GREETINGS, DEAR ARCHBISHOP CRAIG! THINKING OF YOU WHILE I'M PRESENTLY WORKING ON MY BOOK «THE PRESENT TESTAMENT VOLUME TEN».
COME STA OGGI AMORE? WHILE LISTENING TO THE BOOK OF ST. MATTHEW, I PONDERED OVER CHAPTER 5 VERSES 44-48. I FOCUSED ON VERSE 48 WHERE JESUS SAYS "BE THEREFORE PERFECT, JUST AS YOUR FATHER WHO IS IN HEAVEN IS PERFECT." THROUGH THE YEARS, I HAVE HEARD MANY PEOPLE SAY "I AM NOT PERFECT" OR "NO BODY'S PERFECT." BUT JESUS CALLS US TO BE "PERFECT", IN REGARDS TO LIVING GOD'S VERSION OF HOLINESS. IF IT WERE NOT POSSIBLE FOR US, THE LORD WOULD NOT HAVE TOLD US TO BE PERFECT. BY LIVING WITHIN GOD'S VERSION OF HOLINESS, WE AS IMPERFECT CHILDREN, ARE GRANTED THE GIFT OF PERFECTION BY ALMIGHTY GOD. TI AMO! BELLA BARBIE
SENT SUN, MAR 6, 2016 6:27 PM-READ SUN 3/6/2016 8:56 PM

GREETINGS, DEAR ARCHBISHOP CRAIG! OH, WHAT A GLORIOUS ENLIGHTENMENT AFTER MASS TODAY! I WILL NOT GO INTO DETAILS, BUT I WAS VERY PLEASED WITH SOME OF THE RESPONSES AND REACTIONS AFTER I MENTIONED ST. BARNABAS' REQUEST FOR LA TOYA TO LECTOR. WE WILL SEE WHERE THE LORD WILL LEAD US NEXT SUNDAY. ST. BARNABAS' MASSES ARE 5 PM ON SATURDAYS AND 8:00 AM AND 10:00 AM ON SUNDAYS. PLEASE ENJOY THE REST OF THIS BLESSED SABBATH DAY. *ALLELUIA!!! BELLA BARBIE*

SENT SUN, MAR 6, 2016 6:27 PM-READ SUN 3/6/2016 8:56 PM

O BLESSED ARCHBISHOP CRAIG, DURING THIS HOLIEST PERIOD OF THE YEAR, ALMIGHTY GOD, THE LORD JESUS, HAS GRACED ME WITH THE GIFT OF EXPERIENCING THE DEPTH OF THE ACT OF DIVINE ORCHESTRATED AND ORDERED BETRAYAL. MY GOD HAS GRANTED ME THE GIFT OF EXPERIENCING THE BETRAYAL OF A LOVED ONE, AS HE EXPERIENCED NOT SO LONG AGO. THE AGONY THAT ENCOMPASSES THE REALM OF BETRAYAL WAS PLACED WITHIN MY REALM OF BLISS ON EARTH. THE REALM OF BETRAYAL PENETRATED MY PLACE OF PEACE DURING THIS CRUCIAL PERIOD OF TIME. I HAVE BEEN GRACED WITH THE PRIVILEGE TO EXPERIENCE A FRACTION OF THE PAIN THAT PERMEATED THE LORD JESUS AS HE WITNESSED THE BETRAYAL AND ABANDONMENT OF HIS DISCIPLES. *TI AMO! BELLA BARBIE*

THE BETRAYAL: THE BETRAYER

BARBARA SPEAKING TO THE BETRAYED LORD JESUS

MY LORD, MY HOLY GOD, LET US WEEP AS ONE BETRAYED ESSENCE, FOR OUR BETRAYAL WILL AVAIL MUCH DURING THIS MOST BLESSED PERIOD OF TIME. MY LORD GOD, LET ME WELCOME THE REALM OF BETRAYAL AS YOU DID, NOT SO LONG AGO. I BLESS YOU, O SACRIFICIAL GOD AND LAMB, FOR CONSIDERING ME WORTHY OF EXPERIENCING THE DEPTH OF AGONY THAT ACCOMPANIES THE ACT OF BETRAYAL BY A LOVED ONE. MY LORD, MY HOLY GOD, MAY YOU CONTINUE TO CRADLE MY BETRAYER, SO THAT HE TOO, MAY EXPERIENCE THE DEPTH OF OUR ETERNAL LOVE.

BARBARA SPEAKING TO THE LORD JESUS

MY LOVING AND MERCIFUL GOD, I WILL PRAY FOR THE BETRAYERS TODAY, AS YOU PRAYED FOR THOSE WHO BETRAYED YOU IN THE PAST. MY HOLY FATHER AND GOD, FORGIVE MY BETRAYERS, FOR THEY KNOW NOT WHAT THEY DO. MY LOVING GOD AND FATHER (THE LORD JESUS), I HAVE EXPERIENCED THE DEPTH OF BETRAYAL BY A LOVED ONE, AS YOU HAVE EXPERIENCED, BY THOSE WHOM YOU SUFFERED AND DIED ON THE HOLY CROSS FOR. MY LORD AND HOLY GOD, MY PAIN AND SUFFERING HAVE UNITED WITH YOURS, AS YOU AND I CONTINUE

EXHIBITING AN AUTHENTIC LOVE FOR OUR BETRAYERS, FOR OUR LOVE IS EVERLASTING AND TRUE. MY HOLY LORD, I WILL KEEP THE ETERNAL SOUL OF MY BETRAYER WITHIN MY REALM OF TRANQUILITY AND DIVINE FORGIVENESS SO THAT THE GATES OF HELL WILL NEVER CLAIM HIM.

BARBARA SPEAKING TO THOSE WHO HAVE BETRAYED HER THROUGH THE YEARS

I WILL KEEP YOU WITHIN MY SANCTUARY OF HOLY PRAYERS, FOR YOU ARE AMONG GOD'S CHOSEN ONES.
MARCH 7, 2016 AT 6:59 PM BY: BARBARA ANN MARY MACK
SENT MON, MAR 7, 2016 7:35 PM-READ MON 3/7/2016 8:50 PM

GREETINGS, ARCHBISHOP CRAIG! TODAY IS PERRY'S (AMYA'S DAD) BIRTHDAY. AMYA TOOK HIM TO IHOP AFTER SHE GOT OUT OF SCHOOL. I BAKED A CAKE TOO! I'M AFRAID TO GIVE HIM SOME OF IT AT THIS TIME, BECAUSE I HAVEN'T TASTED IT YET. WE INVITED HIM TO COME WITH US TO CHURCH, BUT THEY CHANGED HIS DAYS OFF AND HE DOESN'T FINISH WORK UNTIL AFTER 3 PM. PLEASE SEND UP A VERY SPECIAL PRAYER FOR HIM. HE LOVES AMYA SO MUCH! SHE GIVES HIM A REASON TO KEEP STRONG IN THE MIDST OF HIS MANY TRIALS. AMYA, BEING A TEENAGER, SHE CRAVES FOR MORE PRIVACY AND PRIVATE TIME WITHOUT EXCESSIVE CONVERSATION OR ACTIVITY FROM ADULTS. I UNDERSTAND THIS VERY WELL. LA TOYA AND PERRY STILL CRAVE THEIR LITTLE GIRL'S ATTENTION. WE HAVE TO GIVE THEM ENOUGH SPACE TO GROW, BUT NOT TOO MUCH TO CAUSE A GAP IN COMMUNICATION. **AMORE, BEAUTIFUL BARBIE**
SENT MON, MAR 7, 2016 7:51 PM-READ MON 3/7/2016 9:43 PM

BUONA SERA, DEAR LOVED ONE (CRAIG)! FROM MY YOUTH, I HAVE BEEN PLACED IN THE PRESENCE OF MANY WHO WERE CAPTURED BY THE UNINVITED INTRUDER (AN EVIL SPIRIT). OH HOW FRIGHTENED I WAS! TO WITNESS THE PRESENCE OF AN EVIL SPIRIT WHICH HAD TAKEN POSSESSION OF PEOPLE WHO WERE/ARE A PART OF MY LIFE. EVEN AS AN ADULT, THE PRESENCE OF THE EVIL SPIRIT WITHIN THE CAPTURED PERSON FRIGHTENED ME. BUT, WITH THE PRESENCE OF OUR OMNIPOTENT GOD, WHICH ENCOMPASSES AND PROTECTS MY WEAK BEING THROUGHOUT EACH DAY, I AM ABLE TO FACE THE EVIL SPIRITS THAT PERMEATE THE CAPTURED BEINGS. IN SOME CASES, THE LORD'S HOLY LOVE THAT FLOWS THROUGH MY OBEDIENT BEING, HAS CAUSED THE UNINVITED EVIL SPIRITS TO DEPART FROM THE CAPTURED ONES. IT IS A TERRIFYING EXPERIENCE TO BE IN THE PRESENCE OF EVIL IN THE FORM OF A LOVED ONE OR ACQUAINTANCE.
MAY THE PEACE OF ALMIGHTY GOD'S HOLY LOVE, ENCOMPASS YOU THROUGHOUT ETERNITY.

THE EXECUTION OF AN EXORCISM

GOD, THE HOLY SPIRIT, SPEAKING

DIVINE LOVE ALONE, DRIVES OUT THE INTRUDER (EVIL SPIRIT).
MARCH 7, 2016 AT 10:26 PM BY: BARBARA ANN MARY MACK
SENT MON, MAR 7, 2016 10:45 PM-READ MON 3/7/2016 11:18 PM

SUBJECT: AMATO, CRAIG PADRE
O AMATO (CRAIG PADRE),
SONO ANCORA ACCETT ARE FRECCETTE CONTI NUO DI SATANA CHE SI RIVOLGONO A VOI
QUEST O È "MOLTO APPROSSIM ATI VA" E "DOLOROSO"!!!
MA, NE VALE LA PENA!
E LA VOLONTÀ DI DIO! CIAO! BELLA BARBARA

THIS IS WHAT I WROTE IN ITALIAN. PARDON IF I EXCLUDED OR INCLUDED SOME WORDS.

O BELOVED ONE (FATHER CRAIG), I AM STILL ACCEPTING SATAN'S CONTINUOUS DARTS THAT
ARE INTENDED FOR YOU. THIS IS VERY ROUGH AND PAINFUL, BUT YOU ARE WORTH IT! IT IS
GOD'S WILL!
GOOD BYE! BEAUTIFUL BARBARA
SENT TUE, MAR 8, 2016 5:10 PM-READ TUE 3/8/2016 9:27 PM
HI TI AMO!

THOSE WHO DESIRE TO FOLLOW ME, SAYS THE LORD

THOSE WHO DESIRE TO FOLLOW ME, THEY HAVE TO TAKE UP THEIR CROSSES DAILY. THERE
ARE NO EXCEPTIONS, *SAYS THE LORD GOD*

ALMIGHTY GOD SPEAKING

THERE ARE NO EXCEPTIONS!!!
MARCH 11, 2016 AT 9:05 PM BY: BARBARA ANN MARY MACK

HIS WORD IS HIS HOLY WORD

BARBARA SPEAKING

GOD DOESN'T "SUGARCOAT" THINGS. HIS WORD IS HIS HOLY WORD, FOR HE IS "UNCHANGING"!

ALMIGHTY GOD SPEAKING

I AM "UNCHANGING", MY CHILDREN! ABIDE IN MY "UNCHANGING HOLY WORD" AT ALL TIMES. FOR YOUR ETERNAL DESTINATION DEPENDS ON YOUR ALLEGIANCE TO ME, *SAYS THE LORD*

MARCH 11, 2016 AT 9:22 PM BY: BARBARA ANN MARY MACK
SENT FRI, MAR 11, 2016 9:34 PM-READ SAT 3/12/2016 7:06 PM

ALLELUIA! O BELOVED ARCHBISHOP CRAIG. I PRAY THAT YOU HAVE A BLESSED AND HOLY DAY. BELOW IS TODAY'S FB POSTING. *TI AMO, BELLA BARBARA*

ALLELUIA! ALL YE NATIONS AND LANDS OF EARTH. ALLELUIA!!!

LET US JOIN TOGETHER AS ONE FUSED ESSENCE, AS WE GIVE PRAISE, GLORY AND HONOR TO THE LORD JESUS, THE SACRIFICAL LAMB OF OUR ETERNAL GOD AND FATHER! FOR HE IS WORTHY TO BE PRAISED! HE IS WORTHY TO BE ACKNOWLEDGED EVERY DAY! HE IS WORTHY TO BOW BEFORE, THROUGHOUT EACH BLESSED DAY! HE IS WORTHY TO SING CONTINUOUS SONGS OF PRAISE TO! HE IS WORTHY TO REJOICE IN EVERY DAY! HE IS GOD, OUR HEAVENLY FATHER'S, ONLY BEGOTTEN SON! HE IS THE ETERNAL LIGHT! HE IS THE LIVING BREAD OF LIFE! HE IS THE LIVING WATERS THAT KEEP THE BELIEVING ONES SUSTAINED IN THE MIDST OF THEIR DIFFICULT AND DARK TIMES! HE IS KING OF KINGS! HE IS THE VICTORIOUS LORD OF LORDS! HE IS MY HOLY REDEEMER AND SPOUSE! HE IS ALMIGHTY GOD! *ALLELUIA!!!* GIVE HIM PRAISE! PRAISE! AND MORE PRAISE, ALL YE NATIONS AND BLESSED LANDS, FOR HE IS WORTHY TO BE PRAISED AT ALL TIMES!!! *ALLELUIA!!!*

MARCH 11, 2016 AT 3:50 PM BY: BARBARA ANN MARY MACK
SENT FRI, MAR 11, 2016 8:14 PM-READ SAT 3/12/2016 7:06 PM

GREETINGS, DEAR ARCHBISHOP CRAIG! ATTACHED IS THE COVER OF MY FORTHCOMING BOOK "THE PRESENT TESTAMENT VOLUME NINE". I AM PRESENTLY GOING OVER MY GALLERY FOR "THE PRESENT TESTAMENT VOLUME NINE". MY PUBLISHER EMAILED IT TO ME THIS MORNING. SO FAR, THERE ARE SOME MINOR CORRECTIONS THAT I HAVE DISCOVERED. I ALSO RECEIVED THE COVER PROOF FOR THE BOOK. I APPROVED THE COVER PROOF. I HAVE TO GO OVER THE GALLEY AGAIN AND FILL OUT THE CORRECTIONS FORM. HOPEFULLY I CAN TAKE CARE OF THIS BEFORE THE WEEK IS OVER. THIS BOOK CONSISTS OF 412 PAGES. IT WILL BE COMPLETED IN GOD'S HOLY TIME.
GODITI LA TUA GIORNATA, CRAIG PADRE ENJOY YOUR DAY, FATHER CRAIG!
TI AMO! BELLA BARBARA
SENT SUN, MAR 13, 2016 4:33 PM-READ SUN 3/13/2016 5:04 PM

GREETINGS, DEAR ONE! COME STA OGGI? LA TOYA AND I ARE EN ROUTE TO GET MY MONTHLY B12 INJECTION. I ALSO HAVE A 2:30 APPOINTMENT WITH MY SLEEP APNEA NURSE. HOPEFULLY EVERYTHING WILL GO SMOOTHLY TODAY. I WAS UP UNTIL A LITTLE AFTER 5 AM TRYING TO RETRIEVE MY COMPLETED MODIFICATION FORM FOR MY GALLEY. I FINISHED IT YESTERDAY, BUT I WAS UNABLE TO LOCATE IT IN MY SAVED FILES. HOPEFUL I WILL BE ABLE TO FIND IT TODAY. MY PUBLISHER SERVICE ASSOCIATE JUST EMAILED AND PHONED ME TO SEE IF I HAD COMPLETED THE GALLEY MODIFICATION FORM. IF IT'S GOD'S HOLY WILL, I WILL SEND IT IN TODAY. THIS IS HIS GREAT AND HOLY LITERARY WORK, NOT MINE. THEREFORE, I HAVE TO MOVE AT THE PACE THAT HE INSTRUCTS ME. ENJOY YOUR BLESSED DAY, AND TAKE VERY GOOD CARE OF YOUR VALUABLE SELF. *TI AMO, BELLA BARBARA*
SENT SUN, MAR 13, 2016 4:33 PM-READ SUN 3/13/2016 5:04 PM

I LOVE YOU, LORD JESUS!!! GODITI LA TUA GIORNATA, CRAIG PADRE
SENT SUN, MAR 13, 2016 4:33 PM-READ SUN 3/13/2016 5:04 PM

GREETINGS! O HIGHLY FAVORED SON (ARCHBISHOP CRAIG) OF OUR ETERNAL GOD AND FATHER. THE LORD HAS TRULY BLESSED US! FOR HE HAS CHOSEN YOU AND I, TO DELIVER HIS LIFE SAVING MESSAGES TO THOSE WHOM HE HAS PLACED IN OUR LOVING CARE. LET US REJOICE, O BLESSED ONE! MY PUBLISHER EMAILED ME THIS MORNING TO TELL ME THAT MY GOD DICTATED BOOK "THE PRESENT TESTAMENT VOLUME NINE-IT IS WRITTEN" HAS PASSED THE FINAL STAGE OF THE PUBLICATION PROCESS AND HAS BEEN SENT TO THE PRINTER. ALLELUIA!!! HE SHARED WITH ME EARLIER, THAT HE WANTS THIS BOOK COMPLETED DURING THIS LENTEN AND EASTER SEASON.

I BLESS YOU, O RIGHTEOUS GOD AND FATHER, FOR YOUR HOLY WORD AND WILL HAVE MANIFESTED AGAIN!!! ALLELUIA!!! REJOICING BARBIE

SENT SUN, MAR 13, 2016 4:33 PM-READ SUN 3/13/2016 5:04 PM

TI AMO, DEAR ONE! IF IT'S GOD'S HOLY WILL, WE WILL SEE YOU AT YOUR 12:30 PM MASS TOMORROW. SO FAR, LA TOYA IS SCHEDULED TO LECTOR AT OUR TENEBRAE SERVICE ON WEDNESDAY AND EASTER VIGIL MASS. *CIAO! BELLA BARBIE*

SENT SUN, MAR 13, 2016 4:33 PM-READ SUN 3/13/2016 5:04 PM

I LOVE YOU, LORD JESUS!!!

THANK YOU, DEAR ARCHBISHOP CRAIG, FOR YOUR WONDERFUL GOD ORCHESTRATED SERMON TODAY! IT WAS VERY MOVING AND INSPIRING! OUR FAITHFUL GOD IS PLEASED WITH HIS CHOSEN BELOVED SON.

AMORE, FAITHFUL BARBARA! GOD'S SENT CONTEMPORARY MESSENGER AND BRIDE

SENT SUN, MAR 13, 2016 4:33 PM-READ SUN 3/13/2016 5:04 PM

GREETINGS, DEAR ARCHBISHOP CRAIG! COME STA OGGI? BELOW IS MY LATEST FB POSTING. AMORE, BEAUTIFUL BARBARA

JESUS LIVES!!!

BARBARA SPEAKING

JESUS LIVES AND REIGNS IN HEAVEN AND ON EARTH! LET US GIVE HIM CONTINUOUS PRAISE EVERYONE! *ALLELUIA!* I LOVE YOU VERY MUCH, MY LORD AND VICTORIOUS GOD! *ALLELUIA!* GIVE HIM PRAISE!

MARCH 12, 2016 AT 7:14 PM BY: BARBARA ANN MARY MACK

SENT SUN, MAR 13, 2016 8:10 PM- READ SUN 3/13/2016 9:53 PM

BUON GIORNO, DEAR ONE!

I SIT BACK AND ENJOY THE GOODNESS OF THE LORD

BARBARA SPEAKING

OH HOW GOOD AND LOVING YOU ARE, MY HOLY GOD. I SIT BACK AND ENJOY YOUR VISIBLE GOODNESS IN THE LIVES OF MY FAMILY, FRIENDS, ACQUAINTANCES AND STRANGERS. I SIT BACK EACH DAY AND WITNESS YOUR GLORY IN A TANGIBLE MANNER. OH HOW WONDERFUL

YOU ARE, O HOLY GOD AND SPOUSE OF MINE! OH HOW GRACIOUS AND KIND YOU ARE, MY HOLY GOD AND HEAVENLY FATHER! MY LORD, YOU EVEN EXPRESS YOUR GENUINE LOVE FOR THOSE WHO HAVE ABANDONED AND DENIED YOUR HOLY POSITION AS GOD, THE ONLY BEGOTTEN SON. MY HOLY GOD, I WILL IMITATE YOU AS I TRAVEL IN THE MIDST OF THOSE WHO DENY AND REJECT YOU. I WILL WEEP FOR THEM, AS YOU WEEP FOR THEM, MY LORD. I WILL PRAY FOR THEM, AS YOU HAVE COMMANDED US TO DO, O HEAVENLY CREATOR OF ALL THAT IS GOOD AND HOLY. I WILL IMITATE THE GOOD THAT COMES FROM MY ORIGIN AND GOD AS I WITNESS THOSE WHO DENY YOU, O LOVING AND HOLY ONE. I WILL IMITATE THE HOLY ESSENCE (ALMIGHTY GOD) THAT ROAMS THE EARTH DURING THIS TRAGIC PERIOD OF TIME. I WILL IMITATE YOU, O LORD, AS I SIT BACK AND ENJOY YOUR HOLY PRESENCE IN OUR MIDST TODAY. FOR YOU ARE GOD, THE HOLY ONE.

MARCH 12, 2016 AT 2:42 AM BY: BARBARA ANN MARY MACK
SENT SUN, MAR 13, 2016 8:10 PM- READ SUN 3/13/2016 9:53 PM

HI! I PRAY THAT YOU HAD A WONDERFUL RELAXING DAY IN THE MIDST OF YOUR VERY BUSY SCHEDULE, DEAR ONE (CRAIG). BELOW IS GOD'S MESSAGE FOR ALL.
LOVE ALWAYS! BARBARA, GOD'S FAITHFUL MESSENGER AND SCRIBE

GOD, THE GREAT AND HOLY ETERNAL JUDGE

BARBARA SPEAKING

MY BROTHERS AND SISTERS,GOD IS THE ONLY FINAL JUDGE: BUT, CAN YOU HANDLE THE JUDGMENT OF ALMIGHTY GOD?
FOR HE JUDGES YOUR ETERNAL SOUL!!!

ALMIGHTY GOD SPEAKING

I AM THE FINAL JUDGE, MY CHILDREN, *SAYS THE LORD*

MARCH 14, 2016 AT 7:55 PM BY: BARBARA ANN MARY MACK
SENT MON, MAR 14, 2016 8:02 PM-READ MON 3/14/2016 8:53 PM

PLEASANT DREAMS, DEAR ONE!!!

MY CALVARY

BARBARA SPEAKING

I HAVE REACHED MY CALVARY, FOR THE SAKE OF THE ETERNAL SOULS OF MY LOVED ONES. *ALLELUIA!* THANK YOU, O LORD, FOR GRACING ME WITH THE STRENGTH AND COURAGE, TO CLIMB THE HILLS THAT LED TO MY SWEET CALVARY. I HAVE MADE IT TO MY PLACE OF TRIUMPH AND VICTORY! I HAVE MADE IT WITH THE HELP AND GUIDANCE OF JESUS, MY CRUCIFIED SAVIOR AND GOD. I MADE IT WITH THE DIVINE STRENGTH THAT DESCENDED IN THE MIDST OF MY HOLY ASSIGNMENT OF LOVE. I WILL CLING TO THE VICTORY THAT I HAVE OBTAINED, WHICH IS THE MANIFESTATION OF A SUCCESSFUL DIVINE ORDERED TASK OF LOVE. I HAVE COMPLETED THE ASSIGNMENT THAT YOU HAVE FOUND ME WORTHY OF, MY LORD. I HAVE REACHED MY CALVARY WITH THE GRACE AND MERCY THAT FLOWED FROM YOUR HOLY ESSENCE, AS I CLIMBED THE SPIRITUAL HILLS THAT LED ME TO MY CALVARY, MY DIVINE ORCHESTRATED ASSIGNMENT OF LOVE. *ALLELUIA!!!*

MARCH 13, 2016 AT 9:38 PM BY: BARBARA ANN MARY MACK

SENT WED, MAR 16, 2016 3:44 AM- READ WED 3/16/2016 8:24 PM

A DIVINE SUCCESS! GREETINGS, DEAR ARCHBISHOP CRAIG!

COME STA AMORE? SO FAR, I AM HAVING A VERY BUSY DAY FOR THE LORD. I HAD A 10:30 AM APPOINTMENT WITH SOMEONE WHOM THE LORD EXHIBITED HIS HOLY PRESENCE TO THROUGH LA TOYA AND ME. I LEARNED IN THE MIDST OF OUR MEETING THAT THE INDIVIDUAL IS OF THE JEHOVAH'S WITNESS FAITH. ALTHOUGH THOSE OF THAT FAITH DO NOT READ RELIGIOUS LITERATURE OTHER THAN THEIR OWN, THIS INDIVIDUAL LOOKED THROUGH MANY OF MY PUBLISHED BOOKS AS SHE LISTENED TO THE REVELATION OF MY CONVERSION FROM THE JEHOVAH'S WITNESS FAITH TO THE CHRISTIAN FAITH. SHE ACTUALLY READ SOME OF MY PUBLISHED WRITINGS WITH PATIENCE AND AUTHENTIC INTEREST. THIS WAS MY FIRST MEETING WITH THE YOUNG LADY. I DID NOT KNOW THAT SHE WAS OF THAT FAITH UNTIL THE LORD REVEALED IT TO ME AS WE SPOKE. IT IS SO WONDERFUL HOW THE LORD EXPRESSES HIS LOVE BY SENDING HIS CALLED AND CHOSEN ONES TO ME, SO THAT I MAY ENLIGHTEN THEM WITH HIS HOLY TRUTH. WE SPENT MORE TIME DISCUSSING MY DIVINE ASSIGNMENT FOR THE LORD, THAN WHAT SHE AND I MET FOR. LA TOYA AND I KNEW THAT THE LORD SENT THE YOUNG LADY TO ME, WHEN SHE REVEALED THAT SHE WAS OF THE JEHOVAH'S WITNESS FAITH. PERHAPS THIS MEETING MAY LEAD HER TO THE LORD'S REALM OF HOLY TRUTH, AS MY PREVIOUS MEETINGS DID WITH OTHERS. LA TOYA AND I WERE AMAZED OVER THE YOUNG LADY'S ATTENTION AND INTEREST IN WHAT WE SHARED WITH HER PERTAINING TO MY CONVERSION AND MINISTRY. AS A FORMER STUDIER OF THAT FAITH, I KNOW HOW ADAMANT PEOPLE OF THAT FAITH ARE WHEN IT COMES TO DISCUSSING ANOTHER BELIEF. I USED TO BE THE SAME WAY. IT IS EVIDENT, THAT THE LORD WAS IN THE MIDST OF THAT MEETING. PLEASE KEEP HER IN YOUR PRAYERS AS WELL. IF IT'S GOD'S HOLY WILL, SHE IS ONE OF HIS CHOSEN

ONES, FOR SHE HAS BEEN CALLED BY ALMIGHTY GOD THROUGH ME TODAY. *ALLELUIA!!!* LET US GIVE THE GOOD LORD THE HIGH PRAISE THAT HE IS WORTHY OF. *ALLELUIA!!!* I AM PRESENTLY WORKING ON MY MANUSCRIPT FOR "THE PRESENT TESTAMENT VOLUME TEN-WORDS OF A MESSENGER". I COMPLETED THE CONTRACT A COUPLE OF WEEKS AGO, AND I AM WORKING ON THE COMPLETION OF THE MANUSCRIPT. I CREATED A FRONT AND BACK COVER DESIGN TO SEND IN SEPARATE FROM THE INTERIOR TEXT. EVERYTHING HAS TO BE SENT IN ON SEPARATE FILES, INCLUDING THE IMAGES. THIS IS VERY TIME CONSUMING, BUT SPIRITUALLY REWARDING. I AM PRIVILEGED AND HONORED TO HAVE BEEN CHOSEN FOR SUCH A HIGHLY FAVORED TASK OF DIVINE LOVE. OH HOW BLESSED WE (GOD'S CHILDREN) ARE! *ALLELUIA!!!* *TI AMO! BELLA BARBARA*

SENT WED, MAR 16, 2016 3:44 AM- READ WED 3/16/2016 8:24 PM

BUON GIORNO, DEAR ARCHBISHOP CRAIG! IT HAS ARRIVED!!! *"THE PRESENT TESTAMENT VOLUME NINE: IT IS WRITTEN".* UPS DELIVERED MY BLESSED GOD DICTATED BOOK ON TUESDAY, ONE BUSINESS DAY AFTER IT WAS SENT TO THE PRINTER DEPARTMENT. *ALLELUIA!* O BLESSED BELOVED SON OF OUR GOD WHO KEEPS HIS HOLY PROMISE AND WORD. I RECEIVED MY COMPLIMENTARY COPY ON TUESDAY. AFTER LOOKING THROUGH THE BOOK, I CALLED MY PUBLISHER TO GIVE THEM THE OK TO HAVE THE BOOK GO LIVE. I RECEIVED MY REVISED GALLEY LAST THURSDAY. MY PUBLISHER ASSOCIATE ASSISTANT (PSA) AND I WENT OVER THE MINOR ERRORS AFTER I VIEWED THE REVISED GALLEY BETWEEN 4 AND 5 PM. AFTER WE COMPLETED THE FORM VIA PHONE AND EMAILS, A REVISED GALLEY WAS UPLOADED TO MY COMPUTER. AFTER I LOOKED OVER THE CORRECTIONS IN THE REVISED GALLEY, AND IT MET MY APPROVAL, I SENT IN THE SIGNED APPROVAL FORMS FOR THE REVISED GALLEY AND THE BOOK COVER PROOF. WE COMPLETED EVERYTHING WITHIN A COUPLE OF HOURS THAT DAY. I RECEIVED AN EMAIL THE FOLLOWING MORNING STATING THAT EVERYTHING PASSED THE FINAL PUBLICATION PROCESS, AND THAT MY BOOK WAS SENT TO THE PRINTER DEPARTMENT. JOY AND EXCITEMENT PERMEATED MY BLESSED BEING WHEN I SAW THE BOOK IN ITS COMPLETED FORM. I REALLY LIKE THIS BOOK BECAUSE IT REVEALS GOD'S VERSION OF HOLY LOVE FOR HIS BLESSED CALLED AND CHOSEN LITTLE CHILDREN. WE ARE TRULY BLESSED, DEAR ARCHBISHOP! WE ARE TRULY BLESSED! HE IS A GOD OF HIS HOLY WORD. HE REVEALED TO ME THAT MY (HIS) BOOK WOULD ARRIVE SOMETIME THIS WEEK. THIS IS THE FASTEST THAT MY (GOD'S) BOOK WAS DELIVERED TO ME. OH HOW BLESSED AND PRIVILEGED WE ARE, DEAR ONE! LET US GIVE OUR FAITHFUL GOD CONTINUOUS PRAISE AND ACKNOWLEDGMENT! FOR HE HAS MANIFESTED HIS HOLY PRESENCE AND POWER AGAIN! *ALLELUIA!!!* LET US REJOICE AS ONE FLESH AND ONE BLESSED AND IGNITED SPIRIT, FOR WE HAVE BEEN CHOSEN!!! *ALLELUIA!!! TI AMO! BELLA BARBIE*

SENT WED, MAR 16, 2016 3:44 AM- READ WED 3/16/2016 8:24 PM

GREETINGS, DEAR ARCHBISHOP CRAIG! COME STA? I AM PRESENTLY AT THE COMPUTER WORKING ON MY FORTHCOMING GOD DICTATED BOOK "*THE PRESENT TESTAMENT VOLUME TEN*": "*WORDS OF A MESSENGER*". I RECEIVED THE COMPLETED COPY OF '*THE PRESENT TESTAMENT VOLUME NINE*": "*IT IS WRITTEN*" FROM MY PUBLISHER YESTERDAY. I AM ALMOST READY TO SEND IN THE COMPLETED MANUSCRIPT. I AM GOING OVER IT A COUPLE OF TIMES BEFORE I EMAIL IT TO MY PUBLISHER. I TELL YOU, THIS DIVINE WORK FOR THE LORD IS KEEPING ME VERY BUSY AND OUT OF TROUBLE. ATTACHED IS A PHOTO OF MY VERY GOOD FRIEND BRENDA. SHE AND I HAVE BEEN MORE THAN SISTERS FOR OVER FORTY YEARS. OUR COMMUNICATION HAS NEVER BEEN INTERRUPTED THROUGH THE MANY YEARS. SHE ALSO TRULY BELIEVES IN MY POSITION AS A MESSENGER OF OUR GREAT AND HOLY GOD. BRENDA AND I CAN DISCUSS ANY AND EVERYTHING WITH EACH OTHER WITHOUT BEING CRITICIZED OR JUDGED. I CAN TRULY SAY THAT I LOVE HER. WE HAVE BEEN THERE FOR EACH OTHER, EVEN IN THE MIDST OF OUR DIFFICULT TIMES. SHE TOO, IS CAPTIVATED OVER THE CATHOLIC FAITH, EVEN THOUGH HER FAMILY SOMETIMES VERBALLY OBJECT TO HER CHOICE OF DENOMINATIONS. I ASK YOU AT THIS TIME TO KEEP BRENDA AND HER THREE SONS IN YOUR DAILY PRAYERS. SHE IS REALLY TRYING TO PLEASE THE LORD. SHE HASN'T GONE THROUGH CONFIRMATION YET, BUT I AM SURE SHE WILL SOON. ENJOY THE REST OF YOUR BLESSED DAY AS YOU RELAX YOUR BELOVED ESSENCE. *AMORE, FOREVER AND EVER! BEAUTIFUL BARBIE*

BELOW ARE TODAY'S GOD DICTATED PASSAGES

MY LORD, IT FEELS SO GOOD TO BE *LOVED BY YOU!*

BARBARA SPEAKING

OH, THE JOY AND BLISS THAT ENCOMPASS MY BLESSED DIVINELY LOVED ESSENCE THROUGHOUT EACH DAY! MY IGNITED SOUL REJOICES IN GOD, MY SAVIOR, AS I BOW WITHIN HIS HOLY ESSENCE AND PRESENCE! DANCE! O IGNITED BLESSED SPIRIT OF GOD'S CHOSEN MESSENGER AND BRIDE (BARBARA), DANCE WITHIN THE ESSENCE OF GOD, THE HOLY ETERNAL ONE, AS YOU JOIN HIS BLESSED CALLED AND CHOSEN ONES! DANCE! O BLESSED SPIRIT OF THE WEAKENED ONE (BARBARA), AS YOU MOVE WITHIN THE HOLY ESSENCE OF THE VICTORIOUS LORD JESUS THROUGHOUT EACH BLESSED DAY. DANCE! O WEAKENED SPIRIT OF MINE, AS YOU REJOICE IN THE HOLY ESSENCE (ALMIGHTY GOD) WHO WEAKENS YOU WITH THE POWER OF HIS HOLY LOVE AND ALLEGIANCE. DANCE! O BLESSED SPIRIT OF ALMIGHTY GOD'S FAITHFUL BRIDE AND QUEEN (BARBARA), AS YOU REJOICE WITHIN THE SPIRITUAL REALM THAT HOUSES YOUR FIRST AND LAST LOVE (GOD, THE BLESSED AND HOLY TRINITY)!!! YES, MY LORD! IT FEELS SO GOOD TO BE LOVED BY YOU!!!
MARCH 17, 2016 AT 3:49 PM BY: BARBARA ANN MARY MACK

BARBARA SPEAKING

FUSED WITH THE DIVINE SPIRIT OF GOD, MY CREATOR, I SOAR IN THE MIDST OF THIS TROUBLED PERIOD OF TIME. FUSED WITH THE DIVINE SPIRIT OF GOD, MY SAVIOR, I REJOICE IN THE MIDST OF THIS TRAGIC PERIOD OF TIME. FUSED WITH THE HOLY ESSENCE THAT SURROUNDS ME DAILY, I BOW IN THE PRESENCE OF GOD, THE HOLY TRINITY. REJOICE! O BLESSED SPIRIT OF MINE. REJOICE IN THE DIVINE SPIRIT (ALMIGHTY GOD) THAT FORMED YOU NOT SO LONG AGO! REJOICE IN THE PRESENCE OF GOD'S CALLED AND CHOSEN SONS AND DAUGHTERS! REJOICE IN THE MIDST OF GOD'S HOLY ANGELS! REJOICE IN THE MIDST OF GOD'S HOLY SAINTS! REJOICE! REJOICE! REJOICE! O BLESSED IGNITED SPIRIT OF MINE. REJOICE IN THE PRESENCE OF THE WORLD!!! *ALLELUIA!!!*
MARCH 17, 2016 AT 4:35 PM BY: BARBARA ANN MARY MACK

MY LATEST FACEBOOK POST

MY BROTHERS AND SISTERS! LET US APPRECIATE ALL THAT THE LORD HAS BLESSED US WITH, AND BE GRATEFUL FOR THE THINGS THAT HE HAS SAVED US FROM. *ALLELUIA!!!*
MARCH 16, 2016 AT 3:34 PM BY: BARBARA ANN MARY MACK

BEHOLD THE LAMB OF GOD! THE SLAUGHTERED LAMB: THE OBEDIENT LAMB: THE VICTORIOUS LAMB! THE SAVING LAMB OF GOD, THE VICTORIOUS FATHER!!!

BARBARA SPEAKING

MY BROTHERS AND SISTERS! BEHOLD JESUS! THE LAMB OF THE ONLY ETERNAL LIVING GOD AND FATHER OF ALL THAT IS GOOD AND HOLY. BEHOLD JESUS! THE SLAUGHTERED LAMB OF GOD, THE ETERNAL COMPASSIONATE AND MERCIFUL CREATOR AND FATHER OF ALL THAT IS GREAT AND GOOD. BEHOLD JESUS! THE OBEDIENT LAMB OF GOD, THE ETERNAL FATHER OF THE BLESSED CALLED AND CHOSEN ONES. BEHOLD JESUS! THE VICTORIOUS LAMB OF GOD, THE ETERNAL GRACIOUS FATHER OF ALL THAT IS CONTINUOUS AND BLISSFUL. BEHOLD JESUS! THE SAVING LAMB OF GOD, THE ETERNAL FATHER OF ALL THAT IS GLORIOUS AND RIGHTEOUS. BEHOLD JESUS! THE TRIUMPHANT LAMB OF GOD, OUR VICTORIOUS CREATOR AND FATHER. BEHOLD! BEHOLD! BEHOLD! BEHOLD HE, THE VICTORIOUS LAMB OF GOD, OUR FATHER, AS HE ROAMS IN THE MIDST OF THIS BLESSED ERA. BEHOLD JESUS, OUR VICTORIOUS KING, AS HE TRIUMPHS AGAIN, THROUGH HIS SENT MESSENGER AND BRIDE (BARBARA)! BEHOLD JESUS! THE SAVING, OBEDIENT, SLAUGHTERED AND VICTORIOUS LAMB OF GOD, THE

FATHER, AS HE MOVES WITHIN THE BLESSED BEING OF BARBARA, HIS SENT MESSENGER AND BRIDE! BEHOLD, MY BROTHERS AND SISTERS, BEHOLD! BEHOLD THE DIVINITY THAT EMITS FROM GOD'S CHOSEN VESSEL (BARBARA) AS SHE MOVES WITH THE GUIDANCE OF HER HOLY CREATOR AND GOD! BEHOLD! O BLESSED GENERATION, BEHOLD! BEHOLD THE GOODNESS OF THE LORD AS HE MOVES IN YOUR BELOVED MIDST TODAY, FOR HE STILL LIVES!!! HE IS IN OUR BLESSED MIDST! *ALLELUIA!!!* BEHOLD! O BLESSED BROTHERS AND SISTERS, BEHOLD!!!

MARCH 17, 2016 AT 5:23 PM BY: BARBARA ANN MARY MACK

I WILL REJOICE IN THE MIDST OF MY FLOWING TEARS

BARBARA SPEAKING

I WILL REJOICE IN THE PRESENCE OF GOD, OUR SAVIOR'S MIGHTY THRONE ON HIGH! I WILL REJOICE IN HIS HOLY PRESENCE AS I WEEP FOR THE SOULS OF THOSE WHO ARE SERVING FALSE GODS AND HOPES. I WILL REJOICE AS I DANCE IN THE MIDST OF DIVINITY ON EARTH! I WILL REJOICE IN THE PRESENCE OF HE, ALMIGHTY GOD, WHO HAS SAVED THE CHOSEN ONES FROM THE REALM OF ETERNAL DAMNATION. I WILL REJOICE AS MY TEARS FALL FOR THOSE WHO HAVE DENOUNCED JESUS, OUR CREATOR AND SAVING GOD! I WILL NOT LET MY FLOWING TEARS STOP ME FROM PRAISING ALMIGHTY GOD, MY FIRST AND LAST LOVE! I WILL NOT LET MY FLOWING TEARS INTERRUPT MY CONTINUOUS PRAISE! *ALLELUIA!* O SAVING CREATOR AND GOD (THE LORD JESUS, GOD, THE HOLY FATHER'S ONLY BEGOTTEN TRIUMPHANT SON), *ALLELUIA!!!*

MARCH 17, 2016 AT 5:50 PM BY: BARBARA ANN MARY MACK

MY HOLY ASSIGNMENT AND MISSION IS NOT IN VAIN, MY LORD

BARBARA SPEAKING TO ALMIGHTY GOD

OH HOLY GOD! OH HOLY ORCHESTRATOR OF MY DIVINE ASSIGNMENT OF LOVE! OH GRACIOUS KING OF KINGS! OH GRACIOUS LORD OF LORDS! OH HEAVEN SENT BLISS AND ECSTASY THAT ENCOMPASS MY BATTERED ESSENCE THROUGHOUT EACH BLESSED DAY! OH SOURCE OF ENERGY THAT PERMEATES MY SENT ESSENCE OF ALLEGIANCE UNTO YOU! OH GIFT TO THE WORLD! OH LIGHT THAT PERMEATES THIS GENERATION OF DARKNESS! OH HELP IN MY TIMES OF NEED! OH LIFE FORCE THAT IGNITES MY BLESSED SOUL! I HAVE WITNESSED THE GREAT SPIRITUAL BENEFIT THAT WAS RELEASED FROM YOUR MIGHTY THRONE OF FULFILLED PROMISES AND PROPHECIES. MY LORD GOD, I BOW IN THE MIDST OF THE MANIFESTATION OF EVERY FULFILLED PROMISE AND PROPHECY THAT DESCENDED FROM YOUR HOLY THRONE OF RIGHTEOUSNESS. MY LORD, BY YOUR HOLY WORD, I HAVE WITNESSED THE VISIBILITY OF

YOUR HOLY PROMISE AND WORD. MY LORD, MY FAMILY AND FRIENDS HAVE WITNESSED AND HEARD OF THE FULFILLMENT OF YOUR HOLY PROMISE AND WORD THAT YOU REVEALED TO ME NOT SO LONG AGO. MY LORD, I CAN SEE AND FEEL THE PRESENCE OF YOUR HOLY WORD AS I BOW IN THE MIDST OF YOUR DIVINE PRESENCE. MY LORD, MY HOLY GOD, THE VISIBILITY OF YOUR HOLY WORD REVEALS THE TRIUMPHANT ACT, THAT CONFIRMS THAT MY DIVINE ASSIGNMENT IS NOT IN VAIN. MY LORD GOD, MY HOLY ASSIGNMENT FROM YOU HAS EMITTED THE PRESENCE OF "SUCCESS" AND "DIVINE COMPLETION". *ALLELUIA!!!*
MARCH 17, 2016 AT 6:57 PM BY: BARBARA ANN MARY MACK

THE TRIUMPHANT ENTRANCE: MY VICTORY, *SAYS THE LORD!*

ALMIGHTY GOD SPEAKING

I WILL DO IT AGAIN, *SAYS THE LORD!* I WILL ENTER THE REALM OF VICTORY THROUGH THE HUMBLED AND WEAK BEING OF MY CHOSEN MESSENGER AND BRIDE (BARBARA), IN THE MIDST OF MY CHILDREN TODAY. I WILL ENTER THE REALM THAT HOUSES DIVINE VICTORY IN THE MIDST OF THIS CHAOTIC PERIOD OF TIME. I WILL ENTER THE REALM THAT HAS BEEN BLESSED BY GOD, THE ETERNAL HOLY TRINITY! I WILL ENTER THIS BLESSED PERIOD OF TIME WITHIN THE OBEDIENT ESSENCE (BARBARA) THAT MINGLES WITH THOSE WHOM I HAVE SENT HER TO. COME! O BLESSED GENERATION. COME AND WITNESS THE GLORY THAT WILL ENCOMPASS THE ESSENCE OF SHE (BARBARA) WHO REPRESENTS HER CREATOR AND GOD. COME AND WITNESS THE DIVINITY THAT SHE REVEALS, AS SHE ENTERS THE REALM OF VICTORY WITH MY TWO EDGED SWORD OF HOLINESS. COME! O INVITED GUESTS OF MINE. COME AND WITNESS ALL THAT I HAVE REVEALED TO MY CHOSEN VESSEL AND BRIDE (BARBARA) THROUGH THE YEARS! COME! ALL WHO SEEK A VISIBLE SIGN OF MY HOLY PRESENCE IN YOUR BLESSED MIDST TODAY! COME, MY WORTHY CHILDREN! COME AND WITNESS MY TRIUMPHANT ENTRANCE; MY VICTORY, AGAIN, *SAYS THE LORD!!!*
MARCH 18, 2016 AT 3:30 AM BY: BARBARA ANN MARY MACK

THE FEAR THAT COMES WITH *"THE VICTORY"*

BARBARA SPEAKING TO THE VICTORIOUS JESUS

MY LORD GOD, MY HOLY TRIUMPHANT KING OF KINGS! MY SACRIFICIAL LAMB OF GOD, THE ETERNAL FATHER! MY HOLY ETERNAL SPOUSE AND CREATOR! VICTORIOUS JESUS! VICTORIOUS IMMANUEL! VICTORIOUS SAVIOR AND GOD! I, YOUR HOLY HEAVENLY FORMED AND SENT MESSENGER AND BRIDE, AM READY TO EXPERIENCE THE DIVINE FEAR THAT COMES WITH VICTORY AND CONSUMMATION. I AM READY TO EXPERIENCE THE DEPTH OF DIVINE FEAR

THAT FLOWED THROUGH YOUR OBEDIENT HOLY ESSENCE AS YOU CONSUMMATED YOUR DIVINE ASSIGNMENT OF LOVE. MY LORD GOD, I AM READY TO EXPERIENCE THE FEAR THAT COMES WITH A COMPLETED ASSIGNMENT OF LOVE THAT WAS GIVEN TO US BY GOD, OUR HOLY FATHER. WITH YOUR HOLY PRESENCE, MY LORD JESUS, I WILL BOW IN THE PRESENCE OF OUR HOLY GOD AND ORIGIN, AS I WALK THE ROAD THAT LEADS TO THE DIVINE FEAR THAT ACCOMPANIES A "JOB WELL DONE". I AM READY TO EXPERIENCE THE GRACE THAT ENCOMPASSES THE OBEDIENT MESSENGER OF GOD, OUR HOLY FATHER AND ORIGIN. MY LORD GOD, I AM READY TO ENJOY AND WITNESS THE DIVINE ECSTASY THAT ACCOMPANIES THE REALM OF DIVINE FEAR. I AM READY TO EXPERIENCE THE JOY THAT FLOWS FROM THE REALM OF FEAR THAT REVEALS DIVINE COMPLETION AND SUCCESS! MY LORD GOD, I AM READY TO EXHIBIT THE BLISS THAT EMITS FROM THE REALM OF DIVINE FEAR, FOR IT IS GOOD!!! IT IS HOLY!!! IT IS A SIGN OF ALLEGIANCE TO ALMIGHTY GOD, THE ONE AND ONLY FIRST LOVE OF THE BELIEVING ONES! IT IS A SIGN OF REVERENCE FOR ALPHA AND OMEGA! IT IS A DIVINE FEAR THAT KEEPS THE BELIEVING ONES FAITHFUL AND HOLY. IT IS A FEAR THAT ELEVATES THE WEAK ONES IN THE MIDST OF THIS ONGOING SPIRITUAL WAR ON EARTH TODAY. MY LORD, I WILL CLING TO THE REALM OF DIVINE FEAR AS I LOOK FORWARD TO ETERNAL ECSTASY AND BLISS IN SWEET PARADISE. *ALLELUIA!* LORD JESUS. *ALLELUIA!!!*

MARCH 18, 2016 AT 8:04 PM BY: BARBARA ANN MARY MACK

SENT SAT, MAR 19, 2016 10:07 PM- READ SAT 3/19/2016 10:09 PM

TI AMO!

AT LAST!!!

BARBARA SPEAKING

AT LAST! AT LAST! AT LAST!!! IT, THE COMPLETION OF THE MYSTERY AND REVELATION SURROUNDING *"THE GREATEST STORY EVER TOLD"*, HAS FINALLY ARRIVED IN THE MIDST OF THE INVITED GUESTS. THE REVELATION THAT REVEALS GOD'S HOLY PRESENCE IN THE LIVES OF HIS CHOSEN MAIN CHARACTERS (CRAIG, BARBARA, LA TOYA AND AMYA) IN *"THE GREATEST STORY EVER TOLD"* HAS MANIFESTED IN THE PRESENCE OF THE INVITED GUESTS. WE, GOD'S MAIN CHARACTERS, HAVE BEEN PREPARED FOR THE DIVINE RELEASE OF GOD'S GREAT AND HOLY LOVE STORY, IN THE MIDST OF HIS CHOSEN AND BLESSED INVITED GUESTS. THE BLESSED FORETOLD ERA HAS DESCENDED IN THE MIDST OF THE ANTICIPATED ONES. OH WHAT AN EXCITING EXPERIENCE IT IS! TO WITNESS DIVINE FORETOLD ELEGANCE IN THE MIDST OF THIS TRAGIC PERIOD OF TIME. OH HOW EXCITING IT IS! COME! ALL YOU WHO HAVE BEEN INVITED TO THIS GREAT AND HOLY ERA. COME AND WITNESS THE PROMISED GLORY THAT ENCOMPASSES A FULFILLED PROPHECY IN YOUR MIDST TODAY! COME! O INVITED GUESTS. TAKE YOUR PLACE WITHIN THE REALM THAT RELEASED THIS BLESSED ERA AND

TANGIBLE DIVINE ORCHESTRATED LOVE. COME! O WELCOMED ONES. COME! FOR THE TIME, YES, THE BLESSED FORETOLD TIME, HAS ARRIVED!!! *ALLELUIA!!!*
MARCH 19, 2016 AT 9:50 PM BY: BARBARA ANN MARY MACK
SENT SAT, MAR 19, 2016 10:07 PM- READ SAT 3/19/2016 10:09 PM

LET US ENJOY THE BLESSING OF EXPERIENCING ANOTHER PALM SUNDAY. THE TRIUMPHANT ENTRANCE INTO GOD'S HOLY REALM OF SALVATION THROUGH OUR VICTORIOUS LORD JESUS! *ALLELUIA!* O BLESSED ARCHBISHOP CRAIG. *ALLELUIA!!! TI AMO! TRIUMPHANT BARBARA*

BEHOLD! BEHOLD! BEHOLD, O INVITED GUESTS! BEHOLD THE MANIFESTATION OF *THE TRIUMPHANT LORD!*

ALMIGHTY GOD SPEAKING TO HIS INVITED GUESTS

BEHOLD! ALL YOU WHO HAVE BEEN INVITED TO PARTAKE IN ONE OF MY GREATEST LOVE STORIES! BEHOLD ONE OF MY GREATEST WORKS! BEHOLD THE MANIFESTATION OF "THE GREATEST STORY EVER TOLD"!!! BEHOLD "THE GIFT OF LIFE" IN YOUR BLESSED MIDST TODAY! BEHOLD "DIVINE TANGIBILITY" IN YOUR BLESSED MIDST TODAY! MY INVITED CHILDREN, "BEHOLD ME, *SAYS THE LORD GOD!!!*"
MARCH 20, 2016 AT 2:53 AM BY: BARBARA ANN MARY MACK

MY FACEBOOK POSTING

MY BROTHERS AND SISTERS, LET US PAUSE AND REFLECT ON THE GREATNESS OF PALM SUNDAY! JESUS' TRIUMPHANT ENTRANCE INTO JERUSALEM, OUR VICTORY OVER SPIRITUAL AND ETERNAL DEATH.
MARCH 20, 2016 AT 3:20 AM BY: BARBARA ANN MARY MACK

BEHOLD!-PALM SUNDAY

OH WHAT A GLORIOUS CELEBRATION TODAY! *ALLELUIA!!!*
THANK YOU VERY MUCH FOR THE AWESOME CELEBRATION OF GOD'S TRIUMPHANT ENTRANCE INTO JERUSALEM, DEAR ARCHBISHOP CRAIG. OH HOW WONDERFUL IT WAS! ALMIGHTY GOD AND I WERE VERY PLEASED WITH OUR BELOVED ONE'S EXPRESSION OF HIS AUTHENTIC LOVE AND ALLEGIANCE. OH HOW EXCITED WE (ALMIGHTY GOD AND BARBARA) WERE DURING THIS PALM SUNDAY CELEBRATION. MY FAMILY AND I HAVE NEVER EXPERIENCED PALM SUNDAY'S CELEBRATION IN THE MANNER THAT YOU INVITED US TO BE A BLESSED PART OF. I WILL TREASURE THE PALM BRANCHES THAT YOU BLESSED IN THE PRESENCE OF

ALMIGHTY GOD. WE GAVE AMYA'S DAD ONE OF THE PALM BRANCHES. WE USUALLY GET ENOUGH BRANCHES TO GIVE TO OTHERS WHO DO NOT OR CANNOT MAKE TO CHURCH ON PALM SUNDAY. I WILL PLACE MY BRANCHES ON OUR FRONT DOOR AND IN MY SANCTUARY IN MY ROOM. THANK YOU FOR INCLUDING US IN THE GET TOGETHER AFTER MASS. THE LORD WAS VERY PLEASED WITH EVERYTHING THAT HE PLACED WITHIN YOU AND ME TO SHARE WITH HIS INVITED GUESTS TODAY. THIS HAS TRULY BEEN A "MEMORABLE EXPERIENCE".
TI AMO! BELLA BARBARA
SENT- SUN, MAR 20, 2016 6:22 PM-READ SUN 3/20/2016 8:03 PM

ENJOY THE REST OF THIS BLESSED HOLY WEEK, DEAR ARCHBISHOP CRAIG!!! ALLELUIA!!!
WITH ALMIGHTY GOD'S ETERNAL BLESSINGS AND LOVE, BARBARA

THE VICTORY: WE DID IT LOVE (ALMIGHTY GOD, CRAIG AND BARBARA)!!!

BARBARA SPEAKING

WE DID IT! WE DID IT! WE DID IT LOVE (ALMIGHTY GOD AND CRAIG)!!! LET US CELEBRATE AS ONE FUSED SANCTIFIED ESSENCE OF LOVE! WE HAVE ENTERED THE BLESSED REALM THAT REVEALS A DIVINE SUCCESS, MY LOVE (ALMIGHTY GOD AND CRAIG)! WE HAVE EXHIBITED THE PRESENCE OF A GOD ORDERED AND ORCHESTRATED UNION IN THE PRESENCE OF THOSE WHO WERE INVITED BY GOD, THE HOLY ETERNAL ONE. WE HAVE DEMONSTRATED THE POWER AND PRESENCE OF GOD'S HOLY TRUST WORTHY WORD, IN THE PRESENCE OF THOSE WHO WERE CONSIDERED WORTHY TO BEHOLD DIVINITY IN THEIR BLESSED MIDST TODAY. WE HAVE EXHIBITED THE HOLY PRESENCE OF GOD'S FULFILLED PROPHECY THAT WAS REVEALED TO ME, HIS CONTEMPORARY MESSENGER AND BRIDE. OH WHAT A BLESSED PRIVILEGE! OH, WHAT A GLORIOUS HONOR! TO HAVE BEEN CHOSEN BY ALMIGHTY GOD HIMSELF, TO CARRYOUT A MINISTRY THAT BRINGS JOY AND EXCITEMENT TO THOSE WHO WITNESS AND HEAR OF THIS GOOD NEWS. THIS GOD ORCHESTRATED EXPRESSION OF SPIRITUAL AND PHYSICAL UNITY! OH HOW EXCITING IT IS! TO WITNESS THE MANIFESTATION OF THAT WHICH WAS SPOKEN TO ME BY ALMIGHTY GOD HIMSELF! ALLELUIA! O GRACIOUS LORD AND KING. ALLELUIA!!! OH WHAT A TRIUMPHANT ENTRANCE INTO THE REALM THAT HOLDS THE DIVINE KEY, TO THE CONCLUSION AND MANIFESTATION OF "THE GREATEST STORY THAT WAS EVER TOLD"! OH HOW EXCITING IT IS!!! ALLELUIA!
MARCH 20, 2016 AT 11:49 PM BY: BARBARA ANN MARY MACK
SENT MON, MAR 21, 2016 11:39 PM-READ TUE 3/22/2016 12:06 AM

GREETINGS, DEAR ARCHBISHOP CRAIG! COME STA OGGI? BELOW IS TODAY'S PASSAGE FROM THE LORD FOR ALL. CIAO! BELLA BARBIE

REMAIN MEEK, HUMBLE, AND GRATEFUL IN MY HOLY PRESENCE, FOR I AM, *SAYS THE LORD*

ALMIGHTY GOD SPEAKING

IMITATE ME AT ALL TIMES, MY CHILDREN, FOR THAT PLEASES OUR HEAVENLY GOD AND FATHER, *SAYS THE LORD*. FOLLOW MY REALM OF MEEKNESS AS YOU VENTURE THROUGHOUT EACH BLESSED DAY. REMAIN HUMBLE IN MY HOLY OMNIPRESENT SIGHT, FOR I, THE LORD, AM IN YOUR BLESSED MIDST THROUGHOUT EACH BLESSED DAY. EXHIBIT THE GIFT OF GRATITUDE AS YOU ENJOY THE GLORY THAT ENCOMPASSES YOUR CHOSEN BEING THROUGHOUT EACH GOD SENT DAY. ENJOY THE GIFT OF LIFE THAT I HAVE PROMISED AND FULFILLED IN YOUR GRATEFUL PRESENCE, MY CHILDREN. FOR I, THE HOLY LORD GOD, AM IN YOUR BLESSED PRESENCE THROUGHOUT EACH DAY. EXHIBIT THE REALM OF APPRECIATION AS YOU EXPERIENCE THE GOODNESS OF YOUR LORD GOD IN THE PRESENCE OF YOUR FAMILY AND FRIENDS. EXPRESS THE GIFT, THE HEAVEN SENT GIFT OF GRATITUDE, AS YOU ENJOY THE GENEROSITY OF THOSE WHOM I HAVE PLACED IN YOUR PRESENCE. EXHIBIT THE GIFT OF HUMILITY IN THE PRESENCE OF THOSE WHO DESIRE TO WITNESS MY HOLY HUMBLE PRESENCE THROUGH YOUR BLESSED ESSENCE. EXHIBIT MY GIFT OF MEEKNESS IN THE PRESENCE OF THOSE WHO OBSERVE THE ACTS OF MY CHOSEN ONES. EXHIBIT MY VERSION OF MERCY AND KINDNESS AS YOU EXHIBIT YOUR KNOWLEDGE OF YOUR CREATOR AND HOLY GOD IN THE PRESENCE OF THE IGNORANT ONES. MY CHILDREN, EXHIBIT ME THROUGHOUT YOUR TRAVELS, FOR YOU ARE MINE, *SAYS THE LORD GOD!!!*

MARCH 21, 2016 AT 8:10 PM BY: BARBARA ANN MARY MACK

SENT MON, MAR 21, 2016 11:39 PM-READ TUE 3/22/2016 12:06 AM

PLEASANT DREAMS, DEAR ONE! BELOW IS MY LATEST FACEBOOK POSTING.

AMORE, BELLA BARBARA

ENTER MY REALM OF HOLINESS, O CLERGY! SO THAT YOU MAY WALK IN THE LAND OF THE LIVING WITH ME FOREVER, *SAYS THE LORD GOD!!!* FOR IN THE LAND OF THE LIVING, YOU WILL EXPERIENCE THE DEPTH OF MY VERSION OF HOLINESS AT ALL TIMES. THERE ARE NO, NO, NO EXCEPTIONS, O CLERGY, *SAYS THE LORD GOD!!!*

MARCH 21, 2016 AT 11:29 PM BY: BARBARA ANN MARY MACK

SENT MON, MAR 21, 2016 11:39 PM-READ TUE 3/22/2016 12:06 AM

CPSIA information can be obtained
at www.ICGtesting.com
Printed in the USA
BVOW10s1414240416

445227BV00017B/19/P

9 781524 601218